DATE DUE

			PRINTED IN U.S.A.

National Sports Policies

NATIONAL SPORTS POLICIES

An International Handbook

Edited by
Laurence Chalip, Arthur Johnson,
and Lisa Stachura

Greenwood Press
Westport, Connecticut • London

Library of Congress Cataloging-in-Publication Data

National sports policies : an international handbook / edited by
   Laurence Chalip, Arthur Johnson, and Lisa Stachura.
         p.   cm.
      Includes bibliographical references (p.   ) and index.
      ISBN 0–313–28481–4
      1. Sports and state.   I. Chalip, Laurence Hilmond.
   II. Johnson, Arthur T.   III. Stachura, Lisa.
   GV706.35.N38   1996
      796'.06'9—dc20   95–25327

British Library Cataloguing in Publication Data is available.

Library of Congress Catalog Card Number: 95–25327
ISBN: 0–313–28481–4

First published in 1996

Greenwood Press, 88 Post Road West, Westport, CT 06881
An imprint of Greenwood Publishing Group, Inc.

Printed in the United States of America

The paper used in this book complies with the
Permanent Paper Standard issued by the National
Information Standards Organization (Z39.48–1984).

10 9 8 7 6 5 4 3 2 1

Contents

Introduction: Thinking about National Sports Policies   vii
    Laurence Chalip

1. Australian Sports Policy   1
    Peter J. Farmer and Steve Arnaudon

2. The State versus Free Enterprise in Sports Policy:
    The Case of Brazil   23
    Lamartine P. DaCosta

3. Sport and Government in Canada   39
    Donald Macintosh

4. The People's Republic of China   67
    Cao Xiangjun and Susan E. Brownell

5. Communist Sports Policy: The End of an Era   89
    Jim Riordan

6. Sport in Cuba   116
    Paula J. Pettavino and Geralyn M. Pye

7. Sports Policy in France   139
    Alain Michel

8. Sports Policy in Germany   161
    Klaus Heinemann

 9. Sports Policy in Hungary   187
     Gyöngyi Szabó Földesi

10. National Sports Policy in India   212
     M. L. Kamlesh, Packianathan Chelladurai, and Usha Sujit Nair

11. The Governmental Sports Policy of the State of Israel   241
     Uriel Simri, Gershon Tenenbaum, and Michael Bar-Eli

12. Italian Sports: Between Government and Society   253
     Nicola Porro

13. Sports Policy in Japan   286
     Yuji Nakamura

14. Sports Policy in Norway   317
     Berit Skirstad and Kristin Felde

15. Sports Policy in Spain   346
     Nuria Puig

16. Sport in the United Kingdom   370
     Barrie Houlihan

17. Sports Policy in the United States   404
     Laurence Chalip and Arthur Johnson

Index   431

About the Editors and Contributors   437

Introduction: Thinking about National Sports Policies

Laurence Chalip

This handbook is the first to bring together a collection of essays describing national sports policies. These essays are useful for more than the specific information they give about the policies of particular countries. Taken together, they provide a foundation for the comparative study of sport and the policies through which sport is developed and administered. This introduction presents a framework for thinking critically and comparatively about the essays that follow.

There is an interesting intersection of thought among sociologists who argue that reality is socially constructed (e.g., Berger and Luckmann, 1967) and political scientists who contend that policy analysts should employ interpretive forms of analysis (e.g., Dryzek, 1982). If we invent our social worlds, then what we take for granted is particularly significant, because whatever is taken for granted is not discussed and thus rarely subject to change. These are the basic assumptions, the unexamined values, the consensual attributions, and the agreed expectations that drive our social (and policy) systems. The implication is that it is just as important for policy analysts to probe what is not said as it is for policy analysts to scrutinize what is said.

As useful as this formulation may be (cf. Chalip, 1985; Spector and Kitsuse, 1977), it suffers from the limitation that the policy analyst is required to identify elements that are invisible. They are invisible, even to the analyst, precisely because they are taken for granted. This is why cross-national studies of policy are so useful. Cross-national studies provide the kinds of contrasts and comparisons that help to illuminate assumptions, values, attributions, and expectations.

Another nation's differing premises and perceptions can become the ground on which one's own national presuppositions stand out in juxtaposition.

Just as it can be profitable for the analyst to note what is not said during policy debate, it is useful to observe what is not much discussed by those who study policy. We convey a great deal about our assumptions and values as scholars and analysts by the volume of effort we devote to specific policy topics. What we ignore may, in the end, alert us to the subtle biases that undergird our scholarship and analyses. That is why it is so significant that national sports policies have been so infrequently studied or compared. Indeed, although policy journals are filled with studies of education, welfare, military, environmental, tax, health, and criminal justice policies, studies of national sports policies are relatively rare. This lack of analysis is even more telling in the face of clearly articulated calls for such studies (e.g., Rutten, 1993; Stokvis, 1982), and the number of articles and monographs demonstrating the value of sports policy research for our understanding of national political cultures (e.g., Brownell, 1991; Chalip, 1991; Jarvie, 1993; MacAloon, 1984; Macintosh and Whitson, 1990; Riordan, 1977; Wilson, 1994), political economy (e.g., Johnson and Frey, 1985; Noll, 1974), and processes of policy analysis (Chalip, 1995).

It is interesting to speculate about the scholarly inattention to sports policy. In common parlance, sport falls under the rubrics of "play" and "game." If sports are merely play, they would seem to be less significant than matters of clearly instrumental concern, such as education, social welfare, or national defense. If sports are merely games, they would seem to be less worthy of concern than crime, public health, or environmental quality.

Yet, ironically, the ways we conceive and implement sport may be fundamentally tied to those same policy concerns. The ways we construct sport programs are closely aligned to the ways we seek to educate and socialize our children (McCormack and Chalip, 1988; Watson, 1977). Sport has been used as a tool for nation-building (McHenry, 1980; Macintosh, Bedecki, and Franks, 1987) and diplomacy (Macintosh and Hawes, 1993). Sport can affect public health (Blair, Wells, Weathers, and Paffenbarger, 1994; Martinsen and Stephens, 1994) and the environment (Bale, 1989). Indeed, it has been shown that our sense of community is determined, at least in part, by the nature of sports programs and opportunities that our policies afford (Chalip, Thomas, and Voyle, 1992; Stone, 1981). Thus, the study of sports policies can tell us a great deal about our most instrumental policy concerns. Certainly, sports policies deserve far more scholarly attention than they have obtained so far.

The chapters in this handbook describe varying degrees and kinds of government involvement in sport. Often the level of involvement is substantial; in many nations, the sport portfolio is one of the most prestigious a government bureaucrat can obtain. Nevertheless, as the chapters show, the phenomenon of extensive government involvement in sport is relatively recent, having arisen primarily in the post–World War II era. This may further explain the relative paucity of scholarly work on national sports policies. The phenomenon is too new for there yet to be a tradition of academic examination and critique. However, the phenomenon's very recency suggests its significance. There seems to be something about sport's symbolic potential and pragmatic utility that has attracted increasing attention by policymakers during the latter half of the twentieth century. Why? And with what consequences?

Yet the fact that government focus on sports is relatively new in no way implies that local, national, or international concern with sports is new (cf. Dunning, 1993; McIntosh, 1981). Indeed, the various structures initially developed to provide and administer sports at each level were nongovernmental in nature (Thoma and Chalip, 1996). As governments came to be involved with those systems, they had to accommodate them and, sometimes, transform them. This situation has sometimes engendered a tension between public and private sports authorities as each vies for jurisdiction—a matter that has become more complicated with the advent of the European Union and the changing national structures of the former Soviet bloc.

Sport systems, particularly at local levels, initially developed in distinctive ways. For example, locally administered school systems have been pivotal components of the U.S. sport system but far less significant in Europe. Conversely, most European countries have developed a more extensive system of sports clubs than is found in the United States. Similarly, in some countries, sports clubs may provide many sports to members, while in others each club may focus on provision of a single sport. These components of national systems are outgrowths of incremental adaptations of local systems.

One interesting, though often confusing, outcome of these adaptations is the lack of comparability of components that, on the surface, would seem to be similar cross-nationally. For example, in most American sports, the terms *club* and *team* are synonymous, while training *squads* are subunits of the club or team. However, in other countries, particularly those whose systems derive from Britain, there may be no *a priori* relationship among club, team, and squad. It is quite possible in such a setting for an athlete to belong to a club, compete for a different (sometimes selected) team, and train with a squad that is unaffiliated with either the club or the team. Thus, two nations might develop seemingly similar policies regarding sports clubs, but the practical implications of those policies might differ substantially. In a system like the United States', the policy would affect clubs, teams, training squads, and thus athletes simultaneously; in a system like New Zealand's, it might not. The important lesson for comparative sports policy research is that similar names for units of a sport system may mask substantive differences that must be distinguished if policy comparisons are to be meaningful.

Potential pitfalls extend beyond the comparison of structural elements. Governments may have grounded their policies in very different legitimations, which may generate subtle yet telling differences in policy implementation. For example, Canada's concerns for nation-building generated a focus on Olympic sports and the development of elite competitors. On the other hand, several

European governments have sought to promote health through the physical activity that sports generate. They have therefore applied substantial resources to the promotion of sport for all programs rather than to the development of programs to select and train a few elite competitors.

Official legitimations for sports policies may, in fact, be misleading. In most cultures, it is difficult to argue against legitimations framed in terms of personal or national well-being. Thus, there may be substantial rhetoric about the purported values of sports for personal or community health. Indeed, the escalation of government involvement in sport has been tangibly abetted by the subtle reframing of sport from a "want" to a "need" (McIntosh, 1986). Nevertheless, the national pride associated with successful international sport performances by national athletes and teams has, in fact, been one of the most potent driving forces for sports policy development (Chalip, 1987, 1995).

The critical evaluation of policy legitimation and implementation is, perhaps, one of the more interesting challenges facing analysts of sports policies. One might ask whether a particular legitimation is tenable. For example, is it reasonable to claim that sports enhance health when sport providers are becoming increasingly concerned about sports injuries (Kraus and Conroy, 1984), eating disorders precipitated by sport (Garner and Rosen, 1991), and the use of drugs by athletes (Tricker and Cook, 1990)? Similarly, although sport is frequently asserted to be a useful tool for cultivating national pride and a sense of national identity, there is no evidence that it is either a necessary or sufficient instrument for those purposes. There is substantial evidence that international sport successes can trigger momentary nationalistic celebrations (Chalip, 1987), but there is no evidence of any long-term residual benefit.

It may be even more useful to extend critical evaluation to policy design and implementation. For example, if a government seeks to use sport for nation-building, the analyst might ask what mechanisms it has put into place to leverage its international successes. Are there plans or procedures for using athletes, teams, or events to promote national pride?

Conversely, the analyst might search for unintended outcomes of policies designed to promote success in international sport. For example, policies designed to promote participation in sports contested on the international calendar can accelerate the breakdown of indigenous cultures by enticing children away from their indigenous games (Whitson, 1983). The effort to promote national unity could kindle ethnic tension (cf. Glassford, 1976).

Similarly, consider the claim that sport can promote economic development. In fact, most claims of economic benefits from sport are at best unsubstantiated and at worst inaccurate (Crompton, 1995). Perhaps more egregiously, it is rare for policies to incorporate elements that foster the leveraging of public sport investments. For example, De Knop (1992) reports Belgian data showing that the demand for sport as part of the tourist experience increased 1300 percent between 1967 and 1989. Yet, despite the significance of this growth for the promotion of tourism and its associated economic benefits, the planning of public sports investments has been only meagerly blended with tourist development strategies.

The analyst may find comparable shortcomings in policies that link sport to national public health campaigns. If policy legitimations assert that sport is to serve public health or promote socialization, it makes little sense to concentrate resources on highly competitive programs that discourage participation by all but the most physically gifted. If the benefits are to accrue from mass participation, then an array of programs reasonably targeted at multiple market segments would have to be provided. Furthermore, the programs should be designed to optimize the benefits asserted. Opportunities for socialization would have to be structured into programs, and the levels of physical activity would have to be sufficient to promote fitness while minimizing the risk of injury. Finally, the levels of competitiveness should not be so great as to discourage participation by the uncompetitive or to encourage overtraining by the enthusiastic. These are matters of policy (cf. Palm, 1991); the kinds of programs required are substantially different from the highly competitive programs that typify most sports delivery systems. The benefits to be obtained from sport depend not on provision of sport per se; rather, the benefits depend on the nature of program design and implementation.

As with nonsports policies, poor linkages among policy legitimation, policy design, and policy implementation may be a consequence of the political processes by which sports policies are formed. The fact that governments have had to contend with an array of established sports organizations has constrained the policy options. Existing sports organizations at local, regional, and national levels are stakeholders, each bringing its own agenda and objectives to the policy arena. Thus, policymakers have had to contend with an array of demands, claims, and contentions. The chapters that follow describe a number of the resulting policy tensions.

Elite sports often contend with programs that seek to promote mass participation in sport. Sometimes this is a consequence of different stakeholders vying in the public arena. Sometimes it is because governments must implement their programs through existing sports organizations whose primary commitment is to elite sports. There may be a similar tension between spectator sports and participative sports. Spectator sports typically have a higher profile, but participative sports may serve a broader constituency.

Sometimes, sports policies conflict with other policy goals. For example, in some countries, sport's impact on the environment has been a matter of intense policy concern. What effect do sports facilities have? How can detrimental environmental impacts be minimized? Can sports programs be designed to strengthen public appreciation and concern for the environment?

In the final analysis, a great deal of the contention about sports policies pivots on contests over resources. One of the derivative concerns for policymakers is to find adequate means to fund sports programs and subsidies. Governments have instituted an array of alternatives, including tax exemptions, tax-based revenues, public lotteries, and merchandising.

The chapters in this handbook provide snapshots of sports policies in sixteen countries and in addition, describe the transformation of sports policies in the former Soviet bloc. Taken together, they illustrate the breadth and variety of government involvement in sports. In so doing, they provide a useful beginning for the comparative study of national sports policies.

REFERENCES

Bale, J. (1989). *Sports geography.* London: E. & F. N. Spon.

Berger, P., and Luckmann, T. (1967). *The social construction of reality.* London: Allen Lane.

Blair, S. N., Wells, C. L., Weathers, R. D., and Paffenbarger, R. S., Jr. (1994). Chronic disease: The physical activity dose-response controversy. In R. K. Dishman (ed.), *Advances in exercise adherence* (pp. 31–54). Champaign, Ill.: Human Kinetics.

Brownell, S. E. (1991). The changing relationship between sport and the state in the People's Republic of China. In F. Landry, M. Landry, and M. Yerles (eds.), *Sport . . . the third millennium* (pp. 295–302). Sainte-Foy, Quebec: Les Presses de l'Universite Laval.

Chalip, L. (1985). Policy research as social science: Outflanking the value dilemma. *Policy Studies Review, 5,* 287–308.

Chalip, L. (1987). Multiple narratives, multiple hierarchies: Selective attention, varied interpretations, and the structure of the Olympic program. In S. P. Kang, J. MacAloon, and R. DaMatta (eds.), *The Olympics and cultural exchange* (pp. 539–576). Seoul: Hanyang University Institute for Ethnological Studies.

Chalip, L. (1991). Sport and the state: The case of the United States. In F. Landry, M. Landry, and M. Yerles (eds.), *Sport . . . the third millennium* (pp. 243–250). Sainte-Foy, Quebec: Les Presses de l'Universite Laval.

Chalip, L. (1995). Policy analysis in sport management. *Journal of Sport Management, 9,* 1–13.

Chalip, L., Thomas, D., and Voyle, J. (1992). Sport, recreation and well-being. In D. Thomas and A. Veno (eds.), *Psychology and social change* (pp. 132–156). Palmerston North, New Zealand: Dunmore Press.

Crompton, J. L. (1995). Economic impact analysis of sports facilities and events: Eleven sources of misapplication. *Journal of Sport Management, 9,* 14–35.

De Knop, P. (1992, July). New trends in sports tourism. Paper presented at the Olympic Scientific Congress, Malaga, Spain.

Dryzek, J. (1982). Policy analysis as a hermeneutic activity. *Policy Sciences, 14,* 309–329.

Dunning, E. (1993). Sport in the civilizing process: Aspects of the development of modern sport. In E. G. Dunning, J. A. Maguire, and R. E. Pearton (eds.), *The sports process: A comparative and developmental approach* (pp. 39–70). Champaign, Ill.: Human Kinetics.

Garner, D. M., and Rosen, L. W. (1991). Eating disorders among athletes: Research and recommendations. *Journal of Applied Sport Science Research, 5* (2), 100–107.

Glassford, G. (1976). *Application of a theory of games to the transitional Eskimo culture.* New York: Arno.

Jarvie, G. (1993). Sport, politics, and South Africa (1948–1989). In E. G. Dunning, J. A. Maguire, and R. E. Pearton (eds.), *The sports process: A comparative and developmental approach* (pp. 265–279). Champaign, Ill.: Human Kinetics.

Johnson, A. T., and Frey, J. H. (eds.) (1985). *Government and sport: The public policy issues.* Totowa, N.J.: Rowman & Allanheld.

Kraus, J. F., and Conroy, C. (1984). Mortality and morbidity from injuries in sports and recreation. *Annual Review of Public Health, 5,* 163–192.

MacAloon, J. J. (1984). La Pitada Olimpica: Puerto Rico, international sport, and the constitution of politics. In E. M. Brunner (ed.), *Text, play, and story: The construction and reconstruction of self and society* (pp. 315–355). Washington, D.C.: American Anthropology Association.

Macintosh, D., Bedecki, T., and Franks, C. E. S. (1987). *Sport and politics in Canada: Federal government involvement since 1961.* Kingston, Ontario: McGill-Queen's University Press.

Macintosh, D., and Hawes, M. (1993). *Sport and Canadian diplomacy.* Kingston, Ontario: McGill-Queen's University Press.

Macintosh, D., and Whitson, D. (1990). *The game planners: Transforming Canada's sport system.* Kingston, Ontario: McGill-Queen's University Press.

Martinsen, E. W., and Stephens, T. (1994). Exercise and mental health in clinical and free-living populations. In R. K. Dishman (ed.), *Advances in exercise adherence* (pp. 55–72). Champaign, Ill.: Human Kinetics.

McCormack, J. B., and Chalip, L. (1988). Sport as socialization: A critique of methodological premises. *Social Science Journal, 25,* 83–92.

McHenry, D. E. (1980). The use of sports in policy implementation: The case of Tanzania. *The Journal of Modern African Studies, 18,* 237–256.

McIntosh, P. C. (1981). The sociology of sport in the ancient world. G. R. F. Luschen and G. H. Sage (eds.), *Handbook of social sciences of sport* (pp. 25–48). Champaign, Ill.: Stipes.

McIntosh, P. C. (1986). GOs, NGOs and QUANGOs: From wants to needs. Maxwell Howell Address to the North American Society for Sports History.

Noll, R. G. (ed.) (1974). *Government and the sports business.* Washington, D.C.: Brookings.

Palm, J. (1991). *Sport for all: Approaches from Utopia to reality.* Schorndorf: Verlag Karl Hofmann.

Riordan, J. (1977). *Sport in Soviet society.* Cambridge, UK: Cambridge University Press.

Rutten, A. (1993). Policy analysis and utilization process: The interplay between sport policy and applied sociology of sport. *International Review for the Sociology of Sport, 28,* 331–353.

Spector, M., and Kitsuse, J. I. (1977). *Constructing social problems.* Menlo Park, Calif: Cummings.

Stokvis, R. (1982). Conservative and progressive alternatives in the organization of sport. *International Social Science Journal, 10,* 197–208.

Stone, G. P. (1981). Sport as a community representation. In G. R. F. Luschen and G. H. Sage (eds.), *Handbook of social sciences of sport* (pp. 214–245). Champaign, Ill.: Stipes.

Thoma, J., and Chalip, L. (1996). *Sport governance in the global community.* Wheeling, W.V.: F.I.T.

Tricker, R., and Cook, D. L. (eds.) (1990). *Athletes at risk: Drugs and sport.* Dubuque, Iowa: William C. Brown.

Watson, G. G. (1977). Games, socialization and parental values: Social class differences in parental evaluation of Little League baseball. *International Review for the Sociology of Sport, 12* (2), 117–148.

Whitson, D. (1983). Pressures on regional games in a dominant metropolitan culture: The case of shinty. *Leisure Studies, 2,* 139–154.

Wilson, J. (1994). *Playing by the rules: Sport, society, and the state.* Detroit: Wayne State University Press.

1

Australian Sports Policy

Peter J. Farmer and Steve Arnaudon

INTRODUCTION

The Australian sports ethos is unique in the world. In a relatively small country (in population terms), over 150 sports are actively played, many of them at the pinnacle of international competition. At the Barcelona Olympic Games (1992), Australia was ranked in the top ten nations, and it sports a range of world champions in non-Olympic sports. Almost 40 percent of the population are registered members of sporting clubs, and Australian Rules Football matches in Melbourne regularly draw crowds of 100,000 or more. Australians are avid recreationalists and flock to beaches, fun runs, and ski fields in ever increasing numbers. Corresponding to this level of activity is a greater level of television coverage of sport than in virtually any other nation. To be an Australian and not have some involvement in sports is almost considered unpatriotic.

Yet, there are a growing number of concerns about Australian sports—issues such as the increasing number of Australians who are physically inactive; the lack of physical education within school systems; a range of access and equity issues, particularly for disadvantaged sections of the community; and the ever present need to keep up with international sports technology, particularly when,

This chapter is dedicated to the late Darryl Chapman, associate professor at the University of New England at Northern Rivers. Chapman held positions as the assistant director of the NSW Department of Sport and Recreation, the technical committee of the Australian Coaching Council, and many technical and editorial committees attached to the National Rugby League Coaching Scheme. Darryl Chapman represented Australia in Rugby League in 1959–60.

in the main, Australia competes out of season in world championships and Olympic Games.

The Australian policy response to these mixed influences has in itself been mixed. Surprisingly, there was virtually no governmental support of sport in Australia until the early 1970s. The support that was then forthcoming was largely a response to perceived failings in the national sports system. In fact, it has only been since the mid-1980s that Australian sports policy, at the public and private levels, has come of age and been recognized as a legitimate area of public expenditure requiring an integrated policy approach to fulfill specific objectives. These objectives, as elsewhere in the world, are identified as the two "Ps" of *performance* and *participation*. The means by which government policy meets these objectives reflects the cultural and sporting diversity at the national level and the "give it a go" ethos of the community.

ORIENTATION

Australia has varied terrains, such as desert, tropical rain forest, mountains, plains, and beaches. The continent stretches from the Indian Ocean in the west to the Pacific Ocean in the east, the Arafura and Timor Seas in the north, and the Antarctic Ocean in the south, covering some 3 million square miles.

From an historical perspective, Australia has a long and interesting cultural heritage through its Aboriginal population, but a relatively short modern history since being "discovered" by Captain James Cook (1770). It was first colonized in 1788 (Larcombe, 1970, p. 4). Since this initial settlement, comprised primarily of convicted felons, rapid growth and expansion has resulted in a population from the four corners of the Earth.

By 1900 Australia's first Parliament had been established and was granted autonomy in 1901. Although officially recognized as an independent and sovereign nation, Australia was still tied to Great Britain through monarchy, policy, and common interests in sport.

Currently, Australia's population is approximately 17 million, of predominately European ancestry, especially from Great Britain, Scotland, and Ireland. After World War II, massive immigration from Greece, Italy, and other southern European countries occurred. More recently, Australia again experienced a shift in its immigration pattern, with an increasing proportion being from Southeast Asian communities. Australia is said to be a true "melting pot" of populations and cultures.

Government

Australia has a three-tiered political system consisting of the federal or commonwealth, state, and local levels. The first tier is the Commonwealth. This level comprises representatives from six states and two territories, with the federal capital and seat of government in Canberra (Australian Capital Territory).

The federal system is a social-representative democracy composed of a legislative and executive branch. Political authority, however, appears to be squarely in the hands of the popularly elected party, with the executive being the prime minister and cabinet. This federal government has a significant influence and impact on the daily lives of all Australians, regardless of location or status.

The state government level is similar in operation and function to the federal system. Governance is generally through two elected, representative parliamentary units, overseen by the popularly elected political party under the leadership of the premier and cabinet. The third level is the "local" or "council" level. The community structure recognizes a mayor and alderman as the legally constituted representatives. There are three predominant political entities—Labor, Liberal, and National or Country parties—although various smaller parties and independent members are often represented. Each state and territory appoints a minister responsible for sports and recreation. Coordination is maintained through regular meetings of the Sport and Recreation Ministers' Council. New Zealand and Papua New Guinea sports ministers attend these meetings as observers.

SPORT: AUSTRALIAN STYLE

Australia is a product of its unique history and heritage, diverse citizenry, and social democratic political system. These elements have had a direct impact on sport and its development. From its early history, Australians have been uniquely involved with all types of sports activities. Although in its formative years, as reported by the Reverend John Dunmore Lang (1833), Australia was a country whose pastimes were "gambling, rough sports and the drinking that usually accompanied them" (Pearson and O'Hara, 1977, p. 49). The history of Australian sport has been refashioned in its own image and for its own purposes. Games were imported principally from Britain and Ireland. Games such as soccer, horse-racing, cricket, and even Australian Rules had been played in England and Ireland for centuries.

As early as the 1870s, with a population of 2 million compared with England's 23 million, Australian cricketers beat England's cricketers. This was only the beginning. Before long, Australia's rowers or "scullers" beat England and the rest of the world on the Thames, and its rifle shooters trounced the Americans at Philadelphia in 1876. Boxing, evident from the "First Fleet" (1788), created legends known throughout the world, such as Larry Foley, Young Griffo, Les Darcy, and Lionel Rose. In fact, the 1908 title fight between Jack Johnson and Tommie Burns was hailed as the largest "gate in the world to date" (Baker, 1965, p. 184).

As an emerging nation so far removed from Europe and North America, Australia has consistently striven for equality and acceptability. This was brought out by Dunstan (1973), who charged that Australia had produced more world champions than any other country in "boxing, running, cycling, swimming, tennis, football, cricket, rowing, squash, surfing, horse-riding, sailing and golf. . . . Yet even here the enthusiasts are at work with a suitably chilling determination'' (p. 58). In every sport, Australia has produced household names, not just in Australia, but throughout the world. Names such as Jack Brabham, Sir Donald Bradman, Ron Clarke, Margaret Court, Betty Cuthbert, Les Darcy, Herb Elliot, Dawn Fraser, Lew Hoad, Majorie Jackson, the Konrad, Rod Laver, Lionel Rose, Ken Rosewall, Frank Sedgman, and Shirley Strickland are indicative of the men and women who became household names after achieving international success in sport. A 1962 *Sports Illustrated* report ranked Australia sixth out of thirty-four nations; however, after weighting the scores, on a per capita basis, Australia ranked first (Daly, 1985, p. 2). Australia has achieved a presence in sport that very few countries achieve in any endeavor. This essence was captured by Horne (1971) when he stated:

Sport to many Australians is life and the rest shadow. Sport has been the one national institution that has no knockers. To many it is considered a sign of degeneracy not to be interested in it. . . . Australia's success at competitive international sport is considered an important part of its foreign policy. (p. 37)

STRUCTURE OF AUSTRALIAN SPORT

Although producing a plethora of outstanding teams and individuals, Australia's sports tradition has not always been as deliberate and purposeful as it is today. From the outset, individuals or groups succeeded despite the lack of an organized sporting system.

The System: The Sports Club Organization

This system, adapted from the English model, was designed to make sport and sports participation available to the working "classes." It consists of a local, state, and national organizational structure in each sport. At the grass-roots level are the 30,000 or so local sports clubs, with an elected executive responsible for conducting local competitions, coaching, development in local schools, and fund-raising. In some sports, a regional organization, responsible for regional competitions, is apparent (especially in country areas). The club system varies from sport to sport in size and strength, being particularly strong in lawn bowls, golf, and tennis. Other sports, such as volleyball and swimming, rely more heavily on a competition system organized through schools.

State bodies are elected from local/regional representatives and are responsible for the conduct of state competitions and championships, talent identification and development, fund-raising, marketing, public relations, event promotions, and selection of the state team for the national championships. These bodies serve as a liaison with the state government.

National organizations are usually composed of an executive committee drawn from the various state organizations. They are involved in organizing and conducting national championships, liaising with the international/parent body, marketing and promoting national events, fund-raising for national teams, selecting and developing talent, selecting national teams for international events, and liaising with the federal government.

Other elements in this schema are the umbrella organizations, such as the Australian Olympic Committee, the Australian Commonwealth Games Association, and the Confederation of Australian Sport. Although school sport could be considered an umbrella organization, it is fused into the structured framework already presented.

The Australian Olympic Committee (AOC), formed in 1920, serves as Australia's liaison with the International Olympic Committee. As such, it is responsible for the selection, preparation, outfitting, transportation, and participation of teams in the summer and winter Olympic Games. It operates through affiliated councils in each of the six states. The ten-member executive committee operates via subcommittees or commissions responsible for medical, forward-planning, constitution, financial, sponsorship, solidarity, and team justification matters. The AOF works closely with governments that provide supplemental funding above the funds raised through the AOF's sponsorship and marketing activities. The Australian Commonwealth Games Association, established in 1929, like the Australian Olympic Committee, is responsible for the coordination and preparation of the Australian team that competes in the quadrennial British Commonwealth Games.

The Confederation of Australian Sport, created in 1976, represents over 100 Australian sports-related organizations. It has become, according to Stewart (1985), a ''voice for sport and to undertake lobbying activities . . . act as a liaison point for government agencies, to encourage general participation in sport and the raising of national levels of fitness, to advance the development of sports administration and upgrading of sports coaching standards, and initiate and/or conduct research'' (p. 36). This structure affects a top-down approach, with the local groups generally doing little to affect the national level. This is representative of the pyramid-based model of sport which is typical throughout the world (Figure 1.1).

Since the early 1970s, development of Australian sport has been the result of both business and the sports club system with substantial government assistance.

Professional Sport

Professional sport in Australia's early days focused on such activities as boxing, footraces, horse-racing, greyhound racing, wrestling, and sailing. In fact, any sports activity that involved waging or gambling would fit in this category. More recently, however, the number and variety of professional sports activities have increased to include Australian Rules Football, Rugby League, Tennis, Cricket, Basketball, Baseball, Soccer, Golf, Horse-racing, Greyhound Racing, Trotting or Harness Racing, Road-Racing, Surfboarding, Sailboarding or Windsurfing, Off-Shore Racing or Yachting, Professional Wrestling, Cycling, Stock-

Figure 1.1
A Model of Pyramid-Based Sport

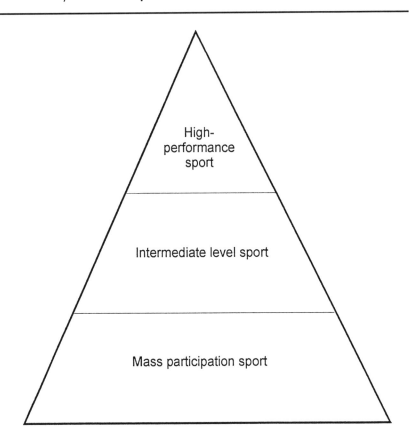

Car Racing, Motorcycling, Auto-Racing, Skiing, Bowling (Ten-Pin), Power-Boat Racing, Triathlon, and Gliding.

Professional sports do not generally receive direct governmental assistance and are not the focus of any specific legislation, other than that relating to the regulation of the horse-racing industry. Australian professional sport is self-sufficient and self-funding. According to Stewart (1985), ''(the) annual gross revenue of the Victorian Football League (VFL) is about $A40 million, the National Soccer League (NSL) about $A6.5 million and the National Basketball League (NBL) about $A3.5 million'' (1985, p. 45).

Sport and sports-related events taking place in Australia are financed primarily by Australian business and organizations. Examples are the World Cup (Cricket), initially sponsored by Mr. Kerry Packer; and the Winfield Cup (Rugby League), sponsored by the Winfield Company. In a number of states, revenues generated from horse-racing are used to support state sports programs, while more recently, some states and territories have established health foundations that have directed tobacco taxes toward sporting organizations and events. Professional sports, from the perspective of development, receive financial help from bodies such as the Australian Sports Commission. Over 100 sports are assisted through the Commission's Sports Assistance Scheme. In the case of "professional" sports, such assistance is directed toward administration, talent identification, junior development, and the like, rather than toward the elite end of the sport, which is funded by private sponsorship.

Notable Sport Events

Annually, Australia supports a number of sporting events that attract international sponsorship, participation, and mass interest. For all intents and purposes, these events are self-supporting. Examples of these well-known events are:

- The Melbourne Cup annual horserace staged in Melbourne, Victoria. Likened to the Kentucky Derby, all Australia stops to view and bet on this 100+ year old racing spectacular.
- VFL Grand Final Annual Australian Rules Club Final held in Melbourne, Victoria, similar to the NFL Superbowl. More than 100,000 people view this local spectacle, as well as millions of people around the world.

Other events include:

- Australian Open: Tennis; Melbourne, Australia
- Australian Grand Prix: Auto-race; Adelaide, South Australia
- Winfield Cup: Rugby League; Sydney, New South Wales
- Australian Open: Golf; alternate sites in Australia
- Stawell Gift: Professional Foot-Race; Stawell, Victoria
- City to Surf: 14 kilometer Road-race; Sydney, New South Wales
- Sydney-Hobart Yacht Race: Off-Shore Racing; Sydney, New South Wales
- Test Matches: These are international competitions between a variety of countries particularly in Cricket and Rugby League

In the recent past, Australia has hosted such international mega-sports events as the Olympic Games (1956); British Commonwealth Games (1962 and 1982); America's Cup (1987); World Cup Track and Field (1977); World Cup Cricket (1992); World Netball Championships (1992); and World Youth Soccer Cup (1993).

Foreign Athletes and Coaches

Since the beginning of Australian sport, there has been a tradition of foreign players and coaches working and making their name in the Australian community. Imports initially from New Zealand and Great Britain were involved in the professional sports of soccer, cricket, and Rugby League. Recently, foreign penetration has been substantial in the National Basketball League (NBL), which limits foreign national basketball players to two for each club in the league. A number of highly ranked athletes and coaches have also been attracted to Australia from East European countries in sports as diverse as track and field, cycling, rowing, and weightlifting. The growing strength of Australian sport is also seen in surfing, golf, tennis, rugby union, and soccer, whose athletes compete full time in international circuits. Australian coaches and administrators are highly regarded and eagerly sought after by Asian countries.

GOVERNMENT AND SPORT

Australia, Greece, and Great Britain are the only three nations whose teams have competed in all Olympic Games. Historically, federal government assistance for international sport competition was limited. The only federal government-oriented assistance before the 1970s came in the form of facility construction during the Depression; assistance in preparation for the 1938 and 1962 Commonwealth Games; and the staging of the 1956 Melbourne Olympic Games (Jacques and Pavai, 1976, p. 46).

Support for sport was seen to be the province of local government, which has traditionally provided considerable assistance for sporting facilities (e.g., swimming pools) and passive recreation (e.g., children's play equipment). At the federal level, John Gorton, Liberal prime minister in 1972, summed up the reason for the government's nonsupport of sport: ''On the question of sporting activities . . . the government does not believe it should enter into these matters but that the running of sporting activities should be done by the sporting bodies concerned'' (Going for Gold, 1989, p. 56).

The election of the Labor party and its prime minister Gough Whitlam in late 1972, saw the first ongoing federal support for sport through the establishment of a sports portfolio—the Department of Sport and Recreation. The purpose of this action was to provide Australia's citizenry with the opportunity for mass sports participation.

In 1975 the Bloomfield report entitled ''The Role, Scope and Development of Recreation in Australia,'' commissioned by the Whitlam government, produced recommendations pertaining to mass and elite sport participation. An additional report, prepared by Dr. Allan Coles (1975), identified the need to develop a center of excellence to cater to Australia's elite athletic community.

A Liberal/National coalition government under the leadership of Malcolm Fraser came to power in 1975 with a mandate to decrease government spending in many areas, including sport. From 1975 to 1979, spending for sports dropped from $A7.4 million to $A5.8 million. This budget decline coincided with a decline in Australia's international sports reputation. This decline can be illustrated by the triumphs of the 1956 Melbourne Olympic Games, where Australia won thirty-six Olympic medals, thirteen of which were gold, compared with the Montreal Olympic Games (1976) where only five medals were won and none of them gold.

The Montreal "debacle" served notice that Australia's sport had declined and was in need of repair. Australia "was the land of Bradman and Lindrum, of swimmers, athletes, tennis players and cricketers. Why were there so few heroes and heroines now? Why were Australians no longer winning?" (Daly, 1985, p. 2). Was the system at fault? Although the club system of Australian sport was still going strong, most sports operations were underfunded and administered on an ad hoc basis using volunteer "kitchen table" administration and untrained coaches. By the international standards of the 1970s, this situation was not unusual, but if sport was to survive and prosper, the system had to change. Something had to be done and quickly if the trend was to be reversed. Australia could no longer rely solely on its "natural" advantages (e.g., a good climate and ready access to inexpensive nutritional foods) in an increasingly competitive and sophisticated world sports scene.

Over the next quadrennium, a series of events provided the impetus for government support of sports at various levels. Apparently, after Australia's dismal performance at the Montreal Olympic Games, a parliamentary investigation into amateur sport and the government's role in its development was conducted. During this same period, the Confederation of Australian Sport, a national body representing Australian sport, developed its "Master Plan for Sport" (1980). This plan involved the federal government formulating a national sports policy and the requisite financial support.

During this same period, at the state government level, entities responsible for sports and recreation were developed, such as departments for sport. In some cases these bodies were also responsible for racing. This trend began in Victoria in 1972, and other states quickly followed suit. Regardless of form, states began to play their part in offering the Australian people the opportunity to participate in sports and recreational activities.

Another important element was introduced at the time of the XXII Moscow Olympic Games (1980). As a result of the Australian government's support of the Western boycott, poor results in the Montreal Olympic Games (1976), and the support of sports advocate and former minister in charge of sport, Robert J. Ellicott, the minister of home affairs and environment, the Australian Institute of Sport was developed (1980) in Canberra. It was born out of a $A2.7 million federal grant.

Beginning with only seven sports, the Australian Institute of Sport (AIS) was charged with assistance in developing Australia's elite athletes. Financial and political support for sport was again a reality. Questions of "elite versus mass participation," "centralization versus decentralization," and "immediate versus long-term results" now became the central themes in Australian sports policy. The Institute was hailed by many as a panacea for Australian sport. However, the early 1980s were not accompanied by any significant programs to promote sports participation or by an integrated approach involving national sporting bodies and state authorities. Although "the formulas" were reasonably good, the level of funding, after adjustment for inflation, declined during the early to mid-1980s. This trend was reversed in 1988–89. Since that time, there has been a substantial increase in federal funding, largely through a revamped Australian Sports Commission (ASC).

During this period, the federal government developed and introduced a range of programs, through the Australian Sports Commission, to revise the standards of Australian sport and to increase the participation base of sport. These included:

- The Sports Assistance Scheme providing support to most of the 122 registered national sporting organizations in areas such as administration, coaching, development, and international competition.
- An increase in the Australian Institute of Sport programs from seven to twenty-one sports.
- The National Coach Accreditation Scheme which has now accredited over 100,000 coaches.
- A range of school sports programs under the banner of AUSSIE SPORT, which now reach some 2 million children in 90 percent of Australian schools.
- The National Sports Foundation to encourage tax-deductible private donations to sports.
- The AUSSIE ABLE program to provide assistance for athletes and organizations supporting athletes with disabilities.
- The Australian Athletes Scholarship Scheme to assist world-ranked athletes with the additional costs involved in maintaining these levels.
- The Women and Sport Program to provide research, awareness-raising, marketing and training advice, and generally to work toward gender equity in sport.
- The National Sports Information Center.
- The National Sports Science and Sports Medicine Center.
- The National Coach Scholarship Program.
- The National Sports Research Program.
- The Australian College of Sports Education.

The institutional base of federal support has also changed with the amalgamation of the Australian Institute of Sport (AIS) and the Australian Sports Commission. In 1989 the independent Australian Sports Drug Agency was established to conduct wider drug testing, in and out of competition. As an independent organization, the Drug Agency is able to conduct drug education campaigns.

The Drug Agency is now funded by the federal government to budget $A2 million per annum. Along with these federal initiatives the states organized their own programs. For example, New South Wales has developed state and regional academies/institutes, a state elite squad, youth sport programs, and coaching initiatives to support the sporting efforts within their state.

Today, sport in Australia is being supported at all levels of government. At the local level, the priority is the construction and maintenance of recreational and sporting facilities. State and territory authorities have focused on participation efforts, which include facility enhancement and athlete and coach development, while still developing their elite athletes and academies. At the federal level, some financial assistance has been available for the development of community sporting facilities. Federal sports policy has had two major objectives: to promote and encourage community participation in sports, and to significantly improve Australia's sporting performance at the elite level (Australian Sports Commission: Strategic Plan, 1991 to 1993).

These responsibilities are evidenced in the information supplied to the parliamentary Inquiry into Sports Funding and Administration in 1989, which publicly disclosed the level of government funding. It was estimated that aggregate government funding for sports and recreation was $A900 million. This was broken down as follows:

- Local—73.0 percent or $A660 million
- State/territory—21.0 percent or $A185 million
- Commonwealth (federal government)—6.0 percent or $A55 million (Going for Gold, 1989, p. 10).

Economic Impact of Sport

During the 1980s, sport was recognized as having an economic value or contributing to the economy. According to the Department of the Arts, Sport, the Environment, Tourism, and Territories (DASETT), through information contained in the 1989 document entitled "Economic Impact of Sport and Recreation-Household Expenditure":

6.5 percent of a total weekly household expenditure or $A31.18 of $A477.91 was on sport and recreation . . . in the total economy, sport and recreation accounts for between 19.2 and 22.6 percent of total private consumption and between 8.6 and 10.1 percent GDP. It is estimated that household participation in sport and recreation activities contributed between $A22 and $A26 billion to the Australian economy and that about 600,000 people were employed in Australia. (Going for Gold, 1989, p. 11)

Recent studies emphasize that "Elite sporting events make a contribution to economic development . . . not only the initial expenditure but the expenditures

Table 1.1
Commonwealth Assistance for Sport and Recreation

Year	Expenditure and Total Sport and Recreation (Australian $'s in Millions)
1970/71 - 1979/80	49.9
1980/81 - 1989/90	266.1
1990/91 - 1995/96	429.1

generated by that initial expenditure, i.e. the multiplier effect'' (Going for Gold, 1989, p. 12).

Studies were undertaken in anticipation of hosting the 1996 Olympic Games in Melbourne. This information postulated a national economic gain of $A12.2 billion; 86 percent of this gross economic gain ($10.5 billion) would flow to the host state. The economic benefit would last longer than a decade. Federal government revenues would have been increased by $2.6 billion. The host state government revenues would be increased by $254 million, and local government revenues by $160 million. Finally, spending by international and interstate visitors of $2.4 billion was forecast for this event. Other benefits that often accrue to Olympic host cities are new and improved facilities and infrastructure that benefit the community after the Olympic Games have concluded. Overall, this event could have provided a major boost to the tourism and convention industries, encouraged investment, opened new trade markets, increased sports participation, and substantially enhanced the status of the host city in the international community.

Federal Government and Sport

The federal government has approached the development of sport through the adoption of a model that represents sport in Australia. This model involves the elements of elite sport and mass participation in a hierarchical structure that promotes the idea that the ''larger the base, the higher the peak''

Federal Expenditures

In the early years of government financial support, sport was ''regarded as a froth bubble industry, in much the same way tourism was regarded a decade ago'' (Going for Gold, 1989, p. 8). In recent years this attitude has changed dramatically, as is evidenced by the Commonwealth budget expenditures for sport. The federal government expended some $326,758,000 from 1978–79 to 1991–92 (see Table 1.1).

A recent feature of federal funding has been the use of four-year planning and funding cycles. The first of these programs, titled ''Next Step,'' was introduced in 1988–89 following the outcome of the "Going for Gold" parliamentary inquiry. It provided for $230 million over four years but was terminated one year early, to be replaced by the "Maintain the Momentum" program. This program, which is now aligned to the Olympics' four-year cycle, will provide $293 million to Australian sport largely through the Australian Sports Commission (ASC).

The Australian Sports Commission

The Australian Sports Commission was incorporated by amendments to the Australian Sports Commission Act in 1989 along with the Australian Institute of Sport. The objectives of the ASC, as set out in this legislation, are:

- To provide leadership in the development of sport in Australia.
- To encourage increased participation and improved performance by Australians in sport.
- To provide resources, services, and facilities to enable Australians to pursue and achieve excellence in sport while also furthering their educational and vocational skills and other aspects of their personal development.
- To improve the sporting abilities of Australians generally through the improvement of the standard of sports coaches.
- To foster cooperation in sport between Australia and other countries through the provision of access to resources, services, and facilities related to sport.
- To encourage the private sector to contribute to the funding of sport to supplement assistance by the Commonwealth (Australian Commission Act, Number 12, 1989).

The Australian Sports Commission is composed of five divisions (Figure 1.2): Australian Institute of Sport, Professional and Technical Services, Sports Development and Policy, Marketing and Communications, and Corporate Services. The Australian Sports Commission budget for the 1992–93 financial year was $63 million. This was allocated among the five divisions of the Commission as follows:

- Australian Institute of Sport provided scholarships (usually twelve months) for athletes in twenty-two sports who generally "live-in" receiving high-level coaching, competition, and sports services support. It also provided short (one- to two-week) camps for national teams under the National Sports Program—$22.7 million.
- Professional and Technical Services—medicine, science, information, research—$5.0 million.
- Sports Development provided grants for over 100 national sporting organizations, as well as broad-based participation programs, such as Aussie Sports, programs for children, and support for the Australian Coaching Council—$23.9 million.

Figure 1.2
Organizational Structure of the Australian Sports Commission

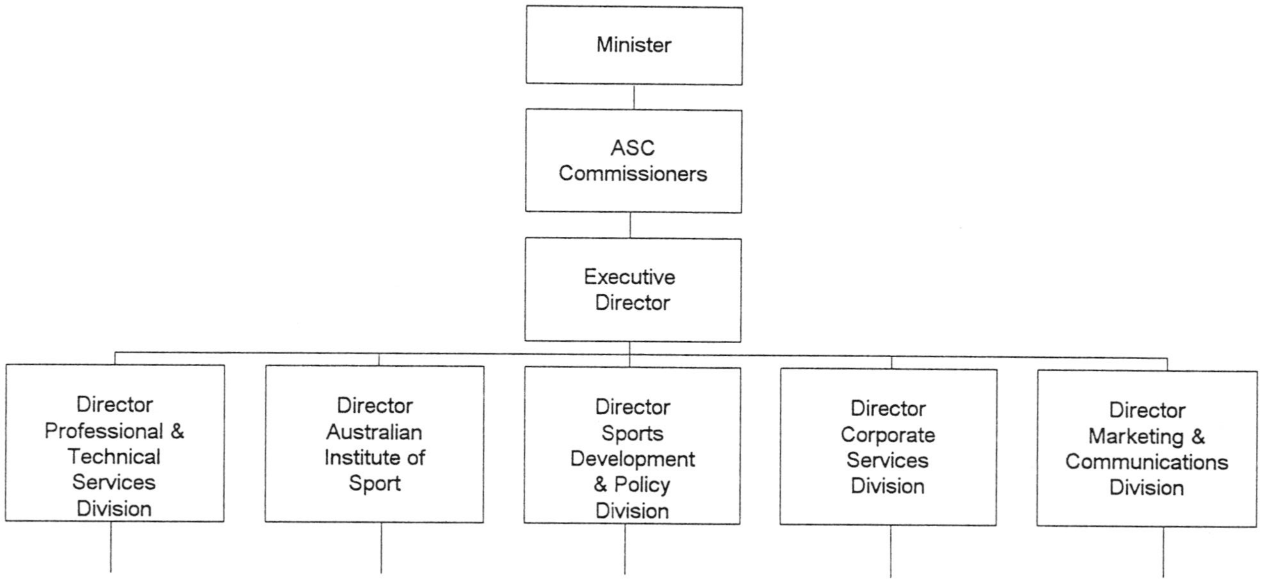

- Sports Science & Medicine Center
  - Physiotherapy
  - Medicine
  - Psychology
  - Biomechanics
  - Physiology & Nutrition
- National Sport Information Center
- National Sports Research Center

- Elite Sports
- Intensive Training Centers
  - State Institute Liaison
  - Scholarships
  - SS/SM Coordination
  - ALS Regional Units
  - NSF & STEP
- Athlete Development, Education & Welfare
- Scholarship Sports

- Sports Development
  - NSO Liaison
  - Sport Development Plans
  - Funding Agreements
  - AOC Liaison
  - Events
  - Games Assistance
  - Disabled
  - Sports Participation
  - AUSSIESPORTS
  - Veterans
  - Policy & Coordination
  - Secretarial
  - Women in Sport
  - SOORS/SRMC
  - Australian Coaching Council

- Commercial & Accounting
  - Planning, Budgeting & Review
  - Personnel & Services
  - Facilities
  - Residence Management
  - Computer Services
  - Internal Audit

- Marketing
- Public Relations
- Publications
- Australian Sports Foundation
- ALS Shop

- Marketing and Communications—marketing, public relations, and publications—$0.8 million.

- Corporate Services—facilities maintenance, computing, personnel, finance, evaluation—$10.5 million. (Australian Sports Commission: Unpublished budget material)

POLICY GOALS

The objectives of the ASC are increased participation and improved performance of Australians in sports. The ASC has abandoned the traditional pyramid structure of sports development in favor of an approach that recognizes the following:

- Involvement in physical activity and sport in a nonthreatening environment during primary school is the best means of attracting sports participants. Thus, the Aussie Sport program evolved.

- Involvement in organized sports through a strong sporting club system is the best means of retaining lifelong sports participants. Hence, the Commission developed programs to attract, train, and retain sports volunteers and to develop strategic planning within sporting clubs.

- Access and equity are important considerations either within or outside the club system. Hence, a range of programs, including Aussie Able, the Women and Sport program, Masters Sport, and Aboriginal Sport, were established.

- A professional approach to sports administration and management is necessary at all levels of sporting organizations in order to maximize the efficiency and effectiveness of the sports delivery system. Hence began the programs of assistance to sport through the Australian Coaching Council, the Australian College of Sports Education, and the National Sports Information Center.

- Investment must be made in "cutting edge" developments sport, with management of the outcome of such investment progressively devolved to sports for implementation. Hence began the programs of the National Sports Science and Sports Medicine Center, and the National Sports Research program.

- Elite athletes, and those who aspire to become such, should be given every encouragement to reach their potential, particularly through access to the best available coaching, sports science and medicine, and international competition. Hence evolved the various state institutes/academies, as well as support to national sporting organizations for their coaching and competitive programs.

- The overall approach to sports delivery in Australia should be conducted within a framework that discourages the use of performance-enhancing drugs, encourages corporate sponsorship of sport, and endeavors to foster closer international relations through sport.

The organizational and program structure of the ASC is designed to facilitate the implementation of these policy goals in cooperation with national sporting organizations and state and territory sports authorities. In respect to foreign policy goals, the Commission endeavors to ensure that Australian athletes have access to high-level international competition in a manner that assists their development while fostering closer international cooperation through sport. The Commission is also mindful of its responsibilities to assist in the development of broad-based participation in sports in neighboring countries and in developing countries. In association with the Australian Olympic Committee, it operates the Oceania Training Center at the AIS, which brings athletes and coaches from various Pacific Ocean nations to the AIS for intensive training and development. The Commission is also fostering the international use of the highly successful Aussie Sport program, with a major pilot project currently being undertaken in South Africa. The concept is also being fostered through the Commonwealth Heads of Government Working Party on the Future of Sport in the Commonwealth.

The Australian College of Sports Education is being used as a vehicle to assist in the development of sports in the Asian region by way of intensive short courses for Asian sports administrators and coaches. During 1993, courses were being provided for sports administrators from Indonesia and the Pacific Island nations.

EVALUATION OF POLICIES AND PROGRAMS

Australia's results at the 1992 Barcelona Olympics were the best since the "home" Olympics in 1956 and places the country squarely in the top ten nations in Olympic sports success. Currently, Australia has world champions in a range of non-Olympic sports such as Rugby League, netball, squash, and surfing. The Aussie Sport program is reaching some 2 million children, and there are over 100,000 registered coaches under the National Coach Accreditation Scheme.

The ASC has embarked on a full and progressive evaluation of its programs involving external review by the Department of Finance. Thirty-one sports were selected for an in-depth analysis, including twenty-five of the highly funded sports, as well as a controlled group of six lesser funded sports. The analysis indicated a noticeable trend in improvement in elite performance in recent years, with a close correlation between performance levels and funding levels. The analysis also showed that elite athlete development requires a complex and interrelated set of programs. It is apparent that the two areas of particular importance were international competition and coaching. Of the thirty-one sports reviewed, twenty-one clearly demonstrated improved international performance in world standards from 1976 onward, taking into account changes in the strength of international competition. Twenty-two of those sports clearly improved their international performances after the substantial increase in federal funding in 1988. The analysis also showed that the depth of Australia's elite level talent has improved since 1988.

In the area of sports participation the evaluation was hampered by a lack of time series, or baseline data, particularly in the period before 1985. Nevertheless, analysis showed that most sports have reported an increase in registration and/ or participation at all levels from junior and senior to elite. Children's attitudes to sport have become more positive over the last decade, this change being attributable in some degree to the Aussie Sport program. The level of coach accreditation also clearly mirrors the apparent benefit of increased government funding of the ASC's programs.

Although the independent evaluation has been overwhelmingly positive in terms of the impact of ASC programs on both "performance" and "participation," there is still some cause for concern. First, the statistical basis for determining levels of participation has not been comprehensive and needs to be addressed both by the Australian Sports Commission (ASC) and the Australian Bureau of Statistics. Indeed, the ASC is currently developing and refining a comprehensive computerized package on sports registration and participation which has been used on a trial basis with Australian gymnastics. Second, the link and impact of sport participation on fitness and health are still tenuous. Again, this is due to inadequate recordkeeping and unsatisfactory statistical analyses. Until longitudinal data are available on these subjects, it will be difficult to develop policy parameters that will provide substantive proof that sport is indeed a preventative health measure and consequently worthy of additional funding. Until that time, the federal sport budget will likely continue to represent just one-half of 1 percent of the federal health budget.

CONCLUSION—THE SPORTS POLICY DEBATE

The fluctuations of government interest in sports as a legitimate area of public policy over the past twenty years can be summarized as

- An initial interest (early 1970s) in sport as an access and equity issue associated with the social reform of the nation.
- A decline in the late 1970s associated with economic rationalism.
- A renewed interest in the early 1980s, perhaps panicked by distressing international sports results.
- A coming of age of sports policy in its own right in the late 1980s, spurred by the activities of the Confederation of Australian Sport and the Australian Olympic Committee. More significant, however, was the emerging sophistication of the sports movement itself, through the numerous national sporting bodies and their constituents.

While Australians have a deep passion for sport, which is reflected in their spending patterns, governments have nevertheless grappled with the necessity for a public involvement. This issue is reflected in a comparison of the level of public funding of the arts and culture to the funding of sport. Whereas public funding for the arts has long been seen as a means of portraying Australia's image and sophistication, sport funding has not had the same priority in domestic or international policy.

It has sometimes been said that the Australian sports industry is about a decade behind the tourism industry or the culture industry in articulating its position and worth to society. Consequently, it has only been in recent years that a clear position has emerged. This position has been based on quite daunting statistics, some positive, some negative, which collectively galvanized the sector into action. For example:

- There are 6.5 million registered members of sports clubs; only 31 percent of men and 22 percent of women were regularly participating in organized sporting activities (DAS-ETT, 1991).

- Seventy-three percent of men and women participate in some form of physical exercise. Only 6 percent of men and 4 percent of women exercised at a level considered to have a training effect on the heart and lungs (National Heart Foundation, 1993).

- Thirty-six percent of Australian school students do not participate in organized sports (Australian Sports Commission, 1991).

- An estimated 6.0 percent (161,000) of all hospitalized persons were admitted due to cardiovascular disease. Of these, 63 percent did not exercise, with a further 27 percent exercising at a low level (Bureau of Statistics, 1992).

- An estimated 280,000 people are employed in the sport and recreation industry, of which some 66,000 are within sporting organizations producing a revenue of over $300 million per annum (DASETT, 1991a).

- Household expenditure on sports amounts to an estimated 2 percent of discretionary expenditures (Australian Bureau of Statistics, 1991a).

- Some 1.1 million Australians provide voluntary services to sports, with a total unpaid contribution of $1.6 billion per annum (DASETT, 1989).

- A range of international sporting events produce significant economic benefits. For example, the Grand Slam Australian Tennis Open provides direct income to Melbourne of some $20.4 million annually. This figure rises to $33.8 million, when multipliers are applied (National Institute of Economic and Industry Research, 1990).

These and other indicators are being used to demonstrate that sport is a significant contributor to the national economy. While sport is growing in terms of participation and associated benefits, there is still significant room for increased socioeconomic benefits through the sector. Against this background, the key to much of Australian sports policy can be linked to four significant events in the late 1980s.

- The parliamentary inquiry into sports funding which recommended substantial increases in federal funding of sport.

- Legislation to establish the Australian Sports Commission, incorporating the Australian Institute of Sport, and to establish a separate Australian Sports Drug Agency.

- The conviction within the federal government arising from the above that its sports policy must be strategic, long term, and matched by a funding commitment.

• The conviction among sports program managers that a sophisticated and professional approach to sports management was the way to ensure that the increased funding was not wasted.

There is no longer a debate in Australian sporting circles as to whether funding for sport is a government priority. It seems certain that the pattern of four-year funding cycles of sport, set against strategic plans of organizations such as the Australian Sports Commission and accompanied by a regular evaluation process and review, is now part of the ongoing scene for Australian sports. The sports policy debate has shifted to the key issues concerning distribution of funding, namely, selective versus broad based; centralized versus decentralized; elite versus participation.

The Australian Sports Commission provides financial assistance to over one hundred sports, but the top forty sports receive 92 percent of the funding. There is a hierarchy of support for sports starting with the top eight who have scholarship programs under the Australian Institute of Sport, as well as Intensive Training Centres located in state capital cities. There are twenty-two sports, including the above eight, which have scholarship programs through the Australian Institute of Sport. There are an additional eighteen sports that receive over $100,000 per annum to assist in their administration, coaching, competition, and development. This mixture of support is designed to provide a balance between targeted and broad-based support. Quite clearly, it has not satisfied everyone's needs. Concern is sometimes expressed that the targeting favors Olympic sports at the expense of some traditional Australian sports with large numbers of participants. In recent years, however there has been a move toward inclusion of more non-Olympic sports within the AIS program.

The initial establishment of the AIS in Canberra as a centralized center for sports excellence in Australia has gradually been supplanted by an integrated national approach under which various AIS programs are now located in state capital cities, as, of course, are the various state institutes of sport which receive federal financial assistance through the Intensive Training Centre program. The essential policy dilemma is to ensure that the individual athlete can train within a living environment that is most conducive to his or her performance, and yet ensure that economies of scale are achieved by co-locating sophisticated equipment and expertise (for example, in areas like the sports sciences and coaching) to ensure that the athletes get the best possible assistance. The ever present danger in the Australian federal system is that state parochialism will break down this integrated national approach so that the ''goal'' becomes that of producing the best state athletes rather than the best national athletes.

Under the current four-year strategic plan and funding cycle for the ASC, there has been a slight shift toward participation programs such as Aussie Sport, the Volunteer Enhancement Program, and Club Development strategies. The balance between elite- and mass-sport is always unstable in that, with limited funds, there is always a tension between funding for international competitors to produce world champions, and funding participation in programs to derive national health and socioeconomic benefits. Policymakers consider the current mix within the Australian system to be appropriate, particularly given the substantial level of funding at state and particularly local government levels for various sport and recreation participation projects. A more pressing problem is that much of the facility provision is at the local government level and is often not accompanied by sufficient training and attention to key matters of facility maintenance and management. These issues are now being addressed by the Confederation of Australian Sport.

In short, Australian sports policy has gone through a significant transition in recent years. The results speak for themselves both in international competitiveness and increased sport participation. It is clear that more needs to be done, particularly in relation to participation levels and their associated benefits. There are also some distributional issues within the funding regime that have not been adequately addressed. There is now agreement at virtually all levels that sports funding and program management should operate on a four-year cycle. In normal circumstances, these issues would be reviewed in earnest in 1995–96. However, with Australia receiving permission to host the Olympic Games in 2000, and the potential benefits accruing from this opportunity, the review process may be delayed until early next century.

REFERENCES

Australian Bureau of Statistics. (1991). *Household Expenditure Survey.* Canberra, Australia: Australian Government Publishing Service.

Australian Bureau of Statistics. (1992). *National Health Survey 1989–90.* Canberra, Australia: Australian Government Publishing Service.

Australian Commission Act, Number 12, 1989, Commonwealth Government Printing Australian Encyclopedia. (1981). The Grolier Society of Australia (pp. 191–192). Sydney, New South Wales.

Australian Sports Commission. (1986). *Strategic Plan; 1986–87 to 1987–88.* Canberra, Australia: Australian Government Publishing Service.

Australian Sports Commission. (1991). *Sport for young Australians.* Canberra, Australia: Australian Government Publishing Service.

Baker, S. J. (1965). *The pacific book of Australiana.* Sydney, Australia: Angus & Robertson.

Bloomfield, J. (1974). *Review of activities; the role, scope and development of recreation in Australia.* Department of Tourism and Recreation, Australian Government Publishing Service, Canberra, A.C.T.

Daly, J. (1985). *Structure.* In Department of Sport Recreation and Tourism & Australian Sports Commission (eds.), Australian Sport; A Profile (p. 13). Canberra, Australia: Australian Government Publishing Service.

Department of the Arts, Sport, the Environment, Tourism and Territories. (1989). *Economic impact of sport and recreation—the volunteer sector.* Canberra, Australia: Australian Government Publishing Service.

Department of the Arts, Sport, the Environment, Tourism and Territories. (1991a). *The Australian recreation sport and fitness industries—economic and employment characteristics.* Canberra, Australia: Australian Government Publishing Service.

Department of the Arts, Sport, the Environment, Tourism and Territories. (1991b). *Recreation participation survey,* February 1991. Canberra, Australia: Australian Government Publishing Service.

Dunstan, K. (1973). Sporting obsession. In M. Turnbull (ed.), *Hammond Innes introduces Australia.* Sydney, Australia: Collins.

Going for Gold. (1989). The first report on an inquiry into sports funding and administration. Canberra, Australia: Australian Government Publishing Service.

Horne, D. (1971). *The lucky country.* Sydney, Australia: Collins.

Jacques, T. D., and Pavai, G. R. (1976). Sport in Australia. Sydney, Australia: MacGraw-Hill Book Co.

Larcombe, Frederick A. (1970). *History of botany; 1788–1979.* Sydney, New South Wales: Halstead Press, p. 4.

National Heart Foundation of Australia. (1993). *Risk factor prevalence study (Survey No. 3, 1989).* Canberra, Australia: Australian Government Publishing Service.

National Institute of Economic and Industry Research. (1990). *The economic impact of the Ford Australian Open at the National Tennis Center.* Melbourne. Canberra, Australia: Victorian Government Publishing Service.

Pearson, K., and O'Hara, J. (1977). The flavor of Australian sport. In D. Mercer (ed.), *Leisure and recreation in Australia.* Malvern, Australia: Sorret.

Stewart, B. (1985). Financial support. In Department of Sport, Recreation and Tourism (ed.), *Australian sport: A profile.* Canberra, Australia: Australian Government Publishing Service.

2

The State versus Free Enterprise in Sports Policy: The Case of Brazil

Lamartine P. DaCosta

Sport in Brazil is managed through a hybrid and fragmented public–private system in which the government and private organizations function jointly to provide, develop, and govern athletes, programs, facilities, and events. The twenty-seven states and 45,000 municipalities act as local supporters. In comparative terms, this structure might be labeled either democratic or authoritarian in different stages of Brazilian history (Donnelly, 1991).

In-depth studies of this institutional composition, however, have emphasized the distinctive nature of sports policies in Brazil. Although Brazil has the eighth largest gross national product among nations, its extreme social inequalities give it the appearance of a Third World country. In short, the management of the Brazilian sports sector by the state is of much concern to political interests, with sports policies representing a mechanism of cooptation rather than a social intervention process. Conversely, local communities and groups play a supportive role in sports practice, not depending on explicit government proposals and directives (DaCosta, 1987, pp. 21–69).

Since research in sports policy seeks mostly to discern relations among sport, culture, ideology, and state, this case may illuminate cross-national comparisons (Chalip, 1991). Therefore, this study aims to provide an overview in which the above-mentioned relations are clearly connected. The central focus, then, is the nature of sports development as a purposive and end result of local culture and initiatives. In adopting the cultural criticism as an approach, one may interpret experience by means of descriptions in order to reach the means of that experience (Alexander and Seidman, 1991).

Table 2.1
Historical Development of Brazilian Sport

Phases	Purposes	Development in Brazilian Sport
1850 - 1900	Community Initiative	♦ Founding of sports clubs by immigrants ♦ Physical Education First Regulation ♦ Soccer as a social, elite sport
1900 - 1920		♦ First Physical Education Faculty ♦ Soccer as a popular sport; club professionalism ♦ Participation in Olympic Games ♦ Popular sport promotions
1930's		♦ First worker's sport clubs ♦ Athletes' professionalism in soccer
1941 1942	Government Control	♦ Government regulation and control in sport ♦ Government intervention in sport for workers
1970's		♦ First evaluation of government interventions ♦ Sport-for-all campaigns ♦ Revision of 1941 Law of Sport ♦ Boom of physical education facilities & health clubs
1980's	Backlash of Private Initiative	♦ Deregulation of sport by government ♦ Diversification of professionalism
1990's		♦ Sport as constitutional right ♦ Professionalism legal rights ♦ Sport-for-all in local promotions ♦ Increase of sponsorship ♦ Profit or non-profit organizations ♦ Autonomy versus independence

NATIONAL GOVERNMENT AND THE SPORTS SYSTEM

A sketch of phases into which the history of Brazilian sport may be divided is set out in Table 2.1, framing the knowledge to focus cultural and enterprise approaches.

Sports activities in Brazil were initiated by European immigrants in the second half of the nineteenth century, similar to those in the United States, Argentina, or Chile. While the first German sports club was founded in 1848 in Cincinnati, another one of the same kind appeared in Joinville, a village located in the southern part of Brazil. By the end of the nineteenth century, nearly 300 German sports and recreation clubs were founded in Rio Grande do Sul alone, a southern state of the Brazilian Federation (Oliveira, 1987).

In addition to this effort, Italian immigration to Brazil, especially in rural areas, followed previous German colonies in preserving their cultural traditions by means not merely of religion, but of traditional games gatherings. This tendency is still recognized today in many Brazilian regions, perhaps because 30 percent of the total population of 145 million are of German and Italian extraction. Although the search for cultural identity through games and sports was much less important in other major ethnic groups, notably Portuguese (the most influential one), African, and Spanish, a tradition based in sports clubs was firmly established in the country. A parallel to this assertion was drawn by Perlman (1977), an American sociologist, who ascertained that 8 percent of the shantytowns' population in the Rio de Janeiro urban area were active members of local sports clubs, primarily dedicated to soccer practice and competitions. This classic study of the behavior of low-income people also suggests that the high proportion of adhesion to social, political, and religious associations (approximately 68 percent of the supposed marginal population of Rio de Janeiro) resulted essentially from self-protection and group identity.

One possible meaning of collective self-esteem, observed as much among the underprivileged as among affluent groups of Brazilian society, refers to sport as a factor in cultural development. This transcends the usual focus on development of sports by means of institutional measures. As a presupposition, this feature of sport is discussed by Chalip, Thomas, and Voyle (1992) in relation primarily to wealthy countries' environments, as well as by Rudiger Dohrman (DaCosta, 1992), focusing on the low-income populations of South America. Thus, the cultural value of sport may be considered paramount, as well as possibly the leverage of sport development in Brazil.

Table 2.1 emphasizes the community predominance in sports development initiatives from the 1850s to 1941 when the dictatorial government of Getulio Vargas established normative control of sport. Actually, the federal Law of Sport, issued in that year, is usually considered to be the first policy of sports development in Brazil. Until then, government interventions were unimportant and concentrated on physical education and military training, But after 1941 and for more than six years, sports played an active role in promoting the nationalistic spirit of the population as a factor of legitimizing the regime (Faria Junior, 1987).

An effort had also been made to adapt the existing private federations of sports discipline, professional soccer included, to fascist ideology, dominant during the 1930s, until 1942 when the dictatorial government joined the Allies in the Second World War. Contrary to later experiences in Eastern Europe and Cuba, the first sports policy in Brazil primarily mobilized and reordered the leadership and managerial levels of sports practice and competitions, allowing the clubs to maintain much of their freedom. This conception assumed the need to preserve local cultural tradition as was stated by Joao Lyra Filho, a lawyer dedicated to sports sociology and chief author of the final text of the 1941 act (DaCosta, 1987, pp. 30–46).

Apart from this concession, the drive of corporatism and the propensity of government to integrate the nation and to mobilize massive support by means of sport came about in the early 1940s. Under the control of the federal government, two new institutions designed to centralize and conduct labor-sport activities were created—one for industrial and another for commercial employees.

This intervention openly attempted to replace the preexisting and autonomous clubs by establishing sports facilities centers and unified competition programs. The Law of Sport was a legitimatizing instrument purporting to increase leisure sport possibilities for workers and their families. Both systems of labor sport survived the Vargas era, passing through the alternation of democratic (1945–64) and authoritarian (1964–85) periods of government. In the 1990s, under a new phase of full representative rules, those two systems jointly reached 15 million participants per year in sports activities. This achievement compares well with sports participation in other developing countries (DaCosta, 1991).

Toward Internationalization

Whether totally or partially controlled by the state, Brazilian high-performance sport obtained its best results in the postwar period under both democratic and authoritarian regimes. But this relative success occurred at the same time as the economic boom experienced by the country during the 1950s, 1960s, and 1970s. This could explain a sort of independence of sport in spite of interventions carried on by different styles of government. Effectively in this phase of economic growth euphoria, Brazil became world champion in soccer on three occasions and a major international power in basketball and volleyball. Brazil's ranking in swimming, yachting, judo, and track and field in the Olympic Games and other international competitions was just below that of the leading nations.

Another accomplishment was the 100 percent increase in the total number of sports clubs between 1960 and 1969, reaching a total of roughly 40,000 units. These data were published by a national survey and assessment carried out during 1969–70. Findings included the 135 percent increase in industrial output of sports goods and equipment, and the outstanding expansion of Physical Education courses for teachers and sport coaches—from 9 in 1964 to 56 in 1971. Despite this growth, the study concluded that sports in Brazil were motivated more by community concerns than by a desire for excellence in major competitions (DaCosta, 1971, pp. 158–159).

From the 1980s to 1990s, with the slowing economic growth, Brazil's participation and success in international sport competition declined.

Another sign of declining motivation and success is the export of athletes, coaches, and managers, which Brazilian sport has been experiencing since the 1980s. It has been estimated that 1,500 professionals currently work in foreign countries, although this figure has not been confirmed by federal government officials.

The majority of participants in national soccer and volleyball teams (ranking among the world's best in the 1990s) has public contractual links with foreign clubs and other sports entities. International bidding for the expertise and excellence of Brazilian sport comes primarily from the Middle East, Africa, and Western Europe. An outstanding example of this is African soccer which

Table 2.2
Brazilian Sport History—Main Functional Focuses

Level	Function	Mean	Ends	Focus
Government	Regulation	Ideology	State power increase	Politics
Top sport	Management	Politics	Development of sport	Economy
Community-based sport	Action	Cultural identity	Development through sport	Culture

emerged as a new international power thanks largely to its long-term involvement with Brazilian coaches and managers.

This emigration otherwise has been partly prevented by the increase of sponsorships in the 1980s and 1990s. Unlike most Third World nations, Brazil's professional athletes are supported by private or state-owned corporations acting independently of federal, state, and local governments. At Barcelona in 1992, according to public declarations by the National Olympic Committee, most of the 310 Brazilian Olympic athletes were sponsored by business enterprises.

Nature of Government Involvement in Sports

The evidence briefly described here reinforces the preliminary assumption that a tension exists between free enterprise and government in guiding, controlling, and developing sport through Brazilian history. Furthermore, this tension suggests a three-level structure in which government oscillates its interventions focusing on politics, while the focus of professional sport is on economy. Community-based sport, in turn, focuses on culture. Table 2.2 exhibits a synthesis of this analysis.

Despite the downsizing of elite sports in the 1990s, the potential of Brazilian amateur and professional sport seem to be expanding. There is a lack of current data; the survey of 1969–70 has not been updated. Nevertheless, indirect evaluations may reveal strengths. For example, the number of facilities for Physical Education continued to increase steadily from 56 in 1971 to 122 in the early 1990s.

In comparison with other countries, the estimated total of 150,000 professionals for Physical Education and sports teachers and coaches should make Brazil second to the former Soviet Union and third to the United States in the area of manpower. This fact seems to be also related to the health club (Academia de Ginastica in Portuguese) boom in Brazil. In the selected examples of São Paulo (population 11 million) and Rio de Janeiro (population 8 million), this rapid growth has significance in itself: from negligible figures in the early 1990s the number of health clubs reached approximately 7,000 units in the urban center of São Paulo and 5,000 in Rio de Janeiro. In addition, Sport-for-All has expanded, either through campaigns (1970s–80s) or through local governmental or private promotions (1990s). This movement may be considered one of the most important in international relations (Palm, 1991).

The relevance of informal sports may also be inferred: In all seven states of the Brazilian Federation which included sports promotion in their constitutions during the 1970s and 1980s, the explicit purposes were informal and "for youth" practices rather than practices favoring high-performance sport (Melo Filho, 1989). Economic crisis might have influenced this shift.

The concern with sports promotion has engendered the necessity to understand participants' reasons for doing sport. In one scientific study with participants of health clubs in Rio de Janeiro, 70 percent declared that they joined workout classes seeking social relations, while 61 percent looked for fitness improvement (DaCosta and Bittencourt, 1987). Similar results were found using a sample from a low-income group of active participants in a Sport-for-All event that took place in São Paulo: 76.5 percent in a total of 600 individuals expressed the preference for making friends among other alternative reasons for their participation (Takahashi, 1984).

On the other hand, the extent of activities in classical forms of sport, which emphasize competition, specialization, and spectatorship, may also be evaluated by indirect evidence. For example, the number of sports federations now total at least 359, although only 239 were reported in the 1969–70 survey. This increase roughly corresponds to more differentiation of sport in Brazil.

Soccer continues to be favored in both amateur and professional sport activities, followed by volleyball, judo, swimming, and basketball, according to the 1969–70 survey. The change in the 1990s is the diversification of professionalism, which was previously concentrated in soccer but is now accepted in any sports discipline.

Diversification, moreover, offers one explanation for the increasing trend of sports practices using seashores during the 1990s. Although not confirmed, there are an estimated 1.5 million participants in surfing, bodyboarding, beach volleyball, and other water and sand sports.

GOVERNMENT POLICIES

After nearly a century of governmental nonparticipation in sports, the turning point in Brazilian sport history came about. In 1941 the authoritarian federal administration issued the Law of Sport, which represented an explicit and tight control of federations and other bodies other than local clubs and associations. Similar controls were imposed earlier on education, health, and social security.

According to Manhaes (1986), frequent conflicts with government proceeded from professionalism in elite soccer clubs as well as from many federations in seeking international affiliations in the 1930s. The result was increased governmental intervention. In summary, the 1941 Law of Sport imposed a threefold system as follows (Lenk, 1942):

Structural Order

- Clubs as private entities, representing local community traditions and commitments, with directors working on a voluntary basis; free choices and diversity in sport practice.
- Leagues of one or more sport disciplines at municipal levels supported by local clubs; private and representative bodies dedicated to organizing competitions and establishing norms and guidelines for federations.
- Federations of one sport discipline in each state, representing municipal leagues or clubs, in the absence of a league in a particular municipality.
- Confederation of one or more sports disciplines already joined in federations; national representation and international affiliation.
- National Olympic Committee as an autonomous organization representing all confederations in view of the International Olympic Committee rules, affiliations, and events participation.

Functional Order

- Community and amateur sports activities as the core of a National Sport System.
- Separate competitions for professional athletes in the same league, federation, or sport discipline.
- Specific and isolated branches of clubs, federations, and confederations for students, workers, and military sports practice and competitions.

Administrative Order

- Overall orientation, control, and incentive of sports practice by a National Sport Council, with members nominated by the president of the republic. State orientation, control, and incentive by a Regional Sport Council, with members nominated by the state governor.
- Federal and state financial aid to selected sports bodies on a case-by-case basis.
- Administration of justice, with special sports courts for institutional or athlete relations.

Except for eventual confrontations involving particular interests, this pyramid-shaped arrangement, self-regulated at the bottom and tightly controlled from the top, was workable under either authoritarian regimes or private initiatives. This interpretation is drawn from experiences in four decades of the 1941 Law of Sport under different styles of government.

With a procedure of casual subsidies accepted and manipulated by major sports bodies, the cooptation nature of the 1941 regulation persisted. Even with the 1975 reform of the Law of Sports, the basic rationale of the 1941 law remained. The new law served only to suppress excesses of control and centralization. That may be the reason why interpreters refer to ''modernization'' rather than ''restoration,'' when referring to the 1975 reform law (Tubino, 1989a).

During the 1975–85 period, the federal government and many states officially declared certain "sports policies." Three national plans overlapped the 1975 Sport Law during this ten-year period. These plans established the following (Tubino, 1989a, 1989b):

• International charts and declarations of physical education, sports, and recreation yielded the central concepts for planning propositions to be accomplished jointly with the 1969–70 national survey.

• Sport-for-All became a major priority for federal and state governments.

• Sport Lottery was created to finance "development" but not "to subsidize" sport.

• "Investment" was made feasible as part of incentives in planning formulations.

With this innovative framework, the original 1975 National Plan was actually a technical document defining objectives, priorities, government roles, strategies, and budgets. In addition, the political support of those proposals was expressed by public announcements made by the minister of education and culture (Braga, 1975). A similar presentation is found in the next two national plans issued up to 1988, and elaborated, by coincidence, in the middle of a transition between authoritarian and democratic rule.

Moreover, sports policies in the 1990s may be described as a deregulation phase brought about by the political and social changes of the 1980s. In other words, the nature of deregulation since 1975 is likely to maintain the basic structure of the old sports system, whereas the functional and administrative orders have been progressively dismantled.

Whether a result of the autonomy tradition of Brazilian sport or a rejection of cooptation, the 1988 constitution adopted two radical positions. It assumed that sport was a citizen's right while restoring the autonomy of all sports entities.

A comparative study of constitutional declarations found that twenty-seven countries regulated sports practice. In different ways those constitutions include sports among other civil rights, but none removed the government from sport (Parente Filho, Melo Filho, and Tubino, 1989).

This Brazilian reform, however, remained incomplete, requiring additional laws. Throughout the 1990s, it became clear to government leaders that the deregulation process had a bottom line. Consequently, the first legal act concerning sports issued in 1993 sought to effect a balance between "autonomy" and "liberty," as expressed by the act's leading proponent, Arthur Coimbra (Presidencia da Republica, 1991).

The 1993 Law of Sport also included the following premises:

• The autonomy of sports entities has a fundamental and prior choice between a community-based or nonprofit organization and a private business enterprise.

- Sports entities' managerial guidelines are appropriately attained by a democratic voting system in the case of a community or by a capital owners' division of rights in the case of a business enterprise.
- The professional contracts of athletes in profit-oriented organizations must cover workers' legal rights with protection clauses for beginners.
- The subsidies to the sport sector are available only to social projects, with priority given to projects involving cultural identity and underprivileged youngsters.
- The relations between sports bodies are dependent on discipline in national and international processes of affiliation and eligibility. These essential conditions are to be promoted by entities in their own interest utilizing juridical and self-regulating procedures. The government's role is to subsidize and to set limits to free enterprise in sport.

The Brazilian government's policies in the 1990s permit independence while restraining autonomy (Dworkin, 1989). Independence is limited however, in order to prevent misconduct and bias; specifically, focus is on violence in sport competitions, drugs, or conflicts in affiliation and eligibility (Coimbra, 1991). This explains why the 1993 Law of Sport proposed a system of warranty for sports entities, shared by the government and the National Olympic Committee, as a guarantee of international regulations. In addition, this legal act maintains the old pyramid-shaped structure by means of government financial support at the municipal and state levels.

DISCUSSION OF GOVERNMENT SPORT POLICIES

One productive approach to government sports policies in Brazil is to describe and analyze the nature of relations between the government and sports entities. Historical evidence indicates that cooptation has produced a sports system marked by long-term stability in a political environment where instability prevails.

Published discussions relating to every law of sport in Brazil have examined forms of governmental power exertion and deregulation. Latin American and Brazilian intellectuals point to patrimonialism, a dominant feature of government political and bureaucratic authority in countries with Spanish and Portuguese cultural backgrounds (Velez Rodriguez, 1984).

The phenomenon of contradictory values mutually tolerated in a single culture is a Brazilian peculiarity (DaCosta, 1988), although it is a feature of the cultures of other postmodern countries as well (Rosenau, 1992). In the case of sports policies in Brazil however, it appears that community-based sports blend values in a manner that the government respects patrimonially. As a consequence, sports laws and plans emerge from collective aspirations, but they perform somewhat independently of both sport and community development needs.

An empirical investigation of the three national plans completed between 1975 and 1985 found a very low correlation between actual federal expenditures and expenditures proposed by the plans. Distribution of financial aid submitted to a mapping review showed that activities and promotions were brought primarily to specific geographic areas and social sectors controlled by major political parties (DaCosta, 1987, pp. 30–69).

In the early 1980s, the Center of Political Studies, University of Michigan, prepared a study of the influence of elite personages in Brazil (McDonough, 1981). In this research, linkages between government and elites such as politicians, industry leaders, priests, landowners, military leaders, and bankers were located by mutual relationships, in a manner similar to a sociogram. It was demonstrated that the Brazilian power structure was complex and multidimensional, with elites attempting to reconcile tradeoffs between economic accumulation and social equity, political order and liberty, and secular and sacred norms of community.

In light of McDonough's findings (1981), top sports leaders and government functionaries might be seen in the same network of relations. Not surprisingly, the behavior of these social actors in past historical stages, especially in soccer and volleyball, mirrored the successful performance of Brazilian industry with notable similarity to its Japanese counterparts. Both of these national industrial sectors, with protectionism supporting them, became world leaders in comparative growth during the first half of the twentieth century. The contrast between Brazil and Japan, however, lies in the appropriation of largesse which is inconsistent in Brazil.

Because of what McDonough calls ambiguities in Brazil, associating authoritarianism with free enterprise, as often occurs in the sports sector, presents no conflict. Tavares de Almeida (1988) described this apparent paradox as "neo-corporatism," when examining the fragmented and multifaceted social relations of the largest and most populated country in South America.

INTERVENTIONS IN PROFESSIONALISM

In Brazil, grass-roots sports can be compared to German sports, and Brazilian elite sports can be compared to Russian sports. Both Russian and Brazilian elite sports began as an aristocratic and exclusive leisure activity. According to Orlov (1988), the first club dedicated to major competition in Russia was established in Tiarlevo in 1888. Concentrating on track and field, members were drawn from St. Petersburg's social elite. Brazil's pioneer competitive club, devoted to rowing, made its appearance in Rio de Janeiro in 1874. Membership in that club represented a status symbol (DaCosta, 1980).

In 1886 the rowing championship in Rio de Janeiro involved six clubs as competitors. The press considered it the most important social gathering of that city. By the end of the century, there were similar rowing regattas in four different locations of the country (Penna Marinho, 1970). After that, several sports disciplines and entities were progressively added, and soccer replaced rowing as an elite occupation. Elite clubs began to combine soccer with other sports and to seek new performers. That was the beginning of professionalism in Brazil because most newcomers were working-class members who received money for their participation.

By the 1920s, soccer stood as the most popular sport in Brazil. Elite clubs had professional teams, and labor relations were handled through informal agreements. By the 1930s this arrangement became less viable because of unpaid debts. This brought about the most important crisis in Brazilian sports by the end of the decade, leading ultimately to governmental intervention.

It follows, therefore, that sports policies in Brazil can be explained in functionalist terms. Table 2.2, for example, is a functionalist overview since the sports system is broken down by its needs. In contrast, Table 2.1 describes the actions and unintended consequences of the same system in terms of specific purposes.

Several resolutions issued by the National Sport Council after its creation by the 1941 Law of Sport are functionalist. These resolutions regulated professionalism in Brazil during the 1942–83 period (Conselho Nacional de Desportos, 1983), with only minor effects. Tubino (1988a, 1988b) and Melo Filho (1988) viewed professionalism in Brazilian sport essentially as a matter of symbolic violence, with human rights placed in jeopardy during this period. More precisely, from the 1920s to 1990s, professional athletes in Brazil remained primarily commercial products, for they could not interfere in clubs and corporate transactions.

The 1993 Law of Sport gave the right of autonomy to amateur and professional athletes in sports practices. This law defined the exercise of this right as follows:

- Any sport contract requires the signatures of athletes involved as part of any business arrangement. Wage control procedures are to be developed by the major national entity of the athletes' sport regulatory body.

- Only the athlete may authorize changes in contractual terms that are valid for a maximum of three years.

- Only the athlete may authorize transfers from one sports entity to another.

- For foreign exchanges, the norms from international major entities prevail in each sports discipline, with athletes involved in negotiations.

- After three years of a contract's duration, the athlete is free to choose other commercial relations.

- Nonprofessional athletes more than thirty years of age are not permitted to participate in competitions among professionals.

In summary, sports professionalism in Brazil, using a functional interpretation, began as a social interaction springing from aristocratic and conservative behaviors. Professionalism in the 1990s may be considered within the framework of deviance amplification: a process in which the extent of deviance is exaggerated, constructing or uncovering social control measures by government agencies. This framework generates a crucial question: To what extent do Brazilian government policies in sports deal with tradeoffs or reflect cooptation?

ANALYSIS OF POLICY GOALS

To answer this question, we must examine policies and goals, giving attention to their consequences. The 1941 Law of Sport did not include expected outcomes or objectives; it was essentially a normative instrument for the improvement of relationships, concerned primarily with a structural, functional, and administrative framework of order. To some of the original lawmaking proponents, this statutory control of sport was equally a guarantee for local and cultural sports preservation.

Whether related to a desire for local autonomy or to a tendency toward isolation by community-based sports, local clubs in Brazil kept their historical feature—social gathering—through recreational sport. This fact was brought out by the 1969–70 national survey, which found a low participation level in competitions in addition to a high number of small clubs in every region of the country. From an average of 478 participants per club, only 49 participants had experienced some kind of contact with another sports body (DaCosta, 1971, p. 171).

Apart from formal competitions, Brazilian sports history indicates a preference for participation in nonformal sports activities. Popular sports promotions in streets, beaches, and parks were launched in the early 1920s: the creation in 1923 of "The Saint Silvester Race" in São Paulo City was a significant example. A private initiative, this competition was the first running event to take place in a downtown area of a large metropolis. The event continues in the 1990s, enjoying international prestige. Another such example is the "public recreation project" that Frederico Gaelzer introduced into the city of Porto Alegre in 1927. This innovation regularly offered games, physical activities, and cultural events in streets and squares, whereas they had previously taken place in closed places such as schools and clubs.

As described by DaCosta (1986), this pioneering work reflected a tendency that had already been in evidence in unconventional soccer games played on areas of waste ground in Brazilian cities. Gaelzer's initiative was characterized by the transformation of physical activities based on rules and standards into alternative forms of practice, with emphasis on participation rather than competition. In order to provide access and encourage participation, public places were adapted and equipment was simplified. Unusual for the period, women's volleyball was organized in public roads, and discarded materials such as old car tires were adapted to replace toys and standard games equipment.

Similar things happened in subsequent periods. DaCosta's 1986 report alludes to Holiday Sports in the 1930s, Leisure Streets in the 1940s and 1950s, popular competitions in the 1960s, and Sport-for-All campaigns in the 1970s. In the last-named campaigns, 25 percent of Brazil's municipalities took part. (Comparatively, the first European Sport-for-All campaigns did not occur until the end of the 1960s.) An assumption derived from each of these Brazilian sports campaigns is that they were motivated by the free initiatives of individuals and groups—not against, but apart from governmental guidelines and direction.

These presumed self-governing functions sometimes are found to be in conflict with the 1939 policy which did not mention unconventional forms of sport. At the time, the goals were summarized by one single expression: "to promote." Statements that included "to promote" referred to

• physical fitness of the population
• sports practices in all regions
• emphasis on mass sport
• development of sports expertise to improve national representation
• expansion of leisure sports opportunities.

After 1970, the sports policies of the federal government were more consistently enforced, although ultimate governmental aims still seem as amorphous as the above listing. Subsequent national plans developed until 1985 repeated the same themes, but replaced the verb "to promote" with the term *guidelines,* as can be seen in official documentation (Ministerio da Educacao e Cultura, 1981). All national plans proposed between 1975 and 1985 had similar content in spite of different text.

After a time lag of almost a decade during which constitutional and institutional reforms were made, the federal government's power of intervention reappeared in the 1993 Law of Sport. In this act the term *principles* was used rather than *guidelines.*

The national sports policy in the 1990s finally took its shape from a statement of rights as follows:

• Equal rights for all in sports participation
• Freedom of choice and association
• Sports promotion as a duty of the state
• Differentiated approaches and legal rights for professionals
• Incentives to promote cultural sports
• Free market competition in commercial sports initiatives
• Quality of life and fitness development as major goals at local levels
• Full decentralization of sports insofar as federal and state governments are involved in order to provide autonomy to municipalities and to support local initiatives
• Democratization of decisions when citizens are affected
• Autonomy within the limits of public interest and guaranteed by principles of free enterprise.

Although the above principles indicate a consolidation of public service sport systems, past experience does not assure the absence of patrimonialism. Nevertheless, because of unprecedented powers granted by the Brazilian federal government, tradeoffs are likely to be handled by the dynamics of free enterprise. To this historical and purposive interpretation may also be added the probability of an increasing emphasis on the role of foreign relations in future references and goals.

THE ROLE OF SPORT IN THE NATION

From the broad perspective, sports policy in Brazil may be closer to the former Eastern European socialist bloc nations than to other developing nations. Hungarian sports sociologist G.S. Földesi (1990) speaks of this possibility. In her analysis of the so-called communist bloc government's role in sport, she concludes that politics has an important role but has failed to influence sporting activity as it has other spheres of culture.

REFERENCES

Alexander, J. C., and Seidman, S. (1991). *Culture and society.* Cambridge, England: Cambridge University Press.

Braga, N. (1975). *Politica Nacional de Educacao Fisica e Desportos* (pp. 3–37). Brasilia: Ministerio da Educacao e Cultura.

Chalip, L. (1991). Sport and the state: The case of the United States of America. In F. Landry (ed.), *Sport . . . The third millennium* (pp. 243–250). Sainte-Foy, Quebec: Les Presses de l'Universite Laval.

Chalip, L., Thomas, D. R., and Voyle, J. (1992). Sport, recreation and well-being. In D. R. Thomas and A. Veno (eds.), *Psychology and social change* (pp. 132–156). Palmerston North, New Zealand: Dunmore Press.

Coimbra, A. (1991). A modernizacao da Practica do Esporte no Brasil. In Presidencia da Republica. *Projeto de Modernizacao do Esporte no Brasil* (p. 13). Brasilia: Governo do Brasil.

Conselho Nacional de Desportos. (1983). *Normas Basicas sobre Desportos.* Rio de Janeiro: Palestra Edicoes.

Cristan, M. L. (1990). Politicas Publicas para os Esportes no Brasil. *Revista Brasileira de Ciencias do Esporte 11,* 3: 186–189. São Paulo.

DaCosta, L. P. (1971). *Diagnostico de Educacao Fisica e Desporto no Brasil.* Rio de Janeiro: Fename.

DaCosta, L. P. (1980) *Esportes* (pp. 42–44). Rio de Janeiro: Block Editores.

DaCosta, L. P. (1986). Sport for All in Brazil. *Olympic Message, 16,* 17–24. Lausanne.

DaCosta, L. P. (1987). *Organizacao Esportiva Brasileira: Crise e Mudanca de Paradigmas.* Rio de Janeiro: Universidade do Estado do Rio de Janeiro—Tese de Livre Docencia.

DaCosta, L. P. (1988). *Valores e Moral Social no Brasil* (pp. 679–685). Rio de Janeiro: Universidade Gama Filho-Tese de Doutorado em Filosofia.

DaCosta, L. P. (1991). *Saude e Exercicio Fisico: uma Atividade Empresarial.* Brasilia: Ministerio da Saude.

DaCosta, L. P. (1992). *Sport for All in Peru—Report to GTZ.* Eschborn: Deutsch Gesellschaft fur Technisch Zusamenarbeit Gmb.

DaCosta, L. P., and Bittencourt, A. (1987). Perfil preliminar do usuario de academias de ginastica. *Homo Sportivus, 4:* 72–78.

Donnelly, P. (1991). Sport and the state in socialist countries: A commentary. In F. Landry (ed.), *Sport . . . The third millennium* (pp. 303–307). Sainte-Foy, Quebec: Les Presses de l'Universite Laval.

Dworkin, G. (1989). *The theory and practice of autonomy* (pp. 3–20). New York: Cambridge University Press.

Faria Junior, A. G. (1987). Professor de educacao fisica licenciado generalista. In V. M. Oliveira (ed.), *Fundamentos Pedagogicos da Educacao Fisica* (pp. 15–33). Rio de Janeiro: Livro Tecnico Editora.

Földesi, G. S. (1990, May). *From mass sport to the Sport for All Movement in the socialist countries in Eastern Europe.* Paper presented at the World Congress on Fitness, Nutrition and Sport for All. Chicago.

Lenk, M. (1942). *Organizacao da Educacao Fisica e Desportos* (pp. 91–101). Rio de Janeiro: Ministerio da Educacao e Cultura.

Lucas, J. A. (1992). *Future of the Olympic Games* (p. 61). Champaign, Ill.: Human Kinetics.

MacAloon, J. J. (1991). The turn of two centuries: Sport and the politics of intercultural relations. In F. Landry, (ed.), *Sport . . . The third millennium* (pp. 31–44). Sainte-Foy, Quebec: Les Presses de l'Universite Laval.

Manhaes, E. D. (1986). *Politica de Esportes no Brasil* (pp. 80–87). Rio de Janeiro: Graal Editora.

McDonough. P. (1981). *Power and ideology in Brazil* (pp. 85–106). Princeton, N.J.: Princeton University Press.

Melo Filho, A. (1988). Por um Estatuto dos Atletas. In M.J.G. Tubino (ed.), *Repensando o Esporte Brasileiro* (pp. 35–41). São Paulo: Ibrasa.

Melo Filho, A. (1989). Introducao. In Parente Filho (Org.), *Esporte, Educacao Fisica e Constituicao* (pp. 17–20). São Paulo: Ibrasa.

Ministerio da Educacao e Cultura. (1981). *Diretrizes Gerais para a Educacao Fisica e Desportos* (p. 24). Brasilia: Secretaria-Geral do MEC.

Oliveira, P. G. (1987). *A imigracao alema e a introducao do Punhobol no Rio Grande do Sul.* Santa Maria: Universidade de Santa Maria—Dissertacao de Mestrado.

Orlov, R. (1988). Cuando Hay lo Que Recordar. *Panoramo Olimpico, 3* (46): 10–11.

Palm, J. (1991). *Sport for All—Approaches from utopia to reality* (pp. 32–56). Schorndorf: Hofmann Verlag.

Parente Filho, M.S., Melo Filho, A., and Tubino, M.J.G. (1989). *Esporte, Educacao Fisica e Constituicao* (pp. 21–29). São Paulo: Ibrasa.

Penna Marinho, I. (1970). *Historia Geral da Educacao Fisica* (p. 165). São Paulo: Cia Brasil Editora.

Perlman, J. (1977). *O Mito da Marginalidade.* Rio de Janeiro: Editora Paz e Terra.

Presidencia da Republica. (1991). *Projeto de Modernizacao do Esporte no Brasil* (pp. 13–15). Brasilia: Governo do Brasil.

Rosenau, P. M. (1992). *Post modernism and the social sciences* (pp. 3–24). Princeton, N.J.: Princeton University Press.

Takahashi, G. (1984). Respostas de uma Comunidade Carente a um Programa de Ativ-
idades Nao-formais. *Comunidade Esportiva, 25,* outubro, 50–60.

Tavares de Almeida, M. H. (1988). *Repensando o Esporte Brasileiro* (pp. 6–25). São
Paulo: Ibrasa.

Tubino, M. G. (1988). *Repensando o Esporte Brasileiro.* São Paulo: Ibrasa.

Tubino, M. G. (1989a). *A Interpretacao do Esporte na Educacao Brasileira.* Rio de
Janeiro: Universidade Federal do Rio de Janeiro—Tese de Doutorado.

Tubino, M. G. (1989b). A constituicao e o Direito ao Esporte. In M. S. Parente Filho,
(Org.) *Esporte, Educacao Fisica e Constituicao* (pp. 47–51). São Paulo: Ibrasa.

Velez Rodriguez, J. (1984). Tradicion Patrimonial y Administracion Senorial en America
Latina. *Revista da Universidade de Medellin,* 2(44): 81–136.

3

Sport and Government in Canada

Donald Macintosh

INTRODUCTION

Canada is a vast country, second in size in the world only to Russia. In contrast, its population is relatively small—approximately 27 million people—fewer than live in the state of California. Most Canadians reside in close proximity to the United States—the majority in central Canada (the provinces of Ontario and Quebec), strung along the northern side of the Great Lakes and the St. Lawrence Seaway and River. It is not surprising, then, that Canada's culture and economy are greatly influenced by the United States. Its historical roots, however, are largely in Europe: the majority of its peoples came originally from Europe; its legal system was borrowed from France (for civil law in the French-speaking province of Quebec) and Great Britain (in the rest of the country); and its system of government, that of a constitutional monarchy, has its foundations in Great Britain. But because the British North America Act of 1867 divided legislative powers between the federal government and the respective provinces, Canada's style of governance can best be described as a liberal democracy, within a federalist system of power sharing.

   Given these historical imperatives, most sporting practices in Canada have their origins either in Europe or in the United States. Canada's "national" sport—hockey—however, is an indigenous one, and there is great interest in the game, especially the National Hockey League (NHL). Indeed, Saturday night hockey telecasts in the 1960s were consistently rated as the most popular programs in Canada (see Macintosh, Bedecki, and Franks, 1987, chap. 4). The two Canadian teams—the Toronto Maple Leafs and the Montreal Canadiens—were "national" institutions with avid followings—the Maple Leafs across most of English-speaking Canada, and the Canadiens, in Quebec and among many francophones in the rest of the country.

But commencing in 1967, the NHL gradually expanded from six teams to encompass most of North America (sixteen teams in the United States and eight in Canada). This expansion inevitably led to a watering down of the talent in the league. There was also a corresponding shift in team ownership and management from that of a community base to control by corporations and wealthy entrepreneurs, and an increase in control of the NHL by American interests (see Clark and Hutchinson, June 2, 1991). Gradually, the player rosters of NHL teams changed from being predominantly Canadian to include many Europeans and Americans. In 1966–67 (the year before the first expansion), 91 percent of the players in the NHL had been born in Canada. But by 1991–92, 17 percent of the NHL player roster were American and 12 percent were from Europe (Scher, October 12, 1992, p. 34). The collapse of the Soviet Union accelerated this transformation. Twelve of the first twenty-one players selected in the 1992 NHL draft were from Russia or Eastern European countries (Scher, October 12, 1992, p. 37). As a result of these developments, along with dissipation of fan interest over eight different cities across the country, the NHL has become a much less important symbol of Canadian identity.

Other professional sports also dominate the public interest, and it is here that the ubiquitous influence of American television in Canada can be seen. The National Football League (NFL) and the American and National Baseball Leagues are followed slavishly by many Canadians. Major league baseball increased greatly in popularity when it expanded into Canada—the Montreal Expos (in 1969) and the Toronto Blue Jays (in 1977). The Blue Jays franchise became one of the most successful in North America, establishing a league attendance record of over 4 million fans in 1991, and winning the World Series in 1992 and 1993. (It is notable that none of the players on this winning team was Canadian, and none of them lived year-round in Toronto.) This was an historical event—the first time a non-American team had accomplished this feat. (See Kidd, 1991, for a discussion of the "Americanization" of Canadian sport.)

Canadian football, which had its origins in both British rugby football and "American" football, but which has retained some of its own unique features, has been able to maintain some semblance of a unique Canadian identity. This game is played in many schools and postsecondary institutions across the country, and the Grey Cup game, held each fall to determine the championship of the Canadian Football League (CFL), has been seen by some as a celebration of Canadian nationalism. Ironically, the managers, coaches, and "star" players are drawn largely from the United States.

The CFL, however, has recently fallen on hard times. In the mid-1980s, its lucrative Canadian television contract was reduced substantially because of the declining viewer popularity of Canadian football with respect to the NFL and other professional televised sport from the United States. Since that time, the

CFL has been in constant financial difficulty, with franchises up for sale and dire predictions of closing down some teams. Teams in Calgary, Hamilton, Ottawa, and Regina have all, at one time or another, been close to financial insolvency. For instance, in 1992 the financially troubled Hamilton Tiger-Cats were saved only after they received a $700,000 line of credit from the Hamilton-Wentworth regional government by a narrow Council vote of 13 to 12 (Marron, July 10, 1992, p. C12).

One of the most successful franchises in the CFL, the Toronto Argonauts, was purchased in 1991 by a consortium headed by multimillionaire Bruce McNall, the owner of the NHL franchise in Los Angeles. His coup in attracting Notre Dame superstar Raghib "The Rocket" Ismail to the Argonauts was credited with saving, at least temporarily, the CFL from collapse (Brunt, July 6, 1992, p. D1). This optimism was short-lived. McNall sold his majority interests in the NHL Kings, the Argonauts were sold to TSN Enterprises, and Ismail moved to the NFL.

The CFL expanded into the United States in 1993, with the addition of the Sacremento Gold Miners. Teams that were granted expansion franchises for 1994 include the Las Vegas Posse, Shreveport Pirates, and the Baltimore CFL Colts. Other cities are expected to follow suit. Whether a unique Canadian game could survive expansion into the United States is a moot point. Specifically, will the expansion into the United States trigger a reciprocal NFL expansion into Canadian cities like Toronto, Vancouver, and Montreal? It is also important to consider whether Canadian rules and Canadian player quotas will survive the expansion.

On the few occasions that the federal government has expressed concern over the incursions of American professional sport into Canada, nothing in the way of concrete legislation has been forthcoming. Consternation over the NHL's control over young Canadian hockey players, and an outcry when Vancouver and Quebec were denied NHL franchises in the league's first expansion, led Ronald Basford, a Member of Parliament from Vancouver, to introduce in 1966 a private member's bill "to bring the operation of all professional sporting leagues within the purview of the Combines Investigation Act" (HC *Debates,* June 13, 1966, p. 6364). The Combines Act was designed to prevent unfair trade practices in the country, but Basford's amendment to bring professional sport under its purview was defeated in the House of Commons. (See Jones, 1976, for an analysis of this episode.)

Attempts by American interests in the early 1970s to establish CFL franchises in the United States were seen by Health and Welfare Minister John Munro as "an erosion of Canadianism" (Goodman, 1981, p. 140), and he said his government would act to prevent it. Nothing came of these proposals. However, in 1974 the World Football League (WFL) was established in the United States and announced that it intended to locate one of its franchises in Toronto. The federal government responded by introducing legislation that would bar foreign football leagues from entering Canada. While this legislation was before the

House of Commons, the owner of this new WFL franchise, John Bassett, Jr. (ironically, a Canadian himself), backed down, bitterly denouncing the government and saying he would move his franchise to Memphis. A federal election was called shortly thereafter, and the legislation died on the floor of the House of Commons (Goodman, 1981, pp. 167–168).

Since 1974, the federal government has shown little interest in legislation to control professional sport in Canada. Its focus has been almost entirely on what was known at that time as amateur sport. It did, however, amend its Competition Act (legislation passed in 1985 to replace the Combines Investigation Act) in 1986 to include sport and specifically, to prohibit the undue restriction of player movement (Adams, September 26, 1992, p. A20). However, no action has been taken against any professional teams or leagues since the passage of this amendment.

Soccer has increased greatly in popularity in Canada, at least in part because of the great influx of immigrants from Europe after World War II. It has become the most widely played summer sport in Canada, and has attracted a great number of young men and women to its ranks. But, as has been the case in the United States, professional soccer has yet to attract sufficient fan interest to establish itself on a sound financial basis in Canada. Similarly, basketball is played widely all across the country, but several attempts since World War II to establish professional basketball in Canada have been unsuccessful. Televised accounts of the National Basketball Association (NBA) and the National Collegiate Athletic Association championship tournaments, however, have recently attracted an increasing audience in Canada. Finally, Vancouver and Toronto received NBA franchises in 1994.

Educational institutions are the main outlet for competitive sports opportunities for Canadian youth. Here, a wide range of sports are offered at the secondary and postsecondary levels. In the 1980s, however, there was a substantial increase in the number of elite sport clubs for youthful competitors, especially in Olympic events such as skiing, skating, aquatic sports, gymnastics, and track and field. In contrast to its neighbor to the south, Canadian collegiate and interuniversity sports have been relatively free of the commercialization and professionalization that have characterized such programs in the United States. With the exception of men's basketball, football, and hockey programs at some Canadian universities, postsecondary sports competition has been athlete centered, accommodating the athletic aspirations of bona fide full-time students.

The physical activity patterns of Canadian adults, however, reflect an interest in less competitive activities. Figure 3.1 lists the ten most popular physical recreation activities for adult Canadians in 1988, with comparable percentage figures for 1981. Not only were a greater percentage of adult Canadians active in 1988 compared to 1981 (see Figure 3.1), but also there was a statistically significant and substantial increase in energy expenditure by adult Canadians over this same time period (Stephens and Craig, 1990, p. 9). This was in spite of a tendency to opt more often for less strenuous activities in 1988 (see the

Figure 3.1
Participation in Physical Recreation Activities, 1981 and 1988 (Age 10+)

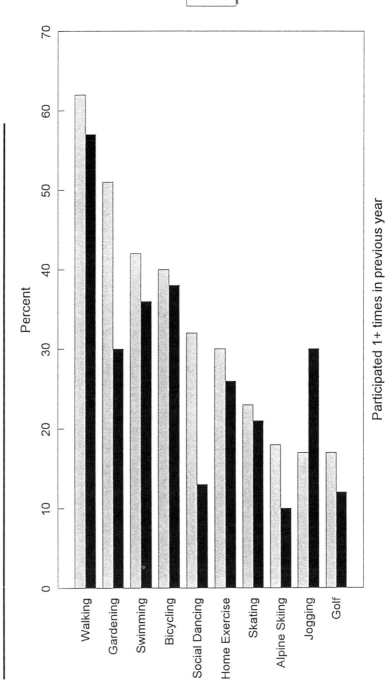

Participated 1+ times in previous year

Adapted from *The Well-Being of Canadians: Highlights of the 1988 Campbell Survey.* 1988. Gloucester, Ontario: Canadian Fitness and Lifestyle Research Institute. Reprinted with permission.

decline in jogging in Figure 3.1). The 1988 survey also revealed that 80 percent of the Canadian population spends, on average, a total of three or more hours a week at physical recreation for at least nine months of the year (Stephens and Craig, 1990, p. 8; see this reference for a comprehensive picture of the Canadians' well-being).

This overview of sport in Canada provides a framework for a more specific examination of federal government involvement in sports since World War II. A number of themes run through this exposition. The promotion of national unity and a desire to preserve a distinctive Canadian identity in the face of a cultural invasion from the United States have been central motives in this involvement. In matters of international relations, the Canadian government has used sports not only to project an image of Canadian culture abroad, but also to further its wider foreign policy goals, particularly within the Commonwealth. A concern for the fitness and well-being of all Canadians was another early motive for federal government involvement.

But the federal government soon learned that sports could be used successfully to promote national unity and project a Canadian identity abroad only if the country's athletes could compete with the best in the world. Consequently, there was a growing emphasis on developing a corps of elite athletes to represent Canada in international sports competitions at the expense of sports for all and equity in participation opportunities among all Canadians. This elite emphasis also led to a penchant to use sports to legitimize the government of the day and to further the careers of individual politicians.

When the Progressive Conservative party returned to power in 1984, it brought with it some of the neo-conservative ideologies of the 1980s—the privatization of publicly owned corporations and a downsizing of government bureaucracy. This included threats to decrease government funding for national sports organizations (NSOs).

It is not surprising, then, that conflicts and tensions have arisen over federal government involvement in sport. These themes and tensions are found in the examination of federal government sport policies and programs that follows and are raised again in the discussion. These policies and programs were directed almost exclusively toward nonprofessional sport.

THE EARLY YEARS

The federal government's active involvement in the promotion of sports is a fairly recent phenomenon. Through most of its history, it was content to impose regulatory measures governing sporting practices, and it directed its limited efforts mainly toward fitness and mass participation. But a number of post–World War II forces and events led the federal government to change its posture. The Soviet Union's decision to use sports to promote its socialist ideology abroad had a profound impact on international sport. To this end, the Soviets developed a corps of elite athletes. The spectacular success of these athletes in international sport, and particularly in the Olympic Games, caused many Western industrialized countries to modify their Victorian attitudes toward sports, which included an antipathy toward state-supported athletes, and to see the potential of sports to promote not only national unity, but the government of the day as well. Soon, most Eastern bloc socialist and many Western industrialized nations followed the Soviet example.

Even more important was the Soviet Union's ability to usurp Canada's traditional role as the premier hockey nation in the world. This realization was brought to the country's attention dramatically when the Soviets beat the Canadian team in the 1954 World Hockey Championships. That this was no fluke was made clear in the 1956 Winter Olympics, when the Soviets won the hockey gold medal while Canada placed third behind the United States. These concerns spilled over to a more general malaise about all of Canada's international sport performances, which was manifested in the press and in the House of Commons. At the same time, a small but devoted number of physical educators and fitness advocates were urging the government to take action on the perceived poor level of physical fitness in the nation. These two concerns came together with some larger social and economic forces that were characteristic of the expanding welfare state in Western industrialized nations. In Canada this led the federal government to enact, in 1961, a bill to encourage fitness and amateur sport. (See Macintosh et al., 1987, chap. 2, for a more complete discussion of these developments.)

For the first few years following the passage of the bill, the federal government was content to play a passive role in promoting fitness and amateur sport. It entered into cost-sharing agreements with the provinces, and through the auspices of the National Fitness and Amateur Sport Advisory Council, a body established in the new legislation, it dispersed funds to National Sports Organizations (NSOs) to use as they saw fit. But the expected improvement in Canada's international sports performances did not materialize, and the outcry in the press and in the House of Commons continued unabated. These concerns coincided with a national unity crisis in Canada in the late 1960s (one of a long string of such crises). Canada's prime minister, Pierre Trudeau, was seeking ways in which he could counter two strong divisive forces in the country. One was a growing nationalism and demands for more powers and independence in Quebec. The other came from the rest of the provinces—an anglophone nationalism, fanned by threats of separation by Quebec, and a perceived threat of American economic and cultural domination. There were also demands for more power sharing and greater autonomy in the largely anglophone western Canadian provinces. In a campaign speech in 1968 at Selkirk College in Castlegar, British Columbia, Trudeau mentioned sports in connection with culture, maintaining that they could play a role in promoting national unity. This was not a new idea, for the theme of the first Canada Games, held in Quebec City in 1967, was ''Unity through Sport.'' In this speech, Trudeau promised that, if reelected, he would establish a federal task force on sport.

A CHANGING FOCUS

The report of the Task Force on Sports for Canadians was tabled in the House of Commons in February 1969, and its recommendations became the basis for a new direction for federal government sports policy, *A Proposed Sports Policy for Canadians,* issued by Health and Welfare Minister John Munro the following month. Although this document contained a great deal of rhetoric about mass participation in sports and recreational activities, its recommendations were directed largely toward elite sport. The federal government did not renew its sports and fitness cost-sharing agreements with the provinces, in part because it believed it was not getting enough credit for these programs, and in part, because of the continued debates with the provinces over federal-provincial jurisdiction. Instead, it moved toward creating a number of arms-length agencies, designed to improve Canada's international sport performances. Such improvements were seen to be necessary if sports were to play a role in promoting national unity.

Consequently, the federal government established a National Sport and Recreation Centre (NSRC) in Ottawa to house NSOs, and provided them with office space and secretarial support, as well as printing, translation, audiovisual, library, and computing services. The government also provided the NSOs with travel monies for national championships and annual meetings, and salary support for executive directors (Canada, 1992, p. 288). During 1970–90, the NSRC was to receive $62 million from the federal government to support these activities (Canada, 1992, p. 289). In 1972 the government created two separate divisions within the Fitness and Amateur Sport Directorate: Recreation Canada and Sport Canada. This second arm allowed it to deal more directly with elite sports.

In the same year, the government announced that the Fitness and Amateur Sport Directorate would be upgraded to the status of a branch, with an assistant deputy minister reporting directly to the deputy minister of health. Sport Canada commenced to provide monies to support the salaries of the technical staff of the NSOs that were housed in the NSRC. The government also increased substantially its funding for the NSOs; the Fitness and Amateur Sport budget grew from approximately $6 million in 1971–72 to almost $39 million in 1978–79. By this time about four and one-half dollars were being allocated to sport for every dollar to recreation and fitness (Macintosh et al., 1987, p. 85). In another step that was indicative of the increased stature of sport within the federal government, Iona Campagnolo was appointed as the first minister of state for fitness and amateur sport in September of 1976.

According to the Task Force on Sport report, inadequate coaching was one of the barriers inhibiting the development of elite athletes. Consequently, in 1970 the government established another agency called the Coaching Association of Canada (CAC) and housed it in the NSRC. Government funding of the CAC rose to about $1.5 million in 1978–79. In 1976 CAC, in cooperation with respective provincial government agencies, formally introduced its National

Coaching Certification Program (NCCP) and went on to develop a comprehensive five-level national coaching certification program. The NCCP was so successful that in the 1980s it became the model for similar programs in a number of countries around the world.

There was considerable backlash in many circles over the Task Force Report's preoccupation with elite sport. As a result, in 1969 Health and Welfare Minister Munro hired a consulting firm, P. S. Ross and Partners, to undertake a study of the issue of mass sport and fitness programs. One of this firm's key recommendations that the government acted on was to establish an arm's length agency designed to motivate Canadians to lead more physically active lives, using awareness education and motivation strategies. This agency, called Sport Participation Canada but better known by its official motto, "ParticipACTION" has been a most successful venture. Its clever 15-second television spot commercials, financed largely by private companies and corporations, have become synonymous with a physically active lifestyle in Canada. Public awareness has risen steadily to a point where almost 90 percent of those surveyed in a 1992 Gallup poll were aware of the ParticipACTION name and logo. Of those surveyed, 90 percent said that they believed the ParticipACTION program was useful and working well (Russ Kisby, President, Sport Participation Canada, personal communication, October 7, 1992). A great deal of the credit for the increase in Canada's physical activity levels during the 1980s must go to ParticipACTION. Government contributions to this agency totaled only $15.4 million during the period 1971–91 (Canada, 1992, p. 289); the estimated total value of the free advertising contributed by the private sector over this same time period was approximately $210 million (Russ Kisby, President, Sport Participation Canada, personal communication, October 7, 1992).

Another step that the federal government took in 1969 was to establish the Canada Games on a permanent basis. The first Canada Games, which, as noted above, were held in Quebec in 1967, were planned largely by federal government officials. But in order to generate more interest in the Games, and in order to get the provinces more involved, a Canada Games Council was established, including federal and provincial sport officials as well as appointees from the Sports Federation of Canada (representing all the NSOs). The official goal of the Canada Games was "to provide a national development competition of high calibre for maximum numbers of athletes from all provinces and territories" (Canada Games Council, 1979, p. 9). But another motive of the federal government was to promote national unity.

Another positive outcome of the Canada Games, which have been subsequently held every two years (alternating between winter Games and summer Games) in smaller cities all across Canada, has been the legacy of sports facilities left in the host communities. The cost of these facilities had been borne in approximate equal amounts by the federal, provincial, and municipal governments, respectively. By 1991 thirteen Canada Games had been held, with total federal government contributions of $56 million, split almost evenly between winter and summer Games (Canada, 1992, p. 287). These funds were matched by both the participating provincial and local governments.

The federal government's contribution of $2.3 million toward the cost of hosting the Pan-American Games in Winnipeg in 1967, according to federal government officials, sparked interest among Canadians for hosting international sporting events (Canada, 1992, p. 287). Certainly, since that time, bidding for international sports events has become a common civic enterprise in Canada, and federal and provincial governments have poured millions of dollars into a number of such successful bids (see Macintosh and Whitson, 1992, for a discussion of the political, economic, and social issues surrounding the staging of major games in Canada).

Putting the Canada Games on a permanent footing forced the provincial governments to develop sport arms in their recreational and culture departments. Along with provincial sports-governing bodies, the provincial governments began to commit personnel and funds to the selection and training of athletes so that they would fare well at these Games. This was to lead to the creation of large sports bureaucracies in the more populous and prosperous provinces. This was ironic, because in the 1960s and early 1970s, the provinces had championed mass sports and recreation programs and were critical of the federal government's efforts to promote elite sport. Still, the provinces maintained their constitutional right to have primacy in matters pertaining to mass sports and recreational programs. Because of this stance, the federal government changed the title of Recreation Canada to Fitness and Recreation Canada in 1977. After the provincial governments refused to participate in discussions of Iona Campagnolo's 1979 green paper, entitled *Toward a National Policy on Fitness and Recreation,* the federal government conceded that recreation was indeed exclusively a provincial responsibility. The following year, Fitness and Recreation Canada was quietly changed to Fitness Canada.

The federal government's efforts to enhance Canada's international sport stature paid off in the second half of the 1970s. Canada improved its standings substantially in the 1976 summer Olympics that were hosted in Montreal, moving from twenty-first in 1972 in Munich to tenth place overall in the unofficial standings in Montreal (Canada, 1992, p. 291). Still, Canadians were disappointed when Canadian athletes failed to win a gold medal at these Olympics. The Montreal Olympics subsequently became best known for the exorbitant deficit incurred, and the political and financial scandals surrounding the planning and building of the facilities involved. In 1973 the federal government had introduced legislation to allow the sale of Olympic stamps, coins, and lottery tickets. This legislation was passed in Parliament only after the prime minister had received written assurances from the city of Montreal and the province of Quebec that the federal government would not be responsible for any debt incurred from the Montreal Games. The Olympic Lottery subsequently raised some $235 million in net revenue for these 1976 Games. In 1976 Loto-Canada replaced the Olympic Lottery, and proceeds from this lottery were used to help finance the

Olympic debt and to provide monies for the federal government's commitment to the 1978 Edmonton Commonwealth Games, as well as to support other aspects of high-performance sport (Canada, 1992, p. 291).

In 1979 the short-lived Progressive Conservative government made good on one of its election campaign promises and turned the rights to its sport lottery over to the provinces. In return, the federal government was to receive payments from the provinces of $24 million a year, which it intended to use to help finance the arts and sport.

In 1981 the new Liberal government announced that it intended to create a sports pool, and in 1983 it incorporated the Canadian Sports Pool Corporation under a new act of Parliament to support the arts and culture, medical and health research, sport, and the Calgary Olympics. The federal government claimed that its new Sport Select pool was different than a sport lottery, but the provinces were of the opposite opinion, and there was much acrimony between the federal government and the provinces over this issue.

When the Progressive Conservative party returned to power in 1984, it withdrew the Sport Select pool. (It had not been a financial success anyway.) In exchange, the provinces agreed to pay the federal government $100 million, which was used as part of the federal government's contributions to help finance the 1988 Calgary winter Olympics (Canada, 1992, pp. 293–295).

Canadian athletes fared extremely well at the 1978 Commonwealth Games, held in Edmonton. For the first time in the history of these Games, Canada finished first, ahead of its traditional rivals, England and Australia. These Games were skillfully televised by the CBC, and were watched with great pride and satisfaction by millions of Canadians all across the country. Canadian athletes, in a show of gratitude for the federal government's efforts, paraded Fitness and Amateur Sport Minister Iona Campagnolo on their shoulders around Commonwealth Stadium at the conclusion of the Games. The federal government contributed about $12 million toward the capital costs of these Games, which were staged within the budget projections of about $70 million (Baka and Hoy, 1978, pp. 7–8).

HOCKEY DIPLOMACY

One of the major preoccupations of the Task Force on Sport was concern over Canada's continued poor performances in international hockey. Indeed, in his campaign speech at Selkirk College, Trudeau had deplored the country's showing in international hockey. As a result, even before Munro had released his new sports policy, the government put in place another arm's length agency called Hockey Canada.

Hockey Canada was given two mandates: to manage and develop Canada's national team; and to foster and develop hockey in Canada. Although its efforts to get Canada's national hockey team back to the top of the World Championships and the Winter Olympics never were quite successful, Hockey Canada did put in place an historical hockey confrontation—the "Summit" series—featuring the best of Canada's professional players against the Soviet Union. This match-up between the two most powerful hockey nations in the world was held in the fall of 1972, with four games in each country.

Team Canada won the Summit series with a dramatic last-minute goal by Paul Henderson in the eighth and deciding game in Moscow, with what seemed in retrospect the whole of Canada following the game on television. It was a memorable event that did much to restore the Canadians' pride in their national game and the country's international hockey prowess.

The format of the series was subsequently changed to include the top six hockey nations in the world under the title of the "Canada Cup." The Canada Cup series has been held periodically ever since and has continued to hold the rapt attention of most Canadians. The 1972 Summit series marked the beginning of the use of sport in Canada's diplomatic endeavors. Rapprochement with the Soviet Union was one of Trudeau's foreign policy objectives when he was returned to power in the federal election of 1968. In an exchange of visits that he held with Soviet Union President Alexei Kosygin in 1971, hockey relationships became a subject of discussion. Both leaders realized that hockey formed a common bond between the two countries and that it could be used to strengthen relations between them. When negotiations by Hockey Canada and the Canadian Amateur Hockey Association with the International Ice Hockey Federation to resolve the impasse over Canada's demand that it be able to use NHL players in the World Championships commenced the following spring, the Department of External Affairs (DEA) offered its services to this end.

Although Canada was not successful in its demand, and consequently refused to return to the World Hockey Championships, this impasse led, with the help of Canada's diplomats abroad, to arranging the Summit series with the Soviet Union. Given the political importance of the series, and in order to attend to the myriad of diplomatic details that were involved, DEA established an international sport desk in 1972. Although this desk was to work in relative obscurity until the mid-1980s and was involved largely in low-level activities such as sports exchanges and diplomatic formalities in international sports affairs, it was a most significant event. In the words of Eric Morse, who held the post of head of this international sports desk through the second half of the 1970s and the first half of the 1980s, "The 1972 [hockey] series was seminal for External's [DEA] appreciation of sport as an element of Canadian international relations" (Morse, 1987, p. 18). The reader is referred to Macintosh and Greenhorn (1993) for more details of this episode.

THE TAIWAN CONFRONTATION

Despite this low level of diplomatic activity at the sports desk in DEA, international sports matters were to occupy the Canadian government at the highest level on a number of occasions in the 1970s. As part of his new approach to Canadian foreign policy, one that was articulated in the document, *Foreign Policy for Canadians,* Trudeau developed what was to become known as the Third Option. This strategy rejected the status quo in Canadian-U.S. relations and sought to wean the country away from excessive dependence on the United States. Part of this new approach was the recognition of the People's Republic of China as the sole legal government of China. As a result, the Canadian government became embroiled in an acrimonious debate with the International Olympic Committee (IOC) over the right of Taiwan to compete in the 1976 Montreal Olympics as the Republic of China, and to fly its flag and play its national anthem. The IOC considered this refusal to be a breach of Canada's agreement to admit all countries that received official IOC invitations. On the other hand, Canada saw Taiwan's participation under these conditions as a violation of its foreign policy. In this imbroglio, the IOC mustered the support of many Western industrialized nations, particularly that of the United States.

At the last minute, however, both the IOC and the Canadian government modified their respective positions somewhat and reached a tense compromise. But Taiwan would not accept the final compromise, which meant that it would have been able to fly its flag and play its national anthem, but not compete under the name of the Republic of China. Instead, Taiwan withdrew shortly before the Games started, making much political capital of the incident at home and with its allies. Canada had stood by its "One-China" policy in the face of international condemnation, but it paid a price in its image, both at home and abroad. (See Macintosh, Greenhorn, and Hawes, 1992, for a detailed account of this incident.)

THE BOYCOTT ERA

Shortly after this dispute had been resolved, Canada was faced with another international political dispute in connection with the Montreal Olympics. The Black African nations had united to oppose apartheid in South Africa and as part of this campaign had attempted to isolate South Africa in the world of international sport. Although many nations had cooperated in this boycott, some nations, in particular white Commonwealth ones that held traditional sporting ties with South Africa, did not. New Zealand was particularly intransigent. In protest over that country's decision in the spring of 1976 not to cancel a tour of South Africa by its national rugby team, the All-Blacks, the Black African nations threatened to boycott the Montreal Olympics to protest New Zealand's participation. When none of the parties involved in the dispute (Canada, the IOC, and New Zealand) took any action, twenty-two Black African nations withdrew in protest on the eve of the Games.

This withdrawal caused considerable embarrassment to the Canadian government, but it was even more concerned over a similar boycott of the 1978 Commonwealth Games, which were scheduled for Edmonton. A boycott of that magnitude would have been very damaging to those Games, because the Black

African nations and their Third World Commonwealth country allies make up a much larger portion of the competitors than is the case in the Olympics. More importantly, such a boycott would have been very damaging to Canada's image as a leader in the Commonwealth in the fight against apartheid in South Africa. Consequently, the Canadian government and in particular, the DEA, went to considerable ends to prevent such a boycott.

One of the most important measures that Canada undertook was to engineer the passage of the Gleneagles Declaration at the Commonwealth Heads of Government meetings in London in June 1977. The Gleneagles Declaration called on all Commonwealth nations to take every practical step to discourage sporting contacts with South Africa. Prime Minister Trudeau played a central role in getting this unanimous accord, using his considerable diplomatic skills and charisma to good effect at the negotiations that preceded the agreement, which were held in Gleneagles, Scotland. Considerable diplomatic work remained to be done before Canada could be assured of Black African nations' attendance in Edmonton, but the Gleneagles Declaration was central to the ultimate success of these efforts. In the end, there was almost full attendance at the Games, and, as noted above, they were most successful ones. (See Macintosh, Greenhorn, and Black, 1992, for a full account of these events.)

The 1980s were heralded by one of the most traumatic events in the annals of Canadian sport—the boycott of the Moscow Olympics. In response to the Soviet invasion of Afghanistan in December 1979, U.S. President Jimmy Carter threatened to impose a number of sanctions against the Soviet Union if it did not remove its armed forces from that country. A boycott of the 1980 Moscow Olympics was one of these sanctions. To this end, Carter set about to get support for his boycott from his allies and other countries around the world. The Conservative government of Joe Clark, which had made improved relations with the United States a part of its mandate, was willing to go along with the Olympics boycott, as well as to impose other economic and cultural sanctions against the Soviets. But the Clark government was defeated in the federal elections in February 1980, and Pierre Trudeau and his Liberal government were returned to power.

In the meantime, the Soviet Union had not withdrawn from Afghanistan, and Carter set out to make his threat of a Moscow Olympics boycott a reality. In light of his earlier position with regard to relations with the United States, Canadian sports officials and athletes were hopeful that Trudeau would reverse the Clark government decision. But they were to be disappointed. In April of 1980, the new Liberal government announced that it would support the United States on this measure, and that although it would not prevent the Canadian Olympic Association (COA) from sending a team to Moscow, it was withdrawing its funding and its moral support for the event. In the previous month, the Olympic Trust of Canada, an organization that the COA had established in 1970 to raise money from the corporate sector (ironically, so that it could maintain some independence from government), decided that it would withdraw funding for the 1980 Summer Olympics. The COA was left in an untenable position, and in April its members voted to support the boycott, in spite of a plea at the meeting from a contingent of Olympic athletes.

The decisions by the federal government and the Olympic Trust were seen in some quarters as bowing to U.S. government and corporate pressure. (Many of the companies that contributed to the Olympic Trust were subsidiaries of American corporations.) The end result was that many Canadian athletes who had trained for years for the Moscow Olympics were denied an opportunity to compete, and some of them would never get another opportunity to participate in the Olympics. In retrospect, most politicians and sport officials condemned the boycott. It, along with the other sanctions imposed, had no effect on the Soviets, who were not to withdraw from Afghanistan for another ten years, and then only after strong domestic pressure. (See Macintosh and Hawes, 1994, chap. 5, for a full exposition of events surrounding the Moscow boycott.)

A GROWING FEDERAL GOVERNMENT PRESENCE

The federal government was successful in the 1970s in its efforts to improve Canada's international sports performances. The NSOs flourished; they grew in size and effectiveness, but at the same time their traditional autonomy from government was gradually eroded because of the greatly increased financial presence of the federal government. At a time when the majority of their finances were coming from the government, and when the salaries of their professional administrative and executive officers were being largely paid from the same sources, the NSOs' opposition to federal government wishes in what became known in the 1980s as high-performance sport became increasingly muted. This trend toward government dominance in sports policymaking continued in the 1980s.

Assistance to Canada's high-performance athletes originated in a recommendation from the 1971 National Conference on Olympic '76 Development, calling for financial aid for elite athletes and coaches. As a consequence, in 1972 Sport Canada initiated an "Intensive Care" program to provide monies for potential medal winners at the 1972 summer Olympics in Munich. Later that year, the Canadian Olympic Association (COA) launched a program called Game Plan '72 to provide financial support for Canada's high-performance athletes. This program was supported by both the provinces (at least in principle; only Ontario and Quebec did eventually contribute monies) and the federal government. But in 1974 the IOC changed its eligibility rules so that athletes could accept lost-time income to compensate for salaries lost while training. When the federal government felt that it could not risk public criticism of making payments directly to athletes, the COA took over this and some other direct-aid programs, while the government assumed financial responsibilities of the original Game Plan operations. In 1975 the provinces agreed among themselves to terminate their involvement in Game Plan '76. The year after the Montreal Olympics, the federal government took over all responsibilities for Game Plan, including a grants-in-aids program for student athletes. The COA confined its role to financial assistance to club athletes who were not supported by the student aid program. In 1979 Sport Canada consolidated all the athlete aid programs under the aegis of the Athlete Assistance Program (AAP).

The criteria for AAP increasingly became tied to performance rather than need, and athletes were differentially paid according to world rankings in their respective international sport organizations, according to an A, B, or C classification. Sport Canada also began mailing AAP checks directly to the athletes rather than through the athletes' respective NSOs, as had been the practice previously. The NSOs resented this step, maintaining that this was their responsibility, and further diminished their autonomy. By 1989 the federal government was expending approximately $4.5 million to support 840 high-performance athletes (Dubin, 1990, p. 605).

Sport Canada also initiated a policy whereby high-performance athletes who wished to receive AAP support were required to sign an agreement with their respective NSOs which outlined their training obligations as well as abiding by Sport Canada policies. Although the extent to which athletes were required to sign this agreement varied greatly from athlete to athlete and from NSO to NSO, it still caused much resentment among many athletes and created tension between athletes and their respective NSOs. This athlete agreement policy also helped bring the issue of athlete rights to the forefront. (See Beamish and Borowy, 1988, for a discussion of the Canadian AAP.)

Another important measure that Sport Canada took in the early 1980s was the imposition of quadrennial planning on the NSOs involved in Olympic sports. This planning exercise had its immediate origins in a commitment by the federal government in 1983 to set aside an additional $25 million to be used specifically by the ten Winter Olympic sport organizations to ensure that Canada would have a "Best Ever" performance at the 1988 Calgary Olympics. This was the first time that the federal government had committed funds to NSOs for a period longer than one year. Along with this commitment, however, came a requirement that these ten NSOs develop a four-year plan to improve their technical and administrative capacities to produce better high-performance athletes. A review of ten "successful" Olympic sports organizations undertaken in 1981–82 revealed that no model or system for the development of high-performance athletes existed in most NSOs.

Canada's success at the "attenuated" 1984 Olympics in Los Angeles (Canada won forty-four medals, its best performance ever in the summer Olympics) did not escape government notice. The federal government announced that it would extend its "Best Ever" Winter program to the 1988 summer Games in Seoul, and set aside an additional $38 million to be used by summer Olympic NSOs to enhance their capacity to win medals in Seoul. Both the Quebec and Ontario governments also made political capital of Canada's outstanding performance at the Los Angeles Olympics. At respective receptions held to honor their own

1984 Olympic athletes, each premier announced that he would establish ''Best Ever'' programs to provide financial aid to provincial athletes to excel in the 1988 Olympics. One Toronto newspaper labeled Ontario Premier Bill Davis a ''medal exploiter.''

These events set the stage for the introduction of quadrennial planning, whereby Sport Canada invited each Olympic sport NSO to participate in an elaborate planning process leading up to the 1988 summer and winter Olympic Games. Although there was a pretense of choice, the NSOs were aware that the amount of government funding that they would receive over the next four years would be dependent on their ''successful'' participation in this exercise. This planning process, which was renewed for the quadrennial, 1988–92, was to raise a number of issues in the respective NSOs, including the conflict between mass and elite sports programs, the proper role of volunteers versus professional staff in the planning process, the degree to which administrative and athlete services should be centralized, and the extent to which this process was simply imposed by Sport Canada. These issues are discussed at some length in Macintosh and Whitson (1990).

Government contributions to sports continued to rise rapidly in the early 1980s. Sport Canada's budget escalated from $21.7 million in 1979–80 to $40.4 million in 1982–83, during a period when government expenditures were under close scrutiny (Macintosh et al., 1987, p. 152). This level of support led to concern over the extent to which the government was supporting NSOs. The election of the Conservative government in 1984 led to a move to privatize many government functions and crown corporations. This spilled over to sports when, in 1985, the minister of state for fitness and amateur sport, Otto Jelinek, announced that by 1988 sports organizations would have to depend on nongovernment monies for at least 50 percent of their funding. Government support of the NSOs had reached a point where some were receiving as much as 90 percent of their funds from the federal government. Jelinek established a Sport Marketing Council to help the NSOs reach this goal. This Council was to assist the NSOs to better market their ''products,'' that is, sports, and to educate and sensitize the private sector to the advantages of high-performance sport as a marketing vehicle.

Although Jelinek's goal of 50 percent was not reached by 1988, it was reiterated in the government's 1988 sports policy document, *Towards 2000: Building Canada's Sport System* (Canada, 1988). Some of the higher profile NSOs, with athletes who could command the attention of the advertising media, did make some progress toward raising a greater percentage of their budgets from the private sector. But the government never did make good on its threat to reduce its contributions to sport, probably because they represented such a small proportion of total government expenditures. In addition, it had higher priorities in its privatization drive.

The culmination of federal government efforts to promote high-performance sport came with the staging of the 1988 winter Olympics in Calgary. These

Games were most successful from a number of aspects. Canadian athletes won five medals and finished among the top eight competitors nineteen times, both "best ever" performances for Canada (Canada, 1992, p. 296). ABC, an American television network, paid US $309 million for the American television rights alone, a record amount for the winter Olympics (Irwin, 1988, p. 35). The nightly worldwide telecasts showed the city of Calgary in its best light.

The Calgary Games were also a financial success, finishing debt free. Of course, in contrast to the widely touted "profit-making" 1984 Los Angeles Games, government financial support of the Calgary Olympics was very substantial. The federal government estimated that it contributed $300 million to the $800 million total cost of the Games, of which $225 million was in direct expenditures (Canada, 1992, p. 296). Provincial expenditures amounted to some $130 million, while the city of Calgary committed $43 million (Kee, 1990, p. 55). For the first time in the history of major games events in Canada, a legacy fund was put in place that would generate enough interest to support the yearly operating costs of the new Olympic sport facilities once the event was over. Some of the sports facilities that had been built for previous major games in Canada (most notably, those for the 1976 Montreal Summer Olympics) had subsequently been prohibitively expensive to operate, and thus had become either "white elephants" or sites for professional sport franchises and pop entertainment extravaganzas. The federal government and the Calgary Olympic Organizing Committee each contributed $30 million to this legacy fund, and the Calgary Olympic Development Association was established to administer the distribution of the monies once the Games were over (Macintosh et al., 1987, p. 179).

Federal and provincial cabinet ministers were conspicuous by their presence at the Calgary Games, especially at the figure skating events, where Canadian athletes figured prominently. Fitness and Amateur Sport Minister Otto Jelinek was seen on television around the world when he participated in the closing ceremonies, which featured many former world champion figure skaters in an "on-ice" show. (Jelinek himself won the gold medal in figure skating pairs at the 1962 World Championships in Prague.) At the conclusion of the Calgary Olympics, Jelinek announced that the "Best Ever" winter sport program would be extended, with a further contribution of $32 million from federal government funds (Canada, 1992, p. 296). This announcement was made in spite of his avowed goal of raising more money for sports from the private sector.

SPORT AND APARTHEID

Although Canada's encounters in international sport in the 1970s were mostly reactive and were tied up with the Cold War politics of those times, its international activities designed to ensure the success of the 1978 Edmonton Commonwealth Games were connected with its wider political goals of championing the causes of Third World countries, particularly those within the Commonwealth. One of these causes was the fight against apartheid in South Africa. Indeed, shortly before the Edmonton Games, the federal government announced that it would disallow visas for all South African athletes and sports officials wishing to enter Canada to participate in sports competitions. This was the final step that ensured the participation of Black African nations in Edmonton. Before this time, Canadian NSOs had been discouraged from sending athletes to South Africa or competing against them in Canada, on penalty of losing associated federal government funds for the event.

The sport sanctions that Canada applied against South Africa in the 1980s were part of the strategy of most Commonwealth nations to use sport as one of the weapons to break down apartheid in South Africa. The sanctions played a role in Canada's wider Commonwealth goals, one of which was to replace Great Britain as the acknowledged leader of the Commonwealth. Margaret Thatcher's Conservative governments of the 1980s took a dim view of tightening economic and social sanctions against South Africa, a position that was not popular with the Third World Commonwealth countries. To this end, Canada was forced to take a moderate position. There was much opposition at home, both in government circles and from the public at large, to imposing significant economic sanctions against South Africa. On the other hand, the lobby against further sport sanctions was relatively weak. This was an important factor in the Canadian government's focus on sport sanctions in the fight against apartheid. (For a full account of these events as well as the role of sport in Canada's larger foreign policy goals, see Macintosh and Hawes, 1994.)

In 1985 the secretary of state for external affairs, Joe Clark, issued a formal policy statement that "reaffirmed Canada's support for the Commonwealth policy limiting sporting contacts with South Africa," and at the same time, set guidelines for Canadian NSOs in interpreting the policy (Canada, July 29, 1988). This policy prevented sporting contacts not only between Canada's high-performance athletes in South Africa and Canada, but in other countries as well. If Canada's athletes knew that South Africans were going to participate in an international sport event abroad, they were required to withdraw or face the loss of government funding. This policy had actually been in force in the Fitness and Amateur Sport Branch since 1982, but the statement by External Affairs was a sign that sport was to play a bigger part in Canada's international affairs. Professional athletes, however, were not included in this ban, and this omission was to cause the government considerable embarrassment.

In the summer of 1988, Joe Clark was preparing to host a meeting of the Committee of Commonwealth Foreign Ministers on Southern Africa (CCFMSA) in Toronto. Much to his embarrassment, the news media picked up on the fact that South African professionals were likely to compete in the annual Players' International men's tennis tournament in Toronto at the same time as he would be chairing the CCFMSA meetings. After hurried meetings among officials from External Affairs, Employment and Immigration, and Fitness and Amateur Sport, Clark and Fitness and Amateur Sport Minister Jean Charest announced that the government's policy would be tightened to deny visas to professional athletes on South African passports seeking to compete in Canada. Despite demands from sport apartheid activists, this ban was not extended to South African professional athletes who possessed "passports of convenience" (passports from other countries) or green (immigration) cards from the United States.

SPORT INITIATIVES IN THE COMMONWEALTH

Another important development at this time was the joint announcement by Joe Clark and Fitness and Amateur Sport Minister Jean Charest in October 1987 that Canada intended to put sport to greater use in promoting its image abroad and to strengthen the country's influence in the international sports movement. To this end, a new International Relations Directorate was established in Fitness and Amateur Sport, and External Affairs committed additional funds and personnel to the sports section in its Cultural Affairs Division. That Canada intended to put more emphasis on sports in its international diplomacy initiatives was made clear when Joe Clark proposed to the CCFMSA that it should take action to provide assistance to the Commonwealth Games Federation (CGF) and to help develop sports in Third World Commonwealth countries. This was consistent with Canada's wider goals of exerting leadership in the Commonwealth by providing technical and financial assistance to the "have-not" nations. It also signaled that sport, and particularly the Commonwealth Games, played a significant symbolic role in holding together an already fragile Commonwealth.

Consequently, a Working Party on Strengthening Commonwealth Sport was formed at the Commonwealth Heads of Governments meetings in Kuala Lumpur in October 1989. Under the chair of Canadian Roy McMurtry, and with assistance from government officials in Ottawa, this Committee prepared a final report that was approved at the Heads of Government meetings in Harare in October 1991. The final report focused on specific ways in which funds and sport expertise could be transferred from developed to undeveloped countries in the Commonwealth, and on ways in which the Commonwealth Games themselves could be sustained. (See Working Party Final Report, July 1991, for details of these recommendations.) To these ends, Clark committed Canada to providing $1 million per year for a five-year period.

Despite these and other initiatives in Third World countries that were taken by the expanded sports section of External Affairs, the federal government announced in February 1992 that as part of its efforts to "streamline" (i.e., reduce) the government bureaucracy, the Cultural Affairs Division (which included sport) in External Affairs would be eliminated, and its functions would be assumed by other departments. The sports section was to be subsumed by the International Relations Directorate in Fitness and Amateur Sport. A consolidated international sport unit made sense from an organizational viewpoint, but leading Canadian sports officials and organizations protested, pointing out that moving sports out of the powerful External Affairs Department indicated a lower priority for sports in international relations. Government officials responded by assuring the sports community that External Affairs would still play a coordinating role forthcoming important international sports matters. (See Macintosh and Hawes, 1994, chap. 10, for a full exposition of this development.)

CRISIS IN SPORT IN CANADA

If the Calgary Olympics can be seen as the zenith of high-performance sport in Canada, the 1988 summer Games in Seoul might well be seen as its nadir. Canada's athletes did not perform as well as expected at these Olympics, winning only ten medals and finishing nineteenth in the unofficial medal count. As a result, there was much soul searching among Canadian sports officials once the Games were over. Much more traumatic, however, were the events surrounding the 100-meter final. Ben Johnson won the event in Olympic record time, scoring a convincing win over his arch-rival from the United States, Carl Lewis. But shortly after Canadian Prime Minister Brian Mulroney had phoned to congratulate him, it was announced that Johnson had failed to pass his drug urine test. After the instant jubilation over this "Canadian" victory, the nation was thrown into gloom and despair. For some time, Canadians could not believe that Johnson had taken steroids. This disbelief was fostered by Johnson himself, who continued to deny that he was guilty.

Recriminations and counteraccusations about prior knowledge of drug taking among Canada's high-performance athletes reverberated at many levels of sport and government, and sports and government officials hastened to cover their tracks. But the public concern was too great to be ignored, and the federal government was forced to initiate a public inquiry. This inquiry was conducted by Charles Dubin, a respected Ontario Court justice who had conducted other public inquiries. After a parade of witnesses at this inquiry, it became clear to Canadians that not only had Ben Johnson been guilty of taking illegal drugs, but also that drug use was widespread among the country's athletes, and not just at the top level of sport.

One of the first government reactions was expressed by the House of Commons Committee on Health and Welfare, Social Affairs, Seniors, and the Status of Women in June of 1989, when it struck a Sub-Committee on Fitness and Amateur Sport to examine the federal government's most recent sports policy document, *Towards 2000: Building Canada's Sport System,* as well as the report that Dubin was to submit to the federal government. *Towards 2000* had all but ignored the drug issue and ethical values in sport in its rush to chart a course toward even better international performances by Canada's high-performance athletes in the 1990s. This was the first time in Canada's history that a House of Commons Standing Committee had taken on the task of studying the proper role of the federal government in sport.

In his subsequent report to the federal government, tabled in the House of Commons in June 1990, Dubin declared that there was a moral crisis in high-performance sport in Canada. He put much of the blame on the heavy-handed involvement of the federal government and its preoccupation with winning medals (Dubin, 1990). The first federal government response was a quick one. In August of the same year, it issued a report that imposed penalties on the persons whom Dubin had implicated in his report, and put forward a Proposed Policy Framework for Doping Policies. The federal government assumed that those NSOs whose officials and athletes had been named by Dubin would take the action against them that the federal government proposed.

The federal government then began to prepare a more comprehensive report on the Dubin Inquiry Report, and this stage involved inviting submissions and briefs from interested persons and sports organizations. In December 1990 the Sub-Committee on Fitness and Amateur Sport tabled its report in the House of Commons. In January 1991 the federal government issued its second response, announcing its intention to set up a new anti-drug organization that would co-ordinate and administer all Canadian anti-drug initiatives. At the same time, the federal government established a Minister's Task Force on Federal Government Sport Policy (Canada, 1992, p. 297).

In May 1992 this Task Force submitted its report, *Sport: The Way Ahead* (Canada, 1992), to Fitness and Amateur Sport minister Pierre Cadieux. In reporting to the minister, former senior public servant Cal Best, who chaired this Task Force, stated that: "Sport must above all be based on ethical values. It must become athlete-centered, community-based and more accessible in a better harmonized system where shared leadership goes hand-in hand with clearly defined accountabilities" (Fitness and Amateur Sport, May 7, 1992, p. 2). This quote set the tone for the Task Force Report, which, if its 117 recommendations were implemented, would represent a completely new direction for high-performance sports in Canada. It would entail a much lower profile by the federal government and correspondingly more responsibility on the part of NSOs for sport policymaking, would result in a truly national sport plan for Canada, and would focus much more on the values and outcomes of sport for the participants and much less on winning medals. The implementation of the Task Force recommendations would also mean a widening of opportunities in sport for those who are currently disadvantaged in the Canadian system—women, francophones, persons from working-class backgrounds, as well as special needs populations. It must be noted, however, that government sports policy documents have promised much the same on several previous occasions.

Canada did rebound from its disappointing performance at the 1988 Seoul Olympics. After exceeding their 1988 Calgary medal performance at the Albertville winter Games in 1992, Canadian athletes won eighteen medals at the Barcelona summer Games, the most Olympic medals ever won by Canada (excluding the truncated 1984 Los Angeles Games). These performances did serve to boost the morale of Canada's high-performance athletes, which had been severely battered by the Ben Johnson scandal.

DISCUSSION AND ANALYSIS

The federal government's changing motives over the past thirty years, and both the positive and negative consequences of its involvement in sport, nicely illustrate what Bruce Kidd (1980) has coined the dilemma of state intervention in sport. On the one hand, there have been some very positive outcomes. Canada now has a corps of high-performance athletes that are capable of competing successfully in most international sport events. The publicity that the high-profile athletes in this corps have received has served to counter to some extent the "North Americanization" of the NHL, the incursion of major league baseball, and the ubiquitous presence of sport from the United States on Canadians' television screens and in their newspapers. In these ways, federal government intervention has helped to inspire pride and promote national unity, fulfilling at least in part Prime Minister Trudeau's vision of sport as a unifying force in Canada, and projecting a unique Canadian identity through the medium of sport.

This federal government involvement has also helped to create a well-articulated support system for Canada's high-performance athletes: a large sports bureaucracy housed in a centralized national sports administration center; sophisticated sports science, sports medicine, and physical therapy services for high-performance athletes; a well-developed and nationwide coaching certification program; a financial support system for high-performance athletes, coaches, and technical and administrative staff; and a number of high-performance training centers across the country. This system has been the envy of many other countries and has been a model for the development of sports in Australia.

One of the few successful joint federal-provincial sports ventures has been the Canada Games. Besides helping to stimulate interest and promote competition among promising young athletes, the monies spent by all three levels of government on these Games have left a considerable legacy of sports facilities. These facilities have contributed greatly to an increase in sports participation by the average Canadian in the moderately sized communities in which these Games have been hosted. This is in contrast to many of the edifices built for major international sports events in larger cities in Canada, which have been ill-suited for use by the average sport participant. Cases in point are Olympic Stadium and the Velodrome built for the Montreal Olympics, Commonwealth Stadium for the Edmonton Commonwealth Games, and the Saddledome (hockey arena) built for the Calgary Winter Olympics. These stadiums have become largely venues for professional sports and events staged by concert entrepreneurs. Large operating expenses make them inappropriate to use by most Canadian athletes. For example, Calgary Olympic Park, built for $62 million to host the Winter Olympic downhill skiing, luge, and bobsled events, also is not well suited to community sport use, and has become largely a training and competition site for high-performance athletes from Canada and other countries that excel in winter Olympic sports.

Governments in Canada are increasingly supporting the costs of the construction of expensive sports facilities, not only for major international games, but also for stadiums such as the SkyDome in Toronto and B.C. Place in Vancouver. This development is symptomatic of the government strategy in uncertain financial times and the present neo-conservative atmosphere in Western industrialized nations. Government support of the construction of expensive sports facilities is justified because it stimulates the economy, providing new jobs and profits for the private sector—the ''trickle-down'' theory of economics or ''Reaganomics.'' It is also one of the few types of government expenditures that meets the approval of the general public. Despite protests from the activist group, ''Bread Not Circuses,'' about the wisdom of the expenditure of hundreds of millions of dollars to host the 1996 Olympics in Toronto in the face of growing poverty and increasing homelessness, the bid went ahead with the support of the public and the local government, with financial support from both the province and the federal government.

Shortly after the news that the Toronto Olympic bid had not been successful, it was revealed that the interest on the $345 million debt on the new Toronto SkyDome was costing the Ontario taxpayers approximately $31 million a year. The cost of building the SkyDome, which was originally projected to be $150 million, ballooned to $578 million. Massive cost overruns by the private-sector consortium that had managed its construction were said to account for this debt, which had been guaranteed by the provincial government. In the meantime, the major benefactor of the SkyDome, the Toronto Blue Jays baseball team, had no responsibility for the debt and continued to make a profit from its lucrative franchise in Toronto.

In the euphoria surrounding the Toronto Blue Jays' 1992 World Series victory, there was little questioning of the wisdom of Ontario taxpayer support of the SkyDome. However, residents in Quebec, who are still paying taxes on the debt accumulated in the 1976 Montreal Olympics, would most likely have a different view of public contributions to the construction of massive sport stadiums. (See Macintosh and Whitson, 1992, chap. 8, for a more extensive discussion of the issue of public support of the construction of massive sport stadiums.)

As noted earlier, the Canada Games helped stimulate the growth of sports bureaucracies in most of the provinces, and although this provincial presence has had many of the same positive benefits of federal government involvement, it has also led to friction between the two levels of government. Although the provinces have been willing to cede responsibility for international sport to the federal government, they have not done so with regard to the *development* of high-performance athletes. This conflict, of course, is set in the wider demands by the provinces for more powers in Canadian federalism. The result has been confusion and competition over responsibilities for high-performance sport.

Although the creation of a national plan for sports in Canada, one that would rationalize the respective roles of the provinces and the federal government, has been on the agenda ever since the early 1970s, such a plan has never materialized. It received top priority once again in the federal government's 1992 sports policy document, *Sport: The Way Ahead* (Canada, 1992). This step is essential if there is to be a well-articulated plan for the development of high-performance athletes in Canada, one that would clearly delineate the respective provincial and federal responsibilities in these endeavors, and would take into account the many community-based elite youth sports clubs that play a central role in the development of athletes in many sports. The tendency of both federal and provincial politicians to use high-performance sports to legitimize the government of the day and to promote their own careers has also mitigated against the development of such a plan.

The federal government's preoccupation with medal production in international sports events has also pushed to the background other of its often stated goals—those of providing for more equal opportunities in high-performance sports for women, francophones, and people from working-class backgrounds. Women made little progress in the 1980s in penetrating the ranks of the senior executive and technical staff in the national sports bureaucracy, or in membership on NSO Boards of Directors and Executive Committees, despite the establishment of a Women's Program in Fitness and Amateur Sport at the start of the decade. Women are still highly underrepresented at the coaching and administrative levels of high-performance sports, not only in the NSOs but also at the university level. Nor has the percentage of female competitors at the national, collegiate, and secondary school levels improved much in the last decade (see Macintosh and Whitson, 1990, chap. 6).

Similarly, little progress has been made in including more francophones as administrators, coaches, and athletes in the high-performance sports system. Francophones still typically make up only about 12 to 15 percent of these cohorts, while they represent about 24 percent of the Canadian population at large. In the case of the inclusion of persons from working-class backgrounds, there is some evidence to support the claim that there are actually fewer high-performance athletes from such backgrounds today than at the start of federal government intervention in the early 1970s. This is despite much rhetoric in federal government documents on sports policy, especially about equity for females and francophones. (See Macintosh and Whitson, 1990, chap. 7, for an analysis of these equity issues.)

FUTURE DIRECTIONS

The Ben Johnson affair was instrumental in bringing to the attention of the Canadian public the consequences of a federal government sports policy predicated on winning medals. Preoccupation with this goal not only has meant the neglect of equity issues discussed above, but has also contributed greatly to the decline of attention to ethics in high-performance sport that was so succinctly documented by Charles Dubin. The question now is whether Canadians (and their governments) wish to continue to support the production of high-performance athletes. Such expenditures have been justified in the past on the basis of the intangible "public" goods that accrue to all Canadians: contributing to national unity; attaining international stature; increasing the motivation to participate in sport; and supporting individual Canadians in the pursuit of excellence. In the debate that now surrounds federal government involvement in high-performance sport in Canada, these outcomes have to be placed in the perspective of other social needs in Canada.

Sport: The Way Ahead suggests that the government will give up its dominant role in high-performance sports, sharing responsibilities more equally with the NSOs. The Cal Best investigation may well recommend to the federal government that all the negative publicity that it has received over the Ben Johnson affair is not worth the expenditures, and that the government might reconsider its role in high-performance sports. This would be consistent with its stated goal of downsizing its bureaucracy and turning over more of the fiscal responsibilities of high-performance sports to the private sector. Such a move, however, would make the NSOs dependent almost entirely on the private sector in order to maintain their present levels of expenditure. This would cause considerable inequities in the extent to which different NSOs would be able to garner such financial support, and would not be likely to contribute to greater equity and an increased emphasis on ethical values in sports. Government involvement and financial support is a legitimate and important component of high-performance sports, just as it is of other cultural endeavors. However, the federal government's presence needs to be mediated in the policymaking process by all the other legitimate actors—the NSOs, the provincial governments and sports organizations, the athletes themselves, and representatives of the public at large.

The reorganization of sports at the federal level and the development of a model national sports system is not likely to be of high priority to government in Canada. The Canadian voters' rejection in October 1992 of the Charlottetown Constitutional Accord, and the fragility of the federal Conservative and the Quebec Liberal governments will preoccupy politicians and public servants for some time to come. The matter of sports policy is likely to remain on the back burner until the country achieves more political stability.

The dramatic political events of 1989 have caused corresponding changes in international sports circles. The federal government will no longer face the crises that were characteristic of Cold War sports politics. In addition, its sports sanctions against South Africa were withdrawn in the summer of 1991 after the IOC negotiated that country's return to international sport. The early acrimony among the de Klerk government, the African National Congress, and the Inkatha Freedom party has been resolved. Thus, the issue of sports sanctions against South Africa will not likely return to the Canadian foreign policy agenda.

Sport as part of Canada's aid to Third World countries, and particularly those in the Commonwealth, is likely to continue to be of high priority for the federal government. However, the impact of the government's decision in early 1992 to turn over the functions of the sports section in External Affairs to the International Relations Directorate in Fitness and Amateur Sport has yet to be determined. Certainly, establishing a single responsibility for international sports matters will likely result in better coordinated and planned sport aid and program development initiatives in Third World countries. But Fitness and Amateur Sport has been inclined to use these sports initiatives to enhance Canada's stature in international sports circles rather than to meet the country's wider foreign policy objectives. This was one of the causes of friction between the sports section in External Affairs and Fitness and Amateur Sport. (See Macintosh and Hawes, 1994, chap. 10, for a discussion of this issue.)

In the new world of interdependence, other issues will be certain to surface. For instance, transnational business concerns, in their eagerness to use sports to sell goods and services across national boundaries, and their willingness to pay large sums of sponsorship and television advertising monies to this end, will increasingly come to set the agenda for international sports organizations like the IOC. The ''North Americanization'' of sport is likely to change to a ''globalization'' of sport, fanned by an ever increasingly sophisticated world telecommunications network, one that will use space satellites to reach better and cheaper home reception satellite dishes and bypass existing cable television networks in North America. North American professional sports organizations are already contemplating this globalization course. This development will make it even more imperative for the federal government to use sport as a vehicle to promote national pride and to maintain a unique Canadian identity.

REFERENCES

Adams, A. (1992, September 26). NHL entry draft under scrutiny. *Globe and Mail,* p. A20.

Baka, R., and Hoy, D. (1978). Political aspects of Canadian participation in the Commonwealth Games: 1930–1978. *CAHPER Journal, 44* (4): 6–14, 24.

Beamish, R., and Borowy, J. (1988). *What do you do for a living? I'm an athlete.* Kingston, Ont.: Sport and Leisure Studies Research Group, Queen's University.

Brunt, S. (1992, July 6). The main event. *Globe and Mail,* p. D1.

Canada. (1988, July 29). Canada tightens policy on sport contacts with South Africa. News Release.

Canada. (1988). *Towards 2000: Building Canada's sport system.* Report of the Task Force on National Sport Policy. Ottawa: Fitness and Amateur Sport.

Canada. (1992). *Sport: The way ahead.* The report of the Minister's Task Force on Federal Sport Policy. Ottawa: Minister of Supply and Services Canada.

Canada Games Council. (1979). *Canada Games handbook: An outline of policies and organizational procedures.* Ottawa.

Clark, B., and Hutchinson, B. (1991, June 3). Hockey's rich American cousins. *Alberta Report,* pp. 42–45.

Dubin, C. (1990). *Commission of inquiry into the use of drugs and banned practices intended to increase athletic performance.* Ottawa: Minister of Supply and Services Canada.

Fitness and Amateur Sport. (1992, May 7). *News Release.* Ottawa.

Goodman, J. (1981). *Huddling up.* Don Mills, Ont.: Fitzhenry and Whiteside.

House of Commons (HC). (1966, June 13). *Debates.* Ottawa.

Irwin, W. (1988). *The politics of international sport—Games of power.* New York: Foreign Policy Association.

Jones, J. (1976). The economics of the National Hockey League. In R. Gruneau and J. Albinson (eds.), *Canadian sport: Sociological perspectives* (pp. 225–248). Don Mills, Ont.: Addison-Wesley.

Kee, J. (1990, Summer). Hosts and sponsors: Making it work—The Calgary experience. *Inside Guide,* pp. 55–65.

Kidd, B. (1980). *The Canadian state and sport: The dilemmas of intervention.* Paper presented at the annual conference of the National Association for Physical Education in Higher Education, Brainerd, Minnesota.

Kidd, B. (1991). How do we find our own voices in the "New world order?": A commentary on Americanization. *Sociology of Sport Journal 8*(2): 178–184.

Macintosh, D., Bedecki, T., and Franks, C.E.S. (1987). *Sport and politics in Canada.* Kingston and Montreal: McGill-Queen's University Press.

Macintosh, D., and Greenhorn, D. (1993). Hockey diplomacy and Canadian foreign policy. *Journal of Canadian Studies, 28*(2): 96–112.

Macintosh, D., Greenhorn, D., and Black, D. (1992). Canadian diplomacy and the 1978 Edmonton Commonwealth Games. *Journal of Sport History, 19*(1): 26–55.

Macintosh, D., Greenhorn, D., and Hawes, M. (1992). Trudeau, Taiwan, and the 1976 Montreal Olympics. *American Review of Canadian Studies, 21*(4): 423–448.

Macintosh, D., and Hawes, M. (1994). *Sport and Canadian diplomacy.* Montreal: McGill-Queen's University Press.

Macintosh, D., and Whitson, D. (1990). *The game planners: Transforming Canada's sport system.* Kingston and Montreal: McGill-Queen's University Press.

Macintosh, D., and Whitson, D. (1992, December). *Economic, political, and social dimensions of major games bids in Canada: An overview.* Paper presented at the Association for Canadian Studies in Australia and New Zealand Conference, Wellington, New Zealand.

Marron, E. (1992, July 10). Council votes to help Ticats. *Globe and Mail,* p. C12.

Morse, E. (1987). Successfully blending politics and sport. *Champion, 11* (2): 18–20.

Scher, J. (1992, October 12). NHL preview '92–93. *Sports Illustrated,* pp. 34–38.

Stephens, T., and Craig, C. L. (1990). *The well-being of Canadians: Highlights of the 1988 Campbell survey.* Ottawa: Canadian Fitness and Lifestyle Research Institute.

Working Party Final Report. (1991, July). Strengthening Commonwealth sport. Ottawa: External Affairs and International Trade.

4

The People's Republic of China

Cao Xiangjun and Susan E. Brownell

This chapter is the product of collaboration between a Chinese sports scholar from the Beijing Institute of Physical Education and an anthropologist who came to know her during a year of research there.[1] As such, it departs somewhat from the usual discussions of Chinese sports policy. It attempts to present policy from the Chinese viewpoint and to demonstrate how the Chinese assess their own sports policy. The larger part of the chapter was written by Cao and then translated and edited by Brownell. Although it has been considerably rearranged, the wording of the translation is generally faithful to Cao's original Chinese. Cao's contributions were then supplemented by Brownell. The difficulties of working in two languages from different sides of the world precluded the possibility of a truly collaborative effort. As a result, the author of each section is indicated to aid the reader in understanding the shifts in voice and viewpoint. Because Cao did not have the opportunity to read the final version, Brownell takes final responsibility for the content.

NATURE AND STRUCTURE OF NATIONAL GOVERNMENT
(Susan Brownell)

The administrative structure of the People's Republic of China (PRC) is divided into three branches: government, army, and judiciary. In principle, the supreme governmental authority resides in the National People's Congress, a large elected legislative body. In practice, government affairs are controlled by the State Council, a complex organization that oversees over thirty ministries and as many departments, offices, and commissions. It is headed by the post of premier. The "commission" (*weiyuanhui*) is a flexible organization that is designed to horizontally coordinate the vertically organized ministries and other organizations (Schurmann, 1970, p. 175). The State Physical Culture and Sports Commission (*guojia tiyu yundong weiyuanhui,* generally called simply the State Sports Commission) is the state organ most actively involved in sports policy-making. It is linked to the State Education Commission and the ministries of Foreign Affairs, National Defense, Public Health, and Culture (Cao, 1985, p. 207). The head of the commission holds a cabinet-level position. The State Sports Commission was created in 1952, taking over many of the functions of the All-China Sports Federation which was created after Liberation in 1949 (Kolatch, 1972, pp. 99–100).

The All-China Sports Federation (*Zhonghua quanguo tiyu zonghui*) is the "mass organization" responsible for coordinating government organization, organizing the individual sports federations, promoting mass physical culture, and overseeing competition schedules. It also serves as the Chinese Olympic Committee (Cao, 1985, p. 207; Clumpner and Pendleton, 1978, pp. 115–116). There is typically some overlap in the people who occupy the highest positions in the State Sports Commission and the All-China Sports Federation.

Chinese sports policy is issued and administered by these two organizations (see Wu and Que, 1990), and is ideologically guided by the Communist party. In theory, the party is the organized expression of the will of the people; it issues policy directives, but it cannot issue orders. Instead, policy is implemented by organs of state (Schurmann, 1970, p. 110). Hence, "comprehensive documents" (*zonghexing wenjian*) which serve as a "basic path" (*luxian*) or as guidelines (*fangzhen*) are issued by party organs, while specific policies (*zhengce*) are directly issued by the relevant state organ or office itself (Schurmann, 1970, pp. 86–87 n.60).

The structural relationship between the party and the sports administrative organs is often complex. Important links are those people who occupy important party positions (e.g., Central Committee members), as well as positions in the two administrative organizations. The party also has organs within the State Sports Commission, headed by the Party Committee (*dangwei*), which issues the "comprehensive" directives that serve as general guiding principles for the administration of the sports system. These directives have most often been formulated at the National Working Conference on Physical Culture as "reports" (*baogao*) on the state of the sports endeavor, and have then been submitted to the State Council for approval.

In order to understand the origins and implementation of policy in the PRC, it is necessary to understand the importance of these comprehensive directives. Upon reading one of the "comprehensive" documents (*wenjian*), it is often difficult for a Westerner to understand that policy is, in fact, being made. Typically, a summary of the accomplishments in physical culture since Liberation has been followed by a general overview of the current situation and suggestions for the future. These "reports" are published in *China Sports News* (*Zhongguo*

Tiyu Bao) and other publications for dissemination to the public. In Schurmann's analysis, the practice of publishing general, personal statements by leaders paves the way for policy decisions by revealing the thinking of the leaders (Schurmann, 1970, p. 65). Often, policy documents are anticipated by those in the system long before they "come down." (The upper/lower spatial metaphor is used to reflect the bureaucratic hierarchy.) This is because people familiar with the thinking of state leaders have good reason to believe that a document will be issued sooner or later.

This emphasis on the thinking of state leaders also explains the importance placed on the practice of leaders "offering words on behalf of" (*wei ... tici*) important public events by penning inspirational phrases that are often published in the media in the leader's own calligraphy with his signature. The offered words are typically labeled "slogans" in English, but Mandarin Chinese distinguishes these phrases from shouted slogans (*kouhao*) and slogans written on banners and walls (*biaoyu*). Chinese sports histories usually mention the main phrases offered by leaders as a way of characterizing key historic junctures. This seems trivial and irrelevant to the Western reader, who fails to understand that these phrases crystallize the ideological context in which concrete policy takes shape.

In contrast to the comprehensive guidelines issued by the Party Committee, the more specific documents issued by the administrative organs of the State Sports Commission are worded concisely to spell out the hard-and-fast guidelines for implementation. These documents are the basis on which the structure of the sports system is built.

MODERN HISTORY OF GOVERNMENT'S RELATION TO SPORT (Cao Xiangjun)

The First Stage: Establishing the Foundation (1949–56)

In the first period after the founding of the PRC (1949), full-scale reconstruction was undertaken to rebuild the New China on the ruins of the Old China; this was even more true of the development of sports and physical culture. Before Liberation, because the mass of people suffered hunger and cold and lived in dire poverty, they had been deprived, fundamentally speaking, of the right to participate in physical culture. Because of their poor living conditions, their physiques became weak, their countenances wan and sallow, and they were insulted as the "weak men of East Asia."

On this kind of foundation, building and developing a new physical culture was very difficult. However, because of the party and government's emphasis on the physical culture and the national leaders' concern for the health of the people, guiding policies were drafted, the organization and leading organs of physical culture were established, the various physical culture structures were laid down, and a good foundation was laid for the development of physical culture.

In September 1949 the National People's Political Consultative Conference drew up a common program that stipulated in explicit terms: "Promote national physical culture." In October, right after the founding ceremony of the state, the National Congress of Physical Culture Workers opened in Beijing, and the original Chinese National Sports Association changed its name to the All-China Sports Federation. Zhu Du attended the congress in the post of chairperson and made an important speech. He emphatically pointed out: "The physical culture enterprise must definitely serve the people and make the people of the nation train so that they become robust of health and happy of spirit, so that they can take on the arduous task of constructing the New China."

In August 1951 the Government Administrative Council (later the State Council) proclamation, "Resolution on Improving the Physical Condition of Students in Every School Level," indicated that "One of the important tasks of improving students' physiques is to guarantee that students complete their academic duties and to cultivate a modern youth that is physically strong." In 1952 Chairman Mao offered this slogan for the All-China Sports Federation: "Develop physical culture and sports, strengthen the people's physiques," and Zhu Du offered the slogan: "Popularize the people's physical culture and sports, serve production and national defense." In 1954 the Party Central Committee approved the "Central People's Government Physical Culture and Sports Commission Report on Strengthening Work on the People's Physical Culture and Sports," and sent out directives on strengthening physical culture work, which pointed out that "Improving the condition of the people's health and strengthening the people's physiques is an important political goal of the Party."

In 1955, on the occasion of the First National Workers' Sports Games, Liu Shaoqi proclaimed: "Develop physical culture and sports, improve health, serve Socialist construction," and Premier Zhou Enlai spoke these words: "Develop workers' physical culture and sports, promote the enterprise of Socialist construction."

In November 1952 the Government Administrative Council founded the State Sports Commission to take over national physical culture work. Vice-Premier He Long doubled as the chairman of the Sports Commission. In his first work report, he pointed out that in order to guarantee the development of physical culture and sports, sports commissions had to be swiftly established and perfected at each level. He advocated that labor unions, youth leagues, and education bureaus should establish physical culture organs. Thus, each province, municipality, and autonomous region established sports commissions in counties, and corresponding physical culture organs were established in the relevant bureaus of the Ministry of Education, the Central Youth League, and the General Political Department of the Military Commission. Twenty-one industrial systems and individual physical culture associations were founded, linking governmental bureaus and mass groups, and establishing a rather complete system of physical culture organizations and leadership organs. At the same time, at the initiation of Liu Shaoqi, nearly 400 various localities nationwide established National Defense Physical Culture Associations and clubs.

During this period, in order to strengthen the training of physical culture personnel, six institutes and eleven schools of physical culture were built, and thirty-eight high-level normal colleges restored their Physical Education departments. In establishing the physical culture system, the documents on "The System of Physical Culture for Preparing for Labor and Protecting the Fatherland," the "Athletes' Grade System," the "Officials' Grade System," and the "Physical Culture Training Standards" were implemented and disseminated. An unprecedented enthusiasm for exercise welled up among teenagers, and nearly 83,000 people passed the standards of the labor and health systems. In 1951 the first set of broadcast exercises was issued, morning and class-break exercises were launched in the schools, and work-break exercises were launched in offices and enterprises. According to statistics for 1954, 70 percent of office cadres did work-break exercises.

In 1956 Premier Zhou Enlai, in his report at the party's Eighth Representative Assembly, declared: "Speed up the development of mass physical culture and sports, and, on the broad base of mass sports, conscientiously raise the level of sports technique." During this stage, sports performances also improved quickly; in 1956 alone, 671 national records were broken, and China also began to mount the stage of international sports. In 1953 Wu Chuanyu won the championship in the 100 meter backstroke at the World Youth Festival, and the Five-Star Red Flag rose over the international sports arena for the first time. Later, in 1956, China's athletes broke three world records, including Chen Jingkai's breaking of the world lightweight weightlifting record, which was the first time that a Chinese athlete broke a world record.

The Second Stage: Two High Tides, One Low Valley (1957–66)

In this stage China entered all-around, large-scale socialist construction. Certain political upheavals (for example, the spread of anti-rightism, "The Great Leap Forward," and other movements) and economic difficulties (three years of serious natural catastrophes) had definite effects on national, social, and economic development. They also had a negative influence on the development of physical culture. However, since two National Sports Games convened during this stage, sports competition had a compensatory effect on the development of physical culture and sports. Therefore, their development in this stage came in waves.

From 1957 to 1958, when anti-rightism intensified, erroneous slogans such as "The Great Leap Forward" were raised again. For example, the "Ten-Year Development Plan for Physical Culture" drafted in 1958, inappropriately suggested that "within five years two sports fields, one recreation station, one gymnasium, one pool would be built in every county." At that time, this goal was hard to achieve. Afterward, these premature methods were quickly corrected. Preparing for and welcoming the First National Sports Games (1959) initiated the first small high point.

In 1959 the first national sports games since the establishment of the PRC served as a review of the achievements reached in physical culture in the ten years since the founding of the nation. The government attached a great deal of importance to these games, successively issuing two sets of written instructions requiring that the games be carried out well and magnificently and that outstanding performances be made. They also emphasized that "popularizing" and "improving" be linked together, that sports ethics be strictly obeyed, that attention be paid to unity, and that "medals-and-trophyism" be avoided.

Beginning in 1960, there was a three-year period of difficulties, with ill effects on physical culture work. Under the guidance of the "adjust, consolidate, replenish, improve" policy, sports bureaus adopted a series of beneficial measures, such as reducing the number of athletes, focusing on raising quality, placing priority on developing focal sports events, reorganizing physical culture schools and institutes and key spare-time sports schools, and reducing competition. Although the total scale of the physical culture enterprise was reduced somewhat, and fewer activities were undertaken, some progress was nevertheless made through hard effort. For example, in 1960 China's mountain-climbing team climbed Mount Everest from the north slope for the first time; in 1961 the Chinese table-tennis team won three world titles in the twenty-sixth World Cup Table Tennis competition. These performances inspired the morale of the Chinese people and roused the Chinese spirit in the midst of a period of temporary difficulties.

After 1963, the Three Hard Years were past. The national economy took a turn for the better, and physical culture leaders offered a series of guidelines, policies, and measures building on their positive and negative experiences. In mass physical culture, they emphasized the flexible policy of "spare-time, voluntary, small-scale, varied measures suited to the time, the place, and the people" and to improve sports training, they mandated and implemented "sports team regulations," "regulations for sports teams' ideological and political work." They also issued the guideline, "Take spiritual rewards as most important and material rewards as supplementary," requiring that philosophic and sports training be linked together, and emphasizing scientific training and perfection of technique.

During these ten years, sports science research also began to take shape, the scope of international sports exchanges expanded, performances improved, and there were different degrees of development in the training of personnel, physical culture propaganda, arenas, and facilities. Thus, although these ten years had small twists and turns, they were still an important ten years in the history of modern Chinese sports.

The Third Stage: Ten Years of Chaos, Ten Years of Setbacks (1966–76)

The Great Cultural Revolution, which began in 1966, was a huge calamity, bringing disaster to China's socialist project. Physical culture was also devastated; in the midst of the chaos, it was essentially in a suspended state.

In 1971 Premier Zhou Enlai fully affirmed the achievements in physical culture work before the Cultural Revolution at the first physical culture convention since the beginning of the revolution, and stated ''achievement is important,'' encouraging the mass of physical culture workers. Physical culture work gained a short period of recovery.

In 1972 physical culture work again showed some recovery, and a number of important national conferences were convened. In addition, physical culture institutes and schools restored the enrollment of students. In 1974, however, the ''Gang of Four'' launched the so-called Criticize Lin Biao, Criticize Confucius Campaign, and again completely denied the achievements of physical culture and snatched away much of the recently restored work. In October 1976, the smashing of the ''Gang of Four Counter-Revolutionary Clique'' set the nation off on a new Long March.

The Fourth Stage: Brief Recovery, Reform, Giant Strides (1976–present)

After the Gang of Four was overthrown in 1976, China entered a new period of history. In 1976 and 1977 order was brought out of chaos as positive and negative experiences and lessons were reviewed, expectations and rules were put forth, and China continued to make progress.

In 1978 the Third Plenum of the Eleventh Party Congress began to fully correct the leftist tendencies of the Cultural Revolution and the preceding period. The strategic focal point of policymaking was shifted toward socialist modernization and construction.

The ''Ten Years of Chaos'' had pushed China's economy to the verge of collapse, and a more stable political situation was required in order to undertake neglected tasks. With the national economy still being rebuilt, the difficulties in developing physical culture were great.

Under the guidance of the policy of reform and revitalization, the Sixth National Games, held in Guangzhou in 1987, were exciting and successful. Again, a number of world, Asian, and national records were broken. In the organization of the competitions, a series of reforms were carried out. Both the competition system and the point scoring system served the competition structure and the Olympic strategy rather well, helping to stimulate the improvement of sports performances.

AMATEUR AND PROFESSIONAL SPORTS ACTIVITIES IN THE NATION (Cao Xiangjun)

In addition to the state sports commission system, each Chinese factory, mine, enterprise, office, school, village, or physical culture association is also responsible for attracting and organizing the masses to participate in physical culture and sports. In the late 1980s sports sociologists estimated that 300 million people participated in all sorts of physical culture activities.[2] In the ten years from 1979 to 1989 alone, people passed the National Physical Culture Training Standards 312 million times. More and more, physical culture became an integral part of daily life. Twenty percent of workers became physical culture activists, and 70 percent of small towns built recreation centers. Physical culture in the cities and countryside developed vigorously. Along with this, the people achieved widespread improvement in their physical condition. In the present generation of teenagers, all physical indexes show improvement over the previous generation. The life expectancy of the population, which serves as a comprehensive indicator of human health, increased from an average of 35 in 1949 to 57 in 1957, and again to 69 in 1980. In casting off the derogatory label of "the sick men of East Asia," physical culture made a definite contribution.

EXTENT OF THE NATION'S PARTICIPATION IN INTERNATIONAL SPORTS (Cao Xiangjun)

Before the founding of the PRC, in Old China's Seventh National Sports Meet in 1948, only nine athletes participated in the gymnastics competition, and in the entire nation there was not even one set of standard gymnastics apparatus. In Old China, only five records were set for weightlifting, four of which were achieved by overseas Chinese. In international competitions, Chinese athletes were always last. Before Liberation, China failed to place in four Olympic Games, and during participation in nine Far East Sports Meets, China won a total of one gold, and otherwise lagged behind Japan and the Philippines.

After Liberation, China's top athletes saw their status rise in the international sports arena, wiping out the humiliation endured on the playing fields of four Olympic Games. In the past forty years, Chinese athletes have won a total of 354 world championships and broken or surpassed 382 world records, demonstrating to the world China's outstanding sports ability. However, international exchanges were disrupted from 1958 until 1971 by China's withdrawal from the IOC and by the Cultural Revolution.

In 1973 the first middle school sports games and the first Asia-Africa-Latin America invitational competition in table tennis were held since the founding of the PRC. In 1974 a Chinese team participated in the Seventh Asian Games and the First World Middle School Games. Thus, the suspended state of physical culture began to end.

At the Ninth Asian Games in 1982, China for the first time won the most gold medals. In 1986, at the Tenth Asian Games, China continued to hold the championship position, and world opinion praised China as the Asian World Sports Power. The Chinese women's volleyball team won five consecutive world titles, and in table tennis reigned supreme in World Cup competition for twenty years. In the 1984 Olympic Games, Chinese athletes won fifteen gold medals, eight silver, and nine bronze, and were fourth in the gold medal count, attracting worldwide attention and helping to strengthen the understanding and friendship between people from different nations of the world.

Since the founding of the PRC, China has held many major international sports competitions. In 1955 it conducted an international friendship competition in shooting. In 1961 Beijing held the twenty-sixth World Table Tennis Championships; in 1972, the Asian Table Tennis Championships; and in 1973, the Asia-Africa-Latin America Table Tennis Friendly Invitational. In 1990 China successfully held the Tenth Asian Games. This was the first time that all members of the Asian Olympic Council took part in a ''one happy family'' Asian Games. It earned the praise of Asia and the world generally. In 1993 China prepared a bid for the 2000 Olympic Games with the hope of making an even greater contribution to the development of international sports. However, the bid was ultimately lost to Sydney, Australia.

THE INTERNATIONALIZATION OF CHINA'S SPORTS
(Cao Xiangjun)

In 1958 China withdrew from the IOC because of the unsatisfactory resolution of the ''Two Chinas'' question. International contacts were further disrupted by the Cultural Revolution and were not restored until the beginning of the 1970s. In 1971 a team was sent to the thirty-first World Cup Table Tennis Competition in Japan. In October 1971, at the twenty-sixth Congress of the United Nations, the PRC's legitimate seat in the United Nations was restored; following the World Cup, an American table tennis team was invited to China; and in February of 1972, the People's Republic of China and the United States jointly announced that they would restore diplomatic relationships, opening a new page in the history of Sino-American relations. In September of the same year, China and Japan restored diplomatic relations. Table tennis was praised in international sports circles as ''the little globe that moved the big globe.''

As China scored great successes in diplomacy and as international relations improved, the nation climbed onto the stage of international sports. In November 1973, in a special meeting in Teheran of the board of directors of the Asian Games Federation, a resolution was passed by an overwhelming majority to recognize the All-China Athletic Federation as a member of the Asian Games Federation, thus formally resolving the problem of the right of representation. In 1979, at the IOC Executive Committee meeting in Nagoya, a resolution was formulated on the right to represent China. Finally, after twenty-one years of struggle, in November of 1979 at the full session of the International Olympic

Committee, the reported count was sixty-two ballots in favor, seventeen opposed, and two abstaining in the vote on the resolution. It was resolved that the Olympic Committee of the PRC would be called the Chinese Olympic Committee and would be able to use the flag and anthem of the PRC, whereas the Olympic Committee in Taipei was to be called the Chinese Taipei Olympic Committee and was not to use the previously utilized flag, anthem, and emblem.

Since the 1980s, the relationship between China and the IOC has continued to develop. In 1981 China's vice-director of the State Sports Commission, He Zhenliang, was selected as a member of the IOC, and in 1982 the honorary chairman of the IOC, The Lord Killanin, and IOC President Juan Antonio Samaranch visited China and were received by Deng Xiaoping. In 1983 Samaranch personally awarded the Olympic Silver Medal of Merit to the Chinese State Sports Commission, and in 1984 he awarded the Silver Medal of Merit to the chairman of the Chinese Olympic Committee, Zhong Shitong. In the same year, the director of the Chinese State Sports Commission, Li Menghua, visited the general headquarters of the IOC at Samaranch's invitation, where he was warmly received. Samaranch expressed appreciation and gratitude to China for defending the position of the Olympic Movement and for its cooperative attitude. He Zhenliang was then selected as vice-chairman of the IOC, enabling him to exercise even greater influence on international sports. By 1980 many more international sports organizations had solved the "Two China" problem: thirty-eight individual international sports federations and eighteen Asian sports organizations accepted the PRC as a member nation, giving China the opportunity to carry out sports exchanges on a grander scale and a higher level.

In 1979, after the IOC restored China to its legitimate place, Chinese physical culture "broke out of Asia and advanced on the world," contributing to communication between peoples and promoting world peace. China helped construct twenty-nine sports stadiums and gymnasiums and twelve athletes' buildings in twenty-two Asian and African nations, receiving high praise from the IOC and various African nations. In the four years between 1985 and 1988, China carried out 6,037 exchanges with over ninety nations and regions. By the late 1980s China had sent 2,016 coaches to eighty-eight nations and regions to establish friendly relations. The sports in which coaches offered foreign aid were table tennis, badminton, gymnastics, volleyball, basketball, soccer, track and field, weightlifting, cycling, handball, swimming, diving, fencing, the martial arts, and judo. Among the coaches were some who had won world championships or set world records.

At the same time, China also received the expertise and help of many nations in raising its levels of sports technique. As early as the 1950s, Hungary, the USSR, and Japan provided help in soccer, weightlifting, swimming, volleyball, and other sports. Poland sent a sailplane expert who helped build the first sailplane airfield and trained the first group of sailplane athletes. China and Japan mutually cooperated in table tennis and volleyball. Rowing and kayaking benefited from the help of Romanian and Polish experts. The progress in fencing and field hockey resulted from the guidance of West German and Pakistanian coaches. In 1980 alone, China engaged experts from Holland, Romania, Japan, Italy, West Germany, America, France, Australia, Switzerland, Spain, the Philippines, and Pakistan. The experts from these twelve nations lectured or organized coach training classes; some brought teams to train. In 1993 China sent athletes, coaches, and referees in basketball, volleyball, track and field, gymnastics, wrestling, motor events, skiing, and other events to Yugoslavia, Japan, India, Singapore, France, West Germany, America, and the Soviet Union, respectively, to train or participate in training classes organized by international sports organizations.

China is a member of seventy-three international sports organizations and thirty-eight Asian sports organizations; 104 people from China have taken on leadership posts in international sports organizations. The Chinese people are proud of their rise in the international sports arena.

IDENTIFICATION AND DISCUSSION OF GOVERNMENT'S SPORTS POLICIES

Policies of Support for Athletes and Organizations (Cao Xiangjun)

In 1958 three documents, "The System of Technique Grades for Athletes," "for Officials," and "for Coaches" established the system of grades by which athletes, officials, and coaches were to be rewarded with bonuses, salary increases, and food subsidies.[3] This system was revised in 1963, when the State Council also issued Provisional Methods for Subsidizing the Sports Technique of Outstanding Athletes and Concerning the Ratification of Each Sport's National Records and the System for Examining and Rewarding them. In 1978 the State Council also issued a supplementary notice concerning athletes' subsidies, and in 1979 the State Sports Commission and the headquarters of the Labor Bureau issued a provisional notice concerning sports subsidies. These stipulated that each record setter and each contributing coach should receive a subsidy according to their respective grades. The policy was intended to reward outstanding performances and to stimulate improvement at the top levels of sports by providing living and nutritional standards that were sufficient to support improvement.

Since the 1980s, the bonuses and subsidies for athletes have increased. For example, athletes who won gold medals in the twenty-fifth Olympic Games and their coaches could receive 80,000 yuan from the government. When combined with the rewards given by various public sectors, companies, and enterprises, each gold medal winner could receive a bonus of a million yuan. This kind of practice was unknown in the past.

Regulatory Policies (Cao Xiangjun)

The highest management organization in Chinese sports is the State Sports Commission. Under the leadership of the State Council, it is responsible for integrating leadership and supervision for the entire national sports system.
Its duties are:

1. To manage the enterprises, organizations, groups, and schools directly under it, and to lead the work of physical culture and sports commissions at the various local levels.

2. To lead, coordinate, and supervise the sports-related work of each bureau, trade union, and other social groups; to analyze the recommendations, commands, and announcements concerning sports-related problems that these organizations issue or ratify and submit to the State Council; to analyze the circumstances surrounding their implementation; and according to the results of the investigation, to adopt the appropriate measures and to make timely recommendations regarding problems in the development of sports; and to submit them to the State Council for ratification and implementation.

3. To carry out the "labor and defense sports system," develop mass physical culture and sports, organize work for raising the level of sports technique, and to carry out statistical work concerning physical culture and sports.

4. To formulate a nationwide sports competition schedule; to hold national sports competitions; to oversee the organization of sports competitions by each bureau, trade union, and cultural organization; and to ratify national performances and new records in each sport.

5. To be in charge of the sports aspects of international relations; to conduct international competitions in each sport; and to organize the participation of Chinese athletes in international competitions.

6. To formulate and ratify the competition rules in each sport; and to investigate and ratify the teaching curriculum, textbooks, and materials used by each sports organization.

7. To organize sport science research.

8. To organize and carry out sports propaganda work.

9. To draw up the regulations for the system of grades for athletes and officials and the honorary titles, medals and commemorative badges for athletes, officials and other physical culture workers.

Policies Affecting Sports Organizations' Structures and Operations (Susan Brownell)

The Sports Competition System (1958) regulates the organization of sports meets. For every level of sports events, it dictates the particular sports, the number of competitions in a year, the units responsible for organizing the meets, and so on. It also dictates that multisport national games be held once every four years.

State Sports Commission Training Standards (1954 and 1964 under another title; current version issued in 1975, revised 1982) define standards to be used in school tests to gauge the fitness of schoolchildren. The document establishes the physical activities to be tested, the point values for performances, and the overall standards to be met in order to receive an award. The standards are regarded as an important means of assessing the overall success of physical culture policies that target the masses.

Two policy changes in the era of reform had a marked impact on the organization of the sports system. Central Document Number Twenty (1984) laid out specific guidelines for the development of mass physical culture, calling for the "societization" (*shehuihua*—public sector support) of sport (Brownell, 1991, pp. 295–298; Brownell, 1995, pp. 100–108). The result was a rapid increase in corporate sponsorship of sports teams and events. The corporations that contributed the funds were collective enterprises (as contrasted with state enterprises), the increasing number of privately contracted enterprises, joint enterprises, and wealthy overseas Chinese.

The number of teams outside the sports commission system also increased. The People's Liberation Army had always fielded its own team outside the sports commission system; it was supplemented by a number of national industry teams, such as the railway, banking, and petroleum industries. These teams were to provide competition for the sports commission system by decentralizing sports to some degree (Brownell, 1991, p. 297; Brownell, 1995, p. 106). In addition, the popularity and importance of sports increased markedly in the countryside. Peasant sports cadres reported that this increase was not imposed from above, but was essentially a grass-roots response to the encouragement of sports by local leaders under the directive (Brownell, 1995, pp. 146–147, 196–197).

In 1987 the State Sports Commission and State Education Commission approved fifty-five institutes of higher education to create high-level teams. This agreement had important effects on the structure of the sports system. It was designed to forge a closer link between the educational and sports commission systems.

Under the sports school system instituted in 1955 after the Soviet model, athletes were tracked into sports schools from a young age and often received an inferior education. They were unable to score high enough on the National College Entrance exam to get into college; hence their postretirement job possibilities were limited. The number of coaching jobs was limited, and they tended to be offered to retiring star athletes. Average athletes often ended up in factory jobs. As education became more valued in the 1980s, it became harder for teams to recruit prospective athletes. The 1987 document allowed fifty-five designated institutes nationwide to recruit former state-supported athletes and to offer them a number of ways to catch up in their studies (Brownell, 1991, pp. 298–300; Brownell, 1995, pp. 197–201). This had rapid results in increasing lower level sports participation because it made sports a more attractive career option for athletes and their parents. It also improved the quality of college sports, offering yet another alternative to the state sports commission system.

OTHER TYPES OF POLICIES (Susan Brownell)

In 1981 the "Rules for Athletes," "Referees," and "Coaches" set out detailed rules for strengthening socialist morality among sportspeople. These were ideological guidelines directing that sportspeople defend the party, love socialism, work to improve China's physical culture, learn from their peers, obey the leaders, dress neatly, and so on. These documents are important in the party's struggle against the "spiritual pollution" of Western bourgeois liberalism and provide the guidelines for political study sessions.

ANALYSIS OF GOALS OF POLICIES (Susan Brownell and Cao Xiangjun)

The overall goals of sports policy since the 1980s are summarized in Figure 4.1. The most important guiding principles for domestic policy are that physical culture should strengthen the people's physiques, enrich social and cultural life, and serve socialism. These principles date back to the Second Congress of the All-China Sports Federation in 1952, when Mao penned the most ubiquitous phrase in Chinese sports: "Develop Physical Culture and Sports, Strengthen the People's Physiques" (*fazhan tiyu yundong, zengqiang renmin tizhi*). This statement is still regarded as the encompassing goal of socialist physical culture (Cao, 1985, p. 178); it is painted on gymnasium walls and is used in the placard sections at major sporting events.

Domestic and foreign policy goals are regarded as complementary. Top-class athletes should serve the causes of the overall "improvement" (*tigao*) of performance levels and of friendship between nations. In international sports exchanges, China has held to the principles of complete equality of large nations and small nations, mutual respect, and democratic consultation. At the same time, it has utilized flexible tactics to open up new prospects for international activities.

"Improvement" at the top levels of sport is to be combined with the "popularization" (*puji*) of sports among the masses, the main goal of which is to produce productive, healthy, and happy workers. These different goals are expressed in different labels for sporting activities: "sport" (*yundong*) refers to competitive sports, and "physical culture" (*tiyu*) refers to sports and fitness for the masses. Improvement and popularization are complementary processes.[4]

At the National Working Conference on Physical Culture in 1979 it was decided that, on the premise that popularization and improvement are mutually connected, sports commissions at or above the provincial level should view improvement as most important and concentrate on solving the glaring problem

Figure 4.1
Goals of Physical Culture Policy

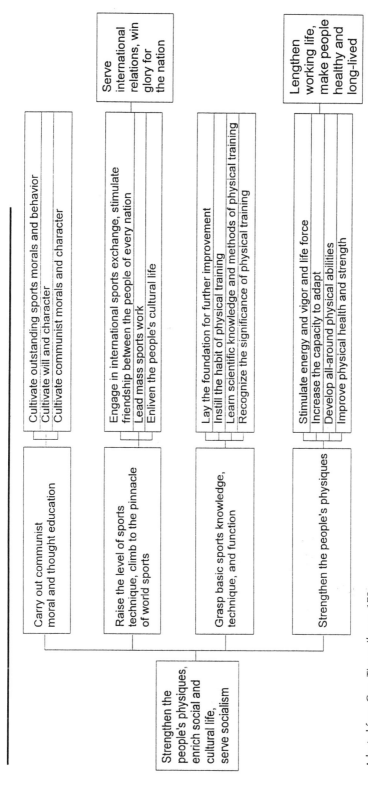

Adapted from Cao, *Tiyu gailun*, p. 178.

of backward sports technique, using improvement to stimulate and promote popularization.

The emphasis on improvement produced striking results in 1979. In that year, China's athletes broke national records 687 times and world records 26 times. In the Fourth National Games, five people broke five world records five times, and three people tied three world records three times.

The Fifth National Games, held in Shanghai in 1983, were also a model of improvement spurring popularization. A total of 8,900 athletes participated in the competitions of this National Games. Two people broke two world records three times, four people tied three world records five times, and sixty-six people and thirty-nine teams broke sixty national records 145 times. Notable among them was Zhu Jianhua, who broke the men's high jump world record twice, once in the preliminaries and once in the finals.

While these games were going on, mass physical culture activities also surged upward. Before the opening ceremonies, over 1 million people watched the spectacular "Vitalize China Torch Relay," about 1.4 million city residents watched the various competitions live, and 600 million watched the live broadcasts. On the day of the opening ceremonies, 100,000 people participated in the "street sports meet," and the organizing committee also invited 265 elderly physical culture workers, former world champions and world record-holders, famous athletes from Hong Kong and Macao, and 314 representatives from mass physical culture to attend and learn from Shanghai's experience in mass physical culture. In addition, the organizing committee also specially organized 100,000 youth into spirit squads.

The entire activity was a celebration of China's revitalization, combining improvement and popularization. As Samaranch, president of the International Olympic Committee, said, "The Chinese government places importance both on improving sports technique and on mass physical culture. I consider that this policy is correct."

CONCLUSIONS: ANALYSIS OF ACHIEVEMENTS OF NATIONAL SPORTS POLICY

Domestic Policy (Cao Xiangjun)

In the half century since the founding of the People's Republic of China, sports policy has followed a winding path. A look at the graphs illustrating the number of national and world records broken demonstrates this vividly (see Figures 4.2 and 4.3). The 1955 physical culture directives from leaders of the party and nation, as well as the relevant government documents, stimulated the development of physical culture despite the poor economic and social base for sports. Because on the whole national politics were stable and economic construction was steadily moving ahead until 1966, physical culture and sports achieved a well-rounded, swift development under explicit goals and guiding

Figure 4.2
Number of National Records Broken by Chinese Athletes

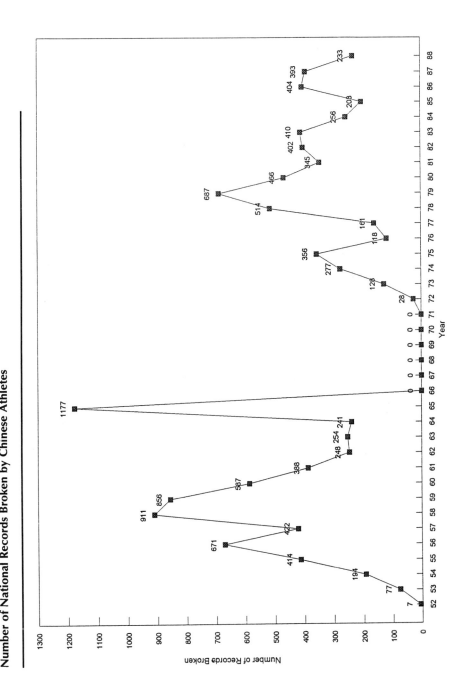

Figure 4.3
Number of World Records Broken by Chinese Athletes

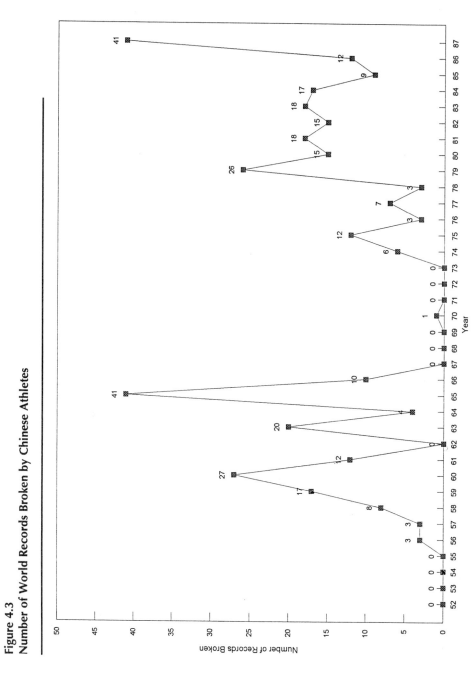

policies that suited the rules of physical culture and sports development. The implementation of the subsidy methods raised the level of sports performance.[5]

The First National Games in 1959 were regarded as successful; in this year alone, 381 people broke 135 national records 856 times and broke world records 17 times, achieving encouraging marks.

This period was followed by the "Three Hard Years" (1960–62). Despite the social and natural disasters of these years, some progress was made as discussed earlier. The success of China's mountain-climbing team at Mount Everest and the victories of the Chinese table-tennis team were important events. These performances provided inspiration and boosted national morale during a particularly difficult period.

After 1962, the improved national economy proved a turning point in China's sports policy. Through a series of guidelines and policies, a second high tide centered around the Second National Sports Games in 1965. The scale of mass physical culture gradually expanded, and the level of sports technique improved swiftly. In 1965 alone, almost 100 million people participated in physical culture activities; national records were broken 1,117 times altogether; and world records were broken or surpassed 41 times. This became the year in which China set the most records.

The years in which the national sports games were held (1959, 1965) were peak years, but in the three years of serious natural catastrophes (1960–62), a low point was reached. Sports activities came to a virtual standstill during the worst years of the Cultural Revolution (1966–73) and began to slowly recover after that. Since the beginning of the era of reform under Deng Xiaoping (1978), sports have rapidly improved. One can well perceive the direct influence of economic difficulties on sports.[6] The data suggest that the guiding ideology of the strategy of combining improvement with popularization suits China's national conditions, as well as the rules of physical culture development.

By examining a cross section of the development of China's physical culture in the past forty years, we can clearly see that fluctuations in physical culture, as a social activity, are intimately connected with social development and reform. First, physical culture is restricted by social, political, and economic factors. When the political situation is stable and unified, and the economy prosperous, then physical culture develops quickly. By contrast, when the political situation is chaotic and the economy in a decline, then physical culture development is greatly slowed down and is depressed. This is a basic rule of the development of physical culture. Second, the various social activities of physical culture also have their own rules of development. These rules are determined by the organization of competitions. Figures 4.3 and 4.4 show that an upward curve in sports performances occurred in the years during which China held a National Games (1959, 1965, 1975, 1979, 1983, and 1987).

China is still surveying the economic lessons of the revisions in the last forty years since the founding of the PRC, making firm strides in reform and learning from the successful experiences of other nations. China continues to strive to make an even greater contribution to the development of world physical culture.

FOREIGN POLICY (Susan Brownell)

In the realm of foreign policy, the PRC learned from the mistakes that led to its withdrawal from the IOC in 1958. Before that time, Chinese representatives had consistently angered the IOC with their insistence on arguing political issues when the IOC charter forbade mixing sports and politics (Kanin, 1978, pp. 36, 44–45, 62–63). Avery Brundage, president of the IOC, stated that he had opposed PRC recognition because he "had not yet met a sportsman from Red China with whom I could discuss athletic matters, but only diplomatic representatives" (Kanin, 1978, p. 44).

After withdrawal from the IOC, China and Indonesia were the main forces behind the organization of the Games of the New Emerging Forces (GANEFO) for Asian, African, and Latin American nations. Challenging the stance of the IOC, President Sukarno of Indonesia said, "Let us declare frankly that sport has something to do with politics" (Kanin, 1978, p. 81). Until it began to fragment with the deterioration in Sino-Soviet relations, GANEFO posed a real threat to the Olympic Movement (Kanin, 1978, p. 84).

With the beginning of the era of "Ping Pong Diplomacy" in 1971, Chinese leaders pursued a different strategy. The phrase "friendship first, competition second" (youyi diyi, bisai dier) became the guiding ideology for international competitions. The appeal of this ideal, and the humility shown by Chinese athletes during competitions, caught the international sports community off guard and captured the international imagination (Hoberman, 1984, pp. 222–225). In contrast with the previous era, Chinese leaders seem to have discovered a way of combining sports with politics that was internationally acceptable; they are displaying considerable sophistication in using sports as a diplomatic tool. As described above, relations with the IOC have improved steadily, especially during Samaranch's term, culminating in Beijing's 1993 bid for the Olympic Games.

With the advent of the era of reform, a new guiding slogan for sports— "Break out of Asia, Advance on the World" (chongchu Yazhou, zouxiang shijie)—would seem to indicate that there has been a shift away from the socialist emphasis on mass sports and the international emphasis on friendship. However, as the slogan indicates, the new vision is that the PRC will play a leading role as Asia becomes increasingly important in world affairs. The 1990 Asian Games were a diplomatic success, bringing together all members of the Asian Games Federation for the first time, with the exception of Iraq, which was excluded at the last minute after the invasion of Kuwait. PRC leaders view the 2000 Olympic Games as a means of marking China's emergence as a world power, capping a fifty-year struggle for international recognition.

NOTES

1. Susan Brownell's research was conducted in 1987–88 while on a Dissertation Research Fellowship funded through the Committee on Scholarly Communication with the PRC (National Academy of Sciences) by the U.S. Information Agency. The writing of this chapter was funded by a Richard Carley Hunt Postdoctoral Fellowship from the Werner-Gren Foundation for Anthropological Research. I wish to thank these agencies for their support. I would also like to thank Professors Gou Jiaxing and Qu Zonghu at the Beijing Institute of Education for introducing me to Professor Cao and arranging for me to attend her course on "A General Theory of Physical Culture."

2. See Kong et al., 1990, pp. 97–98, for a discussion of how the sports population is determined.

3. The policy documents for Chinese sports up to 1982 have been published by the *Guojia tiwei zhengce yanjiushi* (State Sports Commission Policy Research Division) in *Tiyu yundong wenjian xuanbian 1949–1981* (Selected Sport and Physical Culture Documents, 1949–81).

4. Chinese sports ideology emphasizes the complementary nature of improvement and popularization in order to link elite with mass sports. An overemphasis on elite sports would violate socialist principles. The Chinese avoid the word "elite," preferring instead to label their top athletes as *xuanshou* ("chosen hand"), *jianjiang* ("master sportsperson"), *jianzi* ("tip"), *jianer* ("valiant fighter"), or *jingying* ("skilled fighter").

5. The food subsidy was one of the most important early policies. During periods of poor economic conditions, parents often encouraged children to join sports teams for the sole purpose of acquiring the food subsidy. Without the subsidy, it would have been impossible to build a grass-roots base. It is also unlikely that the average family could have provided sufficient food for children to engage in hard training.

6. Many Chinese have criticized sports policy since the 1980s for its elitism. However, it is more likely that under increasing economic prosperity and socialization of sports, opportunities for sports participation are increasing rapidly among the masses at the same time that top-level performances are improving (Cao's assessment).

REFERENCES

Brownell, S. (1991). The changing relationship between sport and the state in the People's Republic of China. In F. Landry, M. Landry, and M. Yerles (eds.), *Sport . . . The third millennium: Proceedings of the International Symposium, Quebec, Canada, May 21–25, 1990* (pp. 295–301). Sainte-Foy: Les Presses de l'Universite Laval.

Brownell, S. (1995). *Training the body for China: Sports in the moral order of the People's Republic*. Chicago: University of Chicago Press.

Cao, X. (1985). *Tiyu gailun* (A General Theory of Physical Culture). Beijing: Beijing tiyu xueyuan chubanshe.

Clumpner, R., and B. B. Pendleton. (1978). The People's Republic of China. In J. Riordan (ed.), *Sport under communism: The U.S.S.R., Czechoslavakia, the G.D.R., China, Cuba*. Montreal: McGill-Queen's University Press, pp. 103–139.

Guojia tiwei zhengce yanjiushi (State Sports Commission Policy Research Division). (1982). *Tiyu yundong wenjian xuanbian 1949–1981* (Selected sport and physical culture documents 1949–1981). Beijing: Renmin tiyu chubanshe.

Hoberman, J. M. (1984). Purism and the flight from the superman: The rise and fall of Maoist sport. In Hoberman, *Sport and political ideology.* Austin: University of Texas Press, pp. 219–231.

Kanin, D. B. (1978). Ideology and diplomacy: The dimensions of Chinese political sport. In B. Lowe, D. B. Kanin, and A. Strenk (eds.), *Sport and international relations.* Champaign, Ill.: Stipes Publishing Co., pp. 263–278.

Kolatch, J. (1972). *Sports, politics, and ideology in China.* Middle Village, N.Y.: Jonathan David Publishers.

Kong X., Niu X., and Qiu B. (1990). A summary of sport sociology research in the PRC. Trans. by Susan E. Brownell. *International review for the sociology of sport* 25(2): 93–108.

Li, T. (1987, November 22). *Tiyu gaigede daitouren* (A leader in the physical culture reforms). In *Tiyu bao.*

Renmin tiyu chubanshe (People's Sports Publishing House). (1973). *Zhongguo tiyu* (Chinese sports). Beijing.

Rong, G., and Editorial Committee. (1984). *Dangdai zhongguo tiyu* (Contemporary Chinese sports). Beijing: Zhongguo shehui kexue chubanshe.

Schurmann, F. (1970). *Ideology and organization in communist China.* Berkeley and Los Angeles: University of California Press.

Tiyu cidian bianji weiyuanhui (Physical culture dictionary editorial committee). (1984). *Tiyu cidian* (Physical culture dictionary). Shanghai: Shanghai Dictionary Publishing House.

Wu, Z., and Que, Y. (1990). Organizational structure of China's physical culture. In H. G. Knuttgen, Ma Q., and Wu Z. (eds.), *Sport in China.* Champaign, Ill.: Human Kinetics Books.

5

Communist Sports Policy: The End of an Era

Jim Riordan

INTRODUCTION

Communist sports policy in Europe is dead. It lives on in China, Cuba, and North Korea. It was not everywhere identical; nor did it feature prominently in terms of national priorities in less economically advanced communist nations such as Albania, Vietnam, and Cambodia. Nonetheless, it did contain certain discernible similarities that marked it off from sports policies elsewhere in both the developed and less developed world. It is these similarities that this chapter examines, as well as the implications of the rapid *volte face* in sport in virtually all the erstwhile communist states following the 1989 revolutions throughout Eastern Europe.

The rapid collapse of Soviet-style communism in Eastern Europe and the resulting collapse of the nine Eastern European nations that subscribed to it (with variations in Albania and Yugoslavia on the totalitarian or "barracks socialism" model) provide an opportunity to examine "communist sports policies" and the impact they had on sports and popular perceptions.

One reason for virtual universal interest in communist sport was that its success, particularly in the Olympic Games, drew considerable attention and admiration. The Soviet Union and the German Democratic Republic (East Germany) provided exciting competition with the United States and West Germany, as did other East versus West, communist versus capitalist sports confrontations.

A less remarkable, though perhaps more far-reaching, aspect of communist sport was the evolution of a model of sport or "physical culture" for a mod-

ernizing community; employing sports for utilitarian purposes to promote health
and hygiene, defense, labor productivity, integration of a multiethnic population
into a unified state, and international recognition and prestige—what we might
call "nation-building." After all, with the exception of East Germany and,
partly, Czechoslovakia, communist development was initially based on an illiterate, rural population. It was this model that had some attraction for nations in
Africa, Asia, and Latin America.

In most communist states, sport has had the revolutionary role of being an
agent of social change, with the state as pilot. In any case, after revolution or
liberation there was rarely a leisure class around to promote sport for its own
disport, as there was in Victorian England.

Partly under the influence of Marxist philosophy which stresses the interdependence of the mental and physical states of human beings, many communist
states emphasized the notion that physical culture is as vital to human development as is mental culture. Consequently, physical culture should be treated
as such both for the all-round development of the individual and, ultimately, for
the health of society. In a classic treatment of this issue back in 1917, the year
of the Russian Revolution, Mao Zedong (1962) actually placed physical culture
before mental culture:

Physical culture is the complement of virtue and wisdom. In terms of priorities, it is the
body that contains knowledge, and knowledge is the seat of virtue. So it follows that
attention should first be given to a child's physical needs; there is time later to cultivate
morality and wisdom.

Sport, or rather physical culture, has had particular social and political significance in the development of communist societies. Sport retained its importance in communist society because it has been more central in their social
systems and has been controlled and directed by the state. The following would
seem to be the main state priorities assigned to communist sport development.

MAJOR PRIORITIES IN SPORTS POLICIES

Nation-building

All communist states face the problems of political stabilization and of economic and social development. Some were confronted with the serious problem
of integrating ethnically diverse populations into a new unified state. A key issue
here is one of nation-building: the inculcation of political loyalties to the nation
as a whole; transcending the bounds of kinship, race, language, religion, and
geographic location. Not only was this a key problem facing postrevolutionary
Russia, China, and Cuba, but it has been equally relevant to postliberation mod-
ernizing societies in Africa and Asia.

What better than sport to help the regimes in such societies promote the building of strong nation-states? After all, sport, with its broad relevance to education, health, culture, and politics, and its capacity to mobilize people (predispose them toward change), may uniquely serve the purpose of nation-building and help foster national integration. It extends to and unites wider sections of the population than probably any other social activity. It is easily understood and enjoyed, cutting across social, economic, educational, ethnic, religious, and linguistic barriers. It also permits emotional release, can be relatively inexpensive, and is easily adapted to support educational, health, and social welfare objectives.

It is here that sports introduced by Westerners in China, Russia, Cuba, and other developing states have some advantages over indigenous folk-games. That is, folk-games are often linked to annual festivals that take place in the various communities. Indigenous sports have served only as a means of expressing tribal or ethnic identity. On the other hand, modern sports have served as a means of expressing national identity. Therefore, it has been the modern sports that the communist nations have promoted.

Integration

Tied to nation-building has been the state-desired aim of integrating a multinational population (often in transition from a rural to an urban way of life) into the new nation-state. Many communist societies were loose confederations of diverse ethnic groups with different colors, languages, traditions, religions, stages of economic growth, and prejudices. Let us take the world's two largest communist countries as examples.

The billion people of China consist of at least a dozen distinctly different ethnic groups: The country is divided into twenty-one provinces and five ethnic autonomous regions. The minorities constitute aborigines (Chaun, Yi, Maio, Manchu, Puyi) and Koreans in the east and Mongol, Turks (Uighurs), and Tibetans in the west.

The USSR was a multinational federation of over 290 million people of a hundred or more nationalities. The country was divided into fifteen Union Republics based on ethnic identity, and many other administrative divisions (autonomous republics, autonomous regions, territories, and national areas). Each schoolday children studied in as many as eighty-seven different languages, and daily newspapers were published in sixty-four languages.

The governments of both these great nations deliberately took Western sports from town to country and, in the case of the USSR, from the European metropolis to the Asiatic interior. They were used to help integrate diverse peoples into the new nation and to promote a patriotism that transcended petty national and ethnic affiliation. In Soviet history, for example, even before the Civil War (1917–21) was over, the new Soviet regime organized the First Central Asian Games in the ancient Islamic center of Tashkent in October 1920. This was the first time in history that Uzbeks, Kazakhs, Turkemenians, Tadzhiks, Kirgiz, and other Muslim peoples had competed in any sporting event together with Russians, Ukrainians, and other Europeans. As Rodionov (1975) made clear later:

The integrative functions of sport are immense. This has great importance for our multinational state. Sports contests, festivals, spartakiads, and other forms of sports competition have played a key role in cementing the friendship of Soviet peoples. (p. 9)

Similarly, in China, the ethnic games festival held in Beijing in September–October 1985 was in the view of Chris Hann (1987)

designed to help integrate the diverse peoples of the state: in this case a rather subtle kind of integration, for it appeared to be predicated on assertions of ethnic difference, but conducive nonetheless to integration in the framework of the socialist state and legitimation of nationality policies. (p. 3)

As we will see, the integrated functions of sport are just as clearly evident when the competitive elements are added. In the case of the USSR, these became important at the end of the 1920s and in China beginning in the late 1970s. Both internally and externally, sport was used to mobilize people in ways that actively contributed to the raising of group consciousness and solidarity—goals explicitly favored by the leadership.

Defense

Since many communist states were born in war and have lived under constant threat of war, terrorism, and subversion (e.g., Cuba, Nicaragua, and Afghanistan), it is hardly surprising that defense has been a prime consideration. Sport, therefore, often assumed a subordinate role under military training. In some countries the system was best described as the "militarization of sport." The role of the military in sport was further heightened by centralized control of sports development. Even before their revolutions, Chinese and Russian military personnel played a prominent part in sports administration, largely because of their countries' geopolitical situation and history of foreign invasion. It must be remembered that both countries have had extensive borders with foreign states—fourteen in the case of China and twelve in that of the Soviet Union. Furthermore, even in relatively recent times, both countries have lost immense numbers of people to wars. For example, China lost 13 million and the USSR some 27 million people in World War II—far and away the greatest human war losses in history.

In both nations, as well as other communist states (e.g., North Korea and Cuba), the sports movement was initially the responsibility of the armed forces. Even recently, communist sport was dominated by instrumental defense needs and by military or paramilitary organizations. All communist nations had a nationwide fitness program with a bias toward military training, modeled on the

Soviet "Prepared for Work and Defense" (GTO) system. (This principle was originally taken from the standards set by Baden Powell for the Boy Scout "marksman" and "athlete" badges.) Thus, in China, as Glassford and Clumpner (1973) attest:

A major component of physical culture in Chinese schools is the military preparation program based on the Soviet GTO system. Route marches of 10 to 20 kilometers, grenade throwing, dashes, mock and real rifle training form the core of this program. (p. 6)

Even in an industrially advanced country like the former East Germany, albeit a "front-line state," it was the Soviet military-oriented fitness system that was employed, particularly for young people. Childs (1978) writes:

The performance objectives of the sport and physical educational programs are based on the requirements of a graded sports badge, the pattern of which was adopted from the Soviet Union. . . . Initially this badge carried the imposing title of "Ready to Work and Defend Peace" and was heavy with militaristic and ideological requirements . . . (it has since become) "Ready to Work and Defend the Homeland." (p. 78)

All communist states, and some nonaligned states as well, have had a strong military presence in the sports movement through armed and security forces' clubs. They have provided military sinecures for more-or-less full-time athletes and at times have established direct military supervision over sport and physical education (such as in the USSR in the periods 1918–22 and 1940–46). Sport and the military were also linked through the Sports Committee of Friendly Arms, set up in Moscow in 1958.

In many communist states, therefore, the armed and security forces have provided many of the funds and facilities that enabled people to take up and pursue a sport. This was especially true for full-time involvement and for sports involving expensive equipment (e.g., ice hockey, soccer, gymnastics, weightlifting, equestrianism). Thus, these forces ensured that as many people as possible were physically fit and mentally alert, and possessed the qualities (patriotism, will power, stamina, ingenuity) that are regarded as particularly valuable for military preparedness (and for internal policing against dissidents and deviants). Furthermore, the military organization of sport appeared to be an efficient and economical way of deploying scarce resources. Similarly, the methods used to direct those resources were more effective coming from paramilitary organizations than from civilian organizations.

Health and Hygiene

Of all the functions of state-run sports in communist societies, the promotion and maintenance of health was always a top priority. In many communist states, sport came under the aegis of the health ministry. Because the development of

Soviet sports was based on a population with a comparatively low health level, and because it has served as a model for most other communist societies, it is instructive to examine briefly the health and hygiene functions of Soviet policy for sports development.

When the Russian communists (Bolsheviks) took power in October 1917, they inherited a semifeudal, illiterate empire. Eighty percent of the population were peasants representing over a hundred different ethnic groups. The country was in a state of war-ruin and chaos. It was a land with a hostile climate, where disease, epidemics, and starvation were common, and where most people had only a rudimentary knowledge of hygiene. The new rulers knew it would take a radical economic and social transformation to alter the situation significantly. But time was short, and able-bodied and disciplined men and women (children too) were urgently needed—first for the country's survival, then for its recovery from the ravages of war and revolution, its industrial and cultural development, and its defense against the likelihood of further attacks.

Regular participation in physical exercise, therefore, was one means—relatively inexpensive and effective—of improving health standards rapidly. It was also a channel by which to educate people in hygiene, nutrition, and exercise. For this purpose a new approach to health and recreation was sought. The name given to the new system was *physical culture.*

The prerevolutionary Western conception of sport and physical education was thought to be too narrow to express the far-reaching aims of the cultural revolution (mental and physical) that was under way. Physical culture was to embrace health, physical education, competitive sport, and even civil defense and artistic expression. Acquisition of that culture was said to be an integral process that accompanied a person throughout life.

As Nikolai Semashko, himself a doctor and the first health minister (also concurrently chairman of the Supreme Council of Physical Culture), made plain in 1928:

Physical culture in the Soviet understanding of the term is concerned not with record breaking, but with people's physical health. It is an integral part of the cultural revolution and therefore has personal and social hygiene as its major objective, teaching people to use the natural forces of nature—the sun, air and water—the best proletarian doctors.

In other words, physical culture was to be a plank in the health campaign, encouraging people to wash, to clean their teeth, to eat and drink sensibly, and to employ a rational daily regime of work, rest, and sleep (hence Semashko's 1926 slogan of ''Physical Culture 24 Hours a Day''—eight hours work, eight hours sleep, and eight hours recreation). The country was in the grip of a typhoid epidemic and had long suffered from such near-epidemic diseases as cholera, leprosy, tuberculosis, and venereal disease. According to Semashko, it suffered from ''dreadfully backward sanitary conditions, the ignorance and nonobservance of rules for personal and public hygiene, leading to mass epidemics of social diseases such as syphilis, trachoma, scabies and other skin infections.''

Physical culture, therefore, was to help combat serious disease and epidemics. The therapeutic value of regular exercise, for example, was widely advertised in the intermittent anti-TB campaigns of the late 1920s. But physical culture was not confined to improving *physical* health; it was regarded as important in combating what the leaders defined as antisocial behavior in town and country. If young people could be persuaded to take up sport and engage in regular exercise, they might develop healthy bodies *and* minds. Thus, the Ukrainian Communist party issued a resolution in 1926, expressing the hope that ''physical culture would become the vehicle of the new life . . . a means of isolating young people from the baneful influence of the street, home-made alcohol and prostitution.'' The role assigned physical culture in the countryside was even more ambitious:

[It was] to play a big part in the campaign against drunkenness and uncouth behavior by attracting village youth to more rational and cultural activities. . . . In the fight to transform the village, physical culture is to be a vehicle of the new way of life in all measures undertaken by the authorities—in the campaign against religion and natural calamities. (Landar, 1972, p. 11)

Even in the 1980s, the name of sport was still being invoked to combat alcoholism and religion (Nekrasov, 1985).

Physical culture, then, stood for ''clean living,'' progress, good health, and rationality. The authorities regarded it as one of the most suitable and effective instruments for implementing social policies. Similarly, the authorities prized the program for its implicit means of social control.

As industrialization got under way at the end of the 1920s, physical exercise, like everything else, became an adjunct of the Five-Year Plan. At workplaces throughout the country, a regime of therapeutic gymnastics was introduced with the intention of boosting productivity, reducing absenteeism from sickness and injury, reducing fatigue, and spreading hygienic habits among the millions of new workers inhabiting bug-infested wooden huts in the villages. This Soviet-pioneered health-oriented system of sport was either imposed on or adopted by every other state that took the road to communism.

Social Policies

Many facets of social policy relevant to sports concern communist states. Some have been referred to above: combating crime, particularly juvenile delinquency; fighting alcoholism and prostitution; and attracting young people away from religion, especially from all-embracing faiths like Islam that impinge on large segments of social life. Another aspect of the use of sports for social policies is that of the social emancipation of women.

Leaders' desire for national recognition through international sports success can be a powerful motivating force for the social emancipation of women. The attention paid by some East European nations to women's sport has sometimes contrasted with the relative neglect in the "enlightened" nations of the West and in developing states. As an East German sports official, Otto Schmidt, has noted, "While other nations can produce men's teams as good as, if not better than ours, we beat them overall because they are not tapping the full potential of their women."

The impact of women's sport is even greater—though emancipation is far more protracted and painful—in communities in which women have, by law or convention, been excluded from public life and discouraged from baring face, arms, and legs in public. Some multiethnic communist countries deliberately used sports to break down prejudice and gain a measure of emancipation for women. This was a conscious policy in communist states with a sizable Muslim population, like Albania, the USSR, and Afghanistan. In reference to women of Soviet Central Asia (bordering on Iran, Turkey, and Afghanistan), a Soviet sports official, R. Davletshina (1976), asserted that "sport has become an effective and visible means of combating religious prejudice and reactionary tradition; it has helped to destroy the spiritual oppression of women and to establish a new way of life" (p. 3). It is a sobering thought that had the grandmothers of such Soviet Uzbek gymnasts as Nelli Kim or Elvira Saadi appeared in public clad only in a leotard, they would almost certainly have been stoned to death.

Western sports officials became increasingly concerned with their athletes' poor showing against communist athletes. This concern, along with the women's movement, heightened interest in women's sports and encouraged Western nations to adopt many Eastern European training methods for their elite athletes. However, the influence has sometimes been the other way. For example, it was the U.S. women's example that encouraged Chinese women to take up weight-lifting and bodybuilding (even boxing) in the early 1980s. Similarly, it was Western women's example that overcame the prejudices of some (male) communist leaders against such sports as women's soccer and long-distance running.

International Recognition and Prestige

For all young countries trying to establish themselves in the world as nations to be respected, even recognized, sport may uniquely offer them an opportunity to take the limelight in the full glare of world publicity. This is particularly important for those nations confronted by bullying, boycott, and subversion from economic and military powers. This has applied as much to the Baltic states in regard to Soviet Russia as it has to Cuba and Nicaragua in regard to the United States. As Fidel Castro (1974) said of imperialist states in regard to Latin America, "Imperialism has tried to humiliate Latin American countries, has tried to instill an inferiority complex in them; that is part of the imperialists' ideology

to present themselves as superior. And they have used sport for that purpose''
(p. 290).

This has put particular responsibility on athletes from communist nations.
Political leaders have seen athletes as encouraging a sense of pride in their team,
nationality, country, and even political system. Not all communist athletes accepted that role, as witnessed by the postcommunist outbursts in post–1989
Eastern Europe. The role that sport has played in communist foreign policy is
dealt with in more detail below.

SPORTS AND FOREIGN POLICY

Ever since the first communist state came into existence in 1917, communist
leaders made explicit the dependence of external sports relations on foreign
policy. It could hardly be otherwise in countries where sport was centrally directed and used in the pursuit of specific sociopolitical objectives, including
those of foreign policy. We have already seen that sport was a political institution run by the state and that overall sports policy was laid down by the
communist government. Decisions of national import concerning foreign sports
policy (e.g., participation in the Olympic Games or in particular states disliked
by the ruling Communist party) were therefore made by the party and government. On occasion it was a supranational body, like the Warsaw Pact, rather
than a sovereign government that has decided policy, as in the case of the Soviet-
led boycott of the Los Angeles Olympics in 1984. For those communist states
in Eastern Europe that had been closely tied to the USSR, it was often the
Soviet Politburo that imposed a ''fraternal'' sports policy on them.

This is not to say that all communist leaderships have acted in accord or
collusion. China and Romania took part in the Los Angeles Games in the face
of Soviet opposition. Cuba and Marxist-governed Ethiopia acted in solidarity
with North Korea in boycotting the Seoul 1988 summer Olympics, while all
other communist states (save Albania which boycotted all Olympic Games up
to Barcelona in 1992) competed.

The role of sport in communist foreign policy varied in importance over the
years, reflecting both shifts in domestic and foreign policies and the rapidly
changing world situation. In the years from 1917 to 1948–49, when the Soviet
Union either constituted the sole communist state in the world or held undivided
sway over the communist movement, it was Soviet policy that dictated communist involvement in world sport. But following the Soviet break with Yugoslavia in 1948 and the communist revolution in China in 1949, the Soviet
monopoly was broken.

On the whole, five major aims seem to have been pursued in communist
sporting relations with the rest of the world: (1) promoting relations with pro-
communist and potentially sympathetic groups, (2) promoting good neighborly
relations, (3) winning support among Third World states, (4) maintaining and
reinforcing the unity of the socialist community and the Soviet ''vanguard''

position within it, and (5) attaining sports supremacy, particularly through the Olympic Games. Some aims were more consistently pursued, and others were pursued in only one phase of foreign politics or with a particular group of communist states. We can consider the pursuit of these state goals as functions assigned to the sports movement and attempt to assess how successfully it has coped with discharging them.

Promoting Relations with Pro-Communist and Potentially Sympathetic Groups

The scope of communist foreign sports contacts has depended on a number of factors, not all of them controllable by the communist leadership. This has been notably so when not only "bourgeois" but also other communist (e.g., Chinese, Albanian, Yugoslav, and Romanian) governments and sports organizations have refused to play, in defiance of the USSR.

After the 1917 Revolution, when the expectations of world revolution dominated Soviet Russia's foreign policy, the tendency was to boycott "bourgeois" sports federations and the Olympics. Instead, they sought to promote sports contacts solely with worker sports organizations rather than with governments. Since the international labor movement and its sports organizations were, however, split into social-democratic and communist factions, Soviet sports ties were mainly confined to "sympathetic" foreign worker clubs. Nonetheless, some attempts were made in the United Front and Popular Front periods (1927–37) to use sport to bridge the gap between the two rival factions—without marked success.

After World War II, the importance of worker sports organizations diminished. The new balance of power in the world, particularly the emergence of several new communist states (including China in 1949) and the vigorous launching by the USSR and its allies of the peaceful coexistence policy in 1953, were key factors in changing sports policy. With the desire by several communist states to measure their strength against the best world opposition, the accent on competing against worker and communist teams lessened, although it did not completely disappear. Examples of the pursuit of such goals were of two main types in the postwar period.

First, there was the promotion of sports contacts with labor organizations abroad, such as those with the Finnish Labor Sports Union (TUL), the French Workers Sport and Gymnastics Federation (FSGT), and the Austrian Workers Sport and Cultural Association. In addition, communist athletes participated in a variety of worker tournaments, such as the annual running and cycling races through Paris and Moscow (sponsored by the French communist newspaper *l'Humanite* and the Soviet government daily *Izvestiya,* respectively). These tournaments included the annual Peace cycling race across Eastern Europe and the World Youth Festival, in whose program sport played a central part.

Second, sports contacts existed with trade and professional associations, such as the International Sports Union of Railway Workers and the International Federation of University Sport (later to stage the World Student Games jointly with the Western-oriented International Union of Students).

Since 1945, however, no serious effort was made to turn either communist or social-democratic sports organizations into alternatives to the existing sports federations, as had happened prior to the war. Nor was "loyalty" to communist sports federations permitted to interfere with sports relations with noncommunist states. The new postwar situation was the result of two important factors.

First, the Soviet Union had broken its isolation. It emerged from the war a victor, its military and political power having penetrated into Central and Eastern Europe. During a time of developing international friction, or Cold War, with two rival blocs confronting one another in a divided Europe, sport became an arena for international competition, for "defeating" one's ideological opponent. In the USSR, domestic sport was now thought strong enough to take on the world; victories over bourgeois states would demonstrate the vitality of communism. During the war, the (Moscow-run) communist Red Sport International had gone the way of the Comintern, being dissolved in 1943. Henceforth, especially once the communist states joined the International Olympic Committee in the early 1950s, most ruling communist parties lost interest in a distinctly different worker sports movement.

Second, with the process of decolonization and steady democratization of both the Olympic movement and bourgeois sport generally (i.e., fewer and fewer sports and clubs being confined to middle-class white males), the belief grew that international sport, particularly the Olympic Games, could be used for peace, international understanding, and the isolation of racist regimes.

Despite these changes of policy, mutual suspicions and wrangling between the communist-social-democratic factions within worker sport survived the prewar period. The social-democratic International Workers Sport Committee was a fervent supporter of U.S.-led efforts to boycott the Moscow Olympics of 1980.

Promoting Neighborly Relations

One relatively stable element in communist sport's role as a diplomatic and propagandist medium was to promote relations with geographically close states and with dependent or newly independent nations in the Third World. This was particularly evident in relations between Cuba and the countries of South America, between China and the rest of Asia, between East and West Germany, and between the Soviet Union and its immediate neighbors in Europe and Asia.

For the Soviet Union, the neighbors in Europe were Norway, Finland, Poland, Czechoslovakia, Hungary, and Romania; immediate neighbors in Asia were Turkey, Iran, Afghanistan, Mongolia, China, and North Korea. Countries whose geopolitical situation brought them within the category of strategically important "neighbors" of the USSR were Sweden and Denmark in the Baltic area; Bulgaria, Albania, and Yugoslavia in the Balkans; Austria in Central Europe; Japan (and following the Seoul 1988 Olympics, South Korea) in the Far East; and several states in the Middle East.

In the 1917–45 period, when the USSR was the sole communist state in the world, contacts with developing states were limited by the hold that imperial powers still had over Africa, Asia, and Latin America. In any case, the USSR's ability to bargain with the superpowers was severely restricted by its weakness and isolation, and by the distrust of other nations. On the other hand, the USSR was less handicapped in dealings with its immediate neighbors, all of whom were relatively weak and vulnerable. Some, like Turkey and Persia, saw it as vital for their survival and independence to pursue neighborly relations with the Soviet Union as insurance against Soviet encroachment and as a warning to other superpowers not to trespass into Soviet border areas.

From the outset, the overall Soviet objective in regard to its neighbors and those states within strategically important areas close to the USSR was, as the historian Max Beloff (1947, p. 21) has written, "to link these (states) to Russia by treaties embodying the three major principles of 'non-intervention', 'non-aggression', and 'neutrality'."

As the revolutionary fires faded in Europe in 1918–19, Soviet leaders began to turn their attention eastward, seeing the East rather than the West as the center of the revolutionary stage. Specifically, the Soviet leaders turned their attention to those states in the imperial colonies of Africa and Asia headed mainly by the national bourgeois as a bulwark against Western colonialism. As the first Soviet foreign minister, Leon Trotsky (1964), put it:

The road to India may prove now to be more readily passable and shorter for us than the road to Soviet Hungary. The sort of army which, at the moment, can be of no great significance in the European scales can upset the unstable balance of Asian relationships, of colonial dependence, give a direct push to an uprising on the part of the oppressed masses, and assure the triumph of such a rising in Asia. (p. 623)

Soviet and later overall communist policy (especially Chinese) was to provide every assistance to national liberation movements in the colonies and newly independent states, including those on their frontiers, even where this conflicted with the interests of indigenous communists. The celebrated case in point was China; millions of communists were slaughtered by Chiang Kai-shek's Soviet-backed Kuomintang forces. It is essential to an understanding of Soviet relations with the rest of the world, including in sport, to bear in mind that from the early 1920s Soviet leaders were concerned less with the export of revolution than with the strengthening of the USSR as a nation-state. They argued that a wider proletarian revolution could only take place *after* socialism was fortified in Soviet Russia. As Stalin (1947) made clear:

The very development of world revolution . . . will be more rapid and more thorough, the more socialism is reinforced in the first victorious country, the faster this country is transformed into a base for the further development of world revolution, in an instrument for the further disintegration of imperialism. (p. 179)

In terms of practical policy, therefore, Stalin sought alliances with "bourgeois" and even "feudal" states that were close to the USSR.

Sports contacts reflected these diplomatic and strategic considerations. Indeed, sport, being "apolitical," was seen as one of the most suitable vehicles for cultural diplomacy. As a Soviet sports leader, Balashov, was later to write,

Sport effectively helps to break down national barriers, to create international associations, and to strengthen the international sports movement. It is an immense social force helping to establish and promote international contacts between national sports associations of countries with different political systems.

There was yet another role assigned to Soviet (and later Chinese) sport from the 1920s: regional contacts with bordering states, especially in the Asiatic part of the USSR, were used to demonstrate the advances made by kindred peoples under socialism.

Contacts with states on the southern and southeastern frontier—Afghanistan, Mongolia, China, and North Korea—developed only in the mid-1950s. Sports agreements with Afghanistan were concluded in 1955, and exchanges took place regularly between Afghan and neighboring Soviet Uzbek athletes, particularly after the entry of Soviet troops into Afghanistan in 1979. Exchanges with Mongolia and North Korea commenced in the mid-1960s when those two nations were preparing for entry into the Olympic Games. Both adopted the Soviet sports structure, including the armed forces and Dinamo (security forces) clubs.

With China, sports relations closely followed the course of the Sino-Soviet dispute. Bilateral contacts, which began only in 1955, were abruptly halted in 1961. After the Cultural Revolution, resumption of political contacts between China and the West, which were said to have been presaged by table-tennis matches in 1971 (the so-called ping-pong diplomacy), was not paralleled by a similar renewal of sports contacts with the USSR. That had to wait until the 1980s when, following world championships in the two countries, tentative efforts were made to improve sports relations. All the same, it was not until 1986 that the first bilateral sports exchange agreement was signed.

Winning Support among Third World States

After the breakup of the colonial empires, particularly since the enthusiastic reinforcement of the peaceful coexistence policy by the USSR and its allies in the early 1960s, with its concomitant East-West contest for influence over the development and politics of the Third World, the communist authorities paid increasing attention to aid to developing countries in sport, economic, and cultural spheres. This sports assistance took the form of sending coaches and instructors abroad, building sports amenities, training foreign sports admin- istrators, arranging tours and displays by communist athletes, and holding sports friendship weeks that often had an unabashedly political character. Much of this aid, including the provision of sports facilities and travel (e.g., to the 1980 Moscow Olympics), was said to have been given free of charge. After all, as Ivanov (1970) put it, "sporting ties are one way of establishing contacts between states even when diplomatic relations are absent" (p. 11).

Given the signal success of the communist states in the Olympic Games, such sporting aid was seen as an effective means of demonstrating the possibilities of the socialist path of development: "The mounting impact of socialist sport on the world sports movement is one of the best and most comprehensible ways of explaining to people all over the world the advantages that socialism has over capitalism" (Talayev, 1973, p. 1). An editorial in the monthly *Sport v SSSR* admitted in 1981 that the USSR spent as much as 2.5 million rubles annually on the sports aid program to Africa, Asia, and Latin America—more than any other country.

A final aspect of communist aid to developing countries has been support for Third World campaigns against racial discrimination in sport. It was the USSR Olympic Committee which instigated moves within the IOC in 1962 to exclude South Africa from the Olympic Games. The moves were successful, and South Africa was unable to compete in the Olympics until it began to dismantle apart- heid in 1992. The communist states also lent their considerable authority to moves to have South Africa banned from all international sports tournaments; it was only Western nations and athletes that continued sporting contacts with the apartheid regime in such sports as golf, boxing, tennis, rugby, motor racing, and horse-racing. Many in the Third World saw the communist states, first and foremost the USSR, as the major champions of their cause in the world sports arenas and forums.

Reinforcing the Unity of the Socialist Community and the Soviet "Vanguard" Position within It

Since sport was centrally controlled in all communist states, it could be wielded for manifestly political purposes. After all, as Orlova (1972) wrote, "sports contacts help to strengthen fraternal cooperation and friendship and de- velop a sense of patriotism and internationalism among young people of the socialist states" (p. 11). From the Soviet standpoint, this enabled Soviet leaders to employ sports to try to integrate the various socialist societies, to bind them to Soviet institutions and policies, and to maintain and reinforce the USSR's vanguard position within the community. Relations tended to reflect the political tenor within the group, with the Soviet Union having to defend (or impose) its "special relationship" as the "first socialist state" and other socialist nations having to strive for compensatory supremacies denied them elsewhere. In the period 1948–56, most of the other socialist states (with Yugoslavia the notable exception) were more or less obliged to learn from the Soviet model, to form Soviet-type administrative structures, to make army and security forces (Dinamo) clubs dominant, and to run fitness programs like the Soviet "Prepared for Work and Defense." This was the case despite the long sporting traditions of Hungary, Germany, and Czechoslovakia, all of which had competed successfully in international sports long before Soviet participation. After 1956, however, the Soviet grip on sport gradually loosened in other socialist states. Albania went its own way, initially following China, while other states resurrected certain national sporting traditions and institutions that had been submerged during the late Stalin era. Thus, after 1988, the Sokol gymnastics movement once again played a major part in Czechoslovakian sport. East Germany pioneered the use of sports boarding schools in the early 1950s. In place of Soviet-dictated exchanges, new bilateral agreements were drawn up and negotiated individually between the USSR and other socialist states.

The sporting ties between the army and security forces clubs were particularly illustrative of the Soviet policy of military integration. These ties at least put a friendly face on some less popular aspects of the Warsaw Pact. A Sports Committee of Friendly Armies (SCFA) was formed in Moscow in 1958, three years after the creation of the Warsaw Pact. It embraced all members of the Pact together with China, North Korea, and North Vietnam. Neither the Pact nor the SCFA included Yugoslavia. Cuba joined the SCFA in 1969; China, Albania, and North Vietnam took no part after 1960. The declared aims of the SCFA were "to strengthen friendship between the armies, improve the quality of physical fitness and sport among servicemen, and to popularize the attainments of army sport" (Romanov, 1973, p. 177).

As a result of the sporting aid given to Cuba by the communist states, Cuba was drawn into the orbit of the system of state socialist powers after a period of isolation and hesitation. The immediate aim was to help harness and build up Cuban skill so that Cuba might make a good showing in sporting confrontations with other American states. In the years 1969–72, "more than fifty Soviet coaches helped train Cuban athletes for the Olympic and Pan-American Games" (Romanov, 1973, p. 90). The subsequent Cuban successes in both tournaments provided ample material for linking sports success with the political system and demonstrating through the popular and readily understandable (particularly so in Latin America) medium of sport, the advantages of the Cuban road to socialism for other Latin American states. Fidel Castro (1976) was later to talk of Cuban Olympic success as "a sporting, psychological, patriotic, and revolutionary victory" (p. 3).

During the 1970s and 1980s, a number of coaches and instructors from socialist states, including Cuba (e.g., in boxing), came to assist Soviet athletes in sports in which the Soviet standard was below world class. As the number of countries within the socialist community built up specialized facilities and expertise, they were increasingly able to help other athletes within the bloc and to gather together on the eve of important international events for joint training (e.g., before the Olympics). These and other forms of mutual assistance and integration were said to have become an important contributory factor in the sports successes of such states internationally. They also demonstrated the leaders' regard for the efficacy of sport as a means of advertising the advantages of socialism and demonstrating the superiority of their system.

It should be borne in mind that special high-level arrangements had to be made for such sports cooperation within Eastern Europe, inasmuch as the free movement of citizens among those countries was never part of their mutual treaty arrangements.

Attaining Sports Supremacy

Whereas other channels were closed to them, sports success seemingly helped countries such as the USSR, China, Cuba, and East Germany attain a measure of recognition and international prestige. Sport was the only medium in which communist societies, including the USSR and China, were able to take on and beat the economically advanced nations. This fact takes on added importance in view of what their leaders have traditionally seen as the battle of the two ideologies for influence over the world. An official Soviet government resolution published in the monthly *Kultura i zhizn* in 1949 claimed that ''The increasing number of successes achieved by Soviet athletes . . . is a victory for the Soviet form of society and the socialist sports system; it provides irrefutable proof of the superiority of socialist culture over the moribund culture of capitalist states'' (p. 5).

Cuba's leader, Fidel Castro, in 1966 looked forward to the day when Cuba could prove the superiority of its national sport, baseball, over that of U.S. baseball: ''One day, when the Yankees accept peaceful coexistence with our country, we shall beat them at baseball too and then the advantages of revolutionary over capitalist sport will be clear to all'' (p. 91).

Despite some setbacks, there is ample evidence that economically advanced socialist states have gone a long way toward achieving their aim of world sporting supremacy, especially in the Olympic Games. They have provided two of the top three nations in the summer Olympics since 1968 (except 1984, when they provided two of the top four despite the overwhelming communist boycott of the Los Angeles Games) and in the winter Games since 1972. Even in the Barcelona summer Olympics of 1992, when the USSR had already broken up (it performed as the ''Unified Team,'' which excluded athletes from the three Baltic states of Latvia, Lithuania, and Estonia) and other East European countries were in disarray, the Unified Team beat its nearest challenger, the United States. The two communist nations, China and Cuba, finished fourth and fifth, respectively.

The Soviet Union dominated the Olympic Games, summer and winter, ever since it made its debut in the summer of 1952 and the winter of 1956. It was challenged only by the German Democratic Republic (GDR) which gained more medals than the United States in the 1976 and 1988 summer Games, and more medals than the USSR in the 1980 and 1984 winter Olympics. The only interruption to communist victory came in 1968, when the USSR took second place to Norway in winter and to the United States in summer, and in the summer of 1984 when the major communist sporting nations did not compete.

China placed fourth in the 1984 summer Games and again in 1992; Cuba has moved steadily up to fifth position in the summer Olympics and consistently won more medals than all the countries of South America put together. The example of East Germany, with a population of under 17 million, is particularly instructive. An overriding problem facing East Germany after the war was that of gaining international acceptance as an independent state. Furthermore, leaders had to contend with attempts to impose Soviet institutions and values on the country, on the one hand, and Western hostility, subversion, and boycotts on the other. The rivalry with West Germany was to become a testing ground for proving the viability of either capitalism or socialism in all spheres, including sport.

Success in sport was seen in East Germany as one means, perhaps the most accessible and "popular" one, of gaining acceptance of the regime and enhancing its image at home and abroad while other channels were closed. It was not easy. In the winter Olympics of 1960, for example, the United States refused visas to East German athletes to travel to Squaw Valley where the Games were being held. The United States and its NATO allies denied visas thirty-five times between 1957 and 1967. In other instances, when East German athletes won competitions, the awards ceremony was canceled. Often, Western officials refused permission for the GDR to display its flag and emblem. But its leadership persisted and quite demonstrably poured funds into sport to try to establish the nation as a world power to be recognized and reckoned with. As Party Chairman Erich Honecker (1976) made clear: "Our state is respected in the world because of the excellent performance of our top athletes, but also because we devote enormous attention to sport in an endeavor to make it part of the everyday lives of each and every citizen" (p. 133). It is impossible to make any study of East German sport without seeing it in the context of two broader concerns: (1) striving to establish the nation as the equal of its fellow German state, the Federal Republic of Germany, and (2) trying to achieve both political and sporting status in the world, above all within the Olympic movement and the United Nations. Final acceptance by the IOC came in 1972 and was followed a year later by membership in the United Nations. Both were the result of twenty-five years of intensive diplomatic activity, both sporting and political. Although the IOC had recognized the East German National Olympic Committee in October 1965 and granted it the right to enter a team separately from West Germany in the Mexico Olympics of 1968, it was only in Munich in 1972 that East Germany possessed its own national team, flag, and anthem. This sporting autonomy and success led to mounting diplomatic recognition of the country throughout the world. Table 5.1 shows the steady change-round in Olympic success between

Table 5.1
Olympic Results, German Democratic Republic and Federal Republic of West Germany, 1952–1988

Games	GDR				FRG			
	Gold	Silver	Bronze	Total	Gold	Silver	Bronze	Total
1952 Summer	--	--	--	--	0	7	17	24
Winter	--	--	--	--	3	2	2	7
1956 Summer	1	4	2	7	5	9	6	20
Winter	0	0	1	1	1	0	0	1
1960 Summer	3	9	7	19	10	10	6	26
Winter	2	1	0	3	2	2	1	5
1964 Summer	3	7	6	16	7	15	12	34
Winter	2	2	0	4	1	0	3	4
1968 Summer	9	9	7	25	5	10	10	25
Winter	1	2	2	5	2	2	3	7
1972 Summer	20	23	23	66	13	11	16	40
Winter	4	3	7	14	3	1	1	5
1976 Summer	40	25	25	90	10	12	17	39
Winter	7	5	7	19	2	5	3	10
1980 Summer	47	37	42	126	--	--	--	--
Winter	9	7	7	23	0	2	3	5
1984 Summer	--	--	--	--	17	19	23	59
Winter	9	9	6	24	2	1	1	4
1988 Summer	37	35	30	102	11	14	15	40
Winter	9	10	6	25	2	4	2	8

the two German states. While West Germany was overwhelmingly successful in the 1950s, the gap closed in the 1960s, and East Germany forged well ahead in the 1970s and 1980s. The united team of Germany came in third at the 1992 summer Olympics, though with twenty medals fewer than East Germany had won at the Seoul Olympic Games in 1988.

East Germany's success in cultivating elite athletes is readily apparent. During the 1980s, calculated in per capita medals, the country won one Olympic or world championship gold medal for every 425,000 citizens. In contrast, the USSR and the United States won approximately one gold per 6.5 million citizens. In short, that means that an East German with sporting talent and ability was sixteen times more likely to reach the top and gain an Olympic or world gold medal than a Soviet or American citizen.

For East Germany, therefore, to quote the West German book, *Sport in der DDR,* we have seen how

Sport has played a vital role in breaching the blockade which, at the time of the Cold War, kept the GDR out of virtually all international relations outside the communist states. Because GDR sport attained international standards and in many areas actually set those standards, world sports organizations were unable to ignore the country. (Schmidt, 1975)

This was an important step toward helping East Germany break out of its political isolation, gain credibility for the communist government with its own people, and be recognized as an independent state. Hence, East German leaders accorded the development of sport and international sports performance high priority. Although not as spectacular, the evolution of Cuban and Chinese sport, since 1960 and 1984, respectively, was dominated by similar considerations— international recognition and prestige.

The communist countries were keenly aware of the advantages that are thought to accrue from sporting (especially Olympic) success, and prepared their athletes accordingly. They believed that the Olympics brought more exposure and prestige, and were, in the view of some communist leaders, *the* measure of a nation's viability.

To sum up, with its control of the sports system, the communist leadership was able to mobilize resources to use sport for what it believed to be salient political functions in foreign policy. It is, of course, impossible to measure the impact of sport on the behavior of states—to discover whether sport can, in fact, ever affect policies, let alone minds and hearts. All that can be said is that sport would no longer seem to be the neutral, apolitical medium that some people once considered it to be.

The sporting gains of communist policy toward developing and neighboring countries are evident and tangible. There have been some successes in the "hearts and minds" campaign among such nations, but the staunchness of friendship and solidarity remains open to question. For example, very few developing states showed solidarity with the Soviet-led boycott of the Los Angeles Games in 1984 or, indeed, with the Soviet armed involvement in Afghanistan. Furthermore, some might argue that Western commercial sport had more of an impact on the popular imagination in Africa, Asia, and Latin America than had communist and Olympic-style sports. It may be that, as far as communist influence was concerned, communist policy was most effective where Marxist-Leninist assumptions were accepted, in a handful of communist countries themselves. Like the space program, it seems more important in establishing national pride and ideological hegemony. Communist sports policy appears to have had markedly less impact outside of states that were already Marxist-Leninist. In the late 1980s and early 1990s, even that bastion crumbled.

THE IMPACT OF THE 1989 EAST EUROPEAN REVOLUTIONS ON SPORTS

Paradoxically, the sporting success of communist nations, particularly of the USSR and East Germany, increasingly undermined the ideological basis of the sports supremacy policy among the populations of Eastern Europe. Many were skeptical of, even hostile to, the world domination policy. This may seem puzzling to some Westerners brought up on the "noble principles of Olympism," but the popular perception in many communist states of communist involvement and success at Olympic sports was very different from the traditional view of Olympism held in the West. One might construct a paradigm of traditional

Table 5.2
Traditional Western and Popular East European Perceptions of Olympism

Western Europe	Eastern Europe
♦ Non-Political	♦ Political/ideological
♦ Amateur/voluntary	♦ State "shamateurism"/coercion
♦ Independent clubs/amateur federations/ university sponsorship	♦ Security/armed forces
♦ Universal/autonomous	♦ Soviet/Russian hegemony
♦ Fair play/open participation	♦ Win at all costs/drug abuse/exploitation of children
♦ Sport for all/self-financing	♦ Distorted priorities in national income dispensation

Western and popular communist perceptions of the Olympic movement and Olympic principles (see Table 5.2).

It may be justifiably argued that Olympic realities never matched the noble aims of Olympism set by Baron Pierre de Coubertin, and have turned from largely amateur-elitist to professional-commercial. But it is the traditional and popular perceptions of Olympism that are referred to here. In the case of Eastern Europe, it will help us to comprehend why the new noncommunist leaderships are rapidly switching resources from Olympic commitment to commercial sport and sport for all, and are dismantling institutions specifically intended for "breeding" champions to demonstrate communism's superiority over capitalism.

To many ordinary people in erstwhile communist countries, the Olympic Games and Olympism represent all that is bad in the old regime's policies: politics and ideology, hypocrisy and sham, paramilitary coercion, Russian *diktat,* drug abuse and exploitation of children, and grossly distorted priorities in the dispensation of national wealth. Let us look more closely at each.

Politics and Ideology

The striving for world supremacy in Olympic sport for political purposes is now utterly discredited. As World Chess Champion Garri Kasparov (1991) has said of the policy, "International victories and titles won by our athletes were supposed to prove 'yet again' the advantages of socialism over capitalism . . . a world chess champion was nothing short of a political post" (p. 3).

As an example of political interference in sport, a Russian journalist, Vladimir Maslachenko (1990), recounts an occasion when he and other journalists were summoned before then Sports Minister Marat Gramov, before they left for the 1982 World Soccer Cup in Spain: "Opening a leather-bound folder emblazoned with the gold letters CCCPSU (Central Committee of the Communist Party of the Soviet Union), he told us exactly what we could and could not say in public" (p. 46).

What no one from any communist country could openly say, owing to strict censorship, was that Dinamo was the sports club sponsored and financed by the security forces, that athletes of Master of Sport ranking and above devoted themselves full time to sport and were paid accordingly, that athletes received bonuses for winning (including dollars), that the national Olympic Committee was a government-run institution whose chairman had to be a member of the Communist party, that communist athletes used drugs, and so on.

Hypocrisy and Sham

Communist party manipulation of sports also involved a great deal of enforced hypocrisy. All athletes, coaches, sports medical personnel, officials, and jour-nalists had to toe the line and, not infrequently "lie through their teeth" if they wanted to keep their jobs and not run afoul of the law enforcement agencies. They had to assert that all communist athletes were amateurs. Instead of having army officer or security forces sinecures, athletes had eternal student status or false registration at a workplace. With the collapse of communism, the veil was being pulled aside. As the leading Soviet male swimmer, Vladimir Salnikov, revealed in early 1989: "We have rid ourselves of hypocritical declarations about so-called amateurism and sports achievements. Professionalism has been recognized and athletes no longer have to compromise themselves" (p. 12).

Sports and the Paramilitary

The world communist sports system has always been dominated by clubs of the security forces and the army (see Table 5.3). Consequently, sports heroes were officially soldiers or police officers, guardians of public order, and role models for a disciplined, obedient, and patriotic citizenry. It is hardly surprising that, during the turbulent revolutions of 1989, the sports clubs sponsored by the paramilitary forces that shored up the old order would suffer by association. Sports heroes in the postcommunist age were to be civilians, not warriors.

Russian *Diktat*

For non-Russians (who made up half the 293 million population of the USSR) and citizens of all the East European states, there existed the irritation of having to put up with a system tailored by Stalin to Russian conditions and imposed from without in contradiction to their own traditions. Sokol gymnastics were banned in Poland and Czechoslovakia after 1948. Youth organizations involved in recreation, like the YMCA (which was very strong, for example, in the Baltic states prior to 1939), the Scouts, and the Jewish Maccabi, were similarly pro-scribed. Pre-1939 Olympic committees were disbanded on orders from Moscow, and their members were often persecuted. As Paal (1990) confirms, Estonia's two prewar IOC members, Friedrich Akel and Joakim Puhk, "were put to death by the NKVD (Soviet precursor of the KGB) for their public activity" (p. 2).

This happened despite the long traditions and often superior standards existing

Table 5.3
Sports Clubs of the Security and Armed Forces in Eastern Europe and the USSR

Country	Security Forces Club	Armed Forces Club
USSR	Dinamo (Moscow, Kiev, Minsk, Tbilisi, etc.)	TsSKA (Central Sports Club of the Army)
Bulgaria	Levski Sofia	TsSKA
German Democratic Republic	Dinamo (Berlin, Dresden)	Vorwarts
Yugoslavia	Dinamo (Zagreb)	Red Star
Romania	Dinamo (Bucharest)	Steaua
Hungary	***	Honved
Poland	Dosze	Legia
Czechoslovakia	Dinamo (Prague)	Dukla Liberec
Albania	Tirana Dinamo	***

in the non-Russian states, both within and outside the Soviet Union. Being tied to the USSR also meant following Soviet foreign policy, including Olympic boycotts. The Soviet Communist party decision to boycott the 1984 Los Angeles Olympics was simply passed down to other members of the Warsaw Pact; no sports or national Olympic committees (not to mention athletes) were consulted. Romania demurred, though hardly for democratic reasons.

Such contempt for national conditions finally provoked mass ire and hatred, expressed violently in the uprisings of late 1989 in Eastern Europe and subsequently in the Baltic states and various non-Russian republics of the Soviet Union. Significantly, many prime targets of the popular outburst were Russian-imposed sports structures and institutions.

Drugs and Child Exploitation

A major reason for the strong anti-elite (i.e., Olympic) sport sentiments in one-time communist states may be found in the revelations in the media, following the 1989 revolutions, of the long-term *state* production, testing, monitoring, and administering of performance-enhancing drugs in regard to athletes as young as seven and eight. It was this mendacity by members of the old regime—loudly condemning drug abuse in the West as a typical excess of capitalism, while concealing its own involvement in a far more extensive program of state manufacture and distribution of drugs (from growth stimulants to growth retardants, anabolic steroids to blood doping)—that brought Olympic sport into question.

Those familiar with communist sport had long known that drug taking was organized at the top and that no athlete was allowed overseas unless he or she had a clearance test before departing. At the Olympics of Montreal and Seoul, as Gromyko (1989) attests, the Soviet squad had a "hospitality" ship used as a medical center to ensure that Soviet competitors were at least "clean" at the last moment. The Soviet coach Sergei Vaichekovsky (Page, 1989), who was in charge of swimming from 1973 to 1982, had admitted that the use of drugs was widespread in his sport, and not just among Soviet swimmers: "From 1974 all Soviet swimmers were using banned substances. I've personally administered the drugs and advised swimmers individually on how to avoid getting caught" (p. 20).

Vaichekovsky also indicated that while the East German method was to give drugs during periods of intensive training, which for swimmers usually comes at the start of the year, Soviet swimmers took them to within a month of major meetings. Other communist sources have uncovered drug-taking and other forms of "doping" in track and field, weightlifting, cycling, rowing, bodybuilding, and gymnastics, including among schoolchildren.

Distorted Priorities

To many, the worst aspect of the old communist system was the misplaced priorities; the gap between living standards and ordinary sports and recreation facilities, on the one hand, and the funds lavished on elite sport and stars, on the other. Valuable resources were used to buy foreign sports equipment and pay dollar bonuses to athletes who won Olympic and international championship medals.

Some journalists have suggested that alongside Olympic medal tables, communist newspapers ought to publish sports amenity comparisons: the 2,500 Soviet swimming pools versus the United States' million plus (Salnikov, 1989); the 120 Soviet indoor skating rinks versus Canada's 10,000 (Druzenko, 1988). Before 1988, the vast majority of communist countries had never held sports competitions for any category of handicapped person. For the first time, some sent teams of physically challenged (the USSR sent thirteen blind men) to the Paralympics in Seoul in 1988.

Bearing these six factors in mind, it should come as no surprise to find that the leaders in the postcommunist period radically changed their scale of priorities. They no longer saw the need to demonstrate the advantages of socialism, since they were trying to distance themselves from the totalitarian system that accompanied the imposition of communism from above.

Such a radical shift of policy is bound to cause a tinge of sadness in those who have admired aspects of communist sport through the years—and not only because it provided good competition with the West. The old system was generally open to talented individuals in all sports, probably more so than in the West. It provided opportunities for women to play and succeed, if not on equal terms with men, at least on a higher plane than Western women. It provided opportunities to many ethnic minorities and relatively small states in Eastern Europe and the USSR to do well internationally and to help promote the pride and dignity that sports success in the glare of world publicity can bring. Nowhere in the world has there been, since the early 1950s, such reverence by governments for Olympism, for Coubertin, for Olympic ritual and decorum. One practical embodiment of this reverence was the contribution to Olympic solidarity with developing nations: to the training of Third World athletes, coaches, sports officials, medical officers, and scholars at colleges and training camps. Much of this aid was free. None of it was disinterested, for it went to those states whose governments generally looked to socialism rather than capitalism for their future. Furthermore, no one outside the Third World did more than the communist nations to oppose apartheid in sport and have South Africa banned from world sports forums and arenas.

In Eastern Europe and the former USSR, the international challenge today is diluted through lack of state support. The free trade union sports societies, as well as the ubiquitous Dinamo and army clubs, have given way to private sports, health, and recreation clubs. Women's wrestling and boxing attract more profit than do women's chess and volleyball. The various ethnic groups (Czechs and Slovaks, Croatians and Serbs, Armenians and Ukrainians) prefer their own independent teams to combined effort and success. Across the Central and Eastern European plain, as far as the Ural Mountains, sports aid and every other aid are at an end. Third World students (in medicine and engineering as well as in sport) have had to go home as their support grants have run out. The ex-communist states have become competitors with other poor nations for development aid from the West.

CONCLUSIONS

The rapidity of post-totalitarian change in all areas, sport included, in Eastern Europe and the one-time Soviet Union would seem to indicate that the elite sports system and its attainments, far from inspiring national pride and patriotism, tended to provoke apathy and resentment. This appears to be more evident in those states—Poland, East Germany, Hungary, Romania, Bulgaria—that had "revolution" and an alien sports system and values thrust upon them which were contrary to their indigenous traditions. A similar mood is apparent in Islamic areas of the old USSR. Sports stars were seen as belonging to a private, elite fiefdom within the overall domain; they were not part of a shared national achievement, let alone heritage. That is not to say that in societies of hardship and totalitarian constraint, and in the face of Western arrogance and attitudes that were sometimes tantamount to racial prejudice, the ordinary citizen obtained no vicarious pleasure in her or his champion's or team's performance. But overall the dominant attitude was not entirely different from Western class attitudes toward sports and heroes which are not "one of their own" (e.g., the ambivalent attitude of many Western workers to Olympic showjumpers, yachtsmen, and fencers).

In countries like the now defunct Czechoslovakia and Yugoslavia, as well as the Slav regions of the old Soviet Union (the Ukraine, Belorussia, and Russia), the patriotic pride in sporting success and heroes appears to have been genuine. One reason for this may be that the socialist revolutions came out of their own experience and had some popular support. The same might be said of China, Cuba, and Vietnam.

That is not to say that communist ideology motivated athletes or that Marxism-Leninism was responsible for Olympic success. A more compelling reason was that the sports system grew up with and was integral to the building of a strong nation-state which generated its own motivational forces and patriotism. The same central control and planned application of resources which initially achieved such remarkable success in constructing the infrastructure of socialist society provided conditions that were more conducive to discovering, organizing, and developing talent in specific sports than in those of the more disparate and private Western systems. It should be added that communist sport was oriented toward *Olympic* success, and its less privileged athletes fared less well in the fully professionalized and commercial sports of the West: soccer, basketball, boxing, rugby, motor racing, tennis, and baseball.

Today, the inheritors of the sports system that evolved during the communist years are faced with a choice of how sharply they should break with the past and adopt a pattern of sport based on market relations. "Westernizers" in Eastern Europe, with public support nourished on a reaction to the communist past and aided by Westerners eager to see the old communist states join the "free" world (i.e., abandon socialism, central planning, and social provision), seem bent on rejecting the past in toto and embracing its antithesis.

Sports in such states may well become a hybrid of the worst of both worlds, retaining the bureaucracy of the old and adding only the exploitation and corruption of some forms of Western sport. The final product may well not inspire admiration. Much the same could be said of the larger reform processes under way.

No doubt, in time, a new sports nationalism will emerge and international rivalries will resume. For the moment, however, it is time to concentrate on more important things. In the immediate postcommunist period the erstwhile communist nations have decided that bread is more important than circuses.

REFERENCES

Beloff, Max. (1947). *The foreign policy of Soviet Russia, 1929–1941*. Vol. 2. Oxford: Oxford University Press.

Castro, Fidel. (1974). Quoted in S. Castanes (ed.), *Fidel. Sobre el deporte*. Havana: El Deporte, 3, 9.

Castro, Fidel. (1976). *El Deporte, 3, 9*.

Childs, David. (1978). Sport and physical education in the GDR. In J. W. Riordan (ed.), *Sport under communism*. London: Hurst (p. 78).

Davletshina, R. (1976). Sport i zhenshchiny. *Teoriya i praktika fizicheskoi kultury, 3, 62*.

Druzenko, A. (1988, November). Olimpiyskaya slava. *Moskovskie novosti, 15*.

Glassford, R. G., and Clumpner, R. A. (1973). Physical culture inside the People's Republic of China. *Physical culture around the world*. Monograph 6, 13.

Gromyko, V. (1989, March 28). Nash styd. *Leninskoye znamya, 2*.

Hann, Chris. (1987, May). *The withering of muscular socialism: physical culture, nutrition and personal responsibility in contemporary China*. Unpublished paper, 3.

Honecker, Erich. (1976). *Report of the Central Committee to the Central Committee of the Socialist Unity Party of Germany*. Berlin, 133.

Ivanov, V. (1970). Sportivnye otnosheniya. *Sport v SSSR, 11, 14*.

Kasparov, Garri. (1991). Too outspoken for a closed society? *Moscow News, 2, 3*.

Kultura i zhizn. (1949, November 1), 11, 5.

Landar, A. M. (1972). Fizicheskaya kultura—sostavnaya chast kulturnoi revolyutsii na Ukraine. *Teoriya i praktika fizicheskoi kultury, 12, 11*.

Mao Zedong. (1962). *Une étude de l'èducation physique*. Paris: Maison des sciences de l'homme (originally published in Chinese in 1917).

Maslachenko, Vladimir. (1990). Ya po-prezhnemu v igre. *Sobesednik, 46, 15*.

Nekrasov, V. P. (1985). Fizicheskaya kultura protiv pyanstva. *Teoriya i praktika fizicheskoi kultury, 9, 37–39*.

Orlova, S. (1972). Sovetsky mnogonatsionalny sport. *Sportivnaya zhizn Rossii, 11, 7*.

Paal, Gounnar. (1990, May 20–25). Increasing Olympic enthusiasm in Estonia. Paper given at the *International Symposium 'Sport . . . Le Troisieme Millenaire.'* Quebec, 2.

Page, Alan. (1989, December 2). Sacked Soviet official admits widescale use of drugs. *The Guardian*, 20.

Rodionov, V. V. (1975). Sport i integratsiya. *Teoriya i praktika fizicheskoi kultury*, 9, 7.

Romanov, A. O. (1973). *Mezhdunarodnoye sportivnoye dvizhenie*. Moscow-Fizkultura i sport, 177.

Salnikov, Vladimir. (1989). Vremya nadyozhd. *A. gumenty i fakty*, 1, 3.

Schmidt, O. (1975). *Sport in der Deutschen Demokratischen Republik*. Bonn, 12–13.

Sport v SSSR. (1981). 6, 39.

Stalin, J. V. (1947). *Voprosy Leninizma*. Moscow: Politizdat, 179.

Talayev, Y. A. (1973). Sport—oblast mirnovo sorevnovaniya. *Teoriya i praktika fizicheskoi kultury*, 1, 8.

Trotsky, Leon. (1964). In Jan Meijer (ed.), *The Trotsky Papers, 1917–1922*. Vol. 1. New York: Paladine Press (p. 623).

6

Sport in Cuba

Paula J. Pettavino and Geralyn M. Pye

THE CUBAN NATIONAL GOVERNMENT AND
THE SPORTS SYSTEM

After the 1987 Pan American Games in Indianapolis, a Cuban newspaper head-line read: ''CUBA: 7.5 medals per Million Inhabitants. USA: 0.70'' (Brubaker, 1992). For the last thirty years, the irony of Cuban sport has been that an island with a population smaller than many U.S. cities has achieved such an astounding measure of athletic success. Despite a limited pool of talent and a notorious weakness in certain sports, Cuba has proven itself to be a sporting powerhouse and has used this strength to the utmost political advantage.

Before the revolution, such great success was limited to selected sports, such as baseball and boxing. In 1959, however, Fidel Castro, the premier Cuban sports aficionado, encouraged sports fanaticism and has since presided over the unprecedented growth and mastery of a long list of international sports. In base-ball alone, in the five years from 1988 through 1992, Cuba amassed a record of 63–1 in regional and world championship tournaments (Brubaker, 1992). In the 1991 Pan American Games held in Havana, the United States won the most medals (352 to Cuba's 265), but Cuba took home the most gold—140 to the United States' 130—and did so in high-profile sports: basketball, baseball, box-ing, and track and field. This was the first time the United States had been beaten in the gold medal tally since the Pan American Games began in 1951 (*USA Today,* 1991). At the Barcelona Olympics in 1992, Cuba claimed a re-spectable sixth place in the medal tally with fourteen gold, six bronze, and eleven silver. Most significantly, perhaps, the Cubans won the gold medal in baseball, an Olympic medal sport for the first time in 1992 (*Washington Post,* 1992b). Clearly, in the area of mass participation and competitive sports, Cuba's revolutionary government has been doing something right. The source of this success lies in the Cuban government and its policies.

The Cuban Government

Cuba's current socialist government is organized according to notions of Marxist-Leninist democratic centralism, with decision making centralized at the national level. Most policies are initiated at the national or executive level through the top bodies of government, such as the Council of Ministers and the Politburo of the Cuban Communist party (PCC). Legislative and administrative functions are divided among the national, provincial, and municipal levels. The role of the Cuban legislatures, the People's Power Assemblies or *Poder Popular,* is limited at all levels. Limited public input into policymaking occurs through mass organizations such as the Confederation of Cuban Workers (CTC), the Federation of Cuban Women (FMC), and the Committees for the Defense of the Revolution (CDRs). Policymaking and funding are centralized in all areas, including sports, where public opinion is reflected through the Voluntary Sports Councils (CVDs) as well as by the CDRs.

History of Cuban Sport

Before the 1959 revolution, in contrast to today, Cuban governments played a relatively minor role in sports. Many sports and their corresponding organizations reflected Spanish, African, and North American influences on the history of this Caribbean nation. In the years just prior to the revolution, the Batista dictatorship took only a limited interest in sports. The 1957–58 budget reveals that a total of 1.75 million pesos—less than 0.5 percent of the budget—was spent on sports-related areas, whereas approximately 25 percent of the budget was dedicated to the military and 22 percent was allotted for administration (Seers, 1975, p. 41).

The General Director of Sports (DGD), the official government body, was formed as early as 1938 (Ginesta Almira, 1979, p. 29). However, state involvement in sports promotion remained limited. In fact, the Batista government refused to pay for the Cuban team to attend the 1955 Pan American Games (Gonzalez Barros, 1966, p. 8). Before 1959, sport in Cuba was characterized by a limited number of facilities and limited access, especially outside of the capital of Havana. Most athletic equipment was imported from the United States. Physical education and sports were almost unknown in public schools. Of the few physical education teachers who were employed, most were not qualified with professional degrees (Gonzalez Alonso, 1985, p. 5). Organized sports were practiced mainly in private schools and clubs, although baseball, boxing, basketball, and cockfighting were more widely enjoyed by Cubans from all classes and of all races. Equality of opportunity, in terms of participation, did not exist. Sport also tended to reflect the racial, gender, and class divisions that characterized Cuban society before 1959. Access to sports was almost exclusively restricted to wealthy, white Cuban males, despite Cuba's early progressive attitude toward nonwhites playing baseball.[1]

By the post–World War II period, Cuban sport was rather commercialized, with professional baseball and boxing well established as potential pathways to money and fame for poor Cubans.[2] In some cases, this path also led to professional sports in the United States. Aside from perpetually strong performances in baseball and boxing, Cuba was virtually unknown in international events. Although by no means the worst sports performer in Latin America, Cubans had won only a handful of international medals before 1959, and those mainly by Cubans who were residing outside of their native island.

Revolutionary Sport

From the beginning, the revolutionary government made a clear commitment to sports. Initially, sports activities were still shared between private and public interests. The main focus of the early years was expanding access to those Cubans who had previously been excluded from sports facilities.

After 1961, centralized control of sports in Cuba grew steadily and all sports are now linked to the government through the National Institute for Sports, Physical Education and Recreation (INDER). INDER has its own budget— around 100 million pesos per annum in 1987, which is between 0.4 and 0.5 percent of the total budget[3] (Powers, 1987, p. 46)—and determines the vast majority of sports-related policies. INDER controls all physical education, specialized sports schools, sports centers, sports teachers and coaches, and the Cuban national teams. In other words, all sports activities are linked to INDER at the municipal, provincial, and ultimately, the national level (see Figure 6.1), with INDER effectively functioning as a subministry accountable to the national government.

By late 1962 professional sports were completely outlawed in Cuba (Arrieta, 1986). Today, a wide variety of sports are practiced in the country, and the vast majority of Cubans participate in sports or physical culture at some point in their lives. Approximately 1.5 million Cubans,[4] or about one-tenth of the population, practice sports on a regular basis (Ruiz Aguilera, 1977, p. 13). The exact number of participants in each sport is not available. Similarly, spectator numbers are unavailable because entrance charges for sports events were completely outlawed by 1967 (INDER, 1985). Nevertheless, baseball, as was the case before 1959, remains the most popular sport in Cuba, in terms of both participants and spectators. Other popular sports include boxing, volleyball, basketball, athletics, and soccer. Cuba has performed well internationally in all these sports except soccer, as well as in weightlifting, water polo, and gymnastics

Figure 6.1
Organizational Structure of Cuban Sports since February 1961

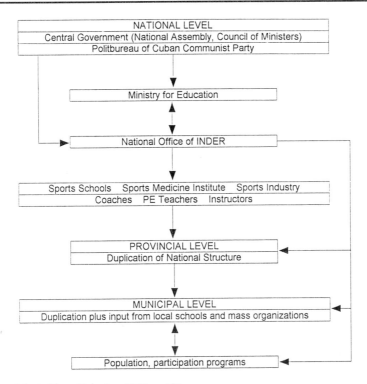

Source: Adapted from Pickering, 1978, p. 156.

(including rhythmic gymnastics). Wrestling and fencing are also quite significant sports in terms of international performance.

This chapter explores the revolutionary government's use of sports and sports policy in the promotion of government interests. Sports aided the government in developing and maintaining military preparedness, especially in a hostile political climate. Furthermore, sports have greatly assisted the government in nation building, socialization, and political integration.

Until recently, sports in Cuba were not a source of revenue for either private interests or the state. The function of sports is more social and political rather than economic. Sports are state funded and therefore a drain on resources that could be spent on more basic needs. More recently, however, several areas of Cuban sports have generated revenue. These are (1) the limited exports of sports goods (Llaneras Rodriguez et al., 1986, p. 128); (2) athletes' winnings; and (3) money earned by Cuban sports professionals working abroad (Brubaker, 1992). Money earned abroad by athletes and coaches is reinvested into the sports system[5] (Gutierrez, 1992). In 1992 Cuba contracted to supply boxing trainers to thirty-six countries, including ten in the Barcelona Olympics (Borges, 1992). The sports industry provides facilities and equipment as well as some employment and a limited amount of export revenue (Llaneras Rodriguez et al., 1986). Overall, sport in Cuba has not been a significant source of revenue. However, the Cubans claim that the sports system has become self-funding (Brubaker, 1992). Indeed, if the trend toward hiring out Cuban sports specialists continues, the system could become a moneymaker as well as an imagemaker.

Cuba first emerged as a world sports power in the 1970s, a record of success that continued into the 1980s and 1990s. Although Cuba boycotted both the 1984 and 1988 Olympic Games, it began the decade credibly, with a strong showing at the 1980 Moscow Olympics. While only eighty-one countries attended these games as a result of the U.S.-led boycott to protest the Soviet invasion of Afghanistan, Cuba demonstrated its continuing strength in world sports, winning eight gold medals, seven silver, and five bronze medals for a total of twenty medals (Kramer-Mandeau, 1988, p. 192).

During the 1980s, Cuba also continued its domination of the Central American and Caribbean Games, finishing first with 271 medals at the 1982 games held in Cuba (see *El Deporte,* 1982). The games cost 12 million pesos to host[6] (Montesinos and Barros, 1984, p. 166). Cuba was again victorious in 1986 and 1990, winning 271 medals in Santiago de los Caballeros, Guatemala, in 1986, and 322 medals in Mexico City in 1990 (Kramer-Mandeau, 1988, p. 167 and Gonzalez et al., 1991, p. 171). Similarly, Cuba continued to be a world power in a number of sports, notably baseball, boxing, women's volleyball, weightlifting, and athletics, and to a lesser extent, wrestling (see *El Deporte* and *Listos para Vencer*). Cuba was a prominent performer at the 1991 World Athletic Championships in Tokyo, finishing twelfth overall (*The Australian,* 1991b, p. 14).

This record of sports strength has been underscored by recent Cuban successes. At the 1983 and 1987 Pan American Games, Cuba finished ahead of Canada and second only to the United States, capturing 163 medals in 1983 and 175 medals in 1987 (Kramer-Mandeau, 1988, p. 181). As host nation for the 1991 Pan American Games, Cuba won 265 medals, 140 of them gold, ten more than the United States (*The Australian,* 1991a, p. 20).

Throughout the 1950s, Cuba never won more than thirty medals in the Pan American Games, and yet since 1971, has never won fewer than a hundred medals in each of the Games. Throughout the 1980s, only the United States won more medals than Cuba in these Games (Dominguez, 1989, p. 150). On a medals won per capita basis, Cuba has long been the best performer in the Western Hemisphere. In amateur baseball, Cuba remains king (Klein, 1987), dominating the sport at the Pan American Games. In 1987 Cuba lost its first game since 1967 to the U.S. team led by pitcher Jim Abbott (Powers, 1987, p. 67). Despite losing six weightlifting medals at the 1983 Games because of drug use (Powers, 1987, p. 67), Cuba proved to be a weightlifting stronghold by winning all the medals at the 1987 Pan American Games in Indianapolis. Cuba's boxers also dominated these games, winning a record ten medals (Moran, 1987, p. C5). By 1991, with the demise of East Germany as an independent country, Cuba became the world's best sports performer on a medals won per capita basis (Fletcher, 1991, p. D6). Cuba won forty-six Olympic medals between 1959 and 1980, compared to fourteen (thirteen in fencing 1900–1904, one in sailing, none by women) before 1959 (McWhirter, McWhirter, and Greenberg, 1980). At the 1992 summer Olympics in Barcelona, Spain, with the most universal representation since 1960, Cuba came in sixth out of 172 nations, with a total of thirty-one medals, behind only the Unified Team (112), the United States (108), Germany (82), China (54), and Hungary (37) (*Washington Post,* 1992b). In the gold medal tally, Cuba ranked fifth and marked its place as an indisputable world sports power.

Since the early 1960s, no foreign investors have been involved in Cuban sports; however, Cuban athletes and coaches have themselves served as a form of "currency." Foreign ties have consisted of athletic and coaching exchanges with the Third World and the former socialist bloc.[7] Between 1961 and 1985,[8] 150 sports specialists, mainly from the USSR, Bulgaria, Hungary, and East Germany, worked in Cuba. (See Table 6.1.) Foreign trade and sports aid, both financial and technical, have always been an important part of Cuba's physical culture economy. In addition, many Cubans received athletic and technical training in Eastern Europe. Initially, much of Cuba's sports equipment was imported from the socialist bloc. Such cooperation was particularly important in military-related sports and in high-performance sport, the latter of which has also received considerable funding. In 1969, for example, Cuba joined the Sports Committee of Friendly Armies and in 1972 signed a five-year sports agreement with the USSR (Lowe et al., 1978, p. 300).

More recently, Cuba has provided significant sports aid and training to Third World countries. Such a cooperative use of sport helped to build on the prestigious reputation that Cuba was cultivating in the international sporting community. Between 1961 and 1985, 853 Cuban sports specialists worked as coaches and trainers in thirty-three foreign countries. Foreign students have also received sports training in Cuba. A total of 163 scholarships to attend the National Institute for Physical Culture (ISCF) were granted to students from thirty-three countries. A further 182 scholarships were awarded to students from thirteen countries to attend Higher Schools of Physical Education (EPEF). In this same period, 53,000 Cubans participated in sports events in foreign countries and 32,000 foreigners competed in Cuba. Between 1963 and 1985, forty-five Cubans graduated from sports-related programs in other countries: thirty-five of these in the USSR, six in the GDR, and two each in Bulgaria and Czechoslovakia (Llaneras Rodriguez, 1986, pp. 54–67).

With the tremendous hardships that peaked in the early 1990s, Cuban sports assistance to other countries began to focus on the "sale" of coaching expertise to rival Olympic programs (Brubaker, 1992). Earlier, Cuba had earned its pay

Table 6.1
Foreign Technical Assistance by Country of Origin

Year	USSR	Bulgaria	Poland	Czech.	Hungary	GDR	N. Korea	Romania	PRC	Other	Total
1961	—	—	—	2	—	—	—	—	—	—	2
1962	14	1	—	3	—	1	—	—	—	—	19
1963	4	1	1	3	—	1	—	2	—	—	12
1964	13	1	—	1	2	1	—	—	2	—	20
1965	2	1	—	1	—	3	—	—	1	—	8
1966	17	3	1	3	3	5	1	—	—	—	33
1967	18	2	2	2	4	3	1	—	—	—	32
1968	14	4	6	3	8	4	1	—	—	—	40
1969	14	6	6	4	6	3	4	—	—	1	44
1970	22	9	6	6	6	3	6	—	—	2	60
1971	28	9	5	6	8	2	2	—	—	1	61
1972	26	18	4	3	10	2	1	—	—	—	65
1973	17	15	3	3	7	—	1	—	—	—	46
1974	21	14	2	2	7	6	—	—	—	—	52
1975	28	10	1	1	7	7	—	—	—	—	54

Source: Pickering in Riordan, *Sport under Communism*, p. 155.

in the propaganda value inherent in such sports exchanges. By the 1990s Cubans were interested in more tangible rewards. As noted earlier, by 1992 Cuba had boxing trainers in thirty-six countries, including ten from other teams that participated in Barcelona (Borges, 1992). In volleyball, Cuban coaching is credited with bringing the perennially defeated Spanish team to the quarterfinals. Cuban coaches are also selling their expertise in wrestling to Venezuela, in track and field and baseball to Mexico, and in baseball to Italy (Rhoden, 1992).

GOVERNMENT INVOLVEMENT IN SPORTS

All sports in Cuba have been state funded since the early 1960s, including free access to sports equipment, facilities, and events. Talented young athletes can enter a wide variety of special sports schools from the early primary level to the tertiary level (see Figure 6.2). These schools provide specialized training and, in many cases, full board free of charge. At the tertiary level, scholarships for living expenses are also provided for athletes.

With all sports, athletes, and facilities controlled by the state, sports regulations generally originate in INDER and relate largely to requirements for entering competitions, such as health passes or eligibility status, or for entry to and maintenance of a position in a sports school. Among the more significant regulations produced by INDER are Resolution 2 (March 15, 1961); Resolution 38 (September 2, 1961); Resolution 67-D (January 4, 1962); and Resolution 83-A (March 9, 1962), all of which relate to the outlawing of various professional sports. Other regulations include Resolution 3 (March 15, 1961), which banned alcohol in Havana's main sports facility, *Ciudad Deportiva;* Resolution 696 (June 25, 1965), which called for the creation of a sports equipment industry; and Resolution 1030 (March 16, 1967), which outlawed all charges for sports competition in Cuba (INDER, 1985). As mentioned above, profit-making from sports was outlawed after 1962. Private clubs were converted to state centers, and teams were organized around neighborhood and employment locales rather than around private clubs.

The centralized structure of the Cuban government is clearly reflected in sports. Although the national office of INDER interacts with the provincial offices, there is limited control at the lower levels because most funding and policymaking originates at the top in the national INDER office. Hence, while provincial INDER offices and the legislative bodies at various levels, together with mass organizations, may play an advisory role in each region, sports policies are generated at the national level and implemented at lower levels of administration.

Given the extensive degree of state control, Cuban sports policies are far too extensive to list in full. Such policies clearly have a significant impact on all sports organizations and operations to some extent. Specific policies related to the various goals of Cuban sports are explored below and range from hours devoted to physical education to leave from work for top athletes. The main

Figure 6.2
Possible Progression Paths through Cuban Sports Schools

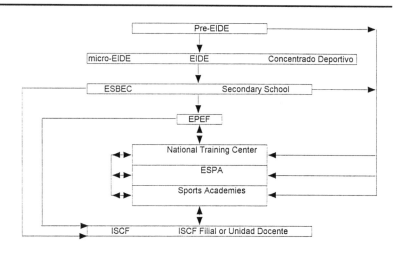

Legend for Abbreviations:

EIDE	School for Sports Initiation, primary level.
ESBEC	Basic Secondary School in the Countryside-sports.
Concentrado Deportivo	Sports Concentration, primary level.
EPEF	Provincial Schools for Physical Education, tertiary level.
ESPA	Higher Education Center for Athletic Perfection, all levels.
Sports Academies	Special Centers for individual sports.
ISCF	Higher Institute for Physical Culture.
Filial or Unidad Docente	A Provincial center of ISCF.

goals of Cuban sports policy since the revolution are (1) to achieve mass participation in physical culture and sports activities, and (2) to produce world-class athletes. Mass participation promotes good health and contributes to productivity and defense. Access to sport is promoted as the right of all Cubans. Sport is also viewed as part of the wider goal of the revolution to encourage socialist values. Top athletes are viewed as positive role models for greater participation in sports as well as being a source of prestige for both Cuba and socialism. All policies relate in some way to one or both of the objectives of mass participation and high performance in sports. The Cuban government has consistently stated that, while medals are very important, popular participation for health is more so: "[n]o importaria que nuestra delegacion fuese la ultima en medallas . . . , si pudieramos tener la satisfaccion de ver un dia que triunfa el deporte como instrumento de la felicidad y del bienestar del pueblo." (Castro, cited in Acosta Diaz, 1979).[9]

ANALYSIS OF GOALS

In theory, the Cuban revolution is dedicated to seeking egalitarianism in all areas of society. In sport an attempt is made to balance equality of access with the attainment of high standards, just as an attempt is made to balance egalitarianism in standards of living with economic development. The twofold objective of high performance and mass participation in sport is based not only on Marxist-Leninist theory, but also on Cuban views about the nature of their society before 1959.

Mass Participation

Cuban leaders claim that physical culture did not exist for the majority of Cubans before 1959. Exclusive clubs denied most Cubans entry on economic and racial grounds. Cuba's leaders also criticize the dominance of U.S. interests in many sports, as well as the corruption and limited government interest in physical culture. Despite the tendency of Cuban leaders to overstate the lack of facilities and to ignore the breakdown of racial restrictions in a few sports, this critique is in large part justified.

Since 1959, Cuban leaders have criticized the inequality and underdeveloped state of Cuban sports and have dedicated themselves to changing these conditions with considerable success. At the beginning of the revolutionary transformation, Cuban leaders worked to remove legal and socioeconomic barriers to participation in sports. With the transition to a socialist and then to a Marxist-Leninist philosophy, the island's leadership pursued a policy of extending access through direct state control. They also sought to radically alter the social structure of the nation and moved to break down gender, race, and especially class barriers to sports participation.

Important factors adding to egalitarianism in sports included the construction of new facilities and the production and distribution of sports equipment. The establishment of the Cuban sports industry in 1965, which grew rapidly (Pickering, 1978, p. 164), extended the amount of sports equipment available. Moreover, by 1988 there were over 9,500 sports installations on the island (Caminada, 1988, p. 5). Although there were certainly problems with work standards and quality control in the sports industry (Caminada, 1988, pp. 8–9), the expansion of facilities and equipment made it possible for growing numbers of Cubans to practice sports or other physical activities.

Cuba's leadership also introduced a wide variety of programs aimed at encouraging participation. In the 1960s emphasis was placed on developing programs for young Cubans. Attention was also directed at providing sports activities in rural regions. These concerns continued into the 1970s and 1980s, along with an interest in competitive sports. Cuba extended its participation programs to include various activities for Cubans of all ages. Programs for sports, exercises, and recreation were steadily developed, improved upon, and expanded. Attitudes, especially those antagonistic to the participation of women, have slowly begun to change, inhibited by the difficulty in raising the educational and cultural awareness of both parents and teachers.

Nevertheless, Cuba has come close to achieving its target of mass participation in sports. Indeed, Cuba has probably progressed further in mass participation than had the Soviet Union, where the dual goals of mass participation, or *massovost,* and high quality, or *masterstvo,* were developed. In a sense, Cubans are duty bound to participate in sports or other forms of physical culture as a sign of their commitment to the revolution.

The policy of mass participation has, however, met with several problems and obstacles. Primary among the obstacles is the prioritization of basic needs and economic expansion over other objectives. The limited availability of resources, intensified by the cessation of Soviet subsidies and the collapse of socialism in Eastern Europe, means that physical culture, including sports (which tends to suffer cuts in times of economic difficulty), will likely receive less funding. In the climate of the 1990s, priority is likely to be increasingly placed on meeting basic needs. The reduced availability of hard currency could result in a reduction of imported sports equipment and perhaps a focus on producing sports items for export rather than for internal use. Unless sports become consistently profitable, these economic problems may well lead to cuts in popular sports programs and training for top athletes. This will make it even more difficult to overcome existing barriers to mass participation such as dropping out after leaving educational institutions,[10] sexism, racism, and bureaucratic inefficiency. Although expanded since 1959, women's participation in organized sports remains well below that of men (Padula and Smith, 1985, p. 87). Facilities and coaching are sometimes below desired standards, reflecting, at times, bureaucratic inefficiency (Caminada, 1988, p. 8).

While the extent of some of these defects, such as racism, is difficult to assess, sexism is clearly evident. *Machismo* and *marianismo*[11] still exist, despite the efforts of the revolution to combat such attitudes. Women are excluded from some sports—such as boxing and baseball—and their number on Cuban teams is still quite small, especially compared to those of the former USSR and East Germany. By 1980, of more than 2.5 million participants in organized sports, only 17 percent were women, who were most strongly represented in gymnastics, horseshoe throwing, volleyball, table tennis, fencing, and athletics (Halebsky and Kirk, 1985). The same disparity is evident in Cuba's national teams. In the 1964 Olympics, only two women represented Cuba; by 1976, there were twenty-six. At the Moscow Olympics in 1980, however, only thirty-six women were in the Cuban delegation of 237 athletes (Slack, 1982).

Although only 5,444 women participated in sports in 1963, by 1976 approximately 1 million women were involved in organized sports. Of these, however, only 200,000, or a fifth, participated outside the school system (Slack, 1982). Despite revolutionary liberation, Cuban women, like those in other societies, found only limited time for sports after working, caring for husbands and children, doing housework, and waiting in queues for rationed goods (Stone, 1981). The lower level of male participation outside of the school system also reflected the fact that the desire to practice sports is weakened outside of the compulsory physical education structure in the school system. The higher numbers of women in physical culture programs might mean that these activities are more attractive to women than organized competitive sports. However, this might also reflect traditional values about the activities suited to and suitable for each gender. Nevertheless, the growth of women's participation in Cuban physical culture, including sports, cannot be dismissed, nor can the fact that Cubans now have the opportunity to participate in many activities from which they were excluded prior to the revolution.

Another likely result of Cuba's development of sports is the benefit of such activities for the health standards of the island's population. This has certainly been a major objective in Cuban policy, but it has been hindered by the nature of the Cuban diet and the difficulty of getting adults in any society to exercise. Since many Cubans are overweight (Paz, 1988, p. 29), it appears that only a proportion of the Cuban people have participated in sporting activities for health reasons, despite this being a goal in Cuban sports policy.

Elite Sports and Athletes

The most visible achievement in Cuba's sports system has been the development of opportunities for those with talent; this is clearly evident in the success of Cuban teams in international sports arenas. Almost all Cubans with athletic ability and aspiration may gain access to specialized training and facilities in sports centers or schools (Feinstein, 1980, pp. F1, F4).

This policy entails several complications, however, notably the tension in balancing bureaucratic and funding emphases between mass programs and elite sports—tensions that have arisen and that were recently raised publicly (Caminada, 1988, pp. 8–9). There is also the problem of athletes receiving certain privileges. For example, athlete access to extra and more varied food may become increasingly irritating for mainstream Cubans as the negative economic effects of changes in the former socialist bloc manifest themselves. Similarly, corruption—especially in terms of advantages for athletes in dealing with the burdensome Cuban bureaucracy—could incur the ire of growing numbers of the population in a period of increasing political and economic isolation and hardship. The ability and willingness of the Cuban system and its people to support elite athletes may be reduced. The elimination of Soviet financial and technical assistance in sports, on which Cuba has been dependent, will add to such pressures. Perhaps Cuba's sports system will show signs of tearing at the seams. The potential unraveling will no doubt be detrimental to both mass participation and high performance in Cuban sports.

For example, athletes may well be asked to accept fewer privileges and to dedicate themselves even more to the revolutionary cause than is already expected. This could potentially lead to demands from athletes to be allowed to retain their winnings, as was the case in the former Soviet Union. Economic and political pressures may weaken the impressive Cuban sports system, together with the varied domestic and foreign policy roles it has traditionally played. Yet, these same pressures could make the use of sport for political purposes more attractive to Cuba's increasingly embattled and isolated leadership.

THE POLITICAL ROLE OF CUBAN SPORT

The economic problems faced by Cuba, together with the antagonism of the Reagan and Bush administrations in the United States, led to an increase in the use of sports for promoting fitness and military preparedness. It is possible that the role of athletes as a vanguard—that is, as role models for the revolution— and the use of sports successes for generating national pride and winning international prestige may be expanded. On the domestic front, there could be an intensification of the use of sports and other forms of physical culture for socialization and perhaps social control. Such uses of physical culture, however, are unlikely to have much impact if discontent grows in the face of economic hardship and political isolation.

Domestic Roles

Military Preparedness

The use of sports as part of military training is common to all countries. In the socialist countries, sports were also encouraged as a way to promote fitness for defense among the population as a whole in the face of often hostile environments. This has certainly been the case in Cuba. In times of perceived or actual security threats, vigilance, including the use of sport for fitness purposes, has increased.

Since the disastrous Bay of Pigs invasion in 1961, Cuba has prepared itself militarily, from the youngest to the oldest, for another attack by the United States. The vigilance of the last three decades was only strengthened by the antagonism of the Reagan and Bush administrations and the various attacks by assorted Cuban exiles.[12] Indeed, the ever-present hostility from the United States led to the formation of military sports clubs to teach civilians basic military skills in combination with recreational activities (Dominguez, 1982, p. 54). Given U.S. policy toward Cuba and the political strength and hostility of Cuban Americans, the use of physical culture for military preparedness will likely be maintained and perhaps increased.

Political Integration

Athletes may also be called upon to broaden their role as sources of national pride and revolutionary role models. The island's sports stars have already played a significant role in the revolutionary process, as has physical culture as a whole. Sport has affected three very important political factors: nation-building, socialization, and political integration.

As Alberto Juantorena said: "Americans live in a country; we Cubans are *building* a country" (cited in Boswell, 1978a, pp. D1, D3). Through sports, Cubans are able to feel personally involved in the process. This creates strong feelings of national pride. People who feel they have helped to create something identify more closely with it. The goal of mass participation was to break down class differences and promote increased cohesiveness. The result, it was hoped, would be a system or network between government and the people, and among the people as a whole, that is mutually supportive. Certainly, the people's participation in numerous sports activities and in policy implementation, including sports, may serve this purpose. On the other hand, the fact that decision making in sports is highly centralized at the highest levels of the state and party structure may have undermined, to some extent, the goal of political integration and national unity.

Socialization through physical culture and the use of athletes as role models may be more effective for unity and cohesion, especially in the long term. Outstanding sportsmen and women become role models for the society as a whole. Cuban athletes usually acknowledge the role of the revolution and the Cuban people in their victories. The most obvious example occurred when Cuban boxing legend Teofilo Stevenson refused the offer of $1 million to retain the love of the Cuban people. Another was when Alberto Juantorena, winner of the 400- and 800-meter races at the Montreal Olympics, dedicated one of his gold medals to his compatriots and gave the other one to Fidel Castro to "share" with them in 1976. Athletes are expected to display such revolutionary commitment as a vanguard for all Cubans. With growing economic problems, ordinary Cubans may be inspired by victories but may be less content to support privileges for athletes. Nevertheless, there is no denying that Cuban national pride is promoted by world-class athletes.

Cuba's capacity to support such "superstars" is quite likely to diminish. Thus, one part of the political socialization process which occurs through physical culture will perhaps be weakened. Moreover, Cuba's current problems may serve to undermine socialization through the promotion of the revolutionary ideology in sport and physical culture at the mass level. Nevertheless, there is considerable social pressure to conform to the revolution's ideology.

Physical culture was regarded as a means to combat old values and promote communist attitudes. While this leads to overt allegiance to the revolution, without repression, socialization cannot guarantee social control. It is also important not to underestimate feelings of allegiance which arise from improved living conditions and the spirit of nation-building, rather than simply through socialization. Socialization through active physical culture and the passive admiration of superstars undoubtedly occurs in Cuba, but no degree of ideological promotion can ensure social control without force. Evidence for this argument appears in the rapid dismantling of socialism in Eastern Europe and the Soviet Union. However, the fact that socialization does occur may become increasingly evident in the former socialist bloc as people accustomed to notions of guaranteed incomes, food, and shelter face the prospect of rising inflation and growing unemployment. It seems improbable that socialization in Cuba will prove any stronger than it has in the former socialist bloc.

Socialization will certainly not lead Cubans to ignore, dismiss, or accept the extreme difficulties they face today. Hence, the role of sport in domestic politics seems likely to be retained, even if limited in its capacity to overcome the problems that the island's population is facing. In foreign policy, however, sport may well have a greater role to play in future years.

Foreign Policy

Sport has traditionally been significant in Cuban foreign policy in the postrevolution period. With the prospect of growing political isolation, this role is quite likely to grow in importance, although funding problems may well undermine this avenue of foreign policy.

In foreign policy, sport serves as a very powerful political tool. Many countries, including Cuba, know this fact very well:

For this land, whose boundaries are set by the sea, sports has become a kind of Cuban equivalent of 19th century American [U.S.] Manifest Destiny. The Olympics are their Oregon Trail, their Northwest Territory, their visible evidence of national accomplishment and a rallying point for morale. (Boswell, 1978b, pp. D1, D7)

Surely the value of a victory in the Olympics, the Pan American Games, or any international sporting contest goes beyond the gold medal. It is but a short distance from an individual athlete in his or her national uniform to the strong symbol of the country being represented (Kanin, 1976, pp. 6–7; Strenk, 1978, p. 460). Consequently, there are many foreign policy uses for sport, some of which are closely interrelated.

Diplomatic Recognition

One of the most concrete uses of sport is as a means of diplomatic recognition or nonrecognition. Sport is a clear but indirect way to communicate often hostile government policy. The most obvious recent examples are East and West Germany, the People's Republic of China and Taiwan, South Africa and New Zealand, and South Africa and the British Commonwealth. Although there are many others, the 1966 Central American Games in Puerto Rico provide a good example involving Cuba and the United States. Cuban athletes were denied visas and air-landing rights by the United States to attend the games. Yet, when the Cuban team arrived by sea on the *Cerro Pelado,* U.S. officials relented and allowed them passage. Cuba's impressive medal tally in those games enhanced the Cubans' political point. The Cubans also made political statements by boycotting the 1984 and 1988 Olympic Games. The tension between the United States and Cuba at the 1987 (Indianapolis) and 1991 (Havana) Pan American Games are further examples. The 1991 Games may also have played a part in Cuba's partially successful attempt to break its isolation in Latin America.

Propaganda

Sport provides a convenient stage for displaying the physical prowess of a country's athletes. There is a clear implication that only a superior social system could produce such dazzling champions. Also implicit is the inferiority of the loser. So important was this function to the socialist countries that meetings were held regularly among the leaders of the propaganda sections of the sports associations of the entire bloc. The 1977 meeting was held in Cuba.

The revolutionary government has not lost the opportunity to capitalize on its sporting successes. After all, many people throughout the world identify Cuba with first the missile crisis, and then with baseball, Alberto Juantorena, or Teofilo Stevenson rather than with Moncada, Granma, or even the Bay of Pigs. To the Cubans, sports success as propaganda is important throughout the world, but nowhere more so than in the rest of Latin America and the developing world. As Castro said:

I can assure you that one of the things most admired by our Latin American neighbors is our sporting successes. We can say that our athletes are the children of our Revolution and, at the same time, the standard-bearers of that same Revolution. (Cited in Pickering, 1978, p. 150)

What gives Cuba more credibility with less developed countries is that Cuba is still one of their own. This position was strengthened even further as Cuba moved into a leadership role, able to provide technical assistance to other countries. "Cuba thus provides a powerful example of the potential of a small country whose resources are rationally deployed under what the Cuban leadership described as a "superior social system" (Casal and Hernandez, 1976, p. 2).

The collapse of most of Cuba's socialist allies means that this propaganda effort may be weakened substantially. The economic chaos in the former Soviet Union and Eastern Europe makes it harder for people and nations to believe Cuba's claims to a superior social system. This also applies to Cuba's own domestic audience. The reduction of technical and economic aid will probably mean that it will be harder for Cuba to maintain its current status as a world-class performer. Nevertheless, prestige in such victories will continue.

Indeed, Fidel Castro made a rare personal appearance at the opening of the 1992 Olympic Games in Barcelona, in conjunction with an extended trip through Spain, a clear show of his political power. Such confidence was in sharp contrast with other Latin American leaders unable to travel because of domestic problems, such as Carlos Andres Perez of Venezuela, Alberto Fujimori of Peru, and Cesar Gaviria of Colombia (Farah, 1992a).[13]

Prestige

Closely tied to propaganda is the function of sports in the search for national prestige. Athletes are a source of pride, and victories are a bonus. Since the mid-1970s, Cuba has been a respected member of the international sporting community. This can be credited not just to the nation's athletes, but also to the government officials and trainers who support the actual contestants. In 1976 Raudol Ruiz Aguilera, a prominent Cuban sports official, was awarded the Philip Noel Baker prize for Scientific Investigation by the International Council for Sport and Physical Education. In Cuba, this was considered a high honor (Mastrascusa, 1976, pp. 14–15).

The hosting of the 1991 Pan American Games is further indication of the level of prestige accorded to Cuba by the international sporting community. Because the Cuban economy had deteriorated drastically since 1987—the year Cuba was awarded the position of host country—the Games did prove to be a further economic burden to the Cuban people. Yet, contrary to what many people expected, especially in the United States, the 1991 Havana Games were highly successful. Once again, in both the Cuban medal tally and in the graciousness shown toward Pan American guests, Cuba further secured its prestige in the eyes of the sporting world.[14]

Whether Cuba is able to maintain its sporting strength and the resulting prestige in the future remains uncertain, just as Cuba's important role in sports cooperation appears to be threatened by economic crisis. Both, however, have been and will remain valuable tools of Cuban foreign policy.

Cooperation

Perhaps the function of sport that carries with it the most hope is that it will encourage cooperation among nations. The assumption is that any contact fosters understanding, perhaps even improved relations. Cooperation, which was especially valuable to Cuba, certainly occurred within the former socialist bloc, but Cuba also extended sports cooperation to less developed countries, such as Jamaica, where the Cubans have built sports facilities, including one for free (Rolo, 1980, p. 11). Jamaicans and many other people from poor countries in Africa and Latin America have also received sports training in Cuba.

Such cooperation is linked to Cuba's commitment to socialist internationalism which, as is evident in the Cuban press, is promoted through sports links. Given the current concerns with domestic problems and the very survival of Cuba's socialist system, it is difficult for Cuba to provide such sports aid free of charge to less developed countries. The upheavals in European socialism may also lead not only to increased antagonism between Cuba and other nations as Cuba becomes more isolated, but also to reluctance to accept sports aid or cooperation from Cuba. With the reduction in aid and equipment from the former Soviet Union and Eastern Europe, Cuba may simply be unable to provide aid to others.

Conflict

Hence, the role of sports as a signal of hostility may increase. Sport has often been a vehicle for the United States to express its hostility toward Cuba and vice versa. Castro hailed Cuba's defeat of the U.S. volleyball team in Los Angeles in 1976 as a "sporting, psychological, patriotic, and revolutionary victory" (Pickering, 1978, p. 147). Similar political hostilities surfaced in abundance at the 1966 Central American Games and over Cuba's boycott of the 1984 and 1988 Olympic Games, the 1987 Pan American Games, and the 1991 Pan American Games.[15]

The intensification of anti-Cuban feelings in the United States and growing Cuban isolation may increase expressions of hostility between Cuba and the United States. Recent examples of such ill-will include the 1992 Torricelli Bill (Farah, 1992b) passed by the U.S. Congress, and Castro's victory in the United Nations against further efforts of the United States to isolate Cuba internationally (*Washington Post,* 1992c).[16] On the other hand, Cuba may seek to use sports—as it has in the past—as a means to expand ties with the United States, particularly with its desire to see the United States' economic blockade lifted.[17] A deepening of hostility, however, seems more likely.

CUBAN SPORT: THE ROLE AND THE RECORD

The purpose of sports in the international arena is invaluable. "International sport is one of the strongest, most direct, cheapest and least dangerous foreign policy weapons a nation can use to set the tone of relations" (Strenk, 1978, p. 457). Cuba appears to have made astute use of this weapon. Today, the tendency to use sports to gain prestige, to imply national stability, and to break political and economic isolation may grow. The capacity to meet such objectives, however, is probably limited. This is even more likely in the case of the Cuban leadership's domestic audience, where the effects of socialization may be further weakened by food shortages (Gunn, 1991, p. 104; Hart, 1991, p. 10). The probable decline in the ability of Cuba's economy to maintain current levels and standards in both elite sports and mass physical culture will make it all the more difficult to realize the political objectives of physical culture. Sports and physical culture cannot solve the more pressing economic and political problems that threaten to bring down socialism in Cuba.

By 1976, only fifteen years into the revolution, Cuba changed from a country that had won only a handful of medals to being one of the top ten medal-winning nations in Olympic Games. Cuba provides the world with a clear example of how a socialist system can help a developing country move from backwardness to excellence in a single area. The phenomenal success of the Cuban sports system is inspirational. Yet, the cost of developing the sports program has been high. Sacrifices had to be made in other areas of society. In a sense, the Cuban government has gotten what it paid for. Determination to invest resources in both the expansion of participation in physical culture and in specialized training for those with talent are the two most important explanations for the state of Cuban sport. Yet, concomitant with this monumental achievement is the tension that arises between those engaging in sport for health and fun, and those who are the sporting elite, the high-performance athletes. Another factor is a high degree of unity of purpose, perhaps relatively easy in a small socialist country with a strong sense of nationalism. With the recent increase in austerity measures, however, cracks may be developing in this unity. Improvements in living standards, especially in food intake and health (Benjamin, Collins, and Scott, 1984, pp. 90, 96–97), are also important factors. Again, in the current economic environment, these factors may apply more to the upper echelon athletes than to Cuban society in general.

Clearly, the island's sporting success, measured both by international performance and participation levels, is a result of the implementation of Cuba's single-minded focus on the sports system. Furthermore, it is a function of Cuba's transformation to socialism, with the all-important concomitant aid from the former socialist bloc. Yet, the rise in per capita Gross Domestic Product (Perez, 1988, p. 357) has been endangered by the elimination of Soviet subsidies, which, in turn, threatens to do considerable damage to Cuba's sports system.

Although the life span of the socialist system in Cuba cannot be predicted, sports will almost certainly suffer. If socialism disappears, it may be hard for any successor governments to ignore completely sports and physical culture in Cuba, as it has become an important part of many Cubans' lives and increasingly has been seen as a right of all people. As is evident in Eastern Europe and the Soviet Union, it is very easy to "throw the baby out with the bathwater." Much has been achieved in Cuban physical culture. While some problems may exist, there are many good features in Cuba's sports system which would be unfortunate losses if the socialist system in Cuba were to collapse.

NOTES

1. Baseball was the one sport that cut across racial and class (but not gender) lines in Cuba. Although the sport may owe its origin to the United States, baseball on the island developed into a distinctly Cuban hybrid. The century-long Cuban love affair with the sport did not decrease in intensity with the revolution and shows no signs of slowing down even now. Baseball provides a clear link between nineteenth- and twenty-first-

century Cuba. It was and is an integral part of Cuban popular culture. For over a century, baseball has gone hand-in-hand with hardship, whether it was the rigors and grinding poverty of the canefields or the austerity of the revolution, relieving it if only for a moment.

2. Until the infamous "color line" was broken in 1947 by Jackie Robinson, only light-skinned Cubans were welcomed in the U.S. major leagues.

3. In 1992 one Cuban peso equaled $0.83 U.S.

4. It is possible that the number of regular participants in sports may now be close to 2 million, for this figure is from 1977.

5. It is not clear how much money athletes and other sports professionals earn or how long this money has been reinvested in sports.

6. In 1982 the Cuban peso approximated $0.80–.85 U.S.

7. Sports exchanges typically include coaching and training, formal study at sports institutions, and the construction of sports facilities.

8. Little has changed in this area since 1985; however, specific figures are not available.

9. "It would not be important if our delegation were the last in the medal tally . . . if we could have the satisfaction of one day seeing sport triumph as an instrument of the happiness and well-being of the people." [Translated by the authors.]

10. This drop in sports participation after leaving school is not unique to Cuba. The problem has also been documented in Australia and, undoubtedly, other countries. See, for example, Australian Sports Commission, 1989, p. 13.

11. *Marianismo* describes the attitude of women who accept the traditional gender stereotypes, roles, and accompanying male attitudes prevalent in *machismo*.

12. In December 1992, three armed Cuban Americans were captured near Cardenas in Matanzas Province, Cuba. According to a statement issued by the Cuban government, the three confessed to being members "of a terrorist organization which operates from the U.S. territory, and were trained and sent to Cuba to carry out violent acts against the revolution" (*Washington Post*, 1992b). Indeed, one of the three was subsequently executed (Estrada, 1992).

13. Interestingly, Castro left Barcelona several days earlier than planned, when rumors surfaced of problems and troop movements at home. The rumors were suspected to be the work of Cuban exiles.

14. Indeed, some representatives of the United States did not comport themselves with similar grace. The U.S. men's basketball team is most remembered for flying back and forth to Miami to avoid staying in Cuba. Ironically, many members of the team contracted diarrhea from the food at the expensive Miami hotel.

15. The details of these incidents are discussed in Pettavino and Pye (1994).

16. The Cuba Democracy Act, or Torricelli law, makes it "illegal for foreign subsidiaries of U.S. companies to sell goods to Cuba and bans vessels that land in Cuba from using U.S. ports for 180 days" (Farah, 1992b). In response, the United Nations General Assembly voted 59–3 (79 abstaining) for a nonbinding resolution calling for an end to the thirty-year American embargo against Cuba. The vote suggests that Washington is more isolated than Havana in international opinion.

17. The most noteworthy examples of Cuba-U.S. sporting ties are boxing matches and exhibition baseball games (not the U.S. major leagues) between the two countries, which have been held fairly regularly in both countries for a number of years.

REFERENCES

Acosta Diaz, L. (1979). *Concurso Nacional de Historia de Deporte, Direccion de Propaganda.* Havana: INDER.

Arrieta, P. (1986, October). Vice president of social sports, INDER. [Interview by Geralyn Pye in Havana.]

The Australian (1991a, August 20). p. 20.

The Australian (1991b, September 2). p. 14.

Australian Sports Commission. (1989). *Youth sport: The next step.* Canberra: Australian Government Publishers.

Benjamin, M., J. Collins, and M. Scott. (1984). *No free lunch: Food and revolution in Cuba today.* San Francisco: Institute for Food and Development Policy.

Borges, R. (1992, August 2). Cubans follow party line, Say it was worth wait. *Boston Globe,* p. 50.

Boswell, T. (1978a, April 8). Cuba's national treasures. *Washington Post,* pp. D1, D3.

Boswell, T. (1978b, April 9). Idle play not in Cuba's game plan. *Washington Post,* pp. D1, D7.

Brubaker, B. (1992, July 12). Cuba's renewed mission: Olympic glory. *Washington Post,* pp. D1, D6.

Caminada, J. (1988, March). "Recuento de un analisis." *El Deporte XX, 203,* 3–6.

Casal, L., and A. R. Hernandez. (1976, November 15–17). *The role of cultural and sports events in Cuba's foreign policy.* [Preliminary Draft Prepared for the Conference on "The Role of Cuba in World Affairs"] Center for Latin American Studies, University of Pittsburgh.

Castro, F. (1966). Cited in L. Acosta Diaz, *Concurso Nacional de la Historia,* 1979.

Champions call for sacking of Soviet state sports committee. (1989, October). *Survey, 12* (9): 15–16.

Cuba 59, United States 3. (1992c, November 29). *Washington Post,* p. C6.

Cubans take all the PanAm gold. (1987, August 14). *Times on Sunday.*

Dominguez, J. I. (1989). *To make a world safe for revolution: Cuba's foreign policy.* Cambridge, mass.: Harvard University Press.

Dominguez, J. I. (ed.). (1982). *Cuba: Internal and international Affairs.* Beverly Hills, Calif.: Sage Publications.

Estrada, Louie. (1992, January 22). Death verdicts in Cuba spur outcry. *Times of the Americas,* p. 1.

Farah, D. (1992a, July 27). Castro's travels connote a tight grip. *Washington Post,* p. A10.

Farah, D. (1992b, December 17). Castro uses stiffer U.S. embargo to justify economic straits. *Washington Post,* pp. A33, A44.

Feinstein, J. (1980, May 25). Cuban refugees ache for shot at "American Great Leagues." *Washington Post,* pp. F1, F14.

Fletcher, P. (1991, July 5). Cuban athletes try to outdo US rivals. *The Washington Times,* p. D6.

Ginesta Almira, W. (1979, April 10). Mas de un medio siglo en el deporte. *Semanario Deportivo Listos par Vencer,* Havana, 17, 877, pp. 28–29.

Gonzalez Alonso, C. P. H. (1985, October). "La formacion de cuadros tecnicos para la

educacion fisica y el deporte en un pais en revolucion (experiencia cubana)."
Cultura Fisica Revista Cientifico-Metodologica del ISCF Havana, 1, 1, pp. 2–23.

Gonzalez Barros, J. (1966, December 4). Baseball. *Granma Weekly Review.* Havana, p. 6.

Gonzalez, G. R., L. Rubalcaba Ordaz, and G. Diaz Cabrera. (1991). *El Deporte Razones de sus Exitos.* Havana: Ediciones ENPES.

Gunn, G. (1991, March). Cuba in crisis. *Current History 90, 554:* 101–104, 133–135.

Gutierrez, B. (1992, January). Interview by Geralyn Pye.

Halebsky, S., and J. M. Kirk. (1985). *Cuba: Twenty-five years of revolution, 1959–1984.* New York: Praeger Publishers.

Hart, K. (1991, April). Will Cuba follow the Kremlin's example? *Swiss Review of World Affairs, 14* (1): 10–11.

INDER Direccion Juridica. (1985). *Fundamentales Disposiciones Legales que Regulan las Actividades Deportivas.* Havana: INDER.

Kanin, D. (1976). The role of sport in international relations. Unpublished doctoral dissertation, Fletcher School of Law and Diplomacy.

Klein, F. C. (1987, November 8). On sports: Pan Am Games. *Wall Street Journal.*

Kramer-Mandeau, W. (1988). *Sport und Korpererziehungauf Cuba Von der Sportutopie eines Entwicklungslandes zum Sportmodell Lateinamerikas?* Koln: Pahl-Rugenstein Verlag GmbH.

Llaneras Rodriguez, M., and 30 collaborators (1986, May). *Cuba 25 Anos de Deporte Revolucionario.* Special Edition of *Mensaje Deportivo, 1*(1), Havana.

Lowe, B., D. B. Kanin, and A. Strenk (1978). *Sport and international relations.* Champaign, Ill.: Stipes Publishing Co.

Mastrascusa, F. (1976, January 6). Un Honor para Cuba. *Listos Para Vencer, 707*: 14–15.

McWhirter, M. D., A. R. McWhirter, and S. Greenberg (eds.). (1980). *The Guinness Book of Olympic records.* Harmondsworth: Penguin Books Limited.

Montesinos, E., and S. Barros. (1984). *Centroamericanos y del Caribe los mas Antiguos Juegos Deportivos Regionales del Mundo.* Havana: Cientifico-Tecnica.

Moran, M. (1987, August 24). Battered American boxers assess effort. *New York Times,* p. C5.

Padula, A., and L. Smith. (1985). "Women in socialist Cuba, 1959–84." In S. Halebsky and J. M. Kirk, *Cuba: Twenty-five years of revolution, 1959–1984.* New York: Praeger Publishers.

Paz, J. (1988, July). Se puede bajar de peso? *El Deporte 20,* 207: 29.

Perez, L. A., Jr. (1988). *Cuba between reform and revolution.* New York: Oxford University Press.

Pettavino, P. J., and G. M. Pye. (1994). *Sport in Cuba: The diamond in the rough.* Pittsburgh: University of Pittsburgh Press.

Pickering, R. (1978). Sport in Cuba. In J. Riordan (ed.), *Sport under communism: The USSR, Czechoslovakia, China and Cuba* (pp. 141–174). London: C. Hurst & Co.

Powers, J. (1987, August 16). US ends Cuba's winning streak, 6–4. *Boston Globe,* pp. 46, 67.

Rhoden, William C. (1992, August 5). You need an Olympic coach? Cuba may have the answer. *New York Times,* pp. A1, B10.

Rolo, M. (1980, August 10). Cuban construction workers finish sports complex in Jamaica. *Granma Weekly Review,* p. 11.

Ruiz Aguilera, R. (1977, June). Humanizing sports. *Cuba Review Sports—Why Cubans Win, 7* (2): 10–20.

Seers, D. (ed.). (1975). *Cuba: The economic and social revolution.* Westport, Conn.: Greenwood Press.

Slack, T. (1982). Cuba's political involvement in sport. *Journal of Sport and Social Issues, 6* (2): 37.

Stone, E. (ed.). (1981). *Women and the Cuban Revolution.* New York: Pathfinder Press.

Strenk, A. (1978, Summer). The thrill of victory and the agony of defeat: Sport in international politics. *Orbis.*

USA Today (1991, August 19). C1.

Washington Post (1992a, January 9). A37.

Washington Post (1992b, August 10). C8.

7

Sports Policy in France

Alain Michel

A multidimensional approach is required to describe the diversity of French sports policy. One needs to not only examine the various forms of government that have formed the France of today, but also the country's history (Enault, et al., 1979, p. 19).

Elected officials have become aware of the importance of physical exercise and sports to the nation's health, and have consequently been concerned with the task of financing sport programs and facilities. At the same time, private organizations have also become increasingly significant in French sports. The goals of a national sports policy are thus confronted with many and varied considerations. The multitude of ethical, political, economic, and social factors, combined with the large number of decision-makers explain the difficulties which arise periodically in defining the main lines of policy.

This chapter identifies the elements that place sport in its present position in France. It first describes the historical development of sport and its organization, and then the methods of financing—government, extra-government and private—are described. Finally, the goals pursued on domestic and international levels, particularly with regard to the status of athletes are discussed. The chapter concludes by highlighting the likely impact of sport at the dawn of the twenty-first century, and evaluating the chances for success on a domestic as well as international level. An overview of present-day research completes this presentation.

FRENCH GOVERNMENT INSTITUTIONS

France is a republic, the characteristics of which are defined in Article 2 of the Constitution of 1958, which founded the Fifth Republic, and which proclaims that it is "indivisible, non-religious, democratic and social." General Charles de Gaulle, upon returning to power in 1958, composed a new constitution wherein the President of the Republic holds the top position in the government. Article 6 stipulates that he is "guarantor of national independence, guardian of the constitution, responsible for the normal functioning of public authorities and for the continuity of the nation." Since 1962 the Chief of State has been elected by universal suffrage for a term of seven years and is eligible for reelection. He appoints and dismisses the Prime Minister who is the head of the "government," that is the Cabinet of Ministers presided over by the Chief of State. The government can initiate a law by submitting a bill for ratification.

The Parliament is composed of two elected assemblies which exercise legislative powers. The first of these is called the National Assembly (577 representatives) elected by universal suffrage by all French citizens aged eighteen and over, for a term of five years. It is housed in the Palais-Bourbon in Paris, and its representatives are aged twenty-three and over. The other assembly is the Senate (321 senators) elected by indirect suffrage for a term of nine years. The Senators are thirty-five years of age and over and convene in the Palais du Luxembourg in Paris.

Up until 1982, France was the perfect example of a country with a centralized administration. All civil service appointments, budget allocations, and administrative decisions came from Paris. All information, problem-solving, and decision-making was referred to the nation's capital.

HISTORY

A brief historical retrospective illustrates the development of French institutions since the Revolution. Historical data also illustrates the different stages of sport development—a process of change which continues today.

Until the end of the eighteenth century, physical education, or sports, hardly existed. At the beginning of the nineteenth century, Francisco Amoros created a kind of exercise that was pedagogical in essence, although military in style. Amoros was a contemporary of the Englishman Thomas Arnold, the German Frederich Ludwig Jahn, and the Swede Per Henrik Ling. In France, the practice of physical activities was limited essentially to canoeing (the future rowing), fencing, horseback riding, hunting, and archery. Gymnastics societies proliferated as well, although legislation at the time limited the number of weekly meetings. In 1851 "gymnastics" was classified as an academic subject. A circular from the Minister of Public Education in 1869 designated gymnastics as compulsory in all teaching colleges, high schools, and junior high schools.

The defeat in 1870 in the Franco-Prussian War was telling, and made the French more aware of the utility of physical exercise. The numerous proclamations and committee meetings to define a method of teaching physical education in schools, demonstrate the interest shown by the various administrations of the Third Republic. The Law of January 27, 1880 made gymnastics compulsory in all primary schools for boys. Two years later, the law was amended to include primary schools for girls.

At the same time, two different movements appeared. The first was at the end of the nineteenth century with the Baron Pierre de Coubertin, who during a speech at the Sorbonne on November 25, 1892, introduced the idea of a "reestablishment of the Olympic Games." In fact, the International Athletic Convention in Paris was behind the restoration of the Games. The second movement was at the beginning of the twentieth century, when naval officer Georges Hebert presented his "natural method" to the international Convention on Physical Education in Paris in 1913.

Organized physical education had its beginnings in 1921, with the creation of a department to oversee physical education attached first to the Ministry of War and later to the Ministry of Public Instruction. In 1928, a subdivision of a government office took over physical education which was still part of the Public Education Department. During the "Front Populaire" administration in 1936, "Physical Education," as it was called, was given over to a subdivision of a government office under the supervision of the Ministry of Health. In addition, "Sports and Youth Activities" were delegated to a government office (the first in history) reporting to the Ministry of Public Education.

During the Second World War in 1941, the Vichy administration created a General Commission on Physical Education and Sports. Its objective was the development of health, physical attributes, and active intelligence.

Upon the Liberation, the ordinances of 1945 legally reinstated the Republic. In 1947 the administration of the Fourth Republic instituted a Department of Youth and Sports attached to the Ministry of National Education.

In 1958 the Fifth Republic transformed this institution into the High Commission on Youth and Sports. In 1963 it was named a full-fledged Ministry, the first of its kind. In 1968, it once again became an office under the authority of the Prime Minister, until the year 1974. "Leisure Activities" later appeared, and combined with "Youth and Sports" to become part of the Ministry of National Education and later of Quality of Life. This department became independent in 1977. It became a Ministry the following year and included Tourism.

In 1981, the office was assigned to the department of Spare Time. Although male-dominated, it was headed by a woman named Edwige Avice, who at first perceived the appointment almost as a snub, but acknowledged that she had to deal with the very real problems of sports and money. In 1984, the title of Ministry of Youth and Sports remained, and there were no additional modifications for the next two years. In 1986 it was renamed a government office for two years before being once again placed under the aegis of the Ministry of National Education, until 1991, when a new Prime Minister was appointed, and it again became a Ministry. These events are consistent with Thibault's (1972) depiction of French sport policymaking in France: "These diverse episodes obviously are not indicative of coherent action. On the contrary, they are proof that physical education as a discipline in teaching remains extremely imprecise" (p. 194).

ORGANIZATION

The nature of the French government and the legacy of history enable us to explain the organization of sports in France. In other countries sports have been either under government control, such as in the former East bloc countries, Cuba, China, and a number of developing countries, or total freedom has been left to powerful sports management organizations, such as in former West Germany, Italy, or the independent leagues of the United States. As Enault et al. (1979) observe, "The French solution is to take a third route midway between liberalism and state control, (which) is more the result of circumstance than an affirmation of will per se" (p. 60).

THE ASSOCIATION LAW OF JULY 1, 1901

This law provides for "liberty of association" and thus encourages individual initiative. The first article stipulates that "association is the agreement through two or more persons to permanently combine their knowledge or activities for other purposes than those of profit-making."

Long before this law was passed, a number of organizations existed. In 1836, the first rowing club was formed; in 1860 gymnastics; and the first skiing club appeared in 1891. Parallel to these single-sport clubs was the creation of multisports organizations. In 1872, the Le Havre Athletic Club was the first to practice athletics and soccer. Then in 1882, the Racing Club of France (RCF) was formed, in 1883 the Stade Français (SF), and in 1906, the Paris Université Club (PUC).

The Law of 1901 has changed since its creation. There are five different types of associations. The first is called an "unregistered association." It cannot own goods or property nor receive funds from the state or from government organizations. The second type is a "registered association" which must respect certain formalities: official registration at the "préfecture" (county courthouse) where its headquarters are located and publication in an official journal. This type of association has the status of a "minor legal entity." This means that it may appear as plaintiff or defendant, purchase goods or property, collect and handle its members' dues, and own or manage the premises necessary for its existence. It may be affiliated with "fédérations" (official leagues).

The third type of association is the "authorized association." It may receive subsidies from the Ministry of Youth and Sports, its departments, or local communities.

The fourth type of association is called "state-approved." Its status is granted by government decree (*"Conseil d'Etat,"* or State Council). Such an association is known as a "major legal entity." It may receive donations and bequests.

Lastly, the "confirmed status association" was named in the Law of December 7, 1987. It is described in the section on legislation.

Alsace-Lorraine enjoys special regulations for associations. In the "departements" (administrative divisions) of Upper Rhine, Lower Rhine, and Moselle, the legal system for associations is basically different from that of French common law. It is derived from provisions in Germanic law which have remained since the annexation of Alsace-Lorraine to France in 1918.

THE FEDERATIONS

The first clubs, called "unions," precursors of the "fédérations" of today, started in 1873, with the "Union of Gymnastics Clubs of France." Later, in 1881, the "Velocipede (Cycling) Clubs" of Angers, Bordeaux, Grenoble, and Lyons appeared. Shortly thereafter the "Union of French Running Societies" was born.

There are three types of leagues. First of all, twenty-one to twenty-three "Olympic single-sport" federations provide for the organization of sports activities in preparation for the Summer or Winter Olympic Games. Next, the "non-Olympic single-sport" leagues organize other sports. They each belong to the international federation of their speciality, in order to deal with matters such as the ratification of records and the application of regulations and their modifications. Finally, the "related" leagues are multisport organizations which can be religious, political, or union affiliated.

A delegation of power is granted by the government to sports leagues. This endows them with a monopoly in their sport and exclusivity in certain fields (the organization of regional and national events, issuance of diplomas, and selection of athletes for international events).

THE FRENCH NATIONAL OLYMPICS AND
SPORTS COMMITTEE

This committee was formed on July 23, 1972 as a result of the merger of two organizations. One was the National Sports Committee (CNS), founded in 1908 by the rowing, boxing, and fencing leagues. It is composed of fifty-nine sports leagues. The other was the French Olympic Committee (COF), created in 1911 and composed of all the so-called "Olympic" leagues.

The French National Olympics and Sports Committee (CNOSF) is the only organization which unites all sports leagues together for one purpose. It claims an efficient form of management, and represents sports with relation to governments and multinational organizations (e.g., UNESCO, the Council of Europe). It is the only structure empowered to deal with the International Olympic Committee (IOC), and is, moreover, holder of the official Olympic symbol and acknowledged owner of Olympic emblems.

The CNOSF is represented in French regional administrative districts by the Regional Olympics and Sports Committee (CROS). These organizations are responsible for achieving objectives defined by their geographical boundaries according to current law. The smaller administrative districts called "Départements" are administered via Departmental Olympics and Sports Committee (CDOS), which deal with different sports associations or clubs and local communities. The CNOSF represents sports groups on the Board of the National Fund for the Development of Sports.

SPORTS IN SCHOOLS AND UNIVERSITIES

Physical Education

Physical education is part of the school curriculum during the compulsory years, that is for children from ages six to sixteen. In 1986, goals were defined regarding "recommendations for physical educational activities in nursery school." Priorities were determined for motor training activities, and coordination and self-expression through movement. Recommendations for activities in water were also included. A decree dated 1990 allows for physical education and art education to take between six and eight hours of weekly instruction.

In elementary school, for children ages six to eleven, the main objectives of physical education (EPS) aim toward hygiene and health while taking into account children's motivation and needs. The teacher's pedagogical procedures stem from observing the child during "real activities" (e.g. during recess) and in his or her own environment. Official pedagogical advisers (from the administrative district or "Department") act as technicians and trainers.

In middle school, for children from ages eleven to sixteen, EPS is taught by specialized personnel. It was originally programmed for five hours per week, but was reduced to three hours in 1973, because of an insufficient number of instructors. It is composed of two parts: the first is basic training, or general physical education, which includes various activities and sports; the second is an optional part, which comprises several specializations, according to programs set up by individual schools. For the first two years of middle school (children ages eleven and twelve years), the objective of this complementary part is to familiarize students with new sports; for the last two years (thirteen- and fourteen-year olds) the objective is to have students compulsory select and regularly practice one or two of those sports.

Two hours per week are allotted to physical education in high school. These are the three years leading up to the Baccalauréat. As far as colleges, universities, and other institutions of higher education are concerned, a decree dating from 1970 allows for the creation of departments for physical education and sports activities. Their responsibility is to set up sports programs, to inform students about them, and to supervise their operation.

Sports

The Sports Union for Primary Education (USEP) was created in 1939. It concerns itself with children in public elementary schools. It was dissolved in 1942 by the Vichy administration and did not reappear until 1946. It is a curricular sports league and educational structure that plays an important role in the development of community life and in the establishment of pedagogical programs. It includes all sports associations of public elementary schools under the Ministry of Education.

Under the aegis of the National Union of Students in France (UNEF), the first sports associations were established by students in 1930. The Office of University Sports (OSU) was created in 1931 to be a liaison and lead and organize competitions. In 1938, it became the Office of School and University Sports (OSSU), a state-approved private organization. It coordinates all sports activities in institutions of secondary, technical, or higher education. The OSSU was dissolved under the Vichy administration, and was reestablished in 1945.

A provisional national committee ran school and university sports until 1962 (Legrand, 1970, p. 187), when the Association of School and University Sports (ASSU) was created.

The Law of October 29, 1975 dealing with the development of physical education provided for the creation of the following organizations: (1) a National Union of School Sports (UNSS), whose aim is to organize and develop familiarity with the practice of sports for students who are members of the sports association of their school, and (2) a National League of University Sports (FNSU), whose mission is to organize and develop amateur competitive sports for students in institutions of higher education.

STATE INTERVENTION

State intervention in sports probably began at the turn of the century with the Law of 1901. There seems to have been a liberal period from the beginning of the century up to the Second World War, and a period of growing State intervention during and after the war (Miège, 1993, p. 52).

During the interim Vichy government between 1940 and 1944, State pressure was especially intense, with the *Sports Charter* and complete government control under the Law of 1901 (Piard, 1972, p. 18). The decree dated October 2, 1943, declared by the government of Algiers, and that of August 28, 1945, reinforced those in effect before June 16, 1940.

The latter decree introduced the important notion of *delegation of powers* granted by the State to groups and federations which in return were obligated to conform to certain statutory regulations.

The Ministry of Youth and Sports is composed of a central administration and decentralized external departments. In addition, the cabinet, communications, and inspection branches report directly to the minister.

Central Administration

The central administration comprises three directorates which are broken down into subdirectorates and bureaus. There are two directorates having "missions" or "objectives": (1) the Sports Directorate, responsible for promoting physical and sports activities from sports at the highest level to sports for the general public or for individual practice, and (2) the Directorate of Youth and Associations. In addition there is the General Administrative Directorate, dealing with operations.

External Departments

There are two external departments. The Regional and Departmental Youth and Sports Directorates pertain to the French administrative districts of "Régions" and "Départements." Each Regional Directorate is headed by a Chief Inspector of Youth and Sports who reports to the Prefect of the Region. The Chief Inspector is responsible for enacting the policies of the Sports Minister. Likewise, in each department, an Inspector of Youth and Sports holds the position of Departmental Chief under the authority of the Prefect of the Department and under the Regional Chief.

The French Public Schools include Schools, National Institutes, or Regional Centers for Public and Sports Education (CREPS). These offices, devoted to training and research, are legal entities and have financial autonomy. Their directors are appointed by the Minister of Sports.

National Institutions

The five national institutions report directly to the Minister of Youth and Sports. Their administration is handled by a Board of Directors appointed by the Sports Minister by renewable decree for a period of three years. The five major French national educational institutions under the aegis of the Ministry of Youth and Sports are described here.

The National Institute of Sports and Physical Education

The National Institute of Sports and Physical Education (INSEP) was created in 1975. INSEP is the product of a merger between the School for Teacher Training in Physical Education and Sports, created in 1933, and the National Sports Institute (INS), created in 1946. The latter was a successor to the well-known Joinville School of 1852. The INSEP is headed by a Dean and comprises four departments: (1) the Department of Top Level Sports, for top athletes, which organizes training programs for the national team, (2) the Training Department for athletes' education, technical preparation, training program, and sports/study program, (3) the Medical Department, which is responsible for injury prevention, laboratory research, and field research, and (4) the Research Department, which is responsible for talent scouting, optimizing performances, and rehabilitation.

The National School of Skiing and Mountaineering

Located in Chamonix, the National School of Skiing and Mountaineering was created in 1943. This institution trains professionals in mountain sports. It has three objectives: (1) education and proficiency training in Alpine skiing and mountaineering, (2) proficiency training for top level French teams, and (3) information dissemination and research.

National School of Sailing

The National School of Sailing (NSS) is located on a seventeen-acre (seven-hectare) estate on the shore of a 24,700-acre (10,000-hectare) bay on Britanny's Quiberon Peninsula. The bay is twenty to sixty-five feet (six to twenty meters) in depth, crossed by slight currents and sheltered from the west winds. The site for the school was decided in 1965 by Maurice Herzog, Sports Commissioner. It was the headquarters for the sailing school of the administrative division (Département) of Morbihan.

The objectives of the National School of Sailing are: (1) to train French national teams, young hopefuls and federations, and (2) to develop tests, research, and technology.

The school's fleet is composed of sailboards (traditional and funboards), sailcraft (solo and double), catamarans, and yachts.

Natonal School of Cross-Country Skiing and Ski Jumping

Located in Premanon, the National School of Cross-Country Skiing and Ski Jumping was founded by the French government and inaugurated in 1970 with the joint participation of two Ministries: the Ministry of Finance and Customs, in charge of its organization, and the Ministry of Youth and Sports in charge of education. It is located in the Jura Mountains, twenty-eight miles (forty-five km) from Geneva, Switzerland. It is at an altitude of 4,000 to 5,000 feet (1,200 to 1,500 meters). It boasts excellent snow conditions, and does not require athletes to adjust their training schedules to acclimatize to the altitude. The school is responsible for: (1) the training of professional instructors in skiing, ski jumping, and particularly biathlon, as well as the training of customs officers and mountain police, (2) the organization of training programs for government offices and the French school system, and (3) the training of French national and regional ski, ski jumping, and biathlon teams.

Table 7.1
Sports Law in France

1945		Official Instructions
1959-1967		Modifications and improvement
1975	*October 29*	1st Sports Law
1984	*July 16*	2nd Sports Law
1985		Sports Lottery created
1989	*June 28*	Law on doping
1991	*January 10*	Law against tobacco & alcohol abuse
1992	*July 13*	3rd Sports Law
1994	*July 27*	State Health Insurance

National School of Equitation

Created in 1972, the National School of Equitation is located in Saumur. Its objectives are: (1) the education and proficiency training of horseback riding professionals on a national level, (2) the organization of preparatory programs for national and international competitions, and (3) the constitution of a center for information and research.

GOVERNMENT PARTICIPATION IN SPORTS POLICY

It was not until 1945 that "official instructions" defined the place that sport was to take in teaching and made it an integral part of physical education. These instructions were modified and improved in 1959 and again in 1967. In fact, it was not until thirty years later that the first law on Sports was voted into effect in France. The legal developments are illustrated in Table 7.1.

The Law of October 29, 1975

The legal aspect of sports appeared with the Law of October 29, 1975, called the "Mazeaud Law," dealing with the "development of physical education and sports." Article One calls this development a "fundamental element of culture (which) constitutes a national obligation." This law, in fact a "Sports Charter" in France, has three sections.

The first section deals with "Physical and Sports Education." It specifies that in primary and secondary education, sports education shall be free and at the State's expense. Secondary sports associations are to be affiliated with a national school sports union (UNSS). A national university sports league (FNSU), with which university sports associations were henceforth to be affiliated, was also created by this law. Education in Science and Techniques in Physical and Sports Activities was approved and organized. The Law of 1963, modified by that of

1967 which defined the profession of physical and sports instructor, was amended to cover all physical and sports activities.

INSEP, under the aegis of the Sports Minister, became the successor to INS and to the National School of Physical and Sports Education (ENSEPS). Its threefold mission is to participate in: (1) fundamental and applied scientific research (pedagogical, medical and technical), (2) continuous education and training of personnel, and (3) the training of national teams and promotion of top athletes.

The second section of the law deals with "The Practice of Physical and Sports Activities." It concerns sports groups formed into associations and those approved by the Sports Minister. The latter may receive State aid for amateur activity only.

The sports groups which employ professional or paid players or athletes may be authorized by the Sports Minister to become "Local Mixed Capital Firms," in other words, joint public and private capital (Article 9).

In addition, Article 11 of the law stipulates that sports federations must include associations, mixed capital firms and licensed members of one or more leagues. The following articles (12 to 14) concern the powers of the sports leagues. In a given sports discipline and for a specific period of time, only one federation may organize regional, national, or international competitions, provided that it meets criteria for competence established by the French National Olympics and Sports Committee (CNOSF). Model statutes were set up to this effect. Finally, in Articles 17 and 18, "the State (which) guarantees the promotion in society of top athletes" creates "a national fund for aid to top athletes."

The final section of the law deals with "Provisions Concerning Sports Facilities." Here it is stipulated that "a decree shall define the conditions under which the partitioning of industrial and residential zones shall include sports facilities." Article 23 stipulates that a decree shall define the conditions under which sports facilities shall be planned in order to ensure their optimal use and availability to all types of users, including senior citizens and the handicapped.

The purpose of the Mazeaud law was to tie sports to physical education by planning for sports initiation for all primary and secondary school students. Under this law sports are directly supervised by the sports minister.

The Law of July 16, 1984

This law solidifies government authority. In its first article, the development of physical and sports activities is in the interests of all and their practice an inalienable right. The State is responsible for education under the sole authority of the Minister of Education. Elite athletes play a social, cultural, and national role of utmost importance.

The first section of the law deals with "the organization of physical and sports activities." Physical and sports education and school and university sports contribute to renewal in the educational system, to the prevention of dropouts, and to the eradication of social and cultural inequality.

Sports groups may benefit from government aid only if they have been State-approved. A sports group affiliated with a league that organizes sports events which generate revenues exceeding a fixed amount and employing paid athletes whose fees exceed a fixed sum, must form a company under the law on commercial enterprises. It thus legally becomes a sports firm or a local mixed capital sports firm. The capital of such a company is composed of non-transferable (personal) shares. Its profits are deposited in reserves; they may not be distributed.

Sports federations contribute to a mission of public service, provided they adopt statutes which conform to a certain type. They have disciplinary powers and may receive help from the State in personnel and finances. They are under the supervision of the Minister of Sports.

Conflicts between licensed league members, sports groups, and leagues are submitted to the French National Olympics and Sports Committee for arbitration. The CNOSF is committed to the equal promotion of different sports disciplines on radio and television.

In business, the "comité d'entreprise" (*Employee Council*) defines the policy for physical and sports activities. In the absence of an employee council, this can be carried out by employee representatives working in conjunction with the CEO.

A national commission for top level sports makes up a list of top athletes from data provided by relevant sports leagues, which is ratified each year by the Minister of Sports. Athletes on the list receive aid in the organization of their studies and through specific assignment during their military service. They may take State competitive exams as applicants for government positions or receive preferential treatment as candidates for jobs in large companies.

A National Committee for Research and Technology in physical and sports activities is supervised by ministers of research, public education and sports.

Sports groups take out insurance policies covering their responsibility for the period of their activity. After consulting the appropriate leagues and communities, a chief plan of sports facilities in the national interest is established.

The second section of the Law of July 16, 1984 concerns "Education and Professions." With the exception of government agents carrying out their duties, no one may teach physical and sports activities for pay as his or her main or seasonal occupation, nor use the title of professor, trainer, monitor, instructor, or any similar title, unless he or she holds a French diploma. State educational institutions and State-approved institutions ensure initial and continuous education of paid managers in physical and sports activities.

Finally, the protection of participants is also provided for by law, as is the inspection of revenue-receiving establishments for physical and sports activities.

From 1985 to 1991

The Finance Law of 1985 created the Sports Lottery under the aegis of the Ministry headed by Alain Calmat, an Olympic skating champion. The Law of December 7, 1987, permits professional or non-professional sports groups dealing with sums of over 2.5 million francs to choose one of three structures: (1) association under the Law of 1901 with so-called "reinforced" status, (2) Local Mixed Capital (private and public) Sports Company, or SEMSL, or (3) Sports-Oriented Company (SOC).

Drafted by State Secretary Christian Bergelin, the law on doping was enacted on June 28, 1989, by his successor Roger Bambuck. The law against tobacco and alcohol abuse, drafted by Claude Evin, Social and Solidarity Minister, and enacted January 10, 1991, provided for the ban of all advertising for tobacco, direct or indirect, as well as of smoking on public premises, as of January 1, 1993. Alcohol and tobacco sponsorship of sports events was forbidden (with the exception of broadcasts from foreign countries). The law provided for fines ranging from 50,000 to 500,000 francs. Sports which were the most affected by the law were golf, horseback riding, and auto and motorcycle racing.

The Law of July 13, 1992

The Law of July 13, 1992 was initiated by Sports Minister Frédérique Bredin. It amends the Law of 1984 and subsequent laws, making them more flexible. Article One concerns the organization of physical and sports activities.

Under this law, professional clubs were required to choose between two statuses: either the mixed capital company mentioned above, enabling the association and the community to hold the majority of the capital, or the sports oriented company, enabling businesses to hold the majority of the capital and management responsibility.

Paragraph 19-2 of the law stipulated that "communities or their groups cannot provide collateral to sports associations and businesses."

A National Committee for Top Level Sports defined the characteristics of athlete, referee and judge in top level sports in all disciplines.

Under this law, a range of measures relative to security in sports facilities and meets were taken. Paragraphs 42-1 and 42-2 set standards and conditions for the authorization of public use of facilities according to strict criteria.

Since the Furiani Stadium accident in May 1992, the law has forbidden access to a sports arena by any person under the influence of alcohol, punishable by a fine ranging from 600 to 50,000 francs. In addition, if such a person is responsible for a violent act, penalties can reach fines of 100,000 francs and two months to two years in prison.

Article Two deals with training and professional matters. It defines the titles of professor, monitor, instructor, and coach and defines the criteria for State-approved diplomas. This article also specifies guarantees in hygiene and security for premises where physical and sports activities are practiced.

After 1993

For years the sports world has been faced with legal problems in conjunction with athletes' remuneration vis-à-vis State Health Insurance. The new Sports Minister, Michèle Alliot-Marie, appointed after the legislative elections of March 1993, was immediately confronted with this problem. The decree of July 27, 1994 defined the rules for the affiliation of athletes to the State Health Insurance Plan. They, like all paid workers, have the right to benefit from the plan.

Three points should be made clear: (1) In all instances, an athlete is able to benefit from State Health Insurance only if he/she is paid. The right to workmen's compensation is subject to the condition that the athlete's pay be legally declared. If the athlete cannot be included within an organized entity, he/she must be declared under the heading of "unsalaried non-agricultural workers" (e.g., monitors, instructors with personal clientele, French Ski School Instructors).

(2) In addition, contributions in the form of salary deductions to State Health Insurance and to the General Social Contribution (CSG)—with a reduction of five percent for expenses in the latter case—are due from athletes benefitting from State Health Insurance. All payments the athletes may receive are subject to deduction, be they salary, bonus, vacation pay, gratuities or any other perquisites in monies or in kind, including commissions on advertising.

The sums paid to athletes for sports competitions are not subject to deduction for State Health Insurance and CSG unless they exceed seventy percent of the daily rate of Health Insurance Indemnities. This rule applies to a maximum of five competitions per month per athlete and per organizer. It applies to State-approved associations employing fewer than ten permanent salaried employees. Contributions to health insurance and CSG are calculated on a fixed basis according to a monthly salary bracket not exceeding 115 times the minimum wage.

(3) "Top Athletes" on the Sports Ministry-approved list benefit from the right to receive "personalized financial aid." Such aid, not exceeding twenty-five percent of annual health insurance indemnities, is exempt from health insurance deductions; but only if granted by the CNOSF. All payment in excess of the aforementioned amount is subject to deductions for insurance and CSG.

FINANCING OF SPORTS

Funding comes from several areas: the government budget, the National Sports Development Fund (FNDS), private companies, the public sector, community treasuries, and also advertising and sponsors.

The Government Budget

From 1975 to 1986, the budget for sports went from .70 percent to .57 percent of the national budget (Paillou, 1986, p. 22). Since then, funds for physical education and sports instructors have been handled by the Ministry of Education. The Youth and Sports budget was only .25 percent of the national budget in 1981. It continued its decline until it represented .19 percent of the total budget in 1991. In 1992, the government budget totalled 1,330 billion francs and 2.84 billion francs, or .21 percent of the total, was budgeted for sports.

The National Sports Development Fund

Article 17 of the Mazeaud Law (October 29, 1975) stipulates that the "government shall guarantee the advancement in society of top athletes," and the next article specifies that "government funds for aid to top athletes shall be granted." These funds were provided through taxes on tickets to sports events in mainland France. Parliament instituted a two percent levy on national lottery tickets in the fall of 1978.

The FNDS was created on March 13, 1979 to replace the previous funding. It is headed by a national committee which is comprised of two sections: (1) top level sports, and (2) sports and facilities for the general public. Local committees determine the distribution of funds to the regions.

Two more sources of funding were added in 1980. The first was a levy of .3 percent on parimutuel wagers at race tracks and off track (PMU). This brought in between 75 and 110 million francs each year until 1985. The second source was the excess yield on the special tax on drinking establishments.

After much debate, the government agreed to the setting up of a new form of lottery, named the Sports Lottery, on October 23, 1984. As of 1985, the large sums yielded from this lottery influenced the government to repeal the .3 percent levy on parimutuel betting (PMU) and to allocate a fixed sum of 20 million francs. The tax on drinking was repealed the same year.

In conclusion, the use of funds is distributed as follows: twenty percent for top level sports, and eighty percent for sports for the general public. This latter portion is divided into two parts: one-third is a national share (subsidies to leagues and funds for sports facilities), and two-thirds is a regional share (funds allocated to regions and distributed by the Ministry and by elected regional Olympic officials).

DEFINITION OF A SPORTS POLICY

Immediately after the war, a plan for school sports facilities was drawn up. It concerned mainly "physical education areas" or basic sports fields with very little attention to stadiums, pools, and gymnasiums. Facilities from 1950 to 1960 were planned to support certain activities. Thus, the swimming pools were designed to satisfy the needs of learning and competition. They were also to be built as inexpensively as possible.

After 1958, the investment budget of the Youth and Sports Ministry was revised with a three-year facilities plan. France's poor results in the Olympic Games in Rome in 1960 led to the drawing up of a new policy to promote sport excellence. Three laws were passed by Parliament, giving France much of its sports infrastructure.

In 1961, for the first time, a real sports facilities policy was put into effect with adequate financing. Funding was provided in three stages: from 1961–65, 1,063 billion francs; from 1966–70, 1,886 billion francs, and from 1971–75, 2,369 billion francs.

Three major types of operations were undertaken. In 1966 and 1972 the Ministry organized a contest called the ''1000 clubs'' and studied projects for the design of small facilities. Another operation was the ''bassins d'apprentissage mobiles'' (BAM). These were ''mobile learning pools'' designed for swimming needs. There were two generations of mobile learning pools. In 1969, fifty autonomous units were built. These BAMs were designed to remain from three to five months in the same spot and enable students aged eight to eleven to learn to swim. The operation's success led to the construction of forty-five new BAMs in 1972. Thus, some 250,000 children received classes in swimming. The third major type of operations was the ''1000 pools''. These were pools with removable roofs. Five hundred fifty pools were constructed, extensions for open-air pools were planned, underwater lighting was put in, and acoustics were improved.

The dearth of facilities, especially indoors, led in 1970 to the implementation on a regional level of procedures permitting the construction of sports facilities such as gymnasiums, multipurpose halls, and locker and shower rooms.

In 1976, a national procedure was established for provision of various types of facilities, such as pools, skating rinks, equestrian rings, and miscellaneous complexes. However, lifestyle changes were starting to appear, with a sharpened sense of how facilities could blend with the environment. ''Leisure centers'' were the result of these changes:

1976	rural multi-purpose halls
1978	1000 playing fields
1980	all-weather fields, ''5000 tennis courts'' with the French Tennis Federation and leisure centers
1985	''Green Plan'' golf course with the French Golf Federation (FGF)
1992	1000 indoor facilities and 1000 100-franc golf courses with the FGF.

Thus the basic needs were fulfilled. Later the trend became one of facilities geared toward leisure, especially concerning swimming pools. An effort was made to improve public relations and atmosphere, to render the sports centers more attractive and comfortable and to facilitate people's access to them. A desire for multipurpose facilities became apparent, and this led to a less rigorous application of standards.

Nevertheless at the same time a need for very specialized facilities was felt. The economic situation resulting from the energy crisis required strict financial management. Research began into bioclimatic architecture and buildings heated by solar energy.

DECENTRALIZATION

In 1982, decentralization laws started taking effect, and the State's role was greatly modified. The Law of March 2, 1982 and the Laws of January 7 and 22, 1983, which concerned the transfer of authority from the State to the Regions, "départements" (administrative divisions) and communities, modified the relationships between the various entities. It is important to note that there was never any reference made to sports. The State thus showed its desire to "continue to assume its responsibilities in this field" (Andreff, 1989, p. 82).

From then on, French communities—the owners of nearly all sports and leisure facilities—became the decision-makers regarding construction. In addition, the system of financing was completely changed with the DGE and the increased financial capabilities the State had with the FNDS (cf. p 29).

Two concepts are noteworthy regarding the laws on decentralization. On the one hand, there has been a changeover in the holding of power, and on the other hand, there are now local decision-makers. The changeover in powers, as defined by the Laws of January 7 and July 22, 1983, implies that communities cooperate with the State in matters concerning their administration and planning. Such changeover in powers is to be accompanied by financial compensation.

The French administrative districts, or "départements," have taken several initiatives on sports facilities. However, the ratio of funds devoted to sports in proportion to the number of inhabitants varies widely and covers very diverse actions. The number of administrative districts having a sports bureau is estimated at forty percent.

Several regions have organized operations to promote top level sports by associating communication campaigns with an emphasis on the image of athletes. The amount of funds is again extremely variable (Miège, 1993, p. 92). Concerning the means to be utilized, local decision-makers, who are civil servants, and local elected officials follow the texts of specific laws. On the one hand, local government employees must respect statutory regulations according to the Law of January 26, 1984. These are different from those of public service. On the other hand, the Law of December 30, 1985 limits these officials from holding several offices simultaneously, be they on a national or local level.

FRANCE AND EUROPEAN INSTITUTIONS

The Council of Europe, created in 1949, and the European Economic Community, formed in 1958, are involved in matters pertaining to sports. Agreements have been adopted by the member states of the Council of Europe in the field of sports. Such was the case in August 1985, a few months after the riot of Heysel, Belgium, when they dealt ''with violence and excesses of the spectators during sporting events, particularly soccer matches.''

On November 16, 1989, an agreement on doping was submitted to member states for signature. Within the Council of Europe, the Managing Committee for the Development of Sports (CDDS), created in 1977, convenes every three years with a view to adopting measures and deciding priorities to be given to sports activities in the European States.

The European Community and its institutions (European Council, Commission, Parliament, and Court of Justice) is a confederation striving toward the progressive integration of member states through the convergence of individuals, goods and services. Thus the European Court has stated that sports remains a community right inasmuch as it constitutes an economic activity—a statement that has met with opposition in international sports circles.

Recent judicial decisions affirm that the principles of freedom of employment across European borders applies to athletes, coaches, and other sports personnel. In addition, the European Parliament has shown its interest in sports by encouraging community initiatives such as the Cycling Race of the European Community, the European Sailing Race, and the European Community Swimming Championships. The first European Games in School Sports were held in Caen in July 1992. The Parliament also contributed to the Olympics in 1992, participating in the budgets of the Albertville Winter Olympics ($5 billion) and the Barcelona Summer Olympics ($7.6 billion).

ANALYSIS OF OBJECTIVES

National Objectives of Sports Policy

The policy of the Ministry of Youth and Sports includes two elements: first, community facilities and the needs of our young people for sports equipment, and second, a partnership between the Ministry and sports groups with a view to an increase in the practice of sports. In 1992, there were three priorities concerning youth: (1) ''Scheduling Contracts'' (CATE) between communities and schools that aim toward children's practicing of sports outside of school time and toward helping incorporate sport into their lifestyle. (2) Town committees made up of children and teenagers enable young people to become familiar with the running of a community. (3) The financing of 20,000 youth programs, called ''Projets J'' (Y programs) facilitates the setting up of youth programs and the creation of 1000 Youth Information Centers called ''points

J'' (Y Spots) for information and orientation to help young people better organize their lives.

As far as sports are concerned, the idea is to create correspondence between the government and sports groups in the running of sports programs in France, thereby creating a partnership between the Youth and Sports Ministry and sports leagues through an agreement on objectives. This is done through: (1) ''J Sports,'' with a plan for 1000 area sports centers set up in priority neighborhoods (''DSQ'' neighborhoods) targeted for social development and available to all young people; (2) aid to sports leagues, representing the major part of credit for aid in the sports sector; (3) aid to small urban and rural sports clubs which are important to the animation of local life in cities as well as towns; (4) ''Sports Tickets,'' created for young people who cannot go away on vacation and to enable sports facilities to remain open; and (5) ''Profession Sports,'' a program begun in 1990 which promotes employment in the field of sports in clubs, associations, and communities. This latter program received government aid for the first three years of its existence only and now is financed independently.

International Targets

In addition to the Olympic Games and various World Cups, France participates in international athletic meets of a geographical and cultural nature.

The Mediterranean Games

The first Mediterranean Games were organized in 1951, in Alexandria, Egypt. Their objective was to bring together the inhabitants of the ''Mare Nostrum.'' The Games are held in a city near the Mediterranean once every four years.

In December, 1986, France was selected for the twelfth Games, and from June 16th to 27th, 1993, these ''regional games'' were held within France for the first time, in the Languedoc Roussillon region. These Games were organized by a group of communities. Eighty percent of the Games' expenses were paid by the communities. The remaining 20 percent was paid by the regional administration, the regional council, and the central government.

The spin-offs of this event were spectacular as regards investments into sports. Cities remained the owners of the facilities. Towns whose supply of hotel rooms increased became major beneficiaries. Mediapartners (the press, radio, and television) covered the events. Public television channels broadcast the competitions and ceremonies and took care of promotion and advertising. The impact on tourism was substantial and the region benefited from three to four extra weeks of visitors.

The Games of the French-Speaking Nations

Over 450 million people speak French throughout the world. In Quebec in 1987, during the second summit meeting of ''French-language-sharing world leaders,'' the decision was made to create the Sports and Cultural Games of the French-Speaking Nations, which would be held every four years. The first Games were held in Casablanca, Morocco, in July 1989, under the aegis of King Hassan II.

The second session was planned for 1993 but was postponed for a year in order to benefit from better organization, which was entrusted to the French National Committee of the Games of the French-Speaking Nations (CNJF), jointly presided over by the Minister of Culture and the French Language, and the Minister of Youth and Sports. This session was held from July 5 to 13, 1994, in the Region of Ile-de-France, in the administrative district (département) of the Essonne and in Paris.

The events cost approximately $11 million. The French government contributed eighty percent of the cost of the Games. The remaining twenty percent was provided by local French communities (10%) and private funding (10%).

Some two thousand athletes and seven hundred artists from forty-four countries were gathered for these Games. There were eight sports events: handball, judo, soccer, table tennis, track and field plus handisports, women's basketball and wrestling.

The IAKS

The French section of the *Internationaler Arbeitskreis Sport-und-freizeit-einrichtungen e.V.,* the operations group for sports and leisure facilities, were officially constituted on October 19, 1994, with its headquarters at the CNOSF (French National Olympic and Sports Committee). This association, founded in 1965, is composed of members from about a hundred nations, and of management comprised of representatives from all the continents in the world. As of today, seven nations belong to this group: Canada, the Confederation of Independent States, Germany, Japan, Norway, Spain, and Switzerland.

CONCLUSION

Sport in France reflects both the attitudes of leaders of all persuasions and the outside influence of all those who have traveled, compared, and endeavored to apply in their own country the means they have discovered of improving the impact of sports. There has been a struggle between the partisans of physical education and the defenders of sports. The reaction of General de Gaulle to France's poor results in the Rome Olympics in 1960, had a strong impact. The intervention of the State in matters of financing for sizeable sports facilities and of aid for the operation of institutions during international meets is proof of the realization by politicians of the importance of results and the image a large number of medals can represent.

However, two phenomena have led to a withdrawal of commitment on the part of the State in matters of budget, and to a rise in the strength of local decision makers. The central powers experienced the constantly rising cost of sports, and the regions and départements became increasingly aware of the identity that sports can offer. All this occurred at a time when decentralization laws were being put into effect.

At the same time, there has been a progression in the practice of sports and leisure activities, with a striving for excellence in performance giving way to an awareness of health, physical condition, and lifestyle achieved through physical exercise carried out not in an artificial setting but in a completely natural one. In the eighties, the desire to protect the environment and the rediscovery of nature benefited this change. From then on, sports practiced in spartan facilities were abandoned for those one could practice in medically supervised, modernized clubs where the individual held priority over the group. The trend is such that sports, once a component of education, have now become an end in themselves.

Regional identity has been strengthened. The goal of local officials has been to optimize their geographical assets as well as their local sports history. Coastlines and mountaintops, green countryside, and rushing streams are attractions to be exploited.

Pioneers of a new kind have appeared, bathing the image of sports in a pleasant and accessible light. Television has given rise to another perception of effort, one without pain and even with a smile. Businesses have shown that they can be original in adapting rules, innovative in their conception of facilities, and creative in setting up a new sort of animation that the traditional sports movement never imagined. New references have appeared, a new demand has been created, and the organization of sports activities by professionals has shaken up a world which until now has resisted change.

The obligation to devote more and more budget funds to sports has resulted in the need for new partners who have demanded a share in power. These past few years have witnessed communication through sports, giving support to those who promote the doctrine that a show belongs to those who organize it. As for the competitors, they now want to recover a certain form of independence as well as a return on their investment in time, while reaping profits from their talents. The resulting trend has been toward decentralization of sport governance.

There is a flexible attitude in sports at present, adapted to the private and public sectors. This attitude is replacing the rigid bureaucratic standards of civil service. The demands of competition require constant adaptation and renewed strategies, elements that are practically ruled out by administrative weight and rigidity. The balance to be found lies between restrictive regulations, which have no place in an international context, and an excessive form of liberalism, where the only thing that counts is results. But the same idea applies to those on the line between their need for constantly higher achievement and their taste for risk in reaching for fame at any price. The quest for the ideal pushes back the limits of those who decline to use technological or chemical means which might tarnish their achievements. We seem to be witnessing irreversible change. We are entering a new era where sports is claiming the place it deserves, by itself, without the help of tutor or benefactor.

REFERENCES

Alaphilippe, F. *Sport et collectivités locales.* Dalloz, 1993.

Andreff, W. *Economie politique du sport.* Dalloz, 1989.

Andreff, W. et Nys J. F. *Economie du sport.* Que sais-je? n° 2294. P.U.F., 1986.

Bodineau, P., and M. Verpeaux. *Histoire de la décentralisation,* n° 2741, P.U.F., 1993.

Bourg, J.-F. *Le sport en otage, La table ronde,* 1988.

Chabaud, L., C. Dudognon, and D. Primault. *Le sport et la Communauté Européenne,* Ed. Dalloz, 1993.

Chappelet, J-L. *Le système olympique.* Presses Universitaires de Grenoble, 1991.

Chazaud, P. *Le sport dans la commune, le département et la région.* Berger Levrault, 1989.

Ehrenberg, A. *Le culte de la performance.* Calmann-Lévy, 1991.

Enault, G., J.-L. Enguehard, A. Lorin, and G. Vanderschmitt. *Le sport en France.* Berger-Levrault, 1979.

Irlinger, P., C. Louveau, and M. Métoudi. *Les pratiques sportives des français.* INSEP, 1987.

Jamet, Michel. *Le sport dans la société.* Coll. Logiques Sociales, Ed. L'Harmattan, 1991.

Legrand F., and J. Ladegaillerie. *L'éducation physique au XIXème & au XXème siècle.* 1970.

Loret, A. *Sport et Management.* Dunod, 1993.

Mathieu, D., and J. Praicheux. *Sports en France.* Fayard-RECLUS, 1987.

Miège, C. *Les Institutions sportives.* Que sais-je? n° 2729. P.U.F., 1993.

Ministère Jeunesse et Sports—Equipements Sportifs et Socio-Educatifs. Ed. Le Moniteur, 1993.

Paillou, N. Journal Officiel n° 8, rapport "Sports et Economie" 22 May 1986.

Piard, C. *Vers une nouvelle politique sportive.* Ed. Amphora, 1972.

Ramanantsoa, B., and Thiéry Baslé. *Organisations et fédérations sportives.* P.U.F., 1989.

Simonnot, P. *Homo sportivus.* Gallimard, 1988.

Thibault, J. *Les aventures du corps dans la pédagogie française.* J. Vrin, 1972.

Thomas, R. *Le sport et les médias.* Vigot, 1993.

Reviews

E.P.S. 11, Avenue du Tremblay—75012 Paris
Revue Juridique et Economique du sport:
        —L'acte unique européen et le sport, n°9, 1989–2
        —Sport-Alcool-Tabac, n° 20, 1992–1.

Periodicals

Journal "L'Equipe," Les Editions P. Amaury, Paris.
La Lettre du Sponsoring et du Mécénat, Ed. des Trois Rives, Paris.
La Lettre de l'Economie du Sport, Ed. Sportune, Paris.

8

Sports Policy in Germany

Klaus Heinemann

HISTORICAL BACKGROUND

When the Third Reich is used as background, sports policy as well as the organization of sports in Germany can only be understood as the political misuse of sport by the state. The Third Reich was run by a centralized leadership to which all life, both public and private, had to be subordinate. This was the case even with sport (Langenfeld, 1988, p. 18).

Before 1933 when the Nazi party took power, sport was characterized by a multitude of organizations and independence from the government. The bourgeois gymnastic and sports movement coexisted with a worker sports movement, and was rich with tradition. Christian sports associations (Deutsche Jugendkraft and Eichenkreuz[1]) had their parallel in Jewish sports organizations. The expression "German gymnastics and sport movement" indicates another peculiarity of German sports. The gymnastic movement started by Ludwig Jahn identified itself as a singular German activity. Sports and gymnastics were to be cultivated in a special "German form" with a special path for German sports.

This structure changed radically following the national socialist revolution. During the early period, several clubs and federations tried to secure their existence through political affirmation, loyalty, and a cheerful and willing integration into the new political order, but without success (Bernett, 1971, p. 19). The bourgeois sports clubs were integrated into a unitary sports association, the Nationalsozialistischen Reichsbund fur Leibesung (National Socialistic Federation of Physical Education in the Reich). Because offices and positions were filled by appointment rather than election, sports clubs and associations lost their democratic legitimation. The most important aim of this national-socialistic sports organization was "to nurture nationalistic socialistic spirit" and to propagate the national socialistic ideology. Sports clubs became important cells of this political indoctrination. Simultaneously, clubs were delegated the important function of improving the health of the population for industrial and military purposes. In their pursuit of total control, the national socialists did not stop even for religious youth groups. Even the Deutsche Jugendkraft (DJK) sports activities were forbidden; the leader of the DJI was shot dead. Later, the sports activities of the Eichenkreuz were forbidden (Bernett, 1992).

Elite sports were used as an instrument to represent the state. Through the Olympic Games of 1936 in Berlin, Nazi leaders attempted to arouse confidence in the state and to distract attention from the government's preparations for an expansionist war (Langenfeld, 1982, p. 32). Between 1933 and 1945, sport was subservient to, and an instrument of, fascist sports policies. This provides the background from which the sports policies of the Federal Republic of Germany (since its foundation in 1949) can be understood.

THE AUTONOMY OF SPORT FROM GOVERNMENT POLICIES

After World War II, the constitution of the Federal Republic of Germany granted clubs and associations organizational autonomy, thus allowing the fundamental principles of independence and self-responsibility. Germany has no federal Ministry of Sport that is authorized to control and regulate sport and sports policy. This did not occur by chance, but is the result of strict separation of governmental sports policy from the autonomous and self-governing German Sports Federation (Deutscher Sportbund) and its member organizations.[2] The principles underlying German sports policy arise from the constitutional maxim that the individual's interests and rights are to be exercised and supported in free and autonomous organizations. This derives from the willingness to secure these rights and from the readiness of society's members to claim those rights (Heinemann and Horch, 1981, p. 127).

The separation of autonomously organized sports and governmental policies, however, does not imply that sports in Germany, in its multiple forms, are not the target of governmental policies. On the contrary, the government summarized its position in its fourth sports report:

Governmental sports policies are in a comprehensive sense, societal policies. It has close relations to health, educational and youth policies but also to ecology, social and structural policies. Governmental support is not a mere act of benevolence. Moreover, it is a self-evident public utility concerning the provision for the future, directed by the respective budget. (Fourth Sports Report of the Government, 1978, p. 10)

The two pillars of governmental sports policy in Germany are autonomy of organized sport, and sports policies of the state as societal policies. Generally, this means that the shaping of sports, except in schools and sport sciences that lie in the hands of the Länder (Federal States), is principally a matter for organized sport itself. The governmental sports policy is one of financial support. In principle, financial aid remains the government's most important means of influence on sports policy.

Two fundamental principles govern the development of sport in the Federal Republic of Germany. First, each citizen must have the opportunity to participate in sport that is

• In a sports facility within easy commuting distance
• At a cost within his or her financial means
• Congruent with his or her temporal, social, and family situation
• In accordance with his or her interests and abilities.

Each citizen should be able to find a suitable opportunity in a club. Second, the government provides the necessary financial support, thereby providing access to sports activities and equal conditions for all. Private investments in the construction of sports grounds and clubs fueled by market forces alone cannot achieve these aims. A return on private investment requires high admission fees that would make sports unachievable for anyone.

With respect to financial support of sport, the state holds that financial support is an aid to self-help and will only be granted if, and to the extent that, after helping themselves, the sport does not have the means to reach its goals; and government sports policy aims to cover all activities in organized sports both within the country, including the construction of sports facilities and the support of sport sciences, and beyond its borders, including participation in international organizations such as UNESCO and the European Council.

A better understanding of how these two fundamental principles underlie the development of sports in Germany requires an examination of three areas: (1) Germany's political order and private sports organizations and their respective responsibilities and spheres of competence; (2) the spheres of competence of public sport administration at three political levels—federal, länder, and communal government; and (3) the problems that result from the separation of governmental sports policy and the workings of state and autonomous sports associations.

THE FEDERAL ORGANIZATION OF THE STATE

Germany is a federal state composed of seventeen länder,[3] of which eleven ''old'' länder (for example, Schleswig-Holstein, Hamburg, Bremen, Hessen, Bavaria) formed the Federal Republic of Germany before reunification and six ''new'' länder (for example, Thuringen, Saxonia, including Berlin) were admitted after the dissolution of the German Democratic Republic. A federal state holds definite and supreme power and as such is not subordinate to the federation.[4] Thus, the länder is responsible for all areas, except for those areas that are stated in the constitution as the responsibility of the federal government. Germany's constitution describes and restricts the duties of the federation, the länder, and their connections. It defines the sovereignty of the länder in cultural matters, including education (schools and universities), research, and sport. Each of the federal states has its own parliament and government and is in charge of framing policy, especially for security, economic development, the education system, and social affairs.[5]

Sports clubs and federations in the Federal Republic of Germany act as autonomous units. Governmental support is aimed at furthering the self-reliance of these autonomous units. According to the federal structure of the Federal Republic of Germany, the federal government, länder, and communities are the primary agents of public sports administration. Responsibilities at the various levels are distributed by constitutional regulation. The delimitation of responsibilities to promote sport is determined in a pragmatic manner after consultation with relevant bodies within the autonomous sports administration system.

THE ORGANIZATION OF SPORTS

The German Sport Federation (Deutscher Sportbund—DSB) was founded in 1950 as an umbrella organization for the German gymnastics and sports movement. It was founded in order to coordinate common efforts in sport, to represent the mutual interest of its member organizations vis-à-vis the government and the general public, and to deal with problems of national and international importance existing beyond the confines of a single discipline. Areas considered significant include the increasing importance of sports in a leisure society; the relationship of sport and the federal government; the creation of new programs in Sport-for-All, recreational sport, and top-level sport; and the building of flexible facilities for multisport, play, and recreation activities (Gieseler, 1988, p. 36).

Figure 8.1 presents an overview of the organization of sports in Germany. They are organized on the basis that the sportsman and sportswoman voluntarily become members of a sports club with the intention of realizing their sporting ambitions. This is the legal basis for all sports organizations, including the sports associations and the DSB (Deutscher Sportbund). These organizations can only represent these interests. Consequently, the sports organization must exclude political functions and not be used to push political aims such as proving the efficiency of a political system, sanctioning violations of the Law of Nations, or guaranteeing the peace. Unfortunately, this principle is not always observed, as was the case with participation in the Olympic boycott in 1984 against Moscow and tentative participation in the Peace movement in the first half of the 1980s.

A sports person is a member of one of the 78,000 sports clubs, 68,000 of

Figure 8.1
Organized Sport in Germany

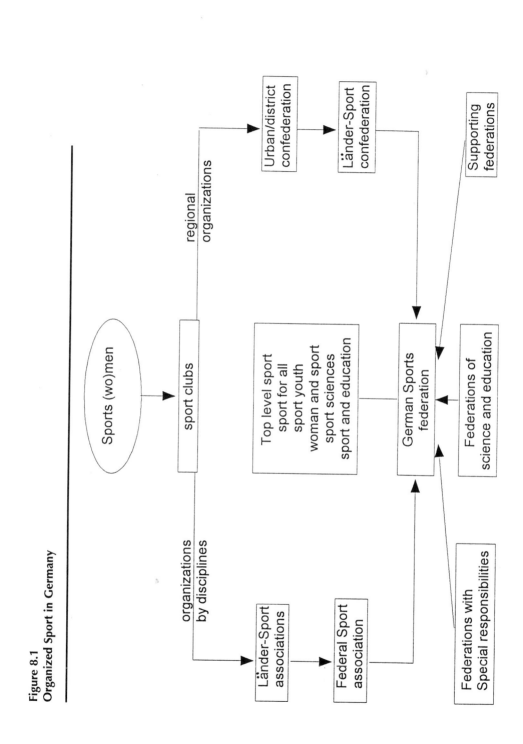

which are located in the former Federal Republic of West Germany, while the remaining 10,000 are situated in the former German Democratic Republic.[6] In principle, German sports clubs

- Are small—70 percent have less than 300 members, and only 5 percent have more than 1,000 members.
- Offer only one sports discipline—65 percent offer one discipline, and only 9 percent offer more than four disciplines.
- Are young (although the oldest existing sports club in Germany was founded in 1816); 32 percent were founded after 1980, and 52 percent were founded after 1960.
- Are managed by volunteers; only 8 percent have paid staff.

The sports person, regardless of discipline, is embedded in the self-administration of sports clubs in two ways: (1) the urban/regional confederation, the so-called Stadtsportbunden, and (2) the federal-sport confederation (Landessportbunde). In addition, the sports person belongs to the sports federation representing the sports discipline they practice.

The federal-sport confederation (Landessportbunde) has similar responsibilities to the German sports federation. However the Landessportbunde's responsibilities are restricted to Germany, and include representing the interests of the sport clubs on the länder level; promoting the training and financial support of instructors, youth leaders, managers, and administrators; and building sports facilities, supporting cultural programs, providing insurance, and so on.

The sports federations, which were founded or reestablished after 1949, are responsible for the rules and regulations of their sports discipline. They represent the discipline internationally via the German Sports Federation (Deutscher Sportbund—DSB) and the National Olympic Committee of Germany. They organize German championships and choose the teams for international competitions. They are responsible for developing elite athletes and technical training and for making the rules in the discipline. The sports federations have national training centers and national coaches hired by the DSB.

The German Sports Federation is the umbrella organization for organized sports. Members are

- The seventeen sports confederations of the länder, including the Federal Sport Confederation of Berlin, the Federal Sport Confederation of Schleswig-Holstein, and the Federal Sport Confederation of Saxony.
- The fifty-four sports federations, including the German Football Federation, the German Wrestling Federation, and the German Tennis Federation.
- The twelve sports federations with special responsibilities, including the General Students Sport Association (Allgemeiner Deutscher Hochschulsportverband—ADH), the Association of Sports Clubs of the Federal Post (Arbeitsgemeinschaft der Postsportvereine), and the German Youth Power (Deutsche Jugendkraft).

- The six federations of science and education, including the German Association of Sport Science (Deutsche Vereinigung fur Sportwissenschaft—DVS),[7] the German Association of Physical Education Teachers (Deutscher Sportlehrerverband—DSLV),[8] and the German Union of Education and Science (Gewerkschaft Erziehung und Wissenschaft).[9]

- The two supporting federations—the German Olympic Society (Deutsche Olympische Gesellschaft—DOG) and the German Sports Association. The objectives of the DOG are to support sports in the Federal Republic of Germany and to promote and further Olympic ideals. The German Sports Association is divided into departments with responsibilities for elite sport; Sports-for-All; women and sport; sport youth and sport science; and health and sport education.

All competitive sports and Sport-for-All are under the auspices of the German Sports Federation (DSB). There are no independent organizations of competitive sport or Sport-for-All in Germany; instead, responsibility lies with the DSB and its member organizations, especially the umbrella organizations. Consequently, different organizational structures have developed to support competitive sports and Sports-for-All. Conflicts arise as these separate organizations compete for funds under the DSB.

Organized sport is structured according to the constitution of the state with respect to decision-making ability, budget, and relations between local and federal organizations. However, sport has no superseding legitimation and thus may not misuse its power to influence public policy. In this respect, it remains undisputed that the DSB may represent the interests of sports policy, sports in schools, and nonorganized sportsmen and sportswomen. In so doing, the DSB is bound to maintain a neutral stance in political party politics.

The German Sports Federation (DSB) is connected via a network of sports organizations as shown in Figure 8.2.

- The German Sport Aid Foundation (Deutsche Sportllilfe—DSH) acts to provide moral and material support to elite sportsmen and sportswomen by providing compensation for their services. The foundation relies on individual and corporate donations, advertising profits, and funds raised through various means (e.g., the sale of postage stamps).

- The National Olympic Committee of Germany (NOC), founded in 1949, carries out the functions entrusted to it by the IOC; chiefly the NOC sends German participants to the Olympic Games.

- The German Olympic Society.

The DSB and NOC are linked to German Sport Marketing Inc. (Deutsche Sportmarketinggesellschaft—DSM) via two representatives who represent all Olympic organizations. The DSM markets the Olympic symbols and emblems in Germany.

In order to evaluate governmental sports policy, keep in mind that all sports clubs and associations are under the umbrella of the German Sports Association

Figure 8.2
Network of the German Sport System

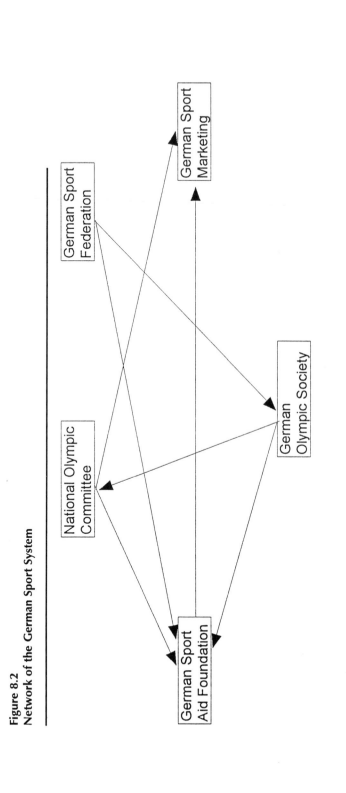

(GSB). The organizations' fragmentation which prevailed prior to the Third Reich no longer exists. The DSB represents a unitary sports movement. This implies that:

- All sports activists are united under one roof (DSB), regardless of social, professional, or religious affiliation.
- The DSB claims to represent and speak for all sports, including leisure, recreational, competitive, and elite sports.
- The DSB and its member organizations claim to be nonprofit organizations. As read in the statutes: "The DSB solely and directly follows nonprofit purposes." Clubs and associations benefit from tax privileges owing to their nonprofit status. Behind this claim for nonprofit status lies the conception that organized sport fulfills public duties. Without the existence of the DSB and its member organizations, sports organizations would have been administered differently and by the government. Organized sport plays a part in fulfilling general public duties and interests and thus becomes a part— through an extraordinary bond—of governmental societal policies.
- Organized sport holds a monopoly. Its monopolistic position implies (1) that organized sport (apart from the school) is the sole provider of facilities for sport practice, and (2) that it is the sole speaker and representative of sport to the state.

  The government accepts organized sport's claim that it represents a unitary sports movement, thus conferring the potential for enormous influence at the local and federal level. This influence arises from the homogeneity and size of sports organizations. Sports organizations, after the churches, are the largest voluntary organizations in Germany. This influence also arises from the large number of interpersonal connections between sport functionaries and decision-making bureaucrats in public sports administration, parliaments, and political parties.

In 1980 the federal government, in cooperation with the German Sport Federation and its member organizations, founded the Management and Administration Academy of Berlin (Fuhrungs-und Verwaltungsakademie—Willy Weyer Akademie, Berlin). This institution offers in-service training programs for managerial and administrative sport staff and organizes conferences on important issues for different sports groups, both domestic and international. Similarly, the German Sport Federation, in cooperation with the Ministry of Education of North-Rhine Westfalia, founded the Coaches' Academy of Cologne (Trainerakademie Koln). This academy is responsible for qualifying coaches for competitive athletes and training programs. In 1992 the federal government, in cooperation with the Olympic Committee of Germany, established the German Olympic Institute (Deutsch Olympische Institute—DOI) to promote the Olympic ideal, to support research on all topics related to the Olympic movement, and to improve communication among scientists, politicians, and sports volunteers.

With regard to sports clubs in the new länder, especially in the former GDR, elite sport functioned as the symbol of the "superiority" of the communist economy and the ambassador of the communist political order. At the same time, elite sport, through international sports successes, was expected to develop

Table 8.1
Facilities in the Former German Democratic Republic and the Federal Republic of West Germany

	GDR	FRG
Sportgrounds	1,218	49,800
Sports Halls	5,888	32,800
Indoor Swimming Pools	205	4,400
Open Air Swimming Pools	709	5,370

national feelings and identification with this artificial state. But Sport-for-All— leisure-time sport—was not promoted in the same way because it could not fulfill these functions. However, Sport-for-All did function to a large extent as an instrument for selection of sport talent or paramilitary education. This can be illustrated by a comparison of the number of sports facilities in the former FRG and the GDR (with populations of 52 million versus 17 million). (See Table 8.1).

The organization of sport also differed in the FRG and the GDR. In the GDR, sport was controlled by the state, whereas in the FRG, sport was controlled by voluntary sports organizations. In the GDR, Sport-for-All was organized in state institutions and organizations such as the army, police, and secret service, or it was organized by state-owned firms. These state-run or -owned institutions, organizations, or firms were responsible for the Sport-for-All programs and paid for sport coaches, facilities, and the like.

The different organizational structures and policies resulted in differences in sports and leisure-time activities. In the former GDR, the percentage of the population who never participated in sports was much higher (70 percent) when compared to the FRG (55 percent), and the percentage of the population who engaged in sports each week was lower by half (12 percent) when compared to the FRG (25 percent). These results can be differentiated by several criteria including, age, gender, education, and profession. It is noteworthy that in both parts of Germany men are more involved in sports than women. These differences in participation are larger in the GDR than in the FRG. In both parts of Germany, the probability of engaging in sports decreases with age, with older people less involved in sports than younger people. In the FRG, gender differences in the age group between sixteen and twenty-nine is rather low (73 percent men versus 57 percent women), but extremely high in the GDR (56 percent men versus 38 percent women).

In contrast to the former GDR's ideology of equal chances for everybody and a "total socialist education," people with higher education and better professional positions engaged in leisure-time activities at a higher rate when compared with a similar population in the FRG. These differences in education and professional position are particularly salient in terms of gender-specific chances to engage in sports in the GDR and FRG. In the former GDR, only 6 percent of women with low education and professional positions (versus 39 percent in the FRG) were engaged in sports, while 49 percent of university-educated women (versus 66 percent in the FRG) engaged in sports.

Within a short time after the collapse of the communist regime and centrally controlled sports, a great number of sports clubs were born. Some of these new clubs were built on the foundations of clubs that had existed before World War II, and some clubs were built using the "insolvent assets" of governmental sports bodies that were taken over and reorganized by sport-ambitious citizens. Three issues had to be faced:

- The question of ownership of many sports grounds remains unresolved, or at least their use by sports clubs is still in question. This is based on the principle that in the communist system private ownership was impossible and many of the sports grounds were used by the army, security services, and the police, or they were used by state-run companies.

- These clubs were not built within the tradition of democratic participation and honorary engagement.

- After reunification, firms, with sports grounds, were privatized. In addition, some properties were returned to their pre–World War II owners. These new enterprises and owners were not always interested in supporting sports and had other uses for the property.

Within a short time after the collapse of the communist regime, five sports federations of the länder, many special associations, and about 10,000 clubs were founded, and a totally new structure developed with the assistance of the "old federal länder." As we evaluate these developments, we can understand both the development efforts and the problems faced by clubs in the new länder.

THE FEDERAL GOVERNMENT'S SPHERES OF RESPONSIBILITIES

Germany's constitution does not explicitly assign the federal government the ability to support sports. According to Article 30 of the German constitution which defines the spheres of jurisdiction, sport lies in the realm of the länder. Only if the matter exceeds the concerns of a single länder does the matter then lie with the federation. In regard to sport, the federal government is chiefly responsible for those tasks that are of central importance to the Federal Republic of Germany and that cannot be accomplished simply by any one of the seventeen länder. The federation represents the entire nation in sport, especially elite sport. It also

- Represents the state, by the sport, at events such as the Olympic Games and World and European Championships.

- Pursues foreign relations by the development assistance of sport in Third World countries.
- Supports nonpublic central organizations that are of importance to the entire federal territory such as the DSB, NOC, and special associations.

Moreover, the federation supports sport in its own sphere of responsibility, including the army (Buneswehr) and federal offices such as the Postal Sports Clubs (Post-Sportvereine).

A number of different ministries and departments are in charge of sport in the above-mentioned spheres:

- The Ministry of the interior supports the construction of sports grounds and sport-scientific research for top competitive sports. The Federal Institute for Sport Sciences is a department within the Home Office.
- The Foreign Office supports sports within the framework of foreign political-cultural affairs.
- The Ministry of Finance and Treasury deals with taxes.
- The Ministry of Defense controls sports in the army, especially the two sports companies and groups in which top athlete-soldiers prepare for international competitions.[10]
- The Ministry of Youth, Family, and Education supports sports for young people and promotes sports as a preventative measure in public health.
- The Ministry of Education and Science controls sports within the educational system.
- The Ministry of Economic Cooperation supports sports within the framework of developmental policy.

The eleven departments within the federal government that deal with sports issues are coordinated by the Ministry of the Interior. The minister is responsible mainly for furthering elite sport, including disabled athletes, and for questions of international sports policies. National sports federations are central to the promotion of elite sports; they provide support for training and competition programs, salaries for full-time managers and national coaches, and maintenance of health care programs for elite athletes. The German Sport Federations receive funds for projects such as coaching seminars or bio-mechanical investigations. The National Olympic Committee for Germany receives federal support for sending their teams to represent the Federal Republic of Germany at the Olympic Games.

The federal government also supports the building of sports facilities. Subsidies are used mainly for permanent federal training centers and Olympic training centers (special institutions for elite sport in Olympic sport disciplines), as well as for recreational sports programs in certain regions (peripheral areas) and sports facilities in institutions of higher learning.

In addition to the funding by the Ministry of the Interior, the Federal Ministry for Youth, Family, Women, and Health channels support to youth activities related to sport, just as the Ministry of Labor and Social Order offers help to sports programs for the disabled.

In addition, public sponsorship in the field of technical cooperation with developing nations is carried out by the Ministry of Foreign Affairs, which offers programs of cultural extension; and the Ministry of Economic Cooperation, which offers programs in developing cooperation.

The extent of support by the federation, 250 million marks in 1992, and its differentiation may be surprising given the fact that the management of sports lies principally in the hands of autonomous sports organizations; and the responsibility for sport is the jurisdiction of the länder. The federal government gives financial aid to the German Sport Federation (DSB) for elite sports and sports for young people; the Management and Administration Academy of Berlin; the Coaches' Academy at Cologne; the NOC of Germany for sending the Olympic team; and the federal special associations for competitive programs and for preparing elite sports for international competition, including the Olympic Games.

The federal government provides financial support for twelve Olympic bases. These bases prepare athletes for the Olympic summer and winter Games. Nearly twenty-five federal performance centers support elite athletes, about 200 federal bases help clubs to support their athletes, and seven special high schools enable young athletes and up-and-coming athletes to obtain education in schools, pedagogical assistance, and access to excellent training facilities. As part of the curriculum at these facilities, athletes are provided with physical checkups, advice from elite athletes, and information regarding drug use and addiction.

As part of their support for sports, the state cooperates with organized sports in providing coaches and sports medicine. For example, the costs are covered for such sports medicine services as physical checkups and advice regarding drugs and addictions. In addition, 120 federal coaches are paid. The coaches are employed by the German Sport Federation (DSB) and are recommended to the DSB by their respective federal sports associations. They report to the president of the respective federal sports association.

The German Parliament (Deutscher Bundestag) possesses its own sports committee in which representatives from major political parties are involved in important questions related to sport. The existence of such a committee underlines the sociopolitical importance of sports in the Federal Republic of Germany.

In the past, the parties of the Bundestag have passed sport-political programs. This link between sport and politics has never been questioned. Moreover, sport's importance has always been highlighted in terms of its impact on the development of the individual, its value as a contributing force in our civilization, and its social integrative power. The fundamental principles of the government's sports policy require that the relationship between sport and the state remains constant. Only the Green Party, which sprang from the ecological movement, takes a different stance toward sport. The Green Party decidedly opposes competitive sport and sees a greater danger to the environment as more people participate in sport.

The Federal Institute for Sport Science (Bundesinstitut fur Sportwissenschaft—BISP) was founded in 1970 in close collaboration with the German Sport Federation, with a charter from the Federal Minister of the Interior, and is located in Cologne. The BISP maintains close and simultaneous relationships—of special importance—with sports federations and scientific institutions and public authorities and facilities in sport, sport science, and sport promotion. The BISP

- Promotes applied scientific research in sport.
- Provides the federal government scientific and technological counsel regarding sport cooperation projects in developing countries.
- Cooperates in planning for the improvement and maintenance of central sports facilities that are owned by the government.
- Operates a national center for sports information and documentation.

INTERNATIONAL SPORTS POLICY

The relationship between the government and the DSB respects the constitutionally secured spheres of duty regarding international sports policy. On the one hand, the government has to safeguard autonomy in sport, while on the other, the DSB has to respect government's responsibility in foreign affairs. Since jurisdictional autonomies are constitutionally secured, it is possible to obtain agreements without having negotiations turn into jurisdictional disputes. Thus, agreements have been reached on such issues as boycotting the 1980 Moscow Olympics in response to the Soviet Union's occupation of Afghanistan, and discontinuing sports exchanges with South Africa to protest that country's policy of apartheid.

All programs related to public sponsorship of sport in developing countries belong under the Interministerial Committee (Ausshub zur Forderung des Sport in Entwicklungslandern). This committee was formed jointly by the German Sport Federation, the National Olympic Committee, the Ministry of the Interior, and the Ministry of Economic Cooperation. The German Agency for Technical Cooperation (Gesellschaft fur Technische Zusammenarbeit—GTZ) operates under the Interministerial Committee and is concerned primarily with long-term projects.

After World War II, sports organizations, in accordance with governmental policies, took a share of the responsibility to overcome Germany's political isolation and to restore its international relations. Sports organizations thus became part of the government's sports policy. The first international contacts were developed in 1915 at the club level after their reinclusion into international federations. A later, but most important, step occurred in 1952 when Germany participated in the Olympic Games in Oslo (winter) and Helsinki (summer).

International representation of sports lies in the hands of each sport's federation, whereas Olympic representation lies in the hands of the National Olympic Committee (NOC). As a result, the DSB has limited responsibility for international sports policy. Prior to the reunification of Germany, the DSB was permanently burdened in its international relations. Two German countries coexisted (the Federal Republic of Germany and the German Democratic Republic), with Berlin holding special status both juridically and politically and belonging neither to the FRG nor to the GDR. That meant that the DSB always had to acknowledge the special status of Berlin and not acknowledge the GDR. Fortunately, this is no longer an issue.

International sports policy sought links to Israel, Eastern European, and Third World countries. International sports policy demonstrated a strong commitment to reparations with Israel, by extensive donations and other support of Israeli sport (e.g., the construction of stadiums); participation in Israeli sporting events (e.g., the Makabi Games and Hapeol Games); and exchange of young people mostly by German Sport Youth (Deutsche Sportjugend).

In the course of "Ostpolitik," or the FRG's policy toward eastern countries after the quartipartite agreement in 1971, the DSB signed sports and cultural agreements with most of the Eastern European and socialist countries.

International sports policy provided extensive assistance to develop sport infrastructures in Third World countries. The primary aim was to help maintain the existing traditional movement culture in those respective countries and to promote access and participation in international sports meetings. This assistance varied from supplying equipment, supporting leisure sports activities, teaching trainers and coaches, constructing educational institutions, and exchanging sportsmen and sportswomen. The Federal Republic of Germany supports sports in approximately seventy countries. The DSB and the NOC carry out the publicly financed development assistance.

Since the 1960s, the DSB has participated in West European independent sports organizations and has represented the interests of its sport in the European Council and the so-called 30 Committees of UNESCO. The DSB's foremost aim was to show that sports are not a governmental instrument, may not be misused for political reasons, and have to be oriented to democratic and free societies.

GOVERNMENTAL SPORTS POLICY AT THE LEVEL OF THE LÄNDER

In accordance with the constitution of the Federal Republic of Germany (Article 30), most aspects of sport are the sole responsibility of the länder. In Germany, the länder holds supremacy in cultural affairs, and sport is understood to be a part of culture. Sport is in the hands of the länder, especially sports at school and sports in general. Financial support is executed via communities for constructin sports and leisure sites, the salaries of trainers and coaches, and work by associations in youth education. The länder's two foremost tasks are sports at schools, including the education of teachers at universities, and research in the field of sports sciences at universities. The länder supports top-level sports in a number of ways, yet its priority is to promote recreational sports both within and outside the sports federations. Responsibility for sports is assigned to various state ministries. In general, the Ministry of Education is responsible for sports in schools and universities, including promoting sports, building sports facilities, and supporting federations. However, a few länder designate the responsibility for school and recreational sports to various other ministries. A major responsibility of the länder is to promote sports facility construction at the community and club level. The länder not only provide financial support, but also offer counseling services in planning and construction of sports, game, and recreational facilities. Furthermore, the länder support elite athletes; construct and maintain regional training centers and instruction centers for the sport federations; and subsidize payment of instructors and administrators. In addition, the länder hold regular training and in-service education of instructors and support projects for young club members.

SPORTS SUPPORT AT THE COMMUNITY LEVEL

At the district and community level, the support of sport is directed mainly toward Sport-for-All and recreational sports. Cities and communities are involved in building and maintaining local sports and recreational facilities and youth centers, and in helping to maintain facilities of private sports clubs. In many cases, the sports clubs have free access to and use of public sports fields, gymnasiums, and swimming pools. City and community sports offices are responsible for the administration, maintenance, and renovation of community sports facilities. In Germany, sports—especially leisure and sports by the general public—are publicly supported, and this support provides for the construction and maintenance of sports grounds at schools and sports clubs.

In 1960 the German Olympic Society passed a so-called Golden Plan that set a target for sports grounds for communities of different sizes. These targets were an appeal to responsible authorities within the Federal Republic of Germany to remedy deficiencies in recreational, playing, and sports facilities. By addressing the problem of inadequate facilities, the German Olympic Society recommended a proposed construction plan costing 6.3 billion German marks. This plan has provided guidelines for communal sports policy for the past twenty-five years. After fifteen years, (West) Germany has constructed a large number of sports grounds:

- 14,700 sports grounds
- 15,900 gymnastic halls

- 3,000 indoor swimming pools
- 2,400 outdoor swimming pools
- 31,000 playing grounds for children.

These sports grounds were set up by communities at costs of more than 18 billion German marks. The costs cover land transfer and investments. These sports grounds generally are open to schools in the mornings and to sports clubs in the afternoons, evenings, and weekends. One advantage of this model is its low cost, since use of these facilities is either free of charge or at a nominal charge. The low cost to the clubs is the chief basis for the realization of Sports-for-All. Most of the clubs are able to provide their sports programs with monthly membership rates of 10 to 15 German marks. Another advantage of this model is its extremely high utilization rate, since schools as well as sports clubs use these sites. However, the federation does not fully support ongoing maintenance costs. In the last budget, more and more of the burden fell on the communities, with the result that already some sports grounds, especially indoor swimming pools, have been closed.

Different bodies coordinate the interests of the communities, the länder, the federal government, and the private sports organizations:

- Districts, cities, and communities have joined forces in national associations such as the German Association of Districts (Deutscher Landkreistag), the German Association of Cities (Deutscher Stadtetag), and the German Association of Cities and Communities (Deutscher Stadte-und Gemeindebund) in order to promote and represent the autonomous system of communal administration.

- Community associations have played an important role in the development of sports. Their recommendations regarding the promotion and construction of recreational, play, and sports facilities at the regional and district level have emerged as a central element of communal sports development.

- The German Sport Conference (Deutsche Sportkonferenz—DSK) was created in 1970 and comprises twelve members from the private sector and twelve members from the public sector, including the länder and community levels, and the political parties represented in Parliament (Figure 8.3). As such, it is an instrument of cooperation of governmental bodies and political parties in sports. It serves to coordinate developmental and promotional activities at all levels.

KINDS OF SPORT SUPPORT

The support of sports by the state operates through multiple channels, and is not limited to financial contributions. It includes a set of allowances that benefit the whole of sport. Sport benefits from:

Figure 8.3
The Institutionalized Network between Sport and State

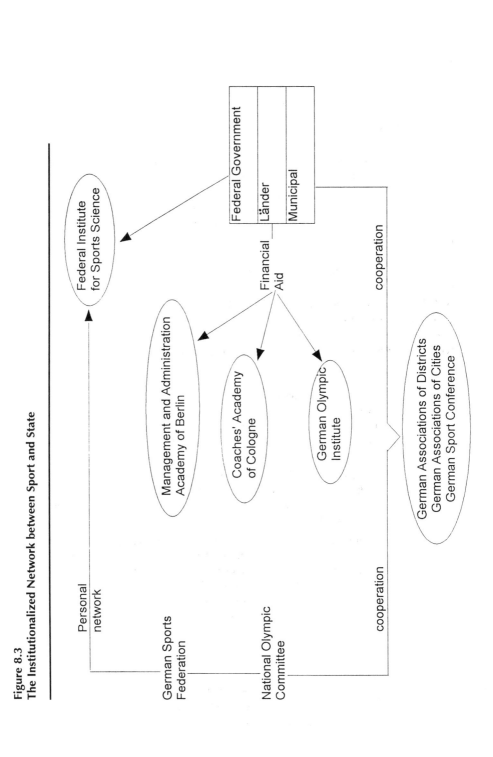

- Abatement of taxes for nonprofit sports clubs and associations. The exemption means that the majority of clubs pay no taxes at all. In addition, contributors can claim a remission on their income taxes for donations[11] to sports clubs and associations.

- Free or specially low prices for the use of sports grounds by clubs.

- Special terms of admission to study at colleges and universities for top athletes—"a bonus"—if the preparation for competition reduces the athlete's proficiency at school or if the athlete's grades do not meet the university's entrance requirements.

- Services for sports with special social tasks, such as sports for disabled people, seniors, children with abnormal social conduct, and ideomotor-disabled children.

- Income from gambling. Lotteries are required to contribute 25 percent of their income for nonprofit purposes.[12] Sports organizations receive 50 percent of this money and thus are heavily dependent on income from gambling.

SELECTED PROBLEMS OF SPORTS ORGANIZATIONS

The state generally supports voluntary sports organized in sports clubs. Sports clubs are widely regarded not only as the ideal suppliers of sport, but also as the purveyors of various cultural, political, educational, and social functions. Because of the state's tremendous support of sports, an adult member of a sports club on average only pays 14 German marks per month. In comparison, an adult member of a commercial sport enterprise would pay up to five times as much. However, in an era of downsized budgets, it becomes more and more difficult for the sports organization to justify this financial support. Support gives sports organizations a competitive advantage over commercial enterprises and has a consequent negative effect on the labor market. Furthermore, tax exemptions for sports clubs (as nonprofit organizations) reduce the state's tax revenues.

In the past ten years, a significant number of commercial sports enterprises (fitness centers, body-building studios, sport schools, etc.), as for-profit organizations, have set up business in Germany. Governmental support is exclusively to the benefit of not-for-profit sports clubs and organizations, which distorts the competition between commercial enterprises and sports clubs (Dietrich, Heinemann, and Schubert, 1990).

Sports clubs are usually restricted to a specific kind of sports discipline and offer a competitive-oriented program at different levels within the sports discipline. In Germany, this traditional concept of the sports club is more attractive to young, middle-class, male athletes. Women, older people, and members of the lower classes are underrepresented in sports clubs. Women and the elderly especially prefer commercial sport enterprises that offer a variety of sports. Membership in sports clubs is approximately 60 percent male and 40 percent female. In comparison, membership in commercial sports enterprise is 25 percent male and 75 percent female. These figures suggest that involvement in sports is dependent on the institutional arrangement and its sport concepts which are influenced by specific sports policies (Heinemann, 1990).

On average between 15 and 20 percent of a sports club's budget is paid either directly or indirectly by the state allocations. In addition, sports clubs receive other indirect support from the state such as the use of sports grounds, especially school grounds which may be used free by the clubs. In addition, sports clubs do not have to pay taxes because of their status as nonprofit organizations. Through these mechanisms, sports clubs have tremendous advantages in the sports market, which gives them economic advantages over commercial sports enterprises.

PROBLEMS OF LEGITIMATION INVOLVING ORGANIZED SPORT AND STATE

So, the question is not only why are there nonprofit organizations in a free market (a substantial amount of literature exists which elaborates on this topic; see Rose-Ackermann, 1986), but also, why is public support necessary? It may even be that nonprofit organizations, like the sports clubs, exist only for their public support. But why does the government subsidize sport, as organized in clubs? In any discussion of these questions, two different forms of legitimation are offered: the concept of neo-corporatism and the ideal of subsidiarity.

Corporatism represents a kind of "cramping" of the state and NPOs by "integration and functional representation of associations into the public sphere" (Heinze, 1981, p. 83). Associations take over governmental tasks and thus obtain a public character. Most evident is the term *Nationalmannschaft* (national team) and the usage of emblems of national representation (crests, banner, national anthem, etc.). Corporate structures develop in a situation where the state, under the claim of being a "social" state, has to take over ever more guaranties and achievements for the people and the economy. Consequently, the need to intervene increases. In addition, sports produce public and meritable goods—national representation, national pride, local identity, health benefits, care for youth, inclusion of fringe, and minority groups—which, because they are neither rival nor excludable (and will therefore not be provided by a free market), must be provided by the state.

Consequently, the development of a "network of relations; a functional entanglement of State and non-public institutions covers the traditional distribution of power" (Alemann and Heinze, 1981, p. 45). The associations relieve the state's obligation to fulfill many tasks. Associations take over the important job of communicating between the administration and groups of people. The state is released from decision making and control. Corporatism represents a kind of negotiated, societal, automatic control that is based on the principle of exchange: the state provides a judicial security and funds to accomplish the functions; the associations fulfill these functions with less expense and bureaucracy than the state because of their different structure of wages and honorary engagement. The state expects a clearly defined return. If this return is not forthcoming, then the association will have to deal with a reduction or a suspension of public support.[13] It is understood that entanglements are partially—personally and organizationally—institutionalized. Such is the case with the advisory councils that are shared by both sides. If part of the costs can be covered by contributions by members, donations, and honorary participation, then it is often less expensive for the state to fulfill its task. If the state alone had to fulfill these functions, then what? In addition, the state makes a concession to the citizens when it subsidizes associations and thus enables them to have more control over the reinvestment of tax revenues.[14]

The principle of subsidiary represents a second form of legitimation of the relationship between state and sports. This principle is based on the idea that all members within a smaller unit—like a sports club—know their desires and interests, and want to realize them responsibly (Nell-Breuning, 1969, p. 1137). According to this thesis, being more directly and closely involved allows people to act in accordance with their needs and to develop more fully as a result. Whenever peoples' needs and interests are perceived and administered from without, the danger of filtering and distortion arises. Accordingly, the state now has to offer financial support where financial means will not suffice but has to refrain from doing anything that may affect the free development of clubs. The principle of subsidiary is kept up by a distrust of bureaucracy and governmental interference. The state only has to check for the adequacy and control of public support for the organizations to prosper. The subsidiary maintains the functions of small organization and lays the foundation for favorable conditions to develop one's self.

If the DSB describes its relation to the state in terms of "partnership subsidiary," then it attempts to link two different kinds of legitimation. The argument is that it fulfills public tasks. This argument finds support in sports organizations, as private clubs present themselves with the insignia of the state at many national and international sports performances.

With further shrinking of the budgets, the extent of the subsidiary in public sport is questioned, but more fundamentally the discussion focuses on whether governmental support is appropriate. Often these two formulas are used as ideological claims that sport tries to realize in relation to the government. In order to realize its interests, sports organizations use all means and instruments of influence at hand. The organization has power through its 23 million members and, most importantly, through the multitude of personnel hookups of functionaries in sport and in government administration as well. Although there is no systematic research yet, there are many examples of this phenomenon. Many leading sports officials (e.g., the presidents of the associations, the chairmen of the clubs) simultaneously hold positions in the parliaments of the communities, in the federal lands and the federation, and in the political parties and public sports administration. The sports organizations have considerable potential for influence at all levels of political decision making and administration. Thus, they are able to carry out their substantial claims concerning financial subsidiary. Phrases like "partnership subsidiary" in relations serve as a justification. So they demonstrate that all is fine, well planned, to the advantage of all, and thus legitimate.

PROBLEMS OF PUBLIC INFLUENCE

Relations and declarations of intent by the partners involved—governmental sports policy and the autonomous sports organization—are presented as jurisdictionally correct in Germany. But often reality looks totally different. Relations between the state and organized sport are not without conflict. Moreover, a tension exists between the sociopolitical aims of the state and the interests of organized sports. What the state gives to sports appears, less and less, to promote self-help in sports. The state pursues and carries out its own intents through financial means. Sport, especially elite sport, is more and more dependent on the state. Through the state's financial support of elite sport, it has become a state-operated system. The state increasingly tries to gain influence and manipulate sport according to its own wants. This may have positive effects in the area of illegal drug use in sport. Parliament has blocked financial support for competitive sports until sports organizations improve drug control.

Increasingly, the state directs sports to assume tasks such as health maintenance, integration of minorities, caring for youth, and social reintegration. The principle of subsidiary, in this sense, is undermined and manipulated in favor of general societal tasks. This is demonstrated by the fact that support is linked to ever more defined purposes and sports organizations are drained of financial means without being bonded to specific purposes.[15] In general, German sports associations and organizations are greatly dependent on the support and aid of the federal government, the länder, and the municipality (Diegel, 1988, p. 68). It is estimated (though such a calculation is not easy to do owing to the different sources of money) that the state pays annually approximately 6.5 billion German marks for sport; about 220 million is paid by the federal government, especially for high-performance sport; 2.5 billion is paid by the länder; and 3.6 billion by the municipality. These figures illustrate not only that German sport has become dependent on public support but also that sports organizations have increasingly become organs of state policy and interest while running the danger of diminishing autonomy.

POLITICIZATION OF THE SPORTS ORGANIZATION

Significant consequences arise when sports obtain funds through sale of services such as advertising and telecommunication rights to others (commercialization) or through federal subvention (politicization). In general, it can be said that changes in the resource structure become incompatible with other characteristic variables of the club which are connected to the traditional concept of financing. They lead to a change in objectives and products and favor a service orientation in the members, increase the tendency toward oligarchy and professionalization—where professionalization comprises an increase in subject matter requirements as well as a wage increase for employees—lead to increased bureaucracy within the club structure, and promote the distinction between the objectives of the organization and the motives of the members. If these changes surpass a certain level, then they can lead to further changes in the resource structure. At the end of this development a type of organization may emerge, which is in exact opposition to the "ideal type of voluntary organization." On the one hand, the following variables are mutually supportive: the connection of objectives and organization to the interests of the members; dependence on the resources of the members; democratic decision structures; goal orientation and grouping of members; high willingness to cooperate; unpaid cooperative work and group character; and mutual stabilization. Conversely, the opposite forms of these variables are also mutually supportive. Because the completion of tasks is no longer bound by the availability of resources from members, the association or rather the managing committee has more flexibility with respect to ways to fulfill these tasks. The dependence on the skills and competencies of the members and on their willingness to sacrifice time or money to the association is much smaller. Services can also be acquired from the market, not just the members. This independence from the members and their willingness to perform services also strengthen the influence of the managing committee (Heinemann and Horch, 1991).

THE RELATION OF FEDERATION, LÄNDER, AND COMMUNITIES

It has become difficult to delineate the spheres of competition among the federation, länder, and communities in their support of sport. The difficulty arises because there is no written legal document that delineates the responsibilities of these three organizational levels of the state (Dellmann, 1981, p. 2). The consequences include permanent conflicts, especially between the länder and the federal government; and negligence of important affairs and issues in sport. The research policy of the Federal Institute for Sport Science provides a good example of the problem. It is the main source for financial support for scientific research in the area of sport. The federal institute is restricted to investigations into high-performance sport. As a consequence, research into recreational sport and Sport-for-All is neglected because these topics are the responsibility of the länder. Unfortunately, the länder do not have the money or the institutional infrastructure for sport sciences. Similarly, sport in vocational schools is extremely neglected as responsibility for professional training is not clearly defined. Increasingly, the federal government is filling the void where responsibilities are not clearly spelled out. At the same time, doubts arise regarding the federal government's role and whether this is still consistent with its constitution. Certainly, the sphere of education and science and the subsidiary of culture are part of the administrative prerogative of the federal lands. But to what extent may we distinguish between sport as education or as culture? Above all, as the länder lack money to adequately meet their tasks, and as the federal government itself financially supports them, then it will not hesitate to use its influence.

CONCLUSIONS

In Germany, sports clubs have a long tradition as voluntary, democratic, and nonprofit organizations. The first, and still existing, sports club in Germany was founded in 1816 (Hamburger Turnerschaft). At the same time, the German gymnastic and sport movement tried to find a "German way" of sport in harmony with the "German character" and in contrast to "English sport." This is one root of the peculiarity of the German sports organization. The other, more important influence was the experience of the Third Reich. As a result of this influence, there is a strict division between the voluntary, nonprofit sports organizations and the state. Sports policy is, in principle, restricted to financial support of sports organizations and a cooperative partnership between sports federations and the state in all public affairs concerning sport. This has positive consequences for sport, for in principle it is possible to offer sports for everyone since the clubs are highly voluntary and economically attractive to members. Without doubt, Germany has a very high rate of participation in sport. However, a private, voluntary, sports organization is selective and increasingly dependent on the state while not always as efficient and cheap as commercial, profit-oriented sports enterprises.

NOTES

1. The Deutsche Jugendkraft (DKJ), founded in 1920, is the sports organization of the Catholic Church, and the Eichenkreuz (EK), founded in 1921, is an evangelical church and part of the CVJM (Christian Association of Young People). In 1991, 500,000 members had enrolled at the DJK and 40,000 at the EK. Although both associations are organized and financed by their respective churches, they consider themselves to be ecumenical.

2. However, some members of sports organizations are calling for a ministry of sport with the view that they can further their interests by lobbying the government. However, these members overlook the fact that such a ministry may threaten the autonomy of sport. The government has rightfully declined to create a department or ministry of sport.

3. In the following, I will use the untranslated word *länder* for these federal states.

4. In principle, Germany has a similar constitution to the US. Länder can be compared with the states in the US system.

5. The federal structure of Germany provides two legislative boards at the federal level—"bundestag," or Parliament, with elected representatives of the people and the "bundesrat" with representatives from federal lands. Laws are passed with the agreement of both houses, the bundestag and the bundesrat.

6. Sport is practiced in 78,000 sports clubs. Every fourth German, whether a baby,

a juvenile, an adult, or a senior is a member of one, if not of several sports clubs. The growth of sports clubs in the past thirty years is impressive. In 1960, 5.3 million members belonged in 29,500 sports clubs; in 1970, 10 million in 40,000 sports clubs; in 1980, 17 million in 53,000 sports clubs; and in 1989, 21 million in 66,500 sports clubs in West Germany.

7. The Association of Sport Science (DVS) represents a union of professors and other academic staff within the various sport science university institutes. The DVS was founded in 1971 to promote the development of sport sciences. The DVS is organized in regional branches, fulfilling its mission through sections (history of sport, sport sociology, motor learning and training, commissions and temporary committees). It is probably unique that this kind of scientific community is integrated into such a community of interest. No union or federation of employees, no union of business economists or political economists (e.g., club of social policy) would seriously consider such a membership. However, this gives the DVS small but important political power.

8. The German Association of Physical Education Teachers (DSLV) is an umbrella organization of physical education teachers at schools, universities, clubs, and federations.

9. This, however, is even more important than a curiosity, for the DSB represents sportsmen and sportswomen—a union-organized group of employees—in the clubs.

10. Doubtlessly, they are a special kind of "state amateurs."

11. The clubs, as sports providers, have an enormous advantage over commercial competitors who pay the value-added tax that corporations pay on their profits. About 11 percent of the income received by clubs originates from donations. Since the donor pays, on average, about 40 percent on income, that means that for every 100 German marks contributed to the club the donor is allowed a reduction of 40 marks on declared income. This is a massive financial subsidy of the clubs.

12. Lotteries and similar games of chance can return only 25 percent on their income to gamblers, while the greatest part is returned to the state; 25 percent of income must be made available for social tasks so that sport and welfare organizations are furnished with funds. One lottery ("Glucksspirale") funnels income solely to sport.

13. A typical example is the pressure that the state exerts on the associations and sports clubs to solve the problem of illegal drug use in sports. The state will only support a "clean" sport.

14. Nevertheless, even the state can fail when attempting to accomplish those duties. Other authors make the point that NPOs developed as a consequence of a failing government. They go on to point out that political decisions are oriented mostly to win political majorities and so are bound to short time intervals, from election to election. In the long run, the tasks that are significant to the maintenance and security of power are not fulfilled satisfactorily.

15. The following event will demonstrate this clearly. In the early 1980s the former president of the German Sports Federation freed the DSB from so-called institutionalized support. Institutionalized support meant that the state supplied the DSB with financial means, but at the same time controlled the usage by submitting them to restrictive and rigid budgetary rules. The alternative to this institutionalized support was support of certain projects (Projektforderung). In this way, the DSB freed itself from budgeting control but is now reliant on these projects. Consequently, the state is provided with a larger measure of influence.

REFERENCES

Alemann, U. V., and Heinze, R. G. (1981). Kooperativer Staat und Korporatismus. Dimensionen der Neokorporatismusdiskussion. In U. V. Alemann (ed.), *Neokor-Poratismus*. Frankfurt/New York: Campus.

Bernett, H. (1992). Sport history: Sport and national socialism—A focus of contempory history. In H. Haaq, O. GruPet, and A. Kirsch, (eds.), Sport science in Germany. Berlin/Heidelberg: Springer.

Bernett, H. (1971). *Sportpolitik im Dritten Reich—Aus den Akten der Reichskanzlei*. Schorndorf: Hofmann.

Dellmann, H. (1981). Schwerpunkt Hochleistungssport: Die Forderung durch den Bund. *Das Parlament 8/2*.

Diegel, H. (1988). Die offentliche Sportverwaltun in der Bundesrepublik Deutschland. In H. Diegel (ed.), *Sport im Verein und Verband*. Schorndorf: Hofmann.

Dietrich, K., Heinemann, K., and Schubert, M. (1990). *Kommerzielle Sportanbieter— Eine empirische Studie zu Nachfrage, Angebot und Beschaftigungschancen im privaten Sportmarkt*. Schorndorf: Hofmann.

Gieseler, K. H. (1988). Grundung, Entwicklung und Strukturen der Sportselbstverwaltung. In H. Diegel (ed.), *Sport im Verein und Verband*. Schorndorf: Hofmann.

Heinemann, K. (1990). *Einfuhrung in die Soziologie des Sports* 3. Schorndorf: Hofmann.

Heinemann, K., and Horch, H. D. (1991). *Elemente einer Finanzsoziologie freiwilliger Vereinigungen*. Stuttgart: Verlag Enke.

Heinemann, K., and Horch H. D. (1981). Organisation im Sport. *Sportwissenschaft* vol. 11/2.

Heinze, R. G. (1981). *VerbandePolitik und NeokorPoratismus*. Opladen: Westdeutscher Verlag.

Langenfeld, H. (1988). Wie sich der Sport in Deutschland seit 200 Jahren organisatorisch entwickelt hat. In H. Diegel, (ed.), *Sport im Verein und Verband*. Schorndorf: Hofmann.

Nell-Breuning, O. (1969). Subsidiaritatsprinzip. In W. Bernsdorf, (ed.) *Worterbuch der Soziologie*. Stuttgart: Enke.

Rose-Ackermann, S. (1986). *The economics of nonprofit institutions*. New York, Oxford: Oxford University Press.

9

Sports Policy in Hungary

Gyöngyi Szabó Földesi

Owing to the political changes in 1989–90, all areas of Hungarian society, including sport, are undergoing transformation. The government's changing relation to sport is a crucial issue in this process. The sport–government relationship no longer operates on a dictatorial basis as it did in the past four decades, but it does not yet function in line with the new, democratic principles. Formed in the spring of 1990, the new government has quickly regulated the forms of central control over sport. The organizational framework of government control has been transformed accordingly. Nevertheless, the new forms, in part, still cover the old content, which is being replaced by a new meaning very slowly. Although a new national sports authority had been set up to manage and coordinate sports affairs, as of 1994 it still had not clarified what relations it would maintain with the sports organizations (federations, clubs, and, in part, the Hungarian Olympic Committee), which have now rid themselves of government control. The new authority has established a national network, but it is not yet clear how this network operates, what functions it has to perform, and how it will develop an appropriate partnership with the local committees in charge of sport.

This description of Hungary's sports policies covers not only the laws, decrees, and rules that regulate the government's relation to sport but also the fields in which this relationship has yet to be regulated and the difficulties caused by the absence of regulation. This chapter deals with how Hungary's new sports model is functioning and not functioning. To provide a realistic picture of sports policies in the transition period, this chapter presents information about both the issues settled in the government's relationship with sport and the problems that have still to be addressed.

THE NATIONAL GOVERNMENT AND SPORTS SYSTEM

The Present and Previous Hungarian Governments

Hungary is a unitary state. Its present government was established in 1989 in the wake of sweeping political changes. Law XXXI of 1989, which is formally an amendment to the Hungarian constitution of 1949 but practically contains the new constitution of a country embarking on the road toward democracy, declares that Hungary is a republic. "The Republic of Hungary is an independent and democratic constitutional state. In the Republic of Hungary all power belongs to the people, which exercises its sovereignty through elected representatives or directly" (*Constitution of the Republic of Hungary,* 2 & [1–2], p. 349).

The Parliament, the nation's supreme organ of state power and popular representation, determines the organization, orientation, and conditions of government, and elects the president of the Republic and the prime minister. The government and its members are responsible to Parliament. The powers of Parliament, however, are limited by the constitution. The idea of the people's sovereignty does not imply any concentration of power. Government is based on the division of powers between the legislative, the executive, and the judiciary. Parliament is surrounded by major supervisory institutions limiting and controlling its power, and the prime minister has a special responsibility for the policy of his government.

Hungary's present government is based on a strong but controlled power (Sári, 1992, pp. 180–184). To understand its relation to sport, one should understand that the present constitution is of a temporary nature: although it was amended on a few occasions, it still left some issues uncovered. There is an element of uncertainty in Hungary's legal system because some laws, decrees, and regulations, which were approved under entirely different political and economic circumstances, are still in force. The past survives even in contemporary Hungarian sport, both in its international ties inherited from the previous governments and in its relationship based on customary law with the domestic institutions. For this reason, we need to examine the previous regime, the so-called socialist government.

Socialist government was introduced in Hungary by Law XX of 1949 of the constitution, which was drafted on the pattern of the 1936 constitution of the Soviet Union. The fundamental principle of the socialist state was the unity and indivisibility of power. All administrative bodies were subordinated to the Council of Ministers. Although, in principle, the central bodies of government had unlimited powers, they were practically instruments of the ruling party.

Hungary's socialist government was based on a one-party system. The

"PARTY," the only party permitted to operate between 1956 and 1989, was the Hungarian Socialist Workers' party, which imposed its will on all government bodies. Although the party declared the principle of democratic centralism, it operated in practice under a centralized, hierarchical regime. It had wider powers than the government bodies, and it operated without any control. The power of the ruling party was not limited by anything. This political structure prevented actual parliamentary government. In fact, Parliament simply rubber-stamped the party decisions. The party enforced its leading role through the Council of Ministers, which controlled all government organs, on the one hand, and through the party organizations which operated in all government organs on all levels of state administration, including the governing bodies of sport, on the other.

The Government's Modern Relations to Sport in Hungary

Hungary was one of the countries where modern sport first emerged. The first sports clubs[1] and national sports federations[2] were founded, and the first championships[3] held, in the second half of the nineteenth century. Hungarian athletes participated in international championships,[4] and Hungarian sports diplomats played a significant role in the foundation of international sports organizations and the development of international sporting life (Kutassi, 1990, p. 111).

The governments of the time maintained strong relations with sports.[5] They popularized modern sports in Hungary and managed Hungarian athletes in the international arena because they realized that sports opened a diplomatic channel for proclaiming the independence of Hungary, which was part of the Austro-Hungarian monarchy between 1867 and 1918. The opportunity to become involved in the international Olympic movement and other international sports federations as an independent state stimulated the country's leaders and motivated the Hungarian sports policy of the time (Földesi et al., 1989, p. 144). Nevertheless, the system of sports administration was established rather late.

Sports affairs (as well as physical education) were under the authority of the Ministry of Religious Affairs and Public Education. The National Council of Physical Education, set up in 1913 under the ministry's auspices, acted as a consulting and advisory body in the subsequent three decades.

In this period, the government placed a relatively strong emphasis on sport. Initially, the central budget set aside a "Physical Education Fund" for the purpose. Later, part of the tax imposed on horse races was channeled to sport. The 1921 Law on Physical Education covered some issues of sport, too.[6]

Physical education and sports were coordinated at the government level because of the post–World War I peace treaty which limited military training in Hungary. As a consequence, the leading political circles tried to use sports as a camouflage for military training. To attain this goal, national sports management was excessively centralized in some fields.[7]

Despite the government's strong influence and the centralization of youth sport, Hungarian sports were organized chiefly on a voluntary basis until the Second World War. The post–World War II years brought sweeping change. The people's democracy and the subsequent socialist regime considered the development of sports a priority task of the government and party, and put sports under central control.

Sports were designed to help achieve certain foreign and home policy goals. These political goals and functions were connected mainly with elite sports. The elite athletes, serving as the envoys of the people, were expected to perform a diplomatic mission: their international successes were meant to prove first the viability, and then the superiority, of the socialist system. The support they received was strongly motivated by political considerations. During the Cold War, they helped their country break out of isolation behind the Iron Curtain. In the subsequent period of peaceful coexistence, they symbolized their country's commitment to peace and enhanced its international reputation, as a kind of compensation for the absence of genuine social and political achievements.

Because of the latter function, sports played an important role in domestic policy as well. Since sport was "liberal and democratic in its principles, and collectivist and nationalist in its inspirations" (Grawátsch, 1989, p. 48), it compensated people for shortcomings that could not be eliminated in another way because they were deeply rooted in the political and economic structure of the communist regime. Elite sport was therefore a surrogate for national identity, which was doomed to be suppressed in the spirit of internationalism; a channel of "mobility," even for the opponents of the ruling party; and "circuses" for the people in a period when even "bread" was in short supply. These functions prevailed in all socialist countries, even if in different ways and with different content, and they remained dominant up to the collapse of the regime. They determined the rule (and supervision) of sport, its financing, and the structure and operation of its organizational system.

The party resolutions, statements, and directives that determined the main trends and tasks in Hungary's political, economic, and cultural life for four decades regularly dealt with sports (and physical education). They determined the place and role of sports in a society "which was building socialism," and specified the main principles and tasks of the sports movement.[8] Although these documents accepted as an axiom the equality of elite sport and mass sport and declared the significance of student sport, in practice priority was given to elite sport, particularly the Olympic branches. In the sphere of government, the party resolutions were legalized by the decrees of the Presidential Council and the decrees of the Council of Ministers.

The resolutions were implemented by the national sports authority, which had operated under the direct control of the government since the early 1950s. The authority established a national administrative network composed of city, district, and county sports committees. The network was topped by the National Office for Physical Education and Sports (hereafter called Sports Office, or NO-PES),[9] which centralized all power in one hand, and directed and controlled all fields of sporting life, including the formally autonomous organizations of civil society. Accordingly, the Sports Office exercised direct political, professional, and financial control over all sports federations, large sports clubs, and even the Hungarian Olympic Committee (HOC).

Financially, the sports federations and the HOC were absolutely dependent on the Sports Office. They either had no budget of their own, or their budget formed an indistinguishable part of the Sports Office budget. The operation of large sports clubs was financed in part by the Sports Office, and in part by state-run institutions and large companies (the so-called base organizations).

The Sports Office exercised indirect control over the smaller sports clubs and organizations through its national network. The party resolutions declared that the decisions of the regional councils for physical education and sports should be binding on all state-run and voluntary sports organizations.

Although the principles that determined the government's relation to sports remained by and large unchanged between 1945 and 1989, they were realized in extremely different forms in the various periods. Before the 1956 revolution, the party's omnipotence was unchallengeable even in sport.[10] In the ten to fifteen years that followed the revolution, central power retained a strong influence on all fields of sporting life.[11]

From the 1970s on, central pressure was gradually eased. Within the given limits, the representatives of professional organizations and local sports organs had a greater say in decision making. Although the structure and hierarchical relations of sports remained unchanged, the party played a weakened role in direction. Professional knowledge increased in importance, and several posts that used to be occupied by party officials were filled by sports experts.

As compared to the other East European countries, Hungarian society, including its sports life, was characterized by a relatively free atmosphere in the early 1980s. This is why the decision that Hungary would stay away from the Los Angeles Olympics in 1984 shocked all Hungarians, especially the youth.

The decision was made by the Hungarian Olympic Committee, with one opposing vote. It was an open secret, however, that the state and party leadership had instructed the Committee. The effects of the measure went far beyond the boycott. Many people realized that, although a process of decentralization had started and some personnel changes had taken place even in sport, they alone were insufficient for a democratic transformation. The latter would require fundamental changes in the basic structure of political power.

Description of Sports Activities

In keeping with the country's traditions and the sports policies of the past four decades, the most popular sports in Hungary are those that are either included in the Olympic program or offer a good chance of achieving spectacular national success. In Hungary, almost all sports are based on amateurism. The only exception to the rule is professional boxing, which reappeared in the early

1990s but has attracted very few participants. The absence of professional sports dates back to the socialist regime which, for ideological reasons, banned them and disbanded the professional sports federations (soccer, boxing) after the Second World War.[12]

According to official data, there are sixty registered sports federations in Hungary (*Sport Értesítő* [Sports Gazette], 1992:4). The Sports Office, however, publishes figures only on thirty-seven branches of sport. In 1991 the largest number of Hungarian sports sections could be found in soccer (1591), hiking (518), table tennis (361), chess (330), handball (329), tennis (275), bowling (218), basketball (173), track and field (152), volleyball (136), karate (121), and swimming (87). The number of registered athletes exceeded 10,000 in six sports (soccer, hiking, handball, tennis, track and field, basketball) and stood between 5,000 and 10,000 in five (chess, table tennis, swimming, karate, volleyball). In nine of the thirty-seven sports, there were fewer than 1,000 registered athletes. The latter category included modern pentathlon (648 club members), in which Hungary is a world power.

In 1991 there were 192,821 registered athletes in Hungary, including 41,652 women. The most sportsmen competed in soccer, hiking, handball, track and field, basketball, chess, tennis, table tennis, and volleyball, and the most sportswomen in tourism, handball, volleyball, swimming, and gymnastics.

As far as nonregistered athletes are concerned, in 1991 most of them were attracted by five-man soccer (328,149), tourism (237,882), track and field (100,932), basketball, handball and volleyball played on smaller than usual grounds (75,324), and table tennis (70,962). Apart from soccer, one-third of these athletes were women. Jogging days were attended by 117,726 athletes (including 38,408 women) and sports festivals by 95,670 (38,140) (*Sportstatisztikai Adatok* [Sports Statistical Figures], 1992).

Anyone can compete in a sports club or attend a leisure sports event virtually free of charge. Until the early 1990s, the facilities were maintained and the experts paid, through various channels, by the government. The emergence of genuine sponsors who finance sport from sources other than state funds is a new phenomenon in Hungary. In some sports courses organized by the state, the participants have to pay a tuition. In 1991 these courses were attended by 85,276 people (including 40,748 women) in the branches of swimming, judo, karate, aerobic, fitness exercise, tennis, body-building, ski, riding, surfing, yachting, yoga, and fencing. These courses are aimed at giving athletes an opportunity to learn new sports and practice old ones. The courses are open to anyone who pays the tuition. (*Sportstatisztikai Adatok* [Sports Statistical Figures], 1991). Surveys have demonstrated that these sports are becoming more popular (Földesi, 1991b, p. 93; Laki et al., 1990, p. 24). Although some private ventures have also emerged in these sports in the past few years, their proportion is still insignificant. About 10 percent of Hungarians are involved in sports more or less regularly (Földesi, 1990, p. 55 and 1991, p. 8; Laki et al., 1990, p. 13; Takács, 1989, p. 4).

From an economic point of view, sport implies expenditure but hardly any revenue for both the government and local authorities. No sports club or branch of sport can finance its costs from revenues. Although revenues have been increasing and the dramatic change is taking place, central subsidies are still of vital importance.

Not even spectator attendance plays a major role in the size of revenues. For culture policy reasons, until recently admission tickets were subsidized; the process of raising ticket prices to true market value is also recent. Although the tickets are relatively inexpensive, only the international first division and some second division soccer matches, basketball and handball matches, and some volleyball matches attract large crowds of fans. In other branches of sports, even the national championships are held in a "family circle" (i.e., the only spectators are the athletes' relatives). Most of the international sports competitions held in Hungary are poorly attended. Some extraordinary events, such as the Formula One Grand Prix race, are exceptions to the rule.

Nor is any income drawn from the television coverage of sporting events. It is still an established practice that Hungarian Television pays nothing for broadcasting rights. On the contrary, the clubs have to pay for their competitions to be broadcast. This practice is expected to remain unchanged in the near future. It is accepted even by the sports clubs, the federations, and the HOC, because the sponsors are usually more lavish if a sports event is broadcast (Schmitt, 1991). Five sports federations (soccer, basketball, volleyball, handball, and water polo) are so pessimistic about the chance of any change in this situation that they have sold the television broadcasting rights to Hungary's Yellow Pages.

Participation and Success in International Sports Competitions

Hungarian athletes participate in international sports competitions on a regular basis and in relatively large numbers. Participation in the Olympic Games is considered by far the most important goal. Hungary's Olympic teams include not only current favorites but also the champions of the future and even some elderly athletes for whom participation is a reward for their successful domestic and international careers.

The Olympic summer Games are always attended by a large Hungarian team. Relative to the number of inhabitants in Hungary, it fares excellently on each occasion. For instance, in the 1992 Olympic Games in Barcelona, Hungary was represented by 235 athletes, who collected eleven gold medals, twelve silver medals, and seven bronze medals, and finished in fourth place five times, and in fifth and sixth places nine times each. In the unofficial points competition, Hungary finished in eighth place. Hungarian athletes excelled mainly in swimming, wrestling, fencing, judo, canoe-kayak, and women's gymnastics (*Barcelona 1992—A XXV. Nyári Olimpiai Játékok könyve* [Barcelona 1992—The Book of the XXVth Olympic Summer Games], 1992, pp. 164–165). The Olympic winter Games are attended by a small Hungarian team with few favorites. The only sport in which Hungarians occasionally succeed is figure skating.

Hungary's top athletes are regular participants in world and European championships. They take part in the world and European championships organized for the various age groups, and in the Youth Friendship competition. Priority is given to world and continental championships in the Olympic sports. In the list of countries ranked by their performance in the European and world championships, Hungary usually belongs to the top field. In the past two years, for instance, it occupied the second, third, and fourth places of the list compiled on the basis of Olympic points (*NOPES Összesített adatok* [NOPES Aggregate Figures], 1991).

The majority of athletes succeeding in the continental and world championships belong to the few "mammoth" sports clubs. Although there are about 4,000 sports clubs in Hungary, in 1990 more than half of the Olympic points were scored by the athletes of four clubs, and more than two-thirds by those of ten clubs. In the recent European and world championships, Hungarian athletes achieved the best results in swimming, canoe-kayak, wrestling, shooting, fencing, table tennis, and track and field (*NOPES Összesített adatok* [NOPES Aggregate Figures], 1991).

Although the results achieved in the non-Olympic sports are rated somewhat lower, Hungarian competitors usually take part in the world and European championships of these sports. In the early 1990s, for instance, Hungarians competed in flipper diving, speedway, car and motorcycle, speedboat, acrobatics and long-distance swimming world championships, and the world competitions of some other less-known sports. In these competitions, Hungarian athletes succeeded less frequently than they did in the Olympic sports, but they scored a few points on each occasion.

Internationalization of Hungarian Sport

Sport in Hungary is based almost completely on native Hungarians, for in the past few decades, foreign athletes, coaches, and managers were not permitted to work here. The ban was initially motivated by ideological considerations and then by financial reasons. The few foreigners who still competed in Hungarian clubs were university students.

The situation changed in the early 1990s. Foreign players can mainly be found in soccer, basketball, handball, and volleyball. Most of them have arrived from Romania (mainly from its ethnic Hungarian community); the successor states of the former Soviet Union, for instance, Russia, Ukraine, and Estonia; and, in table tennis, from China. For them, Hungary is very attractive because the standard of living is much higher there than in their own homeland. These ethnic Hungarians may have emotional and political motives as well. In 1993 there were 100 to 200 foreign athletes in Hungarian clubs. Although their number is increasing, mainly in soccer, they do not play a key role in Hungarian sports.

Penetration by foreign coaches shows a similar trend. Most of them are specialized in the above games and emigrate from the same countries. It happens quite frequently that a sports club signs a contract with a Romanian, Russian, or Ukrainian coach who then brings his former players to Hungary. Now and then, foreign coaches appear in some martial sports (for example, Japanese trainers in judo and karate), but they are usually guest coaches who spend only a brief period of time in Hungary.

While foreign athletes and coaches usually come to Hungary from the East, Hungarians themselves seek to contract with a Western club, even if it has a lower rating than their former club in Hungary. The Hungarian athletes and coaches who contract with Western clubs, or sometimes with clubs in the Middle East or the Far East, represent almost all sports. Their decision is usually motivated by financial reasons; for instance, the chance of being paid in hard currency is most attractive. Athletes are hired mainly in soccer, handball, water polo, and basketball. Coaches usually are hired in the same sports as well as in fencing, track and field, modern pentathlon, swimming, canoe, and kayak. This process started some years earlier than the internationalization of Hungarian sport. In recent years, it has assumed considerable proportions and has caused a loss to domestic sport.

Hungarian sports officials have been present in international sports life for a long time. In the bipolar world order, the Hungarian sports diplomats were perhaps the most popular representatives of the communist bloc in the international sports organizations. They held important offices in some international sports federations and other sports organizations, such as the International Association for the Sporting Press (AIPS), and in some scientific societies. In the organizations that have held an election since the collapse of the communist bloc, almost all of them have been reelected.

In 1993, 120 Hungarians were working in about eighty-five international sports organizations. The highest posts filled by Hungarians were: member of the Executive Board of the International Olympic Committee (IOC), deputy president of the General Association of International Sports Federations (AGFIS), presidents, deputy presidents, and general secretaries of international sports federations (track and field, canoe-kayak, weightlifting, fencing), executive committee members of such federations, AIPS deputy secretary-general, and treasurer of the Intergovernmental Committee for Physical Education and Sport (CIEPS).

Hungary gained an observer's status in the Sports Committee of the Council of Europe (CE) in 1989 and joined it as a full member in the following year. Hungarian sports diplomats are playing an active role in the Committee. For instance, Hungary's delegate to the seventh Conference of the CE sports ministers in 1992 signed an official statement on approving the European Sports Charter and a Code on Sports Ethics.

GOVERNMENT INVOLVEMENT IN SPORTS

Regulatory Policies

Although there are local preferences, regulatory policies are uniform all over the country. The extent and nature of government involvement in sport is regulated by decree No. 169/1991 (XII. 26) (*Sport Értesítö* [Sports Gazette], 1992: 1). Accordingly, since January 1992 the National Office for Physical Education and Sports (NOPES) has been a national authority, operating under the direct control of the government and supervised by a member of the government. In paragraph 2, the decree specifies the tasks and powers of the NOPES as follows:

1. **The Office**
   a. carries out the tasks of central direction in elite, school and leisure sports;
   b. prepares decisions on elite, school and leisure sports for approval by the government;
   c. fulfills the tasks and exercises the powers, without the formulation of legal instruments, related to sports administration and assigned to the Ministry of Culture and Education and the Minister of Culture and Education;
   d. allocates the central funds earmarked for sports policy purposes;
   e. carries out tasks in maintaining international sports contacts.
2. **The Office**
   a. together with the Minister of Culture and Education, provides for the direction and development of sports research, and the education and postgraduate training of sporting experts;
   b. specifies tasks in sports hygiene in cooperation with the Minister of Social Welfare, and tasks in physical education at school in cooperation with the Minister of Culture and Education;
   c. performs regulatory functions in its sphere of authority and directs the organs of physical education and sports under its control.

The NOPES is headed by a president who is appointed by the prime minister. The NOPES president carries out tasks related to the direction of sports. However, the minister's powers of formulating legal instruments in sports administration are exercised by the minister in charge of the NOPES. In 1992 sports fell under the authority of a minister without portfolio. Since early 1993, the minister of the interior has been in charge of sports affairs.

Most of the rules of law regulating the operations of the NOPES were passed either before the democratic change or between 1989 and 1991. This has caused some problems insofar as the new sports authority has essentially new functions, the political, economic and social environment of sport has changed, and several rules of law that regulate other fields have been amended. For this reason, since 1990 a number of former rules have been amended or repealed, and efforts have been made to adjust the regulation of sport to these changes. Consequently, there is a great deal of uncertainty in the regulation of Hungarian sport.

Certain issues remain unexamined, and some rules that are still in effect are inconsistent with the new constitution. The fact that even the Constitutional Court had to deal with the registration and transfer of athletes duly illustrates shortcomings in regulation. In an answer to a petition by two top athletes, the Constitutional Court abrogated, with effect from January 1, 1991, some paragraphs of a 1988 decree of the national sports authority because it found them inconsistent with the Constitution. It reflected the uncertainty of the situation to such a degree that the NOPES president, commenting on the petition, asked the Court to reject it, arguing that the paragraphs referred to limited the athletes' rights to change their clubs in the spirit of an operative, supranational "sports law," which he had to consider superior to national legislation. If Hungary disregarded this "law," he argued, it would be excluded from the international life of the sport concerned (*Sport Értesítö* [Sports Gazette], 1990:10–11).

Since then, the rules of transfer have been shifted to the scope of the sports federations, which adopted new regulations in 1992 on athletes' registration, transfer, and right to compete, and settled the aforementioned issue. This was a matter of decentralization rather than deregulation. Before the system changed in 1989–90, the Sports Office exercised all these rights. The fact that the sports federations have gained control over the rules of transfer indicates their growing autonomy.

Policies Affecting the Structures and Operations of Sports Organizations

In an effort to fulfill its tasks, the NOPES set up a national network of sports administration on January 1, 1992. The network, composed of sports directorates in Budapest and the nineteen counties, is subordinated to the NOPES.

The directorates are financed from the central budget. Their budget and their rules of organization and operation are subject to approval by the NOPES president. Their tasks, albeit regulated by a decree, are not exactly specified and mostly coincide with the local authorities' functions in sport. Their central control is a temporary solution that will remain in effect until a sports law has been enacted (*Sport Értesítö* [Sports Gazette], 1991:11).

The sports directorates are the only organizations subordinated to the NOPES; all the other organizations are independent of it. The relationship between the NOPES and the other sports organizations is characterized by coordination and professional cooperation (see Figure 9.1).

In the four decades before the system's change in 1989–90, all sports organ-

Figure 9.1
Organizational Structure of Physical Education and Sports in Hungary

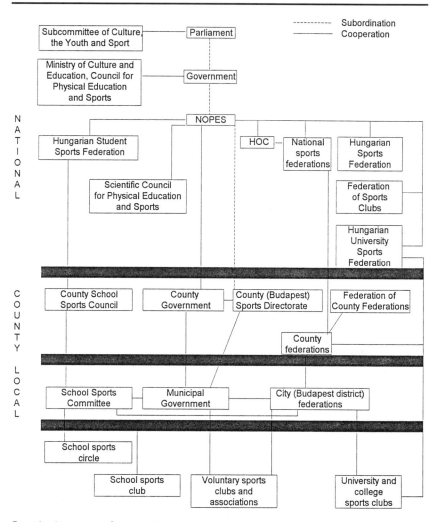

Organizations engaged in sport (Gyenge, 1992).

izations, including the HOC and the national sports federations, were subordinated to the Sports Office. This relationship was changed by the 1989 Law on Association, which was passed outside the sphere of sport. (*Ifjúsági és Sport Értesítö* [Youth and Sports Gazette], 1989:1–2).[13] After the law had come into force, the sports organizations were converted into voluntary organizations, and the Presidential Council of the Hungarian People's Republic passed a law decree on the national sports federations, which is still in force (*Ifjúsági és Sport Értesítö* [Youth and Sports Gazette], 1989:5).

The decree is ambiguous. Although it stipulates that the federation is in charge of directing and supervising work in the branch of sport, it leaves some room for intervention by the Sports Office. For instance, the Sports Office has the right to determine central subsidies that are to be provided for the branch and to supervise their allocation.

Initially, a great many issues remained unsettled in the new relationship between the Sports Office and the voluntary sports organizations, and some of them are still to be settled. In a move to facilitate contacts with the Sports Office and protect their interests, both the sports federations and even the large sports clubs have established national federations, which represent them in their dealings with the NOPES.

The NOPES seems to maintain the best coordinated relations with the HOC. According to the NOPES president and senior sports federation officials, the HOC has become an excellently managed, genuine social organization. The cooperation agreement they concluded proved to be an agreement of equal partners. In the mirror of the mass media, in 1990–92 the HOC had the greatest prestige in Hungarian elite sport.

Policies of Financial Support for Athletes, Sports Organizations, and Other Sports Entities

The prestige of the HOC derives, to no small extent, from the fact that the Committee has the most money in Hungarian sports life. Since 1989–90, the proportion of central subsidies in the HOC budget has decreased from almost 100 percent to 25 percent. In 1990 the HOC drew about three quarters of its income from sponsors, the sale of Olympic lottery tickets, and a share of revenue from gambling (Schmitt, 1990, p. 22).

As the 1992 Olympic Games in Barcelona neared, the number of sponsors kept increasing. The HOC signed agreements with about fifty institutions, including both state-run and private businesses. They became "Official Supporters of the Hungarian Olympic Team." Depending on the size of their contribution, they were awarded a gold, a silver, or a bronze medal. The contracts were generally drawn for the Olympic cycle, so they had to be renegotiated after the Olympics.

Olympic lottery tickets, another major source of income for the HOC, also ceased to yield a profit for a time after the Olympics. The tickets were issued before the Barcelona Games to help finance the Olympic preparations and participation of the Hungarian team. Before the 1996 Atlanta Games, however, this source of income once again became available for the same purpose.

The revenue from gambling, which constituted 15 percent of the HOC's total income in 1990, was withdrawn from sport under a parliamentary decision in early 1993. The measure hurt both the HOC and all sports organizations deriving a benefit from gambling. Parliament was expected to pass legislation on new ways of financing sport. According to the plan, 3 percent of the revenue originating from gambling will be channeled to a National Sports Foundation and earmarked for the purpose of sport. Subsidies from the Foundation will be available through competitive bidding.

Although the uniform system of financing sports from government funds is already a thing of the past, these funds are still channeled to the various organizations, including the HOC, through the national sports authority. The NOPES receives 0.20 to 0.22 percent of the central budget. This is a very small sum, particularly in light of the fact that it also contains the central subsidies allocated to the national sports federations, the Student Sports Federation, and the University Sports Federation.

According to the NOPES president, most of the financial questions related to maintaining sports facilities and the development of sport are not regulated appropriately (Gallov, 1992, p. 3). On the one hand, it is neither regulated by law nor clarified in principle how much should be allocated to which fields of sport from the central budget. On the other hand, legislators have failed to consider how the general laws enacted since the democratic change would affect sport. For instance, the new tax laws grant sport no concessions, not even the modest ones enjoyed in other fields of culture. In contrast with sport, the profit of other cultural fields is exempt from tax, providing that it is reinvested in the same field of culture.

Since the sports clubs do not enjoy such concessions, they try to generate as little taxable revenue as possible. Since the sports clubs, deprived of the former central subsidies, are in any case in deep financial crisis, they have piled up huge personal income tax arrears. Since 1988 all employers in Hungary, including sports clubs, have been obliged by law to deduct in advance personal income tax from their employees' salary. Depending on the size of the salary, the advance tax may go up to 40 percent. Although the advance tax should be transferred to the inland revenue office, several sports clubs use the withheld funds for financing their operations.

The new social security laws had a similar effect: the clubs are in considerable arrears with their payments of social security contribution. Like all employers in Hungary, the sports clubs should pay a monthly social security contribution amounting to 44 percent of their employees' salary. Most clubs, however, lack the funds required for fulfilling this obligation. Given lack of assets and large revenues, they have no means of settling their debts without external assistance. Based on a parliamentary decision made in 1993, some sports received a respite for tax payments until December 31, 1994. This measure, however, does not apply to the social security contributions.

Quite a few clubs and sections have gone bankrupt and have been dissolved. Others were financed by the NOPES to prevent their collapse in the Olympic year. The disorders and contradictions stemming from the absence of rules for financing sport are well illustrated by the fact that, in the interest of Olympic preparations, the NOPES maintained the system of subsidies which dated back to the years of centralized sports management and was declared unsuitable even by the Sports Office.

The absence of regulation has an unfavorable effect on the situation of sports facilities, too. Before the democratic change, the ownership of sports facilities was not a matter of interest since all of them were in state ownership, albeit in different forms of it. What mattered was the right to manage the facilities. In the early 1990s, efforts were made to settle property relations and privatize a considerable proportion of state assets. It turned out that about 65 percent of sports facilities were the property of local authorities and 35 percent were in state ownership. The clubs were deprived of the right to manage these facilities, and the privatization of state-owned sports facilities started. On January 1, 1992, some major facilities (central training camps, People's Stadium, National Sports Hall, Olympic Hall) were converted into autonomous organizations operating under the direct control of the NOPES (*Sport Értesítö* [Sports Gazette], 1992:3).

During this process, quite a few sports facilities were temporarily left without any owner. Since there is no one to finance their maintenance, they are falling into a dilapidated condition. The privatization law fails to oblige the new owner to retain the functions of the facility. Since the NOPES has no right of veto, only a right of comment, it cannot prevent the closing of sports facilities.

In 1990, on the NOPES proposal, the government and Parliament approved a plan for constructing 700 school gymnasiums by 1996. Half of the investment costs are covered from central funds and the other half from local ones. Although the Sports Office and the Ministry of Culture and Education wished to extend the plan to open-air school facilities and swimming pools, Parliament rejected its proposal.

In the absence of comprehensive financial regulation, government provides varying levels of subsidies for the various fields of sport. In 1991, for instance, the NOPES asked for a grant of HUF 541 million from the Ministry of Culture and Education, but it received only HUF 30 million for settling the most crucial problems. In a more important measure, Parliament set aside HUF 500 million in 1991 and HUF 450 million in 1992 from the social security fund for the purpose of promoting youth and leisure sports. The funds were distributed by competition, with the involvement of the Ministry of Social Welfare (*Sport Értesítö* [Sports Gazette], 1991:3–4 and 1992:3). In 1992 the claims exceeded the available funds by fourteen times. Many applicants wished to receive support for maintaining their operation rather than for a special purpose. It remains to be seen whether a fund of similar size will be set aside for sports in future years.

It was with another ad hoc measure in 1992 that Parliament granted the former Olympic champions and, in the second stage, the former world champions a modest pension supplement, regardless of their former job. The measure was initiated by a deputy during the discussion of a bill on national care, and it affects about 150 Olympic and world champions.

A new system of financial support for athletes has to be elaborated. Nor is it regulated according to law by whom the athletes' achievements are "owned." Although the top athletes (belonging to the international and first-class categories) contract with their clubs, it sometimes happens that an athlete signs a contract directly with a sponsor, without involving the club in the deal.

In Olympic sports, the best athletes receive financial support, depending on their performance, from the HOC. The NOPES makes no direct grants to athletes. The sports clubs, however, receive support from the Sports Office, depending on the international results of their athletes. Part of this support is channeled, either directly or indirectly, to the athletes.

At present, the central subsidies cover either a part of or the entire cost of preparing for and participating in the Olympic Games and some European and world championships, as well as the premiums paid to the successful athletes. The principles and the financial rules of premium payments have still to be worked out.

In keeping with the previous legal practice, the top athletes are eligible for medical care in central institutions. The financial conditions of this care have not yet been adjusted to the new economic environment. Some decrees have regulated sports medical examinations (*Sport Értesítö* [Sports Gazette], 1991:1) and sanitary tasks in sports events (*Sport Értesítö* [Sports Gazette], 1991:7).

International Arrangements

The development of Hungary's international sports relations has largely followed the nation's political and economic changes. Hungary maintains sports contacts with 120 countries and has effective cooperation agreements with about 20 of them. Besides sports meetings, these agreements envisage exchanges of experts and experience, training, and joint research. Some of the former agreements were terminated because the partner country ceased to exist (i.e., the Soviet Union, the GDR, and Yugoslavia). To replace them, new agreements have been concluded with Slovenia, the Ukraine, Belarus, Estonia, Lithuania, and Latvia.

The agreements concluded with some other countries (for instance, Angola and Nicaragua) were terminated because Hungary's new political regime no longer considers it its international duty to promote sport in the Third World countries, nor has it funds to do so.

Some agreements concluded for an unspecified period of time are still in effect, but the relationship has become looser for political reasons and because trips to these countries (for instance, Mongolia) have become prohibitively expensive.

Hungary maintains regular sports contacts with nearly 100 countries, without having concluded any formal agreement with them. These countries either lack a national sports authority that could be the NOPES's contracting partner or share the view that regular sports meetings and consultations can be held even without a formal agreement.

Hungary's partners can be divided into three main categories: neighboring countries, countries maintaining traditionally friendly sports contacts with Hungary (China, Cuba, and the North African states), and, in the spirit of a new orientation, the European Community member states.

ANALYSIS OF GOALS OF POLICIES

Domestic Policy Goals

Hungary's current sports policy takes a uniform approach to the various fields of sport, namely, elite sport, school sport, and recreation. In principle, it attributes equal importance to, and aims at developing, all three fields. This goal was inherited from the socialist political regime (Földesi, 1991a). Although at that time it was identified on other levels of the political hierarchy, in other forums, and with another phraseology, the similarity of ideas cannot be denied, not even if the draft sports policy guidelines, which were approved by the government in August 1992 and presented to Parliament in early 1993, carry the title "Guidelines for the Renewal of Physical Education and Sports" (Frenkl, 1992, p. 7).

Hungary's sports policy is based on the principle that sports and physical education are national causes. From the point of view of the moral education of young people, sports and physical education are just as important as intellectual education. The various fields of sport—school sport, recreation, and elite sport—were recognized as equal even in the past. During the socialist regime, emphasis was placed on the unity of elite sport and mass sport, and the importance of physical education. In practice, however, this remained an empty slogan. In 1992 the idea was formulated as follows: "The partial fields of sport, ranging from kindergarten sport to professional sport, form an interactive and interrelated entity, and none of them should be developed to the detriment of others" (*A testnevelés és a sport megújításának koncepciója* [Guidelines for the Renewal of Physical Education and Sports], 1992, p. 2).

According to the guidelines, it should be guaranteed that all useful functions of sport and physical education are achieved. Interpreted in a broad context, these functions include healthy lifestyles, physical fitness, rational leisure-time budgets, fun, promotion of social mobility, medical rehabilitation, fitness for military service, and developing personality. With regard to developing personality, there has been a major shift in emphasis. While "socialist sport" was aimed at evolving a communist personality, the sports policy pursued since 1989–90 gives priority to improving moral qualities and the moral standards of the nation. After some decades of forced internationalism, sport has now been assigned the task of strengthening national consciousness.

In the socialist regime, it was the government's task to finance elite sport, mass sport, physical education, and school sport. The guidelines for the renewal of physical education and sports stipulate that school sport, student sport, and the direct costs of preparations for, and participation in, the Olympic Games and some world competitions should be financed from the central budget. To finance the fulfillment of other central tasks, a public foundation called the National Sports Foundation was to be established.

The goal identified in the guidelines, that national sport standards should be elaborated for the provision of localities (and schools) with facilities, contradicts the intention of "withdrawal." However, it is a major shortcoming of this plan in that it fails to specify any legal or financial basis for implementation.

The Sport-for-All movement is marked by a similar contradiction: in general, it is declared as a central task, but when the concrete goals are determined, it is left out of the program. Under the law, the NOPES "carries out the tasks of central direction in elite, school and leisure sports." In practice, however, it assumes no responsibility for leisure sports and concentrates on elite sport. This is reflected by the short-term goals that determined the direction of action in 1990–92 and that did not even include "Sport-for-All." Short-term goals are related to elite sport in general and to Olympic sports in particular. The implementation of long-term goals was delayed in deference to short-term goals related to Olympic sports.

Economic transformation has brought about a crisis in Hungarian sport. Although this crisis was manifest in several forms in 1990–92, preparations for, and success in, the twenty-fifth Olympic Summer Games functioned as a "superordinate goal," mobilizing the hidden financial and moral reserves of both the sports authority and the voluntary sports organizations, and eclipsing all the other goals. The problems that were swept under the carpet but surfaced again after the Olympics were especially connected with Sport-for-All, school sport, and, to a lesser extent, elite sport. In 1993 priority was given to preserving the assets of Hungarian sport: the facilities, and the clubs and experts training elite athletes.

Goals Relating to Sports Organizations and Athletes

In the short term, priority is given to saving the sports clubs, mainly the "mammoth" clubs training elite athletes and champions of the future. In 1990 the clubs became independent of the national sports authority. Since their transformation into social organizations was not a democratic process initiated from below but a simple measure granting independence to the state-run sports clubs that emerged in the previous, socialist sports model, the financial and part of the legal conditions of their operation are still missing. Although the NOPES has continued to finance these clubs even at the expense of other tasks, its support has proven insufficient. At the same time, central financing implies central control that is inconsistent with the goal that the Sports Office should coordinate rather than control sports life. Nevertheless, both sides have accepted the modified goals, arguing that in the transition period this policy may help prevent losses that could hardly be recovered later.

The meaning of losses has not been clarified, however. Which of the structures, functions, and goals inherited from the previous regime are considered valuable and useful, and which are regarded as worthless and harmful by the new sports policy? What should be preserved and what should be discarded?

When the NOPES speaks about the necessity of providing central subsidies for the sports clubs, it takes a stand for supporting the country's elite athletes through their clubs. It seeks to promote top sports since the amount of financial support depends on the international results of the club members. The concrete terms of support have not yet been specified. The goal is for them to be "more up-to-date," but not even the NOPES has specified what that means.

The plan to set up a National Sports Foundation suggests that the national sports authority wants to make major financial contributions to elite sport, even in the long term. This effort will maintain the government's influence in this field, even if it runs counter to the declared aim of reducing the role of state administration in elite sport.

Although Hungary's sports policy lays special emphasis on school sport, most of the goals specified with regard to sports clubs are related to elite sport. The short-term program makes no mention of the need to "save" the school sports clubs, which are also in a plight, while university sports are neglected even among the long-term goals. The Guidelines for the Renewal of Physical Education and Sports take a somewhat contradictory approach to school sports: paragraph 4/b of the guidelines stipulates that the government will continue to finance school sports through the central budget. Paragraph 5/j, however, provides that the conditions for the operation of sports clubs in primary and secondary schools should be guaranteed by the organizations that are maintaining these schools (*A testnevelés és a sport megújításának koncepciója* [Guidelines for the Renewal of Physical Education and Sports], 1992, pp. 4–6). The state-owned schools are maintained by the municipal authorities who often fail to provide enough money for the purpose because, as they claim, there are insufficient funds in the state coffers. This situation may further aggravate organizational and operational disorders in school sports. Even the fact that the central subsidies earmarked for school sport were channeled to schools through the local sports directorates rather than the Hungarian School Sports Federation was a source of tension because many schools received them belatedly, if at all.

Under the guidelines, there is an invariable, even if temporary, need for the county sports directorates. All this is aimed at strengthening the influence of the governing bodies of sports, and brings about overlaps in direction. Besides the municipal authorities that are in charge of sports administration, the NOPES seeks to maintain a central network of sports administration, which lacks any genuine influence (Kis, 1991, p. 5). Although in early 1993 the sports directorate of Budapest was eliminated, the county sports directorates continued to operate, even under a new name, as regional offices of the NOPES. These directorates are independent of the municipal authorities both professionally and financially.

Foreign Policy Goals

In the first decades of the socialist government, international sports successes were seen as symbols of the superiority of the political regime. Later, a more sophisticated approach was taken to sporting excellence, but success in sports was still considered highly important for the country's international prestige.

The absolute priority given to Olympic preparations after the democratic change may lead to the conclusion that Hungary fosters this tradition, even if on a new ideological basis. As the guidelines submitted to Parliament declare, "The modernization of physical education and sport has the essential aim . . . to foster Hungary's traditions and preserve its prestige in international sports life" (*A testnevelés és a sport megújításának koncepciója* [Guidelines for the Renewal of Physical Education and Sports], 1992, p. 3).

Hungary also continues its tradition of using sports contacts with some countries to help improve political relations and to establish diplomatic ties. In the 1980s Hungarian sports diplomacy played an important role in establishing diplomatic ties with South Korea and Israel. At present, sports relations with Albania (in basketball and the training of experts) are also aimed at improving ties with that country.

With regard to using sports for foreign policy purposes, Hungary, being eager to join the European Community, is placing growing emphasis on developing sports contacts with the EC member states. At the same time, Hungary is not neglecting sports contacts with countries of a different social system, mainly the great powers in sport, such as Cuba and China.

The decision to put those central sports facilities suitable for hosting major international competitions under NOPES control was meant to guarantee conditions for maintaining international sports contacts. The aim that Hungary should be represented in the international sports organizations remained unchanged and was confirmed by the guidelines the government approved in August 1992.

CONCLUSIONS

Compared to other countries of the former communist bloc, Hungary has a successful sports policy since it prevented the collapse of the organizational system of sport. The policy is also successful in light of Hungary's resounding success in the Barcelona Olympic Games, which reflected both the achievements of the former sports policy (which had some essential drawbacks but favored elite sport) and the advantages of the new, democratic social system.

A more thorough analysis, however, reveals grave shortcomings in the country's sports policy. For instance, current policy places excessive emphasis on, and is motivated by, short-term tasks. It is not based on an objective analysis of the situation, and it fails to set genuine guidelines, even though a draft resolution offered by the minister in charge of sports and approved by the government in August 1992 carried the title Guidelines for the Development of Physical Education and Sports. These "guidelines" are nothing more than an eclectic collection of some tasks in sport in the transition period. The guidelines are very difficult to challenge. Although the minister in charge of sport presented them, the guidelines fail to specify who should fulfill the tasks, by what date, and what contribution the government should make. The guidelines are neither a project nor legislation. In fact, there are many similarities between the old party resolutions and the new guidelines both in content and the methods of elaboration and presentation (Frenkl, 1992a, p. 19).

As for its content, the main problem lies in the declaration of the axiom that the partial fields of sport, ranging from kindergarten sport to professional sport, form an interactive entity and "should" be developed equally. Although this idea is not expounded more concisely, the guidelines are based on this axiom. Similarly, the socialist party resolutions emphasized the "integral" unity of elite sport, mass sport, and physical education, but were not taken seriously. The unity of the various fields of sport sounds like a slogan even in the new guidelines. The idea that the modernization of sport is aimed at "improving the health, fitness and moral standing of the nation" is belied by both the guidelines and the actual sports policy.

Although the guidelines specify future goals, this is an insufficient basis for a crisis management plan. Despite the ever-deepening crisis, Hungarian sports policy has no plan for crisis management.

In March 1993 the Hungarian Parliament debated the Guidelines. Contributors to the debate emphasized that

1. Any new program elaborated for the development of sport should duly consider the need for environmental protection.
2. The Guidelines offer only a temporary solution since Parliament should in any case pass a sports law in the years to come.
3. Some issues related to sport (drugs, professionalism, prevention of football hooliganism, integration of young athletes into society) should be regulated by law even earlier. (Minutes of the March 16–17, 1993 session of Parliament)

As for the methods of presentation, it is a justified objection that the Guidelines were put on the agenda instead of a sports bill, which had been in the pipeline for some years. The minister, who had nothing to do with sports administration before January 1, 1992, argued that the sports law should only be enacted after the country's political and economic conditions had been stabilized. For this reason, he suspended the codification of the law, which had been long awaited by the sports community.

The only par excellence sports law designed to regulate physical education and sports in Hungary was passed in 1921. The years of socialist rule were marked by a plethora of regulations aimed at limiting initiative, creativity, and freedom. The regime failed to pass a general sports law because it would have put an end to voluntarism, arbitrariness, and subjectivism. However, repeated reference to the absence of legal regulation in sport does not imply a desire to return to the excessive regulation of the past regime. The process of deregulation started in the reform communist period, just before democratic change. The Hungarian sports community needs a general law that guarantees some level of regulation and encourages the elaboration of long-term sports policies, so that the decline of sport as an important part of Hungarian social life might be reversed.

The causes of the decline in sport are varied, and are related to the economic crisis and the political transformation of Hungarian society rather than to internal problems in the sports field. The internal problems that do exist are largely consequences of the larger societal problems. Underlying causes include a deteriorating standard of living, a shortage of discretionary funds and leisure time, and the grave problems of everyday life, which alienate many common people from sport.

This process is compounded by many politicians' contradictory approach to sports. On the one hand, they do not seem to be genuine advocates of sport, but on the other hand, they realize that, because of the popularity of sport in Hungary, they cannot declare this. Unfortunately, the sports community is not powerful enough to influence the politicians and slow down or halt the decline in sport.

NOTES

1. The first Hungarian sports clubs were established in the following order: Budapest Rowing Club, in 1861; National Gymnastics Club, in 1860; Pesti Skating Club, in 1869; National Shooting Club, in 1871; and National Track and Field Club, in 1875.

2. The first national sports federations were established in the following order: Federation of Hungarian Sports Clubs, in 1885; Hungarian Rowing Federation, in 1893; Hungarian Cycling Federation, in 1894; and Hungarian Track and Field Federation, in 1897. The first national university sports organization in Europe was established in Hungary in 1907; it was the second university sports organization in the world.

3. The first national championships recognized by the national sports federations were organized in the following sports: rowing (1893), tennis (1894), track and field (1896), swimming (1898), cycling (1898), fencing (1900), skating (1900), and soccer (1901).

4. Hungary was among eleven countries that participated in the first Olympic Games in Athens in 1896. The Hungarian Olympic Committee was established in 1885, as the fifth national Olympic committee in the world. At the invitation of Baron Pierre de Coubertin, Ferenc Kemény of Hungary participated in the Olympic movement as early as 1894. Elected to be a member of the International Olympic Committee, Kemény made a great contribution to the rebirth of the Olympic movement.

5. In the 1890s Albert Berzeviczy, under-secretary of state of the Ministry of Religion and Education, played an important role in the establishment of the Olympic Committee, of which he became the first president in 1895. Loránd Eötvös, former minister

of culture and president of the Hungarian Academy of Sciences, was elected as president of the Budapest University Athletic Club in 1907. Former prime minister István Friedrich accepted the post of president of the Hungarian Football Association.

6. The first, and until now the last, law on physical education was enacted in 1921 (Law No. LIII). This law framed the foundation of the Hungarian College of Physical Education (1925), among other institutions.

7. The decree of the minister of religion and education (No.96638/1927/XIII) abrogated the Statutes of the Hungarian Olympic Committee accepted fifteen years earlier, and by so doing, it openly violated the rules of the International Olympic Committee. The Hungarian Olympic Committee was ad interim discontinued. The National Council for Physical Education was rightly accused by several sports institutions and persons because of its centralized policy. This is why in a 1938 press conference, Dr. Lorand Prem, acting president of the NCPE, promised to change the Council's overcentralized policy.

8. The party decisions dealt with timely issues relating to physical education and sport, on the one hand, and prepared the most important changes planned in sport, especially the measures designed to legalize the party decisions, on the other. The party theses analyzed and evaluated the situation in sport from ideological aspects and "clarified" the most important sports concepts and sports theories. Sport and physical education were jointly discussed in all party documents concerning these fields. However, sports belonged to the National Office for Physical Education and Sports, while physical education as a branch of study belonged to the Ministry of Culture and Education. The party theses were made known and "discussed" at all levels of sports organizations. Not only party members but even nonparty people had to be familiar with them.

9. Until 1951, the highest sports authorities (National Sports Committee, 1945–47, National Sports Office, 1948–51) were subordinated to the Ministry of Religion and Education. The first independent sports authority, the National Office for Physical Education and Sports, was established in 1951. It was subordinated directly to the government. Then, over the last four decades, the highest sports authority in Hungary was independent. It was called "Office" and not "Ministry," but its sphere of authority was equal to the Ministry's.

10. The revolution broke out on October 23, 1956, in protest against the authoritarian Stalinist regime imposed on Hungary by the Soviet Union. The revolutionaries demanded that Hungary regain its independence, withdraw from the Warsaw Treaty Organization, and restore multiparty democracy. The revolution was crushed by Soviet tanks in early November, and the new Hungarian government took bloody reprisals against freedom fighters. However, the revolution was instrumental in replacing the tough dictatorship with one that was softer than that of any other country of the former communist bloc.

11. Decisions were made centrally by the highest political and/or sports authorities concerning all important sports-related issues (for instance, the distribution of state subsidies by sports clubs or sports federations, the establishment of international relationships between sports clubs); and in many cases even concerning unimportant issues as well (for instance, who may travel abroad to an insignificant competition, or how many students can be majors in physical education or coaching at the University of Physical Education).

12. According to communist ideology, professionalism was the product of capitalism, and as such it was treated as destructive to socialism. For instance, the Hungarian Football Association made the following decision on November 29, 1948: "The current

situation is intolerable: the spirit of professionalism is not in accordance with the policy of the people's republic building socialism. It has to be changed'' (Földesi, Kun, and Kutassi, 1989, p. 339).

13. The Law on Association (Law No. II), which amended the constitution, was passed by the so-called reform communist Parliament. It is considered one of the major steps toward democratic rule of law.

REFERENCES

A Magyar Köztársaság Alkotmánya. (1992). In I. Kukorelli (ed.), *Alkotmánytan* (pp. 349–373). Budapest: Századvég Kiadó.

A testnevelés és a sport megújításának koncepciója. (1992). A Magyar Köztársaság Kormánya által elfogadott határozattervezet (No. 6586).

Az Országgyülés. (1993). Évi tavaszi ülésszaka március 16–17–iülésének jegyzókönyve, pp. 25007–25087.

Barcelona, 1992. A XXV. Nyári Olimpiai Játékok Könyve. (1992). (L. Harle and L. Ládonyi, eds.). Budapest: Trió Budapest Kiadó.

Földesi, É., Kun, L., and Kutassi, L. (1989). *A magyar testnevelés és sport története.* Budapest: Sport.

Földesi, Sz. Gy. (1989). Leisure time physical activities in Hungary: Socio-economic aspects. In G. Tenenbaum and D. Eiger (eds.), *Proceedings of the ICSS and Maccabiach—Wingate International Congress.* Emmanuel Gill Publishing House, pp. 125–142.

Földesi, Sz. Gy. (1991a). A sportolásra fordított idö Franciaországban és Magyarországon. Budapest. *A Magyar Testnevelési Egyetem Közleményei.* Melléklet I, pp. 1–111.

Földesi, Sz. Gy. (1991b). From mass sport to the "Sport for All" movement in the "socialist" countries in Eastern Europe. *International Review for the Sociology of Sport,* 26 (4): 239–253.

Földesi, Sz. Gy. (1993). The Transformation of sport in Eastern Europe: The Hungarian case. *Journal of Comparative Physical Education and Sport,* in printing.

Frenkl, R. (1992a, September 14). Legyen a sport nagykorú. Budapest: *Magyar Hírlap,* p. 7.

Frenkl, R. (1992b, June 25). Sportkoncepció, sporttörvény. Budapest: *Nemzeti Sport,* p. 19.

Gallov, R. (1992, September 14). Mennyire fontos hazánkban a sport? Budapest: *Nemzeti Sport.* pp. 11–14.

Grawátsch, P. (1989). A szocializmus utolsó mítosza: a sport *Hitel,* 11, pp. 48–50.

Gyenge, J. (1992). *Sportszervezési ismeretek.* Budapest: OTSH, Ifjúsági és Sport Közlöny (1989) III: 1–2, pp. 4–6. Ifjúsági és Sport Közlöny (1989) III: 5, pp. 5–7.

Kis, T. (1991). Sportigazgatásunk szervezeti problémái egy önkormányzati sportszervezö nézöpontjából. Unpublished paper prepared at the Budapest University of Economics. Innovációs Menedzser Szak. II. grade.

Kutassi, L. (1990). A nemzeközi egyetemi sportmozgalom és azolimpizmus. In F. Krasovec (ed.), *A Magyar Olimpiai Akadémia évkönyve* 1990, Budapest: MOA, pp. 135–152.

Laki, L., Lakatos, M., and Újvári, J. (1990). A magyar népesség testedzési és sportolási szokásai. Budapest: *A Magyar Testnevelési Egyetem Közleményei,* 2. pp. 11–30, OTSH. Sportstatisztikai Adatok, (1991). Budapest: OTSH Kézirat.

Összesített adatok. (1991). Budapest: OTSH, pp. 31–43, 37–40.

Sári, J. (1992). Kormányzás—kormányzati rendszerek—kormányformák. In I. Kukorelli (ed.), *Alkotmánytan* (pp. 173–184). Budapest: Századvég Kiadó.

Schmitt, P. (1991). A MOB felépítése, feladata, szerepe a magyar sport rendszerében. In F. Takács (ed.), *Marketing és szponzorálás a sportban.* Budapest: MOB. pp. 21–24.

Sport Értesítö. (1990). V: 10–11, pp. 113–115.

Sport Értesítö. (1991). VI: 1, pp. 12–13; 3–4, pp. 22–23; 11, pp. 161–162.

Sport Értesítö. (1992). VII: 1; 3, pp. 33–36, 40; 49–51.

Takács. F. (1989). A sociological survey of the sporting habits of the Hungarian population. *International Symposium of the ICSS and Maccabiach—Wingate International Congress.* July.

10

National Sports Policy in India

M. L. Kamlesh, Packianathan Chelladurai, and Usha Sujit Nair

India is governed under a parliamentary system similar to that used in Canada and the United Kingdom. It has two parliamentary houses—Lok Sabha, or lower house, and Rajya Sabha, or upper house. The members of the Lok Sabha are elected every five years or less, if and when the ruling government falls. Of the 250 members of the Rajya Sabha—which is not subject to dissolution—12 having special knowledge or practical experience in literature, science, art, and social service are nominated by the president. The rest are indirectly elected by elected members of the legislative assemblies of the twenty-five states and seven union territories of India. The president is elected by members of an electoral college consisting of elected members of both houses of Parliament and legislative assemblies of states in accordance with the system of proportional representation by means of a single transferable vote. The leader of the largest party in the Lok Sabha is invited by the president to form the government. Whenever such a party has a simple majority in the Lok Sabha, formation of a government is quite routine. The leader of the largest party becomes the prime minister with considerable executive authority. The prime minister recommends his or her cabinet to the president, who routinely approves the list. However, when no party has a simple majority, the formation of the government is negotiated with other parties which share similar visions and goals for the country. Under these circumstances, the president is vested with the authority to call on the leader of a specific party to demonstrate that he or she has the support of the majority of the Lok Sabha members.

Following India's independence from British rule, the Indian National Congress, capitalizing on its role in the freedom struggle, held a commanding grip on the electorate, easily winning an overwhelming majority of the seats in both the Lok Sabha and the state legislative assemblies in all states. Over time, however, that dominant influence was usurped by the local provincial parties. The Indian National Congress splintered into two groups in 1969, during the tenure of Indira Gandhi as prime minister of India. At present, no single party in India can be considered "national" in the sense that it could win elections in the majority of the states. Each of the national parties is forced to align with one or more of the state-level (provincial) parties in order to gain influence and win seats in those states.

The formation of the twenty-five states of the Indian Union was based largely on the languages spoken in the locale. Since there are seventeen official languages in India, English has become, of necessity, the common language that facilitates dialogue among people from different provinces. Some of the state-level parties have been formed ostensibly in defense of the local interests and language. In other cases, the parties were formed on the basis of the race of the people. For instance, the two major parties in the state of Tamil Nadu are splinter groups of Dravida Kazhgam, which was formed "to promote and protect the causes of the Dravidian people in the south against the onslaught of the Aryans from the north." As noted earlier, the provincial parties have a strong hold on the electorate in state elections. In the central parliamentary elections, they often sway outcomes by forming coalitions with selected national parties.

India's constitution calls for a secular state, and until recently, the government has assiduously followed this principle. However, the polarization of political parties around religion, caste, and other issues has become increasingly common. Several polls conducted from 1989 to 1993 show fluctuating fortunes for the national and state political parties. Despite social and religious turmoil, the Indian polity remains a primarily secular institution, one that seems to function well. "The Indian election system," said the chief election commissioner, "after the Taj Mahal, is one of the greatest wonders of the modern world" because, though illiterate, caste-ridden, and poverty-stricken, the Indian electorate has shown "wisdom" and fooled "those conducting exit polls."

Nevertheless, religion plays an important role in many other aspects of Indian life. Hinduism is the predominant religion—practiced by 85 percent of the population—followed by Islam, Sikhism, Christianity, Buddhism, Jainism, and others. It should be added parenthetically that the Muslim League, a party of Islam, was in existence even in the early days of the freedom movement. The central government and the national parties have tolerated, and sometimes even supported, the Muslim League. This nonsecular sentiment should be viewed in the context of turmoil, violence, and anguish following the breakup of British India into India and Pakistan.

By virtue of its population of over 870 million people, India is the largest democracy in the world. Despite much internal turmoil, democratic processes have been maintained. Governments have been elected, reelected, and ousted through democratic elections at both the central and state levels. However, the development of India and its standing in the international community has been considerably limited by the size of its population. This is a source of frustration to many in light of the phenomenal growth in the agricultural, industrial, and business sectors of the economy. For example, in 1992 India's gross domestic product grew by 4.5 percent compared to only 1.0 percent growth in the United States. Yet such advances are consistently counteracted by the demands of an ever-expanding population. The population growth of India was 2.1 percent in 1991 compared to 0.7 percent in the United States. This annual increase of 17.75 million exceeds the total population of many countries.

HISTORY OF GOVERNMENT INVOLVEMENT IN SPORT

The government of India (sometimes referred to as the Union Government or Central Government) has taken a leading role in the development of sports ever since independence was gained in 1947. The following brief outline is based on the more comprehensive work of Kamlesh (1988).

The Indian government's first notable engagement in sports was its role as host of the First Asian Games in 1951. Jawaharlal Nehru, the first prime minister of India, tactfully used the first Asiad as a diplomatic tool to bring together the Asian nations. This banding of the Asian nations was the forerunner of what is presently known as the Non-aligned Movement (NAM), a third bloc of nations in addition to the Western and communist bloc countries.

Domestically, the government of India founded the Central Advisory Board of Physical Education and Recreation in 1950 to advise the government on matters relating to physical education in scholastic institutions, including the training of physical education teachers. Based on the Board's recommendations, the Indian government awarded several grants to the existing physical education training institutes to update their programs and improve facilities. Scholarships for research in physical education were also awarded, and guidelines for state governments to follow in specifying requirements for physical education teachers were provided. In addition, the first model institution of physical education, the Lakshmibai National College of Physical Education, Gwalior, was established in 1957. Currently, this college has a branch established at Trivandrum. In 1959 the government launched the National Physical Efficiency Drive to create and promote national awareness about physical fitness among its citizens. In 1965–66, the government also approved the idea of a National Fitness Corps with the goal of developing the fitness levels of the country's youth.

As it began actively promoting physical education and mass sport, the government of India also undertook several measures to promote elite sport. The first step in this regard was the formation of the All-India Council of Sports (AICS) in 1954. The AICS was to function as a liaison between the Indian Olympic Association (IOA), the national sport-governing bodies, and the government of India. This move was spurred by the sport-governing bodies' increasing reliance on the government for financial and technical support. The

AICS was to (1) serve as a coordinating link between the national sports federations/associations and the central government; (2) suggest to the government ways and means to raise the standards of games and sports; (3) make recommendations to the government on the award of grants to sports federations; (4) assist the sports federations in improving their organizational structure and their programs, including coaching of elite athletes; (5) encourage participation in international competitions by selecting specific teams worthy of government support (only those teams/athletes approved by the AICS were eligible to travel and compete abroad); (6) recommend specific plans for the construction of sports facilities around the country; and (7) recommend athletes for the Arjuna award, the highest award for outstanding sports performance.

In its continuing efforts to promote elite sport and following the recommendation of the AICS, the government of India created the Netaji Subhas National Institute of Sports (NIS) at Patiala in 1961. The primary function of the institute was to train coaches in various sports. Since then, the NIS has expanded with three more branches in Bangalore, Calcutta, and Gandhi Nagar. Other landmark events in the government's sports policy include the creation of a separate Ministry of Sports within the broader Ministry of Human Resource Development in 1982 and the establishment of the Sports Authority of India (SAI) in 1984 as the apex body for all of sport in India.

The Union Government encouraged the formation of state sports councils, based on the pattern of the All India Council of Sports to act as a liaison between the state government and the state sports associations. According to local preference, the state sports council may be either a nominated body of experts and bureaucrats—as in Punjab—or a democratically elected organization of various state sports associations and district olympic associations—as in the state of Kerala. In general, the president of the state sports council is either the state minister in charge of sport or a bureaucrat holding the sports portfolio. In order to have effective control over developmental sports activities, some states have replaced the state sports council by a statutory State Sports Authority analogous to the Sports Authority of India.

AMATEUR SPORTS

The task of developing amateur sports rests chiefly with the national sports federations/associations. These associations are voluntary organizations rooted in the state and district units and extending to clubs at the local level. The IOA acts as an umbrella for these voluntary organizations, bringing them together with representatives of the State Olympic Association and the national sports associations. The IOA's mission is "protecting and proliferating" the Olympic movement. Except for a few national sports associations such as the Board of Cricket Control in India, most of the fifty-three national sports associations (NSAs) are compulsorily affiliated to the Indian Olympic Association. Although association is mandatory according to national policy and the Olympic charter, the NSAs enjoy considerable autonomy in the formulation and implementation of developmental policies and action plans. While a few NSAs are financially independent, most receive substantial financial support from the government of India for activities such as the operation of coaching camps for their elite athletes, the organization of national championships for various age groups (senior, junior, subjunior), and the maintenance of their offices. The NSAs also sponsor teams in international competitions, subject to the approval of the Indian Olympic Association and clearance from the Union Government. In this case, the Union Government exerts considerable control. The approval process at times causes undue delay in the movement of national teams for international exposure. In order to systematize the working of the NSAs, the Union Government has issued guidelines from time to time. Regarding this as an affront to their autonomy, most NSAs have adopted a belligerent posture toward the government, often flouting the guidelines. The continuing conflict between the NSAs and the government has adversely affected the development of elite sport.

In addition to national sports activities, the state and district sport associations oversee local sports as well. This arrangement is argued to be problematic in several aspects, however. Since some sports are not popular in certain areas, for example, the club-level organization is quite meager. Another common complaint is that most officials of these sport associations have never played the sport they represent. They are either businessmen, bureaucrats, politicians, or petty officials whose lack of sports experience brings into question their ability to develop effectively the sports under their charge. Thus, it is argued that they are primarily resourceful politicians who simply "patronize" sports rather than provide competent leadership. Perhaps more importantly, the state and district associations are in a constant state of crisis and are heavily dependent on meager government funding. Consequently, they are not able to provide the necessary facilities and equipment to support their units, nor are they able to organize an adequate number of competitions. Being "autonomous," they are unaccountable for their loose organization and poor performance. Finally, they seem incapable of mobilizing resources due to lack of leadership.

At the grass-roots level of the amateur sport hierarchy are the sports clubs. It should be noted that India's club system does not achieve the organizational scope and sophistication of comparable systems in many European countries. Typically, a few individuals interested in playing a particular sport will form a club in their locality, participating in the sport in a recreational and leisurely manner. As they gain some proficiency in the sport, they may seek affiliation with the district sport association and enter a few competitions. If and when they are successful in tournaments, the local public may show greater interest in the club and support it through donations. Some of these clubs have existed for a long time and have produced outstanding athletes. But their success is largely dependent on the initiative and tenacity of the playing members, and, to some extent, that of the local patrons. Most clubs exist in India's urban areas.

In the countryside, which comprises 85 percent of India's population, sports clubs are almost nonexistent, leaving a vast reservoir of untapped sporting talent.

PROFESSIONAL SPORTS

In India, sports are largely an amateur pursuit. However, games like cricket, golf, soccer, billiards and snooker, and lawn tennis have professional leagues that are controlled by the national federations of the respective sports. Government control over professional sports activities is virtually nonexistent.

Some professional sports such as billiards, snooker, and lawn tennis are, and have historically been, dominated by the higher economic strata of Indian society. In contrast, soccer and cricket have a much larger base. Professional soccer, for instance, is the product of club culture and is very popular in the east and in the south. The Mohan Bagan, Mohamedan Sporting, and East Bengal, to mention a few, are famous professional soccer clubs of Calcutta. Professional soccer is also very popular in Goa, with its famous Salgaonkar Club. Quite a number of soccer clubs are owned and operated by large business houses such as JCT, Titanium, and Mahindra & Mahindra, whose players participate at both the amateur and professional level. Their existence and excellence are owed to their professional status and the sponsorship they receive from their employers. In the final analysis, however, the status and standard of professional sports are no match to those found in Europe or the United States.

INTERNATIONALIZATION OF SPORT

India was exposed to the modern sports world through British officers and native feudal princes who frequented Europe during the heyday of the British regime. The rulers of the erstwhile princely states of Patiala, Jaipur, Cooch Bihar, Jamnager, Jodhpur, Baroda, and scores of others were themselves keen athletes and patronized a number of sports never known in India before. In 1920 Harry Crowe Buck, an American and Christian missionary, established the YMCA College of Physical Education at Madras to prepare physical education teachers for schools. This served as a catalyst for the systematic expansion of modern games and sports in the country. Buck is also credited with the formation of the Indian Olympic Association in 1927, which still plays an important role in spearheading the sports movement in India.

In 1920 a contingent of five Indian track and field athletes and a wrestler competed in the seventh Olympic Games at Antwerp, marking the first Indian participation in Olympic sports. After the Indian Olympic Games were conducted in 1923 under British rule, eight Indian athletes were sponsored to take part in the eighth Olympic Games in 1924 at Paris. By this time, field hockey had become a popular sport in the armed forces, and the Indian Olympic Association, competing under the British banner, fielded a hockey team at the ninth Olympic Games in 1928 at Amsterdam. Captained by Dhyan Chand (ever remembered as "Hockey Wizard" all over the world), the hockey team won the Olympic gold. Until the seventeenth Olympic Games (Rome, 1960), the Indian hockey team continued to dominate Olympic competitions, when, for the first time, it lost the gold to Pakistan. So emotionally attached are the Indian people to hockey that they call it their national game. Despite untiring efforts, India's fortunes in the game at the Asiads, Olympics, and World Cups have fluctuated. Except for victories at the twenty-second Olympic Games at Moscow and the World Cup in 1975, the Indian hockey squads have not performed well in international competitions in the last three decades.

Cricket is another major sports event in which India has an excellent track record. Indian teams have won the World Cup, the Sharjah Cup, and many other important competitions in both one-day and five-day tests. World-record holders like Sunil Gawaskar and Kapil Dev are the most recent stars of Indian cricket. The electronic media have helped cricket to become a popular activity among urban youth in India. It is played with gusto in streets and open spaces. The Cricket Control Board of India is probably the richest sports association in India.

Other sports in which Indians have shown credible performances in international competitions—especially in the Asian championships—include archery, track and field, wrestling, boxing, weightlifting, badminton, and lawn tennis. In archery, Limba Ram equaled the world record; in track and field, Milkha Singh broke the Olympic record in 400 meters in 1960; and P. T. Usha dazzled the nation with four golds at 1986 Seoul Asiad. In badminton, Prakash Padukone won in World Cup competitions during the 1980s. In lawn tennis, Leander Paes won the junior title at Wimbledon in 1991. Such performances reflect the efforts and keenness of the Indian people to secure a place in international sports. Unfortunately, however, India has not been consistent in its performance. In particular, Indian volleyball and soccer teams—top-rated teams in Asia during the 1950s and 1960s—have not performed well in recent years.

In order to gain greater international exposure for athletes and to create enthusiasm for competitive sports among the masses, India has made many efforts to initiate and organize international competitions on its own soil. The ninth Asian Games (1982) were held in New Delhi as part of an effort to build a strong foundation for international sports competitions in the country. The infrastructure created for this event has facilitated a competition boom. As a result, more and more international track and field invitational meets are being hosted in New Delhi and elsewhere.

In 1983 the South Asian Federation (SAF) Games were instituted chiefly due to India's initiative. Held every other year, the games bring together India, Pakistan, Nepal, Bangladesh, Sri Lanka, Bhutan, and Maldives, and most recently, Afghanistan and Uzbekistan. The implicit objective is to establish greater solidarity and cooperation among the member countries through the medium of sport. Since the inception of the SAF Games, India has enjoyed acknowledged superiority in most major sports, including track and field, basketball, soccer, shooting, swimming, volleyball, table tennis, lawn tennis, kabaddi, weightlifting, and the like. For instance, at the fourth SAF Games held in Islamabad, Pakistan, in October 1989, India won sixty-one gold, forty-three silver, and twenty bronze medals in eleven disciplines. India's tally at the fifth SAF Games held in Colombo, Sri Lanka, in December 1991 in ten sports disciplines was sixty-four gold, fifty-nine silver, and forty-one bronze. At the sixth SAF Games at Dhaka, Bangladesh, in December 1993, the Indian contingent amassed sixty-one gold, forty-five silver, and thirty-one bronze.

In the Commonwealth Games, Indian athletes have also fared well. At the fourteenth Commonwealth Games in 1990 at Auckland, New Zealand, Indian teams contested in six disciplines: badminton, boxing, bowling, judo, shooting, and weightlifting. In weightlifting alone, their tally was twelve gold, seven silver, and five bronze.

Regarding the government's stance on the internationalization of sport, the national sports policy hints at "a selective approach," one that "concentrates on such of the sports disciplines in which the country has performed reasonably well in the past two decades." The list of disciplines to be funded by the government is not a fixed list, but a dynamic one where additions and deletions are made on the basis of actual performance in the international scene. Keeping fiscal constraints in mind, a realistic assessment of likely achievements in different disciplines is made, informing decisions about actual participation in events like the Olympics and Asian Games. Although winning is emphasized, the government has a fairly liberal attitude on this issue, realizing that participation is important in its own right.

CITIZEN PARTICIPATION

Developing a sports culture and promoting sport as a "mass movement" in a country with such diverse cultural nuances, economic strata, and philosophies cannot be considered the sole responsibility of the government. Participation by individual citizens and private organizations is necessary as well. Unfortunately, the country's social and economic problems are so overwhelming that the average citizen has no time for sports.

Few official surveys of public interest in sports have been conducted. However, several informal studies have been undertaken by physical education students at the master's degree level at various institutions. The data include opinion polls of freshmen at physical education colleges, interviews with scholastic and collegiate heads, and career-preference polls of pre-degree students. Overall, these surveys suggest a negative attitude toward games and sports. Generally, parents and teachers do not encourage young children to play. Rather, participation in sports is regarded as a sheer waste of time, energy, and money. Some children find leisure time constrained by their need to prepare and compete for admission into highly valued fields such as engineering and medicine, while others are concerned primarily with the search for increasingly scarce jobs. Paradoxically, parents and teachers talk in undertones about children's health and fitness, but often they do not allow children to devote time to sports. While the middle and upper classes consciously reject sports in favor of other goals, those in the lower class, especially in the villages, have hardly any concept of physical education and sports. For the common man in India, the bare necessities of life overshadow all other concerns. Thus, the common person's attitude toward sports as a source of health, fitness, and vigor is generally indifferent.

In terms of official educational policy, physical exercise and sports have no specified slots in the school schedule. Seven hours of continuous academics per day, travel time to and from school, and homework leave little time for children to engage in sports. School and college playgrounds are seldom occupied, and at community sports complexes, attendance is low. Even where compulsory physical education and sports programs have been implemented, they do not yield much in terms of health excellence and sport performance, owing largely to minimal interest on the part of academicians and other authorities.

In the case of professional sports—with the possible exceptions of soccer and cricket—the popular response to sport competitions is not very enthusiastic. At times—especially during international sports competitions, such as World Cups—the number of spectators may be quite high. However, not all sports competitions draw the same number of enthusiasts. Traditional sports such as bullock-cart races, bull-chase, weightlifting, tug-of-war, wrestling, kabaddi, kho-kho, and malklamb, which are organized during the seasonal festivals in various regions, attract throngs of rural people as participants and spectators. Yet at other national sports championships and festivals, spectator stands are usually almost empty. More and more people, it seems, prefer to stay indoors and watch sports programs on television. This lack of public interest may be another reason why state and local governments do not feel obliged or compelled to create more sports facilities for their citizens.

The electronic media, especially television, play a significant and growing role in bringing sports closer to the people. The government-controlled television network, Doordarshan, has allotted a separate channel for sport programs, including live telecasts of all important domestic and international sport events. Thus, Indians are more aware of soccer World Cups, cricket fixtures, Olympic Games, Asiads, and the like, than ever before.

Television has several implications for the development of sports culture in India. Telecasts of well-planned fitness programs involving aerobics, calisthenics, yoga, and fitness training regimens for elite athletes have increased the level of sports consciousness. Hard data are not available to assess the impact of this venture, although it is believed that the general population is becoming more aware of fitness and sport. Scholastic and collegiate students in particular have greater exposure to elite and competitive sports through television. A growing number of corporations and industries are sponsoring sports events in exchange for publicity and advertising for their products and services. Finally, the television appearances of top international athletes may serve as a potential motivating force for young children to become involved in sports. However, these processes are somewhat ambiguous and not easily measured in quantitative terms.

At the international level, sports competitions have high financial stakes on account of corporate sponsorships. This trend has had a very positive impact on the sports scenario in India, as Indian corporations have capitalized on the publicity their products and goods can receive through sponsorship of sports. The government of India has recently permitted these industries and businesses to deduct expenditures for sports promotion from their taxable income. Such deductions may include contributions to sports infrastructure, donations to the Sports Authority of India, sponsorship of sports competitions, establishment of sports academies to groom young talent, sponsorship of national sports squads in recognized international competitions, provision of kits to national teams, and the like. This policy gives business houses and private companies a strong incentive to invest heavily in the development of sports.

In fact, the following public-sector businesses have established national academies for various sports that tap talent and train for sport excellence:

Air India	National Academy for Hockey, National Stadium, New Delhi
Steel Authority	National Academy for Handball at Bhilai; Regional Academy for Hockey for Tribal Youth at Rourkela
Central Excise	Tennis and archery at Calcutta
Goodrich	Chess Academy at Calcutta

The following sports academies are to be established in the near future:

Bharat Petroleum	Swimming academies at Madras
Port Trust	Volleyball, athletics, and hockey academies at Bangalore
Vijayawada Corporation	Municipal Badminton Academy

Similarly, Tatas (i.e., TISCO and TELCO) have patronized sports for a long time, employing young athletes, giving them the best opportunities for training, and contributing a great deal to the formation of national teams for international competitions. Through such arrangements, players are assured not only of excellent training facilities and coaching, but also employment. As a result, athletes are able to concentrate on performance knowing that they have secure financial support. Tatas's contribution to the promotion of sports is exemplary. A large number of track and field athletes, cyclists, and archers have enjoyed highly successful careers through their support. The ITC (Indian Tobacco Company) Group of Industries has also been a major sponsor in the national and international track and field competitions held in India, contributing millions of rupees to the identification and training of talented young athletes. The ITC also provides large sums of money, in the form of incentives and awards, to winners of the International Track and Field Championships. In the same way, MRF (Madras), Air India (Bombay), and many other business concerns are now involving themselves in the promotion of cricket, archery, and hockey, respectively. Thus, the business world is increasingly enmeshed with the sports world, with both deriving substantial benefits.

Despite these trends, the economic importance of games and sports to the nation in general is yet to be properly realized. On account of other, more pressing issues, sports as a means of economic development has little priority on the nation's policy agenda. Neither the municipalities of the urban areas nor the village councils (*panchayats*) in the rural areas pay much attention to the development of facilities for games and sports. The state governments do, for their part, encourage sports activities among village folk and provide some financial support, but much more is possible in terms of formal organization. In fact, public participation in sports in economic terms is almost nonexistent, and it is uncertain what the future holds.

GOVERNMENT INVOLVEMENT

Sports and physical education have always been associated with public education which, until recently, was a state responsibility. Now it is shared with other levels of government, but sports continue to be dominated by the state. India's National Policy on Education (1986) contains a Resolution on national sports policy which stresses that the "importance of participation in sports and physical education activities for good health, a high degree of physical fitness, increase in individual productivity, and also its value as a means of beneficial recreation promoting social harmony and discipline is well-established." Reflecting the government's desire to raise the national standards of games and sports, central and state governments have been enjoined "to accord to sports and physical education a very high priority in the process of all around development."

Against this background, and within the framework of the national sports policy, the government of India has developed several "schemes" to provide financial support for athletes, sports organizations, and the construction of sports infrastructure. The central allocation for promotional activities has been raised from Rs. 200 million[1] in the Seventh Five-Year Plan to around Rs. 500 million in the eighth Five-Year Plan beginning in 1991. In a significant policy measure, the government has granted exemptions from import duties on sports equipment purchased by individuals and sports associations, as well as an income tax exemption for awards and prizes won by athletes. As noted earlier, the industrial/ business houses that contribute financially to the promotion of sports are fully exempted from the payment of income tax on expenditures incurred through creation of sport infrastructure, purchase of equipment, operation of sports academies, and sponsorship of teams or individuals. Thus, many sports persons and sports organizations are receiving assistance from both large and small business houses. Many major industrial enterprises are adopting one or more sports disciplines and share the burden of establishing sports academies dedicated to single disciplines.

The central and state governments also give special incentives directly to athletes. For example, 1 to 3 percent of administrative jobs in the government and corporate sectors are reserved for sports persons. Elite junior athletes receive special admissions consideration in college and university courses otherwise beyond their reach, based on the recommendations of the state sports councils.

IMPORTANT GOVERNMENT POLICIES

Grants for Creation of Sports Infrastructure

The government of India assists state governments and local organizations in the construction of modern facilities—such as synthetic athletic tracks and artificial hockey surfaces—by financing up to 50 percent of the project costs, with a ceiling of 5 million rupees. By the end of 1992, 245 projects of such nature had been financed by the government of India in thirty-one states and Union Territories. About 1,752 of these projects are yet to be completed because the state governments or sponsoring organizations cannot meet the 50 percent matching funds required for recipients of central assistance. The state governments are always under greater financial strain than the Union Government. Consequently, higher motivation and greater incentives in this regard are being provided to the state governments for the completion of these projects and the initiation of the new ones. The most salient feature of this policy has been the promotion of a state sports training complex in each state. As of 1994, six such complexes had been approved. By the end of 1990, synthetic tracks for track and field events had been installed at Calcutta, Trivandrum, Lucknow, Gwalior, and Amritsar. In addition, synthetic tracks and hockey surfaces have also been laid at five centers of the Sports Authority of India—namely Bangalore, Gandhi Nagar, Patiala, Calcutta, and New Delhi.

Grants to Rural Schools

According to national sports policy, grants of up to Rs. 100,000 are given to build basic sports facilities in rural schools. No matching contribution is required, and the state governments and schools have only to guarantee that the facilities created with this grant will be maintained. Unfortunately, a large number of schools could not avail themselves of this opportunity because of inadequate space. Nevertheless, from 1991 to 1992, sixty-eight schools received assistance of Rs. 5.8 million for this purpose.

National Sports Organization Program

This program covers three vital aspects of sports development in colleges and universities—considered the backbone of sports endeavors. These aspects are (1) creation of sports infrastructure in universities and colleges, (2) organization of interuniversity tournaments, and (3) scholarships to talented university and college students. The implementing agency of this scheme is the University Grants Commission (UGC). In the first aspect of the scheme, that is, infrastructure development, each project proposed by a university or college is funded on the basis of a 75:25 cost ratio. However, ceilings have been set, such as Rs. 750,000 for the construction of a running track or an indoor stadium/gymnasium, and Rs. 75,000 for the development of playing fields. Moreover, the UGC provides grants to colleges and universities—up to Rs. 150,000—for the purchase of sports equipment of a nonexpendable nature, without any matching contribution required from the recipient institution. Under the second aspect, that is, organization of interuniversity tournaments, financial assistance is provided to the Association of Indian Universities for organizing interuniversity tournaments, for conducting coaching camps to prepare Indian university contingents for international competitions, and for preparing university teams for participation in national championships. With respect to thirteen specified disciplines, the winning universities are awarded Rs. 50,000 as first prize, Rs. 30,000 as second prize, and Rs. 20,000 as third prize. In addition, a trophy is awarded to the winning university along with a cash prize of Rs. 50,000; universities coming in second and third also receive cash awards that are to be utilized for the development of sports facilities. Finally, the Sports Authority of India disperses individual scholarships of Rs. 3,600 per annum to outstanding sports persons. About 300 new scholarships are awarded every year. The scholarships are renewed annually, provided the holders continue to maintain or improve the level of achievements.

Grants to State Sports Councils

This policy is considered crucial to the broad-basing of sports in the country by involving an ever-increasing number of people in sports activities at the grass-roots level. Under this scheme, matching financial assistance is provided to the State Sports Councils for the development of playing fields, stadiums, swimming pools, sports complexes, and improvement of existing infrastructure. The total amount of grants awarded to twenty-five states and seven union territories through this policy was more than Rs. 460 million during 1991–92. Besides this, the national government has also decided to extend financial assistance for the construction of one state-level complex per state, financing 50 percent of the cost of the project, subject to a maximum of Rs. 20 million.

Sports Projects Development Area (SPDA) Scheme

In 1987 the government of India initiated SPDA centers in all states and union territories to provide in-house coaching facilities for talented youth. The program is generally implemented by the central government and the state/UT governments. Each SPDA center covers 80 to 100 developmental blocks that have linkage with the regional centers of the SAI at the national level, and block model centers at the grass-roots level. Each SPDA center caters to a maximum of four Olympic disciplines based on their popularity in the area. In addition, one or two indigenous games are also promoted at the center. The Olympic disciplines generally include track and field, gymnastics, and swimming. The major objective of the program is to serve the rural areas comprising 80 percent of India's population. Fifty percent of the cost of the project—subject to a maximum of Rs. 5 million—is provided by the government of India, and the remainder is financed by the state/UT government. Each SPDA is expected to cost approximately Rs. 10 million. Out of seventy-eight SPDA centers approved, twenty-four were operational as of 1994, and the remaining are likely to become functional during the eightieth Five-Year Plan.

Assistance to National Sports Federations

Otherwise autonomous, the fifty-three national sports associations/federations and the Indian Olympic Association are financially assisted in conducting national championships and organizing coaching camps for preparation of teams for national and international tournaments. The government also subsidizes the purchase of sports equipment by the national sports federations. Limited secretarial support is given through a salary reimbursement for the joint/assistant secretary of a federation. By the end of January 1992, about Rs. 3.78 million had been spent under this policy.

Prize Money for Schools

Introduced in 1986, with the objective of promoting sports in schools, this scheme carries a cash prize of Rs. 10,000 awarded annually to secondary and higher secondary schools winning the district interschool tournament conducted by the School Games Federation of India in the disciplines of athletics, hockey, basketball, volleyball, and football. A maximum of Rs. 90,000 is awarded annually in each district. The award is to be invested by the school management for district promotion of sports, including the construction of playgrounds and the purchase of sports equipment. A basic weakness of the scheme is that the districts are unable to conduct tournaments in all disciplines. Moreover, some schools lack resources and established teams and are unable to participate. This is especially true in the case of rural schools.

Cash Awards to Medal Winners in International Events

Introduced in 1986, awards ranging from Rs. 5,000 to Rs. 50,000 are given for winning medals in specified international sports events in all disciplines included in the Olympics, the Asiad, and the Commonwealth games. These awards are also given in the disciplines of chess and billiards/snookers. The objective is to help the sports persons sustain motivation and maintain themselves with dignity.

Travel Grant to Sports Scholarships/Research Workers

In pursuance of the resolution of the national sports policy of 1984, travel grants are provided to sports scholars and research workers for undertaking specialized training and research abroad, or for attending international academic and scientific conferences with the express objective of promoting and encouraging research and development in sports and physical education.

National Welfare Fund for Sport Persons

The National Welfare Fund for Sports Persons and their families was created in 1982, primarily to assist outstanding former athletes. This financial support is generally in the form of a monthly pension of up to Rs. 1500. Lump-sum grants are also given for medical treatment and injury.

Arjuna Award

This award was instituted in 1961 as the highest national recognition of distinguished persons. The recipient is given a bronze statuette of Arjuna, a scroll, and a cash award of Rs. 40,000 along with a monogram, blazer, and a tie. To be eligible for this award, the candidate should have displayed consistently outstanding performance at the national and international level for the three years preceding the year of the award and excellence in the year of the award. The recipient should also have a high sense of discipline, sportsmanship, and outstanding qualities of leadership. The number of sports persons honored with the Arjuna award through 1994 is roughly 500.

Dronacharya Award

Instituted in 1985, this award is meant to honor and accord recognition to Indian coaches of eminence who have trained sports persons or teams achieving outstanding results in international events during the three years preceding the year of the award. The award consists of Rs. 50,000, a plaque, a scroll, a blazer, and a tie.

REGULATORY POLICIES

Understanding the regulatory policies of the government of India is facilitated by Figure 10.1, which illustrates the organizational structure of sport governance within the country. The development of organized sport in India is controlled

Figure 10.1
Organizational Structure of Sports Administration in India

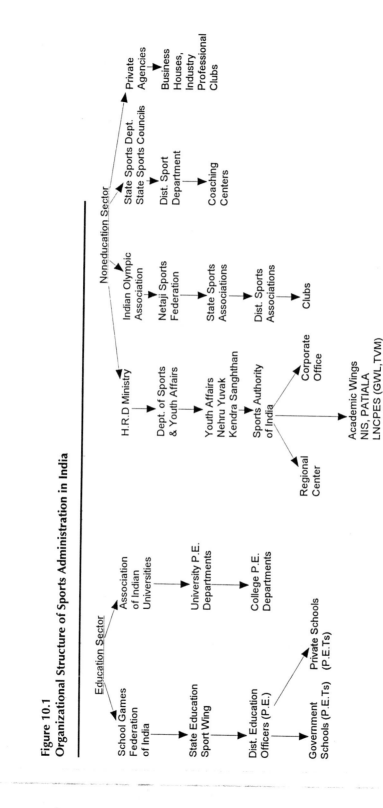

by the education and the noneducation sectors at the top. The hierarchical structure shown in the diagram is basically fixed, but there is overlap as well as very close liaison between some agencies.

In general, government regulations do not specifically aim to streamline the development of sport under the auspices of various sectors. While the government has been issuing certain directives and guidelines for the development of sport, these directives do not have statutory status.

The activities of the sports associations are more or less regulated by the directives and policies of the Indian Olympic Association on the one hand and the respective international federations on the other. The government does not interfere at all in their routines. It does, however, render developmental assistance in terms of both finance and infrastructure. The Sports Authority of India looks after the interests of the government insofar as the working of the sports associations is concerned. The Department of Sports and the Sports Authority of India perform government watchdog functions, overseeing training, talent scouting, organization of competitions, foreign travels of the national teams, elections of the office bearers, and so on. More often than not, conflicts of power arise between the government and the national sport associations. In contrast, the government has considerable influence on sport development within the education sector.

Education Sector

Schools

At the school level, it is mandatory that each school have at least one physical education teacher. The ideal student/teacher ratio suggested by the Central Advisory Board of Physical Education and Recreation in the National Plan of Physical Education (1956) is 250:1. Unfortunately, the state of physical education in the schools—whether public or private—is simply weak.

There are many reasons for the lack of a strong physical education program. In most states, physical education is not a compulsory subject, and as such, the duty of the physical education teacher is confined basically to occasionally preparing teams for interscholastic tournaments. In addition, no regular timetable exists for physical education classes, and most schools, especially those in congested urban areas, are not equipped with playgrounds. Neither the physical education teacher, nor the headmaster, nor any other official in the educational hierarchy is held accountable for the state of physical education and sport in schools. Physical education teachers generally are regarded as mere appendages to the educational system.

A small amount of money is collected from students for a sport fund, but this is completely inadequate to meet needs. Government allocations for sports in schools are literally nil, and physical education is given the lowest priority in both financial and operational matters. A few privately managed schools of the elite category place some emphasis on games and sports, providing regular clas- ses and increased funding for sports competitions. In some states, like Punjab, an effort has been made to make physical education and sport a curricular ac- tivity. However, the outcomes, in terms of mass participation and developing talent, have so far belied expectations. There have been some innovations, such as the establishment of states' Sports Schools in Punjab and Kerala. In a few schools where facilities for certain games and sports exist, sports hostels fully funded by the state and central exchequer have also been established. These efforts have met with some success but do not even come close to meeting demand, given the vastness of the country and size of the population.

At the district education level, one assistant district education officer or an official of the same rank supervises physical education in the schools. This officer is responsible for holding interscholastic tournaments within the district, as decided upon by a committee composed of institutional officials and promi- nent physical education teachers. The coaching and sponsoring of district teams for state meets also falls under the purview of the district physical education officer. At the state level, an officer known as sports organizer or assistant director of public instruction is in charge of coaching and training state teams, conducting state tournaments, and sponsoring state teams for the national cham- pionships. This physical education wing receives a budgetary allocation from Department of Education funds. It also receives part of the school sports fund collected from the students.

Another organization, the School Games Federation of India (SGFI), prepares an annual calendar of national sports events, organizes national school coaching activities, and sponsors teams for international competitions. The SGFI receives financial assistance from IOA and the Union Government at par with other NSAs.

Colleges/Universities

In India, higher education is offered through colleges affiliated to a larger university. While some universities do not have affiliated colleges, the majority of universities are composed of affiliated colleges located in different parts of the region. These colleges may be private or public, religious or secular.

Unlike Western colleges and universities, Indian schools do not encourage or foster competitive sports. The colleges have at least one director of physical education who, in terms of status, salary, and perks, is treated as equivalent with other college teachers. In the absence of regular classes, his main function is to oversee coaching activities and to organize tournaments. With the exception of one or two state systems, sports and physical education are not curricular sub- jects.

The university department of sport/physical education has two functions: (1) to organize sports activities and coaching camps for the university teams and staff, and (2) to conduct intercollegiate tournaments and sponsor university teams for interuniversity championships. Most universities have reasonably good sports complexes that allow them to organize interuniversity tournaments from time to time, depending on other conditions. Funding comes from the main budget of the university, as well as from collections made from the affiliated colleges. In some universities, sports management and teaching are concurrent activities. The workings of the physical education departments are regulated by university statute.

The Association of Indian Universities has a University Sports Control Board that prepares the annual calendar of sports events; provides guidelines for the conduct of interuniversity tournaments; partially finances the interuniversity tournaments; formulates eligibility criteria for the athletes and teams participating in the interuniversity tournaments; sponsors combined-university teams to the national championships; and organizes coaching and arranges sponsorship for the Indian University Teams to participate in the World Universiads. The Association of Indian Universities, though fully funded by the government of India, autonomously frames its own sports policies. Both the School Games Federation of India and the Association of Indian Universities are affiliated units of the Indian Olympic Association and enjoy governmental facilities and favors at par with other sports associations. There is little governmental interference in the working of these organizations.

NONEDUCATION SECTOR

Ministry of Human Resource Development (HRD)

Created in 1985, the HRD integrates all efforts for the development of human potential in the areas of education, youth, women and children, arts, culture, and sports. A Central Advisory Board of Education comprises eminent educators, officials, educational scientists and technologists, and representatives of the states who help the government to frame national policies on education. A committee of this Board has been formed to suggest ways and means to implement effectively physical education and sports in the educational institutions of the country.

The Department of Youth Affairs and Sports, under the charge of a minister of state and headed by a secretary, deals with matters relating to (1) sport infrastructure, physical education, sport incentives, awards, and welfare of athletes; (2) the Sports Authority of India, the national sports federations, and the Indian Olympic Association; (3) the National Youth Federation, Nehru Yuvak Sangathan, the training of youth, youth clubs, financial assistance to voluntary organizations, the National Service Scheme; and (4) coordination, publicity, production, and distribution of literature and grants-in-aid.

The Sports Authority of India (SAI) was instituted by the government of India in 1984 as a registered society with the objective of promoting sports and games in the country. Its role is to manage, maintain, and ensure proper use of various sports facilities and infrastructure created for the Asiad 1982 at New Delhi. The prime minister of India is the president of the Society, and the HRD minister serves as vice-president and chairman of the governing body; the minister of state for sports and youth affairs acts as vice-chairperson. The SAI has four functional wings with specific areas of action:

1. *Academic Wing* for the training of coaches and for research and development in sports, located at Netaji Subhas National Institute of Sports, Patiala.
2. *Academic Wing* for physical education and research and development in physical education, located at Lakshmibai National College of Physical Education at Gwalior (M.P.), and Trivandrum (Kerala).
3. *Operational Wing* for general sports promotion and identification and nurture of young talent.
4. *TEAMS Wing (Training of Elite Athletes and Management Support)* for long-term training of elite sports persons and preparation of national teams in specific disciplines for targeted international competitions.

The SAI has six regional centers, each of which is under the charge of a regional director with an advisory committee to oversee and advise on the implementation of various policies and programs of the SAI. Apart from the academic pursuit of producing competent coaches, four regional centers—located at Patiala, Bangalore, Calcutta, and Gandhi Nagar—also train talented youth and serve as venues for state, regional, and national level sports programs such as the National Sports Talent Contest (NSTC), the Special Area Games (SAG), the Sports Hostel Scheme, and the National Coaching Scheme.

The SAI is also responsible for implementing various central programs such as the Sports Project Development Area (SPDA), the Scholarship Scheme, the Promotion of Sports among Women, and the All India Rural Sports Tournament. The SAI is a medium through which the government of India provides coaching facilities, equipment, personnel, and scientific support to the national federations, as well as controls in such areas as the selection of individuals and teams for the international competitions and their sponsorship. In order to accommodate a variety of views regarding sports promotion in the country, people from various backgrounds—including veteran athletes, journalists, administrators, bureaucrats, sports scientists, statesmen, politicians, and architects—have been nominated to various committees of the Department of Sport and Youth Affairs and the Sports Authority of India. Nearly ideal facilities for coaching and scientific support have been created at various SAI centers. The regional centers of the SAI have direct liaisons with the state sports departments. This proximity helps the state governments to benefit from the central schemes and to receive and utilize central grants easily and quickly.

The Indian Olympic Association and National Sports Federations

Within the ambit of the national sports policy, the government of India provides financial assistance to the national sports associations (NSAs), as do the state governments to the state associations. In addition, the NSAs have been given office accommodations and other facilities at the Jawaharlal Nehru Stadium, New Delhi, which is also the Central Office of the Sports Authority of India. The government of India also has a policy to provide the national sports federations with standard sports equipment at subsidized rates, and it imports the equipment from abroad on their behalf.

As explained earlier, neither the national nor the state governments have administrative or regulatory control over the NSAs and their subordinate state-level organizations. Except for technical matters—for which they are answerable to the respective international federation—the NSAs are completely autonomous. Elections to these sports organizations are held every four years, and in the case of any dispute, the matter is referred to either the Indian Olympic Association (in the case of National Federations) or the State Olympic Association (in the case of State Sport Associations). Twelve years ago, the government of India issued clear guidelines regarding the election of officeholders, terms of office, and conduct of tournaments, but these guidelines were not followed at all. Most of the NSAs considered this action an affront to their autonomy, which is guaranteed under the Olympic Charter.

State Sports Departments

The state department of sports and youth affairs is usually headed by a bureaucrat. It has district centers that are administered by a district sports officer who is generally a senior, trained, professional coach. Each district has a central sports complex and many coaching centers at the block level. Several coaches work under the control of the district sport officer. These coaches impart training to the young and old alike at various coaching centers; help the district sport associations and clubs to prepare teams for competitions; accompany the teams at state or national competitions; and help school and college teams wherever necessary. The coaches and other sports personnel draw salaries from the public exchequer and are permanent government employees. Their appointments, transfers, service conditions, and in-service training are regulated by the state governments.

It must be noted, however, that because of overlapping objectives, activities, and client groups, some friction has arisen between the Education Department and the Department of Sports. The fact that the state sports departments benefit much more from central schemes than the Education Department contributes to the hostility. Furthermore, several of the sports hostels established by the state sports departments are located in schools and colleges, which is a strain on their resources.

The structure of state sports councils varies from state to state. In some states, the state sports council is a democratically elected body representing the district sports councils and state sports associations. In others, it is a purely state-nominated body. The role of the elected state sports councils is much larger, with a stronger hold on the state associations, while state nominated councils have a nominal role. All the state sports associations are required to be recognized by the state sport councils for the purpose of financial grants and coaching camps while the state government plays a regulatory role.

Private Agencies

Professional sports clubs and training centers (*gymkhanas*) have existed for a long time in India and have played a significant role in the development of sports in the country. However, with the exception of cricket and soccer, professionalism is not pervasive. Tennis professionals in India are few, and are a product of private clubs and gymkhanas. The clubs and gymkhanas are self-financing and self-sustaining institutions.

Recently, large business houses and companies have begun to show interest in promoting sports by financing various sports competitions and setting up sports academies. Their major aim is to promote their business interests through the medium of sport. As noted earlier, they receive tax benefits for money spent on sports promotion. There are no regulatory policies governing these private ventures.

Central-State Government Relations

A few states, like Andhra Pradesh and Tamil Nadu, have chosen to establish a State Sports Authority in accordance with the national sports policy. As far as objectives are concerned, there is neither contradiction nor confrontation between the national and the state sport policy. The state governments are free to pursue their own policies in dealing with sports organizations and institutions. More often than not, they lean heavily on central financial support.

Periodically, the Ministry of Youth Affairs and Sports holds a conference with the state governments under the chairmanship of the union minister for human resource development and sports. The agenda items of these conferences are crucial to the development of sports in the states. At one such conference, held on November 18, 1991, state governments were apprised of measures that the central government was taking to help them strengthen various sports promotion schemes. The state governments were encouraged to take optimal advantage of the central schemes, whereupon the central government was requested to be more liberal in awarding grants to the state governments. The state governments also expressed appreciation for the various schemes introduced by the center. The conference put equal emphasis on improvement of infrastructure, orientation for in-service physical educators and coaches, a well-concerted effort for preparing teams for national and international competitions, and scientific support.

Sport, being a state responsibility, is under the complete control of the state governments, and the role of the Union Government is secondary. The Union Government may be characterized as a policymaking and supporting agency, with the states as the executive units. There are, in fact, no written agreements between the central government and the states as far as general sports policy is concerned, although the states are expected to play a major role in sports development. Agreements exist for the implementation of a number of schemes between state and local governments and the central government. For instance, for the establishment of a SAI center as large as the regional center at Bangalore or LNCPE at Trivandrum, or as small as an SPDA or NSTC in a remote place, the state governments are committed to provide buildings, land, and a token financial grant for the establishment of such a center, so that there is a feeling of attachment on the part of the state government. These centers, in fact, form a binding commitment between the state and the central government. The local managing committees of these centers generally are composed of state officials, representatives of sport associations, and senior officers and heads of the respective centers. Day-to-day administration of the center is the responsibility of the center head in consultation with the local managing committee, but the regional centers or the Sport Authority of India/Department of Sports decide on policy matters.

In summary, the central government's directions to the states in matters concerning sports are generally in the form of guidelines that may or may not be followed. Sports are still a low-priority area, and annual budgetary allocations are correspondingly low. Moreover, the states rarely sign any sport protocols with foreign countries; it is only the central government that does so. The more active states manage to get a larger share of monetary assistance from the central government for building infrastructure and importing equipment. Operational aspects of sports and physical education are the prerogative of the states.

ANALYSIS OF VARIOUS POLICY GOALS

With regard to games and sports, the National Policy of Education (NPE) of 1968 emphasized "inspiring the physical fitness and sportsmanship of the average student, as well as those who excel in this department." The need for "playing fields and other facilities" was given priority. The 1979 NPE recognized as physical education sports, games, and athletics, including rural sports, indigenous games, and yoga exercises, as "part of education at various levels," with emphasis on "health and fitness . . . at all stages." "Effort should be made," stated the NPE, "to locate talent among boys and girls and facilities should be provided to enable them to develop their capacities and attain national and international standards of excellence in sports.'' It is significant to note that these policies are mere statements devoid of time-bound action plans and targets. The NPE contains a detailed resolution on national sports policy which recognizes the right of every individual to participate in games and sports, and the necessity of raising the national standards for Indian athletes in international competitions. It enjoins the central and state governments to accord ''a very high priority'' to various developmental aspects of physical education and sports. The implementation of the national sport policy was, in fact, effectively taken up only during the seventh Five-Year Plan, in 1985–86.

Before drafting a program of action for implementing the national sports policy for the next five years and beyond, a review of all the current policies of the union department of sports and the Sports Authority of India was undertaken. State governments, members of Parliament, national sports federations, eminent sports persons, and other nongovernment agencies participated in this review. Broadly speaking, there was a consensus that, while the objectives presented in the 1986 national sports policy are comprehensive, there are serious flaws in the area of implementation, including:

1. Failure to make physical education and sports integral and compulsory parts of the school curriculum.

2. Poor coordination between various government and nongovernment agencies involved in this enormous task.

3. Lack of investment in sports and sport promotion by both the public and private sectors.

4. Financially weak and poorly managed sports bodies at various levels.

5. Lack of quality and reasonably priced sporting equipment and goods.

6. Weak structure of domestic sports competitions.

7. Inadequate media promotion of physical education and sports.

8. Lack of infrastructure and poor utilization of existing infrastructure.

Goals for Domestic Sports

The main goal of the national sports policy is to create a national environment in which physical education and sports enjoy high priority, and young children are encouraged to take part in these activities and remain motivated throughout their careers. The specific goals enumerated in the national sports policy include:

1. Introducing physical education, sports, and games in the daily school timetable as a regular activity.

2. Arranging for teacher training: in addition to regular physical education teachers, the subject teachers are to be oriented in sports.

3. Providing basic infrastructure for sports and games.

4. Providing basic and simple equipment support.

5. Introducing a system of continuous competitive exposure at the school, college, and university level.

6. Providing special incentives, such as concessional marks for class promotion and admission to college for talented young athletes, and employment opportunities in the public and private sectors.

7. Identifying talented athletes and providing coaching and training facilities for them.

These goals are somewhat lofty and do not seem to be commensurate with existing situations such as the growing financial crisis and the population explosion, which inhibit all government efforts to ameliorate living conditions, much less raise the standard of sport. The Action Plan does not suggest any short-term, targeted measures to improve the situation. For instance, no mention is made of (1) the time frame within which physical education and sports should become a regular activity for all schoolchildren and collegiate youth; (2) the content of the training program for the orientation of subject teachers; (3) funding for this gigantic task; and (4) how the 700,000 primary schools in the country will be provided facilities for physical education in terms of playing fields, personnel, and equipment. No clear demarcation of responsibilities among various agencies has been made. Looking at the national policy on sports objectively, the experts insist on an ''urgent need to frame concrete and workable'' policies and achievable goals that promote a better ''standard in health, physical fitness and sports skills'' (Wakharker, 1993).

Goals Related to Sports Organizations and Athletes

The national sports policy has set certain goals for various agencies responsible for developing physical education and sports, as follows:

1. NSAs and their affiliated units at the state level will establish a nationwide network of sports clubs to absorb non-school-going children—especially the rural youth—and school-going children, after school hours, in sports activities. The NSAs will introduce a well-organized competition calendar for different age groups, so that the skills of participating children can be continuously evaluated and tested.

2. The state governments will implement Operation Playfields for the creation of sports facilities in schools, largely in rural areas under various employment generation programs.

3. For team sports such as football, hockey, volleyball, and basketball, establishment of sports academies at both the regional and national level will be undertaken by the central and state governments, or business and industry.

4. The regional centers of the SAI will improve their facilities, and state and university-level centers will be established over a period of time to provide scientific support to all sorts of athletes.

5. A comprehensive plan to upgrade the skills and qualifications of technical officials,

referees, and judges in identified disciplines will be drafted. Workshops and clinics will be organized at the national and regional level.

6. Highly talented junior athletes of various disciplines will receive financial and managerial support for specialized training abroad and personalized coaching at home. To promote and support athletes and sports persons identified for this purpose, the government is considering establishing a self-financing trust that will be professionally autonomous.

The crux of the issue, according to the national sports policy, is the creation of the requisite social and economic sports atmosphere in the country, duly backed by the commitment of all concerned—the central and state governments, the IOA, national and state sports organizations, coaches, and, finally, the athletes themselves. In order to achieve these objectives, numerous measures have already been taken, and many are in the pipeline. The decision of the government of India to encourage holding the National Games every two years at different venues will gradually help upgrade existing facilities and create new ones throughout the country. This will also attract more participants in games and sports. It should not be difficult for the central government to meet these objectives, because it has a strong organizational network through the Sports Authority of India, which has centers throughout the country. The national and state sports associations, however, may not meet expectations, as has been the case throughout the history of sports in independent India.

Foreign Policy Goals

The Indian government, in a sense, has been quite liberal in the matter of foreign policy as it relates to sports. Ultimate responsibility for developing competitive sports, as outlined in the national sports policy, lies with the NSAs and the Indian Olympic Association. The specific goals enumerated in the national sports policy in this regard are as follows:

1. The NSAs need to be encouraged to hold regular national competitions and implement effective plans for preparing national teams for participation in international competitions.
2. National teams should be sent to international competitions only when they have definitely met the standards required for such competitions.
3. The diplomatic priorities of the country should be kept in mind when considering foreign competitions or the organization of international events within the country.

In pursuance of these objectives, the government of India has been concerned with the standards of performance of national teams vis-à-vis the qualifying standards. Interestingly, long-estranged diplomatic ties with countries such as South Africa, Israel, and China are becoming less strained, with positive effects on India's sports scenario. In addition, a growing number of athletes and teams are participating in the SAF Games and Asian Games. India's participation in Commonwealth and Olympic Games is still restricted, however, because the athletes and teams rarely meet the qualifying standards. The government, IOA, and the NSAs have always been conscious of the prospects for success in international sports events. The reciprocal visits of foreign athletes and teams for practice and competitions have increased dramatically.

CONCLUSIONS

Declaration of the national sports policy in 1986, and its Program of Action in August 1992, marked an end to ad hoc approaches to the development of physical education and sports. The NSP is a comprehensive document, specifying precisely the government's intentions and efforts for the improvement of India's sports scenario. A good number of programs have already been implemented—especially those directly financed, controlled, and monitored by the central government; more are at the embryonic stage; and still others are at the conceptual stage. The time elapsed since the actual introduction of the NSP is so brief that it is simply impossible to make an objective assessment of the impact of various policies and programs in terms of concrete achievements. Long-drawn debates and dialogues are still raging over the perforated texture of the NSP. For instance, no concrete measures have been suggested to make sports and physical education an integral part of the learning process at all stages, and to develop low-cost sports and physical education infrastructure in schools and colleges. There is a general feeling that the steps taken by the central government to implement the national sports policy are being thwarted by drastic budgetary cuts in most states. The funds received from the central government are often diverted to other priority areas, and the central sports schemes, which require a 50 percent contribution from state governments, languish for want of financial input.

Physical education is yet to become routine in schools, especially in elementary and primary schools where the maximum exposure to play activities is required. No broad-based participation in sport, as envisaged in the sports policy, can be possible without involving more and more young children in sports activities at a tender age. Unfortunately, this objective has yet to be achieved, despite the publication of a National Plan of Physical Education in 1956. The situation is becoming more and more complicated owing to increasing population and declining resources.

Numerous schemes administered by the Department of Youth Affairs and Sports and the Sports Authority of India have been in place for five to seven years. Schemes such as Special Area Games and Sports and SPDA have begun to pay rich dividends in terms of athletes' performance at the national and international levels. Remarkable achievements in archery, both at the national and international level, are the result of the Special Area Games program. A large number of junior national tournaments are now being won by trainees from the SPDA centers of the SAI. The National Sports Talent Contest Scheme is continuously evaluated and modified, especially in the area of formulating norms and standards in talent selection. The schemes for the construction of infrastructure and sports complexes, and provision of prizes, incentives, and awards have been quite successful. They have certainly benefited a large number of organizations, institutions, and individuals.

It is somewhat intuitive to suggest that the workings of the national sport associations, their subsidiaries, and subordinate organizations cannot be improved by any governmental effort and assistance. The national sport associations comprise diverse populations beset with myriad problems whose objectives and motives are often at odds. Unless more and more sports persons become involved in sports associations and their management, the situation is not likely to change. The government of India is making a strong effort to encourage the club culture, which ultimately will improve the status and standard of the national sport associations. Such benefits may take years to manifest themselves, however. In recent years, the media—especially television—have played an important role in raising sports consciousness among the Indian people, and more and more people are participating in some sort of sports activity. Indeed, the developments outlined in this chapter suggest a growing government emphasis on the development of sports in India.

NOTE

1. The 1995 exchange rate was about 30 Indian rupees to one U.S. dollar.

REFERENCES

Agarwal, J. C., and Agarwal, S. P. (1988). *National policy on education.* New Delhi: Concept Publishing Co.
Annual Report, Part-V. (1989–90). Ministry of Human Resource Development, Government of India, Department of Youth Affairs and Sports, New Delhi.
Annual Report, Part-III. (1991–92). Ministry of Human Resource Development, Government of India, Department of Youth Affairs and Sports, New Delhi.
Annual Report and Audited Accounts. (1988–89). Sports Authority of India, New Delhi.
Annual Report and Audited Accounts. (1990–91). Sports Authority of India, New Delhi.
INDIA, 1990. (1990, September). Research and Reference Division, Ministry of Information & Broadcasting, Government of India.
Kamlesh, M. L. (1988). *Physical education: Facts and foundations.* Faridabad: P. B. Publications.
National Sports Policy. (1985). Department of Youth Affairs and Sports, Government of India, New Delhi.
Program of Action. (1992, August). National Sports Policy, Government of India, Ministry of Human Resource Development, Department of Youth Affairs and Sports, New Delhi.

Right Tracks. (1993). Vol. 1, No. 4. Department of Youth Affairs and Sports, Government of India, New Delhi.

Seshan, T. N. (1993). Urgency of election reforms: A report. *The Indian Express,* New Delhi. December 12.

Wakharkar, D. G. (1993). National Sports Policy 1992: An appraisal. *Research Bi-Annual for Movement, 10* (1): 31–34.

11

The Governmental Sports Policy of the State of Israel

Uriel Simri, Gershon Tenenbaum, and Michael Bar-Eli

Since its very first day of existence in 1948, the state of Israel has been governed by coalition governments, for no party ever succeeded in gaining an absolute majority in the 120-seat Knesset, or Parliament. Up to 1977 the Labour party was the dominant party; from 1977 until 1992 the right-wing Likud-Bloc (made up primarily of the Revisionist-Herut party and the Liberal party) inherited that role. In June 1992 the Labour party returned to power.

The democratic system of government in the state of Israel is highly centralized. Nonetheless, the government's direct involvement in sports has been relatively minor. This is because the government has always had to center its priorities on security problems and on absorption of immigration. Therefore, sports were destined to play a very small role in the political life of the state.

Sport in Israel has been practically free from government control since the very beginning, but it has been linked to political parties. The parties look on the sports organizations (Maccabi, Hapoel, Elitzur, Betar) as a convenient tool for increasing the influence of their political ideology. This link has served to create a very strong parliamentary lobby for the sports organizations, which are all multisport in nature, a lobby crossing the lines of government and opposition.

The Maccabi sports organization was founded in 1912 and has been considered an apolitical organization for most of its existence. However, it has always had strong links to the General Zionist (the Liberal and later the Likud-Bloc) party. In the beginning of the 1950s, three Maccabi members were even elected to the Knesset as part of the General Zionist ticket. The Hapoel sports organization, founded in 1926, has always been linked to the Labour parties, whereas

Elitzur and Betar, dating back to the late 1930s, were connected with the Religious and the Revisionist parties, respectively.

Elitzur is the only sports organization whose athletes do not compete on the Sabbath, but the National Religious party, which sponsors that organization, never had enough power to force the other organizations also to refrain from doing so. Elitzur has come to terms with a number of federations, which enable the religious athletes to schedule their competitions for weekdays.[1]

On the eve of World War II, the General Council of the Jews in Palestine (Hava'ad Haleumi) established a Physical Training Department that would cater to all aspects of physical activity, with the exception of competitive sports. At that time, Maccabi and Hapoel, the two main sports organizations, had no areas of cooperation except in the game of soccer. This was because Maccabi was associated with the general international sports movement, whereas Hapoel was an active member of the international labor sports organization (SASI). The newly created department did not possess enough power to overcome the political structure of the sport system, and therefore its accomplishments were minor.

When the state of Israel was created in 1948, the Physical Training Department was taken over by the new government and placed within the framework of the Ministry of Education and Culture. In 1960, following complaints concerning the organization of Israel's participation in the Rome Olympics, a special government inquiry committee (the Dafni Committee) was established. Its recommendation was to replace the department with a Sport and Physical Education Authority, which would supervise both competitive sports and physical education. In practice, the Authority has had a minimal effect on competitive sports and the autonomous sports organizations and federations. As for physical education, the Authority had no influence in this area until 1986, when the minister of education decided to carry out the mandate that had been bestowed on the Authority twenty-five years earlier.

The Knesset has had a sports committee since the early 1970s. However, its contribution has been quite limited because it is merely a subcommittee of the Committee on Education, with limited power to effect change.

In 1991 a deputy-minister for sports within the Ministry of Education and Culture was appointed for the first time. This appointment came as a result of a coalition agreement, which allocated this position to a member of a minor coalition partner. This appointment has resulted in temporary attempts to obtain more direct governmental involvement and supervision of sports by the Ministry of Education and Culture.

NATIONAL SPORTS BODIES

In 1951 unified national sports federations were established for the first time by Maccabi, the veteran organization, and by Hapoel, which at that time was already the largest and strongest sports organization in the country.

The major sports federations in Israel are:

1. The Olympic Committee of Israel, created in 1951, which is considered to be the umbrella organization of all sports federations.

2. The Israel Football (soccer) Association, created in 1928.

3. The Israel Sports Federation, created by Maccabi in 1931, which supervises all Olympic sports with the exception of soccer, basketball, and tennis. This federation was joined by Hapoel in 1951.

4. The Israel Tennis Association, created in 1949.

5. The Israel Basketball Association, created in 1968. Until that year, basketball was controlled by the Israel Sports Federation, but the enormous growth of this sport demanded the creation of an independent organization.

6. The Eyal-Israel Sport Association is an umbrella organization for twenty-four non-Olympic minor sports, founded in 1987.

7. The Israel Sports-for-All Association, founded in 1982, coordinates the organization of mass noncompetitive sports events through various sports organizations, as well as through municipal and local authorities.

Until several years ago, Israel's sports were strictly amateur. Nowadays top athletes in team games, such as soccer, basketball, team handball, and volleyball, are paid for their athletic activity, although they have not been officially declared professionals. Since 1979 the teams in the top league of basketball (the "National League") have been allowed to hire the services of two foreign players, a decision that was reached by the soccer federation in 1991. As of that year, the top teams in handball and volleyball have been permitted, by their respective federations, to use the services of one foreign player.

ISRAEL IN INTERNATIONAL SPORTS

In July 1948 Israel decided to send two female athletes to the London Olympics, in spite of its ongoing War of Independence. This participation was prevented by a British initiative, which claimed that since Palestine had ceased to exist on May 15, 1948 (the day that Israel was declared a state), recognition of the Olympic Committee of Palestine had been withdrawn, and the state of Israel's Olympic Committee had not yet been recognized. Thus, the IOC disallowed Israel's participation.

The premiere appearance of Israeli athletes in international sport finally took place in September 1948 at the Polo Grounds in New York, where Israel's national soccer team competed against the United States. Within twelve months, Israel also played against Cyprus in an exhibition soccer match and competed against Yugoslavia in the preliminary stages of the 1950 Soccer World Cup.

Tennis and basketball followed soccer into the international arena. Israel's tennis team competed for the first time in the Davis Cup competitions in 1949 against Denmark in Copenhagen, and a year later the women's basketball team participated in the European championship, held in Budapest. The latter, as well as Israel's participation in the European volleyball championship held in Paris in 1951, were to have political significance in later years, serving as a precedent for Israel's claim for integration into European sports. This precedent was possible because at the time certain international federations had no strict continental restrictions, and the European zone was known as "the zone of Europe and the Mediterranean basin."

Israel participated in the Olympic Games for the first time in 1952 in Helsinki, and two years later for the first time in the Asian Games, in Manila. Israel has taken part in all subsequent Olympic Games, with the exception of the 1980 Moscow Games when it joined President Carter's boycott. Following the 1974 Asian Games in Teheran, Israel was forced to end its involvement in Asian sports as a result of political pressure from the Arab states.

Following its expulsion from sports on the Asian continent, Israel decided to pursue integration into the European sports scene. A major obstacle, however, was the objection of the Soviet Union, which continued until the political upheavals in the communist bloc in 1989. (That year Soviet athletes appeared for the first time in Israel, following a twenty-two-year boycott since the end of the Six-Day War.) Since then, Israel has come close to full integration into European sports.

ACHIEVEMENTS IN INTERNATIONAL SPORTS

As long as its athletes were active on the Asian scene, Israel could pride itself on a significant number of medals—eighteen gold, sixteen silver, and nineteen bronze—gained by Israeli athletes in the Asian Games between 1954 and 1974.

In the Olympic Games, Israel was to gain its first medals only when its athletes participated for the tenth time—in 1992 in Barcelona. On this occasion, two Israeli judokas came away with medals—Yael Arad gaining the silver medal in the 61 kilogram class for women and Oren Smadja gaining the bronze medal in the 71 kilogram class for men. Prior to Barcelona, the fourth place gained by the yachtsmen Joel Sela and Eldad Amir in the Flying Dutchman class of the 1988 Olympics had been Israel's top achievement in the games.

Over one-third of the Israeli delegation to the Barcelona Olympics (eleven of thirty-one) was made up of new immigrants from the former communist states of Eastern Europe, but the highest achievement from this group was the sixth place finish of Andre Danisov in the 100 kilogram class in weightlifting.

In team competitions, the outstanding international achievement was the second place gained by the national basketball team in the European Championship in 1979. In soccer, Israel reached the final sixteen teams in the World Cup games of 1970, and in tennis, it ranked among the top sixteen nations in the world between 1986 and 1989.

In July 1992, Israel won its first world title in professional athletics when Johar Abu-Lashin, a Christian Arab from Nazareth, won the lightweight title of the World Boxing Federation. (Abu-Lashin is one of the very few official professionals in Israeli sports. The others are several tennis and soccer players who are playing abroad.) In addition, a number of athletes have won medals in world and European championships: Yael Arad won bronze medals in the judo world championship in 1991 and in the European championship in 1992. Oren Smadja won a bronze medal in the European judo championships in 1992. Oleg Sadihov won a silver and Andrej Danisov a bronze medal in the European weightlifting championships in 1992. Maxim Geller took the silver medal in the 1991 European championships in freestyle wrestling. Amit Inbar was ranked first in the 1991 world ranking in wind-surfing and placed second in the 1992 world championships.

THE GOVERNMENT'S INVOLVEMENT IN SPORTS

The first interaction between the government of the state of Israel and a sports organization occurred less than one year after the state was created. In the spring of 1949, Prime Minister David Ben-Gurion approached the Hapoel sports organization (which was aligned with his own Labour party) and asked that they recommend whether to affiliate the Department for Physical Training with the Ministry of Education and Culture or with the Ministry of Defense. The Hapoel national council decided, by a 60 percent majority, to support affiliation with the Ministry of Education, and Ben-Gurion accepted the recommendation.

The subsequent interaction was of quite a different nature. Hapoel and Maccabi had signed an agreement of cooperation in March 1948, but when the state of Israel was created two months later, the agreement was not enforced by either side. In 1951 two National Olympic Committees, one backed by Maccabi and the other by Hapoel, requested recognition from the International Olympic Committee.[2] Both NOCs were refused recognition, and the possibility that Israel would not be allowed to participate at the Helsinki Olympics of 1952 became imminent.

At the urging of Hapoel, the Ministry of Foreign Affairs intervened, and Maccabi and Hapoel managed to work out a new agreement. According to this agreement, all sports bodies in the state would be run on a parity basis, each side represented by 50 percent of the members. That agreement held for about a dozen years, and only in the early 1960s did the sports federations gradually adopt statutes of a truly democratic nature.[3] As a result, Hapoel gained dominance in practically all national sports federations. It should be added that "nationalization'' in the early 1950s would have, for all practical purposes, given Hapoel the same dominance, as it was aligned with the party in power.

While Israel's sports bodies were searching for ways to become integrated into European sports in the beginning of the 1950s, there was pressure from the government, especially the Ministry of Foreign Affairs, for integration into Asian sports. The official government policy at that time was that since Israel was part of the Asian continent, it should establish links with that continent, despite the fact that Israel was surrounded by hostile Arab states with whom relations of any kind could not be established.

In 1953 the government decided to build a national center for sports and physical education, but it took four years until the Wingate Institute for Physical Education and Sport would open its doors.[4] The Institute, though officially a public institution, is under de facto control of the government, and a substantial part of its budget comes from government sources. The Institute carries out many of the professional operations recommended by the Ministry of Education and Culture and its subdivisions. Its main activities are: (1) provision of scientific and professional sport services to young and adult athletes, (2) education of coaches in all the sport disciplines (for both youth and adults), competitive as well as recreational, (3) development of young talented athletes, and (4) development of educational resources (databases, library, historical museum, audiovisual presentations) for scholars, coaches, athletes, and other groups who have an interest in physical activity, health, and sport.

Following the Sinai military campaign of 1956, while the army reserves were still mobilized, Prime Minister David Ben-Gurion decided to intervene and determine the size of the Israeli delegation to the Melbourne Olympics. He drastically reduced the size of the delegation and included only two delegation heads (one from Hapoel and one from Maccabi), two male athletes, one female athlete, and a basketball official who had been invited by the international basketball federation (FIBA).

The next governmental intervention in the activities of the sports organizations occurred in 1960, with the establishment of the above-mentioned inquiry committee. The newly created Sport and Physical Education Authority placed representatives in all sports federations, who functioned mainly as observers without attempting to initiate major changes. The work of the committee did, however, result in a major political change. Since its founding in 1939, the Physical Training Department had always been headed by a member of Maccabi, the veteran sports organization in the country. However, the new Authority was to be headed by a member of the government Labour party and not by a member of the opposition, to which Maccabi belonged at the time. Reuven Dafni, the chairman of the inquiry committee, became the first director of the new Authority.

The first law enacted in the state of Israel pertaining to sports, or rather to physical activity, was the Law of Public Bathing Beaches. This law, dating back to 1964, authorized the minister of interior to declare each beach a public bathing area and to require municipal and local authorities to maintain these beaches and make them accessible for public use.

In 1967 the Knesset sought to ensure the financial security of Israel's sports movement by enacting a law on sports betting. Up to that time, the betting pools were operated by sports organizations, as well as by a number of newspapers and private businesses. The new law nationalized betting on sports (soccer) results and established the Israel Sports Betting Board to operate it.[5] The Board is composed of twelve members, with six representatives each from the government and the sports federations. Members of the Board are nominated by the minister of finance and the minister of education and culture, with a government representative serving as chairman of the Board.

In the twenty-five-year period from 1968 until 1992, the Board contributed $370 million to sports, thus becoming by far the major source of income of all sports federations and organizations. For example, the Israel Sport Federation receives close to 90 percent of its annual income (the budget of the federation stood at U.S. $17 million for the year 1992) from the betting Board. Since the late 1980s, the Board's annual allocation to sports has risen to $30 million annually, compared to a $12 million budget for sports by the government. The majority of the government's budget, however, does not go to national sports federations and organizations, but rather to municipal authorities.

The Board has also become a major factor in the financing of sports facilities. These facilities include indoor and outdoor stadiums, modern sports centers, and thousands of outdoor courts for all major ball games. Furthermore, the Board has supported the pension fund for soccer players, as well as a special fund for the promotion of outstanding athletes. The State Lottery (Mif'al Hapayis), whose main objective is to support educational and health institutions in the country, has also given substantial financial support to the building of sports facilities in schools, which also serve the communities at large.

In 1970 the minister of education and culture, Yigal Allon, appointed a National Council for Sport and Physical Education. The Council, which was supposed to be of an advisory nature, met twice and thereafter was never called to a meeting, although it was never officially disbanded. In June 1992 the deputy minister of education and culture in charge of sports, Pinchas Goldstein, convened a new Supreme National Council on Sports. Its contribution to sport was marginal in light of the political changes in July 1992, which returned the Labor party to power. Its functions and contribution remain to be determined in the future.

In the soccer season of 1970–71, a bribery scandal received massive attention in the Israeli media and created strong public pressure to investigate the entire sports establishment. Motives for the bribery were, on one hand, to avoid relegation to a lower league and on the other, to influence the outcome of games included in the weekly betting pool. The government appointed an inquiry committee, headed by Supreme Court Justice Moshe Etzioni, to investigate the state of affairs in the Soccer Federation, as well as in the Israel Sports Betting Board.[6]

The Etzioni Committee published its recommendations in September 1971, all of which were accepted (but not fully applied). For example, the committee recommended that representatives of the sports federations be excluded from the Israel Sports Betting Board, a recommendation that has yet to be carried out. It should be pointed out, however, that the Betting Board accepted all of the committee's recommendations and introduced several changes in the betting system.[7]

One byproduct of the bribery affair was the so-called Klinghofer Law, named after the legislator who introduced the bill. According to this law, passed in 1971, it became a criminal offense to bribe or to attempt to bribe an athlete, as well as for an athlete to accept a bribe. In the years that have passed since the enactment of this law, only one related case has been brought before the courts.

In the mid-1970s, the Sport and Physical Education Authority started a drive to develop sports at the municipal level. The official reason given for this move was that the sports organizations were emphasizing competitive sports and were neglecting the general public, to which they had catered in the past. The Authority initiated the creation of sports departments in each municipality and began to subsidize their activities, providing their programs included programs for the underprivileged, the handicapped, and the elderly. The sports organizations, on the other hand, claimed that the purpose of this policy was to undermine their autonomy.

In 1977, following an upset in the elections, the Labour party became part of the opposition. While in power, the Labour party had been satisfied that sports were controlled by a sports organization (Hapoel) aligned with it, but the new ruling party (Likud) faced a national sports movement that was controlled by the opposition. However, the Ministry of Education and Culture was handed over to a coalition partner (the National Religious party), for whom sport was far from a top priority. The new minister found himself in a peculiar situation, being responsible, against his deep religious convictions, for sports activities that took place primarily on the Sabbath. Therefore, he chose not to interfere in the sports structure, and thus Hapoel succeeded in remaining the most influential organization in Israeli sports.

The religious parties, therefore, have not made any significant impact on sports in Israel. Their most substantial contribution was to delay the construction of a municipal stadium in Jerusalem for over fifteen years. This delay was caused by ultraorthodox parties, who organized a successful judicial filibuster in the courts of the state. The stadium was finally opened in 1992.

In 1991 the minister of education and culture made a deputy minister from another minor nonreligious coalition partner, Pinchas Goldstein, directly responsible for sports. Only at that time did the government take serious measures to shake Hapoel's dominant position. That year, the deputy minister proposed, for instance, to change the structure of the Sports Betting Board by reducing the number of representatives from the sports organizations from six to four, but because of the political pressures of the sports organizations' lobby, this measure was not taken. Goldstein's term of office came to an end in June 1992 as a result of the national elections.

As early as 1980, the government forced its hand in an issue with the sports organizations. On May 22 of that year, a few days before the end of the registration period for the Moscow Olympic Games, the Olympic Committee of Israel, under pressure from the Likud government, reversed its previous decision to participate in the Games and joined the Carter-initiated boycott. It was reported at the time that the government had hinted strongly that if the decision had not been reversed, it would change the law of the Sports Betting Board, on whose income the sports movement had come to rely.

Prior to the political upheaval of 1977, the Sport and Physical Education Authority had tabled a Sports Law in the Knesset, which was modeled after a similar French law.[8] The opposition of the sports organizations again proved to be very effective, and as a result of their lobbying, the minister of education succeeded in getting the law adopted by the Knesset only thirteen years later (in 1988), and in a significantly modified version. In the years that followed, the Authority, in spite of relentless efforts, had to be satisfied with only one minor legal achievement—passage of a law regulating scuba diving (1979).

The major items of the new Sports Law called for mandatory certification of coaches and instructors; mandatory health and loss of income insurance of athletes participating in competitive sports; mandatory periodical medical examinations for participants in competitive sports; and prohibition of the use of any narcotic materials. The minister of education and culture was given a number of regulatory powers within the framework of the law.

In order to pacify the sports organizations that opposed this law, the Authority added a paragraph to the law giving the disciplinary committees of the sports federations the status of a legal court, whose decisions could not be appealed in a civil court.[9]

Within the framework of a reorganization of the Ministry of Education and Culture, the Sport and Physical Education Authority and the Supervision of Physical Education in the school system were unified into one administration as of 1986. The major objectives of the newly constructed unit were defined by the minister of education and culture as follows:

1. Dissemination of sports and of recreational physical activities in all spheres of society.

2. Regular physical education instruction in the *entire* school system, and improvement of that instruction.

3. Intensification of extracurricular physical activities for youth within the school system, on a competitive as well as recreational basis.

4. Assistance to the development of sports in the country through the establishment of a proper infrastructure, including professional personnel and facilities.

5. Financial and administrative assistance to sports associations and federations.

6. Professional and scientific services for the nation's sports and physical education programs.

The Authority has made a special allocation of funds for the quadrennial Maccabiah Games and Hapoel Games. The Maccabiah Games are a meeting of Jewish athletes from all over the world, and the Hapoel is the largest open-to-all international event in Israeli sports, with participation from athletes of the highest levels in a large number of sports.

A legal matter in need of clarification is that of the professional/amateur status of Israel's athletes. In spite of the fact that most top athletes in the major sports of the country are de facto professionals, they have not been granted that statutory status. As a result, the state's social security system does not recognize sport as a profession and claims that no legal employer/employee relationship exists among the federations, their clubs, and the athletes, in spite of the fact that between 400 and 500 athletes in the country made a living from sports in 1992. Thus, if an athlete is seriously injured during a game or practice, he or she cannot submit a claim toward any social security benefits, such as for loss of income or for old-age pensions.

Another problem facing the government is the diminishing income of the Sports Betting Board, which reached its peak in the mid-1980s, a phenomenon parallel to that in many European countries. The Board's income lags behind the rate of inflation (about 70 percent between 1988 and 1992), and the federations are demanding that the government increase its financial support of sports.

In the national election campaign of 1992, although sport received more attention than ever before, it was far from a major issue. The New Liberal party, to which the deputy minister of education and culture belonged, spoke out for the creation of a Ministry of Sports, whereas Itzchak Rabin, the leader of the Labour party and candidate for prime minister, opposed it, claiming that the creation of another ministry would be a waste of public funds and that it would be much wiser to spend such funds on direct support of the sports federations and organizations. The New Liberal party failed to gain a single seat in the newly elected Knesset, and the victorious Rabin appointed a new deputy minister in charge of sports (Micha Goldman) from among his own party members.

CONCLUSIONS

This chapter has discussed the direct and indirect involvement of the Israeli government in sports. Direct governmental involvement has thus far been quite limited, despite the efforts of the Likud-Bloc at the beginning of the 1990s. It may be assumed that with the government headed by the Labour party indirect supervision will prevail. However, it remains to be seen whether general trends in Israeli society toward economic and business privatization will contribute to the reduction of governmental involvement in sport, be it direct or indirect.[10]

Many foresee an end to the rule of the national sports organizations, but such an end has been foreseen time and again in the past, and has never materialized.

NOTES

1. Elitzur, for instance, is not active in soccer, Israel's most popular sport, because the soccer federation is unwilling to force its teams to play on a weekday.

2. Jean Leiper (1981, p. 111) is correct in reporting that two Israeli NOCs applied for recognition in 1951, but is wrong in assuming that one was a Jewish and the other an Arab committee.

3. Reshef and Paltiel (1989, p. 313) are incorrect in reporting that from 1948 to 1970 each sports organization received seats on the Israel Sport Federation according to its parliamentary strength. Betar and Elitzur, for instance, had no representation whatsoever up to the mid-1960s. When the parity agreement came to an end, the seats were allocated according to the number of registered athletes, as well as the achievements of these athletes.

4. The Wingate Institute was named after the late General Orde Charles Wingate of the British army. Wingate, who came to Palestine as a young captain in 1936, offered his services, out of his deep religious conviction that the land of Israel historically belonged to the Jewish people, to the official Jewish underground (the Haganah). When his offer was accepted, he started to train elite units. He later went on to liberate Ethiopia (from Italian occupation) and rose to the rank of general. When he was killed behind Japanese lines in Burma in 1942, the Jewish Agency decided that if ever a national school for physical education were to be established, it would be named after General Wingate, who highly valued physical fitness.

5. Until the summer of 1992, betting was done only on the results of soccer games. At that time, the deputy minister recommended that betting on horse races be introduced as well, but the minister of education rejected this proposal.

6. In 1968 the Knesset passed a law to enable the establishment of official inquiry committees, to be headed by a Supreme Court judge. This law gave the committees extraordinary powers, including power to subpoena witnesses and force them to present documents, and power to accept as evidence any material relevant to the topic of the investigation without abiding by the code of courts and their procedures. Relatively few inquiry committees have been set up by the government or by the Knesset since the passage of this law.

7. The changes included, among other things, requiring that the participants in the betting identify themselves, restricting the maximum amount a participant could bet in a given week, and mandating that the major prize be distributed at least once a month.

8. The French law was formulated by the Ministry of Youth and Sports, which was created by President Charles De Gaulle after the French debacle in the Rome Olympics of 1960. It gave the Ministry supervisory powers over the sports movement, in accordance with the French philosophy of centralized government power.

9. This clause was put to the test by the Torten brothers. The brothers had participated, against the orders of the delegation's leaders, in an Olympic sailing competition in 1988 on the holy Yom Kippur (Day of Atonement) and were therefore suspended for five years by the supreme disciplinary committee of the Israel Sport Federation. They appealed to the Supreme Court of the State, claiming that the sports federation had no

jurisdiction over them during the Olympic Games, and their sentence was repealed. No new charges were brought against them by the Olympic Committee of Israel.

10. In the 1992–93 season, private businessmen took over complete financial responsibility of a small number of top teams. Thus, for instance, a Maccabi soccer team is now operated by such a businessman, as is a Hapoel basketball team. The teams, however, remain affiliated with their national organizations.

REFERENCES

Very few references outside the Hebrew language are available on the topics of this chapter. The list contains only sources in the English language.

Efrati, E. (1991). *Toto—Millions for prize money, millions for sports.* Tel Aviv: Israel Sports Betting Board.

Leiper, J. M. (1981). Political problems in the Olympic games. In J. Segrave and D. Chu (eds.), *Olympism* (pp. 104–117). Champaign, Ill.: Human Kinetics.

Reshef, N., and Paltiel, J. (1989). Partisanship and sport: The unique case of politics and sport in Israel. *Sociology of Sport Journal, 6*: 305–318. (*Note:* see reservations of the authors, Note 2).

Simri, U. (1989). Sport and physical education in the State of Israel. In H. Ueberhorst (ed.), *Geschichte der Leibesuebungen, vol. 6* (pp. 567–583). Berlin: Bartels and Wernitz.

Simri, U. (1991). *Sport and physical education in Israel.* Netanya: Wingate Institute.

12

Italian Sports: Between Government and Society

Nicola Porro

NATIONAL GOVERNMENT AND THE SPORTS SYSTEM

The organization and development of sports in Italy began during the second half of the nineteenth century, as it did in most of the other central and northern European countries. In Italy, however, the phenomenon coincided with the political unification of the country, a process imbued with the ideas and interests of the urban middle class of the north but lacking a real popular foundation.

Italy, a land of precocious mercantilism, started industrialization and state-building development late (Tullio-Altan, 1986). It had adopted capitalism early but maintained typically archaic features for a long time with its rural areas heavily subordinated and its urban system, though highly developed, having no real unifying center. The political elites were incapable of establishing a hegemony over the rural classes or over the new working class (Carocci, 1975). The Catholic and socialist movements—the two emergent social organizations in an era of mass populism—did not participate in the construction of the state. A difficult conflict divided the leading classes during the period of King Humbert I's reign and Giolitti's government (between the late nineteenth century and World War I).

Admirers of Great Britain praised the parliamentary system and wished to see the newly formed Italian nation included among the colonial powers. The landed aristocracy, the main supporter of a continental role for Italy, fought for a nationalistic, militaristic, and authoritarian government (the "German paradigm"). The Francophile elite upheld land reform, the confiscation of Church properties for the use of the state, and the celebration of the working citizen. This political conflict—fought among the progovernment liberal elites and the antigovernment social movements—had important symbolic features that influenced the role and development of sports in Italy until World War I.

The Church defended its monopoly of children's education and the lower classes' leisure by obstructing all of the state's interventions in the field of socializing activities.

The socialist movement, whose roots in Italy were more in the rural proletariat than in the urban working classes, took a long time to overcome its bias against the new state. Socialists held on to an old conception of sport as a higher class status symbol or, at least, as a typical middle-class privilege. World War I marked a turning point: mobilization of the whole nation, then the peace (1919), and suffrage were to be the finishing strokes for the fragile leadership of the old liberal elites.

The Catholic party (Partito Popolare) burst onto the political scene, while the socialist movement—though electorally strengthened both by its opposition to the war and by the radical inclinations of the new factory working class—was split in two by the advent of the Communist party (1921). The crisis of the old elites, and the lack of legitimacy caused by the attitudes of the main popular movements toward the state, opened the door to the fascist regime, which came to power in 1922.

Under fascism, physical education and sports were accorded a strategic and instrumental role as a means of nationalist propaganda and widespread social control. Sports also became a field for the "invention of traditions" and for an "authoritarian modernization" (Hobsbawm and Ranger, 1987). CONI (Comitato Olimpico Nazionale Italiano) was instituted in 1933, in order to develop the centralized management of competitive sports according to the political philosophy of the regime.

After World War II and the fall of the fascist dictatorship, the politically oriented mass organizations acquired new importance in socially significant activities. A pervasive party system grew in the late 1950s and the 1960s. Italy's political system therefore falls within the analytical category of party government, which is characterized by a highly fragmented democratic representation and the predominance of legislative power over executive power.

The system, designed after the defeat of fascism, was inspired by the expressed wish of assuring the maximum degree of social and political representation. The proportional electoral system and the patronage policies of party apparatuses have produced, over time, inefficiency and corruption of political personnel, whence came the striking institutional crisis of the early 1990s.

The attempt to modernize institutions had already been pursued in the 1970s, with administrative reform enacted to overcome state centralization and to expand the democratic social base. Regional governments were created, other than those already existing in Sardinia, Sicily, and in some areas of northern Italy. Other local entities were formed in the school and health system, and cities were broken down into defined administrative areas. However, this project of institutional reform—directed to shift the balance of power from the center to the periphery—was slowed down by bureaucratic resistance, political instability, and the declining influence of unions. In the 1990s the reform of the electoral system and, possibly, of Italy's constitutional charter have become of paramount importance in reducing the political parties' power and in controlling the budget deficit.

Modern History of Government's Relation to Sport

Unlike sports in other important European countries, in Italy the social and institutional establishment of a sports movement coincided with the forming of the national state during the second half of the nineteenth century. This movement mirrored two essential features: the exclusion of the most representative political movements of the lower income classes (Catholic and socialist) and the obsessive search for an exemplary "foreign model" (British, French, and Prussian). The origin of Italian sports therefore reflected the internal political conflict in the new nation-state, which was in the throes of political unification.

As a prevailingly urban phenomenon of the northern areas, sports were influenced by educational and ideological models of the political elite of the *Risorgimento* (the patriotic revival of the nineteenth century). From the start, sports represented an arena wherein different political ideas about institutions, hierarchies, and loyalties clashed. Most of the first sports clubs featured shooting, fencing, and mountain climbing and were founded by the leaders of the unification. These same men also introduced physical education into the schools (1878).

In sports, however, the nationalization process has been quite swift and not without significant social influence, as can be seen by the decline of the more popular disciplines practiced in pre-unity years. The establishment and institutionalization of sport follow the same ideological and cultural cleavages that divide the leading classes politically.

The supporters of the "English way" favored socially reserved sports (riding, tennis) and new team games like soccer. This was part of a "civilizing process" (Elias and Dunning, 1986) that fascinated the liberal middle classes despite the absence in Italy of the hubris provided by the British public school system. The "German paradigm" can be found in the adoption of Ludwig Jahn's theories of physical education and in the emphasis on the nation's martial virtues (the practice of shooting and wrestling in collective, noncompetitive, militaristic performances). French influence can be detected in two trends. One trend values physical exercise as a civil religion (the lay celebration of the citizen, according to Hobsbawm and Ranger, 1987). The other initiated the success of competitive cycling (the Giro d'Italia is clearly copied from the Tour de France as well as its "symbolic representation" of the nation space: Vigarello, 1992) and automobile racing (the rallies Targa Florio and Millie Miglia, for example). These kinds of activities reflect behavior patterns that were based on a real cult of mechanics and on a lifestyle open to the influence of futurism, a cultural movement that had one of its main diffusion points in Italy.

Until World War I, voluntary gymnastics and walking associations were ideologically inspired by secular patriotic values. Catholic associations were supported by the Church and its mighty social network (parishes, oratories); the Church was completely hostile to the liberal state. Ideological criticism of sport as bourgeois and competitive prevailed among the socialists (Fabrizio, 1977). Sports management by the fascists between the world wars was utilized to build consensus, nationalistic fervor, and totalitarian control over civil society.

Fascism established a standard case of authoritative political management of physical activity (Hoberman, 1988). (Sport practice, however, had started expanding before Mussolini's advent to power in 1922.)[1] The fascist propaganda slogan "sport for everybody" delineated the regime's answer to emerging social demands. Fascism stressed bureaucratic regulation and direct government control of sports by suppressing amateur associations of political and religious groups not belonging to the party; by imposing on sports systems the rigid corporative model (company clubs, associations organized by sex, age, etc.); by delegating to Comitato Olimpico Nazionale Italiano (CONI) the organization of competitive sports (training, administrative planning of events) as well as the management of designated financial resources. CONI was set up in 1914, as a coordinating organization among various sports federations, some of which represented non-Olympic and noncompetitive disciplines such as "alpinisme." Its inspiring principles however, were the same as those of the Comite International Olimpique (CIO) in the years of the reconstitution of the Olympic movement and of Demetrious Vikelas's (1894–96) and Baron Pierre de Coubertin's (1896–1916) management.

Soon after World War I, an attempt was made in Italy to organize sports associations within a pyramid structure. CONI, having official responsibilities and being recognized as the only interlocutor for state authorities, would be at the top; the national sports federations, which would direct and control the galaxy of voluntary associations, would constitute the base. This project had been supported during the political elections of 1921 by a press campaign promoted by the Gazzetta Dello Sport and, later, by the group of Parliament members elected in the "Blocco nazionale" list.

The objective was to create a mighty and coordinated organization that could be entrusted with the management of military and school physical training. All the voluntary associations were to be involved in the project, and they were supposed to give the state their collaboration in exchange for tax relief and government commitments to a sports facilities development program. The initiative failed for fear that politically oriented groups would get control of the army and exercise ideological influence on the recruits. There was an atmosphere of quasi-civil war following the war veterans' homecoming and the factory workers and peasants revolts of 1919–20.

In 1923 one of the first measures of fascism was the transfer of responsibility for premilitary training to the armed forces authorities. CONI was reconstituted as a body and was delegated to organize competitive sports activities. The fascist state, therefore, promoted a real policy of public intervention in sports. It did not just support the voluntary association network, as in democratic countries (such as France, Britain, and the Scandinavian countries) had done. However, between the 1920s and the 1930s, the question of a more complete and direct regulation of the sports movement was raised in democratic nations. The fascist regime stressed the centralizing feature of CONI (Federation of Sports Federations), overemphasizing and politically using a tendency encouraged by CIO, which preferred to deal with authoritative national interlocutors.

A twofold process can be observed. On the one hand, in the 1930s CONI developed and followed a trend—the nationalization of sport—common to most Western European countries. This was an emerging mass social phenomenon that spread widely. Characteristic innovations were the creation of a professional bureaucracy, the first government measures to support physical training and its introduction into school curricula, and the construction of facilities. On the other hand, a massive presence of party hierarchies imposed itself, aiming manifestly at a propagandistic and ideological management of sport. Hence, there was also a recurring undercurrent of tension between party hierarchies and professional bureaucracy that prevented a complete "fascistization" of Italian sport. The law instituting CONI, passed as late as 1942 in the middle of World War II, reflected the dual nature of that body. CONI felt the effects of the unresolved contradiction between its responsibilities for public service, an outgrowth of the rationalization and bureaucratization of industrial societies, and its subjugation to political and propagandistic exploitation by a regime inclined to consider competitive sport as a privileged instrument and as a showcase for its own successes. This law delineates CONI as a national emanation of CIO, undertaking, among their duties, pedagogic and humanitarian aims (rather anachronistic even by then) contained in Article 24 of the Olympic rules. At the same time, it outlines the Italian Olympic Committee as a public, but not government, agency with tasks of guidance and control over all sports activities "by whomever and wherever exerted."[2]

At the head of CONI is a National Council and a restricted executive committee (Giunta), which actually runs the body. It is led by a president appointed every four years by the people responsible for all the federations (thirty-nine in 1993). The committee works with a group of professionals among whom the general secretary has an operational position. He is, traditionally, a sort of leader of the internal bureaucracy and represents an element of continuity for various administrative bodies.

CONI sets down, carries out, and checks the programs for competitive activities and sports promotion; it also deliberates on the constitution, the dissolution, or the unification of the individual federations, and approves their statutes. It also recognizes individual societies and well-deserving associations as official organizations having title to legal benefits for the promotion of sports and their related activities. CONI fixes the criteria for the distribution of financial, technical, and administrative resources among the federations, the local branches, and the voluntary organizations.

CONI, unlike many public entities created during the fascist period, survived World War II. It was even restructured and reinforced in its role as leader of Italy's sports system through effective connections with the new democratic system. Under the chairmanship of Giulio Onesti (1946–78), CONI was officially confirmed as (1) the coordinating body of all the competitive sports federations ("federation of all federations"), (2) the only representative for international competitive events, and (3) the replacement body for the Ministry of Sports.

Political figures supported by the government parties were usually appointed to head CONI. This practice changed in 1993, when a past general secretary was elected president. Another example of political influence on the Italian sports system is featured by the *enti di promozione*—multisport voluntary organizations that to a certain extent are similar to those existing in northern Europe. In Italy, however, they arose in the 1950s and the 1960s within the main political parties such as the Christian Democratic party and the Communist party. Eventually, all parties and even union organizations developed these multisport associations. In the 1970s they played an important role when many jurisdictions of the central government, including sports promotion and facility construction, were transferred to regional divisions and local municipalities. This reform also stimulated the sports infrastructure boom between the 1970s and the 1980s and helped Italy catch up with the most advanced European countries. In only a little more than ten years, the number of available sports facilities grew from 45,494 to 118,712; gymnasiums from 7,340 to 19,674; indoor equipment for sport and/or tennis from 719 to 3,830 (Nomisma, 1991).

In 1976 CONI recognized the *enti* as official bodies in Italian sports. By such recognition, CONI allowed them access to public financing (especially that arising from gaming pool revenues) and legitimized their position as co-responsible players in the Italian sports system. This recognition represented an important turning point, taking place as it did during a critical political period just after the so-called protest cycle—confrontations started by the student revolt of 1968 and carried on by the wave of strikes in big factories in 1969. The years of terrorism were just around the corner, reaching their climax in 1978, with the murder of Aldo Moro, the most authoritative Italian statesman of that period.

The political elections of 1976 were characterized by the remarkable success of the Communist party, and the possibility of setting up a government of national unity became a reality. This ad hoc coalition of traditional government parties and the communists confronted economic crisis and terrorist attacks. In this setting, the opening of CONI had clear political symbolism. It was considered a progovernment body by voluntary movements, which organized hundreds of thousands of young athletes and often supported "popular sport" as a culture of opposition to conservative government.

CONI's recognition of the voluntary movement occurred as a debate about the "sports model" itself, and the role of a public authority in it developed in the 1980s and the early 1990s. A large part of the CONI bureaucracy was set against centralizing control over the sport movement's base, claiming to keep to the letter of the institutive law of CONI (overseeing . . . "activities by whoever and wherever exerted."). On the contrary, only in the mid-1980s did the sports voluntary movements (*enti*) begin to develop an autonomous battle against the dictatorship of competitive sports, joining the movement of sport for everybody, rooted in central and northern Europe, but still scarcely widespread in Latin countries. By emphasizing their sports character rather than their political identities, these movements progressively rid themselves of patronage from parties and union organizations. From this point of view, an important event occurred in Verona in 1989 when the principal Italian voluntary organizations—self-help, cultural, and sports alike—declared an end to this phase of *collateralismo*, political flanking, and demanded a general reform granting them the autonomy and social function of voluntary associations.

So, in a sense, Law 266 (approved by Parliament in 1991), designating the practice of sports as a citizen's right and bestowing a lighter tax system on nonprofit associations, sanctioned the end of political party patronage over sports movements and voluntary organizations. However, a crisis for the postwar party system led to the electoral reform of 1993 and to a quick replacement of political elites. Hence, the functions and jurisdictions of all the players (CONI, federations, voluntary organizations) were yet to be defined by government law.

Amateur and Professional Sports Activities

In Italy the notions of amateur and professional sports activities should be redefined regarding (1) the development of sport as a mass phenomenon arising from the welfare state culture, (2) the tensions generated by policies related to income and nonprofessional associations, and (3) the proliferation of spectator sport and their related economic interests. Taking into account the influence still exerted in the 1990s by an institutional model based on CONI leadership of the national sports movement, it seems difficult to separate professional practices from amateur ones, unless we refer to outdated distinctions.

In fact, the philosophy of performance that inspired CONI and its sports federations has produced a widespread phenomenon of nonofficial professionalism in many specialties included in Olympic programs. Yet, this scarcely occurs in Italy. Vice versa, typically, professional sports like soccer, basketball, volleyball, and water polo often border between amateur and professional status. The regional championships are an example. This also explains why questions of the legal status of sports associations since the 1950s showed a wider and deeper contrast between a quasi-doctrine of juridical systems plurality (supported by voluntary associations) and the CONI hypercompetitive model, which views the state as the only center of the system. Nevertheless, this long trench war did not discourage the development of sports practice, especially since the late 1970s.

Data gathered by Istat, the Italian Institute of Statistics (*Indagine multiscopo,* July 1990), indicate the volume of sports participation. The number of people practicing sports was estimated at 12,264,000, which is about 22.35 percent of the population who are more than three years old (31 percent of males and 14.1 percent of females).

Samples from 1981 and 1985 show a sizable growth in volleyball and basketball participation. Volleyball, in particular, attracts boys and girls ten to fourteen years old. The growth of this sport is astonishing. In 1981 registered members did not exceed 152,000 (CONI data); however, by 1990 about 600,000 people—376,000 females, 225,000 males—chose to play volleyball. Of these, the largest percentage were members of the youngest age groups.

Perhaps, between the 1980s and the early 1990s, volleyball benefited from the international successes of both male and female national teams,[3] as well as from the achievements of the major Italian clubs in the European competitions. A new impetus was given to volleyball after it became a school sports activity within the schedule of compulsory school programs. A Japanese television series centered on the adventures of three young volleyball players may have further generated interest in volleyball. This series was very popular among the youngest audiences during the mid-1980s.

The Basketball Federation claimed 175,000 adult participants in 1991, up from 112,000 in 1981, and 130,000 girls and boys under twelve in 1991, up from 73,000 in 1981. Gymnastics, fitness, and competitive dance were practiced by a fifth of the total of those doing sports (and by 42 percent of females) and presented a fair distribution across sex and age groups. The 1985 data showed an expansion in tennis participation and appeared well distributed across age groups; it is the chosen "second" sport of the youngest age group. The impressive drop in winter sports and non- and semicompetitive activities (hunting, fishing, and walking) can be explained by the rigorous criteria applied by Istat, which tend to diminish the weight of seasonal sport activities. Swimming—introduced in the schools after the 1970s—diving, and water polo appear well distributed across sex and age groups. An example of a sport in transition is cycling, once associated with expectancies of social mobility by the lower classes and now practiced mainly by the elderly or as a noncompetitive ecological hobby (mountain bike, cycletourism). Data are still few and imprecise regarding new outdoor activities such as trekking, orienteering, hang gliding, rafting, river canoeing, or activities arising from traditional ones, such as free climbing and cross-country riding.

A statistical survey regarding soccer in the early 1990s does not confirm the alleged decline in soccer participation, especially by the youngest age group. A 1992 report edited by the Federazione Italiana Gioco Calcio (FGCI) seemed to disprove a decline in soccer participation based on the relationship between the number of boys aged eight to sixteen (the soccer recruiting period) and the number of federation membership holders. In 1991 the census recorded 3,336,095 boys (due to a decrease in the birth rate in the 1980s); 518,064 boys— an increase—practiced soccer. However, this increase is mostly the result of a bureaucratization of youth soccer practice: the number of registered players has surely increased more than the unregistered players. It follows that the real growth rate for soccer is lower than that for almost all the other team sports, if we consider the trend toward increased sports practice overall in the same period. The number of spectators remains approximately the same, whereas the television commercial market linked to soccer has expanded enormously. We can therefore more properly suppose that soccer has undergone profound changes in television spectatorship rather than passed through a real crisis of participation.[4] Moreover, the growing employment of foreign champions (not only in the top divisions) reinforces this trend, failing to meet the career expectations of young Italian athletes and spoiling the local breeding grounds.

Fitness and gymnastics sports are spread rather homogeneously throughout the country, although the southern regions remain less endowed with sports facilities and equipment and are less competitive in recruiting in the technical sports. Last, but not least, we must examine the distribution of sports practice by area in Italy. It can be observed (Table 12.1) that participation in general concentrates in the northwest (Piedmont, Lombardy, and Liguria), in the northeast (Venetia, Emilia-Romagna), and the central regions, while the variations between areas with a different urbanization rate (Table 12.2) are slight. We get the same results if we include the periphery of the major urban areas.

The pattern of sports spectatorship differs from that of participation. Soccer continues to be the dominant sport watched on TV. (Fifty-eight percent of those interviewed by a sports magazine in 1992 expressed this preference.) Motor-racing and, in some respects, cycling and boxing continue to have a big hold on audiences (not only TV audiences) unrelated to active participation. Sports such as wrestling, fencing, weightlifting, boat-racing, road-walking, target-shooting, skiing, and sailing, while they add to Italy's medal count at the Olympics, have instead a very strong regional base. The same thing applies to ice hockey (which is very popular in the German-speaking alpine region), baseball, badminton, and, partially, to rugby and water polo. A classic alpine sport, downhill skiing has completely lost any local characterization as a result of the winter sports boom among the urban middle classes. Other expensive sport specialties (such as sailing or golf) continue to maintain elite traits.

Lastly, there are some competitive disciplines that have traditionally pertained to the armed forces (equestrian, pentathlon, and some winter sports). The vast area of military sports, however, extends far beyond the mentioned disciplines and constitutes an area where the distinction between amateur and professional practice is very difficult to make.

Table 12.1
Distribution of Sports Practice according to Italian Territorial Zoning

Zoning	(x1000)			
	Participants	Nonparticipants	Not Indicated	Total
North West	3757	10608	159	14524
North East	2652	7238	101	9991
Centre	2427	7966	155	10548
South	2339	10929	266	13534
Islands	1089	5263	116	6468
Italy	12264	42004	797	55065

Zoning	(row percentages)			
	Participants	Nonparticipants	Not Indicated	Total
North West	25.9	73.0	1.1	100.0
North East	26.5	72.4	1.0	100.0
Centre	23.0	75.5	1.5	100.0
South	17.3	80.8	2.0	100.0
Islands	16.8	81.4	1.8	100.0
Italy	22.3	76.3	1.4	100.0

Source: ISTAT. (1990 July). *Indagine multiscopo sulle famiglie. Lo sport in Italia* (Rome: ISTAT).

Participation and Success in International Sports Competition

By utilizing Rostow's table method of Pociello (1981) and Giuntini and Rossi (1990), we can compare the data for the constitution of the international federation with the corresponding data for the Italian one, and even the data of the first world championships (Table 12.3) for the principal sport specialties. These comparisons disprove the thesis—supported by many Italian historians—of a substantial delay in the beginning of the Italian sports movement when compared to other Western European countries (France, Germany, and Britain). On the contrary, since 1860 the sports clubs of Lombardy, the richest Italian region and the first to be politically and culturally integrated in the central European context, represented a real avant garde of continental sports practice. The delay, if anything, concerns the access of the lower classes to most sports specialties. It is true, however, that the late constitution of official sports organizations deriving from the late national unification prevented Italy from being in the forefront in the reconstruction of the international Olympic movement (1894).

Table 12.2
Distribution of Sports Practice according to Town Size

Town Size	Participants	(x1000) Nonparticipants	Not Indicated	Total
Areas of major cities*	2913	10580	240	13733
Chief town of area	1973	7422	147	9542
Periphery of area	940	3158	93	4191
Other towns	9351	31424	558	41333
Over 2000 inhabitants	8614	28728	524	37866
Under 2000 inhabitants	737	2696	34	3467
Italy	12264	42004	798	55066

Zoning	Participants	(row percentages) Nonparticipants	Not Indicated	Total
Areas of major cities*	21.2	77.0	1.7	100.0
Chief town of area	20.7	77.8	1.5	100.0
Periphery of area	22.4	75.4	2.2	100.0
Other towns	22.6	76.0	1.4	100.0
Over 2000 inhabitants	22.7	75.9	1.4	100.0
Under 2000 inhabitants	21.3	77.8	1.0	100.0
Italy	22.3	76.3	1.4	100.0

*Concerning the eleven cities of Turin, Milan, Venice, Genoa, Bologna, Florence, Rome, Naples, Bari, Palermo, and Catania and their metropolitan areas.

Source: ISTAT. (1990 July). Indagine multiscopo sulle famiglie. Lo sport in Italia (Rome: ISTAT).

The gap between south and central-northern Italy, especially until the end of World War I, was wide in terms of participants in sports and the availability of sports. In the northern areas, popular and local games such as pallone (elastic ball), a sort of Basque pelota, survived for a longer time and contended with emerging soccer as the most popular sport in the first decades of the century. Despite these shortcomings and the mere symbolic presence of Italian athletes in the first five summer Olympics (those preceding World War I), the Italians' competitive performance appears very respectable. In fact, if we take as an indicator the number of medals won at the Olympics (1896–1992), Italians have gained 153 gold, 124 silver, and 131 bronze medals. In a medal count, by country, after the Barcelona Olympics, Italy would rank sixth just after Great Britain and France. But these results, especially until the 1970s, reflected the qualified management of a specialized structure (CONI) rather than the wide spread practice of sports.

Table 12.3
Years of Establishment of International and National Sports Federations and First World Championship

Sports	International	National	World Championship
Climbing		1863	
Gymnastics	1881	1869	1903
Shooting	1887	1882	1897 (1)
		1926	1929
Rowing	1892	1888	1962
Skating	1892	1922	1896
Cycling	1900	1885	1921
Motoring		1905	
Motor-Cycling	1904	1911	1949
Football	1904	1898	1930
Aeronautics	1905	1911	1934 (2)
			1950 (3)
			1952 (4)
Sailing	1907	1879	
Swimming	1908	1899	1973
Hockey on Ice	1908	1924	1924
Bob	1908	1925	1924
Track and Field	1912	1906	1983
Wrestling	1912	1902	1929
Fencing	1913	1909	1921
Weight Lifting	1921	1902	1937
Riding	1921	1911	1953
Motor-Boating	1922	1923	1938
Canoeing	1924		1948
Hockey on Field	1924	1923	
Skiing	1924	1913	1931
Table-Tennis	1924	1960	1927
Archery	1931	1961	
Basketball	1932	1921	1950
Baseball	1936	1948	1938
Boxing	1949	1916	1974
Water-Skiing	1946	1950	1949
Tennis	1948	1895	1900
Bowling	1951	1919	1947
Judo	1951		
Fishing	1952	1948	1954
Rugby	1954	1928	
Golf	1958	1927	1958
Diving	1964		1973
Pentathlon		1940	1949

(1)target-firing (2)acrobatics (3)sail-flying (4)motor-flying

Source: C. Pociello. (1981). *Sports et societe* (Paris: Vigot) and L. Minerva. (1982). *Lo sport* (Rome: Editorie Riuniti.)

Italy's national team represents one of the historical powers of world soccer (three times world champion and winner of Olympic and European titles). In this sport, the professional clubs have performed a very important role, since the 1950s, in the internationalization of Italian sport. In the sixteen winter Olympics between 1924 and 1992, Italian athletes have won nineteen gold, nineteen silver, and seventeen bronze medals. The result can be considered respectable especially in view of the fact that Italy only became competitive in the 1970s. (Four gold, nine silver, and eight bronze medals were obtained alone in the 1992 Albertville Winter Olympic Games.) Also, the standing of Italian competitive sport is regularly tested in regional and special category games such as the Mediterranean, University, and Military Games.

Italian Sports and Internationalization

The Italian sports system has been integrated into international circuits for many years. Spectator team sports—mainly soccer, basketball, water polo, volleyball, and rugby—have a long established tradition of recruiting foreign athletes and trainers.[5]

The solid financial strength of Italian professional sports does not reflect the nation's economic realities and market conditions. In the 1950s and 1960s, when Italy's per capita income and gross domestic product were lower than those of countries like France, Germany, and Britain, the Italian spectator sports (especially soccer clubs) could afford to offer enormous fees to lure the most famous foreign professionals. So Italy, which until the 1960s was a land of emigration, has become the Eden of foreign sport professionals.

Industries, too, have been attracted by high returns arising from advertising and sponsorships (say, in cycling, motor-racing, and skiing). In many sectors of motor-racing and sailing, technological joint ventures have been formed between Italian firms (like Ferrari) and highly specialized European, American, and Japanese firms.

At the beginning of the 1990s, two other important factors gave impetus to the increasing internationalization of professional sports. On one hand, Italian clubs began recruiting foreign players beyond the traditional areas (soccer players from Western Europe and South America) to include East Europeans and overseas black athletes (especially in boxing). On the other hand, Italy aligned to EC directives on free circulation of labor, sanctioned by the Rome and Maastricht treaties, changed the system of opportunities in the sports market. The effects of this free flow started to come to fruition in the early 1990s. For example, in professional soccer, national federations have limited the number of foreign players that clubs can engage and have forbidden EC players to play for the national team of the country where they are resident. In fact, there are two main norms, based on political and symbolical arguments: not favoring the superpowers of big soccer and basketball clubs (already very much "internationalized" in terms of athletes and capital) and limiting the impact of innovations on national identifications of teams. These norms seem to be in conflict with the spirit of Rome and Maastricht, which envision a European continent that is less and less divided by nationalistic rivalries. But these utopian views clashed with the hard laws of economic competition, with different development and productivity levels, and with the realities of national identification in the sphere of symbolic perception. In fact, the EC does not want to intervene until more precise norms regarding these matters are issued. While supranational rules are being elaborated, private business enterprises are becoming increasingly active in spectator sports.

These initiatives concern the purchase and sale of radio and TV rights—a sector in which Silvio Berlusconi's mass-media holding (Fininvest) is powerfully present—advertising promotions, sponsorships, and intermediate goods imports.[6] The Fininvest case is of great interest because it is an example of the development of spectator sport linked with big business. This Milanese holding company controls sectors in the commercial distribution, saving and insurance system, building industry, publishing, and advertising in Italy and abroad. At the end of 1991, it could boast an overall turnover of about US$15,000 million. Its entry in the sports system in 1985 had nothing to do with traditional patronage—through sponsorships or shareholding of soccer or other team game clubs by the biggest industrial groups (e.g., the Fiat group, which has always been the patron of the Juventus soccer team in Turin). Berlusconi's holding owns one of the most popular soccer clubs in Italy, the Milan, and controls many sports societies with all the main team games.

It can be argued that spectator sport is the privileged instrument of a business network: Publitalia manages advertising on soccer grounds, TV spots, and sponsorships; Telepiu' (a pay TV company established at the end of the 1980s) is the sole broadcaster, for Italian audiences, of high-performance sports events (e.g., top soccer championship matches and the international tennis competition at Wimbledon); since 1993 Finivest has had the TV rights and the operational organization of Italy's cycling Giro. This business strategy, centered on the relationship between television and spectator sports, is the origin of the expansion of the sponsorship and TV rights market in the 1980s and early 1990s.[7] One of the most ambitious projects of the Berlusconi group—which presents some analogies with the experiences of the Real Madrid in Spain, the Olympique in Marseille (managed by the French tycoon Bernard Tapie), and the Philips clubs in the Netherlands—is the constitution of unique big multisports clubs (Supermilan) able to monopolize spectator sports at the European level.

Between the end of the 1980s and the early 1990s, Berlusconi's model influenced other important Italian experiences. The Ferruzzi group—the second largest Italian industrial group, crushed in 1993 by a serious financial scandal that led to the suicide of its former President Raul Gardini—excelled in the field of basketball, female volleyball, and sailing races. Gardini himself had been a protagonist in 1992, as sponsor and participant, of the America's cup sailing race. Also in Rome a group represented by Maurizio Flammini, a former Formula

One motor racer, is involved with the construction of a multisports society connected with an important television network. The Italian sports system, in terms of commercial import/export, is in good health. Important industrial sectors, from mechanical to nautical and from summer and winter sports, have benefited from broadcasting the successes of Italian athletes and teams in car and motorbike rallies (Lancia, Gilera, Cagiva), famous sailing races (from "Azzurra" to "Il Moro benezia"), and skiing contests.

Italy also has a prominent position in the sports equipment market. According to a study by the Idea-Nomisma research center (1993), in 1991 Italy was positioned fourth in the world with an expenditure of US$5,143 million, after the United States (US$38,844), Japan (US$10,057), and Germany (US$8,478). It is within this ample international context, motivated by the successful formula of European club competitions (e.g., Europe's Champion Cup in soccer, basketball, and volleyball) that the idea is evolving to create championships for "super-clubs" at the continental level. The promoters and sponsors of this project ought to be big financial and industrial groups, like Italy's Fininvest and Holland Philips.

GOVERNMENT INVOLVEMENT IN SPORTS—IDENTIFICATION AND GOVERNMENT SPORTS POLICIES

Financial Support and Subsidy

Italy has neither a Ministry—unlike France, Luxembourg, and Turkey—nor a government agency for sports. Central regulating power is shared by four bodies: (1) the Ministry of Tourism, which exerts a supervisory function over CONI activities;[8] (2) the Ministries of Public Education and Scientific Research, which coordinate and promote sport–physical education in schools and universities, respectively; (3) the Ministry of Defense, which is in charge of sports practice for the military;[9] and (4) the Ministry of Public Health and the Ministry of Public Works, which supervise, respectively, sanitation and structures control.

In Italy, CONI has the largest share of jurisdiction and functions, which in other nations belong to government organs. CONI administers considerable financial resources deriving from the government monopoly on sports betting (soccer and horse-racing, in particular): Law 117 of 1965 assigned 25.8 percent of revenues to the government, and the rest was to be divided between CONI and betting winners. In the long run, these percentages changed in favor of the government (see Table 12.4). In 1991–92, Italians spent US$2,430 million on soccer championship results betting ("Totocalcio"), while US$4,000 million were paid to buy sports events tickets that are subjected to a substantial taxation (about 20 percent of the cost of the ticket).

In 1991 the Italian government's direct contribution to finance the building of large facilities or the organization of international sports events was just 13.5 percent of the money spent for sport in Italy for that year.[10] Similarly, in 1990

Table 12.4
Revenues from Betting on the Results of the Soccer Championship (Totocalcio)
and Their Distribution

Years	Total Revenues (U.S. Million Dollars)	To CONI %	To Government %	To Bets Winners %
1977-78	193.4	35.2	26.8	38.0
1978-79	293.6	35.2	26.8	38.0
1979-80	361.0	28.5	33.5	38.0
1980-81	491.4	35.2	26.8	38.0
1981-82	656.7	35.2	26.8	38.0
1982-83	925.3	35.9	26.2	38.0
1983-84	1172.5	37.2	24.8	38.0
1984-85	1254.9	37.2	24.8	38.0
1985-86	1186.1	37.2	24.8	38.0
1986-87	1433.7	37.2	24.8	38.0
1987-88	1679.6	37.2	24.8	38.0
1988-89	1964.6	32.9	29.1	38.0
1989-90	2116.3	32.2	29.8	38.0
1990-91	2251.4	32.2	29.8	38.0
1991-92	2428.9	29.1	34.4	36.5

the government's direct contribution to the total national budget for sport in France was 39.2 percent; in Britain it was 20.4 percent and in Germany 19.2 percent (Nomisma-Idea Plus, 1993). In none of these countries, however, is there an entity like CONI which is authorized to administer about one-third of betting revenues. It is even possible, therefore, to maintain that to a certain extent in Italy it is sports that finances the government, and not vice versa. Such a state of affairs explains the influence and power of the sports bureaucracy and the position of privilege it enjoys in Italian public administration.

A 1991 law, for example, concedes CONI maximum freedom in human resources management and in the signing of private contracts. At the beginning of the 1990s, CONI controlled a budget of about US$1 billion. Financial resources at the disposal of local authorities are modest. Funding for sport infrastructure is still delivered by Credito Sportivo, an entity founded in 1957 as an offshoot of CONI and judged by many as anachronistic after the decentralizing administrative reform.

Regulatory Policies

The persistent hegemony of CONI, the weak direct involvement of government institutions, and the pressure of interest groups organized in political lobbies constitute the analytical variables that are essential to understand the dynamics of the regulatory process and the difficulties in innovation of sport legislation. The 1968 soccer regulations reform which transformed professional clubs into corporations can only be understood in this framework.

In 1975 CONI suggested in "the blue book" new definitions for jurisdiction among schools (formation activity), promotional entities, and labor unions (promotional and recreational activities), reserving for sports federations the exclusive responsibility for elite sport practices. The idea lying behind "the blue book" was to create a regulatory system at different levels that would eliminate the phenomenon of deceitful amateur practices and convert CONI into a service agency of a new Ministry of Sport. Similarly, school and university sports as well as recreational activities by companies needed clearer "rules of the game," thus distinguishing between amateur practice, semiprofessionalism, and simple promotion.

For a long time sports movements allied with political, union, and religious organizations were in conflict with CONI and argued about the criteria for and size of distribution of funds from betting revenue. Clubs would enjoy all sorts of tax benefits (as nonprofit organizations), welfare services, and health protection (preventative medicine, cure, and rehabilitation) as well as administrative tax advice.[11]

In March 1977 the left-wing opposition parties unsuccessfully proposed in Parliament a draft bill for the institution of a National Sport Service. Instead, it was decided to create a Committee for Sport Development, composed by CONI, promotional entities, and unions. The objective of this committee was to supervise the functioning of decentralizing reform in the sports system, particularly with regard to promotion and infrastructure projects. A plan for privatizing CONI was also advanced at this stage, even by some in government circles, to end the body's anachronistic monopoly sanctioned in 1942 and to give equal standing to voluntary associations. A boycott by CONI bureaucrats and allied lobbyists made it impossible to carry out the necessary reform of regulatory policies.

In 1978, however, the clandestine soccer betting scandal highlighted a deficit in control policies.[12] The scandal, which was uncovered just as the first national law concerning the sports labor market was on the point of being passed, showed once again how Italy was lacking a precise set of rules on the rights and duties of professional athletes. Paradoxically, the failure to acknowledge the professional status of high-performance athletes had made the act not liable to punishment: the penal consequences of the scandal were insignificant. Nonetheless, the juridical discipline in the sports labor market was globally reformed, and the control system was strengthened in compliance with other categories of workers.

In 1978–79 the National Sanitary Service was established, which assigned (only temporarily) to CONI a wide range of functions in relation to sports and preventive medicine. These functions were passed to local authorities in the 1980s and became the focus of conflicts between interest groups (sports doctors) and regulatory local bodies. CONI's board remained divided between those supporting reform and co-management with voluntary associations and defenders of traditional category privileges. Meanwhile, the problem of soccer sponsorships—an unregulated business of the first magnitude—burst. In fact, since the end of the 1970s the dimensions of the sponsorship and advertising market, favored by the success of TV sports, have called for the adoption of new criteria in the definition of users' contracts, fees, and commercial guarantees to prevent financial groups from using the unregulated field of sports sponsorship to avoid taxes.

In 1982 the central government organized a national conference of sports in which the subjects of institutional regulation and decentralization of sports organizations were viewed for the first time in an innovative way. A few months earlier, Law 91 had set new terms for the relationship between clubs and professional athletes. The sports federations were entrusted with the task of establishing guidelines of professionalism for the single disciplines, stressing as necessary criteria for economic retribution, continuity of performance, and association with CONI.

The professional status of athletes, coaches, and technical directors was acknowledged at last by the legal system and regulated (as a form of autonomous or subordinated labor) by a precise law with respect to taxes, health insurance, and social security. At last, Italy's legal system abandoned the distinction between professional and amateur status, advancing the revolutionary "rule 45" approved by the international Olympic committee (Tokyo, 1990).[13]

Another open issue that remains is that of drugs and substances (and other related matters), the use of which is spreading to nonprofessional circles (think of those substances used in the fitness room) and can no longer be simply considered a mere breach of ethical conduct in sport

Policies Affecting the Sports Organizations

The promotion policies enacted by public powers in favor of the sports movement are essentially related to clubs' fiscal treatment, insurance policies, and infrastructure financing. Huge public sports projects—usually in connection with spectacular competitive events (1956 winter Olympic Games, 1960 summer Olympic Games, 1990 World Soccer Cup, 1987 World Athletics, etc.) or with religious and civilian manifestations—have always been justified, in fact, by the aim of reinforcing the infrastructure of the cities involved. In this sense, the funding of huge projects performed a Keynesian function in the economic cycle. These expenditures replaced the modest investment capacities of local entities and indirectly favored spectator sports.

The interventions in sport at the grass-roots level and therefore in voluntary associations appear rather dubious, for to this end a more flexible and smaller infrastructure would be required. As a result, since 1957, Credito Sportivo has distributed $US 2,700 million at low interest for the building and reconstruction of about 12,000 facilities. However, it is only since 1983 that private associations and practicing organizations have had access to this financing.

Better effects on sport associations development came in the 1980s from Decree 616, which in July 1977 enacted the norm for administrative decentralization. By this decree, the town councils—holders among other things of licenses for sports events, plant use permits, swimming pools, and skiing schools—are also the "guarantors" of concessions for the use of fitness rooms and school swimming pools. Moreover, they are the institutional mediators among consumer organizations, school boards, and other interest groups competing for limited financial sources.

In matters of insurance, Casa di Previdenza per gli Sportivi (Sportass)—the body for insurance protection of sports athletes (founded in 1934) which in 1978 became an autonomous public entity—mainly insures athletes against accidents. It has been granted tax exemption status and been given the monopoly on insurance policies for athletes (by law stipulated by their federations).

Until a few years ago, the Italian sports movement was subject to a very complex and costly taxation system, which voluntary and sports associations lobbied to lighten and simplify. Their efforts resulted in the law on revenues generated from amateur activities (1986) and the simplified accounting procedures set for voluntary associations and nonprofit amateur organizations (1991). In the Law of 1986, the revenues from competitive sports activities (provided they are performed as "nonprofit" and with the patronage of CONI or voluntary associations acknowledged by CONI) have been distinguished from the other types of income and are subject to lighter taxation. Prizes for the winners of these competitions, if lower than about US$1,000, are totally tax free. The "voluntary service general law," a "nonprofit" that better defined the nonprofit societies, obliged them to officially certify both their activities and their balance sheet. Thus, the law simplified the tax system of societies with an annual budget lower than 100 million lire (about US$77,000).

Another public entity with indirect promotional responsibilities is Unione Nazionale Incremento Razze Equine (UNIRE), a body for security and selection of race horses which operates under the Ministry of Agriculture. To this purpose, UNIRE carries out an important coordination activity within the different economic sectors involved in racing (racecourse managers, horse race agencies, syndicates of breeders for trotters and gallopers, jockeys and trainers, horse-betting entities), allocating a share of revenue from wages to first-quality breeders and to sector beneficiaries.[14]

Similarly, the government distributes budget resources for the upkeep of seven motor-racing tracks of national interest and supports the organization of spectacular competitions (Italy's cycling Giro, the Rome Tennis Open, Italy's Golf Open, Motor Racing Grand Prix, etc.). In economic terms, the added value produced by the nonprofit sports sector—in large part thanks to public contribution—was over US$2,300 million in 1992.

Intergovernmental and Subgovernmental Arrangements

The administrative reform of the 1970s has produced, as mentioned above, a transfer of jurisdiction in sports matters which has stirred tensions among the players involved (the sports bureaucracy, local authorities, and professional categories, such as sports physicians and financial agents). Decentralization has favored those at the local level who were best equipped and most sensitive to the social demands of sports practice. The massive offer to build structures in the 1980s denotes, for example, the unforeseen feedback effect of the repeal of an old fascist Law of 1934 which (in accordance with the central fascist philosophy) limited the authority of town councils and municipalities in budget affairs. Since 1978, local authorities have been able to obtain loans and build. However, the formidable expansion of structures and facilities in the 1980s has been somewhat limited in its social effects because of unsound criteria in site selection, maintenance management, planning, and diversification. For example, for reasons of political propaganda or in order to support "protected" economic interests, impressive and expensive facilities, too specialized for actually encouraging grass-roots practice, were often built. All this—especially in the southern regions—caused neglect, underutilization, and deterioration of the facilities. Similarly, the implementation of medical assistance for sports practitioners and local programs to benefit groups of people such as the disabled and immigrants—often due to the lack of integration between public health service and social services administration—remain very unsatisfactory at this stage.

The 1992 and 1993 budget restrictions threaten to worsen the situation. In fact, fearing the crack in public finance and having been urged to keep the deficit under control in order to meet their obligations with the EC, the governments of this period started a policy of reducing social spending. Especially after the crash of the financial markets and the devaluation of the lira in September 1992, a program of restraint of public administration debts and of "unproductive" expenditures was being carried out. Actually, there has been a sharp contraction of welfare programs which has caused widespread social discontent (particularly because of the considerable increase in health expenses to be paid for by the citizens) and difficulties for local administrations as expenses are cut, including those supporting voluntary associations and financing for sport facilities. On the contrary, the powers conferred in 1991 by Law 142 to "urban areas" and local administrations (actually never implemented and aimed at beginning sports for everybody) released them from CONI's patronage and encouraged the rising demand for noncompetitive sports practice, including new outdoor activities.

Since the late 1980s, however, especially in the urban centers of the north and center, some interesting developments have taken place among consumers who have taken an active role in the negotiations with the local authorities. A more mature perception of sport and its manifold social and environmental components has also been growing in public opinion, as shown by a popular referendum in Val d'Aosta (1992) whereby almost 80 percent of the inhabitants of the region refused to support the bid for the winter Olympics and the campaign for Milan 2000 Olympic Games.[15]

Other Types of Policies

The school system and the armed forces are two influences in sports policies. It has already been observed that military sport encourages "amateur" practice by granting a completely different and privileged treatment of the athletes belonging to the armed forces and the police, who can profit both by sponsorship and advertising using their image. An important example is given by the ski champion and TV star, Alberto Tomba, officially a mere *carabiniere* (a noncommissioned officer of one the three Italian police bodies). In other words, military sport is concerned with recruiting elite athletes rather than promoting sports practices among the military.

The armed forces, however, have always claimed to have a primary role in physical and sports activities as they are conceived as preparation for national service. Traditionally, they have watched over the disciplines connected with war activities and the political reliability of those involved in sports practices. This dual strategy has produced a system of regulatory policies especially favorable to military sport, practically exempting qualified athletes from draft obligations and offering secure professional positions at the end of their competitive career. Military groups are engaged not only in the traditional army activities of skiing and shooting, but also—under CONI's consent—in very technical specialties (bobsled racing by air force personnel or boat racing by police personnel).

With regard to the school system, since the end of the nineteenth century, the Catholic and Liberal ruling elites in the country have been on opposite sides of the debate on compulsory physical education in schools. As already mentioned, earlier, the fascists made instrumental use of physical education as a premilitary activity. But this issue has been the object of recurring tensions even under democratic coalition governments. The subordinate status assigned to sports in the educational system is attributable to the political and pedagogical hegemony of moderate Catholics, who have little sensitivity to the values of the body and are very careful to conserve Church privileges in voluntary and recreational organizations.

From this point of view, a real breakthrough came in 1979 with the ministry programs for the secondary school, which defined sports activity literally as "a fundamental area of education." This small cultural revolution, however, was delayed because the standards were not applied and school administrations obstructed their implementation. In 1980 an agreement between the Ministry of Public Education and CONI made sports activities an official subject of secondary school education.

In the early 1990s, two issues dominated Parliament's political agenda. The first concerns the reform of superior physical education institutes, which train school teachers and operations staff at the base level. It regards the updating of programs, length of diploma course, and acknowledgment of its university-level status in line with EC norms. The second issue regards the new setting of public education institutions within the "sports model," after the decision by CONI's board to withdraw from the organization, Giochi della Gioventu', a sports event for the young, created at the end of the 1960s for early recruiting of sports talents. Over time the Giochi have not proved effective, and by its withdrawal CONI pointed out the need to devise different selection criteria, to limit the disciplines to the basic ones, and to overcome the competition between regional teams. The issue remains, however, whether school personnel would be capable or effective at recruiting young children into sport.

POLICIES AND THEIR GOALS

Domestic Policy Goals

All authoritative historical research (Fabrizio, 1977; Grendi, 1983; Jacomuzzi, 1973; Pivato, 1991) underscores the influence of politics on Italian sports from the start. Physical education school (1878), besides forming the "soldier citizen," was expected to reproduce the ideas of the bourgeoisie of the Italian Risorgimento. At the end of the nineteenth century, popular gymnastics schools attended by illiterate, lower-income classes exhibited an explicit ideological goal; discipline, nationalism, paramilitary organization, and fealty to class hierarchies represented until Giolitti's time (the early decades of twentieth century) the dominant features of the official sports movement and of "methodical gymnastics" as theorized by Emilio Baumann. This conception was opposed by the pedagogy of Angelo Mosso, a follower of de Coubertin's ideas and advocate of "English sport games," who supported a more leisure-oriented sports approach to social control of the working classes.

In the last years of the fascist dictatorship (1922–43)—after the elimination of socialist and Catholic sports and recreational facilities—sports became a privileged vehicle of symbolic identification with the nation and its regime and of permanent mobilization and political control through an elaborate organizational network.[16]

In the second postwar period, CONI reestablished its hegemony over the sports system by political agreement with government parties. The strategic accord—first in the interest of anticommunist coalitions by center and center-left (with socialist participation) governments—did not leave out the opposition parties and their associates, especially after polarization was replaced by consociation political practices in the 1970s (the "wide understandings").

An important example of spectacular events and the use of "democratic" symbolic manipulation is the Rome Olympics of 1960. In the 1960s, with the economic boom, the successes of soccer clubs and of most popular champions proved to be an important component of the feeling of success that spread over the country.[17] In addition, the larger share of leisure time available favored the consumer's demand for spectator sports and active sports practice.

It took the early center-left governments—between 1963 and 1967—to include sports in the government agenda and within the welfare framework. In the 1960s the Consulta Nazionale dello Sport (a consulting body for sports) came into existence. It urged that the legal status of clubs be defined and that consistent tax breaks be given for sports events (a goal obtained only thirty years later). In 1961 an advanced Institute of Sport Sciences was set up; in 1966 a School of Sport was constituted in Rome. Both are public agencies, subordinate to CONI's directives, with the task of elevating the quality of sports operators and research. In 1964, the Centri di formazione giovanile—promotional agencies for sports recruiting—were set up. Starting from 1966–67, they were called Centri Olimpia and were run by regional sports clubs, while CONI reserved to its CAS (Centri di avviamento allo sport) the task of supporting the individual disciplines among children, six to fourteen years of age.

Acknowledgment of the social role of voluntary movements actually challenged traditional CONI hegemony over the whole sports practice, but it was counterbalanced by the possibility of self-financing through Totocalcio bets. In short, in the mid-1960s the early center-left governments seemed to break with the relative indifference to sport showed by the postfascist governments (1946–63). Their political strategy, however, was based largely on mere money contributions, which were more helpful in granting political consensus than encouraging and supporting the spontaneous growth of sports practice. For the first time in the postwar period, the national economic plan of 1966–70 included an extraordinary intervention for sports facilities in the southern regions and in the underdeveloped northern areas. In addition, booming universities in the 1960s favored important public initiatives in the field.[18] In 1967 a project for building sports facilities in university towns was passed. In 1968 a new statute of sports associations was adopted, which partly enfranchised university sports centers from CONI's control.

At the end of the 1960s, however, the reforming impulse of center-left wing governments declined, and sports matters again were delegated to its traditional institutions. The Olympic failure of 1968 in Mexico City—after the brilliant performances of Italian athletes in Rome (1960) and Tokyo (1964)—exposed CONI to severe criticism, which, however, did not produce innovative effects on the sports system.

In 1975 the ISEFs (the Superior Physical Education Institutes) were shaken by student protests and sit-ins: claims for reform mingled with the fear of a devaluation of the role of professional sport operators and physical education teachers. The government was not able to effectively reform, and CONI—provided with a specialized structure for coaches' training—of course did not encourage reform that might question its role.

For a large part of the 1970s, the weakness of central administrations and the recurring government crises allowed CONI to increasingly act as if it were an "unofficial" Sports Ministry able to intervene in the legislative agenda. Anyway, in 1981 legal recognition of professional sports finally permitted athletes and operators to take advantage of all social security benefits. Also in the early

1980s, the mighty and anarchic system of professional soccer was regulated. In particular, professional players were no longer considered the "property" of their clubs, which, up to then, could speculate on the estimated commercial value of the individual athletes, often evading taxes and compulsory contributions while using the champions' popularity in many profitable ways.

The trade unions' powers of intervention and protection were legally recognized. Between the 1960s and 1970s, while the reformist left and the Communist party itself accepted the idea of sports as a collective right within the spirit of the welfare state, the new radical movements—influenced by neo-Marxist and Frankfurt school thought—submitted competitive sport, defined as "consumeristic and capitalistic," to severe criticism. Actually, CONI's total attention to competitive events and a very fragile "sport for everybody" culture (paradoxically experienced in Italy only within the authoritarian framework of fascism) coincided to slow down the political and organizational emancipation of the sports movement.

So, until the early 1990s, a substantial dual system was set up: CONI versus voluntary movements; a strategy of centralized planning for competitive sport versus an incentive to self-manage base-level practice. Central government tended to mediate the conflict, avoiding binding decisions or siding with one or another of the opposite players. Actually crushed by the cross pressures exerted by the CONI professional bureaucracy (traditionally progovernment) on the one hand, and a voluntary network fortified by a widespread social consensus, on the other, the central authorities mostly developed mediation rather than intervention policies.

Hence came the partial turning point of 1976—with the opening of CONI to promotional associations (the *enti*) and their political linkages—and the laws of 1979 which facilitate the direct intervention of local administrations in the sports system granting them money contributions for facilities and activities, but without abolishing the Credito Sportivo, the old power center controlled by CONI. Moreover, even in symbolic terms, there were clamorous examples of instrumental and liturgical use of spectator sports by institutional powers, from official decorations for winners of international competitions to rhetorical forms of patriotism in highly emotional competitive events. An example was the 1982 World Soccer final in Madrid, won by the Italians against the German team in the presence of top state officials and acclaimed by the people with tears of joy. Anthropologists and semiologists interpreted the tears as a sort of ritual (implicitly legitimated by the institutions) liberating Italy from the torpid period of terrorism and recession of the 1970s.

Athletes and Sports Organizations' Goals

From the start, the amateur sport movement (mountaineering, tennis, equestrian clubs) presented many distinctive traits of elite practice. Until World War I, the most popular and politicized voluntary organizations were gymnastics and walking clubs. Central power gave incentives—such as discounted railway fares—and provided a form of paternalistic support for the takeoff of the first national practicing clubs. No benefit was accorded to clubs that the government did not control or recognize. But by 1910 the religious sports associations— born in cultural and political opposition with the liberal state and gathered in the Federation of Catholic Sport (FASCI)—were already able to compete with the national Federation of Gymnastics.[19]

In the socialist camp, physical culture, which was rigorously uncompetitive, was reduced to a hygienic practice and a means of fighting alcoholism in the countryside. At the outbreak of World War I, gymnastics clubs in the north began an intense interventionist campaign and clashed regularly with Catholic and socialist pacifists. The aims of organizations, which were reconstituted after the war, were generally extraneous to mere sports activity. Before Mussolini seized power (1922) and the repression involving opposition sports associations (1925–26), the socialist movement abandoned its original hostility to competitive sport.[20]

One aspect of fascist sports policies that has been less analyzed is the creation of a sports patronage system financed by industrialists and inspired by the regime of corporate culture. CONI was appointed to oversee high-level competitive activities, while amateur associations were grouped under Opera Nazionale Dopolavoro (entity for recreational activities), under direct control of the party. It was the Opera that administered a wide range of operational services and that supervised sports practice in schools and fitness centers, facilities, and summer camps. The turning of sports into preparatory training for military activity—as in the old "German paradigma" of the early century—and the emphasis on high-level sports performances as an instrument of political propaganda, deprived Italian sports between the two wars of any autonomy and of any attention to the social aims of physical and sports activities.

With the end of the fascist regime after World War II, different sports policies and cultural views were debated. These views were influenced by political parties and the dominant ideologies. So sport, for a long time, felt the effects of the political conflict that Italy experienced (Porro, 1992). A turning point can perhaps be detected in the 1970s, when some sectors of progressive Catholic associations launched "social sport," which was a little different from their former recreational activities and cultural approach. Similarly, leftist associations tried to give ample space to sports in the countryside. In both cases, it appeared evident that the growing demand for sports and fitness had necessitated an adequate public policy to address the problem. But only in the late 1970s and 1980s—when the idea that sport is a "meritorious good" (Mishan, 1982) became widespread—were important legislative innovations launched to favor access to public sports facilities and the growth of mass sports practice. Endogenous dynamics of change, induced by the new assignments of voluntary associations and the crisis of the old bureaucratic model, added to the exogenous crisis of the traditional political membership organizations. Significantly, in 1990

Italian Union Popular Sport (UISP) became Italian Union Sport-for-All, enfranchised from traditional identities and redefined as a social consumer network.

Separate attention ought to be given to hooligan organizations, born at the
end of the 1970s, especially in soccer, but also in other team games. Some
sociologists have viewed a need for social identification with the decline of
political movements of the 1970s. The thesis is disputable, but the appeal of
symbols and jargon of political extremism is quite evident (especially those
using race and regional identity).

Foreign Policy Goals

There are many examples of Italy's use of sports in international politics,
from the boycott of the Austro-Hungarian teams in the years preceding World
War I to the paranoic rivalry with France and Britain during the fascist period.
In reality, all these exasperating confrontations revealed a latent national inferiority complex, probably arising from the country's late unification and one of
the psychological ingredients of consent to the fascist regime. Even after the
defeat of 1943–45, however, national sport "icons"—the cyclists Coppi and
Bartali, the boxer Primo Carnera, the soccer players of "grande Torirlo" (trag-
ically killed in an air accident in 1949), the water-polo winners at the London
Olympics (1948), the successes of throwers and walkers as well as the technological exploits in motor racing—gave international public opinion evidence of
Italy's desperate will to survive.

With the 1960 Olympics, the attempt was made to project an image (even an
aggressive one) of a revived Italy eager to resume an international role more
consistent with its economic potential. The sports victories of Italian athletes,
which were part of this image promotion, reinforced the traditional "results
ethics" of the competitive direction. Again, it was in anticipation of a successful
result that in 1976 the Italian tennis team was permitted to contend (victoriously)
for the Davis Cup against the Chileans, in spite of domestic opposition and
public opinion, and a desire to isolate Pinochet's regime.

Italy resolved the potential conflict between objectives and ethical values in
a Machiavellian way by establishing a precedent that would allow Italian athletes
to participate in the Moscow Games five years later, "overcoming" the boycott
in response to the Soviet invasion of Afghanistan. Only military athletes did not
participate, and the national team paraded without the flag; the competitive results were again very positive at the games' end. It was a compromise choice,
recurrent in Italian diplomacy and at the same time functional given the hyper-
competitive logic of Italy's sports organization model.

The use of sports events for purposes of international promotion can also be
found in the setting up of the 1990 Soccer World Championship, and in the
early stages—even though the initiative precociously fell through—in the candidacy of Milan for the 2000 Olympic Games. In both cases, the image of valor
on the international scene was principally important to economic holdings in-

terested in foreign markets. In fact, industrialists and company consortiums set up COL, the soccer Mondiali 90 Organizing Committee, presided over by the ex-manager of the Fiat group and Ferrari, Luca di Montezemolo. Their strategic objective was to give a new image to "made in Italy," one no longer linked to the traditional sectors of quantity exports (light industry, chemical products, furniture, and furnishing) but to elite goods and services. The organization committee's logo became a sort of status symbol obtained at very high costs, but useful to gain credibility in foreign markets reached by television events (Lanfranchi, 1991). As for the image promoted to tourists, the offer of an "Italian package" was replaced by the promotion of the various cities—and the arts— chosen to play the matches.[21]

The Italian participation in the great sailing races of the America's Cup (sponsored by the Ferruzzi-Montedison industrial group), the introduction of the Benetton clothing holding in Formula One motor racing, and the constant presence of Olivetti in the computerized information management for high-performance sport, meet this strategy. In this way, the commercial is definitively being favored over the more traditional—national image and prestige—competitive means.

Italy's sports policy toward Third World countries is inadequate, consisting only of financing, through the cooperation programs of the Ministry for Foreign Affairs, public works such as stadiums, grounds, gymnasiums, and swimming pools, in Central East African countries (Ethiopia, Eritrea, Somalia), in Albania, and a few other geographic areas. A series of bilateral agreements, often financed by the Italian state, allows Third World coaches in Coverciano, near Florence, and the specialized centers of Track and Field Federation of Formia, Tirrenia, and Sestriere (for high-altitude training).

CONCLUSIONS

Between the late 1940s and the early 1990s, CONI has consistently assured high professional standards and has represented a model of efficiency in Italy's rather lackluster institutional sport services. However, this paradigm of development, founded on the absolute priority of results, has had a negative impact on social sport perceptions, as is shown by the absence of any relationship between actual sports practice and competition results.

The case of Italian sport is one where the government has preferred to bestow permanent responsibility on a specialized entity rather than taking direct policy action. This sports system, through betting revenues, finances the government and even, at least until the early 1990s, the political parties through services offered by politically affiliated associations. So the paradox is that Italian sport has been plagued by both intervention and inadequate policies. The same legal innovations that benefited the sports movement in the 1970s and the following years (juridical recognition of voluntary associations) were never "sports-centered" policies. It is not incidental that the growth of investments and opportunities has been accompanied by an outbreak of jurisdictional conflicts among CONI, voluntary associations, and local authorities over health insurance and structures management (Fedele, 1993). This conflict resulted in the demand for a new sports regulation policy.

Only at the end of the 1980s, especially following on the regulation of voluntary organizations and the shift away from the old patronage system, did the central institutions begin an acknowledgment policy. The most important part concerns the legal status of sportspeople, the tax system of amateur clubs, and the different tasks of CONI and the school system in first recruiting and reopening negotiation for a general law on sports. Unfortunately, many other central issues, such as regulations on substances, clandestine betting, illegal professionalism, and new norms for the colossal advertising market, have not been included in the agenda. Policies for requalifying sports operators (reform of the Superior Institute of Physical Education), setting up new regulations for health and insurance systems, and regulating semiprofessionalism in the military have been demanded for years. It is quite proper to speak of a strategy of omitted regulations, which has ended by producing a situation that has hardly improved.

In 1992 the number of Leviathan CONI employees totaled 3,300,[22] but the employment structure still appears to be greatly unbalanced in favor of high-level sport in contrast with the rising demand for noncompetitive sports practice in Italy as in other Western countries. The large demand for sports for everyone meets the principles of the European Sport Charter which asserts "the right of everybody to sport and fitness," as subscribed to in May 1992 by the twelve EC ministers. In Italy, however, often this social demand is still left to spontaneous development or, even worse, to speculative interests. Public authorities have given little encouragement and support. While acquiring at last the social principle of sports as a "right of citizenship," public officials continue to delegate all actual responsibilities to CONI.

On the other hand, the frustrations suffered by Italian competitive sports between the end of the 1980s and the early 1990s (e.g., the small number of medals won in Barcelona in 1992)—particularly in the individual specialties least sustained by private economic operators (e.g., canoeing, weightlifting, and professional boxing)—witness a crisis in ideas and management that questions CONI's traditional efficiency. In addition, in 1993 a popular referendum sanctioned the abolition of the Ministry for Tourism which was entrusted with the main tasks of overseeing CONI itself. These tasks have been temporarily assigned to the head of government, while calls have again risen for the institution of a real ministry of sport that would completely absorb CONI. This call to transform CONI into a ministry has produced an inevitable conflict with this powerful and large bureaucracy, and this call increases the risk of recreating CONI's hyper-competitive philosophy and poor care for "a sport for everyone." So the debate on CONI's destiny has once more been connected with the future of the Italian political system as a whole.

In the spring of 1993, during the election for the CONI presidency, some influential media, including Italy's largest circulation daily, the *Repubblica,* campaigned against the old president Arrigo Gattai, specifically against his strict centralism and his political alliances. These media critics sought a clear-cut division between competitive and noncompetitive sport management. Such a radical transformation of the traditional Italian sports model is unlikely, but the accession of the "reformist" Mario Pescante to CONI leadership opens the way to a thaw in the relationship with voluntary movements and to important organizational changes. The most rational trend seems to be in the search for a balance between high-performance sport—strengthening CONI's coordinative feature and transferring more resources and powers to the thirty-nine specialty federations—and the pressure exerted by the sports-for-everybody movements. These movements could enjoy a special autonomy, perhaps directly administering part of the available resources. The point, however, is on the one hand to overcome the resistance to change by the most traditionalist CONI sectors, and, on the other hand, to regulate the disorderly galaxy of sports for everybody.

At least half of the traditional promotion entities, linked to old political, union, and religious organizations, should be abolished because they are not representative enough and have survived only thanks to a political exchange system (consensus against resources), which by now has been largely criticized. Some traditional specialties ("tamburello," billiards) or those that arrived in Italy in the 1980s (orienteering, badminton) should be reorganized, acknowledging their autonomy and sustaining their recruiting campaigns.

Finally, a representative system of amateur sports should be devised, a system meant neither to join CONI competitive federations nor sports for everybody mass associations. (This is the case for the new outdoor specialties such as rafting, hang gliding, and free climbing.) So reorganized, entrusted with more responsibilities and enfranchised from the oppressive patronage of CONI, a body specifically in charge of sport for everybody could better promote sports education in the schools. It could also take care of scarcely protected fields, like those of the Third Age, of over a million disabled (in 1991), but with only 3,000 of them practicing some physical activities. (This sector is overseen by a branch of CONI, the Federdisabili.)

Endowing the real protagonists of sports for everybody with wider and autonomous powers, perhaps it will be more feasible to reverse the trend to build huge and hyperspecialized plants, which are useless for mass sport practice; to change the Health Service norms, which appear to be more bureaucratic than effective in the field of prevention and protection; and to keep under control the costs of the private sports market which thanks to the lack of state regulation, is thriving. A reform of CONI—not necessarily its abolition as a leading body of national sport—is therefore politically and strategically essential. However, it requires a courageous and culturally updated view of sport as a mass phenomenon and of its transformational processes.

NOTES

1. A model case is represented by the entry of women into the sports system. This phenomenon began in Italy immediately after World War II erupted, when women had to replace the men engaged in warfare in all their traditional activities, therefore producing an unintentional factual emancipation. For this reason, women in sports cannot be considered a "conquest" of the regime. Similarly, Italian successes in major competitions in the 1920s and 1930s were the product of integration in the international community and of the technical maturity achieved in some disciplines rather than the result of competitive promotion campaigns as touted by the fascist leaders.

2. Such a function clearly exceeds the Olympic spirit and is inspirited rather by reasons of social control, which are typical of the authoritarian state.

3. The men's team became European Champion in 1989 and 1993, World Champion in 1990, and was a three-time winner of the World League.

4. In this respect, the soccer championship of 1992–93 represents a real turning point, with the very expensive purchase, by pay TV, of the right to broadcast a top division match live, even changing the "sacred" timetable of Sunday afternoon matches.

5. The phenomenon dates back to the years between the two world wars when a large number of South American soccer players of Italian origin (*oriundi*) were engaged by top professional clubs and, in some cases, even played for the Italian national team. After World War II, athletes from completely different parts of the world came to play in Italy, attracted by astounding contracts. In the 1960s and 1970s, this phenomenon began to involve the second division teams as well, including technical directors and coaches, and extended to basketball and other major team sports.

6. Silvio Berlusconi, one of the most popular European tycoons of the 1980s and the early 1990s, has made many brilliant business deals which have made him the protagonist of an evident transformation of the Italian economic system. He controls the main private European radio and television companies, which in Italy compete with the three state networks in terms of audience and turnover. They have (alone or jointly) nationwide broadcasting channels in Spain, Germany, and France.

7. Only considering the 1991–92 soccer championship, for example, US$83 million were spent on TV rights in Italy, against US$46 million in Spain; US$39 million in France; US$29 million in Germany; and US$23 million in Britain. As regards the TV rights connected with sports programs in general, in 1992 Italy was third in the world, with an outlay of about US$153 million (USA 1,715 million US$ and France 254 million US$).

8. This ministry, however, was abolished in 1993.

9. This category comprises athletes from the different bodies of the police forces, which were demilitarized in the 1980s.

10. In 1991 the total amount for "sport expenses" was about US$8,000 million; if we include sports clothing expenses, the total would be about US$16,000 million.

11. Since the second half of the 1970s, some important legal provisions—in line with the regulatory approach philosophy of the period—have been adopted, but in an often disorderly way and under the pressure of interest groups linked to political circles. For instance, many sports disciplines were admitted in school programs. Almost at the same time, CONI's employees achieved semiofficial status (as public but nongovernmental officers), with important effects on the personnel structure and policies.

12. In 1978 the top series soccer championship was upset by the discovery of a clan-

destine betting network, called "Totonero." This circuit, which had caused heavy losses to the official betting system ("Totocalcio")—the main financing source of official Italian sport—proved in some cases to be controlled by organized crime. It was ascertained that some matches had been fixed in advance with the connivance of very popular players. The clandestine network was busted by a spectacular police operation: some athletes were arrested in public. The sports court of the Soccer League inflicted severe punishments, including disqualifications and demotions for some teams to a lower rank. In the mid-1980s, however, the phenomenon returned in a similar way.

13. By this rule, CIO allows professional athletes to take part in Olympic Games provided they were not paid directly for their participation.

14. In 1989 betting on horse racing represented 35 percent of the total Italian betting market, for a value of about US$2 billion.

15. The campaign for Milan 2000 Olympic Games had been promoted by a group of Milan businessmen and eminent citizens. They had worked out a plan with no costs to the state, totally self-financed and aimed at reversing the trend to gigantism of the last Olympic Games. The failure of the initiative dates back to January 1993, with the City Council's delay while debating the candidacy, which finally passed despite vocal opposition. Among the objections to the project were fear of new damages to the historical and natural environment and skepticism about the economic advantages of the project. A call for signatures for a petition against the project had already been announced.

16. Moreover, in the last years of the regime, radio and cinema propaganda became intense. The nationalistic and bellicose exaltation of sports champions represented a nonsecondary aspect of the increasing importance attributed to "media network" by the regime, even to the detriment of direct mobilization.

17. Also in the arts, it is meaningful that the harsh representation of Italy in the 1950s, as portrayed by neo-realistic film-making, was replaced by Fellini's *La Dolce Vita*.

18. In the 1960s the university still had an important role in the national sports system. Disciplines such as track and field and rugby, for example, were especially popular in university sports centers.

19. FASCI's success was also the cause of its identity crisis because it fed the concrete need for official recognition by government institutions, generating sharp tensions between moderate and intransigent groups within the movement.

20. Representatives of the Proletarian Association for Physical Education (APEF), founded in 1920 in Milan, successfully joined the proletarian games of Leipzig in 1922 and even won a weightlifting medal at the Paris Olympic Games (1924). A magazine with the title *Sport and Proletariat* was started in 1923, although it did not last long, and the communists created sports-paramilitary organizations to defend against fascist squads.

21. For example, the artistic spots introducing the TV broadcast matches—dedicated to the host cities—were shot by major Italian film directors. The opening ceremony of the championship in Milan in June 1990 corresponds to a spectacular representation of this strategic image, based on three symbolic and at the same time concretely commercial elements: the performances of singers, the high fashion show, and the evocation of the Renaissance folklore.

22. To CONI employees in 1989 one had to add almost 716,000 sports operators, including managers (505,000), coaches (120,000), and competition officers (91,000). There were about 874,000 in 1983 and 531,000 two years earlier (CONI-CENSIS, 1992), with a strong growth in the coaches category.

REFERENCES

Brunelli, M. (1992). Olimpiadi e sponsorizzazioni. *Lettera dall'Italia, 7*(6): 40.

Carocci, G. (1975). *Storia d'Italia dall'Unita a oggi.* Milan: Feltrinelli.

CONI. (1988). *Atti del Congresso Olimpico dello Sport Italiano.* Rome.

CONI. (1982). *Atti della Conferenza Nazionale dello Sport.* Rome.

CONI. (1967). *Attil Coni e le Federazioni Sportive.* Rome.

CONI. (1976). *Il libro azzurro dello sport.* Rome.

CONI. (1968). *Il libro bianco dello sport.* Rome.

CONI. (1971). *Il libro verde dello sport.* Rome.

CONI. (1981). *Quaderni dello Sport, 14*(6). Rome.

CONI-CENSIS. (1994). *I numeri dello Sport.* Rome: Coni-Divisione Documentazione e Informazione.

CONI-CENSIS. (1992). *I numeri dello sport. La practica sportiva in Italia 1981–1990.* Rome: Coni-Divisione Documentazione e Informazione.

Dal Lago, A., and Moscati, R. (1992). *Regalateci un sogno. Miti e realta del tifo calcistico in Italia.* Milan: Bompiani.

Elias, N., and Dunning, E. (1986). *Quest for excitement.* Oxford: Basil Blackwell.

Fabrizio, F. (1977). *Storia dello sport in Italia.* Rimini: Guaraldi.

Fedele, M. (1993). La ridefinizione dei problemi politici. In *I nuovi confini della comunicazione politica.*

Giuntini, S., and Rossi, L. (1990, March). Introduzione a un secolo di sport in Lombardia. *Lancillotto e Nausica, 3:* 7–11.

Goffman, E. (1981). *Relazioni in publico.* Milan: Bompiani. (Original English-language work published in 1959.)

Grandi, B. (1992). Lo sport, gli sponsor, i mass media. *Lettera dall'Italia, 7*(6): 25.

Grendi, E. (1983, August). Lo sport. Un'innovazione vittoriana? *Quaderni storici, 53:* 679–694.

Hoberman, J. H. (1988). *Politica e sport.* Bologna: Il Mulino.

Hobsbawm, E., and Ranger, T. (1987). *L'invenzione della tradizione.* Turin: Einaudi.

ISTAT. (1990, July). *Indagine multiscopo sulle famiglie. Lo sport in Italia.* Rome: Istituto Nazionale di Statistica.

Jacomuzzi, S. (1973). Gli sport. In AA. VV. *Storia d'Italia, V,* (pp. 911–935). Turin: Einaudi.

Lanfranchi, P. (1991). L'Italia e i "suoi" mondiali. Note sull'avvenimento sportivo e d'informazione del 1990. In F. Anderlini and R. Leonardi (eds.), *Politica in Italia 1991* (pp. 243–253). Bologna: Il Mulino.

Lombardo, A. T. (1989). Alle origini del movimento olimpico in Italia. *Ricerche storiche, 19*(2): 297–314.

McLuhan, M. (1964). *Understanding media.* New York: McGraw-Hill.

McLuhan, M., and Fiore, Q. (1968). *The medium is the message.* New York: Bantam Books.

Mishan, E. J. (1982). *Introduction to political economy.* London: Hutchinson.

Nomisma. (1991). *Sport ed economia.* Rome: Fondazione Giulio Onesti.

Nomisma-Idea Plus. (1993). *Sport ed economia.* 2nd Report. Rome: Fondazione Giullo.

Pescante, M., and De Juliis, T. (1990). *L'educazione fisica e lo sport nella scuola italiana.* Florence, Italy: Le Monnier.

Pivato, S. (1991). *I terzini della borghesia.* Milan: Leonardo.

Pociello, C. (1981). *Sports et societe.* Paris: Vigot.

Porro, N. (1995). *Identità nazione, Cittadinanza, Sport, societe e sistema politico nell'Italia contemporanea.* Rome: Edizioni Seam.

Porro, N. (1992). Sport, political system, and sociology in Italy. *International Review for the Sociology of Sport, 4:* 329–341.

Premier Comite Olympique Italien. (1907). *Revue Olympique, 5:* 288.

Salvo, F. (1959). *Dala Magna Charta alla Costituzione italiana.* Palermo, Italy: Palumbo.

Tullio-Altan, C. (1986). *La nostra Italia.* Milan: Feltrinelli.

Valderno, S. G., and Landi, L. (1966). *Sport Enciclopedia* (Vol. 6). Rome: CONI.

Vigarello, G. (1992). Il Tour de France. Memoria, territorio, racconto. *Ludus, 2:* 17–40.

13

Sports Policy in Japan

Yuji Nakamura

The promotion of Japanese sports began in 1961, when the Promotion of Sports Law was enacted following the decision to hold the Olympic Games in Tokyo in 1964. The Games increased the Japanese people's interest in sports, as did the establishment of the National Conference of Physical Strength in 1965. This political support, however, was followed by negative political action. For example, the Japanese government pressured the Japanese Olympic Committee into joining the U.S. government's boycott of the Moscow Olympic Games in 1980.

Similarly, the relationship between politics and sports policies in Japan cannot be ignored. In particular, the government has been striving to promote competitive sports, because they fulfill the human desire for conflict in a socially acceptable way. Furthermore, sports are a vehicle for expressing national pride (as promoted by reciting the national anthem and hoisting the national flag in sports ceremonies).

Urbanization and industrialization in Japan developed rapidly after 1960, leading to an increase in leisure time. As a result, more and more, sports are used for creating pleasure and getting rid of stress, while at the same time increasing exercise among the people. To deal with these new necessities, government had to issue a comprehensive sports policy.

Through a national sports policy the government, political parties, and sports organizing bodies provide measures and programs for sports activities. However, in Japan, except for the Communist party, political parties have not been able to provide concrete sports policies. The Liberal Democratic party (LDP) regards the sports policy of the Ministry of Education, Science, and Culture (hereinafter referred to as the Ministry of Education) as its own policy.

The Japanese political system is a parliamentary cabinet system, and the existence of the cabinet depends on retaining the Diet's confidence. Although each minister is ranked as holding the highest position in each respective ministry and government office, these ministers' positions can be described almost as honorary posts. To a certain extent, administrative bureaucrats, among whom the highest position is that of the ministers' secretariat, can draft policies and laws. Indeed, the education committee is in charge of sports policy in the Diet, but the members of this committee also depend on the sports policy. The Physical Education Bureau is the central authority that provides and enforces concrete plans concerning sports.

Thus, the Sports Bureau holds a position of leadership and authority in its relationships with the Japan Amateur Sports Association (JASA), the Japanese Olympic Committee (JOC), the Prefectural Sports Association, the National Sports Federation Affiliated with the JASA and with the JOC, the education committees at both prefectural and municipal levels, and with special corporations under the supervision of the Ministry of Education.

The Ministry of Education was established after the Meiji Revolution of 1871. Through this ministry, the central government was able to emphasize physical education in school. The Physical Education Division of the Ministry of Education was established in 1928, and as a direct result, a physical education and sports administration system was developed. In Japan, this system is regarded as the basis of the Sports Bureau.

Subsequently, the Physical Education Bureau was established as part of Japan's military buildup for World War II. Although the Physical Education Bureau was abolished temporarily in 1945, it was reestablished at the end of the war. Since that time, the Japanese have recognized this bureau as the Physical Education Bureau. Considering the names and policy contents of the divisions which are the main objects of this chapter, however, the agency will be called the Sports Bureau.

"Social physical education" encompasses all sports except for the physical education provided in schools. Consequently, in education, sports in Japan have traditionally been viewed through a historical perspective. Characteristically, the Sports Bureau regards adult sports as one area of education. In other words, social physical education is viewed as one component of social education. Moreover, this Bureau attaches more importance to school physical education than to social physical education.

The Sports Bureau consists of the Physical Education Division, the Sport-for-All Division, and the Competitive Sports Division. Excluding the chief of the Bureau, these divisions employed seventy officials in 1992. The Sport-for-All Division and the Competitive Sports Division are engaged in all sports policy areas except the administration of physical education in Japanese schools. This administrative structure has made it increasingly difficult for the Japanese people to develop sports activities independently. Rather, this structure promotes sports policy under the control of the Sports Bureau. Therefore, this chapter focuses on the sports policy provided by the Sports Bureau. However, politicians have used the influence of sports with large companies as a means of seeking profit. The government has significant power over the decisions concerning the introduction and abolition of influential sports policies.

Sports policies relating to professional sports have been almost completely ignored in Japan, although, of course, there are a number of very popular professional sports in Japan including sumo wrestling, baseball, golf, boxing, and tennis. Bicycle racing, horse-racing, and motorboat racing are other sports used to promote the construction of public utilities. However, these sports have not directly been the subject of sports policies of the government.

INTRODUCTION TO THE SYSTEM OF
JAPANESE GOVERNMENT

The Japanese Diet consists of the House of Representatives and the House of Councilors, composed of 512 members and 252 members, respectively. Japan's parliamentary cabinet system vests executive power in the cabinet, which consists of the prime minister and not more than twenty ministers of state, all of whom are collectively responsible to the Diet. The prime minister, who is designated by the Diet, must be a member of the Diet and has the power to appoint and dismiss the ministers of the state, all of whom must be civilians and a majority of whom must be members of the Diet.

Japan is divided into forty-seven prefectures, including the Tokyo metropolis. Local government administration is conducted at the prefectural, city, town, and village levels, each with its respective assembly. The prefectural governors and city, town, and village mayors, as well as the members of the local assemblies, are elected by the registered voters within the district concerned. Thus, Japan has three distinct levels of government: national, prefectural, and municipal. The forty-seven prefectural governments (Shi Cho Son) are classified as local governments. Japan's system of intergovernmental relations differs from that of a federal system such as the one operating in the United States.

In practice, local government in Japan is said to enjoy only 30 percent autonomy and at times as little as 10 percent autonomy. In reality, Japanese local government is basically weak and is under the tight control of the central government. This is an especially relevant point when reference is made to the Kikan-Inin-Jimu system (agency-delegated functions). It shapes the basis of relations between the central government and local government. Through this system, the power to execute national administrative affairs is delegated to prefectural governors by the central government.

The system of agency-delegated functions includes such administrative affairs as city planning, welfare, registration of foreigners, issuance of passports, and the taking of the national census. Such affairs occupy most of the office work duties of the prefectures and municipalities. However, within this system the Kikan-Inin-Jimu activities are subject to various restrictions, which even further limit the autonomy of the local governments. A qualified minister of the central government directs and supervises the governor; then a qualified minister and the prefectural governor direct and supervise the heads of municipalities (mayors). Therefore, among the activities of the prefectural governments, about 70 to 80 percent are regarded to be Kikan-Inin-Jimu activities.

In addition to the Kikan-Inin-Jimu system, the various revenues on which the local governments have to rely are controlled to a high degree by the central government. Such revenues include the allocation of local tax grants, national treasury disbursements (subsidies in a broader sense), and local bonds. Nevertheless, the standards set by the central government and the calculation methods it uses for subsidizing local governments tend to be unrealistic, especially as a result of the current rising inflation. As a result, local governments are confronted with the financial problem of "excess burdens." Moreover, the central government provides subsidy programs to guide local governments for the purpose of implementing its own specific policies.

Thus, the position and circumstances of local governments in Japan are deeply integrated with the administrative and financial policies of the central government. This situation was traditionally supported by the political culture which placed the highest value on loyalty and contribution to the central government. However, this political culture has been gradually changing in recent years.

With respect to local politics, remarkable innovations have taken place since the end of the 1960s. The multiple urban and environmental problems that have accompanied Japan's rapid economic growth triggered various citizens' initiatives at the community level. Municipal governments have responded to these initiatives quickly and positively. Despite a continued centralized administrative and financial system, municipal governments have to their credit a number of achievements in policy areas regarding pollution, welfare, and urban planning. Moreover, the prefectural governments are also playing a strategically important role in encouraging the creation of a more decentralized relationship between the national and local governments.

THE CENTRAL GOVERNMENT'S ROLE IN SPORTS POLICIES

As in the days of the Meiji Revolution, the Japanese government does not promote sports policies as goals in themselves but rather tends to use these policies for political objectives. This tendency is especially clear when we consider that as the scale of international sports events becomes larger, the opportunities increase for governments to use these events for political and economic gain.

Nations often use the Olympic Games for purposes of nationalistic self-interest: to advance their foreign policy, to enhance their image and prestige, or to legitimize aggression. In contrast, governments can use the Olympics as a positive means of promoting peace policies. This section discusses the relationship between the Japanese government and its policies on Olympic events, with specific reference to the 1964 Tokyo Olympics, the 1980 Moscow Olympics, and the Resort Development Law.

The Tokyo Olympics of 1964 is said to have started Japan's trend toward Olympic grandeur. At these games, an unprecedented 1 trillion yen were spent on Shinkansen Express lines, massive public works projects, expressways, hotels, and drainage works. Surprisingly, however, only 30 billion yen of this amount was spent on projects directly related to sports. This example shows how the Olympic events can be utilized for economic advancement. Moreover, in the case of the Tokyo Olympics, the strong connections of the Olympic Committee with the Japanese political powers cannot be ignored. Two years before the opening of the Tokyo Olympics, both the president of the Olympic Organizing Committee and the Olympic secretary general were pressured by the government to resign. In the meantime, the government established a replacement position, giving a cabinet member full charge of the Olympics organization. Under the guise of this member's leadership, the government was able to organize, manage, and hold the Olympics in a manner that suited its own goals.

In the case of the Moscow Olympics boycott as well, sports circles bowed to government pressure. In February of 1980, the Japanese government firmly suggested to the Japanese Olympic Committee (JOC) that Japanese participation in the Moscow Olympics be avoided. In May, at an emergency general meeting, the JOC adopted this suggestion as its own. The Ministry of Education placed more pressure on the JOC by announcing it would cut all financial support of the JOC if it participated in the Moscow Olympics. These two examples provide strong evidence that the statement "sports independence from politics" is merely myth.

The Resort Law, promulgated and enforced by the Japanese government in 1987, provided preferential financial treatment to private enterprises involved in the business of golf courses, ski fields, and the construction of other large-scale sports facilities. This legislation both established favorable status in the taxation process for these private businesses and made available to them loans at exceptionally low interest rates. Contrary to what one might think, the primary goal of the government was not to extend opportunities for the public to enjoy sports and leisure through the improvement of sports and leisure facilities. The real government objectives in promoting this law were:

- Through resort and sports facilities development, the government hoped to enhance domestic demand and thereby resolve, in some part, Japan's excessive export record. This was considered one way to resolve the trade conflict with America.

- In the resort development area, the government equated successful development with positive "far-reaching economic effects." Most notably, the government realized the possibility of securing stable employment in regional areas and with the outflow-of-people from overpopulated cities to resort areas hoped to greatly increase revenue in the tourist industry. Generally, the government saw such measures as a resolution to the depopulation problem of Japan.

• The government hoped that, by increasing the number of available resort areas, it would offset the level of citizen dissatisfaction with skyrocketing land prices.

• Such a law provided an avenue for Japan's largest enterprises to spend some of the vast fortunes they had amassed through Japan's economic success.

These examples of the government's economic and politically connected sports policies show that through such policies the Japanese government acts not to promote specific goals but rather to gain political profit.

The government's economic and political goals in promoting national sports policies are well known, but little has been written about the number of citizens who derive enjoyment from sports activities. Many nonelite sports, basically untouched by the administration's rules and regulations, are being enjoyed by citizens throughout Japan. In proportion to the people's increased leisure hours in recent years, citizen demand has increased for information regarding the availability of convenient sports facilities. As a result, Japan has witnessed increased citizen demand for sports policies that are not merely rules enforced by government from above to favor sports organizations connected by Olympic events. Instead, people are demanding policies that create a reasonable sports environment for the citizens.

A sports environment for the citizens can be seen as a system of cooperation among citizens and all kinds of businesses. Until now, people have looked for cooperation between the citizens (consumers of sporting goods and services) and the sporting industry (producers of sporting goods and services including such related industries as sports journalism and sports schools). However, even nonsports-related industries can become involved in creating a favorable sports environment by providing an array of related facilities. Essentially, the government administration must provide public sports facilities and sufficient financial assistance to ensure the continuing involvement of citizens in sports and private enterprise's social contribution to sports. In this respect, the existence of a partnership of citizens, private enterprise, and public administration seems reasonable.

THE CURRENT SPORTS SITUATION IN JAPAN

Table 13.1 shows the level of sports activity participation and frequency in Japan (Leisure Development Center, 1992, p. 24). General exercise and jogging show both a high participation rate and a high average annual frequency.

Golf and skiing are comparatively expensive activities. If we include golfing practice sessions in the total, the rate of participation in golf has risen to 30 percent. This provides clear evidence of the continuing golf boom in Japan.

Gateball croquet, which is especially popular with the older generations, also

Table 13.1
Sports Participation in Japan, 1991

Sports	Participation Rate (%)	Average Annual Frequency (times)	Average Annual Cost (thousand yen)
Exercise	36.8	54.1	3.5
Bowling	34.6	5.9	8.0
Jogging and Marathon	26.0	33.9	5.2
Swimming	24.1	14.6	14.8
Playing Catch, Baseball	21.9	17.0	6.0
Golfing Practice	18.1	19.3	38.9
Badminton	17.0	12.6	2.5
Softball	17.0	12.5	4.0
Skiing	16.6	6.5	116.8
Fishing	16.6	11.0	44.4
Cycling	15.5	26.2	12.6
Volleyball	14.7	20.5	2.3
Table Tennis	14.4	10.0	4.3
Tennis	13.8	20.8	20.3
Golf	13.2	12.6	214.9
Physical Training	13.0	43.2	13.7
Ice Skating	8.7	3.4	6.1
Basketball	7.2	21.5	1.8
Soccer	6.3	20.3	4.4
Aerobics and Jazz Dancing	4.3	28.7	34.7
Japanese Martial Arts	3.9	37.7	17.0
Gateball Croquet	3.2	41.6	11.0
Skin Diving, Scuba Diving	1.2	10.6	107.2
Yachting, Motorboating	1.1	11.4	42.4
Surfing, Windsurfing	0.8	11.1	68.2
Riding	0.7	14.8	21.1
Hang Gliding, Para Gliding	0.4	8.0	158.0

has a very high average annual frequency. Even though gateball is a group sport, the data show that it rates favorably in terms of average annual frequency.

A comparison between baseball and soccer indicates that if the 1990 soccer boom in Japan continues, the participation and annual frequency rates for soccer may overtake those of baseball.

Even though the participation rate of Japanese martial arts is quite low, the data show that martial arts enthusiasts still regularly participate in this sport.

The participation rates of hang-gliding and scuba diving currently are low, but there has been a marked improvement in the sale of related sporting goods. We can expect participation to increase significantly in the future.

Whatever participation and annual frequency rates the chart may show, we must remember that these rates depend on the availability of sports facilities as well as on venue organization.

Sports Facilities

In 1985 the number of sports facilities in Japan totaled about 292,000, approximately twice the number in existence twenty years earlier. Half of this total

Table 13.2
Sports Facilities in Japan, 1985

Owner	School	Public	Job Site	Private (non-profit)	Private (profit)	Total
Number	158,119	60,777	29,332	16,741	27,148	292,117
Percentage	54.1	20.8	10.1	5.7	9.3	100.0

consists of school physical education facilities as shown in Table 13.2 (Sports Bureau, Ministry of Education, 1987, p. 9). Sports facilities, which sports associations control, fall under the category of private nonprofit sports facilities. From 1975 to 1985, the number of private profit and public sports facilities increased remarkably. Table 13.2 presents the most recent figures available (1985) on sports facilities in Japan. (The Ministry of Education refused to provide 1990 data, thereby exemplifying the continuing restrictive character of this ministry.)

Table 13.3 shows the kinds of sports facilities that are ranked highest in Japan (Sports Bureau, Ministry of Education, 1987, p. 12). Outdoor playgrounds, including fields for ball games, gymnasiums (both Judo and Kendo gymnasiums), and swimming pools, make up almost half of the total number of sports facilities.

The Public Availability of School Physical Education Facilities

Physical education facilities provided at public schools are available to the public at night and during the holidays. The availability rate of these facilities is as follows (see Table 13.4): outdoor playgrounds 75.5 percent, gymnasiums 72.3 percent, and swimming pools 24.1 percent. The availability rate of public school swimming pools remains low because of the problem of safety. The availability rate of elementary and junior high schools, which are established by municipalities, is considerably higher than that of high schools (Sports Bureau of the Ministry of Education, 1987, p. 40).

In comparison to other countries, the quality and number of public school sports facilities in Japan fares well. However, in contrast, there is a serious lack of sports facilities available to the general public, especially in crowded cities where land prices are high and there are few available sites. In many cases, few funds are allocated for improvement in existing facilities because of drastically limiting budget measures. Consequently, while the availability of public school sports facilities is essential to the promotion of citizen sports, at present the overall situation is not one in which the schools and the public can cooperate.

Leaders in Sports Promotion

As shown in Table 13.5, sports leaders in administrative organizations who are members of Boards of Education throughout the municipalities consist of

Table 13.3
Ranking of Popular Sports Facilities in Japan, 1985

Ranking	Facilities	Number	Percentage
1	Playgrounds	50,148	17.2
2	Gymnasiums	47,962	16.4
3	Swimming Pools	35,288	12.1
4	Gateball Croquet Courts	25,312	8.7
5	Outdoor Tennis Gymnasiums	25,268	8.6
6	Table Tennis Gymnasiums	12,114	4.2
7	Baseball, Softball Stadiums	9,979	3.4
8	Outdoor Volleyball Courts	8,865	3.0
9	Golf Training Facilities	5,812	2.0
10	Physical Training Facilities	5,797	2.0
	Other Facilities	65,572	22.4
	Total	292,117	100.0

general officials, officials of sports facilities established by municipalities, and part-time leaders of sport. When we speak of sports leaders, we include municipal sports leaders, appointed directors, officials of municipal sports facilities, and part-time leaders of sport. We can also include those people who have attained leadership qualifications from a sports association. In 1987 approximately 276,000 people belonged to this category.

Municipal sports leaders are heavily involved in planning sports promotion policies, in managing various kinds of sports projects, and in leading practical skills classes for the education committee of each municipality. According to 1986 figures, approximately 15 percent of these sports leaders, dispatched directors included, hold a certificate in physical education training. The percentage for full-time sports leaders is 60 percent (Sports Bureau, Ministry of Education, 1992a, p. 1822).

Part-time leaders of sports are located in the municipal education committees, and their actions are regulated by the Sports Promotion Law of 1961. Article 19 of this law states that the part-time leaders of sports are responsible, within their own municipality, for practical skills guidance and for advice to citizens on sporting matters. This is how they fulfill their duty of promoting sports. The education committee endeavors to appoint part-time leaders of sports who are socially confident and have a deep interest and understanding of matters related to sports. Of necessity, individuals also are chosen who are zealous and have sports ability. In 1987, for each municipality there were approximately seventeen part-time leaders for sport.

Sports directors are dispatched from the prefectural Board of Education to the municipal Board of Education in accordance with municipal wishes (Sports-for-All Division, Sports Bureau, Ministry of Education, 1992, p. 16; Meeting for the Study of Sports by Sports Research Group of the Ministry of Education, 1990, p. 168).

Table 13.4
Public Availability of School Physical Education Facilities in Japan, 1985 (public elementary schools, junior high schools, and high schools)

Facilities	Number of Schools (A)	Schools Available for the Public (B)	B/A X 100
Outdoor Playgrounds	39,154	29,575	75.5
Gymnasiums	39,154	28,316	72.3
Swimming Pools	39,154	9,425	24.1

In 1989 a new system was created wherein the minister of education authorizes the projects of sports associations by examining the knowledge and skill of the sports promotion leaders. See Table 13.6. (Sports-for-All Division, Sports Bureau, Ministry of Education, 1992, pp. 12–13; Meeting for the Purpose of Studying Sports Administration, 1990, p. 8). As a result, the number of qualified people in this system is on the increase.

Sports Clubs

An effective sports club is an association managed by individuals who are sports enthusiasts who daily and continuously participate actively in sports. While enjoying sports, these individuals are also endeavoring to improve and maintain their own physical strength and health. Furthermore, they voluntarily act to promote mutual friendship and cooperation among their members.

According to a public opinion poll concerning physical strength and sports conducted by the Prime Minister's Office in 1991, the rate of membership in sports clubs in Japan is only 17.7 percent. The rates of membership in some of the various sports clubs are: golf 14.1 percent, tennis 13.2 percent, baseball 11.5 percent, softball 9.5 percent, and volleyball 8.1 percent.

According to the Report of Research of Sports Clubs in 1985, which was taken by the Japan Sports Club Association, the total number of sports clubs in Japan at that time was about 403,000. Of these, about 35,000 were for those who play sports mainly in public sports facilities. The percentage of sports clubs with fewer than twenty members was 45.8 percent; the percentage of sports clubs with more than twenty members but fewer than fifty members was 41.1.

The establishment of sports clubs does not automatically guarantee their success. The problem at hand is whether or not the managers of sports clubs have the ability to successfully maintain a working relationship between their administration and their members. According to the Report on Research of Sports Clubs:

- 41.2 percent of the municipalities have adopted a sports club registration system.
- 10.5 percent of the municipalities have specific guidelines for establishing sports clubs.

Table 13.5
Leaders in Sports Promotion in Japan, 1986

Kinds	Number Full-Time	Number Part-Time	Total
Municipal Sports Leaders	6,996	4,849	11,845
Dispatched Direcors	596	0	596
Officials of Municipal Sports Facilities (Jurisdiction of Education Committees)	5,820	6,044	11,864
Part-Time Leaders of Sports	0	55,865	55,865
Total	13,412	66,758	80,170

• 24.3 percent of the municipalities actively encourage study and training projects for the sports club leaders.

• 25.2 percent of the municipalities currently utilize dispatch of the sports leader's system.

The number of municipal administrations that are not fully aware of the number of sports clubs in their jurisdiction, or cognizant of the number of club members or club activities, is surprisingly high.

ENTRIES INTO SPORTS ATHLETIC ASSOCIATIONS

Table 13.7 shows the number of registered athletes in sports associations affiliated with the JASA in accordance with their events (Meeting for the Study of Sports by Sports Research Group of the Ministry of Education, 1990, pp. 190–191). Many people belong to sports associations such as tennis, rubberball baseball, judo, and kendo clubs. It must be noted, however, that this figure only represents athletic associations that are directly affiliated with the JASA. Primary and secondary schoolchildren are included in these figures. For example, in rubberball baseball, approximately 400,000 primary and secondary school students and in soccer, approximately 250,000 students are included in the figures.

Measured by the diminished level of competition after the boycott of the Los Angeles Olympic Games by the communist countries and the poor athletic results of Japanese athletes in the Seoul Olympic Games, the level of Japanese international athleticism has declined. The same can be said about Japanese participants in the Asian Games. In 1986 China won 224 medals, and South Korea won 224 medals in the Seoul Asian Games. For the first time in history, the number of medals garnered each by China and by South Korea exceeded Japan's total of 211 medals. Nevertheless, attracted in part by Olympic glamor, the number of Japanese Olympic participants is increasing yearly. In the Barcelona Olympics, Japanese participants won five fewer gold medals than in the Seoul Olympics; however, including silver and bronze awards, the overall number of medals won by Japan increased.

Table 13.6
Sports Leaders System Authorized by the Ministry of Education in Japan, 1991

Kinds	Contents	Number of Qualified
Sports Leaders for Local Communities	In charge of technical guidance at sports clubs or at sports schools, organizing of community sports clubs, guidance on management and planning issues, and operation of events such as sports meetings.	17,792
Coaches for Improving Competitive Skills	In charge of basic and professional guidance on the techniques for a specific sport, training and guidance for activity organizations, and guidance for improving competitive skills according to the skills of individual athletes.	1,973
Sports Teachers at Commercial Sports Facilities	In charge of professional guidance on the techniques of a specific sports, and planning and management of various sports activities, mainly working at commercial sports facilities as professional teachers of the respective sports.	875
Sports Programmers	In charge of basic guidance such as consultation on sports, offering sports programs and various other training methods, working mainly at sports facilities such as private sports clubs.	678
Total		21,318

Note: The above projects are conducted by national sports athletic associations and JASA.

Using the poor performance of some athletes at the Seoul Olympics as a rationale, the Japanese government established a sports promotion fund in 1990, which it used to subsidize the training of Japan's first-class athletes. It further laid down plans for establishing a National Sports Research Center for Japan's top athletes. All this activity indicates that the government now felt more strongly that "the Olympics come first." Increasingly, the government's sports policies are being influenced by the number of medals that its best athletes win.

Recent international sports competitions held in Japan include International Figure Skating Championships, the 12th Asian Games, and the Summer Universiade in 1995. Also, the winter Olympic Games in 1998 will be held in Japan. The decision to hold the 1998 winter Olympics in Nagano involved a serious direct confrontation between environmentalist groups and fiscal and political circles. The environmentalists argued that the event would lead to environmental destruction. The spokesmen for fiscal and political interests emphasized the far-reaching economic advantages of holding this event. The local people of Nagano also were deeply divided by this issue. However, the IOC reached the final decision to hold these Olympics in Nagano. This decision seriously affected the administrative budget of the Ministry of Education. The planned completion by 1996 of the National Sports Research Center was delayed. Because the Nagano winter Olympics have been given preference within the Ministry of Education's budget, the 1993 fiscal outlay for the National Research Center's projects such

Table 13.7
Entries into Sports Athletic Associations, 1988

Associations	Registered Athletes	Associations	Registered Athletes
Athletics	182,000	Rubberball Baseball	1,176,000
Swimming	110,000	Sumo	36,000
Football	675,000	Equestrian	4,000
Skiing	93,000	Judo	1,300,000
Tennis	1,500,000	Fencing	7,000
Rowing	14,000	Soft Ball	283,000
Hockey	9,000	Badminton	160,000
Amateur Boxing	4,000	Archery ("Kyudo")	130,000
Volleyball	825,000	Rifle	6,000
Gymnastic	35,000	Kendo	1,236,071
Basketball	633,000	Rugby	139,000
Skating	7,000	Mountaineering	80,000
Wrestling	8,000	Canoeing	2,000
Yachting	10,000	Archery	12,000
Weightlifting	3,000	Karatedo	11,000
Handball	62,000	Ice Hockey	20,000
Cycling	3,000	Jukendo	80,000
Soft Tennis	738,000	Clay Target Shooting	3,000
Table Tennis	201,000	Naginata	32,000
		Total	9,777,000

Note: The total number of entry members amounted to 6,475,000 in 1980 and 7,838,000 in 1982.

as the construction of a speed skate arena, as well as other facilities, estimated to cost 6.6 billion yen, was drastically reduced.

The construction of the National Sports Research Center is an experimental project whose basis is a 26,000-square-meter building with seven floors and one basement. Its main features are a 100-meter track and an indoor track and field area. The building will also contain a training area for small boat and canoe competition, and it will also provide facilities to use computer and television images for the analysis of Japan's top athletes.

Considering the potential of this center, the delay of its construction, ironically, may have a negative impact on the performances of Japanese athletes at the winter Olympics.

THE SPORTS BUREAU OF THE MINISTRY OF EDUCATION

In the preceding section we have surveyed the current Japanese sports situation. In this next section we look at the sports policies issued by the Sports Bureau of the Ministry of Education, as well as its organization and budgeting.

The Sports Bureau of the Ministry of Education is responsible for the improvement of health and physical fitness of the general public and for the promotion of sports. Sports at the national level also are the responsibility of the Bureau. Relevant programs are facilitated by the Physical Education Division, the Sports-for-All Division, and the Athletic Sports Division of the Ministry of Education.

In this analysis, we omit physical education in schools except when physical education facilities are available to the public. The Physical Education Division is concerned mainly with setting standards for the building of sports facilities. The Sports-for-All Division focuses on life-long sports activities and recreational activities suited to the lifestyle and environment of individuals as well as their state of health and physical strength. The Athletic Sports Division is concerned with reviewing various conditions affecting the improvement of people's competitive power in sports and with the promotion of research activities in sports medicine and science.

The entire budget for construction of sports facilities is actually provided in the form of subsidies (Hojo-kin) from the Physical Education Division. A subsidy means a grant from the national treasury to cover part of the costs of various projects of the local governments (prefectures and municipalities). Subsidies are also available to private organizations and, under certain conditions, even to individuals. This system of subsidies has infiltrated related government policy and Sports Bureau policy. For example, a local government that wants to obtain a subsidy for the construction of sports facilities must submit to the minister of education an Application for Subsidy Grant and Attached Documents, the budget of revenue and expenditure on the construction project, and the site plan for the premises and facilities. Then the local government's plans must be inspected, supervised, and directed by the Sports Bureau in charge of that particular project.

In such cases, the rate of the grant is one-third of the total cost, which is calculated independently by the central government. A formula is used to calculate the subsidy projects expenditure: Subsidiary expenditure = Subsidy projected total floor space × Unit cost of construction × Rate of grant (dictated by the administrative guidelines of the central government—known as Yo-ko). Further subsidiary expenditures are appropriated in the sports administration budget for lighting equipment, clubhouses, fences, and so on, which are seen as necessary for sports activities using public school facilities.

The Sports Safety Association, the Managing of Sports Facilities Association, the Institute of Sports Medicine Science Research, and the Japan Women's Sports Federation are all sports-organizing bodies directed under the supervision of the Physical Education Division.

The budget of the Sports-for-All Division (approximately 2,554,000 yen) is divided into two different categories: subsidy programs and projects concerning direct sports programs and services. Subsidy programs are connected with the local government's promotion of sports activities. The Sports Bureau exercises direct control through an array of meeting and research sessions regarding the activities of the sports leaders in the municipalities. Moreover, the Sports Bureau uses sports leaders as a means of permeating its own policies into different regions, as well as sources for collecting information about the current situation of sports in these regions. Lifetime sports conventions and national sports and recreation festivals are new additions to the Bureau's duties.

The Sports-for-All Division grants 85 percent of its budget for subsidies. Included in the financial assistance given to the prefectures is the amount that the prefectures must give the municipalities in order for them to carry out certain projects. This system seems one of tight supervision. Funds and commendation are passed down in chain-like fashion, from national to prefectural level to municipality. Projects promoting lifetime sports are included in the financially assisted programs of the municipalities. These have been great in number since the second half of the 1980s.

Under the supervision of the Sports-for-All Division, there are ten athletic sports associations (two of which are affiliated with the JASA), eight outdoor activity and recreation associations, six facilities management associations, three gymnastic-related associations, four Budo- (traditional Japanese martial arts) related associations, four professional instructor associations, three aiding bodies, and six other related bodies.

In the budget of the Athletic Sports Division, the percentage of financial assistance from the central government is extremely high. In fact, it is 93 percent of the total budget. Notably, subsidies directed to the JOC total about three times as much as those directed to the JASA. Subsidies to JOC and JASA compose three quarters of the total budget of the Athletic Sports Division.

Under the supervision of the Athletic Sports Division, there are forty-six athletic sports associations (forty-four of which are affiliated with both the JASA and JOC at the same time), two outdoor activity and recreation associations, one facility management association, three Budo-related associations, three professional instructor associations, three aiding organizations, and one related group. Included in these are national sports festivals called *kokutai* in Japanese. Three years before a kokutai is due to take place, working committees are inaugurated in the prefecture that is in charge of the festival and in the municipality in which the festival will be held. The Ministry of Education, JASA, and various central athletic associations work together to start functional preparations for the festival.

The position of president for the working committee is filled by the mayor in the case of the prefecture and by the local head of government in the case of the municipality. The burden for these kinds of expenses, borne by the hosting prefecture, is considerably large. For example, in the case of the thirty-eighth Autumn National Sports Festival held in Gunma Prefecture in 1983, the administration costs totaled 170 million yen, approximately 40 million of which were covered by subsidies from the central government. The costs of various construction for the festival and for environmental maintenance are different for each prefecture and are not included in the calculation of administration costs. In fact, when all additional related costs are included, the total cost of hosting

Table 13.8
Sports Promotion Projects Issues by JASA

Training of Authorized Sports Leaders*	Sports leaders for Local Communities, Coaches for Improving Competitive Skills, Sports Teachers at Commercial Sports Facilities, Sports Programmers, Sports Doctors.
National Liaison Conference of Sports Leaders	Contacts between the representives of each prefecture and those of each athletic association.
Publishing Journals Concerned with Sports	The monthly journal, "Taikyo Jiho (JASA's Current Topics)" in publication since 1951, the "Sports Journal".
National Sports Festivals*	These are held under the auspices of JASA, the Ministry of Education, and host prefecture.
National Festival of Sports and Recreation	The first of these Festivals was held in 1988, and is now an annual event. It is held under the auspices of JASA, the Ministry of Education, the host prefecture, Japan Recreation Association, and the Alliance among National Sports Leaders.
Training of Junior Sports Clubs*	The first Junior Sports Club was established in 1962. Now, there are more than 30,000 Junior Sports Clubs with total members numbering about 1.2 million, including the leaders of the organizations.
International Exchanges	JASA is the member of two world-wide organizations: the International Assembly of National Organization of Sports (IANOS) and the Trim and Fitness International Sports for All Association (TAFISA). There has been exchange competition between juniors in Japan and Korea* since 1969, and in Japan and China* since 1982. As a part of the ODA projects of the Japanese government*, Inspection tours and training sessions to grasp the status of Japan's sports for young people have been carried out for the benefit of youth sports leaders among the ASEAN nations since 1991.
Sports Events	The Central Commemorative Event on the Health and Sports Day, and The International Sports Fair are held annually.
Others	The Research Institute of Sports Science, The Committee for Sports Science, The Sports Medicine Clinic and the management of Youth Sports Centers are related to JASA.

* Subsidies Projects

Note: The assets of the JASA consist of the (1) fundamental property valued at 1,001 yen, (2) movable and immovable properties, (3) profits from these assets, (4) subsidies from the government and their share of the expenses provided by affiliated associations, moreover, the salaries of the JASA's officials are provided by the Athletic Sports Division of the Ministry of Education, (5) projects income, (6) donations, and (7) other income.

such a festival can be anywhere up to, or even exceed, ten times as much as the figure mentioned above.

JAPAN AMATEUR SPORTS ASSOCIATION (JASA)

JASA is a nonprofit corporation that controls amateur sports circles. Table 13.8 shows the various sports programs and services adopted by JASA (Japan

Amateur Sports Association, 1991, pp. 2–13). In the table the asterisk represents subsidies received from the Athletic Sports Division. Since the reestablishment of JOC, JASA has entered a new phase of existence and has devoted its energies to the promotion of national sports.

Japan's Olympic Committee (JOC)

The JOC, which is one of the committee organizations of the JASA, was forced to obey the decision of the board of directors, which was manipulated by the central government. The directors held the view that Japan should not participate in the Moscow Olympic Games. Furthermore, the Japanese international athletic standard has been declining relatively since the Tokyo Olympic Games. As a result of a desire to rectify such problems, JOC was reestablished in 1989, as an organization with the status of a legally recognized corporation. The hope is that JOC will be able to deal effectively with these unfavorable athletic circumstances.

Council for Health and Physical Education

The Council for Health and Physical Education is an advisory body of the Ministry of Education. In the past twenty years, this advisory body has submitted two reports to the Ministry of Education, one was in 1972 and the other in 1989. The report on Sports Promotion Policies corresponded with the point of view that at the citizen level the people's sports orientation should be one of casual activities that help to resolve stress and to improve physical strength. However, in response to the 1989 Sports Promotion Report, there was public criticism that sports promotion policies were neither aligned to the demands of the public nor paid much regard to citizens' needs.

Four specific points of criticism were leveled. The foremost one was that by shifting the responsibility for establishing sports facilities onto local governing bodies the government had broken its promise to take this responsibility itself. In its 1972 report, the government had promised to set up maintenance standards for public sports facilities whereby they would provide one sports gymnasium for every 10,000 people. However, this goal is far from being reached; in fact, the government has laid it aside. The reality for sports facilities is that the budget provided for such purposes has been in a state of decline since the 1982 sports facilities budget peak of 1,178 million yen.

Another criticism blames the government for placing more importance on competitive sports policies than on lifelong sports policies. Moreover, it seems that the government intends to develop competitive sports even further by taking advantage of the financial support available from various private enterprises.

The third critical point raised is that in relation to sports promotion the government mentioned only the positive aspects of sports: namely, the enjoyable impressions evoked through watching sports, the birth of a more active society, the significance of young people's admiration for their sports heroes, and youthful dreams for the future. This dreamlike rendition of sport fails to mention the reality whereby only the top-class athletes receive fame and financial comfort. It also fails to communicate the harsh reality that professional athletes are treated as commodities and used to the full when in good working order but quickly discarded when injured or suffering other misfortunes.

Lastly, many observers of sports promotion policies in Japan see the introduction of private enterprise management and administration of lifelong sports as indicating a relinquishing of the government's responsibility to the nation in this area. A natural result of governmental responsibilities being gradually transferred to private enterprises is that citizens are incurring the burden of providing sports facilities for themselves. Private enterprises increasingly are being encouraged to provide more of the sporting facilities; consequently, prices go up. Sports leaders have become enmeshed in this system.

In March of 1988, in anticipation of the Seoul Olympics late that year, the prime minister had his private advisory committee prepare a report on sports promotion in Japan. Not surprisingly, the information gathered in this report coincided with the 1989 Sports Promotion Report. However, it also found that politicians were using sports too much for political purposes. Like the 1989 report did later, the Nakasone inquiry found that the Liberal Democratic party depended too much on Olympic victories and medals to enhance national prestige and that this sense of dependence had infiltrated the Ministry of Education.

At deliberative councils at the local government level, Councils on Sports Promotion in the prefectures act as advisory bodies for the Board of Education. On the municipal level, there are 683 established Councils on Sports Promotion.

Sports Promotion Fund

The Sports Promotion Fund provided by the central government for the benefit of athletic sports associations that are troubled by inadequate funding was established in the revised budget of 1990. At that time, the government invested 25 billion yen into helping athletic sports associations provide funds for training their top athletes and for their overseas travels and other expenses. In addition, donations from private enterprises totaled 40 billion yen in 1992. These donations are distributed annually among the athletic sports associations for their own use.

The recipients of these funds are sports groups that promote competitiveness among participants by encouraging competitive camps, practice games, and coaches to conduct research on players. Many of these groups are associated with JASA and JOC. Other recipients include top-level Olympic representatives, coaches, international and national competitive sports groups, sports research groups, and teams excelling at the international level. Obviously, Sports Promotion Funds are used primarily to promote first-class competitive sports. These donations are basically a direct reaction to the fact that Japanese athletes won

Figure 13.1
Relationships between the Sports Bureau and other Sports Organizations

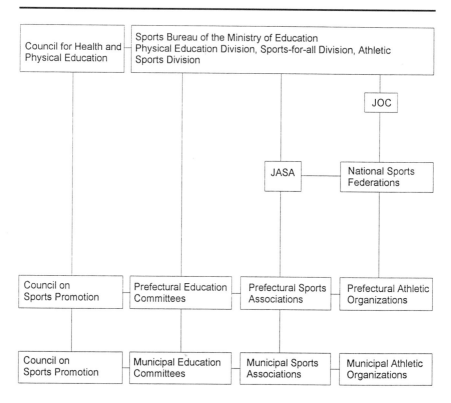

only thirty-eight gold medals at the autumn Asian Games in Peking in 1990. This medal total was twenty less than in previous competitions. Donations came quickly from various sources. These contributions are currently being used at the rate of approximately 150 million yen a year.

In order to distribute these funds efficiently and fairly, the Ministry of Education proposed that a screening committee be put in charge of the task. Although part of a special corporation of the central government, this committee was to act as a single entity. The JOC was strongly opposed to such an idea because it would be shut out of the negotiations for the allocation of funds. Eventually, a compromise was reached. Each of the athletic sports associations must submit an application for use of funds to the JOC, which, in turn, organizes the individual applications collectively and requests the government for allotments at the rate of funds available. Figure 13.1 depicts the relationships of the Council and the Sports Bureau. (Meeting for the Study of Sports by the Sports Research Group of the Ministry of Education, 1990, pp. 216–217).

Table 13.9
Government Offices and Budgets Concerned with Sports Administration

Government Offices	Contents of Projects
Management and Coordination Agency	The Promotion of National Physical Fitness Campaign; Subsidies to the "Foundation for Health and Physical Fitness; Promotion projects in each prefecture and local municipality.
Economic Planning Agency	Coordinates all government policies on leisure; Researches government leisure policies; coordinates government policies on lifestyle and leisure.
Environmental Agency	The maintenance of national parks and the guidance of outdoor activities; Subsidies to prefectures; Training of natural park leaders.
Ministry of Health and Welfare	The maintenance of health and sport facilities; The training of sports leaders; The popularlization of physical fitness; Promotion of aged sports meetings; Sports activities as part of the projects of public welfare.
Agency of Social Insurance	In charge of health care in the workplace; Promotion of health and physical fitness at workplace.
Ministry of Agriculture, Forestry and Fisheries	Oversees projects concerning recreation in the forests; The maintenance of facilities; The promotion of health and physical fitness; Maintenance of skiing areas and sporting grounds.
Ministry of International Trade and Industry	The promotion of sports to related industries; Conducts research on how leisure is related to industry; Subsidies toward the promotion of health and physical fitness undertaken by smaller businesses.
Ministry of Transportation	The maintenance of tourist recreation areas, yacht harbors, and facilities in green tracks; Subsidies to local governments and managers of harbors.
Ministry of Postal Services	The promotion of radio gymnastic exercise; Sponsoring short distance marathon meets; The 10 million Festival of radio gymnastic exercises; Organizing and encouragement of groups advocating radio gymnastic exercises.
Ministry of Labor	Provision of gymnasiums and outdoor facilities for workers; Various kinds of sports meetings, sports classes, and sports exchanges for young workers; subsidy of worker's health maintenance projects and the commission of welfare projects to the groups of working women and youth.
Ministry of Construction	The maintenance of state-operated parks, urban parks, and big scale bicycle roads.

OTHER ORGANIZATIONS, PROJECTS, AND PROMOTION RELATED TO SPORTS POLICIES

Government Offices Concerned with Sports Administration

If we regard sports policies as being concerned with leisure, recreation, and physical fitness activities, then, in addition to the Ministry of Education, eleven other government offices contribute to work related to sports policies. These can be seen in Table 13.9 (Management and Coordination Agency, 1992, pp. 1–44).

Sports Policies of Political Parties

In comparison to political power, sports policies issued by political parties are generally weak. However, circa 1991, the political parties endeavored to issue well-thought-out sports policies. The reason for this keener attention can be attributed to two events: The Olympic Games were going to be held at Albertville and Barcelona in 1992, and Japan witnessed a prolonged and dominating argument over the introduction of a type of soccer pool. (Will soccer pools be accepted or refused?)

The LDP generally adopted the same sports policy as the Sports Bureau of the Ministry of Education. The LDP had been in favor of introducing a type of soccer pool. The Social Democratic party stood in opposition to the growing importance placed on competitive sports, which were so emphasized in the policies of the Sports Bureau and the LDP. Moreover, the Social Democratic party was critical of the introduction of a kind of soccer pool and, instead, proposed the establishment of a Government Sports Office (Sports Ministry), with the intention of unifying all government offices concerned with sports administration.

In 1991 the Communist party announced its own comprehensive sports policy in which it criticized the system of subsidies in sports administration, the intervention of politics in sports, and the commercialization of sports.

The Diet has an Education Committee as a permanent committee in both the House of Representatives and the House of Councilors. These committee members are devoted to discussing sports policy issues. Moreover, an Examining Committee for the Security of Sports Promotion, was established in 1992. This committee was organized primarily so that its members could discuss the introduction of a soccer pool and how this pool would affect the professionalization of soccer competitions.

Officially, according to the Liberal Democratic party, it seriously began to consider sports promotion policies because

- The importance of a healthy sports environment has increased. Such an environment is necessary to bring up future sports leaders, to expand the sports-for-all ideal, and to bring up young people who will work a five-day week.

- It is necessary to discuss how to strengthen and train top athletes toward participation in the Olympics.

- It is necessary to discuss public administration of the Ministry of Education.

In practice, however, the Liberal Democratic party was trying to produce a theoretical arrangement for the introduction of soccer pools. It sought to establish an unshakable sports promotion policy legitimizing the soccer pools as a source of revenues that would probably amount to 100 billion yen.

Donations from private enterprises to Sports Promotion Funds are far from sufficient despite the original high expectations. This inadequacy also contributed to the acceleration of the movement toward the introduction of soccer pools. The essence of this debate follows.

Debate on the Introduction of the Soccer Pools

According to the proposal, soccer pool bets would be placed on the games of the ten teams in the Japan Professional Soccer League. Citizens will be able to purchase pool tickets through convenience stores or city banks. The earnings of these soccer pools are to be delivered to the national treasury and subsequently used to promote sports in Japan.

Gambling sports such as horse-racing, bike-racing, and motorboat-racing exist in Japan. In contrast to these sports, the soccer pools are similar to that of a public lottery. Purchasers of pool tickets predict the results of all the games in the league. Since this is a difficult feat, most purchasers guess incorrectly. In its promotion drive for soccer pools, the Liberal Democratic party emphasized this point.

In contrast, the Social Democratic party opposed the introduction of soccer pools proposed by the Liberal Democratic party. The Social Democratic party's argument points to the influence the soccer pools may have on sports fans who are children. This party also opposed the connection between the Ministry of Education and public soccer pools. In regard to the insufficiency of the Sports Promotion Fund, the Social Democratic party asserted that the central government should spend more money on sports promotion.

From the very beginning of this debate in early 1992, the Japanese Olympic Committee and the Japan Amateur Sports Association presented each political party with a formal request for the introduction of soccer pools.

Sports Promotion Law

The Sports Promotion law enacted by the central and local governments of Japan is the most fundamental law related to sports promotion. It consists of twenty-three provisions and prescribes for councils, leaders, events, availability of school facilities, sports safety, subsidies from the central government, and other related sports issues. Since this law was enacted in 1961, the Ministry of Education has primarily controlled sports promotion policies by following the guidelines of this legislation. It cannot be denied, however, that the Sports Promotion law is out of date. More than thirty years have elapsed since this law was first enacted.

PROFESSIONAL SPORTS AND GOVERNMENT POLICY IN JAPAN

Table 13.10 shows the present status of Japanese professional sports. It includes information on the establishment of sports-governing associations, the number of spectators attending professional sports in 1990, the types of audiences, and the number of professional athletes in 1991 (Japan Professional Sports Association, 1991, pp. 12–13).

Table 13.10
Professional Sports in Japan

Organization	Initial Year of Operation	Number of Spectators	Number of Participating Athletes
Japan Sumo Association	1925	815,428	797
Japan Baseball Machinery	1948	20,629,000	713
Japan Professional Golf Association	1957	1,500,000	1,000
Japan Female Professional Association	1967	585,000	349
All Japan Boxing Association	1976	300,000	1,400
Japan Kick Boxing Association	1966	12,000	Unknown
Japan Professional Bowling Association	1967	100,000	650
New Japan Professional Wrestling Co.	1972	490,000	27
All Japan Professional Wrestling Co.	1972	568,000	20
Japan Central Horse Racing Association	1954	10,680,000	209
National Local Horse Racing Association	1962	13,873,716	665
Japan Bicycle Promotion Association	1957	27,557,000	4,390
National Motorboat Racing Federation	1951	44,000,000	1,602
Japan Small-Sized Automobile Promotion Association	1962	6,887,944	568

Professional baseball, horse-racing, bike-racing, motorboat-racing, and small-sized automobile racing are all blessed with many spectators. With the exception of professional baseball and small-sized automobile racing, the other three professional sports are known as Public Gambling Sports. As such, part of the earnings from these sports is allocated to sports promotion projects such as the construction of sports facilities. Besides the sports mentioned above, Japan boasts professional tennis players, professional skiers, and professional surfers.

The Japan Professional Soccer League ("J League") was inaugurated in May 1993, and came up with new managing systems. For example, the home team is managed and a stadium is built and maintained in a cooperative relationship among a private corporation, local government, and citizens of the district. The name of the team purposely does not include the name of the private corporation to prevent the team from becoming the exclusive possession of the private corporation. Also the home team not only has farm teams, but junior teams as well. This pyramidal coaching system is different from that of school physical education, which has occupied a dominant position of sports promotion in Japan. These managing systems are different from that of professional baseball, which regards teams as a means to profit.

Since the opening of the "J League," professional soccer and baseball are equally matched in popularity in Japan. The economic effectiveness concerning the "J League," such as sponsor fees and broadcasting fees, has attracted considerable attention.

Government Sports Policy Toward Professional Sports

The government, through the Sports Bureau of the Ministry of Education, grants permission for professional sports associations to become corporations, and guides their associations and supervises their management from the very

beginning. The Japan Professional Sports Association, which is an affiliate organization of the Ministry of Education, was established in 1990. This association

- Conducts research and study that furthers the promotion and development of profes-
  sional sports in Japan.
- Officially commends people for their contribution to professional sports promotion.
- Obtains and presents domestic and foreign information on professional sports, publish-
  ing books related to professional sports, and other publicity work.
- Promotes international relations with exchanges through professional sports activities.
- Holds study and research meetings related to professional sports.

The professional sports associations that are affiliated with the Japan Professional Sports Association are shown in Table 13.10.

The Japan Professional Sports Association consists of a member of the House
of Representatives (the president), a member of the House of Councilors (the
vice-president), a chairman of the foundation, representative directors of enterprises (four members), an adviser of an elected special corporation which
supervises the Sports Promotion Funds, a research director from the headquarters
of the Liberal Democratic party, and some officials of professional sports associations.

According to the explanation given by the Sports Bureau, an administrative
official of the Ministry of Education has been given charge of professional sports
for several reasons:

- Professional sports, which require high degrees of playing skills, not only make strong
  impressions on people and give them great pleasure, but they also motivate young
  people to be more interested in sports.
- Professional athletes are now permitted to participate in the Olympic Games.
- It is necessary to provide avenues of exchange between professional athletes and amateur athletes.

The Promotion Conference of the Professional Sports started to function in
1991. This conference involves members of political and economic circles, professional sports contributors recommended by the minister of education, men of
general learning and experience, and members of the mass media.

The policy of commending professional sports contributors has been enforced
since 1990, when the Sports Bureau of the Ministry of Education began awarding the Prize of the Sports Promotion. The Ministry of Education often supports
professional sports, for example, through the Japan Professional Golf Championship. The Ministry awards the winner with the Minister of Education Cup.
This policy of sports commendation characterizes the government's sports policy
toward professional sports. On the other hand, some of the professional sports

associations are wary of government control. Nevertheless, an explicit function of the Japan Professional Sports Association is to attempt to organize their various professional sports groups. Apparently, the government is still groping for an ideal path in connection with its policies toward professional sports.

CHARACTERISTICS AND PROBLEMS OF SPORTS POLICIES IN JAPAN

In Japan, sports policies are developed under the control of the Sports Bureau and are supported by a system of subsidies from the central government. The subsidy system helps narrow the financial gap between rich and poor local governments by facilitating direct liaison and coordination between central and local governments. Nevertheless, it is generally criticized as a factor contributing to the increase of bureaucratic centralization. Critics also point out that the standard for judgment of subsidy allocation is not clear.

Taking 1992 as our sample year, we find that the total budget allocated by the Ministry of Education for sports promotion projects (including the Physical Education, Sports-for-All and Athletic Sports divisions) was approximately 15.1 billion yen. Of this total amount, approximately 14.6 billion yen were used for government-subsidized projects, whereas only 440 million yen were used to finance direct sports project funding. This information underscores the dominance of projects subsidized by the central government. In fact, the Physical Education Division's projects are completely subsidized.

Looking at only the Sports-for-All Division and Athletic Sports Division, we see a total allocation of 5.4 billion yen for sports projects, of which 5.0 billion (93 percent) were spent on subsidized projects. In this respect, we can view local governments and sports associations as subsidized project developers. They are bound up in the systems of subsidies. Detailed conditions for subsidy allocation are set by directive guidelines of the Sports Bureau. For example, to promote youth camps in competitive sports held at the prefectural level, a local sports subsidy fund is available for allocation only if the following guidelines are observed:

- The camp must include three teams, two of which must be athletic and swimming teams.
- A camp must be held twice a year.
- The camp must operate at least six days.
- More than twenty junior and senior high school students must attend the camp.

These criteria also apply even if quasigovernment associations, under the supervision of the Ministry of Education, contribute sports promotion funds.

These kinds of administrative guidelines in the subsidy system have enabled the Sports Bureau to enjoy an elite position among the organizations associated with sports. Furthermore, because of the detailed conditions bound with subsidy allocation, the level of independent creativity and planning of the municipalities, prefectures, and sports associations is severely limited.

For the sake of unhindered implementation of sports promotion policy, local governments and sports associations need to have available a grant that is not bound by awkward conditions. It is therefore imperative that we look toward a change in the role of the Sports Bureau in the allocation of subsidies.

Budget for Sports Administration

It must be asked whether the administrative budget of 15.1 billion yen provided for national sports promotion is sufficient. This is a significant question when we consider that other ministries with sports-related functions have an administrative sports budget of 47.8 billion yen. For example, the Ministry of Agriculture, Forestry, and Fisheries has a more than adequate budget for the construction of skiing fields.

The burgeoning growth of the importance of sports and recreational activities in Japan's national context increasingly makes the ministries responsible to citizens' needs. The public poll concerning physical strength and sports held by the Prime Minister's Office in 1992 showed that more than 30 percent of the people wanted to become sports club members. Many people requested that more sports facilities be available at a lower cost. This same poll also showed that the number of permanent public sports advisors was not sufficient.

Results of Sports Promotion Projects

In 1988 the Administrative Inspection Bureau (which is part of the Management and Coordination Agency) inspected several sports promotion projects of the Ministry of Education and found that the following problems prevailed:

- Sport-for-All promotion projects were not used exclusively by the subject group; there were big differences between projected membership and actual membership; a lack of public relations efforts to promote sports lessons led to failure as there were no participants; lack of sports leaders and lack of interest among new members caused clubs to close down.

- In sports leaders' projects, there were not enough positions made available in the municipalities for sports directors.

- Public sports facilities were closed on public holidays and Sundays; the general public could not use facilities after school hours if school students were using them.

- Planned public sports facilities were constructed in areas where demand was low; users were few.

- The rate of availability of swimming pools was extremely low and remarkably different from the availability rate that the Ministry of Education announced.

- The results of the Ministry of Education survey claimed that out of ninety-five universities, eighty-one (85 percent) were available for public use. However, in reality, the statistic was much lower.
- In the management of National Sports Festivals, JASA was recognized as the main organizer, and the Ministry of Education was found not to have fulfilled its role. The prefectures engaged as sports instructors those people who, they believed, would win the events, thus ensuring their own victories; practice for festival ceremonies encroached on students' general lesson time.

The actual results of sports promotion projects show that there is a large gap between the intended results and the actual results.

The Emphasis on Athletic Sports by the Government

In view of the report submitted by the Council for Health and Physical Education in 1989, it is noteworthy that the government puts so much emphasis on athletic sports compared to sports for all. Also noteworthy are the differences between JOC and JASA as to the amounts of the subsidies and the ways of using the sports promotion funds.

The Sports-for-All policy is emphasized with a view to building up a basis of improvement in athletic sports. Especially after the Seoul Olympic Games, the Japanese government's principal aim has been to acquire as many medals in Olympic Games as possible. The government assumes that the further development of top-level athletes is desirable because they contribute to increasing national strength, prestige, patriotic spirit, and the stability of the present administration.

There is little difference between professional sports athletes and amateur sports athletes at the top level from the point of view that sports activities are their livelihood. Amateur and professional athletes are also similar in that they have high standards of athletic skills. But the question for the future is how the Athletic Sports Division of the Ministry of Education will cope with the relationship between amateur sports, politics, and professional sports.

The 1984 Los Angeles Olympic Games, which were managed using sponsorship from private enterprises, accrued large profits of about $150 million. The introduction of this kind of commercialization by the International Olympic Committee (IOC) has influenced the method of management of the JOC. It is of public concern that the JOC may become a profits pursuing body, because it has strong connections to sponsoring companies that provide its financial basis. These connections allow the private interests an influential voice in JOC activities.

Business and Sports

As in the past, some Japanese businesses still emphasize athletic sports and employ athletes whose activities and skills promote business publicity. However, the regard and treatment of retired athletes tend to diminish. Surprisingly, many of them are placed in unfavorable positions within their companies. Popular athletic events that are sponsored by newspaper publishing companies, television stations, and advertising agencies are very influential in changing the athletic milieu, the manner of management of athletic meets, and the rules involved as well. Business activities as philanthropies also attract considerable attention among people. Some examples of sports industries are the production and selling of sports goods, the management of sports facilities, sports schools, sports journalism, and so on. National expenditure on properties and services related to sports amounted to 4,300 billion yen in 1989. This accounted for 1.1 percent of the nominal gross national product (GNP) (Industrial Policy Bureau, Ministry of International Trade and Industry, 1990, p. 49). The Industrial Policy Bureau of the Ministry of International Trade and Industry is also involved in the sports industries of Japan.

Considering the increase in leisure time and the expected reduction in working hours in the future, we estimate that sports-related industries will be greatly expanded. To cope with the perceived related problems of industry expansion, the Sports-for-All Division set up the Sports Promotion Service Section in 1991. All these points further emphasize the necessity for citizens, businesses, and public administration to establish common rules concerning sports policies.

Activities of the Sports Safety Association

The Sports Safety Association was established in 1971 as a public service corporation in Japan. The association pays compensation benefits when a person has suffered from an accident occurring during sports activities. The current membership of this association is about 8.5 million (Sports Bureau, Ministry of Education, 1988, p. 25).

Establishment of the Resort Law

The Law of Comprehensive Preparations for Regional Health Resorts (generally known as the Resort Law) was enacted in 1987, after which large-scale regional development projects were initiated by energetic private sectors. The target projects of the developments included the construction of sports facilities such as golf courses (3,244 sites in 1985) and skiing grounds (1,669 sites in 1985). However, in the current climate of increased environmental protection activities, reexamination and even abolition of these projects have become more common. Taking this point further, some people are afraid that the natural environment of the Japan Alps area is being destroyed and will be further damaged by the development projects underway for the Nagano winter Olympic Games.

Sports and Business Sponsors

In Japan enterprises such as railways, newspaper companies, television stations, fisheries, and food and drink companies, often own professional baseball teams as a sideline business. Furthermore, many of these enterprises are also involved in the construction of stadiums and in the management and advertisement of their teams. On the other hand, there are associations, such as the Japan Sumo Association, which keep their activities purely independent. Various kinds of enterprises that do not have professional sports teams themselves are involved in sponsoring aforementioned enterprises in pursuit of self-advertising.

If one sport's athletic association decided it would like to hold a large-scale athletic event in which top sports athletes (professional or amateur athletes) would participate, the costs of doing so on its own would be far too exorbitant. (Imagine it holding the Olympic Games!)

When ambitious athletic meets do occur, they provide ample opportunities for a number of enterprises to sponsor such sporting events. Of course, for any enterprise involved, it is merely an attractive opportunity for it to attempt to exploit sports events as a means of advertising their commodity or company. Such actions have led the related sponsored sports to be called Crowned Sports. The name of the enterprise or its commodity is attached to the beginning of the name of the sports event. For instance, the Kirin Beer Company's sponsorship of a soccer game would entitle the event to be named the Kirin Cup Soccer Competition. Almost all games of professional golf in Japan fall into the category of Crowned Sports. The Toyota Cup Competition in soccer is yet another example.

"Crowned Sports" can be found in various popular amateur sports, and the parties concerned seem to welcome this trend. It is appropriate to look specifically at the campaign, "Do your best, Japan!" originally adopted by JOC in 1984. For this campaign, the JOC received the support of fifty private enterprises and financial support amounting to 10,000 million yen (approximately 40 million per enterprise) in a four-year contract from 1989 to 1993. The financial support funds were distributed among the various sports athletic associations in proportion to the level of athletic achievement attained in the Olympic Games and in world championships.

The JOC is planning to establish a public stock corporation, Japan Olympic Marketing (JOM), in order to earn enough money to cover the management costs of the Nagano winter Olympic Games in 1998. The main bodies investing in JOM and their rates of investment are: JOC 25 percent, Nagano Winter Olympic Organizing Committee 25 percent, one advertising agency 22 percent, one business firm 19 percent, and one bank 5 percent. The JOM expects its earnings to exceed 40 billion yen in the period from 1994 to 1998. The main sources of the earnings are expected to be sponsor charges (about 30 billion yen) and products related to the Olympics (hundreds of thousands of yen). With these funds, about half of the direct managing cost is expected to be covered.

Considering the circumstances mentioned above, it is obvious that JOC and sponsoring business enterprises are closely related and that the Olympic Games will give these private enterprises an excellent opportunity to enter into the sports markets. There is no doubt that the enterprises that invest large sums of money in JOM will gain an influential voice in the management details of the Nagano winter Olympic Games. This means that not only the government but also business enterprises use sports as a means of attaining economic goals.

CONCLUSIONS

The government has set up the framework for sports policies in Japan, but its character is administratively directed and bureaucratic. As a result, the Sports Bureau of the Ministry of Education (the Physical Education Division, the Sports-for-All Division, and the Athletic Sports Division) supervises and leads the JASA, the JOC, sports associations, and prefectural and municipal sports policies both directly and indirectly.

The Sports Bureau's comprehensive controls over these organizations are supported by a system of subsidies, which constrain the autonomous sports activities of sports associations, prefectures, and municipalities. However, it cannot be denied that these organizations also depend on the sports policies issued by the Sports Bureau of the Ministry of Education. Inadequacies in sports promotion projects at the citizen level can be attributed to these kinds of situations impacting sports activities.

We cannot sufficiently conclude whether or not the sports administrative budget is adequate for athletic sports or Sports-for-All activities. However, it is a fact that the voices of citizens demanding improvement of and more satisfaction from sports leaders and facilities are on the increase. Moreover, the government is now examining comprehensive sports policies as part of recreation, leisure, and cultural policies. These considerations include the prospective establishment of a Ministry of Sports.

Hence, if the athletic sports promotions are developed in a manner more closely connected with sponsoring businesses, not only will influential businesses increasingly impose their intentions on the holdings and management of athletic games, but they may in fact threaten the continued existence of the JOC itself.

We must not forget that sports industries are related to all activities in the Sports-for-All Division. Therefore, the question of how to establish the relationship of roles among citizens, businesses, and public administration in the future poses an insistent and important problem for current sports policymakers in Japan.

REFERENCES

Administrative Management Bureau, Management and Coordination Agency, Prime Minister's Office. (1991). *Organization of the government of Japan 1992.* Tokyo: Institute of Administrative Management.

Athletic Sports Division, Sports Bureau, Ministry of Education. (1992). *Athletic sports administration in Japan.* Tokyo: Athletic Sports Division, Sports Bureau, Ministry of Education.

Industrial Policy Bureau, Ministry of International Trade and Industry. (1990). *Sports vision toward the 21st century.* Tokyo: Industrial Policy Bureau, Ministry of International Trade and Industry.

Japan Amateur Sports Association. (1991). *Sports handbook.* Tokyo: Japan Amateur Sports Association.

Japan Professional Sports Association. (1991). *The professional sports II.* Tokyo: Japan Professional Sports Association.

Leisure Development Center. (1992). *White paper on leisure.* Tokyo: Leisure Development Center.

Management and Coordination Agency. (1992). *Budgets concerned with the promotion of physical fitness.* Tokyo: Management and Coordination Agency.

Meeting for the Purpose of Studying Sports Administration. (1990). *Commemoration of the first meeting.* Tokyo: Meeting for the Purpose of Studying Sports Administration.

Meeting for the Study of Sports by Sports Research Group of the Ministry of Education (1990). *Sportpia 21.* Tokyo: Meeting for the Study of Sports by Sports Research Group of the Ministry of Education.

Sports Bureau, Ministry of Education. (1987). *Sports facilities in Japan.* Tokyo: Sports Bureau, Ministry of Education.

Sports Bureau, Ministry of Education. (1988). *Physical education and sports in Japan.* Tokyo: Sports Bureau, Ministry of Education.

Sports Bureau, Ministry of Education. (1992a). The list of rough estimates of the Sports Bureau in fiscal 1992. In *The handbook to practical affairs for leading sports.* Tokyo: Gyousei.

Sports Bureau, Ministry of Education. (1992b). Outline of the Sports Bureau Budget in fiscal 1992. *Sports and Health, 24:* 20–22.

Sports-for-All Division, Sports Bureau, Ministry of Education. (1992). *Wave toward the 21st century, Sports-for-All.* Tokyo: Sports-for-All Division, Sports Bureau, Ministry of Education.

14

Sports Policy in Norway
Berit Skirstad and Kristin Felde

INTRODUCTION

The Land and the People

Norway is a small country with just 4.2 million inhabitants, but in terms of square kilometers it is a large country—it covers 386,958 square kilometers. It is the most sparsely populated country in Europe, with 75 percent of the population living in towns and developed areas. One-third of the country is situated above the Arctic Circle. It has been estimated that people have lived there for more than 10,000 years. The topography consists of fjords, mountains, narrow valleys, and large unpopulated areas. The climate is better than one might expect. There is great climatic variation with mild winters along the coast from the Gulf Stream or North Atlantic current.

Norway features many regional variations in language, economics, and sport. In general, costs are high there. Funds are transferred from richer to poorer areas, especially to northern Norway. There are two official written languages, *bokmal* and *nynorsk,* and numerous local dialects. The Sami people who make up 1 percent of the population belong to an ethnic minority who live mostly in the north. They have their own culture, language, and some sports competitions.

Norway is a monarchy and has been independent since 1905. (From 1814 until 1905 it belonged to a union with Sweden, and for 400 years prior to 1814, Norway was ruled by Denmark.) The monarchy became a symbol of unity during the Second World War, and therefore now a great majority of the people wish to maintain it. The late King Olav V was a sportsman, a ski-jumper, and an Olympic sailor. The present monarch, King Harald VII, is also a sailor and involved in sport.

According to the constitution, power is divided among the king, Parliament, and the Supreme Court of Justice. The Parliament is a representative assembly called the Storting; its 165 members are elected for four years. The parliamentary system of government was introduced in 1884. The Storting is divided into two bodies (houses), the Lagting and the Odelsting. Seven political parties are represented in Parliament. To become operative, a law has to be signed by both houses in succession and the king. In the 1989 election, women won 59 of the 165 seats in the Storting. Earlier, in 1981, Gro Harlem Brundtland became the first woman prime minister and is now in her second term. Of Norway's nineteen ministers, eight are women. Women's strong position in Norwegian society has some bearing on women's position in sport as well.

During most of the postwar period, the Labour party has been in power. Norway is known as a socialist democratic state or a welfare state, one of the most comprehensive and universal in scope. According to Kramer (1992, p. 46), Norway has rightly been regarded as a state-friendly society where government is viewed not as an evil but as a necessity. Everyone over sixty-seven years of age in Norway gets a pension, and the sick and the unemployed get social security benefits. Education in Norway is free. Although 88 percent of the population belong to the Evangelical Lutheran Church (the state church), there is freedom of religion. Only 3.2 percent of the population are foreign citizens. Life expectancy is 72.7 years for men and 79.4 years for women. The unemployment rate is low, with a rate of 6.3 percent as of July 21, 1993.

THE CONCEPT OF CULTURE

In the 1970s a broader concept of culture was advocated (Mangset, 1992, p. 19). Before that period, traditional or qualitative culture was the official concept of culture. Traditional cultural activities were defined as theatre, paintings, classical concerts, and opera. The new concept of culture was based on the knowledge that traditional culture belonged to a cultural elite. The new trend was to focus on the culture of ordinary people and on its cultivation in local milieus. Another reason Mangset (1992, p. 248) suggested was that one hoped to educate people to appreciate traditional (real) culture through amateur culture (i.e., the culture of the masses) and its own activities.

Central to this broadened concept of culture was the decentralization of cultural decision making and cultural activities to the individual. The term *cultural democracy* was talked about. Cultural democracy was prominent in the labor movement in the period between the world wars. Norway and Denmark are somewhat alone in viewing sports as part of the cultural policy arena. The broadened concept of culture mirrors the fact that voluntary organizations have a strong position in Norway. In the 1970s, sport became culture. Thanks to North Sea oil, the state's economic situation was such that it became more strongly involved in the new cultural policy (Simonsen, 1990, p. 10). This involvement was initiated from above (from the department level) not from below or from the side (from sports or culture). In Norway, culture is closely tied to the local and regional level (municipalities and counties). It is the municipal administrative level that has the greatest power and that has had the biggest growth in terms of money in the last decade. Much of the authority, including the allocation of money, has been decentralized. The decentralized cultural administrative apparatus has its parallel to the voluntary organizational structure in sport. In 1976 the contact committees were set up as a result. The new politics in sport integrated sport into the local culture. The cooperation between the cultural administration and the contact committees in the municipalities can be seen as (local) corporatism (Mangset, 1992, p. 245).

THE CONCEPT OF SPORT

Norway also has a very broad concept of sport. When Sport-for-All is mentioned, it means sport that all of us can enjoy, no matter who we are, where we are, or whatever our handicaps may be. It even includes elite sport. The ordinary use of the phrase "Sport-for-All" or *Trim* as it is called in Norway, is a rather young phenomenon. It has led to a remarkable increase in sports participation from the late 1960s and onward in all parts of the world. This can also be observed in the membership statistics of the Norwegian Confederation of Sports. The idea of "Trim" (Sport-for-All) may have given Norwegian sports more recognition abroad than influence on Norwegian sport organizations. In 1975 Trim became known when it was introduced at the Conference of Ministers of Sport in Brussels. The NIF did not have the time or the interest to follow up this success, and West Germany took over Norway's role as the promoter of Trim.

Today sport is recognized as a fundamental right and necessity for everyone and no longer a privilege to be enjoyed by the few. We need to exercise our bodies since robots have taken over much of the heavy physical work in factories. Besides, the leisure time at our disposal has increased significantly. The leisure-time industry is the fastest growing industry in Europe (Marchand, 1990, p. ix).

Brief Modern History of the Government's Relation to Sport

Sport in its various forms has been part of Norwegian culture for about 1,000 years. During the Nordic middle ages, *idrott* (sports), a word derived from *id* (activity), and *drott* (power, endurance) were used to describe a number of physical and intellectual skills that characterized an all-round and well-educated person (man). The Vikings highly praised courage, independence, and decisiveness.

The organized sports of today started in the middle of the 1800s with the growth of gymnastic and rifle clubs. In 1861 the National Association to Promote Physical Exercise and Weapons Training was established, and as early as 1863, this umbrella organization received financial support from Parliament. Except in 1882–83 and during World War II, the annual grant to sports has not been interrupted.

Initially, the motivating factor for Parliament's interest in sport was the military significance of a physically fit citizenry. The umbrella organization, under various names, was assigned to the Ministry of Defense until 1929. Then it was transferred to the Ministry of Social Affairs, and the focus became health benefits. For a short period, it belonged to the Ministry of Local Government and Labour. In 1949 sport was transferred to the Ministry of Church and Education, and the focus shifted to educational goals.

Since 1982, sports have been under the Ministry of Cultural Affairs and Science. The name of the department changed to the Ministry of Church and Cultural Affairs in 1989–90, and it changed again in 1990 to the Ministry of Cultural Affairs.

In the beginning, the intrinsic value of sports played only a small role in the history of organized sports in Norway. Their legitimation was the practical outcome of military preparedness, nationalism, and improved public health. Then the "useless" English sports entered the country with their emphasis on competition, performance, and excitement, and that has had a great influence on sports in Norway in this century. Sports and other physical activities are believed to have strong intrinsic value. This belief is based on fundamental questions such as: What are we? Who should we become? What are our opportunities? What is our group identity? The focus on the intrinsic value of sports underlies the march of sports toward the widened cultural concept.

In 1992 the government submitted two separate reports to Parliament, one on sport and one on culture. This was the first special report on sport exclusively. (St. meld. nr. 41, 1991–92). This was done to give a more comprehensive presentation of both culture and sport. In the period 1973 to 1981, four different governments had forwarded culture reports that included certain aspects of sports. The forerunner for these culture reports was a report on "The demands for sport and physical education." This report was not forwarded to Parliament because it was claimed that it was too strongly influenced by the voluntary sports movement and contained too little about public sports policy (Goksøyr, 1992, p. 65).

The first report (St. meld. nr. 8, 1973–74) concerned organizing and financing cultural work and was delivered by a nonsocialist centrist government. The report stressed that the aim for governmental work in sport was "to give all the best possible conditions for sport activities." Physical, psychological, and social health were emphasized, in addition to the intrinsic value of sports. The report was in line with the district policy of the time; local and regional sports facilities were favored instead of huge central facilities. The report stated that a centrally governed sport culture focused on elite achievements would only stimulate a passive attachment to sports as an entertainment phenomenon.

Because of a change of government to the Labour party, a new report was made the same year (St. meld. nr. 52, 1973–74) and appeared in March 1974. This report was much more positive toward elite and top sport, and focused on Sport-for-All, which included the best performers. This report began recognition of elite sport and government-provided scholarships. The third report on new cultural policy in the 1980s (St. meld. nr. 23, 1981–82) was delivered by a Labour party government. Its main message was to strengthen sports organizations in order to avoid commercialization and increase official governing in cooperation with sports leaders. The philosophy of the 1970s was intact, but not the economic premises.

In 1983 a conservative-dominated coalition government accompanied the fourth report (St. meld. nr. 27, 1983–84) on new tasks in the cultural policy. Here we find important changes in the view of cultural policy, especially the role of the marketplace. The free market was expected to compensate for the lack of public funding. All these reports made up official sports policy and created a new debate about the relationship between elite sport and Sport-for-All, which continues today.

On March 23, 1985, the Social Democrats and the rest of the coalition government, except the Conservative party, held a majority, and this led to a question on sports policy in Parliament. Formally, the fight was about the allocation of money from football betting, but this fight was based on opposition to the conservative parties' view on advertisement, liberalization, and the free market. If sport had not been defined as culture ten years before, this fight would never have reached these proportions.

In the beginning, sports leaders were satisfied with the classification of sport as culture. The money the government wanted to give to counties and municipalities was tempting. This concept of culture did more for elite sport than for the sport's role in health and preventive youth work. In this way, artists and sports people became equal. In the more stringent economic times of the 1970s, sports organizations became nervous owing to the large growth in membership. Sports leaders afraid of economic setbacks therefore stressed that sport was much more than just culture.

Central in all these reports has been the position of sport as part of the comprehensive cultural picture. Areas covered include Sport-for-All; respect for voluntary organizations in sports and their autonomy; the economy; the authorities' responsibilities for building and maintaining sports facilities, plus responsibilities for physically inactive people in the population. The discussion about what kind of sports the government should support has always embraced the contrast between Sport-for-All and elite sport.

Organization of Sports

In principle, responsibility for sport is shared. The government is responsible for sports facilities, and nongovernmental organizations (voluntary organizations) are responsible for the activities. This division is not completely followed in practice, and this has caused problems that are discussed later in this chapter. Since culture is not enforced by law in the municipalities, it is important that there be shared responsibilities for government and sports organizations.

Government Structures

National Level

At the national level, the country is divided into 19 counties and 438 municipalities. The Royal Ministry of Cultural Affairs' Sport Department is responsible for matters relating to sport. The Sports Division provides opportunities in sports and physical activities for the whole population. The Sport Department has twenty employees and is divided into two offices, the Sports Division and the Technical Division. The Sports Division is in charge of general sports matters and sports politics, including administering the distribution of the money to sports allocated from the national budget and revenue from the surplus from lotteries and football pools; sports for the disabled; other target groups; and international affairs.

The Technical Division is responsible for advice and guidance in technical matters concerning sports facilities, as well as approval of sports facilities and cultural centers. Approval in detail of sports facilities was given to the counties and the municipalities in 1988, and for cultural centers in 1993.

Regional Level

At the regional level, each county has its own culture administration, with one or two staff members responsible for sport. The Ministry urges the counties to make county plans for sports facilities and preparations for outdoor life in order to get the revenue from gambling. These plans should also include bigger sports facilities in municipalities. In the future, the Ministry will stress planning work, which takes into consideration the demands of the whole population rather than just participants in competitive sport.

Local Level

At the local level, each municipality has a cultural administration in charge of local culture and sports matters. They make recommendations to the counties as to who should receive grants for building sports facilities. It is their responsibility to build and run the facilities within the municipality. They also give grants to local sport clubs. The local cultural administration cooperates with the contact committees run by the voluntary sports organizations.

Nongovernment Structures

National Level

The main nongovernmental structure at the national level is the Norwegian Confederation of Sports (NIF), an umbrella organization for forty-five sports federations (Figure 14.1). NIF engaged 139 persons full time in 1990. The total membership in the NIF, 1,707,873 (NIF, 1993, p. 34), amounts to about 40 percent of the Norwegian population if one does not take into account multiple membership. The central administration of NIF had a staff of forty-eight persons in 1940 (St. meld. 1991–92, p. 58). The highest authority for sports in the nongovernmental structure is the General Assembly of Sports where representatives meet every fourth year. Altogether, 131 representatives meet: 11 representatives from the executive board, 60 representatives from nineteen district associations, and 60 representatives from forty-five sport federations.

After a change in the General Assembly in 1990, the Norwegian Olympic Committee (NOK) was given the operating responsibility for elite sport in cooperation with the national sport federations.

Regional Level

The nongovernmental structure at the regional level is the District Association. The country is divided into nineteen District Associations, and in addition, all special sports have Special District Associations.

Local Level

At the local level there are 12,586 sports clubs, and 5,597 of them are company sports clubs (NIF, 1993, p. 34). The members are usually divided by sex and age, under seventeen and over seventeen years of age. Most sports clubs in Norway are engaged in many sports. Lately, there has been a tendency to establish more specialized sports clubs concerned with only one competitive sport.

Contact committees are a common organization for all sports clubs in the municipality. This nongovernment organizational structure was established in order to coordinate the application for access to sport facilities. The contact committee also works with the allocation of training time, school leisure activities, sport schools, "Fit for the Olympics," Sport-for-All, and information.

Other voluntary organizations run sports activities and include welfare, scouts, church, political, agricultural, and housewives' organizations. In addition, eleven organizations for outdoor activities belong to an umbrella organization called Friluftslivets Fellesorganisasjon (FRIFO). They are concerned with Sport-for-All, the young, and the elderly.

Description of Sports Activities

Sports activities in Norway include play, outdoor activities, and small and large competitions. Studies show that on average people spend thirty-one minutes per day on sports, that is, three minutes more per day than in 1970 (Haraldsen and Kitterod, 1992, p. 93). On average, men spend twelve minutes more than women on sports activities, up five minutes since 1970. Since 1970, women have not increased time spent on sports. This makes the gender difference in time spent on physical activity greater today than in 1970. There has

Figure 14.1
Governmental and Nongovernmental Structure of the Norwegian Sport Organization

Governmental Structure   Non-Governmental Structure

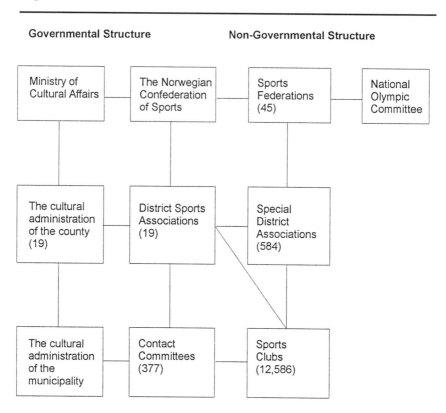

been a trend for older people, sixty-seven to seventy-four years old, especially men, to spend more time on sports and outdoor activities compared to twenty years ago (Haraldsen and Kitterod, 1992, p. 167). On average, men have more leisure time than women. Overall, Norwegian leisure habits show few signs of new trends and changing lifestyles as a whole. The majority of people still participate in the traditional activities of walking and hiking. Since the mid-1960s, membership in NIF has grown strongly. This time period is often called the sport revolution. During this period, it was mainly adults who joined organizations because they wanted to take part in the Sport-for-All movement that started with the Trim campaign in Norway in 1967. This was due in part to the change in sex roles in the 1970s and beyond.

Children and Youth Sports

Children and youth—under seventeen years of age—account for one-third of the membership in NIF. Sports are an essential part of the lives of children and youth in Norway, for through sports children learn about themselves and their own possibilities; get a sense of accomplishment and increased self-confidence; and develop a positive self-image and social sharing. It is also reported that some children experience adult-induced stress in competitions and presentations which can ruin motivation and the sport experience. The dropout rate among children and youth indicates a downside of sport participation wherein some children do not find these activities meaningful.

Sport in the twentieth century took form from English competitive sport. Since 1982, the priority has been all-round quality and variation in sports activity. Thus, activities should be planned so that they improve basic motor skills such as coordination, balance, and rhythm. Further, activities should stimulate children's imagination and creativity. In 1987 a law was passed governing children's participation in sports competition; children under the age of ten could not participate in competition outside the sports club; and children from ten to twelve years of age were restricted to organized competition at the local and regional level.

Sport Schools for Children were implemented, offering extracurricular activities. The requirement was that these activities were well rounded and introduced various types of sport. From being primarily user-oriented, sport for children and adolescents put physical, psychological, and social development at the centre of attention. A 1987 research project on sports showed that 83 percent of those polled cited the local sports clubs' work as important in creating a good environment for raising children.

Research initiated in 1991 by the Norwegian Confederation of Sports (NIF) showed that 65 percent of the eight to eleven year olds and 60 percent of the twelve to fifteen year olds were members of a sports club. This involvement drops to forty percent for the sixteen to nineteen year olds and 32 percent for the twenty to twenty-four year olds. In all groups, more boys than girls are members. It also appears that the boys are more active members than the girls. Furthermore, the boys appear to be more interested in competition than the girls; 28 percent of the boys and 10 percent of the girls mention soccer as their main activity. The data show a tendency for individual sports to lose participants to team sports and outdoor activities to lose participants to indoor activities.

Sport-for-All

More than two-thirds of Norwegians perform outdoor activities such as hiking and skiing in the woods and in the mountains. The Norwegian tradition of walking and skiing is a strong one. This means that most of the physical exercise takes place out of doors and outside sport facilities. The outdoor activities are simple and inexpensive, and require little special equipment. Social anthropologists note the Norwegian tradition in which closeness to nature is considered one of the basic qualities of life. In a recent investigation, the most important reason for taking walks in the woods was in order to "experience the silence and peace in nature" (Aarønaes, 1993, p. 43). Norwegians are brought up believing that fresh air and walking and skiing in the mountains or the forest are important factors in their happiness and self-development.

About 47 percent of Norwegians engage in physical activity, at least once a week, on a regular basis. An additional 15 percent take part less often, and 34 percent claim they do not engage in any form of physical fitness (Aarønaes, 1993). Only 15 percent of the people take part in competitive sports. Track and field, handball, shooting, orienteering, swimming, cycling, sailing, tennis, and rowing are popular sports. In the summers, jogging is the most common form of exercise, involving 18 percent of women and 22 percent of men (Dølvik et al., 1988, p. 37). A poll taken in 1991 shows that 57 percent participate in sporting events during the year and on average participate on sixty-two occasions during the year.

Soccer is without doubt the most popular summer sport in Norway, even if Norway usually does not do well at the international level. The twelve clubs of the National Elite Division attract many hundreds of thousands of spectators during the season. In the fall, the Cup Final is the major soccer event of the year.

Norway has a very good women's football team. They won the world championship in 1991 and the European championship in 1993. Many women report that they go to gymnastic courses and aerobics. Twenty percent of women say that this is their most common form of training.

Sixty-six percent of the sixteen to nineteen year olds and 49 percent of the twenty to twenty-nine year olds do physical activity regularly. The percentage declines drastically to 39 for thirty to thirty-nine year olds. More than 30 percent of physically active people drop out before they are thirty years old. The dropout rate is greater among women than men (Dølvik et al. 1988, p. 43).

Membership in the Norwegian Association for Company Sport has increased considerably lately, and a great potential for growth seems to exist. However, only 20 percent of women are members. According to a research project, 66 percent of physically active people are active in informal settings, alone, or together with friends. The commercial institutes include about 23 percent of the physically active segment of the population (Dølvik et al., 1988, p. 79).

Physically and Mentally Handicapped People

In 1961 the forerunner of the Sport Department in the Ministry of Culture took a first step toward a countrywide action to promote physical activity for mentally handicapped people. It was found that handicapped people benefited from physical activity, and there existed a great need among handicapped people. In 1968 the first course for the training of instructors for the mentally handicapped was conducted. Since that date there have also been organized sports competitions in the summer and winter for the mentally handicapped.

The Ministry of Culture believes that physical activity may be a link in the therapeutic process which prepares each person for everyday life. Furthermore, simple sports competitions could give inspiration and could aid in the development of personality for the individual. In the Paralympics in Barcelona, Norway received thirteen gold, thirteen silver, and seven bronze medals.

Extent of Nation's Participation and Success in International Sports Competition

As a result of rather poor results in the 1984 winter Olympics, a common project of the NIF and NOK was established in 1985. It was called Project '88, or P-88. Since the evaluation of the project was favorable, it continued as *Olympiatoppen* after the Olympics in 1988. At the general assembly, in 1990 the Olympiatoppen received a stronger organization with five employees. The results have improved since the winter Olympics in 1988, when the Norwegian team came home without a gold medal. Four years later, the Albertville winter Games witnessed the greatest Norwegian Olympic performance ever—nine gold, six silver, and five bronze medals. In 1988 Norway won fourteen medals and in 1992, thirty-one medals in the summer and winter Games. The first Norwegian woman won a gold medal in the summer Olympics in Barcelona. In the world championships Norway won eleven gold medals (NIF, 1993, pp. 9 & 22). In 1993 success continued at the World Championships in alpine skiing where Norway won three gold, three silver, and a bronze medal and finished as the top performing nation. Norway has good athletes in skiing, both Nordic and Alpine, and in team sports such as handball and soccer for women.

Thanks to the winter Olympics in Lillehammer in 1994, winter sports received extra funds in the amount of NOK 12 million in 1992 and NOK 9 million in 1993. The support apparatus for elite athletes and team-leader development has been targeted.

Norway has no professional sport, but in soccer it has "nonamateur" players. Norwegians are professionals in football, handball, basketball, ice hockey, boxing, alpine skiing, and cycling abroad. As Hoberman (1993, p. 22) points out, sports—especially winter sports that have a long tradition—have played a role in building national self-respect in Norway.

GOVERNMENT INVOLVEMENT IN SPORT—GOVERNMENTAL SPORTS POLICY

Financial Support for Sport

Norwegian sport is in the middle of an important phase in which national and international impulses and influences are stronger and go deeper than ever before. Volunteerism, support of voluntary organizations, and cooperative solutions have come face to face with professional and commercial undercurrents, mixed with strong individual and differentiated traits (St. meld. nr. 41, 1991–92, p. 10).

There is increasing interest in sport as a separate activity on several levels—as a preventive and rehabilitative factor, a media event, an income source, and an arena for political power plays (Felde, 1991; Hanstad, 1992; Ronglan, 1992).

In Norway, the state finances sports with funds allocated from the national budget (NOK, 10.2 million in 1993) and from a share of revenues from the state's gambling revenues (NOK, 530 million in 1993 from the Football Pools and the National Lotto, Norsk Tipping A/S). The gambling system was introduced in Norway in 1946 as a way to raise money to build new sports facilities after World War II. The establishment of Norsk Tipping A/S, with the Norwegian Confederation of Sports (NIF) and the state as shareholders, has ensured sport a relatively autonomous position. During the period 1946 to 1993, Norsk Tipping A/S has been an important source of financing for sport. Throughout this time, some struggles have arisen between sports organizations and the government regarding the control and distribution of profits from the Football Pools.

The profit from Norsk Tipping A/S has always been held outside the national budget; yet this represents about 95 percent of the government's financial support to sport. Since World War II ended in 1945, both sports and government, regardless of political stripe, have been interested in maintaining sports affairs as a nonpublic sector with a relatively high degree of independence. This was ensured by establishing a financial safety net that has helped confirm the position and status of sport as a leisure-time activity.

Sports' share of the profit from state gambling (Norsk Tipping A/S) is allocated from the budget of the Royal Ministry of Cultural Affairs. To complete and understand the picture of sport's position and autonomy, it is important to know that the total governmental support directed to sports organizations represents only 14.5 percent of the total income in sports organizations at all levels. Sports organizations have to raise about 85 percent of the total income from other sources such as voluntary work, lotteries, kiosk sales, sports meetings, gifts, and sponsors.

In practice, this means that there are few debates in the Parliament about financing sport in opposition to other cultural activities such as professional dancing, music, art, museums, theatre, and opera, which actually get most of their grants from the national budget. In the last few years, representatives from the left—the Socialist party and the Progress party—have argued in Parliament that all proceeds from Norsk Tipping A/S should be allocated to the national budget. However, there is little support for this argument from the majority of representatives in Parliament.

Both lottery and budget funds for sport are administered by the Royal Ministry of Cultural Affairs. The funds are mainly transferred in the form of a grant for administrative support to the working capital of the Norwegian Confederation of Sports and a grant for investment purposes for the construction of sports facilities. Investment grants are distributed by the Royal Ministry of Cultural Affairs to the counties that are responsible for distribution from that point. Compared to other voluntary organizations, Norwegian sports succeeded in obtaining recognition from the government at a relatively early stage (Goksøyr, 1992).

State Gambling Revenues

Proceeds from state gambling revenues (Norsk Tipping A/S) represent about 95 percent of governmental economic support to sports (St. meld. nr. 41, 1991–92), and still this represents only about 14.5 percent of the total income of voluntary sports organization. Figure 14.2 shows the income for the state from gambling from 1981 to 1991. Football Pool income has decreased, but the National Lotto income has increased considerably over the past years. After the year-end adjustments, the accounts for Football Pool and High Score Betting (betting on which games in the upper division score the highest number of goals each week) show a profit of NOK 633 million in 1991, with NOK 427 million (67.5 percent) allocated to sports and NOK 206 million (32.5 percent) allocated to research. Lotto generated a profit of NOK 957 million. Thirty-three percent of this profit, or NOK 316 million, went directly to the treasury, and from there 67.5 percent was distributed to different cultural purposes, excluding sport (Norsk Tipping A/S, 1992, p. 40).

Until 1993 the revenues from Lotto have gone to cultural activities and to research purposes, and the revenues from the Football Pool to sport and research purposes. The sliding scale has changed several times to give sport a higher percentage of the profits.

On January 1, 1993, a new coordination law for the main distribution of state gambling revenues came into effect (Ot. prp. nr. 52, 1991–92) and the structure of the shareholding company Norsk Tipping A/S changed. The company is now totally controlled by the state, which owns 100 percent of the shares. Since 1993, all proceeds from Football Pool, High Score Betting, and Lotto has been shared equally between cultural activities, sport, and research purposes. The new regulation will probably give sports about NOK 100 million more per year if the income from gambling continues at current levels. After year-end 1992 adjustment, the account shows a total profit of NOK 1,590 million to be divided equally—NOK 530 million—between sports, research, and cultural activities (Norsk Tipping A/S, 1993, 0.40).

The new law is a result of pressure from sports organizations which, as Figure 14.2 shows, saw that the income from the football pools had been reduced. The Norwegian Confederation of Sports attributed the reduction to an increase in the number of lotteries in Norway, including the National Lotto which started in 1986. Discussion of the lotteries has led to acrimonious conflicts in Parliament between the Labour and Conservative parties. The new coordinating law was made by the Royal Ministry of Finance in cooperation with the Royal Ministry of Cultural Affairs.

Consumption in Norwegian Sports Organizations, and the Governmental Share of It

Table 14.1 gives information about governmental grants to the Norwegian Confederation of Sports, revenues from state gambling, and grants from other ministries from 1980 to 1991. Figures 14.3 and 14.4 present information about

Figure 14.2
Turnover in the Football Pools, Lotto, and High Score Betting, 1981–1991

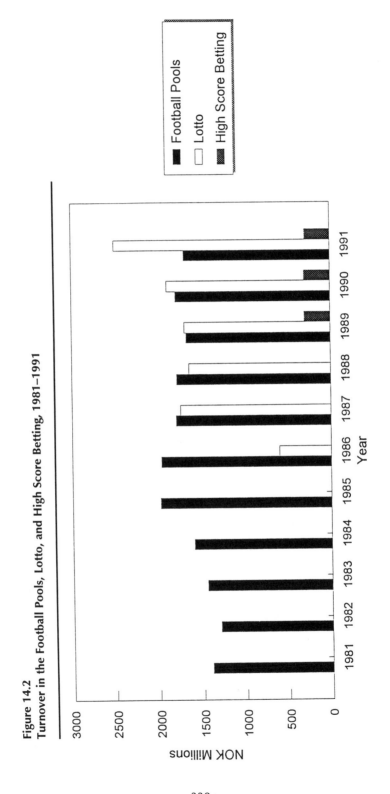

Table 14.1

Grants to National Confederation of Sports from the National Budget, the State Gambling, and other Ministries, 1980–1991

Year	Appropriation on the National Budget 1)	State Gambling 2)	Other Ministries 3)	Total Grants	Translated to 1980 NOK 6)
1980	3,795,000	72,457,627	3,742,194	79,994,821	79,994,821
1981	4,077,500	79,500,000	3,652,796	87,230,296	76,787,232
1982	4,330,000	94,230,000	3,757,729	102,317,296	80,947,223
1983	6,805,000	98,770,000	3,081,230	108,656,230	79,253,268
1984	5,018,000	108,970,000	3,276,587	117,264,587	80,594,213
1985	5,490,000	123,995,000	4,517,255	134,002,255	87,127,601
1986	5,765,000	138,200,000	4,756,500	148,721,500	90,188,902
1987	5,010,000	156,220,000	5,675,481	166,905,481	93,139,219
1988	5,210,000	186,069,480 4)	6,758,138	198,037,618	104,499,870
1989	5,310,000	180,108,000	7,199,250	192,617,250	96,308,625
1990	5,490,000	187,351,515	10,092,950	201,934,465	93,531,478
1991 5)	5,693,000	194,750,000	11,100,000	211,543,000	94,443,055

Notes:

1. Appropriations on the National budget=administrative grants and grants to athletes.
2. State gambling=ordinary transfers and special projects.
3. State subsidies in addition to grants and gambling incomes. These are destined for special projects and granted by several ministries.
4. The heavy increase in state gambling is a result of a change in the distribution law. From 1987 67.5% of the surplus was channelled to sport.
5. The figures from 1991 are budgetary figures.
6. Convention factor=consumptions price index.

Figure 14.3
Voluntary Sports Organizations: Distribution of Expenses

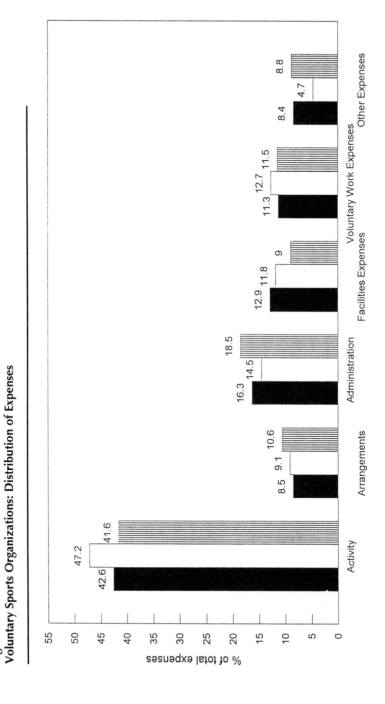

Figure 14.4
Voluntary Sports Organizations: Distribution of Income

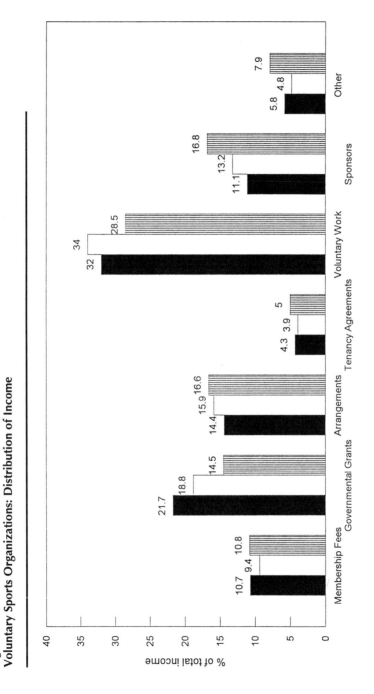

costs and income for voluntary sports organizations in Norway in 1980, 1984, and 1988. From 1980 to 1993, the total income in Norwegian sports organizations increased from NOK 735 million to about NOK 3.5 billion. In 1993 the total grants from the Royal Ministry of Cultural Affairs (including grants from the national budget and profit from Norsk Tipping A/S) to the Norwegian Confederation of Sports was about NOK 228 million. NOK 108 million of the grants was distributed to the forty-five sports federations and NOK 45 million to the nineteen district sports associations.

Sports clubs accounted for approximately 70 percent of total consumption in 1988. Only 8.4 percent of income came from government grants. The rest of the income came from membership fees (12.1 percent), arrangements (18.6 percent), tenancy agreements (6.6 percent), sponsors (12 percent), and voluntary work (41.6 percent).

Government grants for sports clubs decreased from 12.1 percent in 1980 to 8.4 percent in 1988, and income from sponsors increased from 7.1 to 12 percent in the same period. One explanation for this is that the total consumption increased more than NOK 2 billion in this period. Meanwhile, the local communities that allocate money to sports clubs have not been able to increase their grants to the same level because of the economic situation during that period. The authorities give priority to tasks required by law in periods of economic decline. Social, medical, and educational tasks are required by law; sports and culture are not. A second explanation is the reduction of income in the football pools (see Figure 14.2).

The greatest expenses for sports clubs are for activities and arrangements (52 percent). Administrative expenses account for 9.3 percent. Increasingly, administrative work is done by professionals, and this trend will continue in the future (St. meld. 41, 1991–92; NOU, 1988:17; Selle, 1992b).

The government and the Ministry of Cultural Affairs, more than ever before, assert policy objectives for sports and use their control of finances to achieve these objectives. Because of the long tradition of autonomy and self-control and the strong position of the Norwegian Confederation of Sports, it has been difficult for the state or ministry to achieve these objectives. After 1993, the budget process of the National Confederation of Sports began to be scrutinized by the ministry in more detail. Detailed regulations for sports organizations are being established. NIF will have to report how they use money to the ministry. In this way, the government intends to influence the amount of money directed to underdeveloped bodies and parts of the organizations' work.

The National Budget and Grants to Top-Level Athletes

In 1991 the total budget of Olympiatoppen was NOK 30 million. This amount includes government grants through the national budget. In 1993, 100 training grants of NOK 40,000 for a total of NOK 4 million were awarded. The state itself does not review the eligibility of the athletes. All elite athletes in the forty-five sports federations belonging to NIF are eligible for training grants, and these same athletes may receive grants for several years. No tax implications are attached to the training grants. The government grants are supplemented by grants from NOK and money from sponsors.

This represents just a part of the total financial support for top-level sport. In addition, the forty-five sports federations have their own budgets for top-level sport. Top-level sport is so expensive that it absorbs an increasing proportion of available funds, both directly and indirectly.

The main financial income for the top-athlete program comes from sponsors in Norwegian industry and trade. Government sports policy is concerned with ensuring the right of sport to self-determination in the face of strong commercial forces.

Governmental Support from Other Ministries

Sports organizations also get some grants from other ministries such as the Ministry for Health and Social Affairs, the Ministry for Environmental Affairs, and the Ministry of Education, Research, and Church Affairs. In 1991 these grants totaled NOK 11.1 million (St. meld. nr. 41, 1991–92). These grants are based on cooperation with the ministries on special projects such as activities for the disabled, Sport and Fitness, Fit Nation before the Olympics (FIFOL), and sports for immigrants. The number of such grants increased from NOK 3.7 million in 1980 to NOK 11.1 million in 1991.

Municipalities and counties allocate considerably more for cultural purposes, including sport, than the central government. Of total public expenditure for cultural purposes in 1985, the central government provided 38 percent, the county 6 percent, and municipalities 61 percent (Simonsen, 1990, p. 15). This is the result of a new cultural policy beginning in the 1970s. In 1986 a new income system was introduced in the public sector, which involved funds from the central government being transferred to counties and municipalities. The transfers are general framework subsidies. These subsidies are based on the size of the various municipalities and county municipalities and are calculated on the basis of a number of criteria that attempt to take into account such elements as size, density of population, and age structure.

The new income system gives greater freedom of action to municipalities to improve implementation at the local level (Simonsen, 1990, p. 16). This system does not influence sport as much as it influences other sectors.

As in other countries, Norway distinguishes between the private and public sector. Voluntary organizations are neither private nor governmental, but something in between. Since 1988, we have talked about voluntary organizations as a third sector (NOU, 1988, p. 17). When defined as a third-sector organization, it puts voluntary organizations in a special position concerning taxes and value-added taxes (VAT). Voluntary organizations are given exceptions from taxation, through special allowances and reliefs, because of the role of volunteers, who work without pay for idealistic purposes in organizations. If the organization had to comply with the usual regulations for taxes and charges, the amount of voluntary work would decrease. Voluntary work is of great importance to the economy of all voluntary organizations.

In the third sector, many economic values are produced outside the economy of the society. Much of the efforts of the third sector are created through the voluntary work of its members. If this voluntary work were paid, it would have amounted to NOK 9–10 billion (NOU, 1988, pp. 17, 79). Neither the organizations nor the state would have been able to raise this additional money if voluntary work was eliminated. This voluntary work is appreciated from members and is of vital importance to the life of an organization.

Discussions about rules concerning taxes, charges, and VAT for voluntary organizations have led to conflicts between the organizations and the government, and between different political parties in Parliament. If the surplus from voluntary activity exceeds NOK 70,000 per year, the organizations have to pay ordinary taxes and charges according to Norwegian law. A person can earn up to NOK 2,000 working for a voluntary organization before having to pay tax on the income. The Ministry of Financial Affairs is responsible for the tax rules, and Parliament has to sanction the rules. Sports clubs have to pay employers' charges for staff in accordance with Norwegian law. Nonetheless, there exists what we might call a "black economy" in sport as in other sectors of society—that is, payment "under the table" for wages, income, and employers' charges not reported to tax authorities. A research report from 1989 shows that 46 percent of trainers received wages "under the table" and did not pay taxes on them. The report estimated the amount as NOK 450 million per year (Døsen and Gundersen 1989, pp. 68–69). According to the newspapers, taxation authorities, and sports organizations, the increase in problems and difficulties concerning taxation in sport parallels the increase in participation of sport in Norway.

Regulatory Policies and Policies Affecting Sports Organizations, Structures, and Operations

Voluntary sports organizations in Norway are autonomous and have their own regulations and laws. But laws for sports organizations, as for other voluntary organizations, are placed under general Norwegian law. This is because after World War II, sports organizations and the government found a way to finance sports (Football Pools), which ensured that sport would hold a relatively autonomous position. Thus, sport is maintained outside the ordinary national budget (Goksøyr, 1992).

The Norwegian Confederation of Sports has made general regulations for all the main organizations, including the Norwegian Olympic Committee, sports federations, district sports associations, and sports clubs. In addition, there are regulations for the relationship between sport and the media, for the names of sports clubs, and for accounting. Two regulations concern all sports: one is for drugs, and another is for sports activities for children up to twelve years of age. In some specific areas, general Norwegian law regulates sports directly such as in the use, sale, and importation of drugs; professional boxing; tax regulations, charges, and VAT; equity between men and women; and the distribution of funds derived from the state gambling revenues.

Regulations concerning the use, sale, and importation of drugs are of great importance. Norwegian national law states that it is illegal to import and sell drugs. The law of the Norwegian Confederation of Sport maintains that it is illegal to use certain drugs for all members of the organization, and participants in organized sport activities and competitions. The authorities and the sports organizations fight together against the use of illegal drugs in sport. Norway has been, and is still, an active nation in this work internationally.

Professional boxing is forbidden by national law. Thus, Norwegian boxers who want to become professional have to leave the country to practice their sport. Most of them go to Denmark or to the United States.

At all three administrative levels, the goals for public sports policy are realized through cooperation among the municipalities, counties, and central government, and voluntary sports organizations.

Beginning in 1993, the ministry has made appropriations to specific activities and projects for parts of the populations. These appropriations are derived from the sports' share of state gambling revenues. The Norwegian Confederation of Sports (NIF) is opposed to the ministry using these funds to achieve its goals, for according to the NIF this means stronger governmental and political control over the use of the money and over the organization in general. NIF seeks to control grants to voluntary sports themselves.

Other Types of Policies

Construction of Sports Facilities

Today a sports facility is regarded as "an area, place or facility which due to its design and situation, is suitable for sporting activities" (Henriksen, 1992, p. 2). This definition of sport encompasses a wider spectrum of activities and has produced a more differentiated concept of a sports facility. The Report to Parliament no. 41 (1991–92) states that the planning, building, and operating of sports facilities are primarily public responsibilities.

While the division is maintained (it is primarily a public, not a sports club's, responsibility to build and operate facilities), it is still normal for sports organizations to plan, build, and run a number of facilities. However, this division of responsibility must be maintained when facilities are especially expensive to build and operate. About 70 percent of all sports facilities in Norway are built through the cooperation of municipalities and local sports clubs (St. meld. nr. 41, 1991–92). The precise number of facilities in Norway is not known. The Ministry of Cultural Affairs estimates about 10,000 facilities, but this number does not include traditional school facilities. Research is being conducted to register all sports facilities, both public and private, in the country.

The Ministry of Cultural Affairs classifies sports facilities in four categories: neighborhood, municipal, county, and national. In addition, facilities for outdoor life, hiking, and recreating are classified on the basis of intended use (Henriksen, 1992).

Yearly, about 40 percent of the sports' share of state gambling revenues are directed to governmentally supervised construction funds guided by general rules to ensure equal treatment for all applications. Municipalities, counties, and sports organizations can apply for construction funds if they have sanctioned municipal plans with a needs analysis concerning facilities and areas for sports and outdoor recreation. As a rule, municipalities and county municipalities, not clubs, should be applicants for construction funds for large and expensive facilities. There is a sliding scale for subsidies which gives a higher rating to certain parts of the country and to certain types of facilities. Special statutory provisions ensure that all people, regardless of where they live in the country or whether they are rich or poor, have nearly the same opportunity to take part in sports on different levels. The different priorities for subsidies make it possible for poor communities to build sports facilities through increased support from government funds.

Research reports show that interest in physical activity and fitness is increasing, but the arenas for these activities are changing (Dølvik et al., 1988). Traditional sports grounds and sports clubs are no longer the main arena for activity. Only a minority of club members are active in the clubs. The adult part of the population (sixteen years or older) prefers to do their exercise outside traditional sports organizations. The main arenas for activity are neighborhoods, local playing fields and sports grounds, and commercial aerobic and health institutes.

The main cause for this change in trend is practical necessity. People want efficient training without being involved in helping with club activities and taking on leadership responsibilities. The sports movement is going through a process of change and differentiation. New activities are being developed; new values and needs are replacing older ones; and diversity is growing. A primary goal for governmental organizations dealing with sports is to increase the number of sports facilities and organize areas for physical activity in local communities near schools and areas where people live. Particularly for children and the elderly, sports activities must take place in an environment that provides security and enjoyment. In building sports facilities, the government therefore has decided to give priority to local neighborhood facilities in the period from 1993 to 1998.

These facilities must be of a design and size that render it impossible to arrange competitive activities, and they must be located within walking distance from where people live. To increase the building of local community facilities, the government offers to grant 50 percent of the cost of the project to municipalities that give priority to this kind of facility. The Norwegian building regulation states that all public buildings and facilities are to be designed and constructed to provide access to the physically disabled. Sports facilities that are not built in accordance with these regulations will not receive a grant from the construction funds.

The ministry carries out more rigorous inspections of larger and more complicated sports facilities to reduce the need for requirements and extraordinary maintenance, replacements, and so on. In this connection, financial support of rehabilitation and rebuilding of facilities are given priority. There will also be an emphasis on the environmental aspects of architectural design and location of facilities. During the building of the sports facilities for the 1994 winter Olympic Games in Lillehammer, the emphasis was on the environmental and architectural aspects of the facilities. Both the government and sports organizations will put more emphasis and money into these areas in the future. More information, education, and competence are absolutely essential concerning sports facilities.

GOALS RELATED TO POLICIES

Since the beginning of the 1970s, public policy on sport has been based on the principle of Sport-for-All. This principle represents every person's right to engage in sports in relation to his or her abilities, needs, and interests. Furthermore, Sport-for-All has pushed to the forefront the authorities' responsibility to make individual rights a reality, that is, the opportunity to engage in sports. Sport-for-All, as a planning concept, has goals that are too long term and a vision that is too large to serve as a guideline for specific priorities at municipal, county, and central levels. Even so, the government wants to retain Sport-for-All as the main goal of its policy in sport. In addition, the government has adopted a number of specific and more detailed goals (St. meld. nr. 41, 1991–92).

These specific goals state the responsibilities and objectives of public policy on sport in the 1990s. In these goals, we can also recognize three of the government's main policy goals in general—a priority on creating (1) a better life for children and youth; (2) better living conditions for all people, both indoor and outdoor; and (3) activities and employment for the unemployed.

Domestic Policy Goals and Goals Related to Sports— Organizations and Athletes

Through a report to the Parliament (St. meld. nr. 41, 1991–92), the government has listed the national domestic policy goals and the goals related to sports organizations. These goals concern sports policy from 1993 to 2000 and influence action on both the governmental and nongovernmental level. To understand how important these goals and report are, it is essential to know that this is the first time a separate report on sport has been presented to Parliament. The main goals are shown in Table 14.2. With regard to the organizational structure of Norwegian sport, public sports policy goals are to be realized through cooper-

Table 14.2
The Governmental Domestic Policy Goals and Goals Related to Sports Organizations for the Period 1993–2000, Reported to and Accepted in Parliment, October 27, 1992

1. Financial support to sports organizations in order to maintain a uniform level of activity.

2. Children's access to playgrounds and sport facilities in their local communities must be ensured.

3. A greater share of the population must be offered better opportunities to engage in sports, especially vulnerable groups in society.

4. Effort on creating equal opportunities for athletes of both sexes, including those interested in competing in top-level sports.

5. A combined education at extensive sports programs should be offered to younger athletes who have the interest and ability to pursue a career in sports. Such programs should be offered on an equal basis, regardless of income level or where one comes from.

6. Development of sports facilities should be subjected to more specific needs evaluations and long-term economic considerations. Greater attention should be given to the environment and design.

7. A special emphasis should be placed on developing simple facilities that satisfy the need for play, training, and exercise. More money will be allocated to this during 1993 - 1998.

8. International efforts should extol the fundamental values of sport as an independent, democratic, and popular movement with respect to the needs and rights of the individual as well as group interests, and which is on guard against economic, political, and human manipulation.

St. meld. nr. 41 (1991–1992); p. 15.

ation among the municipalities, counties, and central government and the voluntary sports organizations at all three administrative levels. Separate appropriations are suggested for children, particularly for sport schools for both children in general and the disabled. After-school programs and school sports competitions are listed as important activities in cooperation among the schools, the Norwegian Confederation of Sports, and the government.

Separate appropriations are made for children and youth in major cities who are at high risk for antisocial behavior. Finally, the Outdoor Recreation Federation (FRIFO) gets increased support for projects directed primarily toward measures for children and youth. Projects are also available for the elderly and for the recruitment of women leaders and coaches. Government grants for elite support (over the national government) were increased from a total of NOK 2.4 to 4 million in 1993.

Foreign Policy Goals

"International efforts should extol the fundamental values of sport as an independent, democratic and popular movement with respect for the needs and rights of the individual as well as group interest, and which is on guard against economic, political and human manipulation" (St. meld. nr. 41, 1991–92, p. 15).

Throughout the twentieth century, sport has developed into a worldwide phenomenon. The number of participating nations in international sports events, like the Olympics, has increased dramatically, and so, too, has the participation in mass sport and outdoor activities all over the world.

Sport may be characterized as a vast enterprise that demands skillful management and careful professional attention (Segrave and Chu, 1981, p. 165). Thus, there is a need for international communication and cooperation in sports, which has also influenced Norwegian sport. Today regular cooperation takes place with Nordic countries during meetings, and a common strategy has been adopted on international questions of common interest at both the government and nongovernment level.

The Sports Division in the Royal Ministry of Cultural Affairs wants to be an active member of the Council of Europe, Committee for the Development of Sport (CDDS). Experts from both governmental and nongovernmental levels are represented in CDDS. The organization has thirty-five member countries (January 1993), and has headquarters in Strasbourg, France. The focus is on ethical tasks such as violence and misbehavior at sports events; drugs; the economy of sport; assistance to Eastern and Central Europe; exchange of information about sport; and coordination of sports research.

The Council of Europe has adopted two conventions concerning sport: on spectator violence and misbehavior at sports events, and in particular at football matches; and on drugs. The United Nations Educational, Scientific and Cultural Organization (UNESCO) has its own committee working with Physical Education and Sport (CIGEPS). This work is supported by the Nordic countries which coordinate their representation. The European Normative Committee (CEN) involves nearly all European countries, and among other tasks, it is responsible for setting common European standards for sports facilities. The Norwegian Confederation of Sports, the sports federations, and the Norwegian Olympic Committee have their international counterparts.

Norwegian sports have been involved in a developmental aid project for Sport-for-All in Tanzania since 1992, in Zambia since 1989, and in Zimbabwe since 1990 through bilateral agreements. The projects are part of the Directorate for Development Cooperation (NORAD) scheme for support and development of voluntary organizations.

The winter Olympics in Lillehammer in 1994 provided a unique opportunity to present Norway and Norwegian sport to the world. This event was important for the government, the municipality of Lillehammer, and Norwegian sports. As a result, a number of international championships, conferences, and meetings were organized in Norway, providing the nation an opportunity to strengthen its international contacts and position in sports. These contacts gave increased competence to Norwegian sport.

Serious planning of Lillehammer started in 1988, after the IOC made its decision in Seoul. The idea was already born in 1981, but it was kept secret for the first year. From the beginning few people were interested in the idea. People did not believe the idea would come true, but in Seoul it happened after years of intensive work from idealistic people. Since then politicians, media, researchers, sports organizations, Parliament, and people have discussed if, and why, Norway should host the winter Olympic Games. Both locally in Lillehammer and on the national level there was opposition and debate about the project. Media and researchers have been critical the entire time.

The state granted the Lillehammer Olympics NOK 1.4 billion in 1985, NOK 1.8 billion in 1987, NOK 7 billion in 1991, and NOK 7.271 billion in 1993 (adjusted to 1993 NOK). In addition, the budget for the costs of infrastructure such as roads and railroads was NOK 2,533 billion as of June 1993. In 1989, a special division for the winter Games at Lillehammer was established in the Ministry with a staff of nine people, but in 1993 this number began to be reduced. The Lillehammer Olympic Organizing Committee (LOOC) was founded after the IOC charter but adapted to Norwegian conditions. In June 1993, 520 people were employed and 110 were hired on a consultative basis. The Parliament put the greatest emphasis on marketing, economic growth, and new job possibilities as its goal for the Lillehammer Olympics.

Issues of financing, locating the sports facilities, environmental aspects, and the cultural concept produced the most difficult and important debates. The fact that Lillehammer would host the Games mobilized considerable research activity in the field (e.g., Andersen, 1991, Nebben, 1992; Lesjø, 1990; Spilling, 1985, 1991, 1992). The participation of the sports organizations in the process has been studied by Felde (1991) and Hanstad (1992). The debates focused on the direct and indirect costs and benefits of the arrangement, as well as economic, environmental, and social costs.

CONCLUSION

Sports organizations and the government, regardless of its political orientation, have been interested in maintaining sports as nonpolitical, with a relatively high degree of independence. This objective is ensured in part by a financial safety net provided by the proceeds from the Football Pool. This has helped maintain sports as a leisure time activity apart from government policy (St. meld. nr. 41, 1991–92, p. 22).

One reason why Norway has been able to preserve a unified organizational structure in sports is the NIF's influence on the distribution of Football Pool funds. However, the lack of inner cohesion and of real community and unity in sport has made it difficult for the NIF to act with authority in political matters relating to sports. The consequence has been a reduction of the sport organizations' influence.

Different sports cultures with different values have emerged in Norway. The most visible split is Sport-for-All and commercialized sport. The conflict between these two has a long history and is manifested in the way sport is structured with the special sports federations (mainly elite sports) on one side and the district sports associations on the other side (mainly Sport-for-All). An important question for the future is how the variety of sports organizations, often in conflict with each other, can survive within the existing organizational structure. Each time the NIF has considered splitting up, the government has intervened (St. meld. 41, 1991–92, p. 20). The role of the district associations is essential. If they disappear, the NIF will be little more than an umbrella organization.

The winner in the future may be the Norwegian Olympic Committee. The Lillehammer Olympic Committee helped move power in sport away from the NIF to the Norwegian Olympic Committee, and in 1994, one president began to serve for both the NIF and NOK. The formal fusion of the two organizations is to occur in 1996. Only time will tell what effect commercialization will have on Norwegian sports and whether the public's mistrust of elite sports can be minimized.

It is questionable what kind of impact the special report on sport to Parliament will have on the politics and economics of sport, especially when the economy is weak. The responsibility for sport is shared so that government is responsible for the facilities and the voluntary organizations are responsible for sports activities. This sharing of responsibilities is not followed strictly, which creates problems. Voluntary sport organizations are an integral part of public sports policy. Sport is rather autonomous in its relationship to government, but at the same time the two are linked to each other through mutual cooperation. The closer the cooperation with the official bureaucracy, the fear increases that there will be corruption in sport. Thus, only time can reveal how the future relationship between government and sport will evolve.

REFERENCES

Aarønaes, Lars. (1993). Det nyeste om nordmenns friluftsliv. In *Fjell og Vidde* 1: 40–43.

Andersen, T. (1991). *Plassering av OL-anlegg—aktører og innflytelse. En analyse av arealplanprosessen i Lillehammer i 1989.* Lillehammer: ODH.

Dølvik, J. E., et al. (1988). *Kluss i vekslinga. Fritid, idrett og organisering.* Universitetsforlaget.

Døsen, I., and Gundersen, L.M.H. (1989). *Ansettelses-, lønns- og skatteforhold for norske idrettstrenere.* Diplomoppgave ved Bedriftsøkonomisk institutt.

Felde, K. (1991). *Beslutningsprosessen knytta til lokaliseringa av isanlegga for OL på Lillehammer. Ein analyse av idretten sin medverknad i prosessen.* Norges Idrettshøgskole.

Goksøyr, M. (1992). *Staten og idretten 1981–1991.* Kulturdepartementet.

Hanstad, D. V. (1992). *OL på Lillehammer—En prosessanalyse med særlig vekt på overveielser, beslutninger, og tiltak i det politiske system.* Norges Idrettshøgskole.

Haraldsen, Gustav and Kitteroed, Hege (1992). Doegnet rundt: *Tidsbruk og tidsorganisering, 1970–1990: Tidsnyttingsundersoekelsene.* Oslo: Norway: Statistisk sentralbyraa.

Henriksen, M. (1992). *Sports facilities, terms and definitions, capacity and demand.* Royal Ministry of Cultural Affairs, Sports Division.

Hoberman, John. (1993). Sport and ideology in the post-communist age. In Lincoln Allison (ed.), *The changing politics of sport.*

Kirke-og undervisningsdepartementet. (1969). *Innstilling om Behovet for idrett og fysisk fostring fra en komite nedsatt ved kongelig resolusjon 16.desmber 1966. Innstillingen avgitt* 4 July 1969.

Klausen, Bergen, and Martin, Arne. (1993). Construction of the Norwegian image—reflections on the olympic design program. In Puijk (ed.), *OL 94 og forskningen III.* Lillehammer.

Kramer, Ralph M. (1992). The roles of voluntary social service organizations in four European states: Policies and trends in England, the Netherlands, Italy and Norway. In Stein Kuhnle and Per Selle, *Government and Voluntary Organizations.* Great Britain: Avebury.

Kulturdepartementet. (1992). *Forskrifter og bestemmelser om stønadav tippemidlene til anlegg for idrett og friluftsliv.* Oslo, Norway: Kulturdepartementet.

Lesjø, J. H. (1990). *OL saken som beslutningsprosess, rasjonell, segmentert eller anarkistisk?* Østlandsforskning.

Lesjø, J. H. (1992). OL på Løvebakken. In R. Puijk (ed.) *OL-94 og forskningen II.* Lillehammer.

Mangset, Per. (1992). *Kulturliv og forvaltning.* Oslo, Norway: Universitetsforlaget.

Marchand, J. (1990). *Sport for All in Europe.* London: HMSO.

Nebben, K. B. (1992). *En studie av reorganiseringesprosessen i OL-organisasjonen på Lillehammer. Mykskapning eller rasjonell tenkning.* UiO, Institutt for statsvitenskap, hovedfagsoppgave, Oslo.

NIF. (1992). *Årsrapport 1991.* Oslo.

NIF. (1993). *Årsrapport 1992.* Oslo.

NOU. (1988) 17, *Frivilige organisasjoner.*

Norsk Monitor. (1991). *Rapport 1991.* Markeds—og mediainstituttet.

Norsk Tipping A/S. (1992a). *Årsmelding 1991.* Norsk Tipping A/S.

Norsk Tipping A/S. (1992b). *Årsmelding og regnskap 1992.* Norsk Tipping A/S.

Norsk Tipping A/S. (1993). *Arsrapport 1992.* Norsk Tipping A/S.

Ronglan, L. T. (1992). *Makt og avmakt blant særforbund i Norge. En analyse av maktforholdene innen 13 sær-forbund på 1980-tallet, med utgangspunkt i en bytteteoretisk maktmodell.* Norges Idrettshøgskole.

Segrave, J., and Chu, D. (1981). *Olympism.* Human Kinetics, Publishers Inc.

Selle, Per. (1992a). *Idretten og det offentlege: Ein familie?* In Rapport fra Statens Idrettskonferanse oktober 1992. Kulturdepartementet, Idrettsavdelinga.

Selle, Per. (1992b). Frivillig organisering i nve omgjevnader. Lossenter Notat 92/36.

Selle, Per, and Øymyr, Bjarne. (1991). Explaining changes in the population of voluntary organizations: Aggregate or individual data? Lossenter Notat 91/49.

Simonsen, M. B. (1990). *Norwegian Cultural Policy.* Kulturdepartementet, Oslo.

Skirstad, Berit. (1991, October 26). Sport for All movement and women's sport in Norway. Lecture at the Japan Society for Comparative Studies of Dance, Tokyo, Japan.

St. meld. nr. 8. (1973–74). *Om organisering og finansiering av kulturarbeid.*

St. meld. nr. 52. (1973–74). *Ny kulturpolitikk.*

St. meld. nr. 23. (1981–82). *Kulturpolitikk for 1980-åra.*

St. meld. nr. 27. (1983–84). *Nye oppgåver i kulturpolitikken.*

St. meld. nr. 41. (1991–92). *Om idretten. Folkebevegelse og folkeforlystelse.* Kulturdepartementet.

15

Sports Policy in Spain

Nuria Puig

INTRODUCTION

The Spanish Political System

In 1978 a new constitution in Spain established a parliamentary monarchy. Juan Carlos I de Borbon has ruled the country since 1976, succeeding General Francisco Franco, a dictator who seized power in 1939 following a three-year civil war. Prior to Franco's reign, Spain had endured an up-and-down political life, alternating between a republic and a monarchy.[1]

The new constitution established a federal parliamentary structure much like that of the United States. In addition, the constitution takes into account the existence of seventeen autonomous governments (comunidades autonomas, or CCAAs), one for each of the regions that make up the territory of Spain. Each comunidad autonoma has its own president and Parliament. The autonomous communities were set up because of the historical differences in cultural identities throughout the country. Evidence of these differences is that four different languages are spoken in Spain. The most important of these languages, "Castellano," normally called Spanish, is spoken all over the country, although it coexists with another language in some regions. The other three are Catalan, spoken in Catalunya, Valencia, and Les Illes (Balearic Islands); Euskera (Basque), in Euskadi (the Basque country); and Gallego, in Galicia.

The CCAAs are ruled by their respective statutes of autonomy in which they regulate the fields that each one assumes. These are variable. The so-called historical communities (Catalunya, Galicia, Navarra, and Euskadi) have a higher level of responsibility than the others, although they do not have identical situations. Simply put, the central government has exclusive power in international relations, defense, political economics, and taxes. The CCAAs have responsibilities concerning people, specifically, culture, youth, education, social services, and health.

Despite this decentralized structure, Spain cannot be described as a federal democracy; in fact, it can be called the "state of the autonomies." Even today strong tensions continue to inhere in the political model by which the country is ruled. Although certain sectors seem satisfied with the actual system and demand the existence of a strong central government to control the relations between the CCAAs, others demand even greater economic and fiscal autonomy for each of the communities. Arguments about the responsibilities of both government bodies are frequent.

The Spanish political map is also shaped by the existence of the *diputaciones* (provincial county councils) and the town councils. The diputaciones are the government organs of the provinces, territorial entities into which each region is subdivided. They were very important during the Franco era when the existence of different identities in Spain was not recognized and the political structure was completely centralized. The diputaciones were the link between the central government and the town halls. Even though today their existence is controversial, and their dissolution is being contemplated, at the moment they continue and possess a certain range of political power.

The town halls are ruled by the Ley Reguladora de Bases del Regimen Local (Law Governing the Bases of Local Government) of 1985. They have a basic political importance since they have direct contact with the citizens. This importance is even greater when the matters involved affect the people, as in sport. The citizens, individually or through organizations, go to the town halls to report on their needs and aspirations. Thus, the administration of political power in Spain involves complex interrelationships and networks. These complexities have a profound effect on sports.

Legal and Institutional Framework of Sports Policy

The actual Spanish sports system has grown parallel to the political system. Article 43.3 of the Spanish constitution states that the public powers will promote physical education and sport. This article underscores the importance of Spanish public institutions to the development of sport. The historical context during which this policy was formulated is of interest here. After 1975 Spain was leaving behind a stage characterized, among other things, by a serious shortage of collective services such as hospitals, schools, and sports facilities. All eyes looked to Europe where the welfare state policies were being harvested following the Second World War. The authors of the constitution, aware of this situation, hoped to demonstrate democratic changes guaranteeing the quality of life for the people. Both they and the general public regarded sports as one of the basic elements of the quality of life in the society they were beginning to build. In 1980 the General Law of Physical Culture was passed which legislated the lines to be followed until 1990, when a new, more modern Law of Sport, was passed.

Since 1992 the sports policy of the central government has been carried out by the Consejo Superior de Deportes (CSD). This Superior Council of Sports, an administrative organ of an autonomous nature, is attached to the Ministry of Education and Science (MEC). The CSD, together with the CCAA or the Spanish sports federations, works on a national and international level. Although it collaborates in programs of sports promotion, the campaign for the construction of sports facilities in schools, for example, its main job is in the area of coordination in top-level sports and in scientific research of sports. This includes the fight against drugs and strategies against violence in sport (Consejo Superior de Deportes, or CSD, 1992, p. 4; Ministerio de Educacion y Ciencia, or MEC).

At the same time, the Estatutos de Autonomia (Autonomous Statutes) regulate the CCAA's degree of competence with reference to sporting activities. The CCAA seeks to "promote, construct and organize sport facilities, advise and coordinate the sports federations in the CCAA, promote sport organizations in its various forms, organize sport in schools and have legal power over sport in their territory" (CSD, 1991, p. 4; MEC). Currently, only four laws regulate sports at an autonomous level (Castilla-Leon, Catalunya, Madrid, and Euskadi). Although they cannot act in contradiction to the Sport Law of the central government, they contain notable differences. Analyzing them, we notice their different social-political contexts and political intentions (Burriel, 1992). Not all the CCAAs are governed by the same political parties, and in the laws that they formulate, whether in sports or in any other area, different political models are revealed.

This assembly of laws also regulates the responsibilities of the diputaciones concerning sport. Their functions are based on the coordination and assistance of the town halls. The concerns of the town halls are: "The maintenance of the grounds and the construction of sports development, of programmes of sports promotion for all ages, help for the sports clubs in the area, and the maintenance and administration of sports facilities themselves" (CSD, 1991, p. 4; MEC).

Private Organizations

The Spanish Olympic Committee (COE) is concerned with the development of the Olympic movement in Spain, as is shown by Spanish legislation. Although it is a private organization, it is called by law *entidad de utilidad publica* (organization of public utility).[2]

Although the sports federations have private rights, they, too, are called by law *entidades de utilidad publica*. There are fifty-four Spanish sports federations which, following the Spanish political and administrative structure, are subdivided into 600 territorial or regional federations. Each has its own legal entity which works in each CCAA. Among their most important functions are: To organize and control the official competitions throughout the whole state, to develop the preparation of elite athletes and national selections, and to showcase Spain's representation in international competitions.

At the bottom of the hierarchy are about 30,000 sports organizations throughout the country. These are varied in affiliation and purpose, and are becoming increasingly diversified (Heinemann, 1986; Puig and Heinemann, 1992). Thus, while traditional sports clubs continue to be held together by the solidarity of their membership, volunteer work, and an orientation toward improving performance, recognition is given more to those associations that promote the less performance-oriented Sport-for-All. The Sport-for-All clubs are required by the Law of Sport to form a national-level, official body of sports promotion called *Entes de Promocion Deportiva*. At the other extreme are the large professional football and basketball clubs which, since 1992, have a commercial structure called *Sociedad Anonima Deportiva* (Sports Corporations).[3]

The diverse Spanish sports organizations are the "great unknowns." Since no serious studies have been done of them, it is impossible to evaluate their levels of voluntary and professional work, the structure of their financial resources, or their social or sporting impact. Moreover, no study has been made which deals specifically with sports policy. Only some partial investigations have been performed, which allow us to draw a few inferences (Burriel, 1990; García Ferrando, 1986, 1989; Martínez del Castillo et al., 1991a; 1991b; Puig et al., 1985). Sports policy appears to be the result of the confrontation of laws, projects, or proposals with the social, political, cultural, and economic context in which they are developed.[4] In addition, there appear to be some sociological constants that will be examined subsequently.

Sports in Spain: A Pervasive Phenomenon

The People's Attitude Toward Sports

Sports in Spain are not only an activity, but increasingly a way to express many feelings, interests, ambitions, and the like—that is, an authentic social phenomenon that impacts society as a whole.

In 1990, 35 percent of the total population between fifteen and sixty years of age participated in sports in Spain (García Ferrando, 1991). This percentage includes people who say they participate in one or more sports three times or more a week or only on holidays. In total the number of Spanish people between 15 or 60 who practice a sport is about seven and a half million (García Ferrando, 1991, p. 31). Since 1968, there has been a progressive increase in participation in sports (Figure 15.1). However, since 1985, the increase has been only 1 percent. Although in round numbers it appears that we have reached the limit, a deeper analysis shows new phenomena that reflect a greater penetration of sport in society (García Ferrando, 1991, p. 29). In this sense, we must emphasize

Figure 15.1
The Evolution of Sports Practice

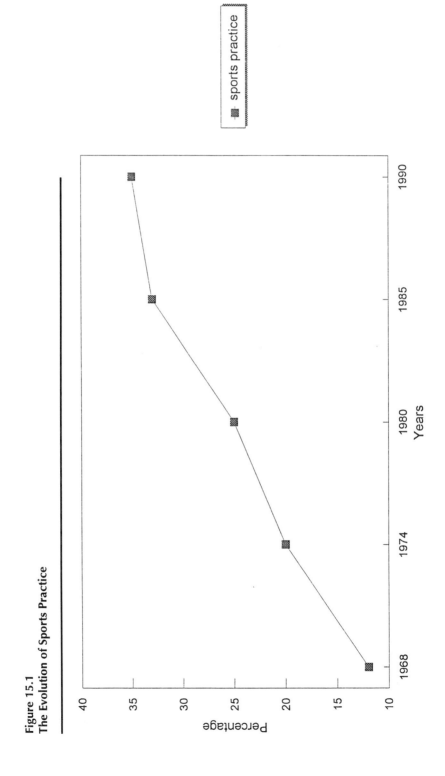

Table 15.1
The Most Practiced Sports in Spain

Order of Sports		% in relation of total sportspeople
1	Swimming	39
2	Football	28
3	Basketball	23
4	Tennis	18
5	Cycling	15
6	Jogging	15
7	Fitness	14
8	Indoor-Football	13
9	Track and Field	9
10	Handball	6
11	Volleyball	6
12	`Pelota`	6
13	Dance/Rythmics	5
14	Table-Tennis	5
15	Hunting	5
16	Skiing	5

Source: García Ferrando. (1991).

that, although the total number of people engaged in sports has not increased, many people have stopped participating and would like to return to sports. A life including sports is highly valued.

With regard to the most practiced sports, they are varied and reflect different sporting tastes (Table 15.1). They range from the so-called traditional sports (dance, jogging) to others that had once been highly restricted from the social point of view (tennis, skiing). To find such different sports among the most practiced is further indication of the increased pervasiveness of sport in Spain.

Different models of sports practice are operative (García Ferrando, 1991; Puig and Heinemann, 1992). While the so-called traditional model (belonging to a club, a code of values based on attaining a result, predominance of young men, etc.) is still prevalent, other models are appearing. In addition, the number of participants in sports has increased greatly, as indicated by federation licenses (membership cards for a federation of athletes at the local, regional, national, or international level). The number of people associated with clubs has not increased as greatly (Figure 15.2). Despite these significant changes, the access to practicing sport and the interest in sport are not homogeneous for all the population. They clearly vary according to age, sex, level of education, and social-professional category.

As noted, there are differences according to age. As the age increases, the percentage of sports practice decreases. However, this is due not to biological

Figure 15.2
Sports Practice and Number of Federation Members

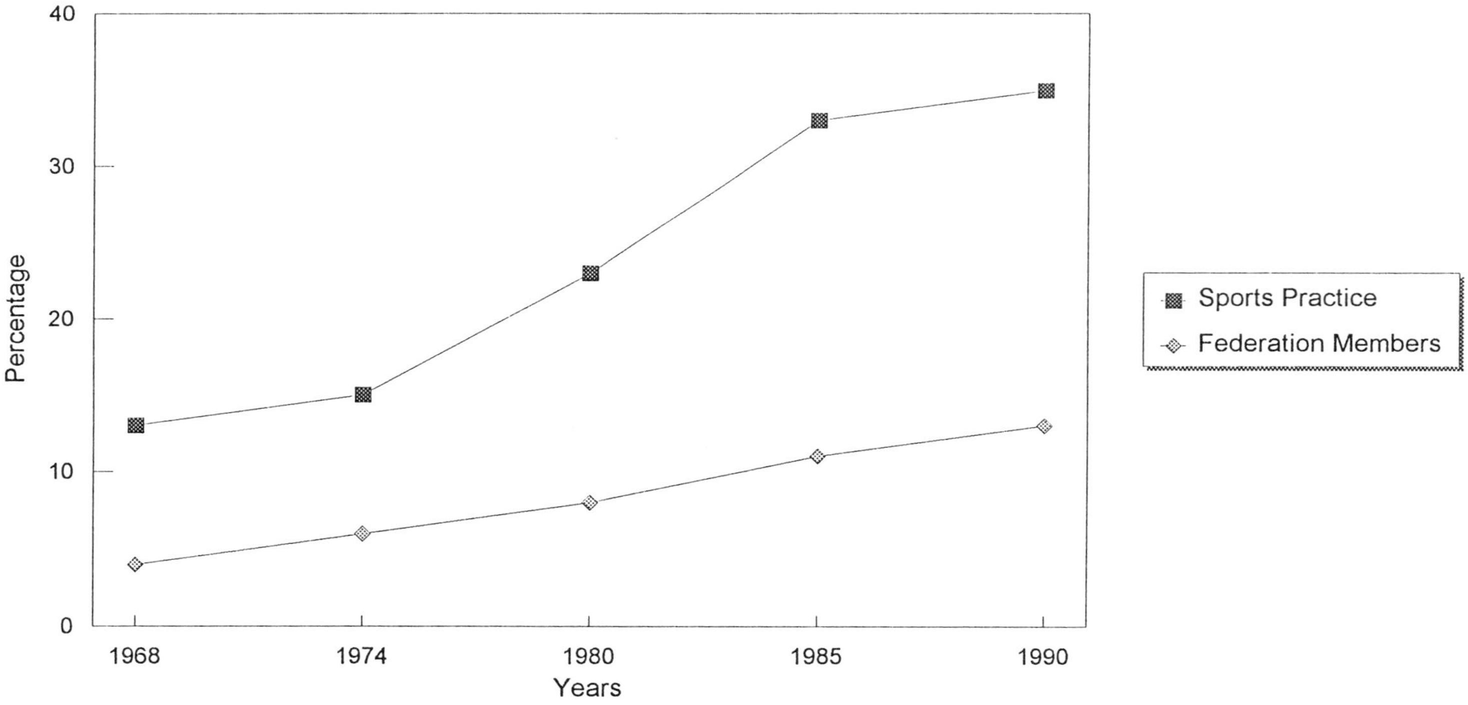

reasons but to what is called the generation effect; that is, older people have had fewer opportunities to acquire a sports habit. As we have seen, the incorporation of sport into the Spanish lifestyle is a recent phenomenon; the era in which older people grew up was less inclined toward sport practice.

The existing relationship between the process of socialization and sports behavior is clearly shown in the case of the female population. Women not only practice less than men but also they do it in a different way. After 1968 a numerical difference was noted between the sports participation of men and women, and these differences did not decrease; they were parallel curves (Figure 15.3). Between 1985 and 1990, however, this tendency changed (García Ferrando, 1991, p. 32). This fact reflects the changes in the traditional stereotypes with regard to gender. Women currently seem more likely to adopt lifestyles that are less conventional, and some of them tend to adopt models of behavior that are not very different from those of men (Buñuel, 1991; García Ferrando, 1990; Puig 1986, 1992a).

Age and sex variables are also influenced by occupation and level of education. Those who have had very little education or only basic education practice less. In addition, housewives, pensioners, and unskilled laborers have a lower level of participation.

Economic and Occupational Impact of Sports

Little information is available on the economic impact of sports in Spain. It is necessary to systematize the statistical sources to begin any detailed investigation (Alonso et al., 1991). Here we can only offer an overall picture based on a few concrete facts.

In 1989 spending on sport by all public administrations represented 0.25 percent of the gross domestic product (GDP), more than half of which was provided by the town halls. In 1985 sport spending was 0.16 percent of the GDP. Thus we can see a significant increase in a short period. At the same time, and despite the deficiency of the available statistical sources, Alonso et al. (1991, p. 35) predict that spending on sports in Spain could reach 1.2 percent of GDP. They base their calculations on existing indirect indicators (Alonso et al., 1991, p. 34).

This increase of money put into sport is also noticeable when we analyze spending per person. A detailed study was carried out in Barcelona (Burriel, 1990) in which it was shown that in 1984 the town halls spent an average of 584 pesetas (pts.) per citizen on sports, while in 1988 the amount increased to 1,251 pts. Another indication is the statistic relative to private consumption. In the 1960s the budget of Spanish families began to be diversified, with more importance being paid to the entry of "amusements, spectacles, education and culture," which is where the Instituto Nacional de Estadistica (INE) (National Institute of Statistics) includes what is spent on sports. However, in the 1980s, this category was replaced with "other goods and services," travel, restaurants, and personal care. This may reflect less spending on sports.

Figure 15.3
Sports Practice according to Gender

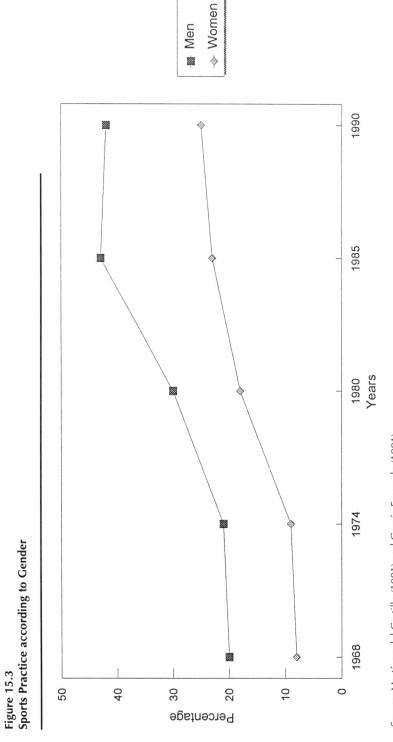

Source: Martínez del Castillo (1991) and García Ferrando (1991).

On the other hand, the figures relative to sports as a source of employment are more exact. Two investigations were recently carried out by Martínez del Castillo et al. (1991b, 1992) at the request of CSD. According to this research, in 1991 the employment generated by the training, teaching, and management sectors was 42,679 jobs. In 1973 there were 9,824 jobs (INE, 1975). The employers in decreasing order were as follows: Ministry of Education, CCAA (specifically, those who had transferred to educational responsibilities and enterprises), 12,151; private companies, 10,742; town halls, 10,400; and sports organizations, 9,386. At the same time, if we consider the "underground" employment produced in these sectors, it can be estimated that the total number of jobs provided could be as many as 49,000. This represents 0.3 percent of the active working population in Spain. Finally, the number of jobs produced directly or indirectly by the sports sector is calculated to be 147,000, that is, 0.96 percent of the active working population of Spain (Alonso et al., 1991, p. 35).

A trend to be considered here is a change in the labor market. In all the fields studied, we can see a diversification in the professional characteristics desired. There tends to be more specialization. In management, we must distinguish, for example, between the manager of a commercial club and the person in charge of some public facilities. In promotion campaigns, specialists are needed for pensioners, handicapped people, marginal youths, and so on. These changes are producing such a deep impact on the system that legislation is expected to follow on the *Reforma de las Ensenanzas y Titulaciones Deportivas* (Reform of Sports Teaching and Titles) (CSD, 1991).

Sport as a Spectacle and Top-Level Sport

Football, traditionally, and basketball, in more recent times, have a function that goes beyond simple entertainment and is converted into a phenomenon of social importance. A match between F. C. Barcelona (usually called "Barca") and Real Madrid leaves the streets empty, alters the hours of work, and cancels all meetings. A victory can also change a normal workday into an unofficial holiday. The winners are applauded when they arrive at the airport, they are accompanied on their triumphal passage through the city, their names are sung out when they are received by the authorities, and so on. Moreover, these great teams form part of a city or region's identity, and their victories become transformed into victories by the groups that support them.[5] This is especially true for Barca and other Catalan teams. Each of their victories is an act of national affirmation; in Catalunya sport and nationalism are strongly interrelated (Hargreaves, 1992).

The professional football and basketball teams invest much money in the buying and selling of players. They contract players from all over the world for astronomical figures. (The purchase of Koeman cost F. C. Barcelona 1,000 million pts. in 1991.) These clubs, as noted, have a commercial structure. Each of the professional leagues has its own legal personality and a certain autonomy.[6]

Until now other sports have had a relatively insignificant role. Spanish athletes in international competitions, on the average, achieved results that were only middling. If the teams had any success, it was considered more of an accident than a result of well-conceived preparation. Since the results obtained in the Barcelona Olympic Games, that is no longer the case. In all, Spain won twenty-two Olympic medals, which put them in sixth place in the medals. The total number of medals in the previous Olympic Games was lower.

To date we can only make educated guesses about the reasons for this improved sports performance. Through an agreement among the CSD, the Spanish Olympic Committee (COE), and Spanish television, a program of private sponsorship for the preparation of the Olympic athletes was created. The Associacion para los Deportes Olimpicos 92 (ADO '92) (Association for Olympic Sports) coordinated the contributions of twenty-one companies who between 1988 and 1992 gave 13,130 million pts.[7] Sixty-five percent of this amount went to the federations, which, together with their usual resources supported the Olympic preparations (Sánchez Bañuelos, 1992). These groups have given the country high-quality sports facilities while building three centers for top-level performance, for exclusive use in developing elite-level sports.

These factors no doubt influenced the results. But we must look deeper to see how they are interrelated with other social or circumstantial factors. To what extent, for example, has the positive vision of sport that is now apparent in Spanish society legitimized the athletes? In the past, many families distrusted a son or daughter who was an athlete; such an attitude no longer exists. This question can be answered when we analyze the preparation plans of each athlete who won an Olympic medal, the places where they were concentrated, the help received from their respective federations, the technical backup provided, the human context of the preparation process, and so on.

Another difficult but important question is: To what extent did the fact that the Olympic Games took place in Barcelona, the host country, influence the results? It is known that "playing at home" is an essential part of winning (Valdano, 1986). Barcelona lived the Olympics with great intensity. Everything in the city was supportive of the athletes; there was a general feeling of happiness and holiday throughout the city. In the facilities where the events took place, there was a lively feeling of expectation with respect to the performances of the Spanish athletes, and there were demonstrations of support. Similarly, the continuing presence of the royal family at all the events was notable, especially the king, who attended all the finals in which a Spanish athlete had a chance of winning.

Each of these questions suggests further profitable research projects.

SPANISH SPORTS POLICY

To understand the current Spanish sports policy, we must see how it has been handled for approximately the last two decades. Present laws, regulatory policies, and relationships with the sports organizations are the result of a process that has evolved in stages. It is clear that there are points of inflection that are more or less decisive in the course of each one of these stages. The most significant was that of October 17, 1986, when the International Olympic Committee chose Barcelona to stage the 1992 Olympic Games. Anything that occurs within the context of the 1983–92 period can be considered a decisive landmark because the Olympic Games were a collective challenge that made it necessary to unite forces and bring to reality all the projects and actions that had been forming during this period.

The stages analyzed are the following:

- 1975–83: This transition period began with Franco's death and was preceded by years of discontent and crisis in structures that were already incapable of responding to the necessities of an industrialized and urbanized Spain. The years of transition to democracy witnessed the construction of a democratic state open to all possibilities, and so there were trials, probes, compromises, and uncertainties.

- 1983–92: This period witnessed the consolidation of the new political model and a period of definition, together with the carrying out of the main lines of economic and social politics. Spain entered into the European Common Market in 1986.

- 1992–present: This period seems intent on new development as already influenced by events from each former stage.

Such stages are not historic moments concerning sport exclusively, but rather should be seen in the light of all recent Spanish history.

1975–83: The Transition Years

Franco died in November 1975. A transition stage toward democracy began that could be considered concluded in 1983 when the second democratic elections were held. This stage was characterized by the dissolution of the previous structures and the construction of a democratic state. In sports policy, as in other aspects of normal life, there was an emphasis on the "participation of citizens" and on the creation of a space for public actions in a social and political context where nothing had previously been defined.

Although the process began in 1975, one important landmark in this stage was the 1979 municipal elections. New democratic councils created the institutional framework for the development of sports policy in Spain.

The years before 1975 were dominated by social urban movements. Spain's urban and industrial development occurred without the state being able to regulate the consequences. Cities grew without urban planning and at the mercy of speculators. The official unions were no more than an appendage to the power structure and did nothing to answer the calls for a better quality of life for workers. Political parties were not legal. While the deficiencies in facilities were increasing (lack of schools, hospitals, sports facilities, urban infrastructure, etc.), Franco's government showed increasing incapacity to regulate the imbalances.

This gave rise to a situation where clandestine private organizations, political parties, and unions created collective platforms that struggled for a betterment of living conditions. At Franco's death, these groups were very important in the early mobilization, and a special emphasis was given to citizen participation in collective affairs. It was precisely this massive support that smoothed the way for the first steps toward Spanish democracy.

At the same time and as a reaction to the state's inefficiency in previous times, public powers were expected to find solutions to many serious problems suffered by the people. Therefore, the public sector placed emphasis on raising the population's quality of life. In reality, and though belatedly, the spirit of the welfare state which had been evident in Europe since the end of the Second World War was being taken up. From the beginning, sport was considered a fundamental part of the collective well-being, and the constitution detailed the obligation of the public powers to promote it.

This whole period is characterized by a constant readjustment between these two important characteristics; the period led to a recognition of the importance of citizen participation, but, at the same time, it was necessary to find a space for the operation of public powers. In sports policy, and in politics generally, such adjustment of powers and responsibilities often caused serious tensions.

At all the various levels of the newly constituted state (central government, CCAA, provincial and local governments), the departments specifically dedicated to sport were strengthened. The progressive importance that sport was gaining could be appreciated by the increase in budgets, as shown by the available data of the central administration, as well as local governments (Puig et al., 1985). In addition, this importance of sport can be seen as part of a generalized appraisal of the so-called personal services (health, social services, education, culture, sports and youth) that also experienced a considerable growth (Puig, 1984).

About 24 percent of Spanish sports facilities were constructed during this period (Martínez del Castillo et al., 1991a). A decisive impetus was given to some of the projects previously established but not yet brought to fruition (Plan Ideal de Instalaciones Deportivas 1968–1973, conclusions of the National Symposia of Sport Architecture in 1974, etc.). Not only were more facilities built but also the main trends toward construction that were to characterize the next period began to emerge. If in previous times the private sector had played a more important role than the public in the construction of facilities, from this time the process began to reverse itself. In this period about 45 percent of the sports facilities were constructed by the town halls, other public bodies, and educational authorities.

In 1980, parallel to this process, the regulatory policy NIDE (*Normativa sobre Instalaciones Deportivas y para el Esparcimiento*) was published. Although these rules on sport and leisure facilities were not legally enforceable, they gave guidelines on methods of constructing sport facilities. They were an initiative of a group of architects who were then working for the Direccion General de Deportes (equivalent to the actual CSD). Worried by the lack of criteria for projects that had to be evaluated for the granting of subsidies, they took as guidelines the regulatory policies existing in other European countries and adapted them to Spanish needs. They are still being used, and what is more, in most CCAAs they have been expanded upon and adapted with greater precision to the characteristics of sport in each region.

The 1980 Ley de la Cultura Fisica y el Deporte (Law of Physical Culture and Sport) and the resolutions that arose from it marked the first attempt to change Spanish sports structures. The federations had had total control—many of them since Franco's death. For the first time, a series of changes was forced through that caused a commotion in Spanish sports policy. At the same time, the way was cleared for greater public participation in sports.

In the allotment of economic resources, the decision to include money for sports in the general state budget is very important. Until that happened, sports had been principally financed from the *quinielas* (a sort of lottery based on guessing the results of the first and second division football matches—football pools in England). This gave sports an uncertain status conditioned by the amount of money wagered. The *quinielas* still exist, and part of the money still goes to the public funds through the county councils. However, its economic importance in relation to the total is limited.

Sports promotion experienced major changes, especially in Sport-for-All. Elite sports maintained the old ways without any fundamental changes. On the other hand, the promotion of sports that would be within the reach of everyone brought about a radical change. The scarcities and lack of continuity in previous initiatives were succeeded by the systematic setting up of programs for the majority. Most of these were done through local councils which received financial assistance from the county councils, the autonomous governments, and the central government. These programs are carried out, either through agreement with local organizations (joint ventures) or through grants to local sports groups.

The increased activity in sports and personal services in general gave rise to an unusual phenomenon in public administration at that time, namely, the appearance of a technical body specializing in sports promotion. This acquired significant weight in public administration—above all municipal—and became the authentic go-between of the population and local powers, while at the same time clearly using their power to promote their own interests (Bourdin and Puig, 1982; Puig, 1984). Moreover, the need to provide instructors with training in accordance with the new needs began to be recognized. However, a policy for sports instructor training was not systematically defined until after 1983.

The sharpest debate about citizen participation and the responsibilities of the public sector in developing sports policy was in the area of municipalities. During these years a lively debate sprang up over the best body to govern its development. The municipal structures were not considered sufficiently flexible to give a rapid reply to the needs of sport. At the same time, citizen participation in decision making was not guaranteed. Many places opted for creating Patronatos Deportivos (Sporting Boards of Trustees) or some similar body that had their own legal personalities within the municipal structure, which permitted them a much more flexible management and made greater participation possible.

Criticism of this formula arose early. With regard to citizen participation, critics quickly pointed out what they considered "a reduction in the autonomy of public powers in making decisions" (Andrés, 1980; Burriel, 1992). Slowly, formulas were being promulgated that built up the autonomy of political power, channeling and regulating citizen participation. The municipal governments had been elected democratically and, in consequence, were the ones that claimed popular representation. The Ley Reguladora de Bases del Regimen Local, set down in April 1985, is clear in this sense: "The forms, methods and participation procedures that the councils establish in exercise of their authority must not, under any circumstances, diminish the powers of decision that correspond to the representative bodies regulated by the law" (Burriel, 1992, p. 43).

The sports structure of the municipality was also criticized for functioning oblivious to other contingencies of municipal life. Some spoke of a power within a power. For some time there were confrontations and debates on this theme. However, this law transformed the general frame of municipal organization, offering forms that, without creating marginal structures, could operate with greater efficiency.

The period ended then, having redefined responsibilities, having established the operational methods and, above all, having witnessed the public powers' efforts to occupy the spaces assigned to them within the legal framework.

1983–92—Legitimization of the Public Sector's Role

The organizational frame through which sports policy would be developed had been shaped in the previous stage. Between 1983 and 1992 the consolidation of the Spanish sports policy model, as well as the complete legitimization of the public power that emerged with democracy, took place. All public institutions and, above all, the town halls had a key role in this process. They took on the responsibility of guaranteeing access to sport for all citizens. They clarified the responsibilities of each one of the institutions involved (CSD, CCAA, provincial governments, and town halls), at the same time establishing relationships with clubs and sports associations. Briefly, during this period the public powers' main objective was to obtain a political return for the efforts made (Burriel, 1990, 1992). Through their performances they tried, on the one hand, to show (at least to give an *image*) that the public sector was necessary in the political system (that is, to provide arguments that *legitimize* its existence) and, on the other hand, to reap the fruits of the efforts made (to get *political profit* particularly in the form of votes, to allow the parties in power to repeat their terms of office).

An important landmark of this time was October 17, 1986—the day Barcelona was designated as the seat of the 1992 Olympic Games by the International

Olympic Committee. This was a decisive factor in carrying forward the projects formulated in the preceding years. In Barcelona and the other subsidiary sites, there was a singular impact, but the country as a whole benefited because of the priority the central government gave to the Olympic project from the start.

The Olympic Games themselves were not the only driving force behind Spanish sports development. In fact, they came at a time when the country was prepared to benefit from an initiative of this kind. Deep changes had been produced which made it possible to absorb and profit from the help that arrived coincidentally with the occasion of the Olympic Games (Puig, 1992b).

The principal investments made during this period were in sports facilities. Of the 49,000 facilities existing in Spain, more than 40 percent were constructed during this time (Martínez del Castillo et al., 1991a). Those responsible for them were, in descending order: local councils for almost 28 percent of the projects; schools in the public sector, 25 percent; and other public agencies (CSD, CCAA) about 2 percent. It should be pointed out that local councils as well as schools in the public sector contributed only partially to the financing of the projects. This was primarily the responsibility of the CSD, CCAA, and provincial governments in proportions that varied according to the particular case. The main responsibility of the town halls and educational authorities was to take the initiative in bringing the projects to fruition as well as paying a part of the financing and providing sites.

It was a time of notable achievements. The most representative was the Anella Olímpica de Montjuic (Montjuic Olympic Ring), the Olympic stadium, Palau Sant Jordi, the Picornell swimming pool, the Institut Nacional d'Educacio Fisica de Catalunya, and the subsidiary Olympic areas in Barcelona. However, it was a time of important projects at all levels including major sports centers, development plans for sports facilities in schools, pavilions, and stadiums in many localities. In reality, the sports facilities were symbols for collective expectations (Puig et al., 1990). They added character to the cities, were "visible" projects that offered a "city image" valued positively by the population, and so brought with them a political return (Burriel, 1990, p. 176).

The construction of sports facilities goes hand in hand with one of the first initiatives to rationalize the procedures: the Censo Nacional de Instalaciones Deportivas (CENID) (the National Census of Sport Facilities). The purpose was to learn the situation of Spanish sports facilities numerically and qualitatively (typology, state of conservation, use, etc.). The fieldwork was done in 1986, and afterward monographical studies were written on each CCAA. The final report about all Spain was published in 1991 (Martínez del Castillo et al., 1991).

Another important clarification was the definition of the legal framework of sports. The outdated 1980 Law was replaced by that of 1990 (Ley del Deporte), which was coupled with the laws of the CCAA and other legal regulations. Sports regulations clearly established the legal status of sports organizations and applied to them nonsports laws which have an effect on sport (Ley Reguladora de Bases de Regimen Local, for instance). The differing forms of sports organizations are regulated. The professional clubs are transformed into Sports Corporations (SADs) that have to fulfill the same duties as any other business. Until then, they had used their sports nature to escape taxation and other economic regulations in spite of the astronomical sums of money involved. Sports organizations not directed at performance may federate to form promotion organizations at the state level, or similar to the *ente di promozione* in Italy. The traditional clubs, for their part, continue to belong to the sports federations.

The development of this new law blended well with the changes that had been produced since the publication of the previous one in 1980. The new law codifies the new realities of sport which the old law did not. In addition to clarifying the responsibilities of each of the public institutions (Consejo Superior de Deportes, autonomous governments, county councils, and town councils), it establishes differences and different levels of responsibility among the various types of existing sports organizations. The most relevant points are those that refer to the big clubs which are changed into limited companies, and to sports associations directed to Sport-for-All. Thus, the law defines the new realities of sport, especially with relation to sports organizations. However, this does not mean that all these organizations are well known. Most Spanish sports organizations are the great unknowns of Spanish sport. We are now seeing important public initiatives in sports promotion. With regard to top-level sport, the program ADO'92 amounted to a revolution in elite sports policy in Spain. The programs of Sport-for-All are also important. The town halls, either directly or by joint venture, contract with sports organizations to carry out programs that tend to cover all groups in the population, although, for the moment, with greater priority given to those of school age (Burriel, 1990).

A great effort is also made to normalize and foster training in sports education. The nine National Institutes of Physical Education are scattered throughout the Spanish territory. Schools for the formation of sports instructors appear, and updating courses for sports professionals organized by public and private institutions are offered for postgraduates.

Sports research is given high priority and support, for they have become an integral part of Spanish social life and the scientific world, after previously being on the sidelines. The National Plan of Research and Development assigned 400 million pts between 1986 and 1992 for sports research. In addition, there are other sources of funds, notably the sports organizations themselves. The CSD and many CCAA assign part of their budgets to sports research—some cases by means of scholarships and grants, and others by hiring professionals for concrete projects. This last procedure is used by some local councils and diputaciones who wish to know and deal with problems of their municipalities at first hand.

If the rewards offered by some organizations and projects financed by banks are added up, the financial investment in sport has been huge, especially taking into account previous scarcity. A definitive valuation has not yet been made.

However, a partial study gives some idea of the fiscal situation (Puig, Rodriguez, and Gusi, 1992, 1992).

This support has apparently resulted in the sudden appearance of diverse scientific associations that are studying different areas of sports science: Federacion Espanola de Medicina Deportiva (1985), Asociacion Espanola de Derecho Deportivo (1990) (Spanish Association of Sport Law), Federacion Espanola de Asociaciones de Psicologia de las Actividad Fisica y el Deporte (1987), Asociacion Espanola de Investigacion Social Aplicada al Deport (1991), and Asociacion Espanola para la Investigacion y Desarrollo de la Historia del Deporte (1991). In some CCAAs, territorial associations of this type also exist.

A stage like this, characterized by big projects and hefty investment, has generally lacked planning. Generally, planning consists of fixing on some goals that, once the project is completed, permit control and evaluation of the results (Burriel, 1990, p. 176). This excludes the organization of the Barcelona Olympic Games, which because of its magnitude and importance did not follow the same ups and downs of sports policy in general. Therefore, it is best to study municipalities, for these play a central role in promoting sports among the majority of the population.

Toward the end of this stage, the consequences of a lack of planning become evident. Sports facilities were built but do not generate profits. They do not always function at maximum capacity, and many of them lack the essentials. Above all, in the beginning of this period, there were doubts that admission fees should be charged to public facilities. The consequence was a skyrocketing public deficit. In addition, the unexpected effects of certain decisions were foreseen. Although it was said to be necessary to encourage associative activities, the management policy of sports facilities or programs to develop sport, which in some places was carried out leaving aside sport organizations, led to more and more precarious conditions for their survival. Moreover, the tremendous growth of commercial organizations should be taken into account. These, owing to growing demand, have drawn clients away from the traditional clubs. Further problems arise from the expansion and ecological impact of sports practiced in nature. Consulting groups have been formed, but their fields of professional operation have not been regulated. Sports service firms have sprung up everywhere and have diversified their offerings beyond the traditional framework of sports facilities. In the natural spaces used by these firms such as the seaside, mounting disturbing signs of degradation are starting to appear. No analysis of the costs and benefits in respect to the economic and social consequences of all this has been made.

At the end of this period, various symptoms of insufficient control start to emerge. Planning is the catchword for policymakers, and those in positions of responsibility are beginning to catch on. Planning is now finally seen as necessary.

In reality, between 1983 and 1992 the principal objective of sports policy (implicit or explicit) was to gain political return from the actions carried out

(Burriel, 1990, 1992). This objective has a fundamental historical importance. Following the period of transition, the public powers have to be legitimized. Thus, they construct visible projects, invest, promote, and bring sports to a population that never had access to them in a systematic way, shaping and debating the aptitudes of each one of them. Entering into these debates are the central government, the CCAA, and the provincial and local councils. It was an active and intense period, and events exceeded planning capacity. Finally, having obtained the desired political advantage and with the appearance of the first danger signals, a new stage began during which future actions in sports policy will probably concentrate primarily on planning and economic rationality.

1993–Present: Planning and Economic Rationality in the Public Sector

Details of a period that has just begun can only be inferred from the situation obtaining at the end of the former stage. Briefly, with the legitimization of the actions and roles of public powers, the time has arrived for efficient management, planning, and research in Spanish sports policy.

The principal lines of actuation are already consolidated, and the biggest projects have been completed. There is a definite legal framework; a network of facilities exists throughout Spanish territory which satisfy the sports needs for everyone including the elite athletes; the promotional programs continue developing while the offer of sports is broadening to encompass all population groups including housewives, disabled persons, and the aged. Finally, the training of specialists is on the right track and starts to cover the different needs posed by each sports activity.

The problem posed now is one of the rational management of resources. Paradoxical as it may seem, until now sports policy has not considered the criteria of economic profit through planning. As has already been pointed out, its object has been to carry out projects that legitimize public powers. Signs of an economic crisis now force a series of changes in the advancing of sports policy. "Economic viability in sports management must be the topmost concern" (Burriel, 1992, p. 45). This change is most evident in the management of sports facilities. If, earlier, there were doubts about charging for access to public facilities, now the models of management used in the private sector are adapted to make such facilities profitable. The local councils cannot allow the accumulated debt to increase.

Also, in the management of the biggest facilities (stadiums, Barcelona Olympic areas, etc.), the town halls have set up municipal mercantile firms that function along private lines. In other cases, the management has been handed over to private firms. This last action has caused negative reactions, for it seems to be returning to privatization, thereby excluding the underprivileged. In a historical context, such privatizing revives serious opposition on the part of certain social forces such as unions, neighborhood associations, and political parties of the left.

In the context of these discussions, the question that arises concerns the best policy to follow regarding sports organizations. Up to now, the tendency had been to grant financial assistance, whether large or small, but without following any concrete policy. The impact of this aid and the capacity of clubs to be autonomous from an economic point of view (self-financing) and to carry forward their activities is, at the moment, unknown. Many questions remain: To what extent have the offers of sporting activities made by public institutions competed with those of the clubs? Have they become more professional and found better ways to interest the public?

To obtain results, it is necessary to plan. Planning means setting definite goals and evaluating the results at the end of the period in question. Serious efforts in planning have just started. In spite of much talk about this need (Martínez del Castillo, 1986), acting on it has only begun under the pressure of compelling historical, social, and economic circumstances. Planning is fairly new to Spanish sports policy. Similarly, research becomes more significant from the moment it supports planning and political decision making (Paris, 1992). Administrations commission certain research to teams of experts. Going beyond a mere description of situation and diagnosis of problems, research is now diversified to include prospects of decisions, behavior, impact, and so on (Burriel, 1992, p. 49).

While the dynamics of the process have generated this situation, undoubtedly the application of the agreements of the Maastrich Treaty in relation to European integration will accelerate the rationalization process already started.

CONCLUSIONS

The results of Spanish sporting policy cannot be evaluated in terms of the objectives achieved through a planning process, for planning has entered into sports policy only very recently. Nevertheless, we can try to predict the changes in sports policy that may come about with European integration. European unity means being able to establish a common dialogue starting from the specificities of each country. Although the similarities are sufficient to set up a union, it is also clear that there are many differences.

The proviso in the constitution requiring that public powers promote physical education and sport may complicate dialogue about the sporting decisions that can be taken from an international perspective. In Spain public assistance for sports need not be justified, for it is established by the constitution. On the other hand, in other countries financing sport is a completely private movement that must be negotiated to get public grants. In this instance, Germany serves as a case in point. Whereas in Spain public funds for the promotion of sport are legal, normal, and expected, such use of government funds in Germany would be seriously questioned. Therefore, if there were a debate on the relationships between public institutions and sport, these two countries would take completely different points of view which, at least in the beginning, would hinder dialogue.

Once democracy has been established, we must ask ourselves whether the generosity of the constitution of 1978 was not a little excessive. The inclusion of public support for sports has an historical explanation. However, today, in a situation of economic recession, such great support of sport on behalf of the public sector causes problems. Although the government must reduce spending, sports could be one of the most affected areas. The public powers could be faced with the fact that they have not fulfilled their obligation. Sports funding cuts would seem to be directed toward the least favored and not the population in general. On the other hand, and perhaps the greatest problem of all, the habit of expecting everything from public institutions has been created and the civil society has lost (or perhaps never had) the capacity to create its own initiatives. As already pointed out, the Spanish sports organizations are weak and little known by the general population.

In the new European atmosphere, the great challenge of Spanish sports policy is to find a balance between the public institutions that sprang up as part of the democracy it helped to build and that of a civil society capable of producing initiatives and having a life of its own without having to fall back on public aid. A middle ground will probably be the result: The public sector will still have to share from its resources but should not superimpose or negate whatever sport initiatives come from the people themselves.

ACKNOWLEDGMENTS

The author wishes to thank A. Camps, J. C. Burriel, and J. Martínez del Castillo for their comments on the original text, and P. Muñoz for the tables, which have improved the quality of this chapter.

NOTES

1. It is not possible to describe all the historical development up to recent times.

2. According to Spanish law, a declaration of public utility (Declaracion de Utilidad Publica) is conferred upon a body corporate either directly by law or by an express act of government when a law exists to make this declaration possible. All associations devoted to health, education, culture, sports, or any other activity designed to foster the general well-being may be recognized as a public utility.

A private entity that has been declared a public utility enjoys the following advantages: (1) the right to include mention of this on all documents; (2) tax benefits; and (3) preferential rights to official credit.

3. According to Spanish law, the Sociedades Anonimas Deportivas (Sports Corporations—SADs) are created by the Sports Law of 1990 whose social aim is to participate in professional sports competitions. SADs may participate only in official professional competitions of a single sport. All clubs or teams that participate in official professional

competitions are obliged to constitute themselves as SADs. For more information, see L. M. Cazorla, (1990).

4. Burriel (1990, p. 10) gives a similar definition of local sport policy: "We can describe a local sport policy as a process of continuous interaction between the local administration—which makes decisions and develops programes—and the social impact of those."

5. John Bale (1989, p. 20) gives similar examples for other countries.

6. Ligas Profesionales (Professional Leagues): In those Spanish federations where nationwide official professional competitions exist, integral leagues will be constituted exclusively and compulsorily by all the clubs participating in such competitions. The jurisdiction of the League covers (1) the organization of official professional competitions; (2) the exercise of disciplinary powers over members; and (3) the exercise of guidance and control of members.

7. On the participation of the different public and private institutions in the Barcelona Olympic Games, see Heinemann (1992).

REFERENCES

Alonso, J., Ruesga, S.; Sáez, F., and Vicens, J. (1991). Impacto económico del deporte en España. *Revista de Investigación y Documentación sobre las Ciencias de la Educación Física y del Deporte* (18): 21–35.

Andrés, F. (1980). Organización de un Patronato Municipal de Deportes. Críticas al modelo original. *Boletín de AETIDE* (14).

Bale, J. (1989). *Sport Geography.* London-New York: L&N Spon.

Bourdin, A., and Puig, N. (1982). Travail social et nouvelles dynamiques locales. *Espaces et Sociétés* (40).

Buñuel, A. (1991). The recreational physical activities of Spanish women: a sociological study of exercising for fitness. *International Review for the Sociology of Sport,* 26, (3): 203–216.

Burriel, J. C. (1990). *Polítiques esportives municipals a la província de Barcelona.* Barcelona: Diputació de Barcelona.

Burriel, J. C. (1992). Perspectivas en el diseño de las políticas deportivas municipales. *Cuadernos Técnicos de Deporte* (5): 37–50.

Cazorla, L. M. (1990). *Las sociedades anónimas deportivas.* Madrid: Ed. Ciencias Sociales.

Consejo Superior de Deportes. (1991). *Proyecto de reforma de las enseñanzas y titulaciones deportivas.* Madrid.

García Ferrando, M. (1986). *La oferta municipal de deporte en la Comunidad Autónoma de Madrid.* Madrid: Dirección General de Deportes.

García Ferrando, M. (1989). *La oferta municipal de deporte para todos en la Comunidad Valenciana.* Valencia: Dirección General de Deportes.

García Ferrando, M. (1990). *Aspectos sociales del deporte. Una reflexión sociológica.* Madrid: Alianza Editorial, Consejo Superior de Deportes.

García Ferrando, M. (1991). *Los españoles y el deporte (1980–1990). Un análisis sociológico.* Madrid: Ministerio de Educación y Ciencia, Consejo Superior de Deportes.

Hargreaves, John. (1992). Olympism and nationalism: some preliminary considerations. *International Review for the Sociology of Sport,* 27, (2): 119–138.

Heinemann, K. (1986). The future of sports. Challenge for the science of sport. *International Review for the Sociology of Sport,* 21, (4): 271–285.

Heinemann, K. (1992). Cost-benefit analysis of the Barcelona Olympic Games. In *International Olympic Academy,* Ancient Olympia (Greece), 32th session.

Instituto Nacional de Estadística. (1975). *Estadística de establecimientos deportivos.* Madrid.

Martínez del Castillo, J. (1986). *La gestión estratégica de la actividad física de tiempo libre a nivel local.* Paper presented in the European Seminar "Gestión deportiva en el ámbito local," l'Hospitalet de Llobregat (Barcelona).

Martínez del Castillo, J., Navarro, C., Fraile, A., Puig, N., Jiménez, P., Martínez, J., and De Miguel, C. (1992). *Deporte, sociedad y empleo. Proyección del mercado deportivo laboral en la España de los noventa. En los sectores de entrenamiento, docencia, animación y dirección.* Madrid: Ministerio de Educación y Ciencia, Consejo Superior de Deportes. Conducted by J. Martínez del Castillo.

Martínez del Castillo, J., Puig N., Boix, R., Millet, L., and Páez, J. A. (1991a). *Las instalaciones deportivas en España.* Madrid, Ministerio de Educación y Ciencia, Consejo Superior de Deportes.

Martínez del Castillo, J., Puig, N., Fraile, A., and Boixeda, J. (1991b). *La estructura ocupacional del deporte en España. Encuesta realizada sobre los sectores de entrenamiento, docencia, animación y dirección.* Madrid: Ministerio de Educación y ciencia, Consejo Superior de Deportes. Conducted by J. Martínez del Castillo.

Ministerio de Educación y Ciencia, Consejo Superior de Deportes. (1992). *El deporte en España.* Madrid.

Paris, F. (1992). Contribution during the Seminar *Desperately seeking relevance: roles for social science in sport policy.* Held during the Olympic Scientific Congress, Málaga (Spain), UNISPORT, July 1992 and coordinated by Professor Laurence Chalip (University of Maryland) and Professor Klaus Heinemann (Universität Hamburg).

Puig, N. (1984). La gestió municipal a Barcelona durant la transició. In *Papers. Revista de Sociologia.* Bellaterra (21): 71–92.

Puig, N. (1986). El deporte y los estereotipos femeninos. *Revista de Occidente* (62): 71–84.

Puig, N. (1992a). Mujeres jóvenes y deporte de alto nivel. Aspectos sociológicos. *El ejercicio físico y la práctica deportiva de las mujeres.* Madrid: Ministerio de Asuntos Sociales, Instituto de la Mujer, pp. 87–95.

Puig, N. (1992b). The influence of the Olympic Games on Sport. In *Olympic Games, media and cultural exchanges. The experience of the past four Summer Olympic Games.* Centre d'Estudis Olímpics, Universitat Autónoma de Barcelona, pp. 95–100.

Puig, N., Burriel, J. C., Masnou, M., and Ibáñez, J. (1990). L'esport com a generador de mobilitat i estructurador de l'espai. In Zaragoza, A. and Puig, N. *Oci, esport i societat,* Barcelona, PPU, pp. 188–203. This article was first published in French (Le sport comme générateur de mobilité et structurant de l'espace) in (1990) *Espaces et Sociétés* (54–55): 119–133.

Puig, N., and Heinemann, K. (1992). El deporte en la perspectiva del año 2000. In *Papers. Revista de Sociologia,* Bellaterra (38): 123–142.

Puig, N., Martínez del Castillo, J., and grupo Apunt. (1985). Evolución de las campañas de deporte para todos en España (1969–83). Ensayo para poder valorar su influencia en la práctica deportiva de los españoles. *Revista de Investigación y Documentación sobre las Ciencias de la Educación Física y el Deporte* (1): 59–105.

Puig, N., Rodriguez, F., and Gusi, N. (1992). La investigació social i l'esport a Catalunya. *Revista d'Etnologia de Catalunya* (1): 54–63.

Rodríguez, F., and Gusi, N. (1991). *La investigació en Ciències de l'Esport a Catalunya.* Barcelona: INEF-Catalunya, research project, not published.

Sánchez Bañuelos, F. (1992). La Asociación de Deportes Olímpicos 1992. *Sistema* (110–111): 143–153.

Valdano, J. (1986). El miedo escénico. *Revista de Occidente,* (62–63): 103–109.

Vazquez, B. (1992). La presencia de la mujer en el deporte español. *El ejercicio físico y la práctica deportiva de las mujeres.* Madrid: Ministerio de Asuntos Sociales, Instituto de la Mujer.

16

Sport in the United Kingdom

Barrie Houlihan

INTRODUCTION

The United Kingdom comprises England, Wales, Scotland, and Northern Ireland; all four countries return elected representatives to the House of Commons, which is one of the two chambers of the Parliament in Westminister, London. Since 1945, with some minor exceptions, elections in the UK have produced majority governments. The combination of an established two-party structure, a simple majority electoral system, and a weak second chamber produces a pattern of government characterized by a strong executive centered on the prime minister and his or her cabinet.

At the central government level, responsibility for particular policy areas is determined largely on a simple functional basis with a series of ministries (also called departments) established for services such as education, defense, trade, and foreign affairs. The functional principle of allocation is augmented by a number of territorial ministries for Northern Ireland, Scotland, and Wales. Responsibility for sport is located primarily in the relatively recently established Department of National Heritage (DNH), although, as will be explained below, there is a broad range of ministries with an interest in sports policy.

Although central government ministries take a key role in shaping national policy, they have few executive responsibilities. A trend that developed during the 1970s to devolve responsibility for service delivery to semi-independent agencies was given additional impetus during Margaret Thatcher's tenure as prime minister. In many policy areas, including sport, the arts, and tourism, important roles are fulfilled by agencies such as the Sports Council, the Arts Council, and a range of Tourist Boards.

Devolution of responsibility for policy implementation to agencies is complemented by a similar pattern of devolution to units of local government (also referred to as local authorities). Unlike federal systems of government, the powers, finances, and responsibilities of local authorities in the UK are determined by Parliament. Consequently, although local government is a major provider of opportunities for sport and recreation, the scope of variation and discretion is limited. Despite the establishment of the Department of National Heritage in 1992, responsibility for sports and recreation at the central government level is fragmented, as Table 16.1 indicates.

Since the mid-1960s, when sport was acknowledged as an identifiable and legitimate concern of government, there has been debate over the status of the responsible minister and over the most appropriate location for the function. Denis Howell was the first member of the government to be designated "Minister for Sport" in 1974. From then until 1991, the function was located within the Department of the Environment (DoE). In many ways, this was a logical choice since the DoE also had responsibility for local government, which was the main provider of public sports and recreation facilities. In addition, the DoE was responsible for land-use planning policy, water and countryside issues, and environmental matters. Yet this location isolated sport from a number of important related policy areas, particularly school sport (Department of Education and Science) and tourism (Department of Trade and Industry). In 1991, as the issue of sports in schools rose on the political agenda, the new prime minister, John Major, transferred responsibility for sports to the Department of Education and Science (later renamed the Department for Education). However, this arrangement was short-lived, for the function was soon transferred again in 1992, this time to its present home in the DNH. As Figure 16.1 suggests, the creation of the DNH was, in part, an attempt to group together a series of related responsibilities. In practice, the development of the hoped-for synergy in policy between tourism, the arts, and sport has, so far, failed to emerge.

Each section of the DNH tends to work independently. The Sport and Recreation Division within the Broadcasting, Films, and Sports Group is a small unit with approximately fifteen policy staff members. As Table 16.2 shows, this small staff covers a very broad range of issues in sports policy.

Even though the creation of the DNH has reduced the extent of interdepartmental liaison required for sports policy issues, coordination still remains extensive. Working groups are established, usually on an ad hoc basis, to deal with issues which cross departmental boundaries. For example, the recent introduction of the National Lottery involved the Home Office (because of its responsibility for the control of gambling), the Treasury (because of its interest in the tax implications), the Department of Health (because health and welfare

Table 16.1

The Pattern of Government Responsibility for Sport in the United Kingdom

Central Government Ministry	Department of National Heritage	Department of the Environment	Department for Education	Ministry of Agriculture, Fisheries & Food
Main responsibilities	Sports Council; antidoping policy; after school sport; sponsorship; international issues; national lottery	Local government organization, functions and finance; land use policy; countryside issues	Sport in the curriculum; community use of school sports facilities	Alternative uses (including leisure) for surplus farm land
Examples of National Government Agencies	Sports Council for England and Wales (soon to be replaced by UK Sports Commission and separate Sports Councils for England and Wales) Foundation for Sport and the Arts The Football Trust	The Countryside Commission The Nature Conservancy Council	School Curriculum and Assessment Authority	
Examples of national non-govermental organizations	Central Council for Physical Recreation British Olympic Association Sports governing bodies British Sports Association for the Disabled	Inland Waterways Amenity Advisory Council Society for the Promotion of Nature Reserves	Physical Education Association English Schools Athletic Association	National Farmers Union Country Landowners Association
Regional Offices of Government ministries or of government agencies	Sports Council regional offices Regional Councils for Sport and Recreation	DOE Regional Offices		MAFF Regional Offices
Local level public bodies including units of local government and local offices/units of central government, and their major responsibilities		Metropolitan Councils responsible for indoor and outdoor sport and recreation provision. County Councils responsible primarily for outdoor/countryside sport and recreation provision. District Councils responsible primarily for indoor sport and recreation provision	Schools, colleges and higher education institutions	National Parks Boards County Councils: land use planning responsibilities

Table 16.1 (Continued)

Home Office	Foreign Office	Ministry of Defense	Welsh, Scottish & Nothern Irish Offices
Control of gambling; crowd safety at sports events; law and order at sports events	Foreign travel of sportsmen, sportswomen, and supporters	Community use of sports facilities	Responsibility for sports policy in each area, though extent of responsibility varies
The Gaming Board The Horse Totalisator Board		Royal Air Force Sports Board	
			Equivalent bodies for Education, Environment and National Heritage
			Scottish Sports Council, Sports Councils for Northern Ireland and Wales
District and County Councils: responsible for licensing stadiums			Range of responsibilities broadly similar to those for English and Welsh local councils

Figure 16.1
The Department of National Heritage: Organization Structure

Ministers

Secretary of State (member of the Cabinet)

Parliamentary Under-Secretary (Sports Minister)

Parliamentary Private Secretary

Departmental sub-divisions	Resources & Services	The Millennium Fund	Heritage & Tourism	Broadcasting, Films & Sports	Arts
Main functions	Finance; personnel; policy review	Oversight of projects to celebrate the millennium	Heritage; royal estates; royal parks; tourism	Broadcasting policy; media; sport & recreation	National lottery; arts policy; museums & galleries; libraries; government art collection

Table 16.2
The Structure of the Sport and Recreation Division of the Department of National Heritage

SARD A	SARD B	SARD C	SARD D
Oversight of the Sports Council; sport for women; relationship with the CCPR and the British Sport Forum	Sport for people with disabilities; sport in the inner city; school sport and community use of school facilities; children's play; anti-doping; ethics in sport; sports performance and excellence	Sports finance; sponsorship; Sports Aid Foundation; tax policy; sports aspects of the National Lottery; Foundation for Sport and the Arts; promotion of sports participation; countryside and water recreation; local government expenditure; facility provision including playing fields	International matters; liaison with the Council of Europe and the European Union; liaison with the British Olympic Association; football policy, including safety at sports grounds and the work of the Football Trust; support for bids to host major sports events e.g. Manchester's bid to host the 2000 Olympic Games

charities were to be partial beneficiaries of the Lottery), and the DNH (because the millennium fund, the arts, and sports are also major beneficiaries).

The DNH has responsibility for the Sports Council, which has a major executive role in sports policy. There are four Sports Councils in the UK, one each for Scotland, Wales, and Northern Ireland, and the Sports Council which combines responsibility for England with a broader, but ambiguous, British responsibility. Each provincial Sports Council is responsible to the relevant territorial ministry—such as the Scottish Office—which is also responsible for providing their funding. While working substantially within government policy guidelines, the Councils have a limited degree of autonomy derived from their status as executive agencies established by Royal Charter. Much of the work of the Sports Council is organized through a series of regional offices that undertake their own analysis of need within the region and prepare a regional strategy. Part of the funding that is received by the Sports Council is transferred to the regions to help support the implementation of their strategies. At present, the Councils have a very broad range of responsibilities. They aim to support sports involvement from the elite level to the foundation/introductory level. They also traditionally support a wide range of sports. The Councils work very closely with the local authorities, governing bodies, and clubs in their region and as such provide an extremely important focus for sport development.

Critics of the Councils argue that they spend too high a proportion of their income on administration rather than on grant-aiding sports projects, and that they spread their activities too widely. Currently, there are proposals to abolish the Sports Council and replace it with two new organizations: a UK Sports Council, which would act on UK-wide issues, and an English Sports Council. It is likely that these new bodies will be established in late 1995 or early 1996.

At the local government level, the distribution of responsibilities for sport and recreation is as complex as at the central government level. The structure of local government and the responsibilities of the different units in the UK vary. In England and Wales, the major conurbations and a number of medium-sized cities (about 0.25 million population) are covered by a series of unitary authorities that deliver all local services. Outside the major cities the most common pattern is a two-tier system of County Councils and lower-tier District Councils. The pattern is broadly similar in Scotland where a two-tier structure (Regional and District Councils) also exists. However, there are significant differences in the pattern of local government between Northern Ireland (also referred to as Ulster) and the rest of the UK. In Northern Ireland, the Northern Ireland Office (a central government department) is much more involved in service delivery than the Scottish or Welsh offices. Because of the corruption of Northern Ireland's local governments by sectarian politics, the Northern Ireland Office is responsible for the oversight of public housing and education. Sports, as well as tourism, are among the small number of significant services left to the local authorities to administer. Table 16.3 indicates the distribution of responsibilities among the different units of local government.

Table 16.3
The Distribution of Responsibilities between Tiers of Local Government in the United Kingdom

Service	England & Wales			Scotland		Northern Ireland District Councils
	Metropolitan District Councils	County Councils	Non-Metropolitan District Councils	Regional Councils	District Councils	
Outdoor sport	◆		◆		◆	◆
Indoor sport facilities	◆		◆		◆	◆
Informal outdoor urban recreation	◆		◆	◆	◆	
Countryside recreation		◆		◆		◆
Licensing sports grounds						◆

Notes: (1) The table indicates the primary provider of the various services and does not indicate exclusive provision. (2) In 1996 the pattern of local government in Scotland and Wales will be altered, creating a series of single-tier authorities. The number of single-tier authorities will also increase. The new English single-tier authorities will replace the existing structure in medium-size (0.25–0.5m population) cities.

In order to provide a complete picture of the government's involvement in sport in the UK, it is necessary to comment briefly on the growing significance of the European Union (EU) (Houlihan, 1994). The various changes in the title of the organization (from Common Market to European Community, and now European Union) indicate clearly the gradual widening of its range of interests. Currently, there are a number of policy areas where the EU is already having or could have a significant impact on domestic sports policy. At one level, the EU has recognized and exploited the value of sports in the development of a sense of "European citizenship," which, for many member states, is part of the progress toward the "ever closer union" referred to in the Treaty of Rome. EU funds have been used to sponsor EU-wide sports events such as the EU Swimming Club Championships in 1987. More significant than these attempts at building a sense of supranational identity is the EU's treatment of sport as primarily an industry that needs to conform to EU regulations regarding, for example, the free movement of labor. This is a particular problem for soccer, where the European Federation (UEFA) has ruled that in international club competitions the number of foreign players that can be fielded is limited to three. Discussions between the EU and UEFA have resulted in the EU's temporary acceptance of the current position, though it is clear that it intends to reopen the question of the free movement of soccer players in the future.

In the UK, the extensive involvement of the government in sport is matched by an extensive and well-organized network of voluntary and not-for-profit organizations comprising mainly the governing bodies of sport, but also the British Olympic Association (BOA), the Commonwealth Games Federation, and the Central Council of Physical Recreation (CCPR). All these organizations jealously guard their independence from government and, while willing to receive the benefits of government funding, are ever alert to government attempts to compromise their autonomy. This is probably best illustrated by the BOA, which the government would like to involve more closely in development and management of the preparation and support of elite athletes. The BOA relies on donations from the public and business to fund the British Olympic team and has always been wary of receiving public money. This wariness was reinforced in 1980 as Margaret Thatcher tried, albeit unsuccessfully, to force the BOA to support the U.S.-led boycott of the Moscow Games. More recently, however, the BOA has begun to work more closely with the Sports Council and will have greater involvement in shaping sports policy when the proposed UK Sports Council is formed.

The Recent History of Government Involvement in Sport

Explaining the evolution of policy is notoriously difficult. It is often tempting to see pattern and intention in what might properly be described as haphazard and serendipitous. This is certainly the case in reviewing the development of government involvement in sport. Travis refers to a nineteenth-century tradition of "identifying *separate* or *specific areas* of failure," the solutions to which "should *not* be seen as a normative planning and management process in a welfare context," but rather as "a scatter of items of isolated legislation" (Travis, 1979, pp. 1–2). In contrast, Hargreaves argues that much, if not most, sports policy can be explained in terms of class tensions and conflict, giving the evolution of policy a coherence resulting from a strategic concern to protect particular class interests and to "rigorously (regulate) the use made of free time through the state repressive apparatus" (Hargreaves, 1985, p. 220). Although the coherence that a class analysis gives to policy development is difficult to establish, it is clear that an examination of the nineteenth-century history of government involvement in sport suggests a number of recurring themes: the maintenance of social stability, the defense of privilege, and paternalism.

These themes were still evident for much of the twentieth-century, although new government preoccupations emerged. The first half of the century was a period during which governmental concern about the fitness of the nation's youth was clearly evident. The consumption of human capital in the First World War and the approach of a second war with Germany were the main stimuli for the passage of the Physical Fitness and Training Act (1937). This Act was followed a few years later by the Education Act (1944) in which the government required local education authorities to provide facilities for "recreation and physical training," thus going beyond simply giving local authorities permission or encouragement to provide sport and recreational opportunities. Important consequences of the 1944 Act were the growth of sports facilities in schools and the appointment of trained physical training/education staff.

By the middle of the twentieth century, legislation designed primarily to control participation in sports was still in evidence. For example, the National Parks and Access to the Countryside Act (1949) was designed to resolve, through the granting of controlled access, the long-running conflict over public access to private land for recreational and sporting purposes. However, an increasing volume of legislation was aimed at promoting sport and recreation. Most of the legislation was permissive rather than mandatory. It allowed local authorities to provide sporting and recreational opportunities but did not require them to do so. Section 19 of the 1976 Local Government (Miscellaneous Provisions) Act is typical as it states that a local authority may "provide . . . such recreational facilities as it thinks fit." It is upon this legislation and similar earlier legislation that the present provision of swimming pools, sports and leisure centers, and outdoor recreational facilities is based. A further characteristic is, as Torkildsen has noted, that "despite . . . enabling Acts of Parliament, governments consistently viewed recreation as a beneficial means towards some other ends" (Torkildsen, 1986, p. 15). These ends included higher standards of personal hygiene, a more socially responsible youth, a fitter workforce, and international prestige.

The emergence of sport as a discrete area of government policy in the 1960s can be traced to three factors. First, as Coalter et al. (1986) note, there was a continuing concern within government with the association between adolescents and urban disorder. The second factor concerned the steady decline in Britain's international sporting success, and "the realization . . . that state-aided sport could help to improve Britain's international sporting performance" (Hargreaves, 1985, p. 221) and hopefully match the early sporting success of East Germany and the Soviet Union (Anthony, 1980; University of Birmingham, 1956). The third factor was the increasing electoral pressure on government—supported by effective lobbying from governing bodies—for an expansion of opportunities for sport and recreation.

The policy themes of the 1960s were located within a broad political consensus characterized by Keynesian economic planning, social democracy, and a welfare state. The economic and political context for sports policy was supportive of notions of service planning, public participation, and equality of opportunity, all of which were important in affecting the shape of policy development for sport. The political perception of sport as an element in the fabric of the welfare state was confirmed in the 1975 White Paper[1] *Sport and Recreation,* which is one of the few attempts by government to provide a comprehensive philosophy of sport and recreation. The White Paper emphasized the capacity of sport to contribute to the "physical and mental well-being of the population and to the reduction of hooliganism and delinquency among young people" (Department of the Environment, 1975, p. 3). It also highlighted the benefits of international sporting success and consequently supported the diversion of "resources to those who are gifted in sport" (1975, p. 18).

The main vehicles for policy implementation were the Sports Council, established in 1972, and the local authorities. During the 1980s, government policy shifted away from promoting "Sport-for-All" and narrowed the focus to the role of sport in tackling urban problems (Hargreaves, 1985). A series of urban riots in the summer of 1981 resulted in a number of initiatives (though many would argue that they were palliatives) involving sport. For example, the Urban Programme, an inner-city development fund, was extended to cover the provision of sporting and recreational opportunities. Similarly, the Sports Council developed an Action Sport Programme designed to provide facilities and Sports Development Officers in inner city areas (Coalter, 1984, p. 26). The program was aimed at inner-city male adolescents, and involved the organization of sports programs that would occupy the target group's free time and deflect their energies into socially approved activities.

The Thatcher governments of the 1980s orchestrated a shift in the dominant political consensus away from welfare state collectivism toward economic liberalism with its antipathy toward public expenditure and preference for market solutions to problems of service provision. With regard to sport, the most pronounced effect of Thatcherism was the privatization of the management of local government sports and leisure facilities, a policy that gathered pace during the 1980s. In addition, the planned restructuring of the Sports Council is intended not only to reduce the number of staff, but also to redefine the successor body so that it focuses more sharply on the needs of the elite and young athletes at the expense of a broader concern with the promotion of mass participation.

Yet Thatcherite economic policy did not displace the more traditional policy themes. The long-standing concern with the problem of "too much" leisure for male urban youths was a major feature of the debate from 1986 to 1992 over the control of soccer spectator violence. More recently, the controversy surrounding the significance of sport and physical education in the newly drafted national school curriculum has focused on the prominence of traditional British team games. While educators emphasize the acquisition of movement skills and the introduction of children to a wide range of individual and team sports, the government wishes to use the sports curriculum to preserve Britain's sporting heritage by concentrating on a narrow range of mainly team games.

Amateur and Professional Sports in the UK

The dilemma facing the government regarding the scope of sports support is exemplified by the current funding policy of the Sports Council. In addition to funding projects that range from the development of "movement literacy" to mass participation and elite development, the Council also funds a very broad range of individual sports. During 1993–94, the Council grant-aided over sixty-five different sports. The breadth of participation by citizens of the UK is also indicated by the inclusion of over eighty different governing bodies of sports in the membership of the CCPR.

Levels of sport participation have risen steadily over the last twenty years. A key factor in this growth is the greater availability of sports facilities owing to the building program of the 1970s. Other factors include the growth in disposable income and car ownership and the successful marketing of sports participation by the Sports Council and the local authorities. In 1990 the government's General Household Survey revealed that the five most popular participation sports were walking (engaged in by 20.1 million, or 45 percent of the 16+ population), swimming (9.8 million, 22 percent), snooker/pool (6.2 million, 14 percent), keep fit/yoga/aerobics (5.8 million, 13 percent), and cycling (4.9 million, 11 percent). The only team sport among the top ten was soccer with 2.1 million participants. In 1987, 70 percent of male respondents and 52 percent of female respondents participated in at least one sport in the four weeks preceding the interview. By 1990, the figures had risen to 73 percent for men and 57 percent for women. Table 16.4 shows that an increase in participation is evident among all age groups, but Table 16.5 indicates that considerable differences exist in the participation levels of socioeconomic groups. The data in Table 16.5 confirm an association between higher levels of disposable income and participation.

Some of the sports that attract large numbers of participants, such as soccer, also attract large numbers of spectators. In general, however, the pattern of spectating bears little relation to the broad pattern of participation. It is not

Table 16.4
Participation Rates by Age Groups, 1987–1990

Age group	1987	1990
16 - 19 years	86%	87%
20 - 24	77%	81%
25 - 29	74%	78%
30 - 44	71%	73%
45 - 59	56%	63%
60 - 69	47%	54%
70+	26%	31%
All	61%	65%

Source: Office of Population Census and Surveys: General Household Survey, 1992.

surprising to find that soccer is the most popular spectator sport, or to find that sports associated with gambling are also high on the list.

Soccer is by far the foremost spectator sport in the UK, yet in the last twenty-five years it has lost almost one-third of its total season attendance. This is part of a longer term decline dating from the 1940s. Explanations for the steady decline are varied and include the growth in popularity of other sports, such as rugby union and league; the widening gap between the elite premier division and the rest of professional soccer; the rise of soccer hooliganism in the 1970s; the progressive restriction on the maximum capacity of grounds; and a series of broader socioeconomic changes such as working patterns and family lifestyles. A number of steps have been taken in recent years to reverse the decline. In Scotland, the league was restructured in the mid-1970s so that the best supported clubs played each other four times a year rather than two. In England and Wales, the league was restructured in the early 1990s, spurring the slight revival in attendance that had begun in the late 1980s.

The sports that have seen significant growth are rugby union, rugby league, motor sports, and basketball. The rise in the popularity of rugby union reflects the increasing success of the governing body in marketing the sport through the media and developing the sport at the grass-roots level. The rugby leagues' revival is more difficult to unravel and is best explained in terms of the beneficial effects of international tournaments (especially against strong Australian teams), the defection of a series of stars from the rival code, and the increasing interest of the media. Motor sport, particularly Formula One, has benefited from the presence of two British stars, Nigel Mansell and Damon Hill, and from the increased interest of television. Finally, basketball has been heavily marketed in Britain for the last ten years, and there are clear signs that the sport is beginning to generate the level of spectator support that will allow the development of teams capable of participating respectably in international competition.

Table 16.5
Participation Rates by Socioeconomic Group (percentages)

Socioeconomic Group	1987	1990
Professional	78%	79%
Managerial	68%	71%
Semi-Skilled	51%	55%
Unskilled	42%	46%
Full-Time Students	89%	91%

Note: Rates are for adults aged 16 or over participating in the four weeks prior to the survey.

Source: J. Mattheson. (1991). *Participation in sport.* General Household Survey, No. 7, supplement B, London: Her Majesty's Stationery Office.

The growth in the number of television channels available in the UK through the introduction of cable and satellite services is increasing the demand for sports programs. One consequence of the rising demand for television programs is that a number of less well-known sports now have an opportunity to present themselves to a national audience and attract spectators from the major traditional sports such as soccer and cricket. The central problem for the major team sports is whether the market can be expanded or is already saturated.

With regard to the significance of sport to the national economy, the sport and leisure sector was one of the fastest growing categories of consumer expenditure during the mid-1980s. Between 1983 and 1989 consumer expenditure on sports goods, broadly defined, grew by 8.4 percent each year. Although this level of growth dropped considerably to just over 1 percent between 1989 and 1992, it still remained a relatively buoyant sector of the retail economy. In 1990 it was estimated that sports accounted for 1.7 percent of the UK's gross domestic product (roughly the same as the motor vehicle industry), for nearly £10 billion of consumer expenditure,[2] and almost half a million jobs. Focusing on the "value-added" by sports industry to the UK economy, a series of recent reports, summarized in Table 16.6 confirm the buoyant nature of the sector and the scale of its contribution not only to the economy as a whole but also to local economies.

The UK and International Sport

The long history of sports participation in the UK is reflected not only in the size of the sports sector of the economy, but also in the level of success of UK sportsmen and women. At the Olympic level, the UK has won five gold medals at each of the last four summer Games, and at the Barcelona Games in 1992 produced Olympic champions in the 100 meter track, 400 meter track, 400 meter pursuit cycling, rowing (coxless pairs), and rowing (coxed pairs). On a simple

Table 16.6
The Economic Significance of Sport: Value-Added

Area	Base Year for Prices	Value Added*
UK	1990	8270.0
Scotland	1990	987.7
Wales	1988	188.3
Northern Ireland	1989	100.5
Wirral (District Council)	1987	14.6
Brackness (District Council)	1987	3.02

*In millions of pounds.

Sources: Adapted from Sports Council. (1993), p. 55; PIEDA (1991); Henley Centre for Forecasting. (1989; 1990; 1992a; 1992b).

medal count for the summer Games between 1968 and 1992, Britain ranks tenth; however, if the medal total is related to population size, then Britain drops to twenty-second place. Britain also recorded notable success in the 1992 Paralympics, where the team accumulated forty gold medals and finished third in the medals table.

While the 1980s and 1990s have witnessed a degree of consistency in terms of achievements in track and field events, this cannot be said of the other major sports played at the international level. In soccer, for example, the national team won the World Cup Finals in 1966, but in the seven tournaments that followed, the team generally failed to find consistent world-class form. In 1970 they were eliminated at the quarter-final stage; in 1974 and 1978 they failed to qualify; in 1982 and 1986 they were again eliminated at the quarter-final stage; in 1990 they were eliminated in the semifinal; and in 1994 they failed to qualify. This erratic performance by the English team is reflected in the team's current world ranking which at eighteenth is down from eleventh in 1993.

The performance of Wales and Scotland has, if anything, been even more erratic. Scotland, whose style of soccer has always promised more than it delivered in terms of international success, has played in five World Cup competitions but has never progressed beyond the first round. Wales has appeared in one competition and Northern Ireland in two, but neither country has performed well.

In rugby union, the English team generally finishes in the top two or three in the annual Five Nations Championship. (The other countries involved are France, Wales, Scotland, and Ireland.) However, against the Australians and the New Zealand team their victories are sporadic. Even the South Africans, emerging from a long period of isolation from top-class competition, managed to beat England in one of the two Test Matches held in 1994. Wales, for whom rugby union is the national sport, has had variable fortunes over the last ten years or so, but in 1994 won the Five Nations Championship, though losing to their traditional rival, England, in the process took the shine off the achievement.

In many respects, the last decade has witnessed a transformation in the fortunes of rugby union as it has progressed from being a sport enjoying modest attendance at club level and equally modest financial success. In 1994 the British Broadcasting Corporation paid £27 million for the rights to the Five Nations Championship for three years. While much of this income is being spent developing the game at the grass-roots and youth levels, it has highlighted a long-standing tension in the sport. The basis of the split in rugby that led to the formation of the two codes, league and union, lies in the vexed question of payment of players and the determination of rugby union to maintain the amateur character of the sport. Over the last ten years there has been a steady movement of top-class players from union to league, with three ''defecting'' in 1994. Hardest hit has been Welsh rugby union, which has witnessed the loss of sixteen players in the last eight years. The newfound wealth of the rugby union governing bodies has reopened the question of player payments with a fresh intensity.

For many supporters of English cricket, the less said about the performance of the national team the better. The condition of the English national summer sport has been subject to endless analysis with little sign of a revival. In the international rankings (1995), England languishes in sixth place, one place behind South Africa which did not play a top-class test match for twenty-nine years. England's ranking for one-day matches is higher at third place, but for the sport's purists this counts for little as it is the five-day test matches that capture the essence of cricket.

Among the other major UK sports, England, Scotland, and Wales have representatives in the top fifteen of the Sony golf rankings, with sixteen players in the top one hundred. However, to put this in perspective, the United States may not have any players ranked in the top five, but it has sixteen of the top thirty places and forty-nine of the top one hundred. UK sports participation and success cannot be measured simply in relation to the Olympic Games, golf, and the major team sports. In mid-1992, the UK had world champion teams or individuals in twenty-three different sports, including angling, croquet, powerboat racing, and wind surfing.

Partly as a result of the range of team sports played professionally and partly as a result of the relative strength of the economy, the UK has been able to attract a large number of foreign athletes into the major team sports of soccer, rugby, and cricket. In soccer, the definition of foreigner is complicated by the fact that UEFA, the European soccer governing body, defines Welsh, Northern Irish, and Scottish players as foreigners when playing for an English team. Nevertheless, most Premier League and First Division clubs will have between one and four foreign players on their team for the domestic league. During 1994, six of the eighteen £2 million plus transfers involved foreign players. The main sources of foreign players are Central and Eastern Europe and English-speaking

Africa. In cricket, most top-class players from the West Indian team and many from India, Pakistan, Australia, and New Zealand play their cricket in England. Each English County team is limited to two or three overseas players and, although there is some criticism of the effect of this policy on the development of English players, the commercial advantages to clubs of attractive overseas sports stars is great. There is a similar balance of trade in players in rugby union and especially rugby league, where there has been a steady stream of Welsh rugby union players moving to English rugby league clubs. Welsh rugby union lost Scott Quinnell and Scott Gibbs to English league sides, and New Zealand lost the immensely talented Va'aiga Tuigamala.

GOVERNMENT POLICY AND SPORTS

Financial Support for Sports

A number of factors affect the government's sport-funding policy. First, there is the definition of sport and recreation as an element of the welfare state which, in the 1980s, was moderated by the Conservative party's antipathy to both public expenditure and local government. Second, there is the tension, particularly evident in Conservative ideology, between treating sport as an aspect of "free time," which should therefore result in minimal intervention by government, and the desire for international prestige. The outcome of this mix of motives is a position in the mid-1990s where sport is funded through a combination of direct public subsidy and state-supported, but essentially commercial, sponsorship schemes.

Direct public subsidy for sport is organized either through the Sports Council or through the expenditure of local authorities. In the financial year 1994–95, the grants to the Sports Councils totaled £67.18 million, fractionally reduced from the 1993–94 level of £67.26 million (approximately 5 percent of the total budget of the Department of National Heritage). A substantial proportion of the income of the Councils (approximately 50 percent) is distributed in the form of grants to governing bodies of sport or to other national sports organizations (such as the British Deaf Sports Council, the National Council for School Sport, and the Young Men's Christian Association). Over the last five years, the Sports Councils have distributed grants to approximately sixty-five different sports each year ranging in size from £1,000 for kendo to £524,900 for field hockey, and including sports as diverse as archery, curling, roller hockey, surfing, and tug-of-war. Part of the British Sports Council grant is distributed nationally, but a significant proportion is distributed through the regional offices as needed to fund a wide variety of projects proposed by schools, universities, voluntary clubs, and local authorities.

The main function of Sports Council funding is "pump-priming" and support for innovative projects. Although the finance that flows into sport through the Councils' grant-aid is an important contribution to the development of sport, it is dwarfed by the volume of investment in sport allocated by local authorities. In the financial year 1992–93, local authorities spent £560 million on revenue support for sport and a further £130 million on capital projects. While these figures are substantial, the pattern of expenditure over the last five years indicates some worrying trends. Although revenue spending has remained broadly steady in real terms, it declined as a proportion of total local authority expenditure from 5.1 percent in 1989–90 to 4.3 percent in 1992–93. In addition, capital expenditures declined in real terms from £300 million in 1989–90 to £130 million in 1992–93, and an increasing proportion (about 30 percent) of capital expenditures are for the refurbishment of existing facilities rather than new provision.

The government's continuing desire to restrain the growth in public expenditures is likely to prevent any increase in direct public-sector expenditures on sport and recreation for the rest of the decade. However, it should be noted that sport, leisure, and recreation services have suffered less severe cuts in public expenditures than many other services, including secondary education and public-sector housing. It should also be noted that the last ten years have seen the introduction of a number of innovative funding schemes for sport designed by government that rely on a mix of public and private sources.

In 1991 the government established the Foundation for Sport and the Arts (FSA), which distributes about £40 million each year for sports projects. The FSA's income is derived partly from a reduction in the tax imposed on gambling on the outcome of soccer matches (the football pools) and partly from a voluntary contribution from the Pools Promoters Association. The FSA distributes financial grants based on the merits of each proposal—a source of irritation to the Sports Council, which argues that FSA decisions should be made with reference to the Council's national and regional strategic plans for sports development.

A second source of grant-aid for sports comes from the Football Trust. During the 1980s, the Trust provided over £10 million to assist local authorities in improving the quality of pitches and providing changing facilities for amateur teams. A reconsideration of the Trust's role was undertaken following the disaster at Hillsborough stadium where ninety-five people died as a result of being crushed during a surge of spectators onto the grounds to watch a Soccer Cup semifinal match. The inquiry that followed made a strong case for all-seat stadiums. The government accepted the report of the inquiry team, as it saw all-seat stadiums as a solution to the specific issue of soccer spectator violence as well as a means to more effective general crowd management. Although soccer is a professional sport, few clubs had the resources to comply with the government's requirement for the phased introduction of all-seat stadiums. The merger of the Football Trust with the Football Grounds Improvements Trust in 1990 was designed to provide the necessary additional finance. The new Trust's funds (about £25 million annually) come primarily from a diversion of 2.5 percent of the tax on soccer gambling, but also from a contribution from the Football Association, soccer's governing body.

The third scheme designed to provide financial support for sport is the national lottery which was introduced in November 1994. The lottery is expected to generate funds for sports totaling between £100 million and £150 million in 1995, rising to £250 million in 1999. Distribution became the responsibility of the UK Sports Councils as of March 1995. During 1994, there was considerable discussion and lobbying over the criteria to be applied when making funding decisions. Initially, the government's preference was to limit the Sports Councils' role and, more particularly, to resist any attempt to make consistency with the Sports Councils' strategic plans a key criterion for a successful application. However, once the government realized the scale of the task, the expected volume of applications, and the problems inherent in the absence of strong guidelines for approval, it reluctantly accepted that the Sports Councils were the only organizations that possessed the necessary administrative capacity and knowledge of the likely range of schemes. In addition, the government grudgingly accepted the fact that if the lottery income was to be used efficiently and effectively, then the Councils' strategic plans provided the logical context for decision making.

At the time of this writing, no grants had been made, but the principles that the Sports Councils will use to guide their decision making have been clarified. In general terms, applicants will be expected, inter alia, to create opportunities for wider participation—especially among currently underrepresented groups— and to raise a proportion of the project funds from other sources, including the private sector or the European Union. Capital projects are preferred to revenue projects, and applicants from professional clubs will have to agree to significant public access.

In addition to the schemes already mentioned, the government has introduced a number of proposals aimed at easing the tax burden on not-for-profit sports organizations and encouraging private-sector sponsorship. Charitable status, with its accompanying tax advantages, is not usually available to sports organizations, even those that do not seek to make a profit. The main stumbling block to granting charitable status has been the concentration of most sports organizations, particularly clubs, on a narrow range of activities for a select group defined by membership. The major exception has been those sports organizations that have been able to claim that their activities are predominantly educational in their nature and directed toward children. For example, the Football Association (FA) Youth Trust was granted charitable status because its objectives were ''to promote the physical education and development of pupils at schools and universities as an addition to such part of their education as related to their mental development and occupation by providing them with facilities to enable and encourage them to play football and other sports.'' However, few sports organizations are so narrowly focused as the FA Youth Trust; consequently, this route to charitable status is rarely successful.

More recently, a number of sports organizations have pursued an alternative route and have been granted charitable status under the terms of the Recreational Charities Act (1958) due to a broadening of their activities to stress the contribution of the organization and its facilities to social welfare. Organizations have to demonstrate that the facilities they provide are available to the public and especially for use by specified groups on the basis of disability, youth, poverty, or other socioeconomic circumstances, and that the facilities will improve the conditions of the selected groups. A number of sports organizations have achieved charitable status through applications based on the 1958 Act, but the numbers are still relatively small.

For most sports organizations, particularly individual sports clubs, a more fruitful opportunity to reduce their tax liability is to seek exemption from the Uniform Business Rate (UBR). The UBR is a property tax that is set by the central government but collected by local authorities. Local authorities have the discretion to waive the UBR due from sports and other community organizations. The Sports Council and the CCPR are actively involved in lobbying for mandatory relief for sports organizations, but the current situation is that the granting of relief varies considerably from one local authority to another.

Although little progress has been made in achieving tax exemptions for sports organizations, the government has introduced a number of schemes designed to help sport obtain sponsorship from the business sector, primarily for sports development activity. "Sportsmatch" is one such example, whereby the government pledges to match sponsorship from the business sector on a "pound for pound" basis. Although the sums involved are comparatively small (£6 million each year for three years up to 1997), the scheme is seen as valuable in increasing the flow of money into sports development. However, business understandably assesses sponsorship decisions in terms of the marketing potential of the investment. Thus, it is not surprising that the bulk of funding has gone to a small number of high-profile sports with more professional administration and marketing, such as tennis, football, rugby union, and cricket. To put the amount of sponsorship devoted directly to sports development into perspective, it is estimated that the total value of business sponsorship in 1990 was £210 million, with four sports (motor sports, soccer, horse-racing, and golf) accounting for 50 percent.

Regulatory Policies

Few policies are designed specifically to regulate sport. In general, the government's preference is to treat sports in the same manner as business or similar voluntary organizations. The element of the general business regulatory framework which is of special significance for sports is that related to "health and safety." The Health and Safety at Work Act (1974) imposes a duty on employers to ensure the safety of their employees. The law is monitored by an executive which has produced two sets of guidance relevant to sports, one for fairgrounds and the other for swimming pools.

The safety of spectators at major stadiums is covered by the Safety at Sport Grounds Act (1975). Following the collapse of a grandstand at the Ibrox Stadium, Glasgow, in 1971, the Act required all major stadiums to obtain a license from the local authority indicating that the facility met standards that ensured the reasonable safety of spectators. In 1987 the Fire Safety and Safety of Places of Sport Act imposed stricter regulations on sports grounds and arenas following the devastating fire at the grounds of Bradford Football Club. The 1987 Act required the management of stadiums with stands with a capacity of over 500 to obtain a fire certificate from the local authority.

The third general area of regulation that impinges on sports is concerned with equal opportunities. The Equal Opportunities Commission, established under the Sex Discrimination Act (1975), is responsible for working toward the elimination of discrimination and providing equality of opportunity between men and women. The main concern of the legislation is employment, although it can also be applied to the provision of sporting opportunities where, for example, the same standard of service has not been provided for both sexes. There have only been a small number of cases relevant to sport in the last twenty years. They have concerned, inter alia, whether a twelve-year-old girl could play for a school soccer team (she could at least until puberty); whether a woman could be part of Oxford University's men's water-polo team (she could not because it is a contact sport); and whether a bar owner was within his rights to prevent a woman from playing snooker because she might rip the table (he was not).

The Race Relations Act (1976) is a parallel act regarding discrimination on the grounds of race. As with the Sex Discrimination Act, the primary concern has been with employment, and there are few cases that relate directly to sports issues. One such case concerned Leicester Rugby Football Club and the local authority that owned the grounds on which they played. Following a decision by three of the club's members to join a tour of South Africa in 1985, the local authority banned the club from using the grounds for twelve months. The club argued that it had expressed its opposition to apartheid and had given the three men literature on the subject. The Court decided that the action of the authority in imposing a ban exceeded the powers of the 1976 Act and that the club had acted properly.

Finally, local authorities have a number of powers and responsibilities under legislation concerned with land-use planning that have occasional significance for sport. Under the terms of the main legislation, the recreational use of land is a peripheral consideration and not subject to statutory requirements. However, in addition to the control of particular uses of land for sporting purposes, local authorities—as the planning authority—have increasingly used their powers to negotiate with prospective developers for the provision of sports and leisure facilities as part of the approval process. The term for such agreements is "planning obligation," which is negotiated outside the terms of the planning consent.

For example, in the county of Hampshire, a planning obligation was agreed to in conjunction with the approval of a prestigious office development. The terms of the planning obligation required the construction, at the developer's expense, of a football pitch, a bowling green, a clubhouse, and a children's play area. The agreement also covered the associated maintenance for one year. Upon completion, the facilities would be transferred to the local authority. Although it is difficult to assess accurately the value of such arrangements, the Sports Council estimated that in 1991 in England the value of sports and recreation facilities was in the region of £40 million.

Local Government and Sports

The primary responsibility for providing facilities and opportunities for mass participation in sports rests with local government. In 1992–93, capital and revenue expenditures by local authorities on sports totaled £690 million. Expenditures grew steadily during the 1970s and resulted in a period of rapid expansion in facility provision. While expenditures have leveled off recently and may well decline slightly in the remaining years of the decade, the impact of past expenditures has been considerable. For example, between 1971 and 1991 the number of swimming pools provided by British local authorities has increased from approximately 500 to more than 1,300. There has been an even more dramatic growth in the provision of sports halls, from about 20 to over 1,500 during the same period. As these figures show, the growth in the significance of local authority involvement has been recent, rapid, and accomplished without the benefit of a statutory foundation of mandatory services on which to base bids for central government funding.

During the late 1960s and 1970s, a number of factors emerged which contributed to the acknowledgment of sports and recreation as a discrete local government responsibility, stimulating local authorities to reflect on the most appropriate administrative structure for service delivery and planning (Veal and Travis, 1979). One important factor was the establishment of the Sports Council in 1972 (and the Countryside Commission in 1968), which did much to stimulate the development of new types of facilities such as sports and leisure centers and country parks. The provision of new facilities was linked to an underlying change in leisure patterns, stimulated largely by a steady rise in disposable income.

A further factor of particular importance for local government was the discussion of structural reform that took place during the 1960s. Part of the debate on reform concerned the appropriate pattern of internal organization for the new, larger authorities. The emerging consensus was that there was a need for a small number of large departments, one of which could cover sport and leisure. The eventual restructuring of local government did stimulate the creation of a larger number of specialist leisure services departments—a trend that peaked in the late 1980s and has since been reversed slightly.

Relative to other local authority services, such as housing planning and education, spending on leisure services has remained remarkably stable as a proportion of total local government expenditure. In 1979 expenditures on recreational activities accounted for 4.8 percent of total local government expenditures; the figure peaked in 1984 at 5.0 percent before dropping back to 4.8 percent in 1993. Thus, spending on recreational and cultural activities by local authorities remained fairly constant during a period of diversity and change in leisure and sports policy objectives.

Clearly, local authorities are strongly influenced by central government policy, particularly when government priorities are supported with additional funding from the Sports Council. In general, sports and recreation services are rarely valued as important in their own right, and arguments for investment are normally couched in terms of the benefits to other policy objectives such as improved health or reduced vandalism. Although this perception is stronger at the central government level, an instrumental attitude to sport and recreation expenditures is also evident among local authorities (Coalter et al., 1986). While part of the stability of local expenditures can be explained by strong popular demand for increased provision, the increasingly common perception of leisure services as an element of economic development is also a factor. During the 1980s, as the government's regional policy—and consequently, funding—was reduced in significance, local authorities became more concerned with marketing their area to investors, and recreational and cultural facilities were considered important in attracting investment. In addition, for many areas tourism has been identified as a potential growth industry, and this has resulted in local expenditures on sports and leisure infrastructure as well as on the promotion of special leisure events such as arts festivals. Figure 16.2 indicates both the variety of policy objectives adopted by central and local governments over the last sixty-five years and which policy or combination of policies was dominant in particular periods.

Northern Ireland (Ulster) is an exception to many generalizations about the pattern of responsibility for sport at the local level and the nature of local policy processes. However, what makes Northern Ireland especially interesting is the explicit use of sport and recreation services as tools for undermining the religious sectarian politics of the province. For much of the 1970s and 1980s, sport and recreation policy was seen as the product of a broad cross-party consensus. As Coalter et al. observed, "it would seem that the apolitical nature of much of the debate concerning leisure policy derives not solely from political apathy, but also from the perceived nature of the realm of leisure. It was regarded by many as an area of personal opinion, freedom and choice, and as such a 'depoliticized' arena, properly outside the realm of adversarial politics" (Coalter et al., 1986, p. 127). It was partly this assessment that encouraged British politicians to make sports and recreation one of the few significant services to be administered by Ulster local authorities, and to attempt to use leisure services

Figure 16.2
Government Policy Objectives and Sports

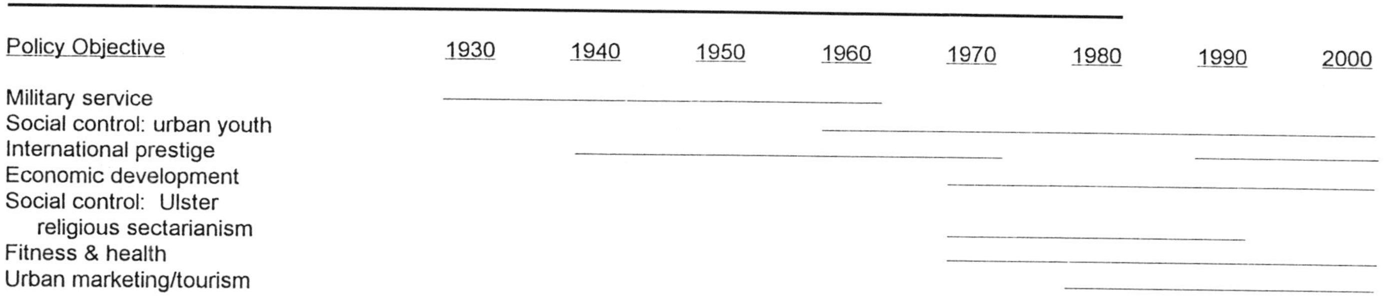

Policy Objective	1930	1940	1950	1960	1970	1980	1990	2000

Military service

Social control: urban youth

International prestige

Economic development

Social control: Ulster
    religious sectarianism

Fitness & health

Urban marketing/tourism

as an instrument to build bridges across the sectarian divide in cities such as Belfast and Derry.

The Local Government (Northern Ireland) Act (1972), which reorganized local government in the province, was the outcome of a compromise between the desire for managerial efficiency and service effectiveness on the one hand and the reality of sectarian politics on the other. Because of the manipulation of key local government services, such as public-sector housing and education and corruption in employment practices, the reorganized structure of local government left few significant services with the twenty-six newly created districts. Most politically sensitive services, such as education and public-sector housing, were to be administered directly by Westminster through the Northern Ireland Office. The new district councils were responsible for the delivery of a narrow range of comparatively minor services such as refuse collection and disposal, burial grounds and crematoria, tourist amenities, and recreation. Within this range, recreation was a relatively important and—in contrast to England and Wales—a mandatory service.

In the early 1970s provision of recreational facilities was far poorer in Northern Ireland than in the rest of the United Kingdom. As Knox points out, "It was not until 1973, with the reorganization of local government and the formation of the Sports Council for Northern Ireland, that the impetus for leisure provision came" (Knox, 1987, p. 79). Knox also makes clear the degree to which the new local authorities relied on the guidance of the Sports Council in matters of the scale, location, and type of facilities to be built. The methods used to determine need and location were a combination of spatial analysis and the notion of a hierarchy of provision throughout the province. This rational approach to location and type was complemented by strong Northern Ireland Office support for investment in leisure, which was perceived as a key means of reducing the level of intercommunal tension.

On the face of things, local government leisure services were in an enviable position. Leisure provision was mandatory, there was strong political and financial support from government, and technical and planning expertise was provided by the Sports Council. Unfortunately, what soon became clear was that the provision of leisure facilities had been subsumed by the weight of sectarian politics, just as the allocation of public housing had before. The location of new facilities in particular was used by the various religious and political factions as a means of seeking sectarian advantage. Location was determined less by rational planning than by the political need to be seen as even-handed in investment in Catholic and Protestant areas. Hence, a new leisure center in a Protestant area would almost certainly be followed by one in a Catholic area (Knox, 1986, 1987).

The consequences of sectarian politics notwithstanding, Ulster has benefited from the high level of investment in sport and recreational facilities to the degree that both Belfast and Derry have levels of provision superior to that found in cities of equivalent size in Britain. What is frustrating for the researcher is the difficulty of determining the impact that the statutory nature of sport and recreation services has had on overall levels of investment.

Sport, the School Curriculum, and the Community Use of Facilities

Two elements of public policy have considerable impact on sport and recreation provision: first, the community use of sports facilities and second, the significance of sports in the school curriculum.

"Community use" (also referred to as dual use) refers to the policy of opening sports and recreational facilities to as wide a public as possible. The policy covers a broad range of facilities, primarily those controlled by local education authorities, but has also been applied to those controlled by private companies, government departments, colleges, and universities. The prime targets for this policy have been the extensive sports facilities attached to schools which generally are open only during the academic term, during school hours, with use restricted to pupils. Ideally, under a community use policy, once the pupils have gone home, members of the local community will be able to utilize the facilities, thus maximizing expensive capital resources.

There are a number of successful community use schemes. In Walsall, for example, a network of community schools is the basis for a hierarchy of provision ranging from simple facilities available at local primary schools, through more sophisticated and specialized facilities at secondary schools, to specially built centers of excellence (Nixon, 1985; Opening Time, 1985). The additional revenue and maintenance costs are subject to an agreement between the education and leisure services departments.

Another element of public policy concerns a recent debate regarding changes in the role of sports and physical education in the curriculum (Houlihan, 1991). The last fifteen years have been characterized by considerable change in the way schools are organized and funded, as well as in the responsibilities of teaching staff. These changes, when combined with other developments in sports, have produced considerable uncertainty about the role of sport in schools. The broadening of the range of sports available to young people both inside and outside school has been accompanied by a decline in the level of participation in the traditional summer and winter sports. In addition, the rapid increase in the number of municipal sports facilities has spurred the growth in "casual" participation in preference to participation organized through clubs. Finally, demographic changes reflect a severe decline in the teenage population in the 1980s. In essence, the competitive clubs in the traditional (mainly team) sports were finding that the steady supply of young players, often introduced to clubs by school physical education (PE) staff, was beginning to diminish.

These developments were reinforced by changes in schools in the 1980s. Of central importance was a series of changes in the school PE curriculum. First, the curriculum was broadened to include a wider range of sports as teachers sought to find a combination of sports that would include the less able. Second, there was a trend to increase the academic content of PE classes through the inclusion of classroom-based activities covering topics such as physiology, psychology, and health and fitness theory. A major aim of this change was to enhance the academic status of PE and sports within the overall school curriculum through a redefinition of sports away from ''sports as skill'' towards ''sports as knowledge'' (see Kirk et al., 1986). The third change was a greater emphasis on the development of the component skills (for example, hand–eye coordination and physical fitness) of sports rather than concentrating on the playing of particular sports.

A series of central government policy changes during the 1980s brought matters to a head. First, the government sought to redefine the teachers' contract and, in the process, provoked a long and bitter dispute. Ultimately, the teachers lost the dispute and had a new contract imposed on them. The details of the new contract and the method by which it was introduced combined to reduce the number of staff hours available for organizing and supervising extracurricular sports. The contract specified both the number of hours that the staff were expected to teach and the number of hours for additional activities such as staff training and meetings. A common consequence was that staff training and meetings were scheduled for the hour following the end of the school day, thus making team training more difficult to organize. Probably of even greater significance was the loss of goodwill among staff, particularly among the non-PE staff, and a consequent decline in their willingness to manage school teams.

The second significant policy change was the introduction of school budgets that made head teachers and school governors more aware of the opportunity cost of transport for out-of-school sport and also for taking children to specialized facilities, such as swimming pools.

The combined effect of all these developments was of serious concern to the governing bodies of sport. As early as 1980, Peter Lawson, the CCPR's general secretary, called for a public inquiry into sports in schools. The Council reflected a range of concerns evident among governing bodies of sports and other interested organizations, which included the decline in team sports, the pressure to reduce the timetable allocation to PE, and the use of non-specialist PE staff to supervise physical education classes. As the decade progressed, these general concerns became focused on the proposed introduction of a national curriculum under the 1988 Educational Reform Act. Three issues related to sports dominated the debate on the curriculum: first, whether PE would be designated as a foundation subject; second, how much time would be allocated to PE; and third, what emphasis would be given to the playing of team games within the PE curriculum.

The government considered the initial specification of the PE curriculum to be too academic and theoretical, and to give too little emphasis to traditional competitive team games: the advisory panel was instructed to reconsider. In 1994 the panel produced its revised specification of the curriculum in line with government instructions. The outcome represented a considerable victory for the sports lobby in general and the CCPR in particular. However, it is too soon to provide an evaluation of the impact of the curriculum and whether it will fulfill the objectives of the major governing bodies in protecting organized team sport. Whether it will result in the eventual production of a cricket team that can beat the West Indies in a Test Series also remains to be seen.

POLICY ANALYSIS

At the domestic level, two policy objectives have dominated in recent years: first, the promotion of mass participation in sports (Sport-for-All); and second, sports as a means of regulating the behavior of the young. The prime responsibility for implementation rests with local government and the Sports Councils, both of which have had to work within the highly restrictive ideological framework of right-wing Conservatism. The policy of privatization had a particularly significant effect on progress toward mass participation in sports.

A consistent policy throughout the sixteen years of Conservative government has been the desire to reduce the size of the public sector through privatization. The most common form of privatization has been the sale of public utility companies such as those concerned with the supply of gas, water, and electricity. With regard to sports and recreation services, the government's preferred form of privatization was the "contracting out" of the management function. Thus, the physical facilities would remain the property of the local authority, but their management would be subject to a process of competitive bidding. The bid would be prepared by the local authority in order to incorporate local policy objectives (e.g., regarding priority groups and pricing policy) into the specification.

The Local Government Act of 1988 introduced the framework for compulsory competitive tendering (CCT) for a range of local government services. In 1989 the terms of the Act were extended by Parliamentary Order to include the management of local authority leisure services. The terms of the Order mandated competitive bidding for leisure services beginning in 1992, with all facilities subject to CCT by January 1993. The Order covered most major facilities and employed a broad definition of management. According to the Audit Commission, CCT is expected to reduce unit costs by up to 20 percent (Audit Commission, 1989, p. 17).

The first round of bidding took place in the early 1990s, with contracts normally running for five years. Most local authorities organized an in-house bid, which meant that the existing management team competed against private companies for the contract to run the facility. For many manual employees the result has been a decline in pay and conditions of service as in-house management teams attempt to cut costs to a level found in the private sector.

As many local authorities approach the end of the first round of contracts, it is possible to assess the impact of the policy on the provision of sports and recreation facilities for mass participation. On the positive side, the advent of CCT has encouraged a greater number of local authorities to think strategically. Indeed, with strong encouragement from the Sports Council, an increasing number of local authorities are preparing strategic plans for sports and recreation. However, the pace of plan production is slow, and for those having strategic plans in place, the extent to which they are used as a basis for constructing the tender specification is limited. Yet even when the client (the local authority) sets explicit targets regarding particular priority groups and sports development activity, it is often the case that these are substantially ignored by the contractor, even when the contract is won in-house. Indeed, recent research suggests that CCT has marginalized sports development activity. According to the Sports Council, "In many cases, sports development objectives are becoming irrelevant to what local authority facilities are actually delivering" (Sports Council, 1993). Part of the problem lies in the client's failure to monitor progress toward the objectives set in the tender specification. The collection of reliable management information by the contractor is often poor, and the capacity of the client to analyze data is often inadequate.

There is a clear tension within many privatized sports facilities between financial objectives and those relating to sports development. The overriding concern of management is to meet income targets even if that means giving priority in bookings to established sports, such as 5-a-side soccer, in preference to the creation of opportunities to develop new sports and activities.

Although the initial assessments of the impact of CCT are generally negative, there are one or two more positive views. In the early days of the policy, the Regional Councils for sports and recreation hoped that local authorities would think more creatively about how they could achieve their policy objectives. The most promising examples to date include a number of schemes that involve closer links between voluntary clubs and local authority sports facilities. In one authority, the local badminton club has agreed to provide coaching for the public (casual user) in return for lower rates for courts; in another, the swimming club has agreed to provide coaching at the sports center in return for cheaper hire rates for club activities. This latter example is becoming widely imitated as clubs offer coaching expertise to the public in exchange for reduced user fees.

Despite these promising examples of innovative cooperation between the public and the voluntary sectors, the key question remains whether CCT will undermine the rapid progress in increasing participation that took place in the 1980s. On the basis of information available so far, it would seem that the quantity of participation may continue to expand, but that the quality of the participants' experience, especially when assessed in terms of choice, may deteriorate.

Within the public sector, a key strategy for increasing opportunities for greater participation in sport is to enable public use of semiprivate facilities through the community use scheme. Although the scheme has a compelling logic and has the support of government, the Sports Council, the CCPR, and many local authorities, the extent of community use is still limited. In order for the policy to operate successfully, three issues need to be resolved, namely, what to share, how to manage the sharing, and how to finance the policy.

Part of the difficulty in resolving these issues is a consequence of the location of responsibility for education and sport within different tiers of local government in the nonmetropolitan areas. Even within the metropolitan districts, agreement has often proved elusive. A second problem concerns the relative importance of the policy of community use to these two departments. For sports and recreation departments, community use is frequently a key element in a community recreation strategy. However, for an education department, the policy is likely to have a much lower priority.

A further problem arises from the Conservative government's policy of transferring responsibility for the financial management of schools from the local authority to schools by calculating individual school budgets. Consequently, decisions about public access to school resources are no longer solely local authority decisions but are now the result of decisions by school-governing bodies. To complicate matters further, the government also passed legislation that makes it possible for individual schools to "opt out" of local authority control and be funded directly by central government grant. Both policies have resulted in schools being less inclined to cooperate with sports and recreation departments, consequently slowing considerably the expansion of community use opportunities.

The long-term prospects for the community use policy are unclear. On the one hand, community use may decline as more schools view their sports facilities as commercial assets to be preserved by excluding nonschool users. On the other hand, the growing financial autonomy of schools may result in an expansion of community use schemes as schools come to see their sports facilities as a potential source of additional revenue and, more importantly, as ways of projecting a positive image of the school to parents and the wider community.

The city of Birmingham illustrates both the problems and opportunities posed by the recent changes. By 1990 the Council had already brokered an agreement between the Recreation and Community Services Department and the Education Department on the basis of a continuation of the city's extensive, and highly successful, community use program. Agreement has been reached on the management structure, which includes a full-time manager for each community use center, and the level to which the Recreation and Community Services Department will reimburse individual schools for additional revenue and materials costs. In contrast to this success, the city has been involved in a long and acrimonious dispute with a school that voted to opt out of local authority control. When Great Barr School obtained grant-maintained status, it terminated the existing community use agreement and asserted its ownership of all sports facilities. Although the minister of state for education eventually ruled against the school, the dispute is indicative of the changed relationship between education and sports services.

As the UK economy emerges slowly from the recession of the early 1990s, there is unlikely to be any return to the levels of public investment seen a decade or two earlier. While the national lottery will inject more money into sports, it remains to be seen what proportion of the fund is directed to expanding participation. The best prospects for achieving the goal of "Sport-for-All" will lie in encouraging closer cooperation between clubs, governing bodies, and local authorities and pursuing an expansion of community use of facilities.

The second major objective of government is a rather more sporadic and less clearly defined concern to employ sports and recreation as a form of social control. This has been asserted as a policy objective, although there is no firm evidence to suggest that there is a positive link between social responsibility (or conformity) and participation in sports. Indeed, the association between soccer spectatorship and violence would seem to suggest that government should at least be wary of assuming that participation in sports leads to civic responsibility.

The White Paper of 1977 (Sport and Recreation) justified additional state expenditures in the following terms: "By reducing boredom and urban frustration, participation in active recreation contributes to the reduction of hooliganism and delinquency among young people." (Department of the Environment, 1975, p. 2). This view was also reflected in the White Paper, A Policy for the Inner Cities, published two years later. From the mid-1970s to the early 1980s, the government supported this policy by channeling finance through the Urban Programme. Later, in the mid-1980s, the government also used its control over the Sports Councils to ensure that 30 percent of its funding was directed to inner cities and identified stress areas (Henry, 1993, pp. 62–63). However, as Henry pointedly notes, the continued allocation of public money for purposes of reinforcing social order "is all the more impressive since there is little evidence to support the assertion that participation in recreation reduces anti-social behavior" (1993, p. 189).

On a number of occasions in this chapter, the centrality of the Sports Council to the development of sports policy has been noted. Yet from the late 1980s the Council has been faced with considerable uncertainty owing to a series of reviews of its status and functions initiated by government. Although it seems that this long period of uncertainty is coming to an end, it also seems likely that the proposed UK Sports Council and the English Sports Council will be required to concentrate their resources on meeting the needs of elite athletes and young people. How the restructuring of the Council will affect its involvement in the promotion of mass participation and the provision of sports opportunities in areas of social stress is, as yet, unclear. It does seem that the central government would prefer that local government take sole responsibility for supporting policy objectives in these two areas, thus leaving the new bodies free to concentrate on improving the quality and performance of UK athletes and teams in international competition.

Indeed, it would seem that the search for international sporting prestige is set to become an increasingly important priority for the future. The current minister for sport has openly expressed his admiration of the elitist selection and training methods of the Australian Institute of Sport. He, along with the prime minister, is also strongly supportive of renewed emphasis on traditional team games in schools. UK sports administrators and government ministers are acutely aware of the extent to which the nation's international sporting status has declined. It was only a generation ago that Britons held key posts in many of the major international sporting bodies, such as the International Olympic Committee, the IAAF, and FIFA. Yet today there are no British presidents of any major international federation. The government clearly sees that the best prospects for a return to the country's former status lie in improving performance in major events and competitions.

CONCLUSIONS

During the late 1980s, the government was led by a prime minister who possessed an open contempt for sports. Margaret Thatcher saw sports more as a source of problems (soccer hooliganism in particular) than as a source of policy opportunities. She also led a government that, in the majority, shared her view and appointed a succession of weak politicians to the post of minister for sport. Sport was one of a series of convenient tools for responding to outbreaks of urban disorder in the early 1980s, but it rarely, if ever, was the subject of positive policy debate. The election of John Major in December 1990 as prime minister and leader of the Conservative party marked a dramatic change in fortunes for sport. Overnight, it lost its pariah status and became the subject of enthusiastic—though admittedly occasional—high-level discussion. Following his election victory in 1992, Major was joined in his cabinet by two other enthusiasts, Kenneth Clarke as chancellor of the Exchequer and David Mellor as the first minister for National Heritage.

Sport has clearly benefited from the prime minister's commitment, most notably in the introduction of the national lottery, but also in the high level of government financial support for Manchester's bid to host the 2000 Olympic Games. The £250 million promised to the city if Manchester's bid had been successful was in marked contrast to Margaret Thatcher's refusal to provide any support for the World Student Games hosted by the city of Sheffield. The changes in the fortunes of sport are to be welcomed, but they reflect the capriciousness of UK politics and the failure of the sports lobby to establish the firm links with political parties and government officials which would guarantee a degree of stability for the policy area. The often repeated observation that government treats sports more as a means to an end than an end in itself is an indication of the weakness of sports organizations in protecting their interests and those they represent. The fortuitous combination of a group of senior government members with a clear agenda for sport can evaporate just as rapidly as it emerged, leaving sport at the whim of the next incumbent of number 10 Downing Street.

The support given by successive governments (with varying degrees of enthusiasm) to the expansion of opportunities for participation in sports is the most notable achievement of the postwar period. In marked contrast, attempts to use sports for purposes of social control have been poorly designed and implemented. Indeed, one could argue that in Northern Ireland the attempt to use sports to bridge the sectarian divide only succeeded in deepening that divide. Sports have always been an important part of the social fabric of the UK, and governments face a delicate balancing act when intervening in the policy area. Few governments have been able to restrict themselves to facilitating greater participation and supporting elite success without also wishing to direct that participation and manipulate the symbolism of elite achievement. In this respect, they are little different from most Western democratic governments. One way in which the capricious and exploitative tendency of government can be checked is through the establishment of an effective sports lobby. Although there are signs of this developing in the UK, there are still too many divisions between key organizations such as the CCPR and the BOA. Yet an effective lobby is the key to ensuring that sport remains part of the social fabric and not merely a convenient policy tool of the government.

NOTES

1. A White Paper is a statement of government policy that may become the basis for proposed legislation.
2. As of May 1995, one British pound was equivalent to approximately $1.54.

REFERENCES

Anthony, D. (1980). *A strategy for British sport.* London: C. Hurst & Co.

Audit Commission. (1989). *Sport for whom?* London: HMSO.

Coalter, F. (1984). Public policy and leisure. In A. Tomlinson (ed.), *Leisure: Politics, planning and people, Vol. 1, Plenary Papers* (pp. 18–33). Brighton: Leisure Studies Association.

Coalter, F. with Long, J., and Duffield, B. (1986). *The rationale for public sector investment in leisure.* London: Sports Council & the Economic and Social Research Council.

Department of the Environment. (1975). *Sport and recreation* (Command 6200). London: HMSO.

Hargreaves, J. (1985). From socialism to authoritarian populism: State intervention in sport and physical recreation in contemporary Britain. *Leisure Studies, 4.*

Henley Centre for Forecasting. (1989). *The economic impact and importance of sport in two local areas: Bracknell and the Wirral.* London: Sports Council.

Henley Centre for Forecasting. (1990). *Sport and the Welsh economy; Sports study 2.* Cardiff: Sports Council for Wales.

Henley Centre for Forecasting. (1992a). *The economic impact of sport in the United Kingdom in 1990.* London: Sports Council.

Henley Centre for Forecasting. (1992b). *The economic impact of sport in Northern Ireland.* Belfast: Sports Council for Northern Ireland.

Henry, I. (1993). *The politics of leisure policy.* Basingstoke: Macmillan.

Houlihan, B. (1991). *The government and politics of sport.* London: Routledge.

Houlihan, B. (1994). *Sport and international politics.* Hemel Hempstead: Harvester-Wheatsheaf.

Kirk, D., McKay, J., and George, L. F. (1986). All work and no play? Hegemony in the physical education curriculum. *Trends and Developments in PE; Proceedings of the VIII Commonwealth and International Conference on Sport, PE, Recreation and Dance.* London: Spon.

Knox, C. (1986). Political symbolism and leisure provision in Northern Ireland local government. *Local Government Studies, 12*(5).

Knox, C. (1987). Territorialism, leisure and community centers in Northern Ireland. *Leisure Studies, 6.*

Nixon, R. (1985). *Working together: the role of education and recreation departments.* Sports Council Recreation Management Conference: Youth. . . . Stepping into leisure. London: Sports Council.

Opening time. (1985). *Sport and Leisure, 26*(2).

PIEDA. (1991). *Sport and the economy of Scotland.* Edinburgh: Scottish Sports Council.

Sports Council. (1993). *The impact of CCT (mimeo).* London: Sports Council.

Torkildsen, G. (1986). *Leisure and recreation management.* London: Spon.

Travis, A. S. (1979). *The state and leisure provision.* London: Sports Council/Social Science Research Council.

University of Birmingham, Physical Education Department. (1956). *Britain in the world of sport.* London: Physical Education Association.

Veal, A. J., and Travis, A. S. (1979). Local authority services: The state of play. *Local Government Studies, 5*(4).

17

Sports Policy in the United States

Laurence Chalip and Arthur Johnson

The government of the United States is characterized by the principles of separation of powers, checks and balances, and federalism. These principles make the structure of American government complex and the policymaking process a confusing one, the outcomes of which are commonly the result of negotiation and compromise among various organizations and individuals with a stake in the resolution of an issue.

The Constitution of the United States identifies three branches of government. The legislative branch is defined as the policymaking branch of government; the executive branch implements laws and public policies; and the judicial branch interprets the law. The Constitution, which was adopted in 1789, is constantly being interpreted and shaped over time, earning it a reputation for being "a living document." Although the Constitution seemingly gives specific functions to each branch of government, the reality is that each branch plays an important role in policymaking. Furthermore, the bureaucracy of the national government (composed of a number of federal agencies) also plays a significant role in policymaking, even though the Constitution makes no mention of a federal bureaucracy.

Therefore, in order to identify national sports policies, it is necessary to examine the policy outputs of each branch of government and the federal agencies. In addition, to fully understand the extent to which government is involved in American sports, it is necessary to recognize that state and local governments also are intimately involved in sports policy and that American democracy is characterized by contradiction in terms of ideology and power.

American federalism has gone through several iterations, but it remains that many of the actions and policies of state and local governments are shaped or influenced by national policies. The national government issues mandates that must be met by state and local governments; its tax policies influence the effectiveness of state and local fiscal actions and options; and in the international arena, the national government has supremacy and thereby is able to limit or expand opportunities for state and local actions.

Although the United States promotes an ideology that extols private enterprise and separation of government and the private sector, the boundary between the private and public sectors is often vague. Tax policies, environmental laws, antitrust regulations, labor laws, occupational safety and health regulations, and a number of other laws and policies directly impact businesses and corporations operating in the United States and may be beneficial or injurious to their success. As a result, private interests spend vast sums of money in an effort to influence the outcome of the public policymaking process, hoping to achieve favorable policy outcomes. This often means that those organizations and individuals with political and financial power disproportionately influence public policy.

Nevertheless, those unhappy with the outcome of a policy debate may challenge that outcome in another political arena, at another time, aided by the principles of federalism, separation of powers, and checks and balances embodied in the Constitution. For example, if Congress passes a law unfavorable to labor interests that the president signs, labor unions or individual workers can challenge that law in the judicial system and may eventually reverse it. Thus, the American public policymaking process is dynamic and rarely conforms to the formal picture contained in the nation's founding documents.

GOVERNMENT AND SPORTS IN THE UNITED STATES

The rhetoric of American public policy historically has been that sport is independent of government. This assertion, however, belies the historical and contemporary relationship between American government and sport at both the professional and amateur levels. Each branch of the government is responsible for policies that have implications for American sports, professional and amateur, despite rhetoric to the contrary (Johnson and Frey, 1985; Wilson, 1994).

American professional sports consist of a rich variety. However, fewer than a dozen sports command tens of thousands of spectators for an event, compensate athletes in hundreds of thousands of dollars in a season or by event, provide a handsome profit to sports entrepreneurs, and boast of longevity. These sports include team sports organized by leagues, the members of which are franchises owned privately by individuals or corporations (e.g., baseball, basketball, hockey, and football), and sports played by individuals (e.g., tennis, golf) organized by a professional association that sanctions events which make up a "tour." An event usually has a corporate sponsor that finances most of an event's costs.

Professional baseball and hockey have their own player development systems.

These "minor leagues" are designed to develop players' skills for competition at the "major" league level. Basketball and football rely more directly on colleges and universities to develop athletic talent. Thus, the vast majority of professional basketball and football players come to their teams directly from the nation's colleges and universities, many of which are publicly funded institutions.

Also, sports such as boxing, horse racing and auto racing qualify as major sports. Boxing, however, commands national attention only for certain championship fights. Similarly, horse racing attracts national attention for a few select races (i.e., the Kentucky Derby), whereas auto racing caters to a more regional market. These sports, therefore, will not be the focus of this chapter's analysis.[1]

Government policy has been of critical importance to the profitability of professional sports leagues and their member-teams. For example, exemptions to antitrust laws—which regulate American business and forbid monopolistic practices—are enjoyed by professional sport leagues in baseball, basketball, football, and hockey. The exemptions, which allow the leagues to pool and then sell as a package their individual teams' broadcasting rights, are worth millions of dollars to the team owners and partially explain their ability to award million-dollar player contracts. The nature of the relationship between the government and professional sports in the United States is one of long standing. The government acts very much as a regulator, as it does for other business operations in the nation. It often serves as an arbiter between labor and management, and among sports organizations and entrepreneurs.

At the amateur level, throughout the twentieth century, the federal government of the United States has sought to limit its involvement. Nevertheless, government involvement has grown incrementally in response to various political and social agendas and particularly in response to the Cold War. In the 1990s, federal policies for amateur sport are manifest in three ways: (1) through implementation of the Amateur Sports Act of 1978, (2) through application of laws to sport that were not explicitly written for sport, and (3) through the work of agencies in the administrative branch of the federal government, particularly the President's Council on Physical Fitness and Sport.

Prior to the Second World War, the federal government took scant interest in amateur sports. During the Great Depression of the 1930s, government work projects created 254 golf courses, 318 ski trails, 805 swimming pools, 1,720 gymnasiums, 1,817 handball courts, 2,261 horseshoe courts, and 3,026 athletic fields. Government projects also built or improved 8,000 parks and 12,800 playgrounds (Clumpner, 1976, pp. 47, 84). However, these projects were part of the government effort to overcome the Great Depression and were not stimulated by concern for the welfare of amateur sports per se.

The first federal policies to promote amateur sports were intended less to promote sports than to enhance Americans' physical preparedness for the Second World War. On May 20, 1941, President Franklin Roosevelt signed Executive Order 8757 to create the Office of Civilian Defense (HEWERS). An advisory board was established which embraced thirteen organizations concerned with physical fitness, including the National Collegiate Athletic Association (NCAA). The HEWERS promoted physical activity via public rallies and literature, as well as through clubs, recreational groups, industrial organizations, and the schools (Applin, 1968, pp. 65–76). The HEWERS program was supplemented by including a Division of Physical Fitness within the Office of Defense, Health and Welfare Services (Drew, 1944, p. 2; Zingale, 1973, p. 72). Although that office was abolished in April 1943, it was replaced by the Committee on Physical Fitness under the Federal Security Agency. However, at the war's end, the Committee on Physical Fitness and the HEWERS program were terminated.

The emergence of the Cold War brought renewed focus on amateur sports. At the national convention of the Amateur Athletic Union (AAU) in 1951, Richard Walsh, representing the State Department, said: "Reports from our embassies during recent months afford positive proof that the Kremlin has mounted a gigantic cultural offensive. It is designed to prove the Soviet line of supremacy . . . in the athletic field" (Walsh, 1951, p. 1007).

As the 1952 Olympics and, thus, the first confrontation between American and Soviet Olympians approached, the popular *New York Times* sports writer Arthur Daley editorialized:

The United States has to have its strongest possible representation just to teach the Red brothers a lesson that can't be excused or concealed. . . . There will be 71 nations at the Olympics at Helsinki. The United States would like to beat all of them, but the only one that counts is Soviet Russia. The Communist propaganda machine must be silenced so that there can't be even one distorted bleat out of it in regard to the Olympics. (1952, p. c3)

The linkage of sport to physical fitness and, consequently, to preparedness for war, generated renewed policy interest in the context of Cold War confrontations. In 1954 Congressman Philip Philbin of Massachusetts asked: "What is the meaning of this rapid advancement of Russia in the world of sports? To what extent is superiority in competitive athletics tied in with national success, prosperity, and invincibility in warfare?" (*Congressional Record*, 1954, p. 13763).

Concerns like these mounted. In 1953, the Kraus-Weber tests concluded that American children were less fit than were their European counterparts (Kraus and Hirschland, 1953). In 1955 Congressman Harley Staggers of West Virginia introduced a concurrent resolution (H. Conc. Res. 19) to express Congress's sense that a civilian physical fitness and training program should be established in the interest of national security. On July 16, 1956, President Eisenhower signed Executive Order 10673, creating the President's Council on Youth Fitness.

During the same era, the State Department sought to counter Soviet uses of sport as a tool of diplomacy (cf. Riordan, 1987) by sending American teams overseas for goodwill tours (Department of State, n.d.). Nine teams were sent in 1955, fifteen teams in 1956, and six teams in 1957. In 1961 Congress passed the Mutual Educational and Cultural Exchange Act, broadening the educational and cultural programs of the Department of State. Although sports teams had been used irregularly and inconsistently in exchanges, an Office of Athletic Programs was now established. In 1963 President Kennedy created an Interagency Committee on International Athletics to provide coordination and advice on sport. That committee advocated increased use of sport to achieve American foreign policy objectives (Clumpner 1976, p. 312), but the use of sport waned under the two subsequent administrations. In 1971 the Harris/Ragan Management Corporation presented a report to the Department of State which concluded that sports should be even more vigorously employed as a tool of foreign relations and as an instrument of diplomacy (Clumpner, 1976, p. 339). The most visible use at that time was the so-called ping-pong diplomacy wherein a table-tennis team was sent from the United States to the People's Republic of China as part of the effort to establish diplomatic relations between the two countries.

During the 1960s, the President's Council on Youth Fitness expanded its activities into sport at all levels. In 1963, by Executive Order, President Kennedy replaced the President's Council on Youth Fitness with the President's Council on Physical Fitness, thus expanding the Council's programs to adults. In 1968, again by Executive Order, President Johnson replaced the President's Council on Physical Fitness with the President's Council on Physical Fitness and Sports (the name it carries to this day), thus making official the Council's growing interest in amateur sports.

Despite the growth of interest in sports policy during the 1950s and 1960s, no legislation specifically aimed at amateur sports was forthcoming until the 1970s. However, American performances at the 1972 summer Olympic Games in Munich were poorer than expected, with the American medal tally falling below that of the Soviet Union for the first time. Moreover, a series of controversies and disqualifications led the popular media to ask whether the American team was properly managed (e.g., "Chaos, Tragedy Overshadowed Munich Athletic Feats," 1972). There was a consequent flurry of legislative activity, including several proposals to nationalize sport governance in the United States.

Two factors bolstered the legislative initiative to nationalize sport governance. One was an historic concern for equity in sports provision. The other was ongoing squabbling between the two largest American sports organizations, the National Collegiate Athletic Association (NCAA), which governed a vast empire of university sport, and the Amateur Athletic Union (AAU), which once governed ten Olympic sports: basketball, bobsled, boxing, gymnastics, judo, luge, swimming, track and field, weightlifting, and wrestling. Thus, the two emerging legitimations for federal sports policymaking were sports development and rationalization of sports administration.

The Kennedy administration during the early 1960s took a strong interest in the development of sports opportunities for all Americans. Working with Bud

Wilkinson, director of the President's Council on Physical Fitness at the time, President Kennedy outlined a plan to use his influence as president to initiate a private foundation to finance development of sports programs and facilities (*Congressional Record,* 1964, p. A1451). Earlier, Senator Hubert Humphrey had advocated a similar plan (*Congressional Record,* 1963, pp. 12392–12400 & 22402–22403).

After President Kennedy's assassination, his brother, Attorney General Robert Kennedy, continued to support the plan. He brought General James M. Gavin, chairman of the Board for the consulting firm Arthur D. Little, Inc. together with President Lyndon Johnson on June 12, 1964 to discuss the idea. A month later, President Johnson wrote to General Gavin requesting that he undertake a study that would provide a detailed plan for a national sports foundation. The resulting report was submitted on January 25, 1965, but was never acted upon (Senate Committee on Commerce, 1973, p. 119).

Just as sports development was becoming more significant to the White House and the Senate, the problems with laissez-faire sports governance were becoming increasingly clear. The long-smoldering feud between the NCAA and the AAU erupted into flames in 1960 when the NCAA accused the AAU of inappropriately interfering with games scheduled between college teams and the Swedish National Basketball Team. The dispute escalated as the NCAA subsequently sponsored creation of new national federations to govern three of the sports then governed by the AAU: basketball, gymnastics, and track and field. In effect, the NCAA was directly challenging the AAU's franchise in these sports.

College athletes were pressured to join the new federations, but were declared outlaw (and thus ineligible for national teams) if they did so. Athletes caught between their collegiate sport careers and their international sport aspirations appealed to their legislators for help. In 1965 Vice-President Hubert Humphrey appointed a five-member Sports Arbitration Board (SAB) to mediate the dispute between the two organizations and to find a permanent solution. The SAB completed its work in 1968 (Senate Committee on Commerce, 1968). However, it failed to resolve the dispute. In 1973 the NCAA forbid its athletes from competing in basketball games against a visiting Soviet team, and also instructed its athletes and coaches not to participate in the upcoming track and field meet between the United States and the USSR.

The fiascoes at the Munich Olympics, the historic concerns for sports development, and legislators' frustrations with squabbling between the NCAA and the AAU made the prospect of nationalized sport governance attractive to some legislators. In 1974 the Amateur Athletic Act (which would have nationalized sports governance) passed the Senate. In part to forestall passage of that Act, President Ford created the President's Commission on Olympic Sports in December of 1974. The Commission presented its final report to President Ford in January 1977. That report recommended that a "central sports organization" should be established with authority over a vertically integrated set of sports associations. The recommendations of the Commission served as the basis for the Amateur Sports Act of 1978, which remains the sole piece of federal legislation regulating the structure and conduct of amateur sport in the United States (see Chalip, 1991, 1995 for further discussion). Remaining applications of federal policy occur as a consequence of application to sport of legislation that was not initially targeted at sport.

THE STATUS OF AMERICAN SPORTS: AN OVERVIEW

Sport is an important aspect of American life. It is used in various ways to market consumer products, promote politicians, entertain the nation, and spend leisure time. The popularity of sports in America is partially explained by its prominence in the nation's educational system, and its coverage in the print and electronic media.

Participation

Sports of all kinds are popular in America. While elite athletes participate at the professional and international amateur levels, tens of thousands more participate in school and university athletics, youth leagues, and adult leagues formed by private entrepreneurs, local communities, or independent organizations.

Estimates of sport participation are complicated by the lack of consistent standards for measurement and by the fact that no organization has a mandate to provide the requisite data. Nevertheless, most indicators suggest that the majority of Americans are not sports participants, and that the percentage of Americans participating in sports may be declining. A United Media Enterprises study of leisure participation among Americans in 1983 found that 66 percent did not participate in any individual sport even as frequently as once a week, and 82 percent did not participate in any team sport even as frequently as once a week (Research & Forecasts, Inc., 1983). A 1993 survey sponsored by the President's Council on Physical Fitness and Sport shows that these percentages did not change substantially during the intervening decade. It further shows that approximately 25 percent of adult Americans get no physical exercise whatsoever (President's Council on Physical Fitness and Sport, 1993, p. 68).

The 1993 study is significant because it was the first effort to identify the nature and scope of nonparticipation in physical activity as an American policy problem. Interestingly, respondents defined as inactive (i.e., those exercising less than twice a week) did not conform to any stereotype. Low levels of participation were not attributable to age, weight, or lack of knowledge about physical activity. Rather, lack of time, lack of interest, and conflicting commitments were stated to be the key obstacles to participation. In communities with a high proportion of poor or unemployed persons, the sense that it was unsafe to engage in physical activities (at least outdoors) was mentioned as a constraint by one-third of respondents.

Table 17.1
The Ten Most Popular High School Sports

Males		Females	
Football	928,134	Basketball	412,576
Basketball	530,068	Track & Field	345,700
Baseball	438,846	Volleyball	327,616
Track & Field	419,758	Softball, Fast Pitch	257,118
Soccer	255,538	Soccer	166,173
Wrestling	233,433	Tennis	136,239
Cross Country	162,188	Cross Country	124,700
Tennis	135,702	Swimming & Diving	102,652
Golf	131,207	Field Hockey	53,747
Swimming & Diving	81,328	Softball, Slow Pitch	41,118

Participation in sports or exercise by children and adolescents has also been deemed to be low. The United Media Enterprises study found that 46 percent of teenagers do not get regular physical exercise (Research & Forecasts, Inc, 1983, pp. 30–31). Meanwhile, school sport participation declined throughout the 1980s as a result of program and budget cuts. For example, track and field participation in schools declined by 40 percent between 1978 and 1990 (Track & Field News Editorial Staff, 1991). By 1987, the decline of school sports and physical education programs had become sufficiently acute that the House and Senate passed concurrent resolutions (which lack the force of law) recommending that the trend be reversed. However, the trend seems to have been reversed in the 1990s, with the National Federation of State High School Associations reporting that the 1993–94 academic year boasted the highest rate of participation in high school sports in fifteen years (High School Athletics Participation Highest in 15 Years, 1995). That study reports 3,478,530 male participants, 2,124,755 female participants, and 11,695 participants in coed sports. The top ten high school sports for males and females, and their participation rates are shown in Table 17.1.

The decline in participation during the 1980s was not limited to school-based programs. Market research data show that between 1980 and 1991, rates of participation in eighteen of the twenty most popular physical activities declined (Warnick, 1993). The only two activities to show increases were walking (a 1.5 percent increase) and golf (a 3.2 percent increase). The modest increases in these two activities may reflect the large post–World War II generation reaching middle age. Subsequent data do not suggest that the general decline in physical activity was reversed during the early 1990s (also see President's Council on Physical Fitness and Sport, 1993). The twenty most popular physical activities and their associated rates of participation are shown in Table 17.2. Note, however, that the participation rates are generously estimated, since an individual

Table 17.2
The Twenty Most Popular Physical Activities

Exercise/Fitness Walking	23.2%
Swimming	23.0%
Exercising in Home	18.0%
Bowling	14.5%
Exercising Away From Home	12.0%
Golf	11.5%
Freshwater Fishing	10.3%
Bicycling	10.2%
Tennis	7.0%
Jogging/Running	7.0%
Aerobics	6.5%
Hiking	6.4%
Hunting	5.2%
Racquetball	4.0%
Rollerskating	3.6%
Downhill Skiing	3.3%
Horseback Riding	3.3%
Water Skiing	3.2%
Saltwater Fishing	2.8%
Ice Skating	2.2%

need only have participated once in the preceding year to have been included as a participant.

Two related factors seem to account for the steady decline in aggregate U.S. sports participation. First, the average age of the population is increasing. As Americans age, they tend to shift their consumption from sports to more passive forms of leisure, particularly the arts (Hofacre and Burman, 1992). Second, the amount of leisure time available to Americans has declined steadily since World War II. An array of studies has found that throughout the second half of the twentieth century, Americans have spent more hours working on the job and in the home (Schor, 1991). The amount of leisure time they have available has consequently continued to shrink. By one estimate, Americans work an average of 320 hours more per year than do their counterparts in France or Germany (Schor, 1991, p. 2). Another study estimates that the average amount of leisure time available to Americans declined by 40 percent—from a median of twenty-six hours per week to slightly less than seventeen hours per week—during the fifteen years between 1973 and 1988 (Harris, 1988). Given these trends, it is not likely that U.S. sports participation will reach levels comparable to those reported in other developed nations.

Spectatorship

Professional games in baseball, basketball, and football are telecast nationally and attract millions of viewers on a regular basis. Similarly, colleges and uni-

Table 17.3
Selected Sport Spectatorship, 1992

Sport	Attendance
Major League Baseball	56,852,000
NCAA Basketball - Men's	29,378,000
NCAA Basketball - Women's	3,397,000
National Basketball Association	18,609,000
College Football	36,199,000
National Football League	17,784,000
National Hockey League	13,786,000

Source: Statistical Abstract, 1994.

versities have their basketball and football games telecast regionally and nationally to millions of viewers. Television is both a means of bringing live sporting events into the homes of millions of Americans and of providing vast sums of money to professional sports entrepreneurs and colleges and universities. Producers of consumer goods therefore are willing to spend millions of dollars to advertise their products during televised sporting contests. This is especially true of sports events that are capable of commanding the attention of the nation, such as the Olympic Games, the Super Bowl, the World Series, and the NCAA basketball championship tournament.

Although television and radio provide access to sporting events for sports fans, millions attend the events in person. In 1992 it was estimated that American sports fans expended $5.5 billion for admission to sporting events. Table 17.3 lists attendance for selected sports.

Economics

Much attention is given to the amount of money that professional sports attract from investors and the exorbitant salaries of professional athletes. For example, franchises in the National Football League and major league baseball are valued well in excess of $100 million. Professional hockey and basketball teams are worth from $30 million to more than $100 million depending on the size of their host city, ownership of their arena and lease arrangements, and television contracts. Players' salaries average more than $1 million annually in baseball and basketball, and more than $500,000 in football. The top players in professional golf and tennis also earn in excess of $1 million. Many players, especially star athletes and those who play in the larger cities, can add substantial sums to their income through product endorsements.

During the 1980s, several efforts were made to estimate the size of the American sports industry (e.g., Comte and Stogel, 1990; Koch, 1986; Sandomir,

1988). The estimates are similar to one another, perhaps because the numbers are derived from the same industry figures. Nevertheless, the data are not firm. The United States has no systematic system for measuring or reporting economic sports data, no agency or organization assigned the task of monitoring the economic performance of sport, and no standard guidelines for measuring sport impacts. Impact assessments are further complicated by unresolved definitional problems. For example, do all sporting goods count or only those used in sport? A large volume of sports gear, such as apparel, is used in nonsport settings. Most estimates seek to delete nonsport uses. Furthermore, what counts as sport? For example, should hunting, fishing, or exercise be included? In most estimates, all of these are included.

Despite obvious limitations in the data, several consistent conclusions emerge. First, sports seem to account for slightly more than 1 percent of the United States' gross national product (GNP), ranking it as one of the twenty-five largest industries in the country. Its most substantial impact on GNP, roughly 32 percent, is generated by sports participation. This includes construction expenditures and fees for participation in sports clubs (e.g., golf, tennis) and leagues (e.g., bowling), sports tourism (e.g., ski holidays), and health clubs. The second largest impact is made by sporting goods, roughly 30 percent. Interestingly, sport as spectator entertainment accounts for less than 25 percent of sport's impact on the GNP. This includes spectator receipts, concession and souvenir sales, media rights fees, advertising, and corporate sponsorships.

Industry data suggest that the sport industry will continue to expand (Rosner, 1989). Projections are optimistic, predicting that the industry will grow faster than the economy in general. Facility construction, sporting goods, advertising, and sponsorships are projected to be the dominant growth categories.

INTERNATIONAL ASPECTS OF AMERICAN SPORT

Each of the professional sports leagues of baseball, basketball, football, and hockey has an international dimension. Their international activities serve one or more of three basic functions: player recruitment and development, marketing, and franchise location. For example, major league baseball has long used Latin America as a source of player talent, and has sponsored leagues in the off-season in the Dominican Republic, Venezuela, and Puerto Rico for player development purposes. It also has a formal relationship with a minor league in Mexico and has recently begun association with an Australian league.

The professional leagues also sponsor tours and exhibition games that have as their primary purpose the promotion of their sport to new markets internationally. A team of all-star baseball players annually travels to Japan to compete in a series of games against Japanese professionals. The National Football League (NFL) sends two of its teams to England during its pre-season to play an exhibition game. From 1991 to 1992 the NFL also sponsored the World League of American Football, which had franchises in England, Spain, Mexico,

Germany, and the United States. This league was more than a minor league for player development. It was intended to develop an interest in American football and perhaps pave the way for the NFL to expand beyond American borders. The National Basketball Association's (NBA) top players comprised the United States Olympic team in 1992. The "Dream Team" gave the NBA international exposure.

Such exposure provides a means to market the sport internationally. Each league has a marketing office that is responsible for selling and controlling the marketing rights to a wide range of memorabilia such as sweatshirts, caps and other sportswear, videos, sports equipment, cards containing players' pictures and autographs, publications, and many other items. Although the revenues obtained from these sales are a small percentage of the total revenues generated by the teams, they are growing and have the potential to increase much more. These marketing activities also create and maintain an interest in the sports and may open the markets to new franchises when the leagues are willing to consider international competition.

Although the National Hockey League (NHL) has its origins in Canada and maintains its league offices in that country, eighteen of twenty-six teams were located in the United States in 1994. It, like baseball, has minor leagues with teams in the United States and Canada. The National Basketball Association will have a franchise in Canada in 1996, and major league baseball has had two franchises in Canada for many years. Although Canadian law prohibits the National Football League from locating in Canada, the Canadian Football League began operations in the United States in 1994. The future may see the NFL, the NBA, and other leagues expand internationally. Existing leagues in other countries (such as basketball in Europe) pose obstacles to such expansion, but international competition by the year 2000 is not out of the question.

Golf and tennis also are internationalized. American players compete in prestigious tournaments overseas, as well as in their own American tour events. In fact, players move fairly easily across national borders in most sports. Many players from Latin America are members of major league baseball teams; American baseball players compete in the Japanese baseball leagues; American basketball players compete in the European leagues; and although NHL players tend to be mostly American and Canadian, many talented Europeans are finding their way into the NHL.

Intercollegiate sports programs in the United States provide strong coaching and facilities in selected sports. In many instances, scholarships are available to cover educational expenses, and talented athletes, including foreign athletes, are heavily recruited. Although reliable figures on the number of foreign athletes at American universities are not available, foreign athletes do participate extensively, particularly in swimming, volleyball, soccer, and track and field. Some also come to the United States to train with elite club programs, particularly in swimming and track and field. Many of these athletes become popular with local fans of their club or university teams, and are cheered by those fans even when they compete for their home countries against the United States in international competition. Nevertheless, the expenditure of American resources on the training of elite foreign competitors has continued to be a matter of popular debate.

GOVERNMENT AND PROFESSIONAL SPORTS POLICY

Until the 1970s and 1980s, American sports history was characterized by the myth of the "purity of sport" (Johnson, 1978), which is the belief that sport is merely "fun and games." Neither its business aspects nor its use as a political tool was fully acknowledged. Indeed, policymakers in Congress and in the courts made decisions (or refused to make decisions) that gave sport a privileged status among American businesses.

American sports policy is developed primarily within the context of American public policy toward business (the private sector). Occasionally, however, Congress singles out sports issues for special treatment. Legal issues that define principles of policy within sport also are brought to the courts for adjudication. Therefore, although no government entity is exclusively responsible for administering American sports, and although it would be misleading to speak of sports policy as if there existed a coherent, systematic approach to sports guided by ideology or some other organizing principle, there is an ever increasing number of laws and judicial decisions that comprise what can be described as American sports policy and sports law (Appenzeller, 1985; Berry and Wong, 1993; Weistart and Lowell, 1979). This is true with regard to amateur athletics as well as professional sports.

American sports policy relative to professional sports can be organized by examining three areas of public policy and law: antitrust law, labor law, and other issues.

Antitrust Issues in Professional Sports

American antitrust laws seek to prevent businesses from engaging in various practices that limit competition, create unfair advantage for one corporation relative to others, or prevent entry by new firms into an existing industry.

American professional sports are dominated by the four team sports of baseball, basketball, football, and hockey. These team sports are organized by leagues. Each league grants a limited number of franchises to team owners. The owners collectively run the league, which is managed by a commissioner. The commissioner is hired by the owners but in theory has vast powers. In truth, the powers of the commissioner are only as great as the owners permit.

Sports leagues attempt to control all aspects of the game, from playing rules and team schedules, to the location and number of league members and labor relations, to facility standards and the marketing of team insignias and sports paraphernalia. In the early history of American sports leagues, the leagues succeeded in exercising their control, especially over the players. This was primarily a result of a series of court decisions that culminated in a Supreme Court ruling, *Federal Baseball Club of Baltimore, Inc. v. National League*, in 1922.

The court ruled that baseball was not engaged in interstate commerce and therefore was not regulated by federal antitrust laws. By extension, other sports were similarly treated. This permitted baseball's "reserve clause" to remain in effect unchallenged for another three decades. The reserve clause made players the chattel of their teams. Players could not voluntarily leave the employ of their teams for another team. Team owners controlled players' movement in the sport's labor market. Players could be sold or traded for other players. In 1946 major league baseball banned eighteen players who, after "jumping" to the Mexican League sought to return to play in the United States. Although one of the players was able to muster a successful challenge to the ban in the lower federal courts, the player and major league baseball settled out of court. Facing eight other lawsuits in 1951, major league baseball sought legislation to codify an antitrust exemption for all sports leagues. Congress failed to act on these legislative proposals in the expectation that the courts would rule against baseball. However, the Supreme Court upheld baseball's exemption in 1953 (*Toolson v. New York Yankees, Inc.*) and again in 1972 (*Flood v. Kuhn*).

Other professional sports leagues that developed in the United States followed the model of baseball. Players' unions occasionally were formed but did not withstand the league's union-busting tactics. With weak unions and a Congress sympathetic to the arguments of team owners and league representatives, those who challenged the practices of the sports leagues and their antitrust exemption were forced to look to the judicial system for relief. With the advent of television and the telecasting of sports contests across the nation, the business aspect of sport and its interstate nature were difficult to deny. Judicial challenges by athletes in these other sports were soon successful. Beginning in 1957, the courts refused to recognize a need for antitrust exemptions in professional football, hockey, basketball, golf, and bowling.

Inexplicably, the Supreme Court has continued to rule that it will not deny an antitrust exemption for baseball. If the exemption is to be removed, Congress should be the decision-making arena. The baseball strike that brought a premature end to the 1994 baseball season renewed the baseball players' association's attack on the antitrust exemption, but with little effect.

With the loss of their antitrust exemption, sports leagues have had to seek congressional assistance when their business practices conflict with the nation's regulatory system (Johnson, 1979, September). For example, sports leagues have created a monopoly for national telecast and broadcast rights to their teams' games. They sell these rights to the nation's television companies for hundreds of millions of dollars. If each team retained control over its telecast rights and sold them to interested networks, some teams would make a handsome profit, others would earn a modest profit, and still others would receive nothing or very little. The sum total would be much less than that received by pooling their rights into one package. The pooling of rights would be a violation of antitrust laws, but Congress granted sports leagues an antitrust exemption for this purpose in 1961. Indeed, the Copyright Act of 1976 explicitly extends federal copyright protection to live sports broadcasts. This grants the team owners the exclusive rights to "perform" them "publicly" (Hochberg, 1985, p. 165).

Similarly, Congress has granted antitrust exemptions to permit league mergers in football and basketball. The consequences are tighter control of the number of league franchises and their location than if rival leagues were competing for markets and fan attention. Thus, local governments often find themselves in a bidding war to retain or to obtain a sports franchise. The team owners can virtually "blackmail" a locality for its presence. The ransom is usually a publicly funded facility for the team to play in, a lease with generous terms (often requiring the payment of token rent and granting most revenue to the team), and frequently, a variety of tax concessions. Similarly, the leagues have imposed extremely high entry fees upon new franchises, when the leagues determine they are prepared to expand.

The United States Congress has been reluctant to take an aggressive posture toward regulating American professional sports. Its activities generally have been limited to congressional hearings. Individual congressmen will introduce legislation hostile to the sports leagues when a league has somehow slighted a city in that congressman's district. The congressman then will seek hearings on some aspect of league operations at which the bill is directed. Often this is baseball's antitrust exemption, but may include league rules concerning franchise relocation, tax issues related to professional sports, or the league's labor relations. The goal is to pressure the league to treat the city in the congressman's district more generously, not actually to enact the legislation.

In sum, although sports leagues—with the exception of baseball—are now considered businesses and theoretically are regulated by the same laws with which other American businesses must cope, certain aspects of their league operations do enjoy special treatment.

Labor Laws

American labor laws demand fair treatment of labor by industry. American workers generally enjoy the right of free movement from one job to another, the right to a safe and hazard-free workplace, and the right to have elected labor representatives negotiate a collective bargaining agreement with management concerning compensation and working conditions.

As noted above, the labor history of American sports leagues has been dominated by management. This has changed since the players' unions have been able to establish themselves on a permanent basis and since they have been able to obtain successful rulings from the federal courts. Although a balance has been achieved, the relationship remains a stormy and antagonistic one. Essentially, the players' associations have been able to establish a collective bargaining framework within which to negotiate salaries and players' rights.

Consequently, players' salaries are very high compared to the average salaries of American citizens. As noted above, average salaries in baseball and basketball exceed $1 million and in football are in excess of $500,000. Salaries are lower in football and hockey because free movement only recently was won for the 1993 season in football, and hockey players still lack the freedom that baseball and basketball players enjoy. Star athletes in baseball and basketball can make as much as $3 million a year. A trend appeared to be emerging in 1992 in which players guarantee a certain percentage of the leagues' revenues in exchange for a salary cap (i.e., a limit is placed on each team's payroll). A salary cap has been accepted in football and basketball and was a matter for negotiation in 1994–95 in the other two sports.

The National Labor Relations Board (NLRB) oversees labor-management relations in the United States and has authority over labor-management relations in the sports industry. However, it often takes the NLRB many months, if not years, to resolve individual cases brought to it. In the case of an athlete, one's playing career (or at least one's peak earning years) may be over in a matter of years. Thus, the NLRB has not been a fruitful arena in which to take grievances. Players and their representatives have instead turned to the courts. The issues have been many and complex, but the most important ones have centered on a player's right to sell his services to the highest bidder.

In sum, labor relations in the sports leagues are controlled by collective bargaining agreements negotiated between the players and team owners. These agreements provide the framework for determining compensation and movement of players and are governed by the National Labor Relations Act.

Other Policy Issues

A number of other issues have been the focus of congressional inquiry, federal agency scrutiny, and judicial decision making. These include issues related to tax policy, immigration laws, sports gambling, copyright protection, migration of sports events from network television to cable and pay television,[2] game violence, player eligibility, and franchise relocation. Parties to disputes in several of these issues have attempted to bring federal antitrust laws to bear, but in most cases unsuccessfully. As a result, it is useful to treat these issues as separate from antitrust issues.

American tax law is quite complex. Corporations, as well as individuals, are required to pay taxes. However, the law treats corporations differently than individuals and treats different types of businesses differently. Tax laws are frequently used for regulatory purposes as well as revenue generation.

Before 1976, American tax law treated team owners very favorably. Owners could claim the monetary losses of their teams in calculating their own individual tax liability, permitting them to reduce their taxable income. When combined with other favorable treatment (i.e. treatment of capital gains when a team is sold, depreciation of player contracts), the sports franchise was an effective tax shelter for wealthy owners.

Over the objections of the Internal Revenue Service, Congress changed the tax law in 1976—as part of a larger tax reform effort—as it relates to the sports industry. In effect, the changes sought to make professional team ownership less attractive as a tax shelter and to undermine the tax advantages of selling a sports team.

In addition to tax policies related to team ownership, federal tax policy has been used by local and state governments to encourage the flow of private money into publicly funded stadium projects. Prior to 1986, individual taxpayers could receive tax-free income from industrial revenue bonds issued by local governments. These bonds were a very popular infrastructure financing mechanism for local governments during the 1970s and 1980s. However, the federal government removed this tax benefit in 1986. In doing so, Congress exempted six cities that were contemplating building stadiums for professional sports teams. As a result, these cities were able to take advantage of this tax policy even after its termination.

Whereas major league teams tend to be located in the larger cities of the nation, minor league teams tend to be located in smaller communities across the country. The teams are closely identified with cities (and states), which often provide the funding for construction of their stadiums and arenas. Sports stadiums and arenas for professional teams at the major league level can cost in excess of $100 million, and only rarely are privately built.

The rationale commonly used to justify public funding of sports facilities is that sporting events attract spectators who spend their money in the community, thus recouping the public investment through increased sales and income taxes as a result of job growth and other economic development. This logic is intensely debated by those who argue that the public investment is never recouped and that public tax dollars should be spent on higher priority items. Another justification of public funding is that a sports team brings a common identity to citizens of a community and promotes community pride. Thus, professional sports, as well as amateur sports, are an important economic development tool for many communities and are used to improve the quality of life of local citizens. Consequently, federal money often finds its way to local and state governments to support the construction of stadiums and arenas in various ways including tax writeoffs, tax credits, and direct grants.

Congress has demonstrated an inclination to be vocal about protecting the American public's access to live professional sporting events, but it has failed to pass permanent legislation accomplishing that. Congress has reacted to unpopular franchise relocations and to television blackouts of football games with numerous legislative proposals and congressional hearings, but no effective legislation. In 1976 the United States House of Representatives created the House Select Committee on Professional Sports ostensibly in response to instability in the major professional team sports. Many believed that the real agenda was to coerce major league baseball to return to the nation's capital, which it abandoned with the relocation of the Washington Senators franchise to Arlington, Texas. Despite extensive hearings and a major report, the Select Committee failed to rally support for legislative action.

In the late 1960s football fans became increasingly vocal critics of the National Football League's policy of "blacking out" telecasts of home games that were not sold out. Congress reacted with temporary legislation in 1973, when the NFL blacked out the 1971 and 1972 Superbowls. The legislation banned blackouts of games sold out seventy-two hours before game time for three years. With the expiration of the legislation in 1975 and the failure to replace it with new legislation, the NFL was again unregulated. In 1976 Congress passed the Copyright Act, which gave the sports leagues the federal copyright protection for the games they produced. However, it also allowed cable stations to retransmit sports broadcasts in return for a token royalty payment.

Some increasingly aggressive cable television companies retransmitted the leagues' sports broadcasts without the leagues' permission and without any significant compensation. The Federal Communications Commission (FCC) had the responsibility of regulating cable companies. Friction between cable television and network broadcasters and sports leagues intensified in the 1970s and 1980s. The courts, rather than the FCC, became the ultimate arbiter in many of the disputes. By the 1990s, the sports leagues embraced cable television by entering into lucrative season packages with them. Today, the issue once again is the extent of "free access" the public will have to televised sporting events. The fear that prime sporting events such as the World Series and the Superbowl will migrate to pay television raises the specter of some type of federal regulation.

AMATEUR SPORT

A number of policy issues impact amateur sports in the United States, with different levels of importance. These policy areas include those that are financial, regulatory, organizational, and a number of miscellaneous issues.

Financial Support

With the exception of sports facility construction during the Great Depression, the federal government has resisted the direct funding of amateur sport. When federal monies are forthcoming, they are typically routed through the United States Olympic Committee (USOC).

Pursuant to recommendations from the President's Commission on Olympic Sports, early drafts of the Amateur Sports Act (in 1978) included provisions for a one-time appropriation of $30 million to the USOC. However, that appropriation was so controversial that it was deleted prior to the bill's passage. Nevertheless, a last minute amendment to a continuing appropriations resolution that same year authorized $16 million to fund the USOC training centers. However, those funds were not subsequently appropriated. It took the American boycott of the 1980 Olympic Games in Moscow to generate a federal appropriation for the USOC. In order to secure USOC cooperation with the boycott, the Carter administration supported and obtained for the USOC a one-time appropriation of $10.2 million.

Since 1981, the USOC has lobbied for additional funds in the form of a tax checkoff. Under provisions of that plan, taxpayers would be able to designate $1 from their income tax refund to be paid to the USOC. However, bills providing for a USOC checkoff have failed.

The USOC has been more successful at the state level. By 1993 it had obtained a tax checkoff provision in nine states: California, Colorado, Delaware, Idaho, Iowa, Kentucky, Pennsylvania, Rhode Island, and Virginia. That program generated over $2 million during the 1989–92 quadrennium (United States Olympic Committee, 1993, p. 43).

The USOC also developed the Olympic Instant Lottery Program, a two-game package of instant scratch-off tickets that it makes available to thirty-five state lotteries. The package gives the state lottery the right to use the USOC's fund-raising logo. The amount of money raised via this program is not publicly specified by the USOC, since it is not provided as a unique line item in any publicly available USOC financial statement.

During the 1980s and 1990s, the USOC has successfully obtained two sources of federal funding: the Combined Federal Campaign and the Commemorative Coin Program. The Combined Federal Campaign provides the opportunity for federal employees to donate to the USOC via a payroll deduction. That program has generated more than 10,000 gifts per year, totaling almost $2 million during the 1989–92 quadrennium (United States Olympic Committee, 1993, p. 43).

Beginning in 1982, Congress authorized the United States Mint to produce Olympic Games Commemorative Coins. The number of coins to be produced each year is limited by the legislation. The legislation includes a sunset provision such that production of coins expires at the end of the next Olympic year. Thus, the legislation has had to be passed again each quadrennium. In 1992 the Act (PL 102-390) limits production and sale to the years 1995 and 1996. It specifies that all profits from sales of Olympic Commemorative Coins shall be paid equally to the Atlanta Committee for the Olympic Games and the USOC.

Scrutiny of USOC balance sheets suggests that income from the commemorative coins has declined during the first three quadrenniums. During the 1981–84 quadrennium, the USOC reported revenues from the coin program of $33,867,860. During the 1985–88 quadrennium, the USOC reported $25,501,538. During the 1989–92 quadrennium, the USOC realized $9,718,000. The decline does not seem to be due to changes in accounting practices, since the USOC's financial statements report no such change. Yet the decline would seem to be a basis for concern to USOC strategists, since the USOC's own projections estimate income of $75 million from the coins during the 1997–2000 quadrennium (USOC, 1988).

Regulatory Issues

Federal regulation of amateur sports has been limited to applications of laws not specifically targeted at sports. These include tort liability, contract laws, agency law, criminal law, and constitutional law. These laws have found application to sport as they have been applied by the courts. Since the American judicial system works on the basis of legal precedent, a substantial body of case law has developed over the years (see Clement, 1988, for an overview).

One piece of federal legislation has had a uniquely pervasive impact on the practice of amateur sport in the United States: Title IX of the Education Amendments of 1972. Title IX states that "no person in the United States shall, on the basis of sex, be excluded from participation in, be denied the benefits of, or be subjected to discrimination under any education program or activity receiving Federal financial assistance." Although Congress did not initially favor including sports programs under Title IX enforcement, the Department of Health, Education, and Welfare contended that sports are integral components of education. Thus, by 1974 the agency required sports programs to meet Title IX provisions. In a 1993 decision applying Title IX, the 10th Circuit of the U.S. Court of Appeals ruled that the law requires that there be no disparity between the percentage of women enrolled at a school and the percentage of athletes who are women (Herwig, 1993). The decision suggests that the courts will interpret Title IX as requiring schools to provide sports opportunities equally for men and women, and that participation ratios will be an acceptable criterion for determining equity.

Organizational Issues

The Amateur Sports Act (PL 95-606) is the only piece of federal legislation that specifies conditions for the conduct of amateur sport. It was passed into law in 1978, consequent on recommendations of the President's Commission on Olympic Sports. It is limited in application to sports that are included on the programs of the Olympic and Pan American Games. It focuses on elite, rather than grass-roots, sports, and it is concerned primarily with rationalizing the administrative structure of amateur sports rather than with mass development of opportunities to do sports.

The Act gives the USOC authority to establish national goals for amateur sports and to encourage attainment of those goals. The USOC is given exclusive jurisdiction over U.S. participation in the Olympic and Pan American Games. The USOC is expected to promote amateur sports and physical fitness, including for women, the handicapped, and racial and ethnic minorities. The USOC is to encourage sports research and to coordinate provision of technical information about sport.

In addition, the USOC must provide for dispute resolution in amateur sports. It is required to maintain provisions to swiftly resolve any dispute involving the opportunity of an athlete, coach, trainer, manager, administrator, or official to participate in international competition. Before the USOC may alter its constitution or bylaws, it must publish a notice of pending changes. Prior to adopting any amendment, interested persons must have at least sixty days (after publication of the notice) to submit their views. The USOC is given the power to determine which sports organization will serve as the national governing body for each Olympic and Pan American sport in the United States. Procedures for doing so are published, as are procedures for handling complaints and for overturning franchises.

The USOC is given exclusive rights to the Olympic symbol, to the title "United States Olympic Committee," to the words "Olympic," "Olympiad," and to the phrase "Citius, Altius, Fortius." The USOC is given the right to allow contributors to use the Olympic symbols. It is required to submit annually to the president and to each House of Congress a report detailing its operations for the preceding year. The report is to include a statement of receipts and expenditures, as well as a description of USOC activities and accomplishments. However, no government agency provides specific oversight. In fact, no person or agency is charged with responsibility for evaluating (or even reading) the report.

The Act specifies requirements for franchise holders (i.e., National Federations, called "national governing bodies" by the Act). Each is required to be autonomous. (Thus, the AAU was forced to drop its franchise in the sports it governed.) A national governing body must be willing to enter into binding arbitration for disputes if the USOC requires such arbitration. Its membership requirements must be nonrestrictive and must provide equal opportunity without regard to race, color, religion, national origin, or sex (except in the case where there are separate male and female programs in a sport). A national governing body must give 20 percent of its governance to athletes (defined as currently active competitors or persons who represented the United States as athletes within the preceding decade) and must provide for direct representation on the board for other organizations conducting programs of sufficient caliber to generate international class competitors in the sport. No officer of a national governing body may be an officer of another national governing body. The amateur criteria established by a national governing body may not be more restrictive than the criteria of its international federation. Each national governing body must provide procedures for resolution of member grievances.

Several duties are delegated to national governing bodies. First, each national governing body is responsible for promoting its sport in the United States, including among women and the handicapped. It must provide coordination among the various organizations with programs in its sport. It must encourage research on its sport and coordinate dissemination of technical information. It must allow an athlete to compete unless the athlete does not meet requirements specified in the law. It must promptly review all requests for competition sanctions and grant such sanctions unless the competition fails to meet requirements specified in the law.

Restricted competitions (e.g., those for students or members of the armed forces) are exempted from USOC and national governing body control. However, any organization sponsoring an international competition must obtain a sanction from the appropriate national governing body.

The President's Council on Physical Fitness and Sport

The President's Council on Physical Fitness and Sport is the oldest and most visible federal agency with responsibility for sports in the United States. However, because it was created by Executive Order (in 1956), it has no legislative standing. Consequently, it exists only with the continued support of congressional budget committees. It is housed in the executive branch under the Department of Health and Human Services.

The Council has been meagerly funded since its inception. Its budget did not exceed $1 million until 1983, and between 1991 and 1995, its budget averaged $1.35 million—only $.05 per capita. The Republican congressional majority elected in 1994 has proposed eliminating the Council. In response, the Council's administration has studied alternative sources of funding, including licensing of its seal.

The Council has no regulatory authority. Its primary functions are information dissemination and fitness promotion. In 1994 its publications list included five informational brochures (one dating from 1963 and none published after 1990), one quarterly bibliography, and one summary of a 1985 youth fitness survey. In the 1990s the Council's primary promotional activity has been ''The President's Challenge,'' a national physical fitness testing program for children ages six to seventeen that is administered by schools that choose to participate. The program consists of five fitness tests (a one-mile run/walk, sit-ups, a sit-and-reach, pull-ups, and a shuttle run). Awards are based on the percentile rankings that students attain on the five tests. The Council estimates that during the 1992–93 school year, approximately 28,000 schools participated and that over 2 million awards were distributed.

The Council also supports the Presidential Sports Award, which it first developed in 1972. The program is administered by the Amateur Athletic Union. The award is available to any individual over six years of age who meets the standards for quantity of sport participation. An individual can claim the award by submitting a self-report log showing that he or she has met the standards in one or more of the sixty-seven sports covered. There is a $6 charge per award.

The Council occasionally seeks to exert some influence on policymaking. Its staff analyses between 1972 and 1974 paved the way for creation of the President's Commission on Olympic Sports. At the end of 1993, as the Clinton administration's health agenda gained momentum, the Council sponsored a two-day strategic planning forum intended to link exercise to the emerging policy initiatives. However, the forum had no discernible policy impact.

Other Federal Involvements with Amateur Sport

Since its inception in 1962, the Peace Corps has sent teachers to developing nations. Some have undertaken coaching duties. It is Peace Corps policy to send volunteers only when the host country requests them and only for the purposes specified by the host country. Throughout the 1970s and 1980s, some countries requested coaches. However, the Peace Corps' mission is not specifically tied to sport, and provision of coaches remains a low priority within the organization.

During the Cold War, the United States Information Agency (USIA) sought to employ sports as a foreign relations tool. In order to promote goodwill toward the United States, the USIA developed the Sports America Program which sent coaches and sport administrators overseas to give clinics and seminars. With the end of the Cold War, the Sports America Program has been scaled back.

The U.S. State Department maintains a sports desk in its International Organizations Department. The sports desk provides liaison and support to the American athletic community on issues involving international travel, events, and competition. It is staffed by a single officer and retains a relatively weak profile within the organization.

Policymakers also have sought to use sport as a social intervention. However, its utility as a policy tool has not yet been favorably recognized. The Crime Bill brought before Congress in 1994 (HR 3355) sought to authorize $125 million for after-school activities (including sport programs) that would give children and adolescents an alternative to gang participation. An additional $50 million was earmarked for the USOC, and $40 million for nighttime sport leagues designed to keep at-risk youth off the streets. That bill failed. Opponents vociferously attacked its sport provisions, ridiculing the very conception of sport as a social intervention. Nevertheless, this initiative is significant because it is the first time that the legislature has seriously considered the possibility that sport could be incorporated into the domestic agenda.

POLICY GOALS AND EVALUATION

Despite the importance of sports to Americans, there has never been a demand for institutionalized, direct government participation in the world of sport. The nation's values and beliefs dictate that federal policy toward sport be fragmented and indirect. Sport is viewed as a tool to achieve other objectives, be it improved health, lower crime, national pride, community identity, or ideological advancement. As such, it has been in the government's interest to ensure the integrity of sport. Although government intervention does occur occasionally, it generally is in reaction to demands from specific interests embroiled in a dispute or in response to public demand for protection from an industry practice deemed to be injurious to the public interest. Consequently, there is no federal agency responsible for professional or amateur sports and no specific subsidy to the industry.

The business of sport, for the most part, is left to its managers and entrepreneurs, who tend to be mostly white males and have historically displayed little concern for the public interest or for their athletes. Congress on occasion has been asked to protect the public's access to live sporting events (i.e., the franchise relocation issue and network broadcasting), and the courts have adjudicated numerous cases involving athletes' rights.

The business of sport has been concerned mostly with the training and control of elite athletes, while mass participation in sport has been left to the schools, local government, and nonprofit organizations. Although the opportunity for enjoying sports is widespread in America, it is not universal and participation rates reflect that fact.

Opportunities for government intervention in amateur sports occurred on several occasions in the past decades, but the federal government has yet to be persuaded that it should be significantly involved in their regulation or administration. Throughout the twentieth century, amateur sports found their way into federal agendas only when they could clearly be linked to other policy concerns. Thus, during the First and Second World Wars, sport was of some policy concern because it seemed to have the potential to improve the fitness of youth and, thereby, the nation's military preparedness. This concern resurfaced during the Cold War. However, the President's Council on Physical Fitness and Sport was the only tangible policy outcome.

Nevertheless, the Cold War did serve to keep amateur sport on the policymakers' agendas. The propaganda value of sport was too pronounced to ignore. Thus, the defeats of U.S. athletes at the hands of athletes from communist nations propelled formulation and eventual passage of the Amateur Sports Act. Yet that Act simply delegates authority for amateur sport to a private organization. Concerns for competitive excellence were insufficient to legitimate direct federal involvement in amateur sport.

With the end of the Cold War, those who might advocate federal support for amateur sport have lost their key legitimation. Consequently, they are seeking to link it to currently popular domestic agendas, such as health promotion and crime prevention. As a policy legitimation, this strategy would seem to be appropriate. It is useful to remember that sport development was first supported in federal programs that were designed to alleviate the effects of the Great Depression. Nevertheless, current federal efforts to balance the budget and to shift responsibility for domestic concerns to state governments are likely to thwart efforts to enlarge the federal role in amateur sport.

The Amateur Sports Act requires the USOC to promote participation in sports. However, the USOC focuses on the development and support of elite competitors. Meanwhile, sport participation in the United States is low and declining. That fact has yet to prompt any serious policy concern. From the standpoint of U.S. policymakers, amateur sport would not seem to warrant any federal commitment.

Those who seek government support for amateur sport have failed to make a persuasive case. Assertions of sport's role in health or in crime prevention have simply not been credible. There is nothing about sport that makes it intrinsically appropriate for addressing the nation's health or crime problems. It might be true that sport programs could be designed to promote wellness or to enhance participants' moral development, but those outcomes would require programs that look vastly different from the ones currently provided (cf. Chalip, Thomas, and Voyle, 1992). The overwhelming majority of American sports programs accentuate competitive excellence, not social or psychological benefits (cf. Devereaux, 1976; Gould, 1987; Webb, 1969). Thus, there is little prospect that amateur sport in the United States will attain the level of policy significance that it has acquired in other Western democracies.

NOTES

1. For several decades, the United States Congress has attempted to federally regulate boxing or to prohibit it as a sport. Despite numerous hearings and investigations, no legislation has been enacted. Boxing is regulated at the level of state government, as is horse racing.

2. In addition to free national and local network telecasts available to all citizens, telecasts via cable and satellite are available to households in certain areas (usually only in more densely populated areas) for a monthly fee. Such "pay television" offers a much wider array of programs and services as compared to free telecasts.

REFERENCES

Appenzeller, H. (1985). Sports and law: contemporary issues. Charlottesville, Va.: Michie Co.

Applin, A. G. (1968). National legislation for health, physical education, and recreation: The Schwert bills, H.R. 10606 and H.R. 1074—A study of why they failed. Unpublished master's thesis, Pennsylvania State University, State College, Pennsylvania.

Berry, R., and Wong, G. (1993). Law and business of the sports industries: common issues in amateur and professional sports. Westport, Conn.: Praeger.

Chalip, L. (1991). Sport and the state: The case of the United States. In F. Landry, M. Landry, and M. Yerles (eds.), Sport . . . the third millennium (pp. 243–250). Sainte-Foy, Quebec: Les Presses de l'Universite Laval.

Chalip, L. (1995). Policy analysis in sport management. Journal of Sport Management, 9, 1–13.

Chalip, L., Thomas, D., and Voyle, J. (1992). Sport, recreation and well-being. In D. Thomas and A. Veno (eds.), Psychology and social change (pp. 132–156). Palmerston North, New Zealand: Dunmore Press.

Chaos, tragedy overshadowed Munich athletic feats. (1972, September 12). *New York Times,* pp. C1, C4.

Clement, A. (1988). *Law in sport and physical activity.* Indianapolis, Ind.: Benchmark.

Clumpner, R. A. (1976). American government involvement in sport 1848–1973. Unpublished doctoral dissertation, University of Alberta, Edmonton, Alberta.

Comte, E., and Stogel, C. (1990, January 1). Sports: A $63.1 billion industry. *Sporting News,* pp. 60–61.

Daley, A. (1952, June 10). Sports of the Times, *New York Times,* p. C3.

Department of State (n.d.). *Tours completed from beginning of program in 1954 through June, 1958, fy–1955 through fy–1958.* Unpublished report, U.S. State Department, Washington, D.C.

Devereaux, E. (1976). Backyard versus little league baseball: The impoverishment of children's games. In D. Landers (ed.), *Social problems in athletics* (pp. 37–56). Urbana, Ill.: University of Illinois Press.

Drew, G. (1944). A historical study of the concern of the federal government for the physical fitness of non-age youth with reference to the schools, 1790–1941. Unpublished doctoral dissertation, University of Pittsburgh, Pittsburgh, Pennsylvania.

Gould, D. (1987). Understanding attrition in children's sport. In D. Gould and M.R. Weiss (eds.), *Advances in pediatric sport sciences* (pp. 61–86). Champaign, Ill.: Human Kinetics.

Harris, L. (1988). *Americans and the arts.* New York: Louis Harris and Associates.

Herwig, C. (1993, July 9). Title IX ruling called monumental. *USA Today,* p. 1C.

High School Athletics Participation Highest in 15 years. (1995, Winter). *NASPE News,* p. 7.

Hochberg, P. (1985). Property rights in sports broadcasting: the fundamental issue. In A. Johnson and J. Frey (eds.), *Government and sport* (pp. 162–170). Totowa, N.J.: Rowman & Allanheld.

Hofacre, S., and Burman, T. K. (1992). Demographic changes in the U.S. into the 21st century: Their impact on sport marketing. *Sport Marketing Quarterly 1*(1), 31–36.

Johnson, A. (1978). Public sports policy: An introduction. *American Behavioral Scientist, 21*(3).

Johnson, A. (1979, September). Congress and professional sports: 1951–1978. *Annals of the American Academy of Political and Social Science 445:* 102–115.

Johnson, A., and Frey, J. (1985). *Government and sport: the public policy issues.* Totowa, N.J.: Rowman & Allanheld.

Koch, J. (1986). The economic reality of amateur sports organizations. *Indiana Law Journal, 61*(9), 1–20.

Krauss, H., and Hirschland, R. P. (1953, December). Muscular fitness and health. *Journal of the American Association for Health, Physical Education and Recreation,* pp. 17–19.

President's Commission on Olympic Sports. (1977). *Final report of the President's Commission on Olympic Sports* (Vols. 1–2). Washington, D.C.: U.S. Government Printing Office.

President's Council on Physical Fitness and Sports. (1993). *Strategic planning forum* (Vols. 1–2). Reston, Va.: Transcription Services.

Research and Forecasts, Inc. (1983). Where does the time go? The United Media Enterprises report on leisure in America. New York: The Newspaper Enterprises Association.

Riordan, J. (1987). Soviet sports diplomacy towards neighbouring and developing nations. Unpublished manuscript, Department of Linguistics and International Studies, University of Surrey, Guilford, England.

Rosner, D. (1989, January 2). The world plays catch up. *Sports, Inc.,* pp. 6–13.

Sandomir, R. (1988, November 14). The $50 billion sports industry. *Sports, Inc.,* pp. 14–23.

Schor, J. B. (1991). *The overworked American.* New York: Basic Books.

Senate Committee on Commerce. (1968). *Sports arbitration board report* (Serial 90–46). Washington, D.C.: U.S. Government Printing Office.

Senate Committee on Commerce. (1973). *Amateur sports* (Serial 93–23). Washington, D.C.: U.S. Government Printing Office.

Track & Field News Editorial Staff. (1991). Track at the crossroads. *Track and Field News, 44*(5), 4–5, 34–45.

United States Olympic Committee. (1988). Unpublished report of the Long Range Strategic Planning Task Force. Colorado Springs, Colo.: USOC.

United States Olympic Committee. (1993). *The 1993 USOC fact book.* Colorado Springs, Colo.: USOC.

U.S. Statistical Abstract, 1994. (1995). Washington, D.C.: U.S. Government Printing Office.

Walsh, R.B. (1951). The Soviet athlete in international competition. *The Bulletin, 25* (652), 1007.

Warnick, R. (1993, April). Demise of recreational opportunities. Presentation to the American Sports Policy Conference, New Orleans.

Webb, H. (1969). Professionalization of attitudes toward play among adolescents. In G. S. Kenyon (ed.), *Aspects of contemporary sport sociology* (pp. 161–178). Chicago: Athletic Institute.

Weistart, J., and Lowell, C. (1979). The law of sports. Indianapolis, Ind.: Bobbs-Merrill Co.

Wilson, J. (1994). *Playing by the rules: sport, society, and the state.* Detroit: Wayne State University Press.

Zingale, D. P. (1973). A history of the involvement of the American presidency in school and college physical education sports during the twentieth century. Unpublished doctoral dissertation, Ohio State University, Columbus, Ohio.

Index

Afghanistan, 101

All-China Sports Federation, 68, 70, 75

All-India Council of Sports (AICS), 214–15

Amateur Athletic Union (AAU), 408–9

Amateur Sports Act of 1978, 410, 423–25

Apartheid, 56–57

Arjuna award, 226

Asian Games Federation, 75

Association Law of 1901, 142–43, 145

Athletes, foreign. *See under names of specific countries*

Australia, 1–13, 16–21; athletes, foreign, 8; coaches, foreign, 8; financial support for sports, 8–11, 12–13, 20; government of, 2–3; international sporting events, host for, 7; professional sports, 5–7; public policy goals, 11; sports, economic impact of, 11–12; sports participation by women, 19; sports participation in, 18, 19; sports performance of, 3–4, 9; sports system, structure of, 4–7

Australian College of Sports Education, 17

Australian Commonwealth Games Association, 5

Australian Institute of Sport (AIS), 9, 13, 20

Australian Olympic Committee (AOC), 5, 17

Australian Sports Commission (ASC), 7, 10, 13, 17, 18, 20

Australian Sports Drug Agency, 10–11

Barcelona Olympic Games, 356, 357, 361

Berlin Olympic Games, 1936, 162

Berlusconi, Silvio, 266, 282 n.6

Bloomfield report, 8

Brazil, 23–36; financial support for sports, 31–32; financial support of athletes, 27; health clubs, 27; history of sports in, 24–26; physical education, 27; professional sports, 28, 32–33; public policy goals, 28, 34–35; Sport-for-All, 27–28, 34–35; sports participation in, 28, 34; sports performance of, 26. *See also* Law of Sport

British Olympic Association (BOA), 378

British Sports Council, 386, 400

Buck, Harry Crowe, 217

Canada, 39–42, 44–65; financial support
    for sports, 45–46, 48–49, 54–56; finan-
    cial support of athletes, 53–54; foreign
    policy goals, 50, 51, 57, 58; govern-
    ment of, 39; intergovernmental rela-
    tions, 62–63; international sporting
    events, host for, 56; professional
    sports, 40–42; public policy goals, 44,
    60, 61–65; sports facilities, 61–62;
    sports participation in, 42–43; sports
    performance of, 45, 48–49, 59–60. *See
    also* Department of External Affairs
Canada Cup, 50
Canada Games, 45, 47
Canadian Football League (CFL), 40–41
Canadian Olympic Association (COA),
    52–53
Carter, Jimmy, 52
Castro, Fidel, 116, 132
Catholic Church, 254, 256, 273, 277
Central American Games, 1966, 131
Chinese Olympic Committee, 76
Clark, Joe, 52, 57, 58
Coaches, foreign. *See under names of
    specific countries*
Cold War, 407, 426
Comitato Olimpico Nazionale Italiano
    (CONI), 254, 267–68, 269, 274, 279–
    81; history of, 255–59
Commercial sport, 107, 108, 118, 343
Commonwealth Games, 58
Communist states, 89–109, 111–14; ath-
    lete and coach exchanges, 102, 103–4;
    foreign policy goals, 96–107; public
    policy goals, 90–95; Sport-for-All, 108,
    sports performance of, 104–6
Competition Act, 42
Confederation of Australian Sport, 5, 9,
    21
Corporate sponsorship. *See under names
    of specific countries*
Council of Europe, 156, 195, 341
Cuba, 116–21, 123–34; athlete and coach
    exchanges, 120, 121, 123, 132–33; ec-
    onomic impact of sports, 120, 121; fi-
    nancial support for sports, 117, 126;
    financial support of athletes, 127–28;
    foreign policy goals, 130–33;

government of, 117; international
    sporting events, hosting of, 132; pro-
    fessional sports, 118; public policy
    goals, 124–33; sports facilities, 125;
    sports participation by women, 126–27;
    sports participation in, 118, 125, 126;
    sports performance of, 116, 120–21;
    United States, conflict with, 133. *See
    also* Communist states

de Courbertin, Baron Pierre, 141
Democracy, cultural, 318
Department of External Affairs (DEA),
    50, 52, 58
Department of National Heritage (DNH),
    370–76
Dronacharya award, 226
Drugs, 111
Dubin, Charles, 59–60

East Germany (GDR), 105–6, 170
Economic development, 392
Elitzur sports organization, 242, 251 nn.1,
    3
Enlai, Zhou, 70, 71, 73
Enti di promozione, 258
European Council. *See* Council of Europe
European Parliament, 156
European Union (EU), 378

Facilities, funding for. *See under names
    of specific countries*
Fascism, 254, 256, 273, 277
Financial support for sports. *See under
    names of specific countries*
Financial support of athletes. *See under
    names of specific countries*
Fininvest, 266
Fitness Canada, 48
France, 139–60; financial support for
    sports, 152–53; government of, 139–
    40; intergovernmental relations, 155;
    international sporting events, host of,
    157–58; political history, 140–42; pro-
    fessional athletes, 152; public policy
    goals, 156–57; sports facilities, 153–
    54; sports lottery, 153; sports system,
    structure of, 142–48

French National Olympics and Sports Committee (CNOSF), 143–44, 150

Gambling, 199, 387
Games of the New Emerging Forces (GANEFO), 86
Gang of Four, 73
German Sports Federation (DSB), 164, 173, 175, 181
Germany, Federal Republic of (FRG), 161–64, 166–67, 169–77, 179–84; financial support for sports, 163, 172–73, 176–79, 182; foreign policy goals, 174–75; government of, 163; intergovernmental relations, 184; Sport-for-All, 167, 170, 177; sports clubs, 179; sports facilities, 176–77; sports lotteries, 179, 185 n.12; sports participation by women, 171, 179; sports participation in, 170–71; sports system, structure of, 171–74
Gleneagles Declaration, 52
Government. *See under names of specific countries*
Great Cultural Revolution, 73, 75
Great Depression, 406
Green Party, 173–74
Guidelines for the Renewal of Physical Education and Sports, 203–4, 205, 206, 207
Gymnastic movement, 161

Hapoel sports organization, 241–42, 245, 248, 250
Hebert, Georges, 141
Hockey Canada, 49–50
Hungarian Olympic Committee (HOC), 191, 199, 209 n.7
Hungary, 187–208; athlete and coach exchanges, 195, 202; commercial sponsorships, 199; financial support for sports, 192–93, 199–201; financial support of athletes, 201–2; foreign coaches, 195; foreign policy goals, 206; government of, 188–89; professional sports, 192, 209 n.12; public policy goals, 190, 203–7; spectatorship, 193; Sport-for-All, 204; sports clubs,

204–5, 208 n.1; sports facilities, 201; sports lottery, 199; sports participation by women, 192; sports participation in, 192; sports performance of, 193–94; sports system, structure of, 196–99; tax policy, 200

Identity, cultural, 25, 44
India, 212–26, 228–39; corporate sponsorships, 221; economic impact of sports, 222; financial support for sports, 216, 219, 222–26, 232; financial support of athletes, 221–23, 225–26; foreign policy goals, 237–38; government of, 212–13; intergovernmental relations, 232–33, 233–34; international sporting events, host of, 218; physical education, 214, 228–29, 234–35; professional sports, 217, 220; public policy goals, 234–38; spectatorship, 220; sports clubs, 216, 233; sports facilities, 223; sports participation in, 219–20; sports performance by, 218; tax policy, 221, 222
Indian Olympic Association (IOA), 215–16, 228, 232
Intergovernmental relations. *See under names of specific countries*
International Olympic Committee (IOC), 51, 75–76, 86, 102, 105
Israel, 175, 241–51; corporate sponsorships, 252 n.10; financial support for sports, 247; government of, 241–42; physical education, 249–50; professionalism, 243, 250; sports betting, 247, 250, 251 n.7; sports facilities, 247; sports performance by 243–45
Italian Olympic Committee, 257
Italy, 253–63, 265–81; corporate sponsorships, 265, 266; economic impact of sports, 267; financial support for sports, 267–68; foreign athletes, 261, 265; foreign policy goals, 278–79; intergovernmental relations, 271–72; international sporting events, host of, 274, 278–79; physical education, 273; political history, 253–55; professional sports, 259, 265, 270, 275–76; public

policy goals, 274–76; spectatorship, 261; Sport-for-All, 259, 276, 281; sports betting, 267, 269, 282 n.12, 283 n.14; sports clubs, 266; sports facilities, 258, 267, 270, 272; sports participation by women, 260, 281 n.1; sports participation in, 260–61; sports performance by, 262–64, 278; tax policy, 259, 267, 271

Jahn, Ludwig, 161, 255
Japan, 286–315; corporate sponsorships, 314; economic impact of sports, 313; financial support for sports, 297, 299–300, 303–4, 310–11; government of, 287, 288–89; intergovernmental relations, 299–300, 302; international sporting events, host of, 297; political parties, 305–6; professional sports, 288, 307–10; public policy goals, 290–91; Sport-for-All, 312; sports betting, 306–7; sports clubs, 295; sports facilities, 290, 292–93, 298; sports participation, 291–92, 296; sports performance by, 296; tax policies, 290
Japan Amateur Sports Association (JASA), 301–2
Japanese Olympic Committee (JOC), 290, 302, 304, 312, 314–15
Jelinek, Otto, 55
Johnson, Ben, 59
Juantorena, Alberto, 129

Law of Sport: 1975, 28–30; 1993, 30–31, 33, 35
Lillehammer Olympic Games (1994), 327, 342
Los Angeles Olympic Games (1984), 97, 107, 111
Lotteries, 48

Maccabi sports organization, 241–42, 245
Major, John, 401
Mazeaud Law, 148–49, 153
Melbourne Olympic Games, 1956, 9, 246

Military training, sport as, 92–93, 121, 128–29, 273, 320
Montreal Olympic Games, 1976, 48, 51
Moscow Olympics, 1980, 52–53, 99, 249, 276, 290, 422

National Collegiate Athletic Association (NCAA), 408–9
National Hockey League (NHL), 39–40
National Institute for Sports, Physical Education and Recreation (INDER), 118, 123
National Office for Physical Education and Sports (NOPES), 190–91, 196–97, 201, 204–5
National Socialistic Federation of Physical Education in the Reich, 161
Norsk Tipping A/S, 328, 329
North Korea, 101
Northern Ireland (Ulster), 392–94
Norway, 317–29, 334–39, 341–44; financial support for sports, 327–36; financial support of athletes, 334–35; foreign policy goals, 341–42; gambling, 328, 329; government of, 317–18; intergovernmental relations, 322, 335; international sporting events, host of, 327; professional sports, 327; public policy goals, 339–43; Sport-for-All, 319, 325–26, 339, 343; sports betting, 328, 329; sports clubs, 323; sports facilities, 337–39; sports history, 319–21; sports participation by women, 323, 327; sports participation in, 323–27; sports performance by, 326, 327; sports system, structure of, 321–23; tax policy, 335–36
Norwegian Confederation of Sports (NIF), 322–23, 328, 334, 336, 343
Norwegian Olympic Committee (NOK), 323, 343

People's Republic of China (PRC), 67–80, 82, 85–86; athlete and coach exchanges, 76–77; corporate sponsorship, 79; financial support of athletes, 77; foreign athletes, 76–77; foreign coaches, 76–77; foreign policy goals,

86; government of, 67–68; international sporting events, host for, 75, 86; political history, 69–73; public policy goals, 70, 77–78, 80–82; sports participation in, 74, 79, 82; sports performance of, 72, 74–75, 82, 85; sports system, structure of, 68–69, 79. See also Communist states

Peace Corps, 426

Physical culture, 69–70, 79, 85, 90, 94–95

Physical education, 140–41, 144–45. See also under names of specific countries

Political history. See under names of specific countries

President's Council on Physical Fitness and Sports, 408, 425–26

Privatization, 201, 250, 303, 364, 380, 397

Professional sports. See under names of specific countries

Public policy goals. See under names of specific countries

Republic of China. See Taiwan

Seoul Olympic Games, 1988, 97

Social security laws, 200

Sokol gymnastics, 103, 109

South Africa, 51, 57–58, 102

Soviet Union (USSR), 44–45, 50, 52. See also Communist states

Spain, 346–49, 351, 353, 355–66; economic impact of sports, 353; financial support for sports, 353, 355, 359; financial support of athletes, 356; government of, 346–47; intergovernmental relations, 347, 348; international sporting events, host of, 357, 361; political history, 357–58; professional sports, 349, 355, 362; Sport-for-All, 349, 359; sports betting, 359; sports facilities, 358, 361, 363; sports participation by women, 353; sports participation in, 349–53; sports performance by, 356; sports system, structure of, 347–39

Spanish Olympic Committee (COE), 348, 356

Spectator safety, 390

Sport and Physical Education Authority, 246, 248, 249

Sport Canada, 53–55

Sport Participation Canada (Particip-ACTION), 47

Sport-for-All. See under names of specific countries

Sports, economic impact of. See under names of specific countries

Sports Authority of India, 215, 228, 230–31

Sports facilities. See under names of specific countries

Sports participation. See under names of specific countries

Sports participation by women. See under names of specific countries

Sports performance. See under names of specific countries

Sports systems, structure of. See under names of specific countries

Squaw Valley Olympic Games, 1960, 105

State Physical Culture and Sports Commission (State Sports Commission), 68, 70, 77–78

Stevenson, Teofilo, 129

Taipei, 76. See also Taiwan

Taiwan, 51. See also Taipei

Task Force on Sports for Canadians, 46–47

Television, 220, 282 nn.4, 7, 383, 421

Thatcher, Margaret, 401

Trudeau, Pierre, 45, 50, 51, 52

United Kingdom, 370–71, 376, 378–92, 394–402; corporate sponsorship, 389; economic impact, 383; financial support for sports, 381, 386–89; foreign athletes, 385–86; government of, 370; intergovernmental relations, 376, 391–92; national lottery, 388; physical education, 395–97; public policy goals, 379, 392, 95–96, 397–400; spectatorship, 381–82; Sport-for-All, 380, 397; sports facilities, 387, 390–91, 395, 397;

sports participation by women, 381, 390; sports participation in, 381, 395; sports performance by, 383–86; tax policy, 388–89; tourism, 392

United States, 404–28; antitrust, 416–18; economic impact of sports, 413–14; financial support for sports, 421–23; foreign athletes, 415–16; foreign policy goals, 407–8; government of, 404–5; labor laws, 418–19; lottery, 422; professional sports, 405–6, 414–15, 416–21; public policy goals, 408, 426–28; spectatorship, 412–13; sports facilities, 406, 420; sports participation in, 410–12; tax policy, 419–20

United States Olympic Committee (USOC), 422, 423–25

Vargas, Getulio, 25

Warsaw Pact, 103
Wingate Institute for Physical Education and Sport, 246, 251 n.4
Women's sport, 96
Worker tournaments, 98
World Football League (WFL), 41

About the Editors and Contributors

STEVE ARNAUDON is director of Sports Development and Policy at the Australian Sports Commission. Arnaudon holds degrees in economics and arts and is the former director of the Sport and Recreation branch of the Federal Sports Department in Australia. He is also a member of the Board of the Australian Coaching Council and a member of the Standing Committee on Recreation and Sport.

MICHAEL BAR-ELI is a senior researcher at the Ribstein Center for Research and Sports Medicine Sciences at the Wingate Institute in Israel. He earned a B.A. from Beer-Sheva University, a M.A. from the Hebrew University in Jerusalem, and a doctorate in sport psychology and sociology from the Deutsche Sporthochschule, Cologne. He has published over forty scientific publications and is president of the Israel Society for Sport Psychology and Sociology.

SUSAN E. BROWNELL holds a Senior Advanced Studies Degree from the Beijing Institute of Physical Education and a Ph.D. in cultural anthropology from the University of California, Santa Barbara. She is the author of *Training the Body for China: Sports in the Moral Order of the People's Republic* (1995) and is an assistant professor of anthropology at the University of Missouri, St. Louis. As a track and field athlete (pentathlon and heptathlon), Brownell was a six-time Collegiate All-American, competed on six American teams, participated in four U.S. Olympic Festivals (including the inaugural event in 1978), and competed in the 1980 and 1984 Olympic Trials. During a year of language study at Beijing University, she was selected to represent Beijing City in the 1986

National College Games, where she won a gold in the heptathlon and two silvers in the relays, thus "winning glory for Beijing."

LAURENCE CHALIP is a senior lecturer with the Faculty of Business and Hotel Management at Griffith University's Gold Coast Campus in Queensland, Australia, where he directs the university's sport management program. He earned his Ph.D. in policy analysis from the University of Chicago. He was a research associate with the International Anthropology Project at the Los Angeles Olympic Games and an executive member of the Seoul Organizing Committee for Olympic Cultural Performance and Research. He has held faculty positions at the University of Chicago, the University of Waikato, and the University of Maryland, where he remains an adjunct member of the graduate faculty.

PACKIANATHAN CHELLADURAI received an undergraduate degree from the University of Madras, an M.A. degree from the University of Western Ontario, and M.A.Sc. and Ph.D. degrees from the University of Waterloo. He taught at the University of Western Ontario and is currently a professor at The Ohio State University. Dr. Chelladurai is a scholar of management science, specializing in organizational theory and organizational behavior in the context of sport, and has contributed numerous books and articles to the sport management literature. He is a corresponding Fellow in the American Academy of Physical Education and the first recipient of the Earle F. Zeigler Award from the North American Society for Sport Management. He has participated in the formation of the North American Society for Sport Management, the European Association of Sport Management, and the Indian Association of Sport Management.

Dr. Chelladurai was a member of the Indian national team in basketball, and of the provincial team in volleyball, as well as coach and referee in both sports.

LAMARTINE P. DACOSTA has a doctoral degree in philosophy and works as a consultant in international institutions for cultural and social relations, health, and sports. Currently he is a professor at the University of Rio de Janeiro and at University Gama Filho. He is also author or coauthor of over twenty books and eighty articles.

PETER J. FARMER is coordinator of the Sport Management Program at Guilford College in North Carolina. Previously, he was chair of the Department of Exercise and Sport Sciences and director of the Sport Management Studies Program at Tulane University in New Orleans, Louisiana. Farmer has also served as a public school teacher, national coach of Mexico, and coach/administrator at the Australian Institute of Sport (1984–1985). As an athlete, Farmer represented Australia as a participant and finalist in the Olympic Games (1976 and 1980) as well as in the 1974 and 1978 Commonwealth Games.

KRISTIN FELDE is a senior executive consultant in the Royal Norwegian Ministry of Cultural Affairs. She has a master's degree in sport management from the Norwegian University of Sport and Physical Education.

GYÖNGYI SZABÓ FÖLDESI received a Ph.D. in sociology from Eötvös Loránd Tudományegyetm University of Budapest, a Ph.D. in the sociology of sport from the Akademia Wychowania Fizycznego of Warsaw and a honorary doctoral degree in physical education at the University of Physical Education of Budapest. She is a professor at the Hungarian University of P.E. in Budapest, president of the Hungarian Subcommittee for the Sociology of Sport, and associate editor of the *International Review for the Sociology of Sport*. She has published four books and sixty articles in Hungarian and thirty in other languages. She has been a pioneer in introducing the sociological approach in sports sciences in Eastern European countries.

KLAUS HEINEMANN received his Ph.D. from the Technical University of Karlsruhe. He is professor of sociology at the University of Hamburg. He has published twenty-five books and nearly 100 articles on a variety of subjects including the sociology and economics of sports. He is editor-in-chief of the *International Review of Sport Sociology*.

BARRIE HOULIHAN is professor of public policy and associate dean at Staffordshire University in the United Kingdom. His most recent books on sports include *The Government and Politics of Sport* (1991) and *Sport and International Politics* (1994). He also has acted as a consultant to the British Sports Council and has helped prepare the regional sports strategy for the English West Midlands.

ARTHUR JOHNSON is professor of political science at the University of Maryland Baltimore County. He earned his Ph.D. in political science at the State University of New York at Buffalo. He is the author of numerous articles on public policy and sport in the United States and *Minor League Baseball and Local Economic Development*. He also is the coeditor (with James Frey) of *Government and Sport: The Public Policy Issues*.

M. L. KAMLESH holds degrees in English and physical education from The Punjab Government College of Physical Education and the Punjabi University in Patiala, India. He has published numerous books and papers, and his research concentrates in sports psychology. He is a coach and referee for cycle polo and an administrative member of archery associations. Kamlesh currently serves as director of the Sports Authority of India at Lakshmibai National College of Education.

DONALD MACINTOSH was a professor and director of the School of Physical and Health Education at Queen's University in Kingston, Canada. He conducted extensive research on sport and public policy in Canada with grants from the Social Science and Humanities Research Council of Canada, and is the author of a number of papers and several books on this topic. His chapter is being published posthumously, following his death in 1994.

ALAIN MICHEL is head of the Department of Sports Economics and Management at the University of Paris Dauphine, where he has directed the masters program in Sports Economics and Business since 1983. He is a noted expert on community sports policy in France, and is engaged in comparative research on international sports policies. Dr. Michel is an accomplished athlete in judo, tennis, and golf. He served as a physical therapist at the Olympic Games in Tokyo (1964) and Mexico City (1968). He resides in Villemanoche, in the Department of Yonne, France and has served as the village's mayor since 1976.

USHA SUJIT NAIR has conducted and presented research in physical education and sports. He is a member of the Board of Studies in Physical Education of Kerala University and a lecturer at the Sports Authority of India, Lakshmibai National College of Physical Education.

YUJI NAKAMURA graduated from the Social Science Department of Waseda University in 1985 and completed a Master Course (1987) and doctoral studies (1991) in political science there as well. He has served as an assistant for the Human Science Department at Waseda and as a full-time lecturer at Utsunomiya University. He is currently a member of the Faculty of International Studies at Utsunomiya.

PAULA J. PETTAVINO received her doctorate from the University of Notre Dame in 1982. She is currently an adjunct professor at the American University in Washington D.C. and Marymount University in Arlington, Virginia. She has lived in Peru and El Salvador and has conducted field research in Cuba. She is coauthor of *Sport in Cuba: The Diamond in the Rough* (1993).

NICOLA PORRO teaches sociology at the University of Roma La Sapienza. He is president of the Scientific Committee of the Italian Association for Sport for All (UISP) and a member of the Extended Board of the International Sociology of Sport Association (ISSA). His previous work on sport includes *L'imperftta epopea* (1989) and *Identita, nazione, cittadinanza. Sport, societa e sistema politico nell'Italia contemporanea* (1995).

NURIA PUIG is a professor of sociology of sport at the National Institute of Physical Education of Catalonia in Barcelona, Spain. She received a degree in modern history from the University of Barcelona in 1973. She holds two doctoral degrees; one in sociology from the University of Paris (1980) and the other in philosophy and sciences of education from the University of Barcelona (1993). She has published numerous articles and books, and currently serves as an associate editor of the *International Review for the Sociology of Sport.* Between 1979 and 1983 she was a member of the Spanish Olympic Committee and between 1968 and 1971, a member of the Spanish ski team.

GERALYN M. PYE received her doctorate from the Flinders University of South Australia in 1991. She is currently a lecturer in Politics at Flinders University. Her work includes many years of field research in Cuba, and she has traveled extensively throughout South America as well. She is coauthor of *Sport in Cuba: The Diamond in the Rough* (1993).

JIM RIORDAN is academic head of the Department of Linguistic and International Studies at the University of Surrey, Guilford, England. He has written several books on sport in the Soviet Union and other Communist countries. He has lived and worked for five years in the USSR and was a soccer player for the Moscow Spartaks.

URIEL SIMRI is a retired senior staff member of the Wingate Institute for Physical Education and Sport, Israel. He specializes in the history and the contemporary history of physical education and sports, as well as in comparative physical education. His writings, which include twenty-five books and over one hundred and fifty papers, have been published in eight languages.

BERIT SKIRSTAD is associate professor at the Norwegian University of Sport and Physical Education, where she established a program in sport and culture management. Since 1993 she has headed the Social Sciences Department. At the national level, she has held executive board positions in skiing, orienteering, parks and recreation, and sport for all organizations and has served as president of the Norwegian Association for Sport Research. Internationally, she is active in the International Orienteering Federation, and has served as secretary-general and president of the Sport and Leisure Committee of the International Council of Sport Science and Physical Education. She is the editor of four books and has been published widely in Norway and internationally.

LISA STACHURA is a Governor's Policy Fellow in the State of Maryland. Her current project involves work on Maryland's Neighborhood Business Development Program at the state's Department of Housing and Community Development. She received a Master of Policy Sciences degree from the University of Maryland Baltimore County in 1995. She is a summa cum laude graduate of Towson State University.

GERSHON TENENBAUM is director of the Ribstein Center of Research and Sport Medicine Sciences at the Wingate Institute, Israel. A graduate of the Zinman College, Tel Aviv University, and the University of Chicago, he has published more than 100 scientific publications, including five books. He is a member of seven scientific societies.

CAO XIANGJUN received her undergraduate degree from the Beijing Institute of Physical Education, as well as a graduate degree in physical culture theory. During her studies she was a member of the women's basketball team, captain of the Beijing City women's handball team, and represented Beijing in the First National Sports Games of the PRC, where the team won the championship. Cao was awarded the title of Master Sportsperson. She has taught at the Institute since graduating in 1963, and in 1991 she became the first woman promoted to Full Professor in forty years. Her publications include numerous articles, monographs, and textbooks such as *General Theory of Physical Culture*—an award-winning publication used in all national institutes of physical education and departments of physical education. Other works include *Concise Edition on the Theory of Physical Culture, Pedagogy,* and *Collegiate Sports Management.* Cao founded the Management Department at the Beijing Institute of Physical Education and became its chair. She is a board member of the Chinese Sports Science Association and is associate director and secretary-general of its Social Science Division, which is responsible for organizing national scientific research activities in the social science of sport.

ISBN 0-313-28481-4

EAN

9 780313 284816

HARDCOVER BAR CODE